D1617284

# The Israeli-Palestinian Conflict: A Documentary Record

The Israeli-Palestinian conflict has generated a vast quantity of documents from many quarters and a plethora of suggestions for its resolution. No comparable regional conflict has been subject to such scrutiny or given rise to such radically different interpretations of the same basic facts. Any serious analysis of the conflict demands a familiarity with its documentary history. This collection, compiled and edited by Yehuda Lukacs, brings together in one volume key documents and statements of position of the parties directly and indirectly involved. It covers the period 1967-90. The book begins with UN Security Council Resolution 242 and ends with documents pertaining to Israel's 1989 West Bank election proposals, Egypt's Ten Point Plan, US Secretary of State, James Baker's, Five Point Proposal for Israeli-Palestinian negotiations, and the Arab Summit League Final Statement, 1990.

This is an unique collection of documents on the Israeli-Palestinian conflict. It is an updated and greatly expanded edition of Dr Lukacs' most successful volume *Documents on the Israeli-Palestinian conflict, 1967-1983* and will be widely read by students and specialists of the Middle East, Jewish Studies, International Relations and World Politics. It will also be an essential handbook for policy makers, government officials and journalists.

*Reviews from the first edition*

"This collection...is an indispensable resource for scholars, students, policy-makers and others interested in analyzing the Arab-Israeli-Palestinian conflict and influencing its outcome." *Journal of Palestine Studies*

"In a field of study so bedevilled by controversy and recriminations, it is refreshing to come upon...(a) fairly well-balance and level-headed volume... This collection does remind the reader of things which, in this period of over-documentation and considerable confusion could easily be forgotten." *Jerusalem Post*

Published with the co-operation of

# The International Center for Peace
# in the Middle East

The International Center for Peace in the Middle East is a non-party, non-sectarian and non-profit organization. It seeks to serve as a focal point for all those, in Israel and abroad — scholars, community leaders, professionals, businessmen and others — actively involved in the quest for peace in the Middle East, regardless of nationality, ideology, religion or political affiliations.

Its purpose is to undertake policy-oriented research, studies, public discussions and other educational programmes in order to develop concrete recommendations and promote activities and educational plans directed towards the achievement of:

A comprehensive peace settlement in the Middle East

Full solution of the Israeli-Palestinian conflict through mutual recognition, self-determination and coexistence

Extrication of the Middle East from Superpower rivalries and the arms race, both conventional and nuclear

Co-operation between the Jewish people and the Arab world

Freedom of conscience and religious tolerance

Equality of social, cultural and political rights — individual and collective — for religious and national minorities

Regional co-operation aimed at developing the areas for the benefit of all its peoples

# The
# Israeli-Palestinian Conflict:
# A Documentary Record

### edited by
### Yehuda Lukacs

Assistant Professor of International Relations, The American University, Washington, DC

The right of the
University of Cambridge
to print and sell
all manner of books
was granted by
Henry VIII in 1534.
The University has printed
and published continuously
since 1584.

## CAMBRIDGE UNIVERSITY PRESS
### Cambridge    New York    Port Chester
### Melbourne    Sydney

Published by the Press Syndicate of the University of Cambridge
The Pitt Building, Trumpington Street, Cambridge CB2 1RP
40 West 20th Street, New York, NY 10011-4211, USA
10 Stamford Road, Oakleigh, Melbourne 3166, Australia
©The International Center for Peace in the Middle East,
Hahashmonaim St. Tel Aviv 67011, Israel 1991

First published 1992

*The Israeli-Palestinian conflict: a documentary record* succeeds
and replaces *Documents on the Israeli-Palestinian conflict
1967-1983* published by Cambridge University Press in 1984
(Hardback 0 521 26795 1)

Printed in Great Britain at the University Press, Cambridge

*British Library cataloguing in publication data applied for*

*Library of Congress cataloguing in publication data applied for*

ISBN 0 521 37561 4  hardback

ISBN 0 521 37597 5  paperback

J&F(jds/les)

# Contents

Contents

Dr. Yehuda Lukacs is Assistant Professor of International Relations and Academic Director of American University's World Capitals Program in Brussels. He is the co-editor of *The Arab-Israeli Conflict: Two Decades of Change*, Westview Press, 1988.

# Preface

In addition to blood, much ink has flowed since the United Nations first turned its attention to the question of Palestine. Since then, the conflict has generated a vast volume of documents and a plethora of suggestions for its resolution. This volume, reflecting the multiplicity of actors involved and the complexity of the issues associated with the resolution of this decades-old conflict, presents key documents and statements of position issued by the various parties to the conflict during the period 1967-1990.

This compendium consists of seven chapters: The first presents international documents—United Nations, European, Soviet, joint Israeli-Arab and Jewish-Arab documents; the second presents US positions; the third contains material pertaining to Sadat's visit to Israel in 1977 and the autonomy negotiations between Israel and Egypt which followed the Israeli-Egyptian Peace Treaty; the fourth chapter documents key Israeli statements of position; the fifth chapter is composed of the election platforms dealing with the Palestinian issue of all the parties represented in the Israeli Knesset following the 1988 elections; and the last two chapters consist of Arab and Palestinian documents respectively.

The first edition of the book came about as a result of a seminar on the Palestine problem, conducted in 1983 by the Tel Aviv-based International Center for Peace in the Middle East, for members of the Israeli Knesset. At that time, a need was expressed by the Israeli legislators who participated in the seminar for a reference book which would contain the essentials of the documentary history of the conflict. Subsequently, an expanded version was published which has served as a book of reference for policy-makers, academics, and molders of public opinion.

My intention was not to present all the documents pertaining to the conflict (which would have required several volumes), but rather to publish those documents most frequently cited by the main actors in the conflict as well as scholars, and those documents which best mirror the changes in the positions and attitudes of the parties towards core issues. The documents in this book are unadorned by commentary or analysis; they speak for themselves. They attest to the deep schism separating the parties over how to resolve the conflict. Since semantics play a vital role in this conflict, any serious analysis of the Israeli-Palestinian conflict demands a thorough familiarity with its long documentary record. One should bear in mind, however, that language is often used by the parties to obfuscate rather than clarify an issue and, hence, any given position is subject to conflicting interpretations by both scholars and protagonists alike. The initial rejection by the US of the resolutions of the 19th Palestine National Council regarding the acceptance of UN Resolutions 242, 338 and the recognition of Israel is a case in point.

The documents presented in this new volume illustrate the myriad of changes that have occurred since the publication of the first edition in 1984. The most noteworthy developments have been the Palestinian uprising, or *intifadah*, which began in December 1987, the PLO's recognition of Israel in November 1988, and the US dialogue with the PLO in December 1988.

The *intifadah* has brought to a stark relief the dilemmas associated with the continued Israeli occupation of the West Bank and Gaza Strip on the one hand, and Palestinian demands of self-determination on the other. It also focused international public opinion on Israeli policies in the West Bank and Gaza. Furthermore, the uprising has shifted the focus from the interstate dimension of the conflict (Israel and the Arab states) to the intercommunal dimension, namely, the strife between the two peoples—Israelis and Palestinians—in historic Palestine. Hence, as seen in this volume, once the uprising started, all efforts at conflict resolution were directed towards the Palestinian problem. For example, Israel's West Bank elections proposal of May 1989, Egypt's ten-point plan and the five-point proposal by US Secretary of State James Baker, respectively, were all presented as an urgent response to the challenge of the *intifadah*. These peace proposals, however, never passed the prenegotiation stage, since the Israeli government collapsed in March 1990 over the issue of negotiating with Palestinian representatives in Cairo, as envisaged by the US Secretary of State.

The PLO's recognition of Israel, acceptance of UN Resolutions 242 and 338, and renouncement of terrorism, as stated in the 19th Palestine National Council meeting in Algiers and subsequent statements by Yasser Arafat clarifying the PLO's stance on these issues, led to another important development. While Israel regarded the PLO's newly adopted positions on recognition and terrorism as merely a rhetorical ploy, the United States, on the other hand, opened an official dialogue with the PLO in December 1988. This was done with the hope of narrowing the gap between Israel and the Palestinians so that a negotiating process could begin. The US-Palestinian dialogue was short-lived, however. It abruptly ended when the PLO refused to renounce the attack on an Israeli beach by Palestinian guerrillas in May 1990. The US, in response, suspended the dialogue with the Palestinian organization in June 1990. United States officials saw the attack as inconsistent with the PLO's pledge to renounce terrorism.

Another important consequence of the *intifadah* has been Jordan's July 1988 announcement of political and administrative disengagement from the West Bank. By formally renouncing any claim it had to the West Bank, Jordan's move paved the way for the PLO to emerge as the undisputed representative of the Palestinians in any negotiations.

For Israel, the *intifadah*, coupled with Jordan's decision to disengage from the West Bank, signalled the end of the "Jordanian option," a policy designed to bypass the PLO in any negotiations over the future of the territories. Consequently, the message to Israel embodied in the Palestinian uprising has been that any solution to the Israeli-Palestinian conflict must entail a recognition of the PLO as the legitimate representative of the Palestinian people, as well as acceptance of the principle of trading territory for peace, according to which a Palestinian state be established in the West Bank and Gaza alongside Israel.

The Israeli government, however, holds firm to its position of refusing to negotiate with the PLO since it believes that the PLO is a terrorist organization determined to eliminate Israel. Also, Israel views the establishment of a Palestinian state in the West Bank and Gaza as not an end in itself, as the Palestinians claim, but rather as a first stage towards the destruction of the Jewish state.

The incompatibility between the Israeli and Palestinian positions means that no progress can take place in the diplomatic arena. Thus, both Israel and the Palestinians face a deadlock in the territories. The Palestinians have demonstrated their resolve to oppose the occupation at any cost, yet they have been unable to force the Israelis out of the territories. Israel, on the other hand, has proven its determination not to allow the Palestinians to gain the upper hand in the territories, yet it has failed to end the *intifadah*.

The documentary record of the Israeli-Palestinian conflict, taken as a whole in the period 1967-1990, reflects the widening gap between Israel, the Palestinians, and the Arab states over how to resolve the conflict. Since 1967 the Palestinians and the Arab states have embarked upon a process which has led, albeit grudgingly, to the acceptance of the reality of Israel. Israel, on the other hand, has yet to move beyond its 1979 peace treaty with Egypt. So far, Israel has not demonstrated its willingness to seriously deal with the Palestinian issue and negotiate with the PLO, a sine qua non for diplomatic progress in the Israeli-Palestinian arena. Moreover, this impasse has also spilled over to US-Israeli relations. As seen in this volume, the US has increasingly displayed its displeasure with the policies of the Israeli government in the territories and with Israel's refusal to move ahead diplomatically. The 1990 crisis in the Gulf further intensified the growing Israeli-American differences.

The linkage between the 1990 crisis in the Gulf (not covered in this volume) and the Israeli-Palestinian conflict seems to have made the prospects of a diplomatic settlement even more remote. The overwhelming Palestinian support of Saddam Hussein's vitriolic rhetoric against Israel has laid yet another layer of mistrust between Israelis and Palestinians. This is bound to make Israel less willing to make territorial concessions. Even Israeli doves now question the sincerity of the 1988 PLO's recognition of Israel. The Palestinians, having given up on the prospects of reaching a diplomatic accord with Israel, see in the leadership of Saddam Hussein a rallying point to channel their frustrations and hopes. Thus, as of 1990, as the resolution of the Israeli-Palestinian conflict becomes more urgent, the prospects of reaching a solution remain as elusive as ever.

Sincere thanks are due to my research assistant Jennifer L. Surwilo for her help in locating some of the documents, to Virginia Mansfield, my able assistant here in Brussels, and to Dr. Gill Thomas of Cambridge University Press for her patience and support. Also, my thanks are due to the International Center for Peace in the Middle East for supplying the platforms of the Israeli parties.

Yehuda Lukacs
September 1990
Brussels, Belgium

# International Documents and Joint Declarations

## 1. UN Security Council Resolution 242 Concerning Principles for a Just and Lasting Peace in the Middle East, 22 November, 1967

**The Security Council**

*Expressing* its continuing concern with the grave situation in the Middle East,

*Emphasizing* the inadmissibility of the acquisition of territory by war and the need to work for a just and lasting peace in which every State in the area can live in security.

*Emphasizing further* that all Member States in their acceptance of the Charter of the United Nations have undertaken a commitment to act in accordance with Article 2 of the Charter,

1. *Affirms* that the fulfillment of Charter principles requires the establishment of a just and lasting peace in the Middle East which should include the application of both the following principles:

(i)   Withdrawal of Israel armed forces from territories occupied in the recent conflict;

(ii)   Termination of all claims or states of belligerency and respect for and acknowledgement of the sovereignty, territorial integrity and political independence of every State in the area and their right to live in peace within secure and recognized boundaries free from threats or acts of force;

2. *Affirms further* the necessity

(a)   For guaranteeing freedom of navigation through international waterways in the area;

(b)   For achieving a just settlement of the refugee problem;

(c)   For guaranteeing the territorial inviolability and political independence of every State in the area, through measures including the establishment of demilitarized zones;

3. *Requests* the Secretary-General to designate a Special Representative to proceed to the Middle East to establish and maintain contacts with the States

concerned in order to promote agreement and assist efforts to achieve a peaceful and accepted settlement in accordance with the provisions and principles in this resolution;

4.  *Requests* the Secretary-General to report to the Security Council on the progress of the efforts of the Special Representative as soon as possible.


## 2.  Questionnaire by UN Special Representative Gunnar Jarring to the Governments of Egypt, Jordan, Israel, and Lebanon, with Replies, March 1969

*Ambassador Gunnar Jarring submitted his questions to the States concerned in the form of separate lists specifically addressed to each Government. Those lists were, however, prepared from a general list applicable to all the parties and that list is, to save repetition, reproduced here. As some questions related to provisions of Security Council Resolution 242 (1967) which applied to only one or some of the parties, the numbers of questions in the specific lists were not always the same as those in the general list. Where the number of the answer differs from that of the question in the general list, the latter number is added in square brackets.*

*Specific lists of questions based on the following general list were submitted by Ambassador Jarring to the Governments of the United Arab Republic on 5 March, of Jordan on 8 March, of Israel on 9 March and of Lebanon on 14 March, 1969.*

### A.  QUESTIONS SUBMITTED BY THE SPECIAL REPRESENTATIVE

Security Council Resolution 242 (1967) sets out provisions and principles in accordance with which a peaceful and accepted settlement of the Middle East Question should be achieved. Some of these provisions would impose obligations on both sides, some on one side, and some on the other. It has generally been accepted that they should be regarded as a whole. The following questions designed to elicit the attitude of the parties towards the provisions of the Security Council Resolution are based on this assumption and are to be understood in the context that each provision is regarded as part of a "package deal".

1.  Does Israel (Jordan, Lebanon, United Arab Republic) accept Security Council Resolution 242 (1967) for implementation for achieving a peaceful and accepted settlement of the Middle East Question in accordance with the provisions and principles contained in the resolution?

2.  Does Israel (Jordan, Lebanon, United Arab Republic) agree to pledge termination of all claims or states of belligerency with Jordan, Lebanon and the United Arab Republic (Israel)?

3.   Does Israel (Jordan, Lebanon, United Arab Republic) agree to pledge respect for and acknowledgement of the sovereignty, territorial integrity and political independence of Jordan, Lebanon and the United Arab Republic (Israel)?

4.   Does Israel (Jordan, Lebanon, United Arab Republic) accept the right of Jordan, Lebanon and the United Arab Republic (Israel) to live in peace within secure and recognized boundaries free from threats or acts of force?

5.   If so, what is the conception of secure and recognized boundaries held by Israel (Jordan, Lebanon, United Arab Republic)?

6.   Does Israel agree to withdraw its armed forces from territories occupied by it in the recent conflict?

7.   Does the United Arab Republic agree to guarantee freedom of navigation for Israel through international waterways in the area, in particular:
(a)   through the Straits of Tiran, and
(b)   through the Suez Canal?

8.   Does Israel (Jordan, Lebanon, United Arab Republic) agree that, if a plan for the just settlement of the refugee problem is worked out and presented to the parties for their consideration, the acceptance in principle of such a plan by the parties and the declaration of their intention to implement it in good faith constitute sufficient implementation of this provision of the Security Council Resolution to justify the implementation of the other provisions?

9.   Does Israel (Jordan, Lebanon, United Arab Republic) agree that the territorial inviolability and political independence of the States in the area should be guaranteed:
(a)   by the establishment of demilitarized zones;
(b)   through additional measures?

10.   Does Israel agree that such demilitarized zones should include areas on its side of its boundaries?

11.   Does Jordan agree that a demilitarized zone should be established in Jordanian territory from which Israel armed forces have been withdrawn?

12.   Does the United Arab Republic agree that a demilitarized zone should be established:
(a)   at Sharm-el-Sheikh;
(b)   in other parts of the Sinai peninsula?

13.   Does Israel (Jordan, Lebanon, United Arab Republic) agree that demilitarization of such zones should be supervised and maintained by the United Nations?

14.   Would Israel (Jordan, Lebanon, United Arab Republic) accept as a final act of agreement on all provisions a mutually signed multilateral document which would incorporate the agreed conditions for a just and lasting peace?

## B. REPLY OF THE GOVERNMENT OF ISRAEL

*(Handed to Ambassador Jarring in Jerusalem by the Minister for Foreign Affairs on 2 April, 1969)*

Jerusalem, 2 April, 1969

Dear Ambassador Jarring,

Israel's position on all the subjects raised in your eleven questions has been stated in detail in my address to the General Assembly of 8 October, 1968, and in the memoranda presented to you on 15 October, 1968 and 4 November, 1968.

I now enclose specific replies in an affirmative spirit to the questions as formulated. It is my understanding that on the basis of the answers received from the three governments you propose to pursue further mutual clarifications in an effort to promote agreement on all the matters at issue in accordance with your mandate. We are ready to join in this process at any appropriate place.

Israel's statements of attitude, including her replies to these questions, has taken into account recent developments in Arab policy including the speeches recently delivered by President Nasser and other Arab leaders. We have noted the specific and emphatic reiteration of their refusal to make peace with Israel, to recognize Israel, to negotiate with Israel, to cease terrorist attacks on Israel or to admit the possibility of sovereign co-existence in any field. It would appear at this time that the effective negation by the UAR of the principles of the Charter and of the Security Council's Resolution is obvious and vehement. We hope that this policy, to which effect is given every day, will change; but these authoritative statements have caused deep concern and have intensified the tension which we would have wished to see relieved.

It is also our view that highly publicized encounters by four member States have weakened the attention which should have been concentrated on the efforts of the parties themselves to move towards agreement. They are causing a duplication and dispersal of effort. They have also encouraged a wrong impression in some quarters that a solution can be sought outside the region and without its governments. Israel recognizes your mission as the authoritative international framework within which peace between the States in the Middle East should be promoted.

I recall the idea which we discussed some weeks ago that the Foreign Ministers of the three governments should meet with you soon at a suitable place to pursue the promotion of agreement. As you will remember, I reacted positively to this idea. I wish to reaffirm that Israel will continue to co-operate with you in the fulfillment of your mission.

Yours sincerely,
(Signed) Abba EBAN

**Answer to Question One:**

Israel accepts the Security Council Resolution (242) for the promotion of agreement on the establishment of a just and lasting peace, to be reached by negotiation and agreements between the governments concerned. Implementation of agreements should begin when agreement has been concluded on all their provisions.

**Answer to Question Two:**

It is the Arab States, not Israel which claimed and originated states of belligerency. They declared themselves for two decades to be in a state of unilateral war with Israel. It is therefore primarily incumbent upon them to terminate the state of war with Israel.

On the establishment of peace with her Arab neighbours, Israel agrees to the termination, on a reciprocal basis, of all claims or states of belligerency with each State with which peace is established. A declaration specifying each State by name would be made by Israel in each case.

The corresponding statement by any Arab State must specifically renounce belligerency "with Israel" and not "with any state in the area". Legal obligations must be specific in regard to those by whom they are bound.

Renunciation of belligerency includes the cessation of all maritime interference, the cessation of boycott measures involving third parties; the annulment of reservations made by Arab States on the applicability to Israel of their obligations under international conventions to which they have adhered; non-adherence to political and military alliances and pacts directed against Israel or including States unwilling to renounce claims or states of belligerency with Israel and maintain peaceful relations with it; the non-stationing of armed forces of such other States on the territory of the contracting States and the prohibition and prevention in the territory of Arab States of all preparations, actions or expeditions by irregular or para-military groups or by individuals directed against the lives, security or property of Israel in any part of the world.

The last stipulation is without prejudice to the fact that the responsibility of Arab governments for preventing such activities is legally binding under the cease-fire established by the parties in June 1967.

**Answer to Question Three:**

Israel agrees to respect and acknowledge the sovereignty, territorial integrity and political independence of neighbouring Arab States; this principle would be embodied in peace treaties establishing agreed boundaries.

**Answer to Question Four:**

Israel accepts the right of Jordan, Lebanon, the United Arab Republic and other neighbouring States to live in peace within secure and recognized boundaries, free from threats or acts of force. Explicit and unequivocal reciprocity is Israel's only conditions for this acceptance. "Acts of force" include all preparations, actions or expeditions by irregular or para-military groups or by individuals directed against the life, security or property of Israel in any part of the world.

### Answer to Question Five:
Secure and recognized boundaries have never yet existed between Israel and the Arab States; accordingly, they should now be established as part of the peace-making process. The cease-fire should be replaced by peace treaties establishing permanent, secure and recognized boundaries as agreed upon through negotiation between the governments concerned.

### Answer to Question Six:
When permanent, secure and recognized boundaries are agreed upon and established between Israel and each of the neighbouring Arab States, the disposition of forces will be carried out in full accordance with the boundaries determined in the peace treaties.

### Answer to Question Seven: [General Question 8]
The refugee problem was caused by the wars launched against Israel by Arab States, and has been perpetuated through the refusal of Arab States to establish peaceful relations with Israel. In view of the human problems involved in this issue Israel has expressed its willingness to give priority to the attainment of an agreement for the solution of this problem through regional and international cooperation. We believe that agreement could be sought even in advance of peace negotiations. We suggest that a conference of Middle Eastern States should be convened, together with the Governments contribution to refugee relief and the Specialized Agencies of the United Nations, in order to chart a five-year plan for the solution of the refugee problem in the framework of a lasting peace and the integration of refugees into productive life. This conference can be called in advance of peace negotiations.

Joint refugee integration and rehabilitation commissions should be established by the governments concerned in order to work out agreed projects for refugee integration on a regional basis with international assistance.

In view of the special humanitarian nature of this issue we do not make agreement on plans for a solution of the refugee problem contingent on agreement on any other aspect of the Middle Eastern problem. For the same reason it should not be invoked by Arab States to obstruct agreement on other problems.

### Answer to Question Eight: [General Question 9]
The effective guarantee for the territorial inviolability and political independence of States lies in the strict observance by the governments of their treaty

obligations. In the context of peace providing for full respect for the sovereignty of States and the establishment of agreed boundaries, other security measures may be discussed by the contracting governments.

**Answer to Questions Nine and Ten:** [General Questions 10 and 13]

Without prejudice to what is stated in answer to Question Eight, it is pointed out that experience has shown that the measures mentioned in Questions Nine and Ten have not prevented the preparation and carrying out of aggression against Israel.

**Answer to Question Eleven:** [General Question 14]

Peace must be juridically expressed, contractually defined and reciprocally binding in accordance with established norms of international law and practice. Accordingly, Israel's position is that the peace should be embodied in bilateral peace treaties between Israel and each Arab State incorporating all the agreed conditions for a just and lasting peace. The treaties, once signed and ratified, should be registered with the Secretariat of the United Nations in accordance with Article 102 of the United Nations Charter.

2 April, 1969

## C. REPLY OF THE GOVERNMENT OF JORDAN

*(Received by Ambassador Jarring in Nicosia on 24 March, 1969)*

23 March, 1969

Your Excellency,

Following are the answers of my Government to the questions which you presented to us in Amman, on Saturday, 8 March, 1969. The answers as numbered, hereunder, correspond to your questions.

These answers explain my Government's position, which position has repeatedly been stated to Your Excellency throughout our past meetings.

May I take this opportunity to express to you my continued sincere wishes for your success in the important mission with which you are entrusted.

Yours sincerely,
(Signed) Abdul Monem RIFA'I
Minister of Foreign Affairs

His Excellency,
Ambassador Gunnar Jarring
Imperial Representative to
  The Secretary-General of
  The United Nations.

### Answer (1)

Jordan, as it has declared before, accepts the Security Council Resolution 242 (1967) and is ready to implement it in order to achieve a peaceful and accepted settlement in accordance with the provisions and principles contained in the resolution.

### Answer (2)

Jordan agrees to pledge termination of all claims or states of belligerency. Such a pledge becomes effective upon withdrawal of Israeli forces from all Arab Territories which Israel occupied as a result of its aggression of 5 June, 1967.

A pledge by Israel to terminate the state of belligerency would be meaningful only when Israel withdraws its forces from all Arab territories it occupied since 5 June, 1967.

### Answer (3)

On 5 June, 1967 Israel launched its aggression against three Arab States, violating their sovereignty and territorial integrity. Agreement to pledge respect for and acknowledgement of the sovereignty, territorial integrity and political independence of every State in the area requires the termination by Israel of its occupation and the withdrawal of its forces from all the Arab territories it occupied as a result of its aggression of 5 June.

### Answer (4)

Jordan accepts the right of every State in the area to live in peace within secure and recognized boundaries free from threats or acts of force, provided that Israel withdraws its forces from all Arab territories it occupied since 5 June, 1967, and implements the Security Council Resolution of 22 November, 1967.

### Answer (5)

When the question of Palestine was brought before the United Nations in 1947, the General Assembly adopted its Resolution 181(II) of 29 November, 1947 for the partition of Palestine and defined Israel's boundaries.

### Answer (6) [General Question 8]

It has always been our position that the just settlement of the refugee problem is embodied in paragraph 11 of the General Assembly Resolution 194 of December

1948 which has been repeatedly reaffirmed by each and every General Assembly session ever since its adoption.

If a plan on the basis of that paragraph is presented for consideration to the parties concerned, its acceptance by the parties and the declaration of their intention to implement it in good faith, with adequate guarantees for its full implementation, would justify the implementation of the other provisions of the resolution.

**Answer (7)(8)** [General Questions 9 and 11]

We do not believe that the establishment of demilitarized zones is a necessity. However, Jordan shall not oppose the establishment of such zones if they are astride the boundaries.

**Answer (9)** [General Question 13]

In case demilitarized zones are established Jordan accepts that such zones be supervised and maintained by the United Nations.

**Answer (10)** [General Question 14]

In view of our past experience with Israel and her denunciation of four agreements signed by her with Arab States we consider that the instrument to be signed by Jordan engaging her to carry out her obligations, would be addressed to the Security Council. Israel would likewise sign and address to the Security Council an instrument engaging her to carry out her obligations emanating from the Security Council Resolution of 22 November, 1967. The endorsement by the Security Council of these documents would constitute the final multilateral act of agreement.

## D. REPLY OF THE GOVERNMENT OF LEBANON

*(Received by Ambassador Jarring in Moscow on 21 April, 1969)*
[*Translated from French*]

In reply to the questionnaire which Your Excellency addressed to me on 14 March, 1969, I have the honour, on behalf of the Lebanese Government, to inform you of the following:

Lebanon is essentially involved in the general context of the Israeli-Arab conflict—and, therefore, in the consequences of the war launched by Israel on 5 June, 1967—because of its brotherly solidarity with the Arab States and of the threats which are constantly directed at it by Israel.

Lebanon is justified in considering, however, that the armistice agreement which it concluded with Israel on 23 March, 1949 remains valid, as indicated in its message of 10 June, 1967 to the Chairman of the Mixed Armistice Commission and as confirmed by U Thant, Secretary-General of the United Nations, in his report to the General Assembly of 19 September, 1967. In that report, Mr. Thant, referring to the actual text of the agreement, said that it could be revised or suspended only by mutual consent. In view of Lebanon's circumstances, now and in the past, the armistice lines have, of course, never been changed. These lines, it should be noted, correspond to the frontiers of Lebanon which have always been internationally recognized in bilateral and multilateral diplomatic instruments as well as by the League of Nations and the United Nations. Lebanon participated actively in the drafting of the United Nations Charter and was admitted in its present form and structure to membership in the Organization. Its frontiers have not undergone any *de facto* or *de jure* alteration as a result of the cease-fire decisions taken by the Security Council after 5 June, 1967.

It may be appropriate to state the above-mentioned facts, more particularly with a view to explaining the nature and character of the only reply which we are in a position to give to the questionnaire sent to us by Your Excellency on 14 March, 1969.

In this reply, which reflects the position taken by Lebanon at inter-Arab conferences, we proclaim Lebanon's support of the position of the Arab States whose territory has been occupied by Israel and which have accepted the Security council's decision of 22 November, 1967.

The present note is consistent with the spirit of the talks which you have already held with various Lebanese officials.

Accept, Sir, the assurances of my highest consideration.

> (Signed)Youssef SALEM
> Minister for Foreign Affairs

## E.    REPLY OF THE GOVERNMENT OF THE UNITED ARAB REPUBLIC

*(Handed to Ambassador Jarring in Cairo by the Minister for Foreign Affairs of the United Arab Republic on 27 March, 1969)*

The memorandum handed to you on 5 March, 1969 during your recent visit to Cairo clearly expresses the realities of the present situation. In its items 1 to 7, the memorandum gives a clear restatement of the position of the United Arab Republic which is based on the acceptance of the Security Council Resolution 242 of 22 November, 1967, and its readiness to carry out the obligations emanating therefrom.

The memorandum also clearly expounds Israel's persistence in rejecting the Security Council Resolution and its refusal to carry out its obligations emanating from it as well as Israel's plans for annexation of Arab lands through war, a policy not only prohibited by the Charter of the United Nations but also violates the Security Council Resolution which specifically emphasizes the inadmissability of the acquisition of territory by war. It has become obvious that Israel, in its endeavour to realize its expansionist aims, is no longer satisfied with the actual rejection of the Security Council Resolution but actively works against it.

The same memorandum also states Israel's expansion plan as revealed by the quoted statements of Israeli leaders. This plan aims at:

1. Annexation of Jerusalem;
2. Keeping the Syrian Heights under its occupation;
3. Occupation of the West Bank in Jordan and its complete domination, practically terminating Jordan's sovereignty in that part;
4. Economic and administrative integration of the Gaza strip into Israel and the systematic eviction of its inhabitants;
5. Occupation of Sharm El-Sheikh and the Gulf of Aqaba area as well as the continued military presence in eastern part of Sinai;
6. The establishment of Israeli settlements in occupied territories.

This Israeli position constitutes a flagrant violation and clear rejection of the Security Council Resolution of 22 November, 1967 and of the peaceful settlement for which it provides.

In the light of these undeniable facts, I find it incumbent upon me to state categorically, at the outset of the replies to the specific questions you addressed to the United Arab Republic on 5 March, 1969, that all the answers of the United Arab Republic, which reaffirm its acceptance of the Security Council Resolution and its readiness to carry out the obligations emanating from it require, likewise, that Israel accept the resolution and carry out all its obligations emanating from it and in particular withdrawal from all Arab territories it occupied as a result of its aggression of 5 June, 1967.

## Question (1)

The United Arab Republic, as it has declared before, accepts the Security Council Resolution 242 (1967) and is ready to implement it in order to achieve a peaceful and accepted settlement in accordance with the provisions and principles contained therein.

## Question (2)

The United Arab Republic agrees to pledge termination of all claims or state of belligerency. Such a pledge becomes effective upon withdrawal of Israel's forces from all Arab territories occupied as a result of Israel's aggression of 5 June, 1967.

A declaration by Israel terminating the state of belligerency would be meaningful only when Israel withdraws her forces from all Arab territories it occupied since 5 June, 1967.

## Question (3)

On 5 June, 1967, Israel launched its aggression against three Arab States violating their sovereignty and territorial integrity. Acceptance by the United Arab Republic to pledge respect for and acknowledgement of the sovereignty, territorial integrity and political independence of every State in the area requires the termination by Israel of its occupation and the withdrawal of its forces from all the Arab territories it occupied as a result of its aggression of 5 June, and the full implementation of the Security Council Resolution of 22 November, 1967.

## Question (4)

The United Arab Republic accepts the right of every State in the area to live in peace within secure and recognized boundaries free from threats or acts of force, provided that Israel withdraws its forces from all Arab territories occupied as a result of its aggression of 5 June, 1967, and implements the Security Council Resolution of 22 November, 1967.

## Question (5)

When the question of Palestine was brought before the United Nations in 1947, the General Assembly adopted its Resolution 181 of 29 November, 1947, for the partition of Palestine and defined Israel's boundaries.

## Question (6) [General Question 7]

We have declared our readiness to implement all the provisions of the Security Council Resolution covering, *inter alia*, the freedom of navigation in international waterways in the area; provided that Israel, likewise, implements all provisions of the Security Council Resolution.

## Question (7) [General Question 8]

It has always been our position that the just settlement of the refugee problem is embodied in paragraph 11 of the General Assembly Resolution 194 of December 1948, which has been unfailingly reaffirmed by each and every General Assembly session ever since its adoption.

If a plan on the basis of that paragraph is presented for consideration to the parties concerned, its acceptance by the parties and the declaration of their intention to implement it in good faith, with adequate guarantees for its full implementation would justify the implementation of the other provisions of the Security Council Resolution.

## Questions (8), (9) [General Questions 9 and 12]

We do not believe that the establishment of demilitarized zones is a necessity. However, the United Arab Republic will not oppose the establishment of such zones if they are astride the boundaries.

**Question (10)** [General Question 13]

In case demilitarized zones are established the United Arab Republic accepts that such zones be supervised and maintained by the United Nations.

**Question (11)** [General Question 14]

In view of our past experience with Israel and her denunciation of four agreements signed by her with Arab States, we consider that the instrument to be signed by the United Arab Republic engaging her to carry out her obligations, should be addressed to the Security Council. Israel should, likewise, sign and address to the Security Council an instrument engaging her to carry out her obligations emanating from the Security Council Resolution of 22 November, 1967. The endorsement by the Security Council of these documents would constitute the final multilateral document.

Cairo, 27 March, 1969

## 3. UN Security Council Resolution 338, Concerning the October War, 22 October, 1973

*The Security Council*

1.   *Calls upon* all parties to the present fighting to cease all firing and terminate all military activity immediately, no later than 12 hours after the moment of the adoption of this decision, in the positions they now occupy;

2.   *Calls upon* the parties concerned to start immediately after the cease-fire the implementation of Security Council Resolution 242 (1967) in all of its parts;

3.   *Decides* that, immediately and concurrently with the cease-fire, negotiations start between the parties concerned under appropriate auspices aimed at establishing a just and durable peace in the Middle East.

## 4. Statement by The European Community Foreign Ministers, Brussels, 6 November, 1973.

*On 6 November the Foreign Ministers of the nine States of the European Community met to discuss the situation in the Middle East. At the conclusion of their meeting they issued a statement of policy.*

**Statement by European Community Foreign Ministers**

The nine Governments of the European Community have continued their exchange of views on the situation in the Middle East. While emphasizing that the views set out below are only a first contribution on their part to the search for a comprehensive solution to the problem they have agreed on the following:

They strongly urge that the forces of both sides in the Middle East conflict should return immediately to the positions they occupied on 22 October in accordance with Resolutions 339 and 340 of the Security Council. They believe that a return to these positions will facilitate a solution to other pressing problems concerning prisoners-of-war and the Egyptian Third Army.

They have the firm hope that, following the adoption by the Security Council of Resolution No. 338 on 22 October, negotiations will at last begin for the restoration in the Middle East of a just and lasting peace through the application of Security Council Resolution No. 242 in all its parts.

They declare themselves ready to do all in their power to contribute to that peace. They believe that those negotiations must take place in the framework of the United Nations. They recall that the Charter has entrusted to the Security Council the principal responsibility in the making and keeping of peace through the application of Council Resolutions Nos. 242 and 338.

They consider that a peace agreement should be based particularly on the following points:

1.    The inadmissability of the acquisition of territory by force.

2.    The need for Israel to end the territorial occupation which it has maintained since the conflict of 1967.

3.    Respect for the sovereignty, territorial integrity and independence of every State in the area and their right to live in peace within secure and recognized boundaries.

4.    Recognition that in the establishment of a just and lasting peace account must be taken of the legitimate rights of the Palestinians.

They recall that according to Resolution No. 242 the peace settlement must be the object of international guarantees.

They consider that such guarantees must be reinforced, among other means, by the dispatch of peace-keeping forces to the demilitarized zones envisaged in Article 2(C) of Resolution No. 242. They are agreed that such guarantees are of primary importance in settling the overall situation in the Middle East in conformity with Resolution No. 242 to which the Council refers in Resolution No. 338. They reserve the right to make proposals in this connection.

They recall on this occasion the ties of all kinds which have long linked them to the littoral States of the South and East of the Mediterranean. In this connection they reaffirm the terms of the declaration of the Paris summit of 2 October, 1972 and recall that the Community has decided, in the framework of a global and balanced approach, to negotiate agreements with these countries.

## 5. UN General Assembly Resolution 3236 Concerning the Question of Palestine, 22 November, 1974

*The General Assembly,*

*Having considered* the question of Palestine,

*Having heard* the statement of the Palestine Liberation Organization, the representative of the Palestinian people,

*Having also heard* other statements made during the debate,

*Deeply concerned* that no just solution to the problem of Palestine has yet been achieved and recognizing that the problem of Palestine continues to endanger international peace and security,

*Recognizing* that the Palestinian people is entitled to self-determination in accordance with the Charter of the United Nations,

*Expressing its grave concern* that the Palestinian people has been prevented from enjoying its inalienable rights, in particular its right to self-determination,

*Guided* by the purposes and principles of the Charter,

*Recalling* its relevant resolutions which affirm the right of the Palestinian people to self-determination,

1. *Reaffirms* the inalienable rights of the Palestinian people in Palestine, including:

   (a) The right to self-determination without external interference;

   (b) The right to national independence and sovereignty;

2. *Reaffirms* also the inalienable right of the Palestinians to return to their homes and property from which they have been displaced and uprooted, and calls for their return;

3. *Emphasizes* that full respect for and the realization of these inalienable rights of the Palestinian people are indispensable for the solution of the question of Palestine;

4. *Recognizes* that the Palestinian people is a principal party in the establishment of a just and durable peace in the Middle East;

5. *Further recognizes* the right of the Palestinian people to regain its rights by all means in accordance with the purposes and principles of the Charter of the United Nations;

6. *Appeals* to all States and international organizations to extend their support to the Palestinian people in its struggle to restore its rights, in accordance with the Charter;

7. *Requests* the Secretary-General to establish contacts with the Palestine Liberation Organization on all matters concerning the question of Palestine;

8. *Requests* the Secretary-General to report to the General Assembly at its thirtieth session on the implementation of the present resolution;

9. *Decides* to include the item entitled "Question of Palestine" in the provisional agenda of its thirtieth session.

2296th plenary meeting

## 6.   Joint Statement by the Governments of the US and the USSR, 1 October, 1977

Having exchanged views regarding the unsafe situation which remains in the Middle East, US Secretary of State Cyrus Vance and Member of the Politbureau of the Central Committee of the CPSU, Minister of Foreign Affairs of the USSR A. A. Gromyko have the following statement to make on behalf of their countries, which are co-chairmen of the Geneva Peace Conference on the Middle East.

1.  Both governments are convinced that vital interests of the peoples of this area, as well as the interests of strengthening peace and international security in general, urgently dictate the necessity of achieving, as soon as possible, a just and lasting settlement of the Arab-Israeli conflict.   This settlement should be comprehensive, incorporating all parties concerned and all questions.   The United States and the Soviet Union believe that, within the framework of a comprehensive settlement of the Middle East problem, all specific questions of the settlement should be resolved, including such key issues as withdrawal of Israeli Armed Forces from territories occupied in the 1967 conflict; the resolution of the Palestinian question, including ensuring the legitimate rights of the Palestinian people; termination of the state of war and establishment of normal peaceful relations on the basis of mutual recognition of the principles of sovereignty, territorial integrity, and political independence.   The two governments believe that, in addition to such measures for insuring the security of the borders between Israel and the neighboring Arab States as the establishment of demilitarized zones and the agreed stationing in them of UN troops or observers, international guarantees of such borders as well as of the observance of the terms of the settlement can also be established should the contracting parties so desire.   The United States and the Soviet Union are ready to participate in these guarantees, subject to their constitutional processes.

2.  The United States and the Soviet Union believe that the only right and effective way for achieving a fundamental solution to all aspects of the Middle East problem in its entirety is by negotiations within the framework of the Geneva Peace Conference, specially convened for these purposes, with participation in its work of the representatives of all the parties involved in the conflict including those of the Palestinian people, and legal and contractual formalization of the decisions reached at the conference.   In their capacity as co-chairmen of the Geneva conference, the United States and the USSR affirm their intention, through joint efforts and in their contacts with the parties concerned, to facilitate in every way the resumption of the work of the conference not later than December 1977.   The co-chairmen note that there still exist several questions of a procedural and organizational nature which remain to be agreed upon by the participants to the conference.

3. Guided by the goal of achieving a just political settlement in the Middle East and of eliminating the explosive situation in this area of the world, the United States and the USSR appeal to all the parties in the conflict to understand the necessity for careful consideration of each other's legitimate rights and interests and to demonstrate mutual readiness to act accordingly.

## 7. Statement on the Problem in the Middle East, Soviet Foreign Minister Gromyko at the UN General Assembly, 25 September, 1979

The Middle East problem, if divested of the immaterial, boils down to the following—either the consequences of the aggression against the Arab states and peoples are eliminated or the invaders get a reward by appropriating lands that belong to others.

A just settlement and the establishment of durable peace in the Middle East requires that Israel should end its occupation of all the Arab lands it seized in 1967, that the legitimate rights of the Arab people of Palestine including the right to create their own state be safeguarded and that the right of all states in the Middle East, including Israel, to independent existence under conditions of peace be effectively guaranteed.

The separate deal between Egypt and Israel resolves nothing. It is a means designed to lull the vigilance of peoples. It is a way of piling up on a still greater scale explosive material capable of producing a new conflagration in the Middle East. Moreover, added to the tense political atmosphere in this and the adjacent areas is the heavy smell of oil.

It is high time that all states represented in the United Nations realized how vast is the tragedy of the Arab people of Palestine. What is the worth of declarations in defense of humanism and human rights—whether for refugees or not—if before the eyes of the entire world the inalienable rights of an entire people driven from its land and deprived of a livelihood are grossly trampled upon?

The Soviet policy with respect to the Middle East problem is one of principle. We are in favor of a comprehensive and just settlement, of the establishment of durable peace in the Middle East, a region not far from our borders. The Soviet Union sides firmly with Arab peoples who resolutely reject deals at the expense of their legitimate interests.

## 8. The Venice European Declaration, 13 June, 1980

*The following is the text of the declaration on the Middle East by the European Economic Community issued at the conclusion of a two-day summit in Venice.*

1.    The heads of state and government and the ministers of foreign affairs held a comprehensive exchange of views on all aspects of the present situation in the Middle East, including the state of negotiations resulting from the agreements signed between Egypt and Israel in March 1979.  They agreed that growing tensions affecting this region constitute a serious danger and render a comprehensive solution to the Israeli-Arab conflict more necessary and pressing than ever.

2.    The nine member states of the European Community consider that the traditional ties and common interests which link Europe to the Middle East oblige them to play a special role and now require them to work in a more concrete way toward peace.

3.    In this regard the nine countries of the Community base on Security Council Resolutions 242 and 338 and the positions which they have expressed on several occasions, notably in their declarations of 29 June, 1977, 19 September, 1978, 26 March and 18 June, 1979, as well as the speech made on their behalf on 25 September, 1979 by the Irish Minister of Foreign Affairs at the 34th United Nations General Assembly.

4.    On the basis thus set out, the time has come to promote the recognition and implementation of the two principles universally accepted by the international community; the right to existence and to security of all the states in the region, including Israel, and justice for all the peoples, which implies the recognition of the legitimate rights of the Palestinian people.

5.    All the countries in the area are entitled to live in peace within secure, recognized and guaranteed borders.  The necessary guarantees for a peace settlement should be provided by the United Nations by a decision of the Security Council and, if necessary, on the basis of other mutually agreed procedures.  The Nine declare that they are prepared to participate within the framework of a comprehensive settlement in a system of concrete and binding international guarantees, including guarantees on the ground.

6.    A just solution must finally be found to the Palestinian problem, which is not simply one of refugees.  The Palestinian people, which is conscious of existing as such, must be placed in a position, by an appropriate process defined within the framework of the comprehensive peace settlement, to exercise fully its right to self-determination.

7.    The achievement of these objectives requires the involvement and support of all the parties concerned in the peace settlement which the Nine are endeavoring to promote in keeping with the principles formulated in the declaration referred to above.  These principles apply to all the parties concerned, and thus the Palestinian people, and to the Palestine Liberation Organization, which will have to be associated with the negotiations.

8.    The Nine recognize the special importance of the role played by the question of Jerusalem for all the parties concerned.  The Nine stress that they will

not accept any unilateral initiative designed to change the status of Jerusalem and that any agreement on the city's status should guarantee freedom of access of everyone to the holy places.

9.    The Nine stress the need for Israel to put an end to the territorial occupation which it has maintained since the conflict of 1967, as it has done for part of Sinai. They are deeply convinced that the Israeli settlements constitute a serious obstacle to the peace process in the Middle East. The Nine consider that these settlements, as well as modifications in population and property in the occupied Arab territories, are illegal under international law.

10.    Concerned as they are to put an end to violence, the Nine consider that only a renunciation of force or the threatened use of force by all the parties can create a climate of confidence in the area, and constitute a basic element for a comprehensive settlement of the conflict in the Middle East.

11.    The Nine have decided to make the necessary contacts with all the parties concerned. The objective of these contacts would be to ascertain the position of the various parties with respect to the principles set out in this declaration and in the light of the results of this consultation process to determine the form which such an initiative on their part could take.


## 9.    Soviet Communist Party Chairman Leonid Brezhnev's Position on Arab-Israeli Peace, 23 February, 1981

*Address before the 26th Congress of the CPSU*

Now about the Middle East problem. In its bid for dominance in the Middle East, the United States has taken the path of the Camp David policy, dividing the Arab world and organizing a separate deal between Israel and Egypt. US diplomacy has failed to turn this separate anti-Arab deal into a broader agreement of a capitulationist type. But it has succeeded in another way: A new deterioration of the situation has occurred in the region. A Middle East settlement was cast back.

What now? As we see it, it is high time to get matters off the ground. It is time to go back to an honest collective search for an all-embracing just and realistic settlement. In the circumstances, this could be done, say, in the framework of a specially convened international conference.

The Soviet Union is prepared to participate in such work in a constructive spirit and with good will. We are prepared to do so jointly with the other interested parties—the Arabs (naturally include the Palestine Liberation Organization) and Israel. We are prepared for such a search jointly with the United States—and I may remind you that we had some experience in this regard some years ago. We are prepared to cooperate with the European countries and with all those who are showing a sincere striving to secure a just and durable peace in the Middle East.

The UN, too, could evidently continue to play a useful role in all this.

As for the substance of the matter, we are still convinced that if there is to be real peace in the Middle East, the Israeli occupation of all Arab territories captured in 1967 must be ended. The inalienable rights of the Arab people of Palestine must be secured, up to and including the establishment of their own state. It is essential to ensure the security and sovereignty of all the states of the region, including those of Israel. Those are the basic principles. As for the details, they could naturally be considered at the negotiations.

## 10.   The Brezhnev Peace Plan, 15 September, 1982 [Excerpts]

As we are profoundly convinced, a just and lasting peace in the Middle East can and must be based on the following principles according both to the general norms of international law and specific decisions of the UN Security Council and the General Assembly pertaining to that problem.

In the first place, the principle of inadmissibility of seizure of foreign lands through aggression should be strictly observed. And this means that all territories occupied by Israel since 1967—the Golan Heights, the West Bank of the Jordan river, the Gaza sector and the Lebanese lands—must be returned to the Arabs. The border between Israel and its Arab neighbors must be declared inviolable.

Second, the inalienable right of the Arab people of Palestine to self-determination, to the creation of their own independent state on the Palestinian lands, which will be freed from the Israeli occupation—on the West Bank of the Jordan River and in the Gaza sector—must be ensured in practice. The Palestinian refugees must be granted the possibility envisaged by the UN decisions to return to their homes or get appropriate compensation for the property left by them.

Third, the eastern part of Jerusalem, which was occupied by Israel in 1967 and where one of the main Muslim holy shrines is situated, must be returned to the Arabs and become an inseparable part of the Palestinian state. Free access of believers to the holy shrines of the three religions must be ensured in the whole of Jerusalem.

Fourth, the right of all states of the area must be ensured to safe and independent existence and development, of course, with the observance of full reciprocity, as it is impossible to ensure the security of some people, while flouting the security of others.

Fifth, an end must be put to the state of war, and peace must be established between the Arab States and Israel. And this means that all sides in the conflict, including Israel and the Palestinian State, must commit themselves to mutually respect each other's sovereignty, independence and territorial integrity, and resolve disputes that crop up through peaceful means, through negotiations.

Sixth, international guarantees of settlement must be drawn up and adopted, the role of guarantors could be assumed, let us say, by the permanent members of the UN Security Council, or by the UN Security Council as a whole.

Such a comprehensive, truly just and really lasting settlement can be drawn up and implemented only through collective efforts with the participation of all sides concerned, including, certainly, PLO—the sole legitimate representative of the Arab people of Palestine.

This is precisely the way of settlement implied in our proposal to convene an international conference on the Middle East, which has gained broad support, also from Democratic Yemen.

I would like to stress that in the present situation the unity of the Arab States in the struggle against the Israeli aggressors is important as never before. The Arabs need this unity like air like water, and the stronger and more reliable this unity is, the sooner, the imperialist intrigues in the Middle East are foiled.

An Arab summit meeting ended the other day. The statement issued on the results of its work has reflected the well-founded alarm and concern about the Israeli aggression in Lebanon and the continuing occupation of Arab lands by it. We positively assess the principles for the settlement of the Palestinian issue and of the Middle East settlement as a whole, which were adopted by the meeting. They are not at variance with what the Soviet Union has been struggling for many years now, and which has been once again expressed by me above in a condensed form."

## 11.  The Soviet Union's Proposals on a Middle East Settlement, 29 July, 1984

Being concerned over the remaining explosive situation in the Middle East, the Soviet Union is profoundly convinced that the vital interests of the peoples of that region, and likewise the interests of international security as a whole, urgently dictate the need for the speediest attainment of a comprehensive, just and lasting settlement of the Middle East conflict.

It is likewise firmly convinced that such a comprehensive, truly just and really lasting settlement can be drawn up and implemented only through collective efforts with the participation of all sides concerned.

Proceeding from this and wishing to contribute to establishing peace in the Middle East, it puts forward the following proposals on the principles of Middle East settlement and ways towards reaching it.

## Principles of Middle East Settlement

1.    The principle of inadmissibility of capture of foreign lands through aggression should be strictly observed.  Accordingly, all the territories occupied by Israel since 1967—the Golan Heights, the West Bank of the Jordan River and Gaza sector, the Lebanese lands should be returned to the Arabs.  The settlements established by Israel in the Arab territories after 1967 should be dismantled.  The borders between Israel and its Arab neighbors should be declared inviolable.

2.    Implementation in practice should be ensured of the inalienable right of the Palestinian people, whose sole legitimate representative is the Palestine Liberation Organization, to self-determination, to creating its own independent state on the Palestinian lands, which will be freed from the Israeli occupation—on the West Bank of the Jordan River and the Gaza sector.  As is envisaged by the decision of the general Arab meeting at summit level in Fez and with the consent of the Palestinians themselves, the West Bank of the Jordan River and the Gaza sector can be turned over by Israel under the control of the United Nations Organization for a short transition period of not more than several months.

After the creation of an independent Palestinian state, it will, naturally, itself, by virtue of the sovereign rights inherent in ever state, determine the character of its relations with the neighbor countries, including the possibility of forming a confederation.

The Palestinian refugees should be granted the opportunity envisaged by the UN decisions to return to their homes or receive appropriate compensation for the property left behind by them.

3.    The eastern part of Jerusalem, which was occupied by Israel in 1967 and which is the site of one of the main Muslim shrines, should be returned to the Arabs and become an inalienable part of the Palestinian state.  The freedom of access of believers to the sacred shrines of the three religions should be ensured all over Jerusalem.

4.    The right of all states in that area to secure an independent existence and development should be really ensured, certainly, with the observance of full reciprocity, as the genuine security of some people cannot be ensured through flouting the security of others.

5.    An end should be put to the state of war and peace be established between the Arab states and Israel.  This means that all the sides to the conflict, including Israel and the Palestinian state, should commit themselves to honor mutually the sovereignty, independence and territorial integrity of each other, to resolve arising disputes through peaceful means, through talks.

6.    International settlement guarantees should be drawn up and adopted, the role of the guarantor could be assumed, for example, by the permanent members of the UN Security Council or the Security Council as a whole.  The Soviet Union is ready to participate in such guarantees.

## Ways Towards Reaching Settlement

Experience has most convincingly demonstrated the futility and at the same time the danger of the attempts at resolving the Middle East problem through forcing on the Arabs all sorts of separate deals with Israel.

The sole right and effective way towards ensuring a radical solution to the Middle East problem is that of collective efforts by all the sides concerned, in other words, talks within the framework of an international conference on the Middle East specially convened with that aim.

In the opinion of the Soviet Union, in convening such a conference it is necessary to be guided by the following provisions.

## Aims of the Conference

The objective of the conference should be to find solutions to all aspects of Middle East settlement in complex. (sic)

The conference should end in the signing of a treaty or treaties embracing the following organically interconnected components of settlement: Withdrawal of Israeli troops from all the Arab territories occupied since 1967, implementation of the legitimate national rights of the Arab people of Palestine, including its right to the creation of its own state; establishing the state of peace and ensuring security and independent development of all the states—sides to the conflict. Simultaneously, international guarantees for the observance of the terms of such a settlement should be drawn up and adopted. All the agreements reached at the conference should make an integral whole approved by all of its participants.

## Composition of Participants.

All the Arab states having a common border with Israel, i.e., Syria, Jordan, Egypt, Lebanon and Israel itself should have the right to participate in the conference.

The Palestine Liberation Organization should be an equal participant in the conference as the sole legitimate representative of the Palestinian people. This is a question of principled significance, as Middle East settlement is unattainable without the resolution of the Palestinian problem, and it cannot be resolved without the participation of PLO.

The USSR and the USA should also be participants in the conference as they play, by force of circumstances, an important role in the Middle East affairs and were co-chairmen of the preceding conference on the Middle East.

Some other states of the Middle East and of the areas adjoining it, capable of making a positive contribution to the settlement of the Middle East problem could be included into the number of participants in the conference with general consent.

**Organizing the Conference's Work.**

Like the preceding one, a new conference on the Middle East should be held under the aegis of the United Nations Organization.

The main form of work of the conference could be working groups (commissions) created from among representatives of all the participants in the conference to examine key issues of settlement (withdrawal of Israeli troops and the border line; the Palestinian problem; the question of Jerusalem; an end to the state of war and establishment of peace; the problem of security of the states, which participated in the conflict; international guarantees for the observance of the agreements, etc.)

If necessary, bilateral groups could be set up to hammer out details of the agreements concerning only these two countries.

To examine the results of the activities of the working groups (commissions) and when necessary in other cases, plenary meetings should be held to endorse its decisions, with the common consent of all the participants in the conference.

At the initial stage of work of the conference, the states participating in it could be represented by foreign ministers, and subsequently—by specially appointed representatives; when necessary the ministers could periodically attend the further work of the conference.

## 12.  Moroccan-Israeli Joint Declaration, Following Prime Minister Shimon Peres' Visit to Morocco, Rabat and Jerusalem, 24 July, 1986

His Highness King Hassan II received Israeli Prime Minister Mr. Shimon Peres in his palace in Ifrane on 22 and 23 July, 1986. During the talks, which were characterized by frankness and which focused mainly on an examination of the Fez Plan, the Moroccan king and the Israeli prime minister thoroughly analyzed the situation in the Middle East and the conditions—in form and content—which could effectively contribute to establishing peace in that region.

His Highness King Hassan II presented and explained the advantages of each one of the components of the Fez Plan, which he believes enjoys a double advantage both by being the only objectively valuable document that could constitute the basis for a just and lasting peace and by virtue of the possibility that it could be met with a consensus among the Arab countries, which no other peace plan or initiative could. Mr. Shimon Peres, for his part, clarified his position on the Fez Plan and presented his own suggestions regarding the conditions which he believes are necessary for the attainment of peace.

Because the meeting was merely an exchange of views and was not at all intended as negotiations, His Highness King Hassan II will inform the Arab leaders and Prime Minister Mr. Shimon Peres will report to his cabinet on the points that were discussed in the course of their deliberations.

## 13.  The Alexandria Declaration by President Husni Mubarak and Prime Minister Shimon Peres, 12 September, 1986

The meeting between President Husni Mubarak and Israeli Prime Minister Shimon Peres in Alexandria on the 11th and 12th of September marks a new era in bilateral relations between Egypt and Israel as well as in the search for a just and comprehensive peace in the Middle East.

The signing of the compromise of the Taba arbitration reaffirms the importance of dialogue and negotiation as a means for settling international dispute away from the spirit of confrontation and violence.  It constitutes a promising model to be followed and built upon.

The Egyptian-Israeli peace treaty reflects a shared commitment to proceed jointly and simultaneously to enforce the structure of peace between the two peoples and the achievement of a comprehensive peace in the region that will bring about a peaceful settlement of the Arab-Israeli conflict including the resolution of the Palestinian question in all its aspects.

President Mubarak and Prime Minister Peres firmly believe that having referred the Taba issue to arbitration, the two countries can now concentrate their efforts on revising the comprehensive peace process.  They view with great concern the effects of the stalemate on the process.

They declare 1987 as a year of negotiations for peace.

They call upon all parties concerned to dedicate this year to intensive efforts to achieve the common and noble objective of a just, lasting and comprehensive peace.

President Mubarak and Prime Minister Peres, together with other concerned parties, will continue their efforts toward a solution of the Palestinian problem in all its aspects and the establishment of a comprehensive peace in the region.

## 14.  UN General Assembly Resolution 41/43 D, 2 December 1986

**The General Assembly.**

*Recalling* its resolutions 38/58 C of 13 December, 1983, 39/49 D of 11 December, 1984 and 40/96 D of 12 December, 1985, in which it, *inter alia*, endorsed the call for convening the International Peace Conference on the Middle East,

*Recalling also* the relevant resolutions of the Security Council,

*Reaffirming* its Resolutions 39/49 D and 40/96 D, in which it, *inter alia*, requested the Secretary-General, in consultation with the Security Council, to continue his efforts with a view to convening the Conference,

*Having considered* the report of the Secretary-General of 14 March, 1986, in which he, *inter alia*, stated that "the obstacles which have so far prevented the convening of the International Peace Conference on the Middle East as called for by the General Assembly still exist", and his report of 29 October, 1986,

*Expressing its regret* that, owing to the negative attitude of some Member States, the difficulties regarding the convening of the Conference "have remained essentially the same", and expressing its hope that those Member States will reconsider their attitude,

*Having heard* the constructive statements made by numerous representatives, including that of the Palestine Liberation Organization,

*Emphasizing* the need to bring about a just and comprehensive settlement to the Arab-Israeli conflict which has persisted for nearly four decades,

*Recognizing* that the persistence of the Arab-Israeli conflict in the Middle East constitutes a threat to security and stability in the region and to world peace, and, therefore, directly involves the responsibility of the United Nations,

*Stressing its conviction* that the convening of the Conference will constitute a major contribution by the United Nations towards the realization of a just solution to the question of Palestine conducive to the achievement of a comprehensive, just and lasting solution to the Arab-Israeli conflict,

*Appreciating* the concern about the exacerbating situation in the Middle East as voiced in a great many statements during the general debate at the current session and at previous sessions,

1.   *Takes note with appreciation* of the reports of the Secretary-General;

2.   *Determines* that the question of Palestine is the core of the Arab-Israeli conflict in the Middle East;

3.   *Reaffirms once again* its endorsement of the call for convening the International Peace Conference on the Middle East in conformity with the provisions of the Resolution 38/58 C;

4.   *Stresses* the urgent need for additional concrete and constructive efforts by all Governments in order to convene the Conference without further delay;

5.   *Endorses the call* for setting up a preparatory committee, within the framework of the Security Council, with the participation of the permanent members of the Council, to take the necessary action to convene the Conference;

6.   *Requests* the Secretary-General, in consultation with the Security Council, to continue his efforts with a view to convening the Conference and to report thereon to the General Assembly not later than 15 May, 1987;

7.   *Decides* to consider at its forty-second session the report of the Secretary-General on the implementation of the present resolution.

## 15. The Brussels European Declaration, 23 February, 1987

*The following is the text of the declaration on the Middle East issued in Brussels by the European Community.*

The member states of the European Community have particularly important political, historical, geographical, economic, religious, cultural and human links with the countries, and peoples of the Middle East. They cannot therefore adopt a passive attitude towards a region which is so close to them nor remain indifferent to the grave problems besetting it. The repercussions of these problems affect the Twelve in many ways.

At the present time, tension and conflict in the Near and Middle East are continuing and worsening. The civilian population is suffering more and more without any prospect of peace. The Twelve would like to reiterate their profound conviction that the search for peace in the Near and Middle East remains a fundamental objective. They are profoundly concerned at the absence of progress in finding a solution to the Israeli-Arab conflict.

Consequently, they have a direct interest in the search for negotiated solutions to bring just, global and lasting peace to the region and good relations between neighbors, and to allow the economic, social and cultural development which has been too long neglected. They have stated the principles on which solutions would be based on several occasions, in particular in their Venice Declaration.

Accordingly, the Twelve would like to state that they are in favor of an international peace conference to be held under the auspices of the United Nations with the participation of the parties concerned and of any party able to make a direct and positive contribution to the restoration and maintenance of peace and to the region's economic and social development. The Twelve believe this conference should provide a suitable framework for the necessary negotiations between the parties directly concerned.

For their part, the Twelve are prepared to play their role with respect to such a conference and will endeavor to make an active contribution, both through the President-in-Office and individually, to bringing the positions of the parties concerned closer to one another with a view to such a conference being convened. In the meantime, the Twelve would request the parties concerned to avoid any action likely to worsen the situation or complicate and delay the search for peace.

Without prejudging future political solutions, the Twelve wish to see an improvement in the living conditions of the inhabitants of the Occupied Territories, particularly regarding their economic, social, cultural, and administrative affairs. The Community has already decided to grant aid to the Palestinian population of the Occupied Territories and to allow certain products from those territories preferential access to the Community market.

## 16.   The London Agreement Between Foreign Minister Shimon Peres and King Hussein, 11 April, 1987

Accord between the government of Jordan, which has confirmed it to the government of the United States, and the Foreign Minister of Israel, pending the approval of the government of Israel. Parts "A" and "B," which will be made public upon agreement of the parties, will be treated as proposals of the United States to which Jordan and Israel have agreed. Part "C" is to be treated with great confidentiality, as commitments to the United States from the government of Jordan to be transmitted to the government of Israel.

### A Three-Part Understanding between Jordan and Israel

—**Invitation by the UN Secretary-General:**  The UN Secretary-General will send invitations to the five permanent members of the Security Council and to the parties involved in the Israeli-Arab conflict to negotiate an agreement by peaceful means based on UN Resolutions 242 and 338 with the purpose of attaining comprehensive peace in the region and security for the countries in the area, and granting the Palestinian people their legitimate rights.

—**Decisions of the international conference:**  The participants in the conference agree that the purpose of the negotiations is to attain by peaceful means an agreement about all the aspects of the Palestinian problem. The conference invites the sides to set up regional bilateral committees to negotiate bilateral issues.

—**Nature of the agreement between Jordan and Israel:**  Israel and Jordan agree that: 1) the international conference will not impose a solution and will not veto any agreement reached by the sides;  2) the negotiations will be conducted in bilateral committees in a direct manner;  3) the Palestinian issue will be discussed in a meeting of the Jordanian, Palestinian, and Israeli delegations;  4) the representatives of the Palestinians will be included in the Jordanian-Palestinian delegation;  5) participation in the conference will be based on acceptance of UN Resolutions 242 and 338 by the sides and the renunciation of violence and terror;  6) each committee will conduct negotiations independently;  7) other issues will be resolved through mutual agreement between Jordan and Israel.

This document of understanding is pending approval of the incumbent governments of Israel and Jordan. The content of this document will be presented and proposed to the United States.

## 17. Speech of President Mikhail Gorbachev on Relations with Israel, 24 April, 1987 [Excerpts]

*The following is a speech given by Gorbachev at a dinner in honor of Syrian President Hafiz al-Asad, Moscow.*

...We express solidarity with the Arabs who refuse to recognize the occupation of their lands. We categorically condemn the discrimination against the Palestinian people denied the right to self-determination and the right of a homeland. In the future, like in the past, we will oppose any separate deals, as they are only holding back and thwarting the search for a genuine settlement.

Israeli leaders are stubbornly clinging to a policy which has no prospects. They are trying to build the security of their country by intimidating its neighbors and are using all means, even state terror, for that purpose. This is a faulty and short-sighted policy, the more so since it is directed against almost 200 million Arabs.

There is another, correct and reliable, way for ensuring a secure future for the state of Israel. It is a just peace and, in the final analysis, good neighborly relations with the Arabs.

Much has been said lately about relations between the Soviet Union and Israel, and a lot of lies have been spread, too. Let me put it straight: The absence of such relations cannot be considered normal. But they were severed by Israel in the first place. It happened as a result of the aggression against the Arab countries.

We recognize without any reservations—to the same extent as with all other states—the right of Israel to a peaceful and secure existence. At the same time, like in the past, the Soviet Union is categorically opposed to Tel Aviv's policy of strength and annexations. It should be plain—changes in relations with Israel are conceivable only in the mainstream of the process of settlement in the Middle East. This issue cannot be taken out of such a context. This interrelationship has been created by the course of events, by Israel's policy.

We are confident that preparations for an international conference on the Middle East involving all the sides concerned should be a focal point for collective efforts to bring about a settlement.

This idea, as you know, has no easy fate—it was not accepted at once. But the past years have demonstrated that it is the only road out of the impasse. Today it would not be an exaggeration to say that a substantial part of the international community of nations favors such a conference. Even the United States and Israel cannot maintain an openly negative stand.

The time has come to start careful and painstaking preparatory work. The permanent members of the Security Council could take the initiative in that matter. The Soviet Union, let me reaffirm, is prepared for honest and constructive efforts on a collective bilateral basis.

During our conversations we discussed these issues in sufficient detail. I cannot but express satisfaction at the fact that Syrian leadership is unswervingly following the course toward a political settlement.

It is absolutely obvious that much will depend in this respect on the political activity and persistence of the Arab states, on coordination between them. We are saddened by disunity, frictions and conflicts in the Arab world which are vigorously exploited by imperialists and their henchmen. Naturally we saw a good sign in the current efforts to restore the unity of the PLO.

Making sacrifices and suffering deprivations, the Syrian Arab Republic has for many years now been courageously resisting aggression, the policy of diktat and neocolonialist plans. Its vanguard positions in the anti-imperialist struggle are indisputable. Its role is indispensable in consolidating the Arab world along the lines of the Middle East settlement, the most important aim of which is the return of the territories seized by Israel and the exercise of the legitimate Palestinian rights.

Now that preparatory work for an international conference on the Middle East is appearing on the order of the day a common Arab stand on that matter is especially important. And here, in our opinion, the activity and authority of the Syrian friends can become a decisive factor.

In conclusion, let me express confidence that cooperation and interaction between the Soviet Union and Syria sealed by the 1980 treaty will continue to successfully develop in the interests of our peoples, for the benefit of peace and progress in the Middle East and the world over.

I wish good health to you, Comrade al-Asad, and to all Syrian guests, and peace and prosperity to the friendly Syrian people.


## 18.   UN Security Council Resolution 605, 22 December, 1987

The Security Council,

*Having considered* the letter dated 11 December, 1987 from the Permanent representative of Democratic Yemen to the United Nations, in his capacity as Chairman of the Arab Group for the month of December,

*Bearing in mind* the inalienable rights of all peoples recognized by the Charter of the United Nations and proclaimed by the Universal Declaration of Human Rights,

*Recalling* its relevant resolutions on the situation in the Palestinian and other Arab territories, occupied by Israel since 1967, including Jerusalem, and including its Resolutions 446 (1979), 465 (1980), 497 (1981) and 592 (1986),

*Recalling also* the Geneva Convention relative to the Protection of Civilian Persons in Time of War, of 12 August, 1949,

*Gravely concerned and alarmed* by the deteriorating situation in the Palestinian and other Arab territories occupied by Israel since 1967, including Jerusalem,

*Taking into account* the need to consider measures for the impartial protection of the Palestinian civilian population under Israeli occupation,

*Considering* that the current policies and practices of Israel, the occupying Power, in the occupied territories are bound to have grave consequences for the endeavors to achieve comprehensive, just and lasting peace in the Middle East,

1.   *Strongly deplores* those policies and practices of Israel, the occupying Power, which violate the human rights of the Palestinian people in the occupied territories, and in particular the opening of fire by the Israeli army, resulting in the killing and wounding of defenseless Palestinian civilians;

2.   *Reaffirms* that the Geneva Convention relative to the Protection of Civilian Persons in Time of War, of 12 August, 1949, is applicable to the Palestinian and other Arab territories occupied by Israel since 1967, including Jerusalem;

3.   *Calls once again* upon Israel, the occupying Power, to abide immediately and scrupulously by the Geneva Convention relative to the Protection of Civilian Persons in Time of War, of 12 August, 1949, and to desist forthwith from its policies and practices that are in violation of the provisions of the Convention;

4.   *Calls furthermore* for the exercise of maximum restraint to contribute towards the establishment of peace;

5.   *Stresses* the urgent need to reach a just, durable and peaceful settlement of the Arab-Israeli conflict;

6.   *Requests* the Secretary-General to examine the present situation in the occupied territories by all means available to him, and to submit a report no later than 20 January, 1988 containing his recommendations on ways and means for ensuring the safety and protection of the Palestinian civilians under Israeli occupation;

7.   *Decides* to keep the situation in the Palestinian and other Arab territories occupied by Israel since 1967, including Jerusalem, under review.

## 19.   UN Security Council Resolution 607, 5 January, 1988

**The Security Council,**

*Recalling* its Resolution 605 (1987) of 22 December, 1987,

*Expressing* grave concern over the situation in the occupied Palestinian territories,

*Having* been apprised of the decision of Israel, the occupying Power, to "continue the deportation" of Palestinian civilians in the occupied territories,

*Recalling* the Geneva Convention relative to the protection of civilian persons in time of war, of 12 August, 1949, and in particular articles 47 and 49 of same,

1.  *Reaffirms* once again the Geneva Convention relative to the protection of civilian persons in time of war, of 12 August, 1949, is applicable to Palestinian and other Arab territories, occupied by Israel since 1967, including Jerusalem;

2.  *Calls* upon Israel to refrain from deporting any Palestinian civilians from the occupied territories;

3.  *Strongly requests* Israel, the occupying Power, to abide by its obligations arising from the Convention;

4.  *Decides* to keep the situation in the Palestinian and other Arab territories occupied by Israel since 1967, including Jerusalem, under review.

## 20.   Security Council Resolution 608, 14 January, 1988

**The Security Council,**

*Reaffirming* its Resolution 607 (1988) of 5 January, 1988,

*Expressing* its deep regret that Israel, the occupying Power, has, in defiance of that resolution, deported Palestinian civilians,

1.  *Calls* upon Israel to rescind the order to deport Palestinian civilians and to ensure the safe and immediate return to the occupied Palestinian territories of those already deported;

2.  *Requests* that Israel desist forthwith from deporting any other Palestinian civilians from the occupied territories;

3.  *Decides* to keep the situation in the Palestinian and other Arab territories occupied by Israel since 1967, including Jerusalem, under review.

## 21.   Statement on the Middle East by President Mikhail Gorbachev Following the Moscow Summit, 1 June, 1988 [Excerpts]

...We noted that there have appeared real aspects related to a political settlement of the Middle East situation.

First, there exists in the world community, also among the permanent members of the Security Council, the awareness of the need for settlement in the framework of an international conference. It is quite a different matter that the question of its content has not yet been elucidated. Then, there is an awareness that there exist the interests of Syria, there exist the interests of the Palestinian people, the interests of Israel, the interests of other countries of the region who are affected by this conflict.

We stand for a political settlement of all issues, with due account for the interests of all sides concerned and, of course, for the principled provisions of the relevant UN resolutions. We are talking about the fact that all the Israeli-occupied lands be returned and the Palestinian people's right be restored. We said to President Reagan how we view the role of the United States, but we cannot decide for the Arabs in what form the Palestinians will take part in the international conference. Let the Arabs themselves decide, while the Americans and we should display respect for their choice.

Furthermore, we ought to recognize the right of Israel to security and the right of the Palestinian people to self-determination. In what form—let the Palestinians together with their Arab friends decide that. This opens up prospects for active exchanges, for a real process. Anyway, it seems to me that such an opportunity is emerging.

I will disclose one more thing: We said that following the start of a conference—a normal, effective conference, rather than a front for separate talks—a forum which would be inter-related with bilateral, tripartite, and other forms of activity, we will be ready to handle the issue of settling diplomatic relations with Israel.

We are thus introducing one more new element. This shows that we firmly stand on the ground of reality, on the ground of recognition of the balance of interests. Naturally, there are principal issues—the return of the lands, the right of the Palestinian people to self-determination. I should reiterate: We proceed from the premise that the Israeli people and the State of Israel have the right to their security because there can be no security of one at the expense of the other. A solution that would untie this very knot should be found.

## 22. Joint Statement by Yasser Arafat and a Group of Five American Jews, Stockholm, 7 December, 1988

*The group of American Jews who are associated with the International Center for Peace in the Middle East were: Ms. Rita Hauser, Ms. Drora Kass, Mr. Menachem Rosensaft, Mr. Stanley Sheinbaum, and Prof. Abraham Udovitch*

The Palestinian National Council met in Algiers from November 12 to 15, 1988, and announced the declaration of independence which proclaimed the state of Palestine and issued a political statement.

The following explanation was given by the representatives of the PLO of certain important points in the Palestinian declaration of independence and the political statement adopted by the PNC in Algiers.

Affirming the principle incorporated in those UN resolutions which call for a two-state solution of Israel and Palestine, the PNC:

1.   Agreed to enter into peace negotiations at an international conference under the auspices of the UN with the participation of the permanent members of the Security Council and the PLO as the sole legitimate representative of the Palestinian people, on an equal footing with the other parties to the conflict; such an international conference is to be held on the basis of UN Resolutions 242 and 338 and the right of the Palestinian people to self-determination, without external interference, as provided in the UN Charter, including the right to an independent state, which conference should resolve the Palestinian problem in all its aspects;

2.   Established the independent state of Palestine and accepted the existence of Israel as a state in the region;

3.   Declared its rejection and condemnation of terrorism in all its forms, including state terrorism;

4.   Called for a solution to the Palestinian refugee problem in accordance with international law and practices and relevant UN resolutions (including right of return or compensation).

The American personalities strongly supported and applauded the Palestinian declaration of independence and the political statement adopted in Algiers and felt there was no further impediment to a direct dialogue between the United States government and the PLO.

## 23.   UN General Assembly Resolution A/43/L.53, Geneva, 14 December, 1988

*Adopted at the Forty-Third Session of the UN General Assembly on the Question of Palestine.*

### The General Assembly,

*Having considered* the reports of the Secretary-General,*

*Having noted with appreciation* the statement of the Chairman of the Palestine Liberation Organization,**

*Stressing* that achieving peace in the Middle East would constitute a significant contribution to international peace and security,

*Aware* of the overwhelming support for the convening of the International Peace Conference on the Middle East,

*Noting with appreciation* the endeavors of the Secretary-General to achieve the convening of the Conference,

---

* See A/43/272-S/19719 and A/43/691-S/20219

** See A/43/PV.78

*Welcoming* the outcome of the nineteenth Extraordinary Session of the Palestine National Council as a positive contribution towards a peaceful settlement of the conflict in the region,

*Aware* of the ongoing uprising (*intifadah*) of the Palestinian people since 9 December, 1987, aimed at ending Israeli occupation of Palestinian territory occupied since 1967,

1. *Affirms* the urgent need to achieve a just and comprehensive settlement of the Arab-Israeli conflict, the core of which is the question of Palestine;

2. *Calls for* the convening of the International Peace Conference on the Middle East, under the auspices of the United Nations, with the participation of all parties to the conflict, including the Palestine Liberation Organization, on an equal footing, and the five permanent members of the Security Council, based on Security Council Resolutions 242 (1967) and 338 (1973) and the legitimate national rights of the Palestine people, primarily the right to self-determination;

3. *Affirms* the following principles for the achievement of comprehensive peace:

(a) The withdrawal of Israel from the Palestinian territory occupied since 1967, including Jerusalem, and the other occupied Arab territories;

(b) Guaranteeing arrangements for the security of all States in the region, including those named in Resolution 181 (II) of 29 November, 1947, within secure and internationally recognized boundaries;

(c) Resolving the problem of the Palestine refugees in conformity with General Assembly Resolution 194 (III) of 11 December, 1948, and subsequent relevant resolutions;

(d) Dismantling of the Israeli settlements in the territories occupied since 1967;

(e) Guaranteeing of freedom of access to Holy Places, religious buildings and sites;

4. *Notes* the expressed desire and endeavors to place the Palestinian territory occupied since 1967, including Jerusalem, under the supervision of the United Nations for a limited period, as part of the peace process;

5. *Requests* the Security Council to consider measures needed to convene the International Peace Conference on the Middle East, including the establishment of a preparatory committee, and to consider guarantees for security measures agreed upon by the Conference for all States in the region;

6. *Requests* the Secretary-General to continue his efforts with the parties concerned, and in consultation with the Security Council, to facilitate the convening of the Conference, and to submit progress reports on developments in this matter.

## 24.   UN General Assembly Resolution A/43/L.54, Geneva, 14 December, 1988

*Adopted at the Forty-Third Session of the UN General Assembly on the Question of Palestine.*

**The General Assembly,**

*Having considered* the item entitled "Question of Palestine",

*Recalling* its Resolution 181 (II) of 29 November, 1947, in which, *inter alia*, it called for the establishment of an Arab State and a Jewish State in Palestine,

*Mindful* of the special responsibility of the United Nations to achieve a just solution to the question of Palestine,

*Aware* of the proclamation of the State of Palestine by the Palestine National Council in line with General Assembly Resolution 181 (II) of 29 November, 1947 and in exercise of the inalienable rights of the Palestinian people,

*Affirming* the urgent need to achieve a just and comprehensive settlement in the Middle East which, *inter alia*, provides for peaceful coexistence for all States in the region,

*Recalling* its Resolution 3237 (XXIX) of 22 November, 1974, on the observer status of the Palestine Liberation Organization and subsequent relevant resolutions,

1.   *Acknowledges* the proclamation of the State of Palestine by the Palestine National Council on 15 November, 1988;

2.   *Affirms* the need to enable the Palestinian people to exercise their sovereignty over their territory occupied since 1967;

3.   *Decides* that, effective as of 15 December, 1988, the designation "Palestine" should be used in place of the designation "Palestine Liberation Organization" in the United Nations system without prejudice to the observer status and functions of the Palestine Liberation Organization within the United Nations system in conformity with relevant United Nations resolutions and practice;

4.   *Requests* the Secretary-General to take necessary action to implement the present resolution.

## 25.   Statement by Soviet Deputy Foreign Minister Vladimir Petrovsky to the UN General Assembly, Geneva, 14 December, 1988 [Excerpts]

*Following is a speech given at the Forty-Third Session of the UN General Assembly on the question of Palestine.*

The peace initiative advanced from this rostrum by PLO Chairman Yasser Arafat, paves the way for solving the conflict, which has clouded the international situation for many years. By stating explicitly its readiness to enter talks with

Israel within the framework of an international conference on the basis of Resolutions 242 and 338 and the wish to coexist with it under conditions of peace and security, and by condemning terrorism in all its forms, the PLO has reaffirmed that it is a serious and prestigious partner in the peaceful talks. It is now up to the other side. We urge everyone to take advantage of the unique chance and, sweeping aside stereotypes and prejudice, to immediately take the road of international dialogue for the purpose of attaining a comprehensive and just Middle East settlement.

One can today state with satisfaction, that the outlines of an integral concept for untying the knot in the Middle East are being discerned in the international community. First, the international legal formula for a settlement based on the Security Council Resolutions 242 and 338 and for ensuring the rights of the Palestinian people to self-determination is shaping up. Until recently, the wide-ranging international agreement on these questions has not been sufficiently supported by the development of the positions of the parties directly involved in the Arab-Israeli conflict.

We regard the conference as a universal and flexible forum which, in our view, is the most effective and reliable machinery for unblocking the Arab-Israeli conflict. It offers the largest amount of various forums for cooperation among its participants. Representatives of all sides involved in the conflict, including the Arab people of Palestine led by their only legitimate representative, the PLO, and the five permanent members of the Security Council, could take part in the conference. The diversity and urgency of the problem could call for some intermediary measures and steps on the way to the comprehensive settlement. However, such measures and stages should be regarded and implemented in the framework of the conference and in a manner linked to the comprehensive settlement. In this connection we see the decisions made at the latest session of the Palestine National Council in Algiers as substantive and highly beneficial for peace process in the Middle East. These decisions made a serious contribution to creating favorable conditions for a transition to practical steps in settling the Middle East conflict. The Soviet Union highly assessed the results of the top Palestinian forum in Algiers and supported the decision of the Palestine National Council to create a Palestinian state under the framework of a comprehensive Middle East settlement. Its central link is an international conference.

The present stage could either become a time of lost opportunities or mark the beginning of a principally new, peaceful period in mankind's development. This fully applies to the Middle East situation. We are convinced that there is also emerging a unique chance to start moving toward peace in this region. It is important not to miss this chance; it is important to grasp without delay the novelty of the situation coming about in the world and to use it to the fullest to overcome the former stereotypes, to progress from rhetoric to calm, businesslike, and well-considered work on building a lasting and just peace in the ancient land of the Near East.

## 26.  Statement by the Soviet Foreign Ministry on the Beginning of the American Dialogue with the PLO, 18 December, 1988

In recent days the Soviet Union was gratified to note a number of important developments which have a direct bearing on the problem of achieving a just peace in the Middle East.

In the development of the well-known decisions of the Palestine National Council session which was held in Algiers last month, the Palestinian leadership in the person of Yasser Arafat, chairman of the Palestine Liberation Organization (PLO) Executive Committee, reaffirmed the Palestinians' readiness to participate constructively in resolving the Middle East conflict.

In his statement during the UN General Assembly session in Geneva, the Palestinian leader gave reasons for the Algiers decisions on the right of Israel, just as that of the Palestinian state, to exist in peace and security, called for talks with Israel within the framework of an international conference under the provisions of Resolutions 242 and 338 of the UN Security Council, and again firmly rejected terrorism in all its forms.

The attitude taken by the PLO leadership is being regarded in the Soviet Union as the reflection of the Palestinian people's genuine striving to put an end to nearly the most protracted and dangerous regional conflict and to agree on the ensurance of equal opportunities for freedom and national independence of all states of the Middle East under conditions of a lasting peace.

An important positive step was also made by the US side. On 14 December President Ronald Reagan stated readiness for a dialogue between US and PLO representatives within the framework of the peace process. The US Administration's decision proceeds from the recognition, at last, of the long-standing reality.

A substantially new situation is taking shape. It opens up the possibility of a real breakthrough in the cause of settling the Middle East conflict and convening, with this end in view, an international Middle East peace conference. The Arab countries involved in the conflict and the PLO are ready for this.

Practically the entire international community, including the UN Security Council member states, and its permanent members, are in favor of convening such a conference. The Soviet Union is known to have always been an active advocate of this idea.

The new situation opens up the possibility for Israel to reassess its stand and, upon abandoning the old stereotypes, to take the road of a joint search for constructive solutions.

The prospect of peace, tranquility, justice, renunciation of attempts to resolve the conflict by force, and of transition to peaceful construction and cooperation is now closer to the Middle East peoples than ever before. It can be realized only through joint, genuine efforts.

With this end in view the Soviet Union will continue to do everything required of it, and is calling on all other countries to support the process of the quickening progress toward this goal.

### 27. "Near East: Chance for a Historic Compromise," Soviet Foreign Minister Eduard Shevardnadze, Cairo, 23 February, 1989 [Excerpts]

*Following is a speech given by Foreign Minister Shevardnadze in Cairo.*

...Our meeting is taking place after a series of very useful, interesting conversations and talks that we have held in Damascus, Amman, and here, in Cairo. At their center, naturally, were the problems of a Near East settlement.

As you know, we have passed on to the leaders of Egypt, Syria, and Jordan personal messages from Mikhail Gorbachev. On the basis of the thoughts contained in these messages and at discussions held in the capitals of three Arab states, including at the meeting with the chairman of the PLO Executive Committee as well as with the Israeli foreign minister, I would like to talk today about the Soviet leadership's vision of the overall context of the Near East conflict and ways of resolving it.

I consider it necessary to express the immediate reservation that we do not know of any magic formula, we are not striving to acquire one, and are not offering universal remedies.

We realize that the conflict that has lasted for decades and given rise to five bitter wars has extremely deep roots and a multitude of difficult aspects.

But what follows from this? Is it the conclusion that the conflict is completely beyond solution? Or that it cannot be resolved by the means that have been used to date?

Before replying, it is essential to reveal the core of the problem that must be resolved. If one frees it of the residue of distorted ideas and hypertrophied emotions, then it is about what should be done to ensure that two peoples can live in one common historical homeland and implement the fundamental provision of international law about the inadmissibility of acquiring territory by use of force.

A fundamental solution was found a long time ago in 1947 in UN General Assembly Resolution 181 that approved a plan for the partition of Palestine. In the realities of today, the task is one of ensuring that the Palestinian people can realize their right to self-determination, that the Arabs should have restored to them the land that was taken away, and that the Israeli state should be guaranteed the right of secure existence within recognized borders.

Reason will not accept the idea that this task cannot be resolved. And the same reason, backed up by bitter historical experience, indicates that no one side in the conflict can achieve its aims by force. Relying on force will inevitably lead to more wars that are increasingly bloody and destructive.

The Near East is a museum of lost civilizations. If a peaceful political and all-embracing solution is not found to the Arab-Israel conflict, the development of events in the region may spiral, becoming twisted by the logic of military confrontation. The region is threatened by an arms race which, sooner or later, may grow into a nuclear catastrophe.

As a result, it cannot be ruled out that Israel and its neighbors will condemn themselves to repeating the path along which East-West nuclear rivalry developed. That they will ascend the predictable rungs of the ladder of nuclear escalation. If this happens, future archaeologists will find yet another layer of buried civilization in the Near East.

At best, the sides will come to realize after a while the need for a compromise settlement and will begin to implement it, but under immeasurably more dangerous and complex conditions than now.

In the Near East, time is on the side of war rather than peace. Preservation of the status quo leads to an explosion rather than tranquility.

I am not saying all this to moralize. We can be said to be sharing our experience, given our knowledge of the consequences of confrontation, dogmatic approaches, and the over-ideologization of interstate relations.

I think that a great deal of what M.S. Gorbachev said in his speech at the 43rd UN General Assembly session may also be applied to the situation in the Near East and its problems.

This applies above all to a realization of the universality and compulsory nature of the principle of freedom of choice. The world community once helped the Jewish people exercise their freedom of choice—to create the state of Israel.

When the Soviet Union voted in favor of this, it expressed its respect not only for the sacred right to self-determination, but also for a people who have left a profound imprint on the history of mankind's endeavors and discoveries.

Israel has no right now to deny freedom of choice to the Palestinian people. By preventing Palestinian self-determination, Israel is by no means strengthening but, on the contrary, undermining both its security as a state and the legitimacy of its own self-determination. In our opinion, the key that can open the way to a Near East settlement is recognition of the principle of a balance of interests as the only possible principle in interstate, international, and interethnic relations.

In fact, any settlement consists of this: establishing through talks a balance of interests as the opposite and antipode of a balance of power.

A balance of power does not and cannot provide security; even military superiority does not ensure security, because any measurements of military might and force are temporary, transient concepts. Only a balance of interests and rights creates a durable and stable basis for states to coexist without conflicts and for normal relations and mutually beneficial cooperation to be maintained and developed between them.

While thinking about this, one cannot help asking how long the Arab-Israel conflict can remain unresolved. Can it really be supposed that any solution is possible other than one that would satisfy the Palestinians and give them the opportunity to exercise their own inalienable right to self-determination?

The pyramids may disappear sooner than the Palestinians' craving for their native hearth. The *intifadah* [the Palestinian uprising], which has gained such a broad scale and intensity, confirms this. And can one really suppose that the other people, the Israelis, will agree to place their own existence under threat?

The world is changing. Today it is changing faster than ever, and politically it is changing in a direction that only yesterday seemed unlikely.

Look how easily we get used to new realities. The destruction of Soviet and US nuclear missiles is perceived as natural, as proper. The mutual inspections of military activity both under the Stockholm Accords and in keeping with the Soviet-US treaty on liquidating intermediate and shorter-range missiles are being carried out in a routine fashion.

In many countries the numerical strength of troops and armaments is being cut, spending on military needs is being reduced. In a couple of weeks the talks on disarmament and confidence-building measures in the military sphere in Europe will begin. They will take place against the background of the implementation of radical reductions in Soviet armed forces.

But in the Near East, as, incidentally, in other places, too, many think as before, that everything can be solved with the help of arms.

Let's be frank: There are people who believe that the great powers are not overly vexed about the lack of a settlement of the Near East situation. Allegedly, they earn quite a lot of money from arms sales in the region, and they are not too worried about the consequences.

I would like to say, in any case, on behalf of my own country that this is not so. Upheavals in the Near East always affect us very strongly. The Soviet people are especially sensitive to anything that happens here, because tension in this region costs us dearly, in all respects, including materially.

Now the hope of a radical improvement in the international climate has appeared, important agreements have been concluded on arms reductions. Ahead of us, more large-scale accords are emerging on reducing military confrontation both in Europe and in Asia. This trend is becoming universal and determinant in present-day developments. But the historical process of disarmament may come to a standstill because of lack of movement in the Near East.

However, there is movement—in the opposite direction; in the direction of accelerating the arms race. The scales of the race are such that they go far beyond the framework of the region.

Judge for yourselves. To date, the scale of direct military expenditures in the region has risen to third place in the world—after NATO and the Warsaw Pact. In 1987 this expenditure amounted to $59 billion. But while in these two military-political alliances an understanding of the danger of being armed to the teeth is taking root, in the Near East, on the other hand, the false idea that is today being rejected everywhere still predominates: the more arms, the more reliable the security.

A military potential has been developed in the Near East that far exceeds its real economic and demographic weight in the world.

Twenty-five thousand tanks, more than 4,000 aircraft in the combat formations of the sides, about 5 million—and taking reserve troops into account, 7 million—people under arms, and $600 billion aimed for a decade at military preparations in the region do not mean that a limit has been set for the arms race. Rather, the reverse.

The region accounts for 61 percent of world arms exports. And the results? They are horrific. The Iran-Iraq war alone, causing the irrevocable loss of 1 million human lives, devoured $500 billion, which is about half of the foreign debt of the developing countries. But even this is not yet all. Weapons such as, for example, shorter and medium-range missiles, which we and the United States are completely eliminating, are appearing in the region. And, incidentally, being deployed in the Near East, they represent a threat both to the Soviet Union and to the countries of Europe, and to the interests of the United States.

It is precisely because the Near East is becoming a very serious obstacle to the further development of the disarmament process with which the majority of the peoples of the world link their hopes for a better future, and is becoming a threat to them, that it is necessary to internationalize the search for a solution, for a Near East settlement.

In the absence of such an approach, however, complications may arise in relations between the Near East and a large part of the rest of the world.

I understand that this argument may not be accepted in the region. It is impossible, however, not to take account of the fact that such a factor has already emerged in politics today, and tomorrow it will begin to operate. It will hardly be useful and convenient for the states of the Near East to set themselves against universal human interests.

Sometimes the following argument may be heard: In order to eliminate the arms race, it is necessary to remove the cause of the conflict. Others, however, say: So long as there is an arms race, there will also be conflict.

This argument may appear academic. In our view, it should be a dual, parallel process; of curtailing the arms race, and, at the same time, a process of peaceful settlement removing the causes of the conflict situation.

For many long years a long list of regional conflicts have been enumerated at all international forums, and time and again the absence of any kind of moves to resolve them has been registered.

And so the Geneva agreements on Afghanistan have been signed, and today there is already not a single Soviet soldier in this country.

The Iran-Iraq war, which lasted for 8 years, is coming to an end, albeit with difficulty. Nevertheless, diplomatic talks are being struck up and are proceeding.

Agreements on a settlement in southern Africa are being concluded, and the go-ahead is being given to implementation of the UN plan to grant independence to the people of Namibia.

The time for the complete withdrawal of Vietnamese troops from Cambodia is drawing near, and many states are beginning to actively cooperate to facilitate peace and national reconciliation in this country.

And fruitful dialogue is being conducted in Central America.

Encouraging news is coming from the Western Sahara, where it appears that a political mechanism to settle the conflict has begun to work.

There is positive movement on the Korean peninsula.

The same can be said of matters concerning Cyprus.

Well, and what can one say about the Near East? For all the noticeable change in the situation, it has to be said: So far, constructive steps have been taken only by one side—by the Palestinians. This, of course, is not enough. Responsive steps by Israel are required.

Will the Near East really lag behind the times and drop out of the general tendency of world politics?

Why should the parties in the Near East conflict not look at the experience of others? After all, there is much in it that is instructive and useful.

In the settlement of each conflict situation, the question of the balance of interests is specifically resolved. In these specific matters, however, general rules can be identified, too.

First, a dialogue between the parties is arranged via intermediaries. The negotiations themselves are also conducted with their assistance. In certain cases the United Nations acts as the intermediary (one typical example of this is Iran and Iraq, and Afghanistan is another); in other cases, groups of countries (Contadora, the support group, the ASEAN countries), or individual states.

Second, the withdrawal of the forces of a country taking part in the conflict is balanced by political treaty obligations safeguarding its interests. This approach can be seen in Afghan, southern African, and Cambodian situations.

Third, a guarantee system is used. The role of guarantors of fulfillment of the agreements is undertaken by the great powers, and also by the United Nations, which monitors the observance by the sides of the conditions of the agreements.

These are not just ideas, but actual components of real agreements in real conflicts.

Profound changes are taking place around the Near East conflict, too. Never before has there been such a wide international agreement, not only that it should be solved politically, but also as regards the path to such a solution.

The UN General Assembly and all the permanent members of the Security Council—the USSR, the United States, Britain, France and China—favor the convening of an international conference on the Near East. The European Community is working actively in this direction. All the Arab sides consider such a forum necessary and see no other way of starting the settlement process.

In effect, it is Israel alone that stands in opposition to this idea, and this cannot fail to arouse doubts about its own statements that it wishes to live in peace with its neighbors.

But all the same, practice shows that in the course of dialogue and negotiations, formulas can be found for solving the most acute and complex questions. I shall say more about this later, based on the experience of our contacts with the Israelis. But at this point I should like to stress: In the Near East, it is not only Israel that is concerned about security problems, but to no less degree, all of its neighbors are concerned. It is understandable, therefore, that all the sides in the Near East settlement, including the Palestinians, would like to have firm guarantees that no attack will be made on them.

It stands to reason that each side has the right to have its own concepts of the reliability of such guarantees. But it seems to us that the already-approved international practice, including the practice of regional settlements, makes it possible to compile a package of obligations and verification measures that can satisfy the most exacting requirements and create the necessary conviction that security is safeguarded.

There is no doubt that future guarantors could make commitments with respect to specific measures that would be taken by them in the event of a threat of violation of the future agreements.

It is, perhaps, premature to talk about this now, but in principle, if one looks to the future, such tasks could be successfully tackled by a regional center for the reduction of military danger.

We cannot see why the parties to a future Arab-Israeli settlement would not be able to employ mutual inspections and on-site inspections [proverka], including inspections of suspect sites with a short advance notice.

They would make it possible to remove those suspicions that are straining the situation more than anything else at the present time, namely suspicions relating to work connected with the possible creation [sozdaniye] of nuclear and chemical weapons.

A decision to declare the Near East a zone free from nuclear and chemical weapons would also assist in this. There is a proposal on this score and it must be promoted.

In the Near East the principle of creating fully demilitarized zones, as well as zones with a depleted military presence along temporary demarcation lines and along recognized borders, has already been used. Such zones can in the future, too, fulfill an important function in terms of preventing sudden attacks and relieving the system of mutual and international verification [kontrol].

There is considerable experience in using international verification mechanisms here, too.

And, of course, it is difficult to count on a dialogue achieving results without precise commitments from the sides that they will neither directly nor indirectly encourage terrorism and other subversive activities against one another in any forms. Commitments on this score should envisage verification measures and cooperation measures that are sufficient to create the appropriate confidence that they are being observed honestly.

I am talking about these elements of a possible settlement to the Arab-Israel conflict in order to show that it is possible to find a balance of interests between the conflicting sides and to satisfy their legitimate demands.

If we examine possible options for resolving one specific problem or other relating to a settlement, then we see that there are many of them. In other words, there are already numerous separate little bricks, elements, with which, given the desire, it is possible to build a firm edifice of Near East peace.

This means that it is a question of a choice between preserving the present situation and searching for a compromise that is acceptable to all.

But it is impossible to preserve the present situation—for anyone, either for the Palestinians, or the Arabs, or for Israel itself. There is essentially no alternative to reconciliation and a settlement. There is none, and not only for military and economic reasons.

In the present-day world, the concept of the humanization of international relations, the universality and indivisibility of human rights, and the primacy of law is asserting itself.

Israel's holding of the Arab territories that were occupied in 1967, the regime that has been established on them, and the actions of the Israeli authorities aimed at suppressing the political and civil liberties of Palestinians will inevitably lead to Israel's isolation in the community of nations, and to a loss of support for it even from its staunchest friends. And just as naturally, the question will arise of the use of sanctions against Israel as a country that is flouting the rights of civilians on a mass scale.

Now, when the PLO has proclaimed its state, accepted UN Security Council Resolutions 242 and 338, and renounced terrorism, Israel no longer has even the appearance of a pretext for refusing to enter into a dialogue with an organization recognized by the international community as the sole legitimate representative of the Palestinian people.

Of course, Israel can continue to brazen it out with its refusal to talk to the Palestinians. But then it must also take into account that very many states in the world may refuse to talk to it, too.

It is a particular feature of the Near East conflict that it is exceptionally complex in its history, in the number of sides involved in it, in its numerous political aspects, and in its psychological intractability. The nature of the conflict suggests that its solution must be all-embracing, based on a multilateral dialogue and on negotiations at several levels simultaneously.

It is for this reason that the firm conviction exists that a Near East settlement should be approached through collective international efforts.

The issue of the form of the international conference on the Near East, what it should deal with, how it should work, and who should take part in it gives rise to discussions.

These are all legitimate questions for each of the future participants in this forum. And, obviously, answers must be given to them that are acceptable to all.

These answers will not appear of their own accord. They must be discussed and compromise variants found. This is the main task today.

In the course of our tour and conversations with representatives of the sides involved in the conflict, we tried, above all, to consult on means of working out the necessary recommendations.

There is no more important task now than to begin specific preparation to convene the international conference. In our opinion, this work should be conducted in the form of flexible and multichannel mechanisms that would be of an authoritative nature.

It is for this reason that we propose conducting it through informal discussions in the UN Security Council, through unofficial consultations between its five permanent members, and through a multilateral and bilateral dialogue between the sides interested in a settlement, conducted either directly or through inter-mediaries. In this way it will be possible to produce a definite understanding, acceptable to all parties, of the basic parameters of the international conference on the Near East. This work, obviously, must have a time limit and be completed in the course of 6 to 9 months.

At the same time, it is essential to remember that at this stage it is a matter of instituting an instrument for a Near East Settlement, not of elaborating its parameters. But even at this stage, it is necessary to resolve matters of principle. These are, in our view, the political and juridical basis of the conference and the participation of the Palestinians in it.

As for all the other aspects of this international forum, it is best to leave them for consideration by the conference itself. The main thing now is to commence the process of peaceful negotiations, without deciding beforehand the forms it may take in the course of the conference itself by the desire and agreement of its participants, and without establishing any linkages between separate elements of possible accords, other than those concerning which the negotiating parties themselves reach agreement.

I have already referred to the existing experience of resolving regional conflict situations. It convinces one that in all events, intermediaries are needed of the sort that will take pains to ensure that the threads of talks and dialogue do not break, and that the talking process proceeds without halts and intervals.

An international conference, in fact, is such a collective intermediary. But not only an intermediary. In setting up something akin to an insurance network guaranteeing the talks against collapse, it will facilitate the resolution of many regional matters.

To start a dialogue and to maintain it is not easy. What is needed here is help from elsewhere.

We would consider it expedient and timely to establish, attached to the UN Secretary-General, the post of his special representative on the Near East, appointing to this an individual of high international standing. He could be involved in the preparation of the international conference at its earliest stage.

If his task is supported by the European Community, by the United States, and by the other great powers, then it will be possible to reckon on success.

We have had the distinct feeling that conditions in the region are growing ripe for a "breakthrough" in the task of setting up a full-scale dialogue on a Near East settlement in the context of an international conference.

We have had a preliminary exchange of views with the other permanent members of the Security Council. As we understand it, all of them would be in principle willing to facilitate the convocation of an international conference, to contribute to its preparation, and to create the prerequisites for its success.

In this context, I would like to recall that, despite differences in approaches, the UN Security Council has played an important role in ending the war between Iran and Iraq. The Council has shown its ability to act in a balanced manner, maintaining its unity. Looking back, we see that the members of the Security Council have acted wisely, having concentrated on achieving the implementation of its first resolution on the Iran-Iraq conflict.

There is no doubt that everyone has noted the changes in the activity of the UN Security Council that have occurred in recent times. In its work at present there is without doubt greater collegiality, and a great striving for consensus.

I think that we have sufficient grounds to assume that the Security Council will be capable of working out balanced recommendations with regard to the organization of an international conference on the Near East.

I would like to recall that the UN Organization has from the very start played a fundamental role in Near East affairs. In essence, everything that it has been possible to achieve here has been done in this organization and with its assistance. It is no coincidence that no one today thinks of an Arab-Israel settlement other than on the basis of Security Council Resolutions 242 and 338.

The United Nations Organization, by its charter, bears responsibility for maintaining international peace and security, and for averting situations that may threaten peace.

The United Nations Organization effectively promoted conclusion of the Geneva agreements on Afghanistan.

Resolution 435 was adopted many years ago, and today we can see that without it, it is hardly likely that a settlement could have been reached in southern Africa nor the path to independence be opened up to the people of Namibia.

The sides involved in the Near East conflict can, we think, rely on the United Nations organization and trust it with the role of mediator. Today there are no reasons for not placing the benefit of one's trust in the Security Council and seeing what recommendations it will work out.

No one will be any the worse for that. It will be the worse for everyone if we miss the chance once again to embark on the road toward a settlement, toward peace in the Near East.

Israel has no need to be afraid of the conference. Not only will its security not suffer, but on the contrary, it will increase as the security of the other states in the region will increase.

Yesterday I said this to Mr. Arens, Israel's foreign minister. In general, I should note that our conversation which, incidentally, was the second in the past 2 months, was very useful, in my view. The exchange of opinions, albeit diametrically opposed ones, helps to work out a true view of the state of affairs.

What we were absolutely unanimous about was the need to continue contacts for the purpose of seeking ways to reach a settlement. A meeting of a group of experts is already to take place in the near future.

On the whole, as I understood Mr. Arens, the idea of an international conference is for the moment not regarded very highly among the Israelis.

We think that it is precisely the conference that offers the chance of a historic compromise between the Arabs and the Israelis.

We would like the Government of Israel to know that if it chooses the conference and agrees to enter a dialogue with the PLO it will permit our two countries to take yet another step forward along the path of restoring full diplomatic relations. The beginning of the conference would become the starting point for the renewal of these relations.

In calling others to dialogue, we ourselves are intent on developing a maximally broad and constructive dialogue with all countries.

The Soviet Union intends to encourage and support in every possible way any positive steps aimed at eliminating differences among Arabs and uniting the Arab countries, and at the establishment by them of a constructive dialogue with regard to a Near East settlement. In particular, we support the idea of conducting meetings between high-ranking representatives of Syria, Egypt, Jordan, the PLO, and Lebanon to speed up the convocation of an international conference.

We welcome the development of contacts between the states of the Near East and the European Community, and with the United States of America. In these questions the Soviet Union speaks out in favor of the elimination of any competition among great powers. The policy of ousting one another from the region should be rejected, and we should go over to constructive cooperation for the sake of peace and calm in the Near East.

The new political thinking by which we are guided in our foreign policy views with paramount importance cooperation between states for the sake of establishing values common to all mankind. The range of these values is being built around the idea of equality of people, nations, and states, of freedom of choice for each individual and for each people.

Violations of human rights and, even more so, of the rights of entire peoples, and any discrimination, on whatever basis, directly detract from values common to all mankind. These values cannot be different for different people and countries.

It is only within this interpretation and context that we speak of the priority of values common to all mankind and of the supremacy of the idea common to all mankind.

We are calling for the renunciation in international relations of the "enemy image". It is, undoubtedly, psychologically not easy to take this step. Within the context of Near Eastern history and realities, such a way of putting the question may even appear naive. But renouncing the "enemy image" does not signify forgiveness of specific actions, crimes. Only, it is implicit here that this is not an emotional but a legal approach. After all, in society we do not regard a person who has broken the law as an "enemy." Thus, also in international relations one should change over to legal terminology.

This is not a formal change. Enemy is an unequivocal category. He must be either conquered or destroyed, or at best one must have nothing to do with him.

The "enemy" concept is not really compatible with the principle of the peaceful settlement of disputes and conflict situations, with the principle of the impermissibility of the use of force. The "enemy" notion is always mutual and always subjective. It is capable only of erecting barriers both in human and interstate relations, which are difficult to surmount. Through them it will be difficult to change over from confrontation to dialogue, to a legal settlement of international relations, to the establishment of the priority of values common to all mankind, for violence cannot at all be included within this range of values.

The new political thinking proceeds from the need to remove ideology from interstate relations. Behind this there is no attempt to call on anyone to give up their convictions, their world outlook, or their values. What I am saying is that no one should impose his views on others.

In the Near East, people are well aware how dangerous each kind of intolerance and the fetishization [fetishizatsiya] of ideological dogmas are.

In the present-day world these phenomena are fraught with the risk of the destruction of civilization. Mankind can survive if it is united by interests common to all mankind and devoted to the principle of freedom of choice.

The new thinking is the ability of a state or society to reassess itself critically, admit past mistakes or erroneous political directives, and effect their revision.

The Soviet Union regards its foreign policy with self-criticism and is prepared to listen to and understand criticism from others. I am confident that our concrete actions in the international arena are a convincing enough proof of this aspect of the new thinking.

It would be good, I think, if a self-critical approach and realistic views took root in world politics.

The history of the Near East knows a host of plans and projects for a settlement. None of them has succeeded so far. Now one can read or hear that we have brought with us a new Soviet plan for a Near East settlement.

We will put it slightly differently: We have come here with a desire to work out such a plan, to work it out with the participation of all the countries of the region and with all the interested states. This plan is already taking shape and form. In the course of Mikhail Gorbachev's forthcoming trips to Cuba, Britain, the PRC, France, and the FRG, the subject of a Near East settlement will be in active political use. In early March we will discuss it with Spanish Foreign Minister Ordonez in his capacity as chairman of the European Community, and US Secretary of State Baker.

A Near East settlement is a subject of priority for us.

For the time being, speaking about the plan, I can definitely say that it is based on the Soviet leadership's priority political directive described by Mikhail Gorbachev in his speech at the 43rd United Nations General Assembly session, a directive aimed at joint creative work of countries and governments for solving international and regional problems.

Following that directive, we are acting now to overcome not only geographical frontiers, but also the borders of past prejudices which today dangerously limit dialogue and restrict contacts. In particular, we are giving up the ideological component of interstate relations.

This does not mean giving up our own values or appealing to others to discard theirs. Just the opposite. But each time we establish a contact that seemed impossible or impermissible only yesterday, we ask ourselves: in the name of what?

In this case, in the name of peace in the Near East. This is an answer formulated in its most general form. Answering more specifically, we say: for preparing an international conference on the Near East.

We have come here with the conviction that at present, precisely the issues of preparing the conference are coming into the fore. Apart from rare and a very few exceptions, the idea of the conference prevails in people's minds, and our conversations here have shown that clearly.

We hope that our current and future contacts in the region will promote it successfully.

Equally, we count on establishing a better understanding and cooperation between the Soviet Union and Near Eastern states...

## 28. Joint Statement by New Outlook and Al-Fajr, New York, 13 March, 1989

*The following was issued at Columbia University in New York at the conclusion of the New Outlook-Al Fajr Conference*

1.    That a just and permanent peace should be established in the Middle East, where all people of the region, including Palestinians and Israelis, will enjoy equal rights and opportunities.

2.    That the reaching of a settlement is contingent on putting an end to the occupation of the 1967 War.

3.    That the settlement of the Israel-Palestinian conflict should be based on mutual recognition of equal national rights to self-determination and on peaceful coexistence.

4.    That a comprehensive settlement should include a solution to the problem of the Palestinian refugees in all its aspects.

5.    That all peoples of the region are entitled to live in their own states, within secure and recognized borders, free from threats and violence.

6.    That all differences should be resolved through negotiations between the legitimate representatives of all parties, the PLO for the Palestinians and the Government of Israel for the Israelis, with the aim of reaching a permanent solution.

7.    That in order for the peace process to be advanced, a moratorium on all acts of terrorism should be declared.  The called for moratorium requires also refraining from establishing new facts by the occupying authorities with the intention of making a negotiated settlement impossible or more difficult.

8.    That negotiations among all parties should be conducted under the auspices of an international peace conference.

## 29.    The Madrid European Declaration, 27 June, 1989

*The following is the text of the declaration on the Middle East by the European Community issued in Madrid at the conclusion of the semi-annual European Community summit, 26-27 June, 1989.*

### Declaration on the Middle East

The European Council has examined the situation in the Middle East conflict in the light of recent events and of contacts undertaken over several months by the Presidency and the Troika (the incumbent Presidency, its immediate predecessor and successor) with the parties concerned, and it has drawn the following conclusions:

1.   The policy of the Twelve on the Middle East conflict is defined in the Venice Declaration of 13 June, 1980 and other subsequent declarations. It consists in upholding the right to security of all States in the region, including Israel, that is to say, to live within secure, recognized and guaranteed frontiers, and in upholding justice for all the peoples of the region, which includes recognition of the legitimate rights of the Palestinian people, including their right to self-determination with all that this implies.

The Twelve consider that these objectives should be achieved by peaceful means in the framework of an international peace conference under the auspices of the United Nations, as the appropriate forum for the direct negotiations between the parties concerned, with a view to a comprehensive, just, and lasting settlement.

The European Council is also of the view that the Palestine Liberation Organization (PLO) should participate in this process. It expresses its support for every effort by the permanent members of the Security Council of the United Nations to bring the parties closer together, create a climate of confidence between them, and facilitate in this way the convening of the international peace conference.

2.   The Community and its Member States have demonstrated their readiness to participate actively in the search for a negotiated solution to the conflict, and to cooperate fully in the economic and social development of the peoples of the region.

The European Council expressed its satisfaction regarding the policy of contacts with all the parties undertaken by the Presidency and the Troika, and has decided to pursue it.

3.   The European Council welcomes the support given by the Extraordinary Summit Meeting of the Arab League, held in Casablanca, to the decisions of the Palestinian National Council in Algiers, involving acceptance of Security Council Resolutions 242 and 338, which resulted in the recognition of Israel's right to exist, as well as the renunciation of terrorism.

It also welcomes the efforts undertaken by the United States in its contacts with the parties directly concerned and particularly the dialogue entered into with the PLO.

Advantage should be taken of these favorable circumstances to engender a spirit of tolerance and peace with a view to entering resolutely on the path of negotiations.

4.   The European Council deplores the continuing deterioration of the situation in the Occupied Territories and the constant increase in the number of dead and wounded and the suffering of the population.

It appeals urgently to the Israeli authorities to put an end to repressive measures, to implement Resolutions 605, 607 and 608 of the Security Council and to respect the provisions of the Geneva Convention on the Protection of Civilian Populations in Times of War. They appeal in particular for the reopening of educational facilities in the West Bank.

5.   On the basis of the positions of principle of the Twelve, the European Council welcomes the proposal for elections in the Occupied Territories as a contribution to the peace process, provided that:

-the elections are set in the context of a process towards a comprehensive, just, and lasting settlement of the conflict.

-the elections take place in the Occupied territories including East Jerusalem, under adequate guarantees of freedom.

-no solution is excluded and the final negotiation takes place on the basis of Resolutions 242 and 338 of the Security Council of the United Nations, based on the principle of "land for peace."

6.   The European Council launches a solemn appeal to the parties concerned to seize the opportunity to achieve peace.   Respect by each of the parties for the legitimate rights of the other should facilitate the normalizing of relations between all the countries of the region.   The European Council calls upon the Arab countries to establish normal relations of peace and cooperation with Israel and asks that country in turn to recognize the right of the Palestinian people to exercise self-determination.

# U.S. Documents

## 1. President Johnson, Statement on Principles for Peace, 19 June, 1967 [Excerpts]

Our country is committed — and we here reiterate that commitment today to a peace that is based on five principles:
— first, the recognized right of national life;
— second, justice for the refugees;
— third, innocent maritime passage;
— fourth, limits on the wasteful and destructive arms race; and
— fifth, political independence and territorial integrity for all.

This is a time not for malice, but for magnanimity; not for propaganda, but for patience; not for vituperation, but for vision.

We are not here to judge whose fears are right or whose are wrong. Right or wrong, fear is the first obstacle to any peacemaking. Each side must do its share to overcome it. A major step in this direction would be for each party to issue promptly a clear, unqualified public assurance that it is now ready to commit itself to recognize the right of each of its neighbors to national life.

Second, the political independence and territorial integrity of all the states in the area must be assured.

We are not the ones to say where other nations should draw lines between them that will assure each the greatest security. It is clear, however, that a return to the situation of June 4, 1967, will not bring peace. There must be secure, and there must be recognized borders.

Some such lines must be agreed to by the neighbors involved as part of the transition from armistice to peace.

At the same time, it should be equally clear that boundaries cannot and should not reflect the weight of conquest. Each change must have a reason which each side, in honest negotiation, can accept as a part of a just compromise.

Third, it is more certain than ever that Jerusalem is a critical issue of any peace settlement. No one wishes to see the Holy City again divided by barbed wire and by machine guns. I therefore tonight urge an appeal to the parties to stretch their imaginations so that their interests and all the world's interest in Jerusalem, can be taken fully into account in any final settlement.

Fourth, the number of refugees is still increasing. The June war added some 200,000 refugees to those already displaced by the 1948 war. They face a bleak prospect as the winter approaches. We share a very deep concern for these refugees. Their plight is a symbol in the minds of the Arab peoples. In their eyes, it is a symbol of a wrong that must be made right before 20 years of war can end. And that fact must be dealt with in reaching a condition of peace.

All nations who are able, including Israel and her Arab neighbors, should participate directly and wholeheartedly in a massive program to assure these people a better and a more stable future.

Fifth, maritime rights must be respected. Their violation led to war in 1967. Respect for those rights is not only a legal consequence of peace. It is a symbolic recognition that all nations in the Middle East enjoy equal treatment before the law.

And no enduring peace settlement is possible until the Suez Canal and the Straits of Tiran are open to the ships of all nations and their right of passage is effectively guaranteed.

Sixth, the arms race continues. We have exercised restraint while recognizing the legitimate needs of friendly governments. But we have no intention of allowing the balance of forces in the area to ever become an incentive for war.

We continue to hope that our restraint will be matched by the restraint of others, though I must observe that has been lacking since the end of the June war.

We have proposed, and I reiterate again tonight, the urgent need now for an international understanding on arms limitation for this region of the world.

## 2. The Rogers Plan: Address by Secretary of State Rogers, Washington, D.C., 9 December, 1969

*Address before the 1969 GALAXY Conference on Adult Education*

I am very happy to be with you this evening and be a part of this impressive conference. The Galaxy Conference represents one of the largest and most significant efforts in the Nation's history to further the goals of all phases of adult and continuing education.

The State Department, as you know, has an active interest in this subject. It is our belief that foreign policy issues should be more broadly understood and considered. As you know, we are making a good many efforts toward providing continuing education in the foreign affairs field. I am happy tonight to join so many staunch allies in those endeavors.

In the hope that I may further that cause I want to talk to you tonight about a foreign policy matter which is of great concern to our nation.

I am going to speak tonight about the situation in the Middle East. I want to refer to the policy of the United States as it relates to that situation in the hope that there may be a better understanding of that policy and the reasons for it.

Following the third Arab-Israeli war in 20 years, there was an upsurge of hope that a lasting peace could be achieved. That hope has unfortunately not been realized. There is no area of the world today that is more important, because it could easily again be the source of another serious conflagration.

When this administration took office, one of our first actions in foreign affairs was to examine carefully the entire situation in the Middle East. It was obvious that a continuation of the unresolved conflict there would be extremely dangerous, that the parties to the conflict alone would not be able to overcome their legacy of suspicion to achieve a political settlement, and that international efforts to help needed support.

The United States decided it had a responsibility to play a direct role in seeking a solution.

Thus, we accepted a suggestion put forward both by the French Government and the Secretary General of the United Nations. We agreed that the major powers — the United States, the Soviet Union, the United Kingdom, and France — should cooperate to assist the Secretary General's representative, Ambassador Jarring, in working out a settlement in accordance with the resolution of the Security Council of the United Nations of November 1967. We also decided to consult directly with the Soviet Union, hoping to achieve as wide an area of agreement as possible between us.

These decisions were made in full recognition of the following important factors:

*First,* we knew that nations not directly involved could not make a durable peace for the peoples and governments involved. Peace rests with the parties to the conflict. The efforts of major powers can help, they can provide a catalyst, they can stimulate the parties to talk, they can encourage, they can help define a realistic framework for agreement; but an agreement among other powers cannot be a substitute for agreement among the parties themselves.

*Second,* we knew that a durable peace must meet the legitimate concerns of both sides.

*Third,* we were clear that the only framework for a negotiated settlement was one in accordance with the entire text of the U.N. Security Council resolution. That resolution was agreed upon after long and arduous negotiations: it is carefully balanced; it provides the basis for a just and lasting peace — a final settlement — not merely an interlude between wars.

*Fourth,* we believe that a protracted period of no war, no peace, recurrent violence, and spreading chaos would serve the interests of no nation, in or out of the Middle East.

## U.S.—Soviet Discussions

For 8 months we have pursued these consultations in four-power talks at the United Nations and in bilateral discussions with the Soviet Union.

In our talks with the Soviets we have proceeded in the belief that the stakes are so high that we have a responsibility to determine whether we can achieve parallel views which would encourage the parties to work out a stable and equitable solution. We are under no illusions; we are fully conscious of past difficulties and present realities. Our talks with the Soviets have brought a measure of understanding, but very substantial differences remain. We regret that the Soviets have delayed in responding to new formulations submitted to them on October 28. However, we will continue to discuss these problems with the Soviet Union as long as there is any realistic hope that such discussions might further the cause of peace.

The substance of the talks that we have had with the Soviet Union has been conveyed to the interested parties through diplomatic channels. This process has served to highlight the main roadblocks to the initiation of useful negotiations among the parties.

On the one hand, the Arab leaders fear that Israel is not in fact prepared to withdraw from Arab territory occupied in the 1967 war.

On the other hand, Israeli leaders fear that the Arab States are not in fact prepared to live in peace with Israel.

Each side can cite from its viewpoint considerable evidence to support its fears. Each side has permitted its attention to be focused solidly and to some extent solely on these fears.

What can the United States do to help to overcome these roadblocks?

Our policy is and will continue to be a *balanced* one.

We have friendly ties with both Arabs and Israelis. To call for Israeli withdrawal as envisaged in the U.N. resolution without achieving agreement on peace would be partisan toward the Arabs. To call on the Arabs to accept peace without Israeli withdrawal would be partisan toward Israel. Therefore, our policy is to encourage the Arabs to accept a permanent peace based on a binding agreement and to urge the Israelis to withdraw from occupied territory when their territorial integrity is assured as envisaged by the Security Council resolution.

## Basic Elements of the U.N. Resolution

In an effort to broaden the scope of discussion we have recently resumed four-power negotiations at the United Nations.

Let me outline our policy on various elements of the Security Council resolution. The basic and related issues might be described as peace, security, withdrawal, and territory.

## Peace Between the Parties

The resolution of the Security Council makes clear that the goal is the establishment of a state of peace between the parties instead of the state of belligerency which has characterized relations for over 20 years. We believe the conditions and obligations of peace must be defined in specific terms. For example, navigation rights in the Suez Canal and in the Straits of Tiran should be spelled out. Respect for sovereignty and obligations of the parties to each other must be made specific.

But peace, of course, involves much more than this. It is also a matter of the attitudes and intentions of the parties. Are they ready to coexist with one another? Can a live-and-let-live attitude replace suspicion, mistrust, and hate? A peace agreement between the parties must be based on clear and stated intentions and a willingness to bring about basic changes in the attitudes and conditions which are characteristic of the Middle East today.

## Security

A lasting peace must be sustained by a sense of security on both sides. To this end, as envisaged in the Security Council resolution, there should be demilitarized zones and related security arrangements more reliable than those which existed in the area in the past. The parties themselves, with Ambassador Jarring's help, are in the best position to work out the nature and the details of such security arrangements. It is, after all, their interests which are at stake and their territory which is involved. They must live with the results.

## Withdrawal and Territory

The Security Council resolution endorses the principle of the nonacquisition of territory by war and calls for withdrawal of Israeli armed forces from territories occupied in the 1967 war. We support this part of the resolution, including withdrawal, just as we do its other elements.

The boundaries from which the 1967 war began were established in the 1949 armistice agreements and have defined the areas of national jurisdiction in the Middle East for 20 years. Those boundaries were armistice lines, not final political borders. The rights, claims, and positions of the parties in an ultimate peaceful settlement were reserved by the armistice agreements.

The Security Council resolution neither endorses nor precludes these armistice lines as the definitive political boundaries. However, it calls for withdrawal from occupied territories, the nonacquisition of territory by war, and the establishment of secure and recognized boundaries.

We believe that while recognized political boundaries must be established, and agreed upon by the parties, any changes in the preexisting lines should not reflect the weight of conquest and should be confined to insubstantial alterations required for mutual security. We do not support expansionism. We believe troops must be withdrawn as the resolution provides. We support Israel's security and the security of the Arab States as well. We are for a lasting peace that requires security for both.

### Issues of Refugees and Jerusalem

By emphasizing the key issues of peace, security, withdrawal, and territory, I do not want to leave the impression that other issues are not equally important. Two in particular deserve special mention: the question of refugees and of Jerusalem.

There can be no lasting peace without a just settlement of the problem of those Palestinians whom the wars of 1948 and 1967 have made homeless. This human dimension of the Arab-Israeli conflict has been of special concern to the United States for over 20 years. During this period the United States has contributed about $500 million for the support and education of the Palestine refugees. We are prepared to contribute generously along with others to solve this problem. We believe its just settlement must take into account the desires and aspirations of the refugees and the legitimate concerns of the governments in the area.

The problem posed by the refugees will become increasingly serious if their future is not resolved. There is a new consciousness among the young Palestinians who have grown up since 1948 which needs to be channeled away from bitterness and frustration toward hope and justice.

The question of the future status of Jerusalem, because it touches deep emotional, historical, and religious wellsprings, is particularly complicated. We have made clear repeatedly in the past 2 ½ years that we cannot accept unilateral actions by any party to decide the final status of the city. We believe its status can be determined only through the agreement of the parties concerned, which in practical terms means primarily the Governments of Israel and Jordan, taking into account the interests of other countries in the area and the international community. We do, however, support certain principles which we believe would provide an equitable framework for a Jerusalem settlement.

Specifically, we believe Jerusalem should be a unified city within which there would no longer be restrictions on the movement of persons and goods. There should be open access to the unified city for persons of all faiths and nationalities. Arrangements for the administration of the unified city should take into account the interests of all its inhabitants and of the Jewish, Islamic, and Christian communities. And there should be roles for both Israel and

Jordan in the civic, economic, and religious life of the city.

It is our hope that agreement on the key issues of peace, security, withdrawal, and territory will create a climate in which these questions of refugees and of Jerusalem, as well as other aspects of the conflict, can be resolved as part of the overall settlement.

## 3.  Memorandum of Agreement Between the Governments of Israel and the United States, September 1975

### The Geneva Peace Conference

1.  The Geneva Peace Conference will be reconvened at a time coordinated between the United States and Israel.

2.  The United States will continue to adhere to its present policy with respect to the Palestine Liberation Organization, whereby it will not recognize or negotiate with the Palestine Liberation Organization so long as the Palestine Liberation Organization does not recognize Israel's right to exist and does not accept Security Council Resolutions 242 and 338. The United States Government will consult fully and seek to concert its position and strategy at the Geneva Peace Conference on this issue with the Government of Israel. Similarly, the United States will consult fully and seek to concert its position and strategy with Israel with regard to the participation of any other additional states. It is understood that the participation at a subsequent phase of the Conference of any possible additional state, group or organization will require the agreement of all the initial participants.

3.  The United States will make every effort to ensure at the Conference that all the substantive negotiations will be on a bilateral basis.

4.  The United States will oppose and, if necessary, vote against any initiative in the Security Council to alter adversely the terms of reference of the Geneva Peace Conference or to change Resolutions 242 and 338 in ways which are incompatible with their original purpose.

5.  The United States will seek to ensure that the role of the co-sponsors will be consistent with what was agreed in the Memorandum of Understanding between the United States Government and the Government of Israel of December 20, 1973.

6.  The United States and Israel will concert action to assure that the Conference will be conducted in a manner consonant with the objectives of this document and with the declared purpose of the Conference, namely the

advancement of a negotiated peace between Israel and each one of its neighbors.

Henry A. Kissinger
Secretary of State
for the Government of
the United States

Yigal Allon
Deputy Prime Minister &
Minister of Foreign Affairs
For the Government of Israel

## 4. Deputy Assistant Secretary of State for Near Eastern and South Asian Affairs, Harold H. Saunders, Statement on the Palestinians. 12 November, 1975

*Before House Foreign Affairs Subcommittee on the Middle East.*

Mr. Chairman, a just and durable peace in the Middle-East is a central objective of the United States. Both President Ford and Secretary Kissinger have stated firmly on numerous occasions that the United States is determined to make every feasible effort to maintain the momentum of practical progress toward a peaceful settlement of the Arab-Israeli conflict.

We have also repeatedly stated that the legitimate interests of the Palestinian Arabs must be taken into account in the negotiation of an Arab-Israeli peace. In many ways, the Palestinian dimension of the Arab-Israeli conflict is the heart of that conflict. Final resolution of the problems arising from the partition of Palestine, the establishment of the State of Israel, and Arab opposition to those events will not be possible until agreement is reached defining a just and permanent status for the Arab peoples who consider themselves Palestinians.

The total number of Palestinian Arabs is estimated at a little more than three million. Of these, about 450,000 live in the area of Israel's pre-1967 borders; about one million are in the Israeli-occupied West Bank, East Jerusalem and Gaza; something less than a million, about 900,000, are in Jordan; half a million are in Syria and Lebanon; and somewhat more than 20-0,000 or so are elsewhere, primarily in the Gulf States. Those in Israel are Israeli nationals. The great majority of those in the West Bank, East Jerusalem and Jordan are Jordanian nationals. Palestinian refugees, who live outside of pre-1967 Israel and number 1.6 million, are eligible for food and/or services from the United Nations Relief and Works Agency (UNRWA); more than 650,000 of these live in camps.

The problem of the Palestinians was initially dealt with essentially as one involving displaced persons. The United States and other nations responded to the immediate humanitarian task of caring for a large number of refugees and trying to provide them with some hope in life. In later years there has been considerable attention given to the programs of UNRWA that help not only to sustain those people's lives but to lift the young people out of the refugee camps and to train them and give them an opportunity to lead productive lives. Many have taken advantage of this opportunity, and an unusually large number of them have completed secondary and university education. One finds Palestinians occupying leading positions throughout the Arab world as professionals and skilled workers in all fields. The U.S. has provided some $620 million in assistance — about sixty-two percent of the total international support ($1 billion) for the Palestinian refugees over the past quarter of a century.

Today, however, we recognize that, in addition to meeting the human needs and responding to legitimate personal claims of the refugees, there is another interest that must be taken into account. It is a fact that many of the three million or so people who call themselves Palestinians today increasingly regard themselves as having their own identity as a people and desire a voice in determining their political status. As with any people in this situation, there are differences among themselves, but the Palestinians collectively are a political factor which must be dealt with if there is to be a peace between Israel and its neighbors.

The statement is often made in the Arab world that there will not be peace until the "rights of the Palestinians" are fulfilled, but there is no agreed definition of what is meant and a variety of viewpoints have been expressed on what the legitimate objectives of the Palestinians are:

Some Palestinian elements hold to the objective of a bi-national secular state in the area of the former mandate of Palestine. Realization of this objective would mean the end of the present state of Israel, a member of the United Nations, and its submergence in some larger entity. Some would be willing to accept merely as a first step toward this goal the establishment of a Palestinian State comprising the West Bank of the Jordan River and Gaza.

Other elements of Palestinian opinion appear willing to accept an independent Palestinian state comprising the West Bank and Gaza, based on acceptance of Israel's right to exist as an independent state within roughly its pre-1967 borders.

Some Palestinians and other Arabs envisage as a possible solution a unification of the West Bank and Gaza with Jordan. A variation of this which has been suggested would be the reconstitution of the country as a federated state, with the West Bank becoming an autonomous Palestinian province.

Still others, including many Israelis, feel that with the West Bank returned to Jordan, and with the resulting existence of two communities — Palestinian and Jordanian — within Jordan, opportunities would be created thereby for the Palestinians to find self-expression.

In the case of a solution which would rejoin the West Bank to Jordan or a solution involving a West Bank/Gaza State, there would still arise the property claims of those Palestinians who before 1948 resided in areas that became the State of Israel. These claims have been acknowledged as a serious problem by the international community ever since the adoption by the United Nations of Resolution 194 on this subject in 1948, a resolution which the United Nations has repeatedly reaffirmed and which the United States has supported. A solution will be further complicated by the property claims against Arab States of the many Jews from those states who moved to Israel in its early years after achieving statehood.

In addition to property claims, some believe they should have the option of returning to their original homes under any settlement.

Other Arab leaders, while pressing the importance of Palestinian involvement in a settlement, have taken the position that the definition of Palestinian interests is something for the Palestinian people themselves to sort out, and the view has been expressed by responsible Arab leaders that realization of Palestinian rights need not be inconsistent with the existence of Israel.

No one, therefore, seems in a position today to say exactly what Palestinian objectives are. Even the Palestine Liberation Organization (PLO), which is recognized by the Arab League and the United Nations General Assembly as the representative of the Palestinian people, has been ambivalent. Officially and publicly, its objective is described as a binational secular state, but there are some indications that coexistence between separate Palestinian and Israeli states might be considered.

When there is greater precision about those objectives, there can be clearer understanding about how to relate them to negotiations. There is the aspect of the future of the West Bank and Gaza — how those areas are to be defined and how they are to be governed. There is the aspect of the relationship between Palestinians in the West Bank and Gaza to those Palestinians who are not living in those areas, in the context of a settlement.

What is needed as a first step is a diplomatic process which will help bring forth a reasonable definition of Palestinian interests — a position from which negotiations on a solution of the Palestinian aspects of the problem might begin. The issue is not whether Palestinian interests should be expressed in a final settlement, but how. There will be no peace unless an answer is found.

Another requirement is the development of a framework for negotiations — a statement of the objectives and the terms of reference. The framework for the negotiations that have taken place thus far and the agreements they have produced involving Israel, Syria, and Egypt, has been provided by the United Nations Security Council Resolutions 242 and 338. In accepting that framework, all of the parties to the negotiation have accepted that the objective of the negotiations is peace between them based on mutual recognition, territorial integrity, political independence, the right to live in peace within secure and recognized borders, and the resolution of the specific issues which comprise the Arab-Israeli conflict.

The major problem that must be resolved in establishing a framework for bringing issues of concern to the Palestinians into negotiation, therefore, is to find a common basis for the negotiation that Palestinians and Israelis can both accept. This could be achieved by common acceptance of the above-mentioned Security Council resolutions, although they do not deal with the political aspect of the Palestinian problem.

A particularly difficult aspect of the problem is the question of who negotiates for the Palestinians. It has been our belief that Jordan would be a logical negotiator for the Palestinian related issues. The Rabat Summit, however, recognized the Palestinian Liberation Organization as the "sole legitimate representative of the Palestinian people".

The PLO was formed in 1964, when 400 delegates from Palestinian communities throughout the Arab world met in Jerusalem to create an organization to represent and speak for the Palestinian people. Its leadership was originally middle class and relatively conservative, but by 1969 control had passed into the hands of the Palestinian fedayeen, or commando, movement, that had existed since the mid 1950's but had come into prominence only after the 1967 war. The organization became an umbrella organization for six separate fedayeen groups: Fatah; the Syrian-backed Saiqa; the Popular Democratic Front for the Liberation of Palestine; Popular Front for the Liberation of Palestine; the General Command — a subgroup of the PFLP; and the Iraqi-backed Arab Liberation Front. Affiliated with the PLO are a number of "popular organizations" — labour and professional unions, student groups, women's groups and so on. Fatah, the largest fedayeen group, also has a welfare apparatus to care for widows and orphans of deceased Fatah members.

However, the PLO does not accept the United Nations Security Council resolutions, does not recognize the existence of Israel, and has not stated its readiness to negotiate peace with Israel; Israel does not recognize the PLO or the idea of a separate Palestinian entity. Thus we do not at this point have the framework for a negotiation involving the PLO. We cannot envision or urge a negotiation between two parties as long as one professed to hold the objective of eliminating the other — rather than the objective of negotiating peace with it.

There is one other aspect to this problem. Elements of the PLO have used terrorism to gain attention for their cause. Some Americans as well as many Israelis and others have been killed by Palestinian terrorists. The international community cannot condone such practices, and it seems to us that there must be some assurance if Palestinians are drawn into the negotiating process that these practices will be curbed.

This is the problem which we now face. If the progress toward peace which has now begun is to continue, a solution to this question must be found. We have not devised an American solution, nor would it be appropriate for us to do so. This is the responsibility of the parties and the purpose of the negotiating process. But we have not closed our minds to any reasonable solution which can contribute to progress toward our overriding objective in the Middle East — an Arab-Israeli peace. The step-by-step approach to negotiations which we have pursued has been based partly on the understanding that issues in the Arab-Israeli conflict take time to mature. It is obvious that thinking on the Palestinian aspects of the problem must evolve on all sides. As it does, what is not possible today may become possible.

Our consultations on how to move the peace negotiations forward will recognize the need to deal with this subject. As Secretary Kissinger has said, "We are prepared to work with all the parties toward a solution of all the issues yet remaining — including the issue of the future of the Palestinians." We will do so because the issues of concern to the Palestinians are important in themselves and because the Arab governments participating in the negotiations have made clear that progress in the overall negotiations will depend in part on progress on issues of concern to the Palestinians. We are prepared to consider any reasonable proposal from any quarter, and we will expect other parties to the negotiation to be equally open minded.

## 5.   "Toward Peace in the Middle East," Brookings Institution Report, December 1975

*The Brookings Report, endorsed by Presidential candidate Jimmy Carter among others, was drafted by a distinguished panel of diplomats and academicians, several of whom later became associated with the Carter administration.*

### Summary
The study group reached five main conclusions.

1.   *U.S. interests.* The United States has a strong moral, political, and economic interest in a stable peace in the Middle East. It is concerned for the security, independence, and well-being of Israel and the Arab states of the area and for the friendship of both. Renewed hostilities would have far-reaching and perilous consequences which would threaten those interests.

2.   *Urgency.* Whatever the merits of the interim agreement on Sinai, it still leaves the basic elements of the Arab-Israeli dispute substantially untouched. Unless these elements are soon addressed, rising tensions in the area will generate increased risk of violence. We believe that the best way to address these issues is by the pursuit of a comprehensive settlement.

3. *Process.* We believe that the time has come to begin the process of negotiating such a settlement among the parties, either at a general conference or at more informal multilateral meetings. While no useful interim step toward settlement should be overlooked or ignored, none seems promising at the present time and most have inherent disadvantages.

4. *Settlement.* A fair and enduring settlement should contain at least these elements as an integrated package:

(a) *Security.* All parties to the settlement commit themselves to respect the sovereignty and territorial integrity of the others and to refrain from the threat or use of force against them.

(b) *Stages.* Withdrawal to agreed boundaries and the establishment of peaceful relations carried out in stages over a period of years, each stage being undertaken only when the agreed provisions of the previous stage have been faithfully implemented.

(c) *Peaceful relations.* The Arab parties undertake not only to end such hostile actions against Israel as armed incursions, blockades, boycotts, and propaganda attacks, but also to give evidence of progress toward the development of normal international and regional political and economic relations.

(d) *Boundaries.* Israel undertakes to withdraw by agreed stages to the June 5, 1967, lines with only such modifications as are mutually accepted. Boundaries will probably need to be safeguarded by demilitarized zones supervised by UN forces.

(e) *Palestine.* There should be provision for Palestinian self-determination, subject to Palestinian acceptance of the sovereignty and integrity of Israel within agreed boundaries. This might take the form either of an independent Palestine state accepting the obligations and commitments of the peace agreements or of a Palestine entity voluntarily federated with Jordan but exercising extensive political autonomy.

(f) *Jerusalem.* The report suggests no specific solution for the particularly difficult problem of Jerusalem but recommends that, whatever the solution may be, it meet as a minimum the following criteria:

— there should be unimpeded access to all of the holy places and each should be under the custodianship of its own faith;

— there should be no barrier dividing the city which would prevent free circulation throughout it; and

— each national group within the city should, if it so desires, have substantial political autonomy within the area where it predominates.

(g) *Guarantees.* It would be desirable that the UN Security Council endorse the peace agreements and take whatever other actions to support them the agreements provide. In addition, there may well be need for unilateral or multilateral guarantees to some or all of the parties, substantial economic aid, and military assistance pending the adoption of agreed arms control measures.

5. *U.S. role.* The governments directly concerned bear the responsibility of negotiation and agreement, but they are unlikely to be able to reach agreement alone. Initiative, impetus, and inducement may well have to come from outside. The United States, because it enjoys a measure of confidence of parties on both sides and has the means to assist them economically and militarily, remains the great power best fitted to work actively with them in bringing about a settlement. Over and above helping to provide a framework for negotiation and submitting concrete proposals from time to time, the United States must be prepared to take other constructive steps, such as offering aid and providing guarantees where desired and needed. In all of this, the United States should work with the USSR to the degree that Soviet willingness to play a constructive role will permit.

## 6. Ambassador William W. Scranton, Statements on Occupied Territories, 23 March, 1976, [Excerpts]

*Address before the U.N. Security Council*

The occupation of territories in the 1967 war has always been seen by the world community to be an abnormal state of affairs that would be brought to an end as part of a peace settlement. Resolution 242, adopted by the Council shortly after the end of the 1967 war that led to the occupation, established the basic bargain that would constitute a settlement. This bargain was withdrawal of Israeli forces in return for termination of all claims or states of belligerency and respect for and acknowledgment of the sovereignty, territorial integrity, and political independence of every state in the area and their right to live in peace within secure and recognized boundaries free from threats or acts of force.

My government has committed itself to do all it can to bring about this settlement and, in the words of Resolution 338, to implement Council Resolution 242 in all of its parts and to further negotiations between the parties concerned under appropriate auspices aimed at establishing a just and durable peace in the Middle East, which is what we are here for. We are engaged at this moment in an effort to regain momentum, as all of you know, in the negotiating process that has brought some unusual progress — and it must bring more.

The second focus of our consideration must be the conduct of the occupation itself. In asking for this meeting, the letter of complaint circulated by the Permanent Representatives of the Libyan Arab Republic and of Pakistan identifes three issues:

— The administration of the holy sites;
— The situation in Jerusalem; and

— Israeli actions in regard to the civilian population of the occupied territories and the Israeli settlements in the occupied territories.

The position of the United States on these issues is clear and of long standing. I propose to review the U.S. position today once more to point out that there are proper principles and there are procedures under international law and practice which, when applied and maintained, will contribute to civil order and will, over the longer run, facilitate a just and a lasting peace.

First, there is a matter of the holy sites and practice of religion in the occupied areas. The deep religious attachment of Moslems and Jews and Christians to the holy places of Jerusalem has added a uniquely volatile element to the tensions that inhere in an occupation situation. The area known to Moslems as the Haram as-Sharif and to Jews as the Temple Mount is of particular sensitivity. Israel's punctilious administration of the holy places in Jerusalem has, in our judgment, greatly minimized the tensions. To my government, the standard to be followed in administering the holy sites is contained in article 27 of the Fourth Geneva Convention Relative to the Protection of Civilian Persons in Time of War. All parties to the Arab-Israeli conflict are signatories of the convention. Article 27 of the convention prescribes, inter alia, that:

"Protected persons are entitled, in all circumstances, to respect for their persons, their honour, their family rights, their religious convictions and practices, and their manners and customs."

With regard to the immediate problem before us — a ruling by a lower Israeli court which would have the effect of altering the status of the Haram — it is our view that Israel's responsibilities under article 27 to preserve religious practices as they were at the time the occupation began cannot be changed by the ruling of an Israeli court. We are gratified, deeply gratified, that the Supreme Court of Israel has upheld the Israeli Government's position.

The status of the holy places is, of course, only one facet, however important, very important, of the problem of the status of Jerusalem itself. The U.S. position on the status of Jerusalem has been stated here on numerous occasions since the Arab portion of that city was occupied by Israel in 1967.

Ambassador Yost said in 1969:

"... the part of Jerusalem that came under the control of Israel in the June war, like other areas occupied by Israel, is occupied territory and hence subject to the provisions of international law governing the rights and obligations of an occupying power."

Ambassador Goldberg said in 1968, to this Council:

"The United States does not accept or recognize unilateral actions by any states in the area as altering the status of Jerusalem."

I emphasize, as did Ambassador Goldberg, that as far as the United States is concerned such unilateral measures, including expropriation of land or other administrative action taken by the Government of Israel, cannot be considered other than interim and provisional and cannot affect the present international status nor prejudge the final and permanent status of Jerusalem. The U.S. position could not be clearer. Since 1967 we have restated here, in other forums, and to the Government of Israel that the future of Jerusalem will be determined only through the instruments and processes of negotiation, agreement, and accommodation. Unilateral attempts to predetermine that future have no standing.

Next I turn to the question of Israeli settlements in the occupied territories. Again, my government believes that international law sets the appropriate standards. An occupier must maintain the occupied area as intact and unaltered as possible, without interfering with the customary life of the area, and any changes must be necessitated by the immediate needs of the occupation and be consistent with international law. The Fourth Geneva Convention speaks directly to the issue of population transfer in article 49:

"The Occupying Power shall not deport or transfer parts of its own civilian population into the territory it occupies."

Clearly, then, substantial resettlement of the Israeli civilian population in occupied territories, including East Jerusalem, is illegal under the convention and cannot be considered to have prejudged the outcome of future negotiations between the parties on the location of the borders of states of the Middle East. Indeed, the presence of these settlements is seen by my government as an obstacle to the success of the negotiations for a just and final peace between Israel and its neighbors.

## 7. President Jimmy Carter, on Middle East Peace, Town Meeting, Clinton, Mass., 16 March, 1977

I think all of you know that there has been either war or potential war in the Middle East for the last 29 years, ever since Israel became a nation. I think one of the finest acts of the world nations that's ever occurred was to establish the State of Israel.

So, the first prerequisite of a lasting peace is the recognition of Israel by her neighbors, Israel's right to exist, Israel's right to exist permanently, Israel's right to exist in peace. That means that over a period of months or years that the borders between Israel and Syria, Israel and Lebanon, Israel and Jordan, Israel and Egypt must be opened up to travel, to tourism, to cultural exchange, to trade, so that no matter who the leaders might be in those countries, the people themselves will have formed a mutual understanding and comprehension and a sense of a common purpose to avoid the repetitious wars and death that have afflicted that region so long. That's the first prerequisite of peace.

The second one is very important and very, very difficult; and that is, the establishment of permanent borders for Israel. The Arab countries say that Israel must withdraw to the pre-1967 borderlines, Israel says that they must adjust those lines to some degree to insure their own security. That is a matter to be negotiated between the Arab countries on the one side and Israel on the other.

But borders are still a matter of great trouble and a matter of great difficulty, and there are strong differences of opinion now.

And the third ultimate requirement for peace is to deal with the Palestinian problem. The Palestinians claim up to this day this moment that Israel has no right to be there, that the land belongs to the Palestinians, and they've never yet given up their publicly professed commitment to destroy Israel. That has to be overcome.

There has to be a homeland provided for the Palestinian refugees who have suffered for many, many years. And the exact way to solve the Palestinian problem is one that first of all addresses itself right now to the Arab countries and then, secondly, to the Arab countries negotiating with Israel.

Those three major elements have got to be solved before a Middle Eastern solution can be prescribed.

I want to emphasize one more time, we offer our good offices. I think it's accurate to say that of all the nations in the world, we are the one that's most trusted, not completely, but most trusted by the Arab countries and also Israel. I guess both sides have some doubt about us. But we'll have to act as kind of a catalyst to being about their ability to negotiate successfully with one another.

We hope that later on this year, in the latter part of this year, that we might get all of these parties to agree to come together at Geneva, to start talking to one another. They haven't done that yet. And I believe if we can get them to sit down and start talking and negotiating that we have an excellent chance to achieve peace. I can't guarantee that. It's a hope.

I hope that we will all pray that that will come to pass, because what happens in the Middle East in the future might very well cause a major war there which would quickly spread to all the other nations of the world; very possibly it could do that.

Many countries depend completely on oil from the Middle East for their life. We don't. If all oil was cut off to us from the Middle East, we could survive; but Japan imports more than 98 percent of all its energy, and other countries, like in Europe — Germany, Italy, France are also heavily dependent on oil from the Middle East.

So, this is such a crucial area of the world that I will be devoting a major part of my own time on foreign policy between now and next fall trying to provide for a forum within which they can discuss their problems and, hopefully, let them seek out among themselves some permanent solution.

## 8. President Carter, Statement on Recognition of Palestinians, Aswan, Egypt, 4 January, 1978

It is an honor and a pleasure for us to be in this great country, led by such a strong and courageous man.

Mr. President, your bold initiative in seeking peace has aroused the admiration of the entire world. One of my most valued possessions is the warm, personal relationship which binds me and President Sadat together and which exemplifies the friendship and the common purpose of the people of Egypt and the people of the United States of America.

The Egyptian-Israeli peace initiative must succeed, while still guarding the sacred and historic principles held by the nations who have suffered so much in this region. There is no good reason why accommodation cannot be reached.

In my own private discussions with both Arab and Israeli leaders, I have been deeply impressed by the unanimous desire for peace. My presence here today is a direct result of the courageous initiative which President Sadat undertook in his recent trip to Jerusalem.

The negotiating process will continue in the near future. We fully support this effort, and we intend to play an active role in the work of the Political Committee of Cairo, which will soon reconvene in Jerusalem.

We believe that there are certain principles, fundamentally, which must be observed before a just and a comprehensive peace can be achieved.

* First, true peace must be based on normal relations among the parties to the peace. Peace means more than just an end to belligerency.

* Second, there must be withdrawal by Israel from territories occupied in 1967 and agreement on secure and recognized borders for all parties in the context of normal and peaceful relations in accordance with U.N. Resolutions 242 and 338.

* Third, there must be a resolution of the Palestinian problem in all its aspects. The problem must recognize the legitimate rights of the Palestinian people and enable the Palestinians to participate in the determination of their own future.

Some flexibility is always needed to insure successful negotiations and the resolution of conflicting views. We know that the mark of greatness among leaders is to consider carefully the views of others and the greater benefits that can result among the people of all nations which can come from a successful search for peace.

Mr. President, our consultations this morning have reconfirmed our common commitment to the fundamentals which will, with God's help, make 1978 the year for permanent peace in the Middle East.

## 9. The Reagan Peace Plan — U.S. Involvement in Mideast Peace Effort, 'A Moral Imperative'. President Ronald Reagan, 1 September, 1982

*Following is the full text of the President's address:*

Today has been a day that should make all of us proud. It marked the end of the successful evacuation of the PLO from Beirut, Lebanon. This peaceful step could never have been taken without the good offices of the United States and, especially, the truly heroic work of a great American diplomat, Philip Habib. Thanks to his efforts, I am happy to announce that the U.S. Marine contingent helping to supervise the evacuation has accomplished its mission.

Our young men should be out of Lebanon within two weeks. They, too, have served the cause of peace with distinction and we can all be very proud of them.

But the situation in Lebanon is only part of the overall problem of the conflict in the Middle East. So, over the past weeks, while events in Beirut dominated the front page, America was engaged in a quiet behind-the-scenes effort to lay the groundwork for a broader peace in the region. For once, there were no premature leaks as U.S. diplomatic missions travelled to mid-East capitals and I met here at home with a wide range of experts to map out an American peace initiative for the long-suffering peoples of the Middle East, Arab and Israeli alike.

It seemed to me that, with the agreement in Lebanon, we had an opportunity for a more far-reaching peace effort in the region — and I was determined to seize that moment. In the words of the Scripture, the time had come to "follow after the things which make for peace."

Tonight, I want to report to you on the steps we have taken, and the prospects they can open up for a just and lasting peace in the Middle East.

America has long been committed to bringing peace to this troubled region. For more than a generation, successive U.S. Administrations have endeavored to develop a fair and workable process that could lead to a true and lasting Arab-Israeli peace. Our involvement in the search for mid-East peace is not a matter of preference, it is a moral imperative. The strategic importance of the region to the U.S. is well known.

But our policy is motivated by more than strategic interests. We also have an irreversible commitment to the survival and territorial integrity of friendly states. Nor can we ignore the fact that the well-being of much of the world's economy is tied to stability in the strife-torn Middle East. Finally, our traditional humanitarian concerns dictate a continuing effort to peacefully resolve conflicts.

When our Administration assumed office in January 1981, I decided that the general framework for our Middle East policy should follow the broad guidelines laid down by my predecessors.

There were two basic issues we had to address. First, there was the strategic threat to the region posed by the Soviet Union and its surrogates, best demonstrated by the brutal war in Afghanistan; and, second, the peace process between Israel and its Arab neighbors. With regard to the Soviet threat, we have strengthened our efforts to develop with our friends and allies a joint policy to deter the Soviets and their surrogates from further expansion in the region, and, if necessary, to defend against it. With respect to the Arab-Israeli conflict, we have embraced the Camp David framework as the only way to proceed. We have also recognized, however, that solving the Arab-Israeli conflict, in and of itself, cannot assure peace throughout a region as vast and troubled as the Middle East.

Our first objective under the Camp David process was to ensure the successful fulfillment of the Egyptian-Israeli peace treaty. This was achieved with the peaceful return of the Sinai to Egypt in April 1982. To accomplish this, we worked hard with our Egyptian and Israeli friends, and eventually with other friendly countries, to create the multinational force which now operates in the Sinai.

Throughout this period of difficult and time-consuming negotiations, we never lost sight of the next step of Camp David: autonomy talks to pave the way for permitting the Palestinian people to exercise their legitimate rights. However, owing to the tragic assassination of President Sadat and other crises in the area, it was not until January 1982 that we were able to make a major effort to renew these talks. Secretary of State Haig and Ambassador Fairbanks made three visits to Israel and Egypt this year to pursue the autonomy talks. Considerable progress was made in developing the basic outline of an American approach which was to be presented to Egypt and Israel after April.

The successful completion of Israel's withdrawal from Sinai and the courage shown on this occasion by Prime Minister Begin and President Mubarak in living up to their agreements convinced me the time had come for a new American policy to try to bridge the remaining differences between Egypt and Israel on the autonomy process. So, in May, I called for specific measures and a timetable for consultations with the governments of Egypt and Israel on the next steps in the peace process. However, before this effort could be launched, the conflict in Lebanon preempted our efforts. The autonomy talks were basically put on hold while we sought to untangle the parties in Lebanon and still the guns of war.

The Lebanon war, tragic as it was, has left us with a new opportunity for

Middle East peace. We must seize it now and bring peace to this troubled area so vital to world stability while there is still time. It was with this strong conviction that over a month ago, before the present negotiations in Beirut had been completed, I directed Secretary of State Shultz to again review our policy and to consult a wide range of outstanding Americans on the best ways to strengthen chances for peace in the Middle East. We have consulted with many of the officials who were historically involved in the process, with members of the Congress, and with individuals from the private sector, and I have held extensive consultations with my own advisors on the principles I will outline to you tonight.

The evacuation of the PLO from Beirut is now complete. And we can now help the Lebanese to rebuild their war-torn country. We owe it to ourselves, and to posterity, to move quickly to build upon this achievement. A stable and revived Lebanon is essential to all our hopes for peace in the region. The people of Lebanon deserve the best efforts of the international community to turn the nightmares of the past several years into a new dawn of hope.

But the opportunities for peace in the Middle East do not begin and end in Lebanon. As we help Lebanon rebuild, we must also move to resolve the root causes of conflict between Arabs and Israelis.

The war in Lebanon has demonstrated many things, but two consequences are key to the peace process:

First, the military losses of the PLO have not diminished the yearning of the Palestinian people for a just solution of their claims; and second, while Israel's military successes in Lebanon have demonstrated that its armed forces are second to none in the region, they alone cannot bring just and lasting peace to Israel and her neighbors.

The question now is how to reconcile Israel's legitimate security concerns with the legitimate rights of the Palestinians. And that answer can only come at the negotiating table. Each party must recognize that the outcome must be acceptable to all and that true peace will require compromises by all.

So, tonight, I am calling for a fresh start. This is the moment for all those directly concerned to get involved — or lend their support — to a workable basis for peace. The Camp David Agreement remains the foundation of our policy. Its language provides all parties with the leeway they need for successful negotiations.

I call on Israel to make clear that the security for which she yearns can only be achieved through genuine peace, a peace requiring magnanimity, vision and courage.

I call on the Palestinian people to recognize that their own political aspirations are inextricably bound to recognition of Israel's right to a secure future.

And I call on the Arab States to accept the reality of Israel — and the reality that peace and justice can be gained only through hard, fair, direct negotiations.

In making these calls upon others, I recognize that the United States has a special responsibility. No other nation is in a position to deal with the key parties to the conflict on the basis of trust and reliability.

The time has come for a new realism on the part of all the peoples of the Middle East. The state of Israel is an accomplished fact; it deserves unchallenged legitimacy within the community of nations. But Israel's legitimacy has thus far been recognized by too few countries, and has been denied by every Arab State except Egypt. Israel exists; it has a right to exist in peace behind secure and defensible borders, and it has a right to demand of its neighbors that they recognize those facts.

I have personally followed and supported Israel's heroic struggle for survival ever since the founding of the state of Israel 34 years ago. In the pre-1967 borders, Israel was barely 10 miles wide at its narrowest point. The bulk of Israel's population lived within artillery range of hostile Arab armies. I am not about to ask Israel to live that way again.

The war in Lebanon has demonstrated another reality in the region. The departure of the Palestinians from Beirut dramatizes more than ever the homelessness of the Palestinian people. Palestinians feel strongly that their cause is more than a question of refugees. I agree. The Camp David Agreement recognized that fact when it spoke of the legitimate rights of the Palestinian people and their just requirements. For peace to endure, it must involve all those who have been most deeply affected by the conflict. Only through broader participation in the peace process — most immediately by Jordan and by the Palestinians — will Israel be able to rest confident in the knowledge that its security and integrity will be respected by its neighbors. Only through the process of negotiation can all the nations of the Middle East achieve a secure peace.

These then are our general goals. What are the specific new American positions, and why are we taking them?

In the Camp David talks thus far, both Israel and Egypt have felt free to express openly their views as to what the outcome should be. Understandably, their views have differed on many points.

The United States has thus far sought to play the role of mediator; we have avoided public comment on the key issues. We have always recognized — and continue to recognize — that only the voluntary agreement of those parties most directly involved in the conflict can provide an enduring solution. But it has become evident to me that some clearer sense of America's position on the key issues is necessary to encourage wider support for the peace process.

First, as outlined in the Camp David accords, there must be a period of time during which the Palestinian inhabitants of the West Bank and Gaza will have full autonomy over their own affairs. Due consideration must be given to the principle of self-government by the inhabitants of the territories and to the legitimate security concerns of the parties involved.

The purpose of the five-year period of transition which would begin after free elections for a self-governing Palestinian authority is to prove to the Palestinians that they can run their own affairs, and that such Palestinian autonomy poses no threat to Israel's security.

The United States will not support the use of any additional land for the purpose of settlements during the transition period. Indeed, the immediate adoption of a settlement freeze by Israel, more than any other action, could create the confidence needed for wider participation in these talks. Further settlement activity is in no way necessary for the security of Israel and only diminishes the confidence of the Arabs that a final outcome can be freely and fairly negotiated.

I want to make the American position clearly understood: the purpose of this transition period is the peaceful and orderly transfer of domestic authority from Israel to the Palestinian inhabitants of the West Bank and Gaza. At the same time, such a transfer must not interfere with Israel's security requirements.

Beyond the transition period, as we look to the future of the West Bank and Gaza, it is clear to me that peace cannot be achieved by the formation of an independent Palestinian State in those territories. Nor is it achievable on the basis of Israeli sovereignty or permanent control over the West Bank and Gaza.

So the United States will not support the establishment of an independent Palestinian State in the West Bank and Gaza, and we will not support annexation or permanent control by Israel.

There is, however, another way to peace. The final status of these lands must, of course, be reached through the give-and-take of negotiations. But it is the firm view of the United States that self-government by the Palestinians of the West Bank and Gaza in association with Jordan offers the best chance for a durable, just and lasting peace.

We base our approach squarely on the principle that the Arab-Israeli conflict should be resolved through negotiations involving an exchange of territory for peace. This exchange is enshrined in United Nations Security Council Resolution 242, which is, in turn, incorporated in all its parts in the Camp David Agreements. U.N. Resolution 242 remains wholly valid as the foundation stone of America's Middle East peace effort.

It is the United States' position that — in return for peace — the withdrawal provision of Resolution 242 applies to all fronts, including the West Bank and Gaza.

When the border is negotiated between Jordan and Israel, our view on the extent to which Israel should be asked to give up territory will be heavily affected by the extent of true peace and normalization and the security arrangements offered in return.

Finally, we remain convinced that Jerusalem must remain undivided, but its final status should be decided through negotiations.

In the course of the negotiations to come, the United States will support positions that seem to us fair and reasonable compromises, and likely to promote a sound agreement. We will also put forward our own detailed proposals when we believe they can be helpful. And, make no mistake, the United States will oppose any proposal — from any party and at any point in the negotiating process — that threatens the security of Israel. America's commitment to the security of Israel is iron-clad. And I might add, so is mine.

During the past few days, our ambassadors in Israel, Egypt, Jordan, and Saudi Arabia have presented to their host governments the proposals in full detail that I have outlined here tonight.

I am convinced that these proposals can bring justice, bring security, and bring durability to an Arab-Israeli peace.

The United States will stand by these principles with total dedication. They are fully consistent with Israel's security requirements and the aspirations of the Palestinians. We will work hard to broaden participation at the peace table as envisaged by the Camp David accords. And I fervently hope that the Palestinians and Jordan, with the support of their Arab colleagues, will accept this opportunity.

Tragic turmoil in the Middle East runs back to the dawn of history. In our modern day, conflict after conflict has taken its brutal toll there. In an age of nuclear challenge and economic interdependence, such conflicts are a threat to all the people of the world, not just the Middle East itself. It is time for us all — in the Middle East and around the world — to call a halt to conflict, hatred and prejudice; it is time for us all to launch a common effort for reconstruction, peace and progress.

It has often been said — and regrettably too often been true — that the story of the search for peace and justice in the Middle East is a tragedy of opportunities missed.

In the aftermath of the settlement in Lebanon we now face an opportunity for a broader peace. This time we must not let it slip from our grasp. We must look beyond the difficulties and obstacles of the present and move with fairness and resolve toward a brighter future. We owe it to ourselves — and to posterity — to do no less. For if we miss this chance to make a fresh start, we may look back on this moment from some later vantage point and realize how much that failure cost us all.

These, then, are the principles upon which American policy towards the Arab-Israeli conflict will be based. I have made a personal commitment to see that they endure and, God willing, that they will come to be seen by all reasonable, compassionate people as fair, achievable, and in the interests of all who wish to see peace in the Middle East.

Tonight, on the eve of what can be a dawning of new hope for the people of the troubled Middle East — and for all the world's people who dream of a just and peaceful future — I ask you, my fellow Americans, for your support and your prayers in this great undertaking.

## 10. Text of 'Talking Points' Sent to Prime Minister Begin by President Reagan. Washington D.C., 8 September, 1982

*Following is the text of what U.S. Administration officials called 'talking points' accompanying a letter sent by President Reagan to Prime Minister Menachem Begin of Israel. The same points were presented to Arab governments as a prelude to Mr. Reagan's peace proposals.*

### General Principles

A.   We will maintain our commitment to Camp David.

B.   We will maintain our commitment to the conditions we require for recognition of and negotiation with the P.L.O.

C.   We can offer guarantees on the position we will adopt in negotiations. We will not be able, however, to guarantee in advance the results of these negotiations.

### Transitional Measures

A.   Our position is that the objective of the transitional period is the peaceful and orderly transfer of authority from Israel to the Palestinian inhabitants.

B.   We will support:

*   The decision of full autonomy as giving the Palestinian inhabitants real authority over themselves, the land and its resources, subject to fair safeguards on water.

*   Economic, commercial, social and cultural ties between the West Bank, Gaza and Jordan.

*   Participation by the Palestinian inhabitants of East Jerusalem in the election of the West Bank—Gaza authority.

*   Real settlement freeze.

*   Progressive Palestinian responsibility for internal security based on capability and performance.

C.   We will oppose:

*   Dismantlement of the existing settlements.

*   Provisions which represent a legitimate threat to Israel's security,

reasonably defined.

* Isolation of the West Bank and Gaza from Israel.

* Measures which accord either the Palestinians or the Israelis generally recognized sovereign rights with the exception of external security, which must remain in Israel's hands during the transitional period.

## Final Status Issues

A.   U.N.S.C. Resolution 242.

It is our position that Resolution 242 applies to the West Bank and Gaza and requires Israeli withdrawal in return for peace. Negotiations must determine the borders. The U.S. position in these negotiations on the extent of the withdrawal will be significantly influenced by the extent and nature of the peace and security arrangements offered in return.

B.   Israeli Sovereignty.

It is our belief that the Palestinian problem cannot be resolved (through) Israeli sovereignty or control over the West Bank and Gaza. Accordingly, we will not support such a solution.

C.   Palestinian State.

The preference we will pursue in the final status negotiation is association of the West Bank and Gaza with Jordan. We will not support the formation of a Palestinian State in those negotiations. There is no foundation of political support in Israel or the United States for such a solution. The outcome, however, must be determined by negotiations.

D.   Self-Determination.

In the Middle East context the term self-determination has been identified exclusively with the formation of a Palestinian State. We will not support this definition of self-determination. We believe that the Palestinians must take the leading role in determining their own future and fully support the provision in Camp David providing for the elected representatives of the inhabitants of the West Bank and Gaza to decide how they shall govern themselves consistent with the provision of their agreement in the final status negotiations.

E.   Jerusalem.

We will fully support the position that the status of Jerusalem must be determined through negotiations.

F.   Settlements.

The status of Israeli settlements must be determined in the course of the final status negotiations. We will not support their continuation as extraterritorial outposts.

## Additional Talking Points

1.   Approach to Hussein.

The President has approached Hussein to determine the extent to which he may be interested in participating.

*    King Hussein has received the same US positions as you.
*    Hussein considers our proposals serious and gives them serious attention.
*    Hussein understands that Camp David is the only base that we will accept for
negotiations.
*    We are also discussing these proposals with the Saudis.

2.   Public Commitment.

Whatever the support from these or other Arab States, this is what the President
has concluded must be done.

The President is convinced his positions are fair and balanced and fully protective
of Israel's security. Beyond that they offer the practical opportunity of eventually
achieving the peace treaties Israel must have with its neighbors.

He will be making a speech announcing these positions, probably within a week.

3.   Next Procedural Steps

Should the response to the President's proposal be positive, the US would take
immediate steps to relaunch the autonomy negotiations with the broadest possible
participation as envisaged under the Camp David agreements.

We also contemplate an early visit by Secretary Shultz in the area.

Should there not be a positive response, the President, as he has said in his letter to
you, will nonetheless stand by his position with proper dedication.


## 11.   Statement by President Ronald Reagan on the Establishment of New Israeli Settlements, 27 August, 1983 [Excerpts]

*The following are excerpts from President Reagan's radio address to the nation,
broadcast from Rancho del Cielo.*

The Middle East peace initiative which we announced almost a year ago is
definitely alive and available to those parties willing to sit down together and talk
peace. We remain committed to the positions we set forth, and we stand ready to
pursue them in the context of the Camp David Accords. Those positions are in the
best long-term interests of all parties. Most importantly, they're the only realistic
basis for a solution that has thus far been presented.

The United States continues to support UN Security Council Resolutions 338 and
242.

The establishment of new Israeli settlements in the occupied territories is an
obstacle to peace, and we're concerned over the negative effect that this activity has on
Arab confidence in Israel's willingness to return territory in exchange for security and
a freely and fairly negotiated peace treaty.

The future of these settlements can only be dealt with through direct negotiations between the parties to the conflict. The sooner these negotiations begin, the greater the chance for a solution.

This Administration, like those before it, is firmly committed to the security of the State of Israel. We will help Israel defend itself against external aggression. At the same time, the United States believes, as it has always believed, that permanent security for the people of Israel and all the peoples of the region can only come with the achievement of a just and lasting peace, not by sole reliance on increasingly expensive military forces.

Unfortunately, the opportunities afforded by our initiative have yet to be grasped by the parties involved. We know the issues are complex, the risks for all concerned high, and much courageous statesmanship will be required. Nevertheless, those complex issues can be resolved by creative and persistent diplomacy. Those risks can be overcome by people who want to end this bitter and tragic conflict. And in the process, the United States will be a full partner, doing everything we can to help create a just and lasting peace.

## 12. US Policy on an International Middle East Peace Conference, 13 January, 1984

*The following is a letter from the US Ambassador to the United Nations Ms. Jeane Kirkpatrick to the President of the UN Security Council Mr. Tinoco Fonseca, 13 January, 1984.*

My government has considered carefully the letter of 5 January that the Secretary-General addressed to you on the question of convening an International Peace Conference on the Middle East. The Secretary-General seeks the agreement of the members of the Security Council on the course of action which he proposes for organizing such a conference.

As you know, the United States voted against General Assembly Resolution 38/58 C which endorsed the holding of this conference. We had earlier opposed the International Conference on the Question of Palestine held in Geneva last summer, from which the idea of a Middle East peace conference originated.

The United States believes firmly that the only path to peace in the Middle East lies in a process of negotiations among the parties based on Security Council Resolutions 242 and 338, a process that the United States has sought vigorously and consistently to encourage, particularly in the Camp David Accords and in President Reagan's initiative of 1 September, 1982. Holding an international conference as recommended by the General Assembly would only hinder this process. It would predictably become a forum for propagandistic and extreme positions, and in the context proposed by the General Assembly and further articulated by the Secretary-General it would very likely yield a one-sided outcome not acceptable to one or more of the parties and therefore inoperable. The net result would be to diminish the prestige of the United Nations as the sponsor of the conference and delay the day when peace will come to the troubled Middle East.

The United States will continue to focus its energies on the task of promoting face-to-face negotiations among the parties directly concerned with the Arab-Israeli dispute. We remain hopeful that this course will bring a just and lasting settlement in the region at the earliest possible time.

You are authorized to inform the Secretary-General of the above views of my Government. The United States considers the recommendation of a Middle East Peace Conference in General Assembly Resolution 38/58 C to be ill-considered and harmful. We would regret any decision using the authority of the United Nations for this purpose, or the use of United Nations personnel and financial resources. The United States has no intention of participating in such a conference or in any preparatory activities for it.

## 13.    Statement by State Department Spokesman Bernard Kalb on the Legitimate Rights of the Palestinian People, 15 February, 1985

There is no contradiction between Resolution 242 and the legitimate rights of the Palestinian people. They deal with different issues and are in fact complementary.

Resolution 242 established territory-for-peace as the internationally accepted formula for resolving the situation arising from the hostilities in 1967. In our view, clear acceptance of Resolution 242 as the basis of Middle East peace negotiations is a necessary prerequisite for the participation of any party in those negotiations.

As a separate but related matter, negotiations regarding the final status of the West Bank and Gaza, in addition to resolving the location of the boundaries and the nature of the security arrangements, must also recognize the legitimate rights of the Palestinian people. The full manner in which those rights will be exercised will become clear as the process of negotiations proceeds. In our view, there should be Palestinian participation at every stage of the negotiating process. In addition, any agreement on the final status of the West Bank and Gaza should receive the prior consent of the inhabitants of those territories.

## 14. Statement by Secretary of State George Shultz on Jordan and the Peace Process, Washington, DC, 19 June, 1985 [Excerpts]

*The following is a statement by Secretary Schultz before the Senate Foreign Relations Committee.*

### Jordan and the Peace Process

...There is a new momentum in the peace process in recent months—a momentum due largely to King Hussein.

Jordan has been actively preparing the Arabs to engage in a process leading to a comprehensive peace. Last fall, Jordan reestablished diplomatic relations with Egypt, thereby reducing Egypt's isolation, underscoring once again Jordan's moderate role and reinforcing the principle that no state should be ostracized or penalized for making peace. This strengthened the Arab moderates. At about the same time, Israeli Prime Minister Peres announced his willingness to enter into negotiations with Jordan without preconditions. Last November, Jordan hosted a Palestine National Council session in Amman—in defiance of Syrian opposition. At that session, King Hussein publicly challenged the PLO [Palestine Liberation Organization] to accept UN Security Council Resolution 242, to abandon the call for an independent Palestinian state, and to embark with Jordan on a path of peace negotiations.

The King's agreement with the PLO on February 11 was a step toward organizing a Jordanian-Palestinian delegation for negotiations with Israel. President Mubarak of Egypt also suggested ways to advance the process. On his visit to Washington, the King gave proof that he is seeking to build on the momentum he has done so much to create.

\* He categorically stated his own desire, and that of his Palestinian partners, for a "peaceful settlement." The Palestinians, he said, "are willing to accept the United Nations Security Council Resolutions 242 and 338 and the principles they contain as the basis for a settlement."

\* He left no doubt that he meant "negotiations amongst the parties to the conflict, in other words, negotiations between the Arab side, in this case a Jordanian-Palestinian delegation, with Israel on the other side," in a supportive international context.

\* He said that the Palestinians are turning away from their previous policies: "The relative futility of armed struggle," he said, "and the burdens of continuing military occupation, suffering and destruction have increased the desire for a peaceful alternative." The King spoke of "proceeding in a non-belligerent environment."

\* He stated that the PLO had accepted the goal of a "Jordanian-Palestinian confederation," which we interpret to mean that the PLO has given up on an independent Palestinian state.

\* He affirmed his desire to move toward peace talks *now*: "this year."

President Reagan, for his part, repeated America's commitment to an active role in the search for peace. He expressed admiration for all that Jordan had done to advance the process. The President acknowledged that Jordan has real economic and security needs. He confirmed that the King can count on the United States for assistance in addressing problems Jordan may face in those areas.

Another important recent step in the peace process has been Prime Minister Peres' speech to the Knesset on June 10, in which he outlined a five-stage plan for direct peace negotiations. The Prime Minister called for:

    * Continued talks between the United States, Israel, Jordan, Egypt, and non-PLO Palestinians;

    * Setting up a small Israeli-Jordanian-Palestinian team to prepare the agenda for an Israeli-Jordanian-Palestinian summit, with US participation;

    * Recruiting the support of the permanent members of the UN Security Council for direct negotiations, without asking them to support in advance the position of one of the sides;

    * Appointing Palestinians from the West Bank and Gaza who will represent the inhabitants of the occupied territories and be acceptable to all parties; and

    * Convening an opening conference within 3 months in the United States, Western Europe, or the Middle East.

We welcome these ideas as a reaffirmation of Israel's wish to negotiate. We will be discussing these ideas with both parties to construct a mutually acceptable approach to negotiations. We have stayed in very close touch with Israel: their officials have come here, our officials have gone there, and we have been in close touch through regular channels. Assistant Secretary [for Near Eastern and South Asian Affairs] Richard Murphy will soon travel to the area again to maintain these contacts and consultations.

Our other peace partner, Egypt, remains vital to progress. Israel sees better relations with Egypt as a key to improving the atmosphere for a negotiating process with Jordan. In May, Egypt and Israel began discussions on a variety of bilateral issues, including the Taba dispute, aspects of normalization, and the return to Israel of the Egyptian Ambassador. The atmosphere at the talks has been positive and constructive, and substantial progress has been made. We believe that Israel and Egypt are making a genuine effort to get their bilateral relationship back on track, and we intend to help them as appropriate.

We are anxious that the present opportunity not slip away, as has so often happened before, with such tragic consequences. But tough problems remain, and we have a long distance to go.

    * The question of Palestinian representation remains unresolved. We must find a formula that all parties can accept. The President has restated our own firm position on the PLO: we will not recognize or negotiate with the PLO unless it clearly and publicly recognizes Israel's right to exist and accepts Resolutions 242 and 338. At the same time, we believe credible Palestinian representatives must participate in every stage of negotiations. Otherwise it would be impossible to achieve the broad

Palestinian support necessary for what would be agreed to in the give-and-take of negotiations.

   \*    Another issue is the structure and auspices of the process. We understand King Hussein's desire for a supportive international context, and we know this is a key question. It remains our firm conviction that, with imagination, an answer can be found that will enhance rather than retard the process.

We are prepared to do what we can to bring the parties together. Before King Hussein's visit here, Assistant Secretary Murphy and I both made trips to the Middle East.

The purpose of Mr. Murphy's trip in April was to discuss what could be accomplished in 1985, which several key players in the region had termed the "year of opportunity." We wanted to encourage that sense of urgency. On that trip he found a general understanding among King Hussein, Prime Minister Peres, and President Mubarak that the next 6 months offer the promise of forward movement. He also found a common realization that the aim is to begin negotiations between Israel and an Arab partner in ways that take account of the political realities facing each party.

My own trip to Israel, Egypt, and Jordan in early May confirmed that the key leaders were serious in their desire to move forward. Everyone understood that the problems ahead are politically very difficult. But I also found a strong desire to find solutions.

Based on our assessment, the President decided that the United States would engage actively in the process at this moment of new opportunity. The goal—again—is direct negotiations between Israel and Jordan, with Palestinian participation. This goal is now agreed.

Thus, something new has been happening. King Hussein has been active; he has been moving; he has taken several initiatives. For the first time in some years, someone on the Arab side is focusing on how to get negotiations started, rather than sitting back demanding guarantees of the final outcome. All parties are now focusing on the practical steps that must be taken, advancing their own ideas on how best to begin direct negotiations. This is a new, positive, and important development.

In the turbulent environment of the Middle East, there are those who oppose the peace process and who use violence to stop it. King Hussein is showing great courage and statesmanship. But there are also many millions of people in the Middle East, and many governments, who want to see stability and peace. And there are millions of people around the world, and many governments, who want the same. They recognize that something new and important is happening; they are moving to support King Hussein's efforts. We in the United States, who are crucial to the peace process, must be responsive as well.

President Reagan and I are heartened by the resolve the King is showing. We are encouraged by the degree to which he has secured Palestinian support. We believe his efforts are genuine, promising, and courageous, and we believe it is essential that America show its support.

### 15.   Statement by State Department Spokesman Charles Redman on the Breakdown of the Hussein-Arafat Peace Initiative, 20 February, 1986 [Excerpts]

We are carefully studying King Hussein's speech.* Without question, it is an important commentary on the peace process.

It's obvious that we have embarked upon a period of reflection on the part of all parties. The reason for this is equally clear and is laid out in considerable detail in the King's speech. The PLO leadership has been unable to meet the King's challenge to accept UN Security Council Resolutions 242 and 338 which the King termed "the basic cornerstone for achieving a just and peaceful settlement."

The PLO leadership has been unable to agree to negotiations with the State of Israel and unable to end violence while negotiations are underway.

Most assuredly, King Hussein has not abandoned his commitment to peace. Neither has the Government of Israel. For our part, we intend to continue our efforts to help the parties advance toward our shared goal of direct negotiations for a just, durable, and lasting peace in the Middle East.

...[L]et me first point to the King's exact words. I quote: "When it is clearly on the public record that the PLO has accepted Resolutions 242 and 338, is prepared to negotiate peace with Israel, and has renounced terrorism, the United States accepts the fact that an invitation will be issued to the PLO to attend an international conference."

That quotation is an accurate statement of our position and expectations under these specific circumstances discussed with Jordan at that time. The PLO has now failed the King's test, and history moves on.

The record is clear that the PLO leadership has failed to seize the opportunity offered it, and all parties will now have to find another basis to move toward the undiminished imperative of a negotiated peace, including a resolution of the Palestinian problem.

---

\* Hussein's speech of 19 February, 1986.

## 16. Statement by President Ronald Reagan on an International Peace Conference, Washington, DC, 18 February, 1987

*The following is a statement made by President Reagan prior to Prime Minister Shamir's departure from the White House.*

It's been a pleasure to have an old friend, Prime Minister Yitzhak Shamir of Israel, back to the White House. His visit symbolizes the close and special relations between our countries. His visit has provided an opportunity for in-depth discussion, and I'm pleased to report our discussion went well.

High on our agenda, of course, was Middle Eastern peace and our search for a constructive approach to Arab-Israeli reconciliation. We talked about the dangers that threaten Israel and its neighbors and efforts being made to bring a degree of stability to that troubled region. Measurable progress, we both agree, is vital. Peace cannot be built in an environment where there is no hope.

In our discussions, we agreed again that the road to peace lies through bilateral negotiations between Israel and its neighbors, including representative Palestinians. We reviewed the diplomatic discussions over the last two years which we have conducted with Jordan, Egypt, and Israel—all of whom share a strong desire to end the conflict that has plagued the Middle East.

Our goal now is setting in motion a process accepted by Israel and its neighbors which can lead to a comprehensive peace settlement. We believe this requires direct, bilateral negotiations. And reasonable means of starting such direct negotiations, including an international conference, should be considered. But the United States remains ready to be an active partner in any serious peace effort.

## 17. Speech by Secretary of State George Shultz Before American-Israel Public Affairs Committee, Washington, DC, 17 May, 1987 [Excerpts]

So now there seems to be discussion of a possible new opening toward peace. So I am going to spend some time with you looking at it from a US point of view, and saying, "let's evaluate it," and let's ask ourselves, "What is making peace all about?" Well, to me it's really simple. It's sitting down with people who want to make peace, and who are qualified and ready to negotiate. That's how you make peace. So you have to look for people who are qualified and ready, so let's ask a few questions.

Is the PLO qualified?

*Audience*: No.

*Secretary Shultz*: Hell, no! Let's try that on for size. PLO?

*Audience*: Hell, no!

*Secretary Shultz*: You got it! Look at what they've just done. Their alliance involves the most violent and radical elements around, and they just put it together again. They showed once again that they don't want peace; they want the destruction of Israel, so they're not qualified.

Palestinians? Certainly. They have to be part of peacemaking. There are Palestinians who know that the only answer is through a non-violent and responsible approach to direct negotiations for peace and justice. We have to continue to find them, help them, and support them.

How about the Soviet Union?

*Audience*: No. No.

*Secretary Shultz*: Could it be a constructive presence?

*Audience*: Hell, no!

*Secretary Shultz*: Yes. It could be. And there have been some interesting developments recently, but are they now a constructive presence?

*Audience*: No.

*Secretary Shultz*: No. Look what they do. They encourage the PLO to turn ever more radical and rejectionist. They align themselves with the worst terrorists and tyrants in the region. They refuse to re-establish diplomatic recognition to Israel. Their treatment of Jews and the practice of the Jewish religion in the Soviet Union is not acceptable by any standard, let alone the Universal Declaration on Human Rights and the Helsinki Final Act, to which they are bound by their own signature.

We can all welcome the release of heroes like Natan Shcharansky, but as he is the first to say, the emigration of Soviet Jews is in no way proportionate to the desire and the right of Jews to leave. So if the Soviets want to be a part of the peace process, as they say, let them step forward and qualify themselves.

King Hussein has qualified himself. He is serious and committed to peace. He has rejected the rejectionists. He has stated his readiness to pursue—these are his words—"a negotiated settlement in an environment free of belligerent and hostile acts." He has dealt straightforwardly with Israel. He has courageously established relations with Egypt, enhancing the welcome process by which Egypt's role in the Arab world grows even as Egypt solidifies its peace with Israel.

He has recognized that only bilateral, face-to-face negotiations, can do the job. The name of the game is direct, face-to-face negotiations. He has shown great concern and solid support for the Palestinian people. He is for including Palestinians in the Jordanian delegation—not independent, include them with Jordan. And he has said that the international conference he advocates will not impose any solution or veto any agreement made by the negotiating parties. All this undeniably represents progress. We welcome it, and we are for it.

Now, let me say a little more, from the standpoint of the United States, what we are for and what we make of all this. First of all, we are for a strong Israel, and for the strongest, permanent link possible between the United States and Israel. We believe, among other things, that the underpinning of movements toward peace is to make it crystal clear to everybody that there is no military solution as far as the enemies of Israel are concerned. They can't get there that way.

We are for, in the strongest terms, the treaty of peace between Egypt and Israel. With the passage of time and serious efforts on both sides, that relationship, born of Camp David, represents the brightest hope for peace in the Middle East. Egypt is our friend, and we honor the role it has taken for peace and justice. I think we made a further step in the Taba agreement.

We are for the President's September 1 [1982] initiative. It's not a plan—it's an initiative. That is our position, and we will take it to the table as our view; just as we recognize, when we get to those face-to-face negotiations, others will come with their own views and no doubt differing views. But that represents the view the United States will take unto that table.

We are for the effort to achieve real improvement in the quality of life on the West Bank and Gaza. This program has made progress in recent years. It draws sustenance from the diplomatic activity in the peace process and contributes to creating an atmosphere in which negotiations can take place. And we consistently stand for the principle that the only reliable way to achieve peace is through face-to-face negotiations between Israel and its Arab neighbors.

The United States believes it is important to explore all possible approaches to this objective, to see whether any of these approaches, including an international conference, would lead immediately to direct negotiations.

I might say we are also careful not to intervene in domestic Israeli politics. I have the highest regard for and the closest relationship with both Prime Minister Shamir and Foreign Minister Peres, and for that matter many other Israeli leaders. We are working with all of them to reach an agreed position on recent developments, and I want to say that I know, knowing them all as I do, that all of them are dedicated to peace. All of them are.

Now, this Administration remains committed to helping Israel in its quest for peace and security, as we always have. That has been a steady, constant commitment of the United States, and it has helped time after time after time. We are still here. The same steady friends, working together with Israel, and you on the basis of the same principles.

But important developments have in fact occurred that have led us, consistent with our established policies, to look carefully at the idea of an international conference. I say carefully, cautiously, skeptically, but nonetheless with open minds and willing spirits. The answers are worth working through, even if this idea fails, like so many others on which we have worked. No one should ever be able to claim that a failure to advance the cause of peace resulted from the lack of effort on the part of the United States. For any approach to warrant consideration, we would have to insist that, in addition to leading promptly and directly to face-to-face negotiations, it also would not interfere with, impose its will on, or veto work of the bilateral negotiating parties; include Palestinians in the negotiations, only in a Jordanian-Palestinian delegation; and require all of the negotiating participants to accept UNSC Resolutions 242 and 338, and to renounce violence and terrorism.

Now, sometimes in our policy about the PLO, we use the words, "and recognize Israel's right to exist." Frankly, I cringe a little bit when anybody says that or when I say it, although it is part of our policy. Of course, Israel has a right to exist. It has a right to prosper. It has a right to peace.

Now, if such a conference were ever to take place, only states would be represented and involved. They should have diplomatic relations with all of the parties that come to the table. And it should be clear that the rights of any party to remove itself from the conference or the negotiations is there if such rules or understandings are not observed. Now, there recently has been progress towards such a negotiating format which would offer serious prospects of reaching an agreement between the parties on peace. So, as far as we are concerned, we have to, as I said, look this over carefully, skeptically, but look it over. It may be that there is a genuine opportunity to bring about direct talks. If so, we have all been striving for that.

I might say all across the spectrum of Israeli politics there is a desire to have direct talks. Everybody is in favor of that. Once direct talks have been achieved, an important psychological obstacle would have been overcome, irrespective of the results. We have to insist that there is no predetermined result or plan, so each party can advocate its preferred approach, including the approach that is represented in the Camp David Accords.

As far as the Soviets are concerned, it's impossible to know whether they want to be spoilers or whether they want to be constructive. I must say they couldn't do a lot worse than they're doing now—encouraging the PLO and the radicals to reunite. So we'll have to see about that.

And, of course, I think we also need to remind ourselves, as the statement I made at the outset underlines, that a lack of progress has its own dangers, including increased and deepening bitterness and the continued and potentially explosive tension that we know is there in the region. I believe that as we look at this, as I said, carefully and skeptically, we need to take out an insurance policy, in terms of the close working relationship which is there between Israel and the United States, as long as we agree on that basic structure—and we're ready to walk away from the idea or walk away from a conference, if it fails—then, we can pursue this road without too great a risk. But we can only pursue it if we are able to do so in partnership with the Government of Israel, and we will make no moves unless we are assured of that.

So let me summarize the present initiative accurately. The President and I are not committed to an international conference, and we are not asking others to commit themselves now to the idea. We believe, however, that Jordan is sincere and that a real opportunity has been presented for progress. We are not interested in disrupting Israeli politics in the process. To the contrary, as I said, we will proceed only with the support of the Government of Israel. We have our own views, however, and we will state them in the same spirit in which we have worked with Israel for many years. We believe the present circumstances clearly call for a fair and thorough effort to develop an acceptable plan, however dubious we may be of the general idea. If no acceptable understanding emerges, so be it. We will try again another way, but let us try. Let us use our ingenuity and courage so that we accomplish whatever progress toward peace is achievable.

Israel has fought many wars in its short history. Let us continue to do everything we can to avoid another while safeguarding forever Israel's security and prosperity.

## 18. "Toward Arab-Israeli Peace," Report of A Study Group, The Brookings Institution, Washington, DC, 1988 [Summary]

The Study Group on Arab-Israeli peacemaking was able to reach broad agreement in seven areas.

### 1. Urgency
Arab-Israeli peacemaking deserves to be high on the agenda of the next administration. A prolonged impasse in the peace process could endanger American national interests. Recent violent clashes between Israelis and Palestinians are vivid reminders of the explosive situation in the region. At the same time, possible openings toward peace have been created. In short, both dangers and opportunities exist.

### 2. New Realities
A newly elected president will not be able to get his bearings on the Arab-Israeli conflict simply by evoking the formulas of the past. UN Security Council Resolutions 242 and 338, the Camp David Accords, and President Ronald Reagan's proposal of September 1, 1982, contain some useful building blocks. But a serious policy cannot be developed simply by stringing these formulations together. New realities in the region require that other approaches and concepts be considered as well.

Among the most important of the realities which will confront peacemakers are the following: the Israeli-Palestinian confrontation has now come to the fore as the most urgent and complex part of the Arab-Israeli conflict; demographic trends provide a strong incentive to Israelis to reach an agreement with their Palestinian neighbors which will keep Israel secure, democratic, and predominantly Jewish; the idea of a settlement with Israel is no longer a taboo in the Arab world; and the Soviet Union is becoming more active in the region.

## 3. The American Role

We would like to see a steady, high-level commitment of American resources to the Arab-Israeli peace process. American leadership can help to create the atmosphere in which negotiations can take place. The United States can also assist in bridging differences on both procedural and substantive issues.

Given the prolonged stalemate in the peace process, attention must now be paid to rebuilding the foundations for a negotiated settlement. Since both Israel and the United States will have new governments in place early in 1989, a special effort will be required to develop a relationship of trust if the peace process is to advance. Consultations must take place with other parties as well before a judgment can be made on when and whether the circumstances are ripe for moving into formal negotiations.

## 4. An International Framework for Negotiations

Convening an international conference on the Arab-Israeli conflict is the most widely supported approach to negotiations. While we have some reservations about such a forum, we believe that the idea should be explored seriously by a new administration. Indeed, the effort to organize a conference could help to precipitate the political decisions necessary to negotiate a settlement. If a conference is convened, it should not impose its views on the negotiating parties or be empowered to veto the results of bilateral negotiations.

On the controversial issue of Palestinian participation, we have concluded that Palestinians should be represented in any negotiations with Israel by spokesmen of their own choosing, whether in a joint Jordanian-Palestinian delegation or in some other configuration. The United States should have no objection to the participation of Palestinians who are on record as being prepared to coexist with the state of Israel, are committed to peaceful negotiations, can contribute to that objective, and renounce the use of force. Palestinians are unlikely to come forward to negotiate with Israel without having the implicit or explicit endorsement of the Palestine Liberation Organization.

## 5. Basic Principles for Arab-Israeli Peace

We believe the United States should formulate a strategy for promoting Arab-Israeli peace based on the following points:

- In order to achieve broad Arab-Israeli peace, both Israel and the Palestinians must be directly involved.

- A recognition that the area defined as the former mandate of Palestine west of the Jordan River is home to both peoples is essential to a reconciliation between Israelis and Palestinians.

- Israelis and Palestinians will have to work closely with the Hashemite Kingdom of Jordan, a majority of whose citizens are Palestinians, in shaping a peace agreement. Negotiations must encompass the political and economic relationships among the three parties.

- Under international sponsorship, Israel and Syria should be encouraged to negotiate peace based on the principles of UN Resolution 242.

## 6. Transitional Steps

Within these guidelines, we believe that some form of transitional arrangements must be part of the next phase of Arab-Israeli peacemaking. The atmosphere for peacemaking would be significantly improved by the following sorts of steps, some of which could either precede formal negotiations or be part of an interim agreement:

- ceasing all forms of violence;
- ending the state of belligerency and economic and diplomatic boycott between Israel and its Arab neighbors;
- minimizing the Israeli military presence in populated areas of the West Bank and Gaza;
- placing substantial authority in the hands of West Bank and Gaza Palestinians, especially with respect to land, water, economic activity, and political organization; and
- halting new Israeli settlements and land expropriation in the occupied territories.

The United States should also support free elections to municipal councils as an essential step that would allow Palestinians to select their own leaders for purposes of self-government and as possible participants in a Palestinian negotiating delegation.

For Palestinians to find merit in them, these interim measures must be seen as part of an ongoing process that leads to negotiation of a comprehensive peace that meets Palestinian political aspirations. For Israelis to support them, they must be compatible with Israel's assessment of its security interests and be judged as having intrinsic merit.

A transitional arrangement should also be negotiated for the Golan Heights that would enhance mutual security there, return territory to Syria, and establish a new relationship of non-belligerency as a step toward an overall peace settlement.

## 7. A Long-Term Vision of Peace

We believe the United States is uniquely positioned to articulate a vision of how Israelis, Palestinians, and other Arab parties can attain their rights to security and to self-determination through a political formula based on ideas of peaceful interchange, political pluralism, and the exchange of "territory for peace" as envisaged in UN Resolution 242. Federal or confederal arrangements that would reflect distinctive national identities, while at the same time permitting political and economic linkages among the individual political units, might be an appealing formula.

We envision a future in which borders would not be physical barriers; citizens of one political entity could live safely, and with recognized rights, elsewhere in the region; and economic transactions and movement of individuals would be subject to few restrictions. A regional economic plan with international support should complement such a political settlement and help to ensure its viability.

Jerusalem will be internationally recognized as Israel's capital under any future peace agreements. But Jerusalem is the center of Palestinian aspirations as well. Therefore, a peaceful Jerusalem should remain a unified city, with guaranteed freedom of worship and access, and political arrangements should be found that reflect the nature of the city's population.

Finally, we want to emphasize that the details of an Arab-Israeli peace settlement should not be dictated by the United States or any other outside party. From the standpoint of American interests, the important point is that any agreement be durable. The United States will doubtless benefit by a widening of the scope of Arab-Israeli peace. How that is done is less important than that it be done, and that the process start soon.

## 19. "Building for Peace: An American Strategy for the Middle East," The Washington Institute for Near East Policy, Presidential Study Group, 1988 [Executive Summary]

When the next president enters office, he will be confronted by a Middle East in transformation. The Iraq-Iran war is ending; the Arab-Israeli conflict is reverting to its inter-communal roots; and the arms race is escalating to a new, more dangerous level.

As the region adjusts to these new realities, the next president will need to proceed with caution, acting to reshape the political environment between Israel and the Palestinians, stabilize the Middle East military balance and help construct a postwar framework of stability in the Gulf.

### US Policy and the Arab-Israeli Conflict

*1. The Regional Environment*
The dominant features of the Arab-Israeli environment are likely to be an intractable communal conflict, a potentially dangerous inter-state conflict and a regional leadership unwilling or unable to take the risks necessary to make a negotiated settlement possible.

*The inter-communal conflict between Palestinians and Israelis, manifested in the uprising, has now become a chronic problem, rendering peacemaking both more urgent and more difficult.* Israel now feels it can take fewer risks for peace; the Palestinians seem to believe they can achieve more than is possible or, from the United States viewpoint, desirable; and Jordan appears to have retreated to the sidelines.

*The inter-state conflict between the Arab states and Israel now threatens to become increasingly dangerous and volatile.* Syria remains determined to achieve "strategic parity" with Israel and insists that the conflict can only be resolved by force. The spread of ballistic missiles and chemical weapons throughout the region, combined with possible realignments in the Arab world following the end of the Iraq-Iran war, pose a growing threat to the stability of the post-Camp David security environment.

*As a result of these twin challenges, inter-communal and inter-state, the management and resolution of the Arab-Israeli problem will have to be an important part of the next president's foreign policy agenda.*

*However, quick breakthroughs will be extremely difficult; to make peace in this environment will be virtually impossible. But to build for peace while coping with the dangers of continuing conflict will be essential.*

The immediate task of the next president should be to help create the conditions for an eventual negotiation rather than attempting to bring that negotiation about in short order.

2. *Reshaping the Political Environment*

Another ambitious American plan for solving the Palestinian problem is not only likely to fail but will also be counterproductive. *The US cannot make peace for these parties; it can only assist them once they are willing to do so.*

Traditional American diplomacy which seeks to produce a breakthrough to negotiations should therefore give way, initially, to efforts to reshape the political environment by encouraging the emergence of a Palestinian leadership willing to coexist with Israel and by supporting the Israeli leadership in taking steps which make this more possible.

This process should aim to create an environment in which Israel, the Palestinians and Jordan are able to negotiate a stable solution—one that provides tangible security and recognition for Israel, self-government for the Palestinians and stability for Jordan. Any Palestinian entity which emerges from such a negotiation would have to have its authority heavily qualified by the security requirements of Israel and Jordan. That is why previous administrations have developed four basic principles, proven effective in negotiating peace between Israel and Egypt, which we believe should continue to guide American peace-making:

\* The legitimate rights of the Palestinians should be secured through direct negotiations.

\* The principal participants in the negotiations must be Israel, Palestinian representatives and Jordan.

\* Any Palestinian participant must accept UN Resolutions 242 and 338, renounce terror and recognize Israel's right to exist.

\* There should be a prolonged transitional period in which the intention of the Palestinians to live in peace with Israel and Jordan could be tested.

Once all the parties are ready to accept these principles, active American diplomacy will become critical in helping them negotiate a settlement. But the conditions for reaching agreement on these principles simply do not exist in the current environment. The first task of US diplomacy is to lay the foundation upon which negotiations can be built. This will require the next administration to focus on three elements:

- *Encouraging the Emergence of a Responsible Palestinian Leadership.* For nearly ten months, the Palestinians have demonstrated a willingness to resist Israel but they have not yet shown an ability to convince Israelis that they are ready to live in peace. *They need to produce a leadership capable of clearly communicating and delivering on a commitment to coexist in peace with Israel.*

The PLO has repeatedly failed this test, but it is now under pressure to accept longstanding American conditions for a role in the peace process. In this environment, it would be a mistake for the next administration to retreat from its conditions —acceptance of UN Resolutions 242 and 338, renunciation of terror and recognition of Israel's right to exist— and send the signal that something less might be acceptable.

However, the next administration will also have an opportunity to encourage the political dynamic already underway in the Palestinian community. As a result of the *intifadah*, the inhabitants of the territories have gained legitimacy from resisting Israel. But they also have a stake in coexisting *with* Israel. For the time being, their leadership is radical in its rhetoric and influenced by Islamic fundamentalists. But they are under growing pressure to translate the uprising into tangible political gains and are showing signs of impatience with the PLO's apparent inability to deliver. As the initial euphoria of the uprising dissipates, the chance to ease the military occupation might become sufficiently attractive to make conciliation toward Israel an acceptable first step.

These factors provide an opportunity for Israel and the US. By emphasizing Palestinian rights, while working with Israel to give gradual, concrete and meaningful expression to them, it may be possible to encourage the emergence of a responsible Palestinian partner which would be capable of demonstrating its commitment to live in peace with Israel.

The US could encourage this process by:

* Standing fast on American conditions for dealing with the PLO.

* Stressing the American commitment to Palestinian rights in the context of Israeli and Jordanian security.

* Urging the Palestinians in the territories to take responsibility for their political future by foregoing violence and engaging in a political process that addresses Israel's concerns.

- *Working with Israel.* Israel is our most important partner in this process, not just because of our moral and strategic interests in its well-being, but also because it is in control of the West Bank and Gaza. Assuring Israel of the fundamental nature of the new administration's support is essential if the ripening process is to develop. *One of the president's first tasks should be to affirm this relationship of trust based on strong relations, close consultation and an ironclad commitment to Israel's security.*

Once this is achieved, it should also be possible to engage the new Israeli government in a dialogue about how to produce a more constructive relationship with the Palestinians. Israel should be urged to look beyond the immediate public order problem and consider the measures it might adopt to promote the emergence of a responsible leadership.

The process we have in mind could include:

* A Palestinian willingness to reduce the level of violence and disorder coupled with an Israeli readiness to ease the restrictions imposed in response to the *intifadah.*

* As the process evolved, Israel and the Palestinians could be encouraged to undertake more significant confidence-building acts: the Palestinians articulating their vision of a future in which Palestinian aspirations are accommodated to the reality of Israel and its security concerns; the Israelis liberalizing controls on economic and political activity.

* Ultimately, if the ripening process proves successful, Israel might be convinced to permit free elections in the territories to produce a representative Palestinian leadership. Negotiations could then take place to establish a transitional regime for the territories which would assume authority over certain aspects of self-government.

*The onus is on both sides to find a way out of the vicious circle.* To the extent that both sides seek to replace violence with political dialogue, there is much that the next administration can do to encourage them.

This process could infuse a sense of dynamism into a situation currently characterized by stalemate, helping to create a framework for an eventual negotiation on the more controversial aspects of self-government (control of land, water and security) and on the final status of the territories—a negotiation in which Jordan would also have to be involved.

- *Preserving a Role for Jordan.* While the transitional arrangements we are suggesting ask very little of Jordan, negotiations on the final status issues will require Jordan to be a central participant. *Only Jordan can provide the anchor for an emerging Palestinian entity, some of the guarantees of a stable settlement that Israel will need, and the gateway to the Arab world for the Palestinians.* Jordan is no longer a sufficient partner for peace—there must be a responsible Palestinian participant as well. But Jordan does remain a necessary partner in any final status negotiations.

3.  *Stabilizing the Military Balance*

*Stabilizing the ongoing conflict between Israel and the Arab states will need to be a higher priority* for the next administration than it has been in previous years. Maintaining the balance of power in favor of parties willing to make peace is a prerequisite for a successful diplomacy. Preserving Israel's military superiority is the only way to ensure Israel's security and discredit the Arab war option.

In this context, Syria's continued search for "strategic parity" and its insistence on resolving the conflict by military means is generating a growing risk of war. Moreover, the Syrians pose a major threat to the peace process through their ability to manipulate elements within the Palestinian community and intimidate Jordan.

The next administration will need to maintain a dialogue with Damascus, if only to keep a channel open in the event of Syrian-Israeli tensions. At the same time, its Middle East strategy should include specific steps aimed at circumventing and overcoming Damascus's intransigence on the peace process and deterring its belligerence toward Israel. Steps should include:

* Strengthening Israel's deterrent by advancing strategic cooperation, by signalling Syria that the next administration will not restrain Israel if Damascus launches a surprise attack and by helping Israel develop an anti-tactical ballistic missile defense.

* Discouraging Iraq from returning to its previous rejectionist alignment with Syria.

* Bolstering the Egypt-Israel peace treaty.

Another Arab-Israeli war contains far greater geostrategic consequences for the United States than a continuation of the Palestinian uprising. *The risk of such a war has now increased significantly as a result of the Middle East arms race which has entered a new, destabilizing phase.* With the introduction of large numbers of surface-to-surface missiles into Arab arsenals and the proliferation of chemical warfare capabilities, the rewards for a surprise attack on Israel are growing and the incentive for Israel to preempt is increasing.

*The Arab-Israel conflict is slowly but surely moving back to a hair-trigger environment.* This will require the next administration to focus its attention on measures, beyond deterring Syria, that may help to slow the arms race and reduce misunderstandings, including:

* Engaging the Soviet Union, China and the West Europeans in talks designed to restrict the flow of missiles and missile technology to the Middle East. Pressure will also have to be exerted on Argentina, Brazil and North Korea who are supplying and improving missiles systems in the region.

* Brokering tacit understandings between Israel, Saudi Arabia, Iraq and Egypt about patterns of missile deployment, nature of warheads, command and control, and communications in crisis. Though the task will be sensitive, a community of interest may exist in avoiding an unwanted conflict with devastating potential for civilian populations.

* Mobilizing international opinion against the use of chemical warfare and strengthening support for international norms that have been seriously undermined by Iraq's use of chemical weapons.

4.   *The Soviet Union and the Arab-Israeli Conflict*

Under Mikhail Gorbachev, Soviet diplomacy in the Middle East has become increasingly active. While taking advantage of Moscow's new collaborative spirit, *the next president needs to greet a Soviet desire to play a peacemaking role with both skepticism and openness.*

Before inviting the USSR to play a role in the peace process, the US should urge Moscow to demonstrate by its behavior in the following areas a genuine commitment to conciliation:

* Restraining Syria by restricting the supply of advanced Soviet weapons and by continuing to emphasize that the Soviet Union will not support any attempt to resolve the conflict by military means.

* Demonstrating Soviet support for Israel's security by reestablishing full diplomatic relations, by allowing for the possibility of territorial compromise rather than a return to the 1967 borders, and by making a clear statement in support of Israel's continued survival and security. Greater relaxation of controls on emigration of Soviet Jews would also constitute a signal of Soviet good will toward the Jewish state.

* Demonstrable and consistent efforts to moderate the positions of Syria and the PLO toward peace with Israel.

* Moderating Soviet voting behavior in the United Nations, where Moscow currently supports maximalist Arab positions on all issues.

*An international conference to settle the Arab-Israeli conflict is a negotiating forum that holds little advantage for the United States.* What value there was in such a conference has diminished with Jordan's withdrawal from a primary role in the peace process. However, the Soviet Union is likely to orchestrate Arab and international pressure on the next administration to pursue a conference.

Unless it is strictly confined to the role of an umbrella for direct negotiations, the international conference will not be conducive to reaching a settlement. Therefore, the next administration should continue to challenge Moscow to demonstrate that the conference is a useful tool for resolving the conflict.

Soviet "new thinking" should improve the chances of enlisting Moscow in an effort to stabilize the region's military balance. Limiting the proliferation of ballistic missiles and missile technologies, discouraging the use of chemical weapons, and preventing the outbreak of a Syrian-Israeli war are all interests that the Soviet Union should share with the US. The next president should give priority to engaging the Soviet Union in a dialogue on these subjects, recognizing that selective cooperation with Moscow can be an important element in a strategy designed to manage conflict as well as an important method for testing Soviet intentions.

5. *Implementing US Policy: Appointing a Special Emissary*

The next president will need to demonstrate his commitment to peacemaking while clearly indicating that the US is looking to the parties themselves to recondition the political environment. One of his first acts should be the dispatch of a special emissary to the Middle East with instructions to:

* Express to the new Israeli government the president's desire to work in close

consultation on the peace process and his unshakeable commitment to Israel's security.

* Begin the sensitive process of discussing with the region's leaders the need to control the arms race.

* Emphasize the new administration's commitment to a process designed to reshape the political environment rather than seek a procedural breakthrough to negotiations.

* Express to friendly Arab leaders the president's concern for their interests.

The emissary will need to avoid creating inappropriate expectations in the region or generating plans for grand solutions once he returns.

## 20.   "A Statement for Palestinians," Secretary of State George Shultz, East Jerusalem, 26 February, 1988

I have a statement for Palestinians. Palestinian participation is essential to success in the peace process. I had hoped to carry this message to East Jerusalem this evening and to hear firsthand from leading Palestinians about your aspirations and your point of view. Peacemaking is difficult. Peace has its enemies. Even small steps toward peace can be significant in moving beyond mistrust and hatred. In a small way, I wanted to do that this evening.

All the peoples of this land need to be able to look to a future of dignity, security, and prosperity. New respect for rights and new readiness for political change must replace old recrimination and distrust.

The United States is for positive and rapid change. Fundamental considerations guide our approach.

First, Palestinians and Israelis must deal differently with one another. Palestinians must achieve control over political and economic decisions that affect their lives. Palestinians must be active participants in negotiations to determine their future. Legitimate Palestinian rights can be achieved in a manner which protects Israeli security. Israeli security and Palestinian security are necessary conditions for a better future for Palestinians, as well as for Israelis.

Second, these moves must be part of a broader effort to reach a comprehensive settlement. Israel and the occupied territories do not exist in isolation. Jordan, Syria, Lebanon, and Palestinians living outside the territories have concerns which need to be resolved. In moving toward a comprehensive settlement, Resolutions 242 and 338, in their entirety, must be the basis for negotiations.

Third, what we are seeking must be achieved through negotiations. Negotiations work. Negotiations produce agreements which meet the fundamental concerns of all parties. Experience shows you that you can have an agreement with Israel, and it will be kept by Israel.

Fourth, the start of negotiations must be soon, and the pace of negotiations must be rapid, so that results can be achieved with equal rapidity.

The human resources and potential of Arabs and Israelis are boundless. They have energy and drive which, if not directed against each other, can be marshaled collectively to explore science and technology, literature, and the arts. This region, which nurtured three great world religions, carries within it a powerful and moral force. Islam, Christianity, and Judaism can work together in creating a more durable, moral, and spiritual world for all of us.

Our vision is of Israelis and Palestinians living together in peace in this land; where the rights of each are respected; where the energies of all are directed at peaceful purposes; where security and trust exist. Israelis and Palestinians need to see in each other the embodiment of their own dreams. They will realize that the fulfillment of their own dreams is impossible without the fulfillment of the other side's dreams. They will see that dreams rooted in reality are dreams which can be fulfilled.

Opportunity knocks loudly on your doors. Now is the time to get to work. We have a workable plan, and we are ready to commit our efforts to it. The time is right, together, to make decisions of historic importance. Let us translate our dreams into the reality of peace, rights, and security for all.

## 21.  US Senators' Letter to Secretary of State George Shultz, 3 March, 1988

*The following letter to Secretary of State Shultz, was drafted by Senators Carl Levin (D-MI) and Rudy Boschwitz (R-MN) and was signed by thirty senators.*

Dear Secretary Shultz:

We are writing to express our support for your effort to break the dangerous Middle East stalemate, a stalemate that has led to the current cycle of violence and counterviolence.

We support your mission of peace, which is based on United Nations Security [Council] Resolution 242 (as restated in Resolution 338), a resolution which has been at the foundation of United States diplomacy in the region through five Administrations and which has been endorsed by Israel and most of the Arab parties to the conflict.

The meaning of this resolution is clear. It requires the Arab states to accept Israel's right to "live in peace within secure and recognized boundaries, free from threats or acts of force..." It requires Israel to withdraw from some of the territories occupied during the 1967 war. It can be summarized in three words: land for peace.

Unfortunately, with the exception of Egypt, no Arab state has demonstrated willingness to implement this formulation. To one degree or another, the Arab states have resisted recognition of Israel and peace with it. As for the Palestinians, they not only refuse to recognize Israel, they have refused to meet with you during your visit. For some 50 years, those who have indicated a willingness to negotiate with Israel have paid with their lives. Others have been intimidated.

Israel, for its part, has manifested its commitment to Resolution 242 and the "land for peace" formula in a tangible way. In return for Egypt's recognition of Israel and its acceptance of peace, Israel returned the Sinai peninsula to Egyptian sovereignty including the oil fields located therein.

Successive Israeli leaders have declared their dedication to the Camp David Accords including Resolution 242's "land for peace" formula and have indicated that it would apply to the West Bank of Gaza. According to this formulation, Israel would contemplate the relinquishing of territory in exchange for a peace treaty guaranteeing Jordanian and Palestinian recognition and acceptance of Israel.

That has always been our understanding.

Accordingly, we were dismayed to read in the *New York Times* of February 26 [1988] that Prime Minister Shamir had said that "...This expression of territory for peace is not accepted by me."

We hope that the Prime Minister's statement did not indicate that Israel is abandoning a policy that offers the best hope of long-term peace. Israel cannot be expected to give up all the territory gained in 1967 or to return to the dangerous and insecure pre-'67 borders. Resolution 242 does not require it to do so. On the other hand, peace negotiations have little chance of success if the Israeli government's position rules out territorial compromise.

We are also disturbed by reports that Jordan may be backing away from the idea of a joint Jordanian-Palestinian delegation that would negotiate with the Israelis at a peace conference. These accounts indicate that Jordan may insist on an independent PLO presence at the negotiating table.

We believe that it is only through compromise by both sides that we will achieve Middle East peace.

We applaud your effort to get the peace process moving and share your determination to build a Middle East where every nation and people can live in peace, security and, ultimately, even friendship.

Sincerely,

*Democrats*
Brock ADAMS (WA), Kent CONRAD (ND), Alan CRANSTON (CA), Thomas DASHLE (SD), Dennis DeCONCINI (AZ), Christopher DODD (CT), James EXON (NE), Wendell FORD (KY), John GLENN (OH), Bob GRAHAM (FL), Tom HARKIN (IA), Daniel INOUYE (HI), Bennett

JOHNSTON (LA), Edward KENNEDY (MA), John KERRY (MA), Frank LAUTENBERG (NJ), Patrick LEAHY (VT), Carl LEVIN (MI), Howard METZENBAUM (OH), George MITCHELL (ME), Daniel MOYNIHAN (NY), Donald RIEGLE, Jr. (MI), Timothy WIRTH (CO)

*Republicans*

Rudy BOSCHWITZ (MN), William COHEN (ME), Robert KASTEN, Jr. (WI), Mitch McCONNELL (KY), Warren RUDMAN (NH), Alan SIMPSON (WY), Lowell WEICKER, Jr. (CT)

## 22. Letter from Secretary of State George Shultz to Prime Minister Yitzhak Shamir, 4 March, 1988

I set forth below the understanding which I am convinced is necessary to achieve the prompt opening of negotiations on a comprehensive peace. This statement of understandings emerges from discussions held with you and other regional leaders. I look forward to the letter of reply of the government of Israel in confirmation of this statement.

The agreed objective is a comprehensive peace plan providing for the security of all the states in the region and for the legitimate rights of the Palestinian people.

Negotiations will start on an early date certain between Israel and each of its neighbors which is willing to do so. These negotiations could begin by May 1, 1988. Each of these negotiations will be based on United Nations Security Council Resolutions 242 and 338, in all their parts. The parties to each bilateral negotiation will determine the procedure and agenda of their negotiation. All participants in the negotiations must state their willingness to negotiate with one another.

As concerns negotiations between the Israeli delegation and the Jordanian-Palestinian delegation, negotiations will begin on arrangements for a transitional period, with the objective of completing them within six months. Seven months after transitional negotiations begin, final status negotiations will begin, with the objective of completing them within one year.

These negotiations will be based on all the provisions and principles of United Nations Security Council Resolution 242. Final status talks will start before the transitional period begins. The transitional period will begin three months after the conclusion of the transitional agreement and will last for three years. The United States will participate in both negotiations and will promote their rapid conclusion. In particular, the United States will submit a draft agreement for the parties' consideration at the outset of the negotiations on transitional arrangements.

Two weeks before the opening of negotiations, an international conference will be held. The Secretary-General of the United Nations will be asked to issue invitations to the parties involved in the Arab-Israeli conflict and the five permanent members of the United Nations Security Council. All participants in the conference must accept United Nations Security Council Resolutions 242 and 338, and renounce violence and terrorism. The parties to each bilateral negotiation may refer reports on the status of their negotiations to the conference, in a manner to be agreed. The conference will not be able to impose solutions or veto agreements reached.

Palestinian representation will be within the Jordanian-Palestinian delegation. The Palestinian issue will be addressed in the negotiations between the Jordanian-Palestinian and Israeli delegations. Negotiations between the Israeli delegation and the Jordanian-Palestinian delegation will proceed independently of any other negotiations.

This statement of understandings is an integral whole. The United States understands that your acceptance is dependent on the implementation of each element in good faith.

## 23.	"This is the Plan," Secretary of State George Shultz's Peace Proposal, 18 March, 1988

There are few fixed rules for resolving conflicts. Each conflict has a unique history and unique characteristics. Each party to a conflict has its own dreams, concerns, and fears. The task is to find the right inducements to draw the parties off the battlefield and into the negotiating room. The success of negotiations is attributable not to a particular procedure chosen but to the readiness of the parties to exploit opportunities, confront hard choices, and make fair and mutual concessions.

In the Arab-Israeli conflict, negotiations work. They provide the means for parties to learn to deal with each other. They produce durable and realistic agreements that meet the fundamental concerns of the parties. Experience shows that Arabs and Israelis can make agreements and keep them.

The United States has launched an initiative designed to produce negotiations— direct, bilateral Arab-Israeli negotiations to achieve comprehensive peace. Our concept is based on all the provisions and principles of United Nations Security Council Resolution 242, which is the internationally accepted framework for negotiations. In the case of the West Bank and Gaza, the initiative involves a two-stage interlocked set of negotiations designed to produce rapid and fundamental change in the way Arabs and Israelis relate to each other.

The United States is a firm and consistent supporter of direct, bilateral negotiations between Israel and all of its neighbors as the means to achieve a comprehensive peace. At the same time, the United States has always been willing to consider any approach that could lead to direct negotiations, including an international conference.

In recent months, some parties have focused on a specific kind of international conference—one that would have an authoritative role or plenipotentiary powers. In January of this year, the United States vetoed a resolution in the United Nations Security Council that called upon the Secretary-General to convene such a conference. The United States made clear its belief that this kind of conference would make real negotiations impossible. It would be a vehicle for avoiding meaningful negotiations, not promoting them.

The issue confronting the parties in the Middle East, therefore, is not whether an international conference should or should not be convened. That misses the point. The Arabs require a conference to launch negotiations; without a properly structured conference, there will be no negotiations. But the wrong kind of conference should never be convened. The United States will not attend that kind of conference. No sovereign state would agree to attend the kind of conference that would presume to pass judgment on issues of national security.

The issue is whether the moment is here to negotiate an end to the Arab-Israeli conflict, whether each party is ready and able to confront hard choices and make difficult decisions, and whether the requirements of the parties are amenable to a procedural blend that satisfies minimal demands.

The strength of the American approach is its integrity; no individual aspect of it can be extracted, finessed, or ignored without sacrificing its balance. The conference we support launches a series of bilateral negotiations and, thereafter, may receive reports from the parties on the status of negotiations, in a manner to be agreed by the parties. All conference attendees will be required to accept Security Council Resolutions 242 and 338 and to renounce violence and terrorism. The conference will be specifically enjoined from intruding in the negotiations, imposing solutions, or vetoing what had been agreed bilaterally.

The United States is committed to this integral concept for beginning direct, bilateral negotiations. We will not permit any aspect of our proposal to be eroded, compromised, or expanded beyond its meaning. In particular, we will not permit a conference to become authoritative or plenipotentiary, or to pass judgments on the negotiations, or to exceed its jurisdiction as agreed by the parties.

The ingredients for a peace process are present. There is an unacceptable and untenable status quo. There are competing parties willing to shed illusions and temper dreams to the underlying realities. And there are realistic and achievable ideas on the table that meet the fundamental concerns of everyone.

Our task is also clear. We must act with integrity, resolve, and tenacity to bring Arabs and Israelis off the battlefield and into negotiations. The initiative put forward by the United States—two interlocked stages of direct negotiations launched by a properly structured international conference—is realistic and compelling.

This is the moment for a historic breakthrough, and this is the plan. The time for decisions is now.

## 24.   Arrival Statements by Secretary of State George Shultz During his Visit to the Middle East, Cairo, 3 June, 1988; Amman, 4 June, 1988; Tel Aviv, 5 June, 1988

### Arrival Statement, Egypt, June 3, 1988

We start with fundamental questions. What is the Arab-Israeli conflict? It is the competition between two national movements for sovereignty on one land. The conflict is not the fault of one party or the other, no party has sole responsibility for resolving it. There are no cheap or painless fixes. No one can avoid taking difficult steps.

The continuation of the conflict today stems from the inability of Arabs and Israelis to lay aside prejudices, hatred, and overblown dreams in favor of a negotiated settlement. The fate of Zionism and Palestinian nationalism are interdependent, although many on both sides refuse to recognize this. Instead of a political dialogue among Arabs and Israelis, there is a growing tendency to sharpen differences and avoid compromise.

Negotiations work. Leaders who seize opportunities and pursue policies of accommodation achieve results. Nowhere has this been proven more dramatically than in Egypt, which recovered occupied territory and campaigned actively to advance the cause of Palestinian rights through negotiations. Others fail—those who refuse to confront reality, who reject any opportunity to move ahead, and who cling to old visions and dreams as though they were immutable laws of nature.

No one can be ensured against all possible outcomes in advance of negotiations. Those who seek such guarantees in advance rule out the possibility of making real headway today—and perhaps forever. Only a new realism and sense of responsibility can break Arabs and Israelis out of the self-destructive pattern they are locking themselves into. The recognition that dreams and reality need to be reconciled as a first principle for peace in the Middle East.

In formulating ideas for bringing about negotiations, the United States has been guided by the need to address the needs and requirements of Arabs and Israelis. We have been guided by practical aspects of Middle East reality.

**First,** there is room—physical space—for Israelis and Palestinians to live side by side, as neighbors, in Israel, the West Bank, and Gaza. Arabs and Israelis are not engaged in a winner-take-all competition. A fair settlement is possible, even though people have difficulty conceiving how to achieve it. It is not too late for a settlement.

**Second,** Israelis and Palestinians are locked into mutually reinforcing cycles of hatred, which sometimes lead to actions that contradict norms they have established to guide their own behavior. Discrimination and segregation are incompatible with the values of democracy, freedom, and liberty; violence and terrorism are incompatible with political rights, responsibilities, and obligations.

**Third,** both sides fear entering a process in which the outcome is not known in advance. But a creative process is what is needed, and such a process requires an interplay between transitional and final status negotiations. Just as a transition can provide confidence in possible ultimate outcomes, so the existence of negotiations on the final status can make transitional arrangements work well. The idea of a transitional period, linked to final status talks, was conceived for just such a purpose.

**Fourth,** both sides ignore emerging global realities which require a new look at old concepts. Their definitions of political rights and obligations, boundaries, and sovereignty are outdated. An appreciation of new global realities can help resolve this conflict. Borders today are permeable and porous, indifferent to the ballistic missile, and indifferent to the desire of any sovereign to shut out the outside world.

A thorough reassessment of security concepts is required. Some may need to change; others may not. But one thing is clear: the location of borders is less significant today in ensuring security than the political relations between neighbors. Peace is the real answer to the problems of security.

So, it is illusions which need to be shed but not hopes and aspirations. In a region where visionaries of millennia past shaped the moral and intellectual course of history, it is not too much to hope that visions of today be directed toward accommodation, reconciliation, and peace of tomorrow.

These are among the issues I will want to discuss with our friends in the region. We need to maintain momentum and commitment toward a comprehensive peace. If we are all prepared to confront reality and face up to the challenges ahead, I am confident we can succeed.

## Arrival Statement, Jordan, June 4, 1988

Any settlement of the Arab-Israeli conflict must be based on three fundamental elements.

**First,** the basis of any negotiating process is Resolution 242 and its call for the exchange of territory for peace. The provisions of Resolution 242 apply to all fronts. There can be no genuine peace without an equitable settlement of the land issue, and there can be no settlement of the land issue without true peace.

**Second,** there can be no settlement without addressing legitimate Palestinian political rights. The Arab-Israeli conflict is more than just a dispute over boundaries. It involves identity, aspirations, legitimacy, and history.

**Third,** there must be Palestinian-Israeli accommodation. This is not a matter of winner-take-all, in which one side can win everything it wants. Palestinians and Israelis must learn to treat each other decently, respect their mutual right to live in security, and fulfill their political aspirations.

This is not an easy agenda. The obstacles we face are formidable. But if we are to succeed—and I think we can succeed—we must address our efforts to the things that matter. I am sure our talks today will keep us on the right road to achieve the goal we seek: a just and comprehensive peace.

### Arrival Statement, Israel, June 5, 1988

People ask, "Why am I traveling again?" The answer is clear. The Arab-Israeli conflict persists; it cannot be wished away. It requires the strength to face reality and the vision to come up with practical solutions to problems.

Today in the region, demographic and economic problems are becoming more serious. The proliferation of longer range missiles and chemical weapons threatens to make future conflicts that much more destructive. Indeed, the next war—let us not have a next war; I know that Israel wants peace and will work for peace—will be unlike any conflict we've seen before, involving more casualties and proving harder to contain. These realities increase the stakes dramatically for regional parties and lay to rest the notion that time works in favor of accommodation.

In light of these realities, movement toward peace and accommodation would seem logical. But, instead, the trend runs in the opposite direction.

* Extremism is spreading. Extremists sow hatred and violence, close off options for political accommodation, and hamper the ability of governments to pursue moderate policies.

* Psychological horizons are narrowing rather than expanding. The distinction between the desirable and the possible is being erased. Illusions are becoming substitutes for reality. Prejudice and hatred are overwhelming tolerance and dialogue.

* Palestinians and Israelis are viewing the conflict as threatening their very existence as a people; each fearing the other side is out to destroy it completely. Who will be the first to make gestures of coexistence and accommodation?

A strong and stable Israel is an essential building block for peace. We will always work with you for a strong and stable Israel. The peace treaty with Egypt shows that negotiations can work. We will always work with you to find the way to a constructive negotiation process. Now is the time for further progress toward peace.

This is not idle talk or speculation. The United States has put forward a plan to bring about negotiations. I am back in the region to try to make that plan work. No party has the luxury to turn aside a chance to negotiate. Every party must take up serious challenges of peace.

* For all parties, the challenge is to rise above their fears and prejudices and accept a negotiating process that offers hope for a more peaceful future. That

process must be based on UN Security Council Resolutions 242 and 338, including the exchange of territory for peace, and on the need to accept a creative process of negotiations involving the interplay between transitional arrangements and final status. Transitional arrangements can provide confidence in final outcomes, just as negotiations on final status can make transitional arrangements work well.

* For Israelis, the challenge is to see that security based on strength must allow for a fair and just accommodation with Arabs. The continued occupation of the West Bank and Gaza and frustration of Palestinian rights is a dead-end street. The belief that this can continue is an illusion.

* For Palestinians, the challenge is to forge an effective political program to replace slogans and violence. The basis of Palestinian thinking must be the willingness to engage, directly with Israelis, to accept Israel's existence and the necessity of its security requirements. The belief that this can be avoided or that violence can end Israeli occupation is an illusion.

* For the Arab states, the challenge is to shape the environment of the region in a responsible way that will facilitate rather than hinder a settlement. This calls for a realism, not rhetoric; for practical steps, not slogans; for sensitivity to the constraints operating on all of the parties; and for recognition that much has already been achieved in the way of Arab-Israeli accommodation and that these achievements have come only through direct negotiations. The denial of these realities is an illusion.

These are challenges that can and must be met. And they are challenges no more or less formidable than others which Arabs and Israelis separately have confronted in the past. The shape of the future of this region will be determined by the ability of Arabs and Israelis to work together to meet the common challenge of forging a lasting peace for themselves and their children.

## 25. Address by Secretary of State George Shultz Before the Washington Institute for Near East Policy, 16 September, 1988

Decision time is approaching in the Middle East. In Israel and Lebanon, within the Palestinian community, and in the Gulf, choices will be made that will have a profound impact on the politics of the region and on the chances of settling conflicts peacefully. These decisions must be based on a dispassionate and cold look at reality.

For nearly nine months, the United States has highlighted a simple but far-reaching reality in the Arab-Israeli conflict. The status quo between Arabs and Israelis does not work. It is not viable. It is dangerous. It contains the seeds of a worsening conflict that threatens to inflict even greater losses on all sides in the future.

The Arab-Israeli conflict is not static. Today, potentially far-reaching changes are taking place. But the fundamental nature of the conflict, and the principles for resolving it, have not changed. Indeed, continuity and constancy appear even more important in the process of resolving this conflict. The challenge facing the next Administration will be to shape change by building on the fundamental constants. This will serve US interests and enhance the prospects for peace.

**What is the shape of the Middle East today?**

— The Palestinian uprising in the West Bank and Gaza has not altered the fundamental nature of the Arab-Israeli conflict. It's a reminder that comprehensive peace requires peace between Israelis and Palestinians, and it's a reminder that the status quo serves the interests of no party.

— Jordan's disengagement from the West Bank hasn't ended Jordan's involvement in the peace process. Jordan has its own interests to pursue.

— Jordan's border with Israel is the longest of any, and much of its population is related by family ties to residents of the West Bank and Gaza. The shaping of Jordan's role in negotiations and in a settlement are among the key issues that need to be assessed by all parties.

— Israel's upcoming elections only highlight the intense and continuing debate within that country about peace. People are taking a hard look at the prospects for peace, and they are asking hard questions: Should Israel trade land for peace? Will continued occupation affect the democratic and Jewish nature of the State of Israel? What should Israelis do about Palestinian rights? Are other Arabs ready to accept Israel as a neighbor and make peace?

— The options before the Palestinians also have not changed. Palestinians are grappling with tough choices. Should they renounce terrorism and violence and choose a political course toward peace? How should they move beyond empty slogans toward realistic and responsible positions to give new life to the peace process?

— Elsewhere in the region, change and constancy are key words. In Lebanon, a new president is scheduled to be elected, amidst hopes that this will give a push to the process of national reconciliation. All Lebanese recognize the dangers that would result from a failure to elect a president according to the constitution.

— Iran and Iraq are now negotiating under UN auspices to bring an end to eight years of bloody and destructive war in the Gulf. The results of these talks will have a profound influence on the entire region.

— Ballistic missiles and chemical weapons continue to proliferate. The use of chemical weapons by both sides in the Gulf war, and Iraq's use of these weapons against the Kurds, are grim reminders of the dangers these weapons pose to the conduct of international relations.

— In Afghanistan, Soviet troops are withdrawing. The people of Afghanistan look forward to the end of Soviet intervention.

So, the fact of change is less important than the uses made of change. The Arab-

Israeli conflict does not stand still. But there are enduring realities that point to a method for resolving the conflict.

The Arab-Israeli conflict is not intractable. Negotiations *can* bring about peace. No matter what new situations or difficulties Arabs and Israelis face as they approach negotiations, one thing is certain once they get there: They will confront some enduring realities that shape the rules of the negotiations and the outlines of a fair settlement that negotiations can be expected to produce.

What are the principles that underlie a comprehensive settlement of the Arab-Israeli conflict?

The existence, security and well-being of Israel are the first principles of any settlement. Israel has the right to exist, and it has the right to exist in security. We will do our utmost to ensure it.

The requirements of security need to be understood clearly. These include military hardware, defensible geographic positions and technological know-how. The United States has cooperated with Israel on these elements, and that cooperation will continue. But these are not the only critical components of Israel's security.

Real security results from resolving political differences that continue to fuel conflict. The location of borders is important, but more important is what crosses those borders—ideas, goods, people, instead of armies and weapons. Borders need to be secure and recognized, but political differences between neighbors also need to be resolved through compromise.

Palestinian political rights must also be recognized and addressed. Palestinians want more than the basic necessities of life. They want, and they are entitled to, political participation, and influence over political and economic decisions that affect their lives. This can occur if opportunities for peace and dialogue are seized.

A third enduring reality is that the history, security and destiny of Israelis, Jordanians, Palestinians and Egyptians are inextricably bound together. Jordan is a vibrant and heterogeneous society, with a strong national identity of its own. It is not a Palestinian state. An enduring settlement must reflect the reality that strong, open relations will need to exist among Israeli, Palestinian, Jordanian and Egyptian peoples.

A critical and enduring reality is that negotiations work. Ten years ago, Egypt and Israel forged a treaty of peace that has survived enormous strains. They continue to demonstrate that dialogue and negotiations resolve differences between peoples, far better than war and violence.

American efforts to bring about negotiations are rooted in these enduring principles. Our approach seeks a comprehensive and durable settlement, grounded in United Nations Security Council Resolutions 242 and 338. It calls for direct negotiations, launched—if required—through an international conference. It requires acceptance of 242 and 338 and renunciation of violence and terrorism.

As regards the West Bank and Gaza, our approach highlights the need for a transitional period to help the parties adjust to working with each other to implement an agreement. It recognizes the relationship in time and substance between the transitional period and final-status agreement. It affirms the right of Palestinians to participate actively in every stage of negotiations. And it reflects the strategic reality of Jordanian-Palestinian interdependence.

This has been the American approach to negotiations. The purposes of this effort have been clear.

**First**, the objective is comprehensive peace between Israel and all its neighbors, achieved through negotiations based on United Nations Security Council Resolutions 242 and 338. This will require the exchange of territory for peace. It will require recognition that sovereignty cannot be defined in absolute terms. Today, borders are porous. Openness is required for the free movement of ideas, people and goods. There will need to be a border demarcation, but not a wall established between peoples.

The territorial issue needs to be addressed realistically. Israel will never negotiate from or return to the lines of partition or to the 1967 borders. But it must be prepared to withdraw—as Resolution 242 says—"from territories occupied in the recent conflict." Peace and security for all sides are at stake.

**Second**, peace between Israel and its neighbors will need time and growing mutual good will to succeed. In the case of the West Bank and Gaza, this means there must be a transitional period. All sides need to deal with one another gradually in the light of an agreement freely negotiated. All need time to adjust to a new situation. Palestinians need to achieve rapid control over political and economic decisions that affect their lives. Israelis need time to adjust to a new situation, one in which Palestinians—not Israeli military government officials—administer the West Bank and Gaza.

The concept of transition is vital and far-reaching. Many of its elements have already been worked through and accepted by Israel. These transitional arrangements are extensive and dramatic. They can be implemented quickly.

Such transitional arrangements will benefit from the interplay with final-status negotiations. Each party needs to know the principles that will define the final settlement. As those principles are hammered out in negotiations, they will enhance the transitional arrangements themselves. Each element strengthens the other. This is the essence and benefit of interlock between transitional arrangements and final status.

Direct negotiations are at the heart of this negotiating process. No party should be expected to trust its vital national security interests to any mechanism except direct talks. How better to engage an adversary, take his measure, assess intentions and probe for openings than to square off across the table? Direct talks work.

In the Arab-Israeli conflict, an international conference may also be necessary to ease the entry of the parties into direct negotiations. This conference would also be in a position, at the right time, to deal with important region-wide issues, such as economic development, joint resource sharing and humanitarian concerns. But only the right kind of conference should take place, one that helps launch and support direct negotiations without interfering in them.

Palestinian participation is required at every stage of the negotiations. Palestinians have a vital stake in the outcome of negotiations. They must have a say in the negotiations themselves, and they must approve the outcome.

Participation involves responsibilities, however. There are no free rides. All parties must demonstrate their desire to make peace. They must be creative and reliable. They must adhere to internationally-accepted principles and norms. For Palestinians, this means acting credibly and pursuing goals that are achievable.

No participant in a peace process can wave the flag of justice in one hand, and brandish the weapons of terrorism in the other. All participants must renounce violence and terrorism. Each must agree to negotiate on the accepted international basis of Security Council Resolutions 242 and 338.

There are also no free rides for outside parties that want to play a role in settling the conflict. Both the United States and the Soviet Union consider a settlement of the conflict to be in their national interest. But the Soviets will need to confront some difficult choices.

There is no longer any excuse for the Soviets to avoid such important steps as resuming full diplomatic relations with Israel, nor is there justification for preventing Jews who wish to emigrate from doing so. The sooner these things are done, the better for the peace process.

The challenge of Arab-Israeli peacemaking in a time of change is to find the right mix of fundamental realities and creative ideas. The question is how to assess some of these ideas at this time.

Peace cannot be achieved through the creation of an independent Palestinian state, or through permanent Israeli control or annexation of the West Bank and Gaza. At the same time, each party is free to bring any position it chooses to the negotiating table. Israelis are free to argue for annexation. Palestinians are free to argue for independence. The United States will not support either of these positions during negotiations.

The status of the West Bank and Gaza cannot be determined by unilateral acts of either side, but only through a process of negotiations. A declaration of independent Palestinian statehood or government-in-exile would be such a unilateral act. Palestinians need to decide whether to remain a part of the problem in the Middle East, or become part of the solution. History will not repeat itself. Practical, realistic steps by Palestinians are required.

An attempt by Israel to transfer Palestinians from the West Bank and Gaza would also be a unilateral act to determine the status of those territories. The United States would oppose this vigorously. Such a policy does not provide a solution to the problem, nor does it bring negotiations any closer.

It is also not acceptable to shift the focus from what Palestinians or Israelis need to do to advance the peace process, to what the United States should do. This applies to those who urge that the United States should support Palestinian self-determination.

The United States cannot accept "self-determination" when it is a code-word for an independent Palestinian state or for unilateral determination of the outcome of negotiations.

To expect the PLO to accept Resolutions 242 and 338 as the basis for negotiation is not to ask it to make a concession. Those resolutions lay out basic principles which the international community has decided must be reflected in a peace settlement. In addition to these, the legitimate rights of the Palestinian people—including political rights—must also be addressed. It is through acceptance of these principles—not through any action by the United States—that the Palestinians can participate fully in determining their own future.

In the Arab-Israeli conflict, there is no objective reality and no immutable set of circumstances that cannot be shaped by decisions for peace. During the period ahead, such decisions are required. Israelis and Palestinians themselves must condition the environment for negotiations. They can start down the road to accommodation and reconciliation. Violence has distracted people from establishing achievable objectives. Political debate must replace violence.

Concrete actions on the ground are required. Palestinians must renounce terrorism and violence. They must accept the right of Israel to exist in peace and present themselves as a viable negotiating partner. They cannot murder or threaten other Palestinians who maintain contact with Israeli authorities.

For its part, Israel has the responsibility to maintain law and order in the West Bank and Gaza. But, Israel must also find a way to respond to expressions of Palestinian grievances. It cannot claim there is no one to talk to, while suppressing political expression and arresting or deporting those who speak out—even those who speak in moderate terms.

There must also be actions on the regional level. The peace treaty between Egypt and Israel is a strategic anchor of the entire peace process; it must constantly be enhanced. Relations between Israel and other Arab states must start down the road to normalization. Relations between people don't need to await the formality of a treaty. Israelis and Arabs should find ways to talk to each other now, even before treaty relations exist.

The conditions under which refugees live in the region must also be addressed. Poverty is no ally of peace. The continuing existence of refugees does not make the case for Palestinian nationalism stronger. Palestinian refugees can live in better conditions even while the search for peace continues. Arabs and Israelis, together with the international community, must shoulder this responsibility.

Finally, there must be a change of attitude throughout the region. The way people think affects the way they act. Cynicism, skepticism and pessimism about peace must be shaken. The conflict must be seen to be resolvable. Once there is the will for and belief in a settlement, the benefits of peace will be seen to outweigh the real but transitory risks of achieving it.

So, fundamental realities persist, even in the midst of change. The goals of the peace process have not changed, nor have the principles of negotiations.

Indeed, the only thing that needs to change is the willingness of people in the Middle East to move the peace process forward. Israelis, Palestinians, Jordanians, Syrians and Lebanese can make peace happen. The Egyptians are more than ready to do their part. So are we, and so are others around the world. The opportunities today are greater than before, and so are the risks of doing nothing. To make peace, the parties must exploit the new opportunities created by the current ferment. And they should start now.

## 26. Statement by State Department Spokesman Charles Redman on the Resolutions of the 19th Palestine National Council, 16 November, 1988

After reviewing the outcome of the Palestine National Council, there are signs that there are Palestinians who are trying to move the PLO in a constructive way. That's encouraging and should continue. But measured against the requirements of the negotiating process, more movement on key issues will be required. And measured against the positions the PLO must adopt in order for the United States to engage in dialogue with it, the results of the PNC session fall short of meeting those requirements. The reference to Resolutions 242 and 338 is an advance over previous efforts by the PNC. Nevertheless, it is ambiguous both in its placement in the text and its meaning. Possibly implied or indirect reference to Israel's right to exist is not sufficient. Recognition must be clear and unambiguous. And the statement on terrorism is a restatement of previous positions. It's still performance that counts.

## 27. Statement by the State Department on the Rejection of PLO Chairman Yasser Arafat's Visa Application to the US, 26 November, 1988

The 1947 United Nations Headquarters Agreement obligates the United States to provide certain rights of entry, transit, and residence to persons invited to the United Nations headquarters district in New York City.

The Congress of the United States conditioned the entry of the US into the UN Headquarters Agreement on the retention by the US government of the authority to bar the entry of aliens associated with or invited by the United Nations "in order to safeguard its own security."

In this regard, US law excludes members of the PLO from entry into the United States by virtue of their affiliation in an organization which engages in terrorism. The secretary of state is vested by law with the discretion to recommend to the attorney general that the prohibition against a particular PLO member be waived.

The United Nations General Assembly in 1974 invited the Palestine Liberation Organization to participate as an observer at the General Assembly. The United States acknowledged that this UN invitation obligates the US to accord PLO observers entry, transit, and residence; therefore, visa waivers have been issued to such individuals as a routine practice. As a result, a PLO Observer Mission has been in operation at the UN since 1975. The PLO, therefore, has had, and continues to have, ample opportunity to make its positions known to the membership of the United Nations.

On November 24, 1988, we received an application from Mr. Yasser Arafat, chairman of the PLO, for a visa to attend the United Nations General Assembly session in New York City as an invitee. The Secretary of State has decided not to recommend a waiver of ineligibility in this case; the visa application, therefore, is not approved.

The US government has convincing evidence that PLO elements have engaged in terrorism against Americans and others. This evidence includes a series of operations undertaken by the Force 17 and the Hawari organizations since the PLO claimed to forswear the use of terrorism in the Cairo Declaration of November 1985.

As chairman of the PLO, Mr. Arafat is responsible for actions of these organizations which are units of Fatah, an element of the PLO of which he also is chairman and which is under his control. The most recent sign of Mr. Arafat's associations with terrorism was the presence at the Algiers session of the Palestine National Council (PNC) this month of Abu Abbas, a member of the Executive Committee of the PLO who has been convicted by the Italian judicial system of the murder of an American citizen, Mr. Leon Klinghoffer.

In summary, we find that:

—The PLO through certain of its elements has employed terrorism against Americans.

—Mr. Arafat, as chairman of the PLO, knows of, condones, and lends support to such acts; he, therefore, is an accessory to such terrorism.

—Terrorism and those involved in it are a serious threat to our national security and to the lives of American citizens.

—The Headquarters Agreement, contained in Public Law 80-357, reserves to us the right to bar the entry of those who represent a threat to our security.

The United States firmly believes that Palestinian political rights must be recognized and addressed. A comprehensive settlement of the Arab-Israeli conflict is achievable through the peace process that already has brought significant progress.

Palestinian participation is required at every stage of the negotiations required to achieve peace, justice and security. Participation requires responsibilities, however. All parties must demonstrate their desire to make peace, they must adhere to internationally accepted principles and norms. No participant in a peace process can wave the flag of justice in one hand and brandish the weapon of terrorism in the other. All participants must renounce violence and terrorism.

The outcome of the PNC session in Algiers produced signs that there are Palestinians who are trying to move the PLO in a constructive way. That is encouraging and should continue. It is unfortunate that the blight of terrorism still afflicts the Palestinian cause and leaves no alternative to decisions such as the one the secretary has taken today.

## 28. Statement by State Department Spokesman Charles Redman on Yasser Arafat's Speech to the UN, 13 December, 1988

The United States listened carefully to Mr. Arafat's speech. The speech contained some interesting and some positive developments. But it continued to be ambiguous on the key issues which must be clearly addressed in order for the United States to enter a substantive dialogue with the PLO.

Those issues are: acceptance of Resolutions 242 and 338; recognition of Israel's right to exist, and rejection of terrorism in all its forms. These issues must be addressed clearly, squarely, without ambiguity. That didn't happen and, as a consequence, the speech did not meet our conditions.

As we've said before, it was again obvious in the speech today, there are clearly those in the PLO who are trying to move in a constructive way. As I said, we saw some interesting and some positive developments in this speech. And so we would encourage further developments in that direction.

## 29. Address by Ambassador Vernon A. Walters to the 43rd Session of the UN General Assembly, Geneva, 14 December, 1988

The search for peace in the Middle East has been a constant feature of United States policy. American efforts helped bring about the disengagement of forces agreements between Israel and Egypt, and between Israel and Syria. American efforts helped bring about the Camp David Accords and the Egyptian-Israeli

Peace Treaty. The United States remains an active, committed partner in the search for a comprehensive settlement achieved through negotiations.

In helping willing parties negotiate their differences, the United States has always kept in mind a simple, but abiding reality—namely, that no outside party can want peace more than the parties themselves want and need peace. As such, the United States has always opposed efforts to impose solutions from the outside, concentrating instead on eliciting movement from the parties on the critical issues involved in the negotiations. It is for these reasons, that the United States will vote against the resolutions submitted during this debate.

In seeking to advance the prospects for negotiations leading to a comprehensive settlement, this year the United States advanced a set of proposals that represent the core requirements of a successful process of accommodation:

—The objective is a comprehensive settlement of the Arab-Israeli conflict through negotiations.

—There is no substitute for direct negotiations between the parties concerned. The parties to negotiations must accept to negotiate with each other.

—An international conference may be useful insofar as it helps launch and support direct negotiations; but a conference must not pre-empt or substitute for the direct negotiations.

—The United Nations Security Council established the basis of the negotiating process in Resolutions 242 and 338. Each party may have other positions and preferences that it wishes to bring to negotiations, consistent with 242 and 338; but none can limit or avoid accepting 242 and 338 as the basis of negotiations.

—Negotiations must proceed in an atmosphere free of terrorism, violence and intimidation.

These are valuable and enduring principles that need to be at the core of efforts to resolve the dispute. Additionally, there should be a period of transition between the status quo and a final settlement. This transitional period will help build confidence among the parties that negotiations work. It will give the parties time to adjust to a new situation. It will allow the parties to deal with each other differently, gradually, in light of an agreement freely negotiated.

Movement toward peace starts with movement by the parties. Each side needs to adopt constructive policies aimed at realistic and pragmatic progress toward peace.

For Israel, the choice is clear, albeit difficult. In order to achieve the security it deserves and requires, Israel must face up to the need for withdrawal from occupied territories and to the need to accommodate legitimate Palestinian political rights. The extent, shape and form of these issues need to be hammered out through negotiations; but they must be addressed squarely.

For Palestinians, the choice is equally clear, and equally difficult. In order to achieve the political rights they deserve and require, Palestinian demands will have to accommodate the reality of Israel's existence and security needs, and they will have to commit themselves to negotiations with Israel.

For the other Arabs, the choices are equally important. Jordan, Syria and Lebanon have a conflict with Israel to resolve through negotiations. Their conflict will not be solved otherwise. Other Arab states can help by sending signals of acceptance and reconciliation to Israel. They must talk to Israel. The absence of dialogue means continued stalemate.

For outside parties, support and encouragement are the necessary elements. A role for outside parties in peace making is not a right; it must be earned. It is time for the Soviet Union to restore full diplomatic relations with Israel. It is time for the Peoples Republic of China to recognize Israel. The parties need support to bring them together, and the international community can provide that support.

These fundamental elements of a successful peace process can be encouraged through accommodation and reconciliation between Israelis and Palestinians. This is not an easy task to accomplish. It is very difficult for the parties to overcome prejudices and blind spots about each other; it is sometimes equally difficult for the international community to lay aside political preferences and expediencies and to adopt a realistic course toward a comprehensive settlement. But the international community must speak with a realistic, pragmatic voice.

We must tell the parties that their dispute is resolvable. We must tell them that we are tired of this conflict and tired of their unwillingness to make fair compromises. We must tell them the time has come to agree that a negotiated settlement is required.

So let us channel the energy that has gone into this debate in a positive, realistic direction. Unbalanced resolutions are not the answer. One-sided statements are not the answer.

The answer is commitment to comprehensive peace. The answer is negotiations based on Security Council Resolutions 242 and 338. The answer is renunciation of violence and terrorism. My government stands ready as always to assist in moving ahead in the search for peace.

## 30. Statement by Secretary of State George Shultz on Dialogue with the PLO, 14 December, 1988

The Palestine Liberation Organization today issued a statement in which it accepted UN Security Council Resolutions 242 and 338, recognized Israel's right to exist in peace and security and renounce terrorism. As a result, the United States is prepared for a substantive dialogue with PLO representatives.

I am designating our Ambassador to Tunisia as the only authorized channel for that dialogue. The objective of the United States remains as always, a comprehensive peace in the Middle East. In that light, I view this development as one more step toward the beginning of direct negotiations between the parties which alone can lead to such a peace.

Nothing here may be taken to imply an acceptance or recognition by the United States of an independent Palestinian state. The position of the US is that the status of the West Bank and Gaza cannot be determined by unilateral acts of either side, but only through a process of negotiations. The United States does not recognize the declaration of an independent Palestinian state.

It is also important to emphasize that the United States commitment to the security of Israel remains unflinching.

### 31.   Statement by President Ronald Reagan on Relations with the PLO, 14 December, 1988

The Palestine Liberation Organization today issued a statement in which it accepted United Nations Security Council Resolutions 242 and 338, recognized Israel's right to exist, and renounced terrorism. These have long been our conditions for a substantive dialogue. They have been met. Therefore, I have authorized the State Department to enter into a substantive dialogue with PLO representatives. The Palestine Liberation Organization must live up to its statements. In particular, it must demonstrate that its renunciation of terrorism is pervasive and permanent.

The initiation of a dialogue between the United States and PLO representatives is an important step in the peace process, the more so because it represents the serious evolution of Palestinian thinking toward realistic and pragmatic positions on the key issues. But the objective of the United States remains, as always, a comprehensive peace in the Middle East. In that light, we view this development as one more step toward the beginning of direct negotiations between the parties, which alone can lead to such a peace.

The United States' special commitment to Israel's security and well-being remains unshakable. Indeed, a major reason for our entry into this dialogue is to help Israel achieve the recognition and security it deserves.

### 32.   Statement by President George Bush Following his Meeting with President Husni Mubarak, Washington, DC, 3 April, 1989

Well, it was a special pleasure for me to welcome our good friend, President Husni Mubarak, to the White House this morning. Our personal relationship goes back several years, from the days we were both Vice Presidents; then through my visit to Cairo in 1986; and then our most recent meeting in Tokyo in February. I am glad for this early opportunity to discuss with President Mubarak the vital interest of my administration in moving the peace process forward.

Egypt's pivotal role in the Middle East and our strong bilateral partnership remain keys to achieving that goal. President Mubarak's visit is particularly timely. For over 15 years, Egypt has been our partner in the peace process. And 10 years ago, Egypt and Israel signed their historic Treaty of Peace. Egypt's continued commitment to expanding that peace is a source of great encouragement for all of us who seek a comprehensive resolution to the Arab-Israeli conflict.

The reemergence of Egypt as a respected leader of the Arab world attests to President Mubarak's statesmanship and ability, as well as to Egypt's wisdom in pursuing the path of peace. In our discussions, we talked—spent a considerable amount of time talking about the Middle East peace process. We share a sense of urgency to move toward a comprehensive settlement through direct negotiations.

Ten years of peace between Egypt and Israel demonstrate that peace works. And it can work for Israelis and Palestinians as well. There's a need now for creativity, demonstrable commitment, and the application of sound principles. Creativity in order to look again at old problems, and then devise imaginative ways of solving them; commitment to face the challenges and risks of making peace rather than throwing up our hands and giving up; and adherence to sound principles, like the United Nations Security Council Resolutions 242 and 338.

A new atmosphere must be created where Israelis and Arabs feel each other's willingness to compromise so that both sides can win. Violence can give way to dialogue once both sides understand that the dialogue will offer political gain. Egypt and the United States share the goals of security for Israel, the end of the occupation, and achievement of Palestinian political rights. These are the promises held out by a sustained commitment to a negotiated settlement towards which a properly structured international conference could play a useful role at an appropriate time.

We also had a chance to review some important elements of our own bilateral relationship. They've been sealed at the highest levels, these special ties that we have with Egypt. They're forged by the global imperatives of peace, stability, and development in the region. They are strong and flexible, reaffirmed by every administration, and resilient to withstand turbulent times for the region and for the world.

President Mubarak enjoys our full support as he implements courageous reform measures to strengthen Egypt's economy for future generations. And under the inspired stewardship of President Mubarak, Egypt has grown in stature and in strength, and we in the United States welcome this development. We are proud of our partnership with Egypt, and I look forward to working closely with President Mubarak in carrying out our common vision of peace, stability, and development in the Middle East.

## 33. Statement by President George Bush Following his Meeting with Prime Minister Yitzhak Shamir, Washington, DC, 6 April, 1989

Well, Prime Minister Shamir and I have had a very productive meeting. My message to him and, through him, to the government and the people of Israel was clear. We are friends, strategic partners, and allies. And the mutual interests that bind together the people of the United States and Israel are broad and deep. The Prime Minister and I dedicated ourselves to maintaining and, where possible, improving the relationship between our two countries. Both of us are committed to this goal.

Throughout the world, old enemies are finding ways to talk to one another and to end conflicts in a manner that preserves the basic interests of all concerned. This can and must happen in the Middle East. The Arab-Israeli conflict can be resolved. Peace, security, and political rights can be attained through direct negotiations. The status quo serves the interests of no one.

In this spirit, I reiterated to Prime Minister Shamir the resolve of the United States to assist the parties of the Middle East in their pursuit of a comprehensive settlement of the Arab-Israeli conflict. Our responsibility as friends and as partners in the search for peace is to help develop approaches that enhance peace prospects. Problems do not resolve themselves, leaders acting with courage and vision solve problems. Menachem Begin and Anwar Sadat demonstrated this truth a decade ago at Camp David. Today's leaders can afford to do no less.

I reassured the Prime Minister that the fundamental basis of our approach to a Middle East settlement has not changed. The United States is committed to a comprehensive peace achieved through direct negotiations based on UN Security Council Resolutions 242 and 338. This remains the building block for a viable negotiation for a durable settlement. This is our goal. With regard to final status issues, I reaffirmed to the Prime Minister that we do not support an independent Palestinian state, nor Israeli sovereignty or permanent occupation of the West Bank and Gaza.

To move the peace process forward, I discussed with the Prime Minister, as I had earlier this week with President Mubarak, an ambitious but realistic approach. Progress will require meaningful steps to reduce tensions, political dialogue between Israel and Palestinians, and clear indications that all concerned are prepared to think creatively about key substantive issues. Israel has an obligation to contribute to this process, but it cannot be expected to assume the entire burden. The Palestinians, the Arab states, and other interested parties must demonstrate that they, too, are willing to make peace a reality.

I stressed that no peace process can succeed in a political vacuum. I believe it is in Israel's interest to engage in a serious dialogue with Palestinians that address their legitimate political rights. The United States believes that elections in the territories can be designed to contribute to a political process of dialogue and negotiation. We urge Israel and the Palestinians to arrive at a mutually acceptable formula for elections. And we plan in the days and weeks ahead to work toward that end.

In negotiations, Israel understands that Palestinians will be free to bring their own positions and preferences to the bargaining table. The Prime Minister assured me that Israel is committed to negotiating an agreement on final status that is satisfactory to all sides. And he made it clear that interim arrangements on Palestinian self-rule are not the end of the road, but are directly linked to a broader political process that includes negotiating and concluding and agreement on final status.

I'm encouraged by the Prime Minister's assurance that all options are open for negotiation. The Prime Minister and I agreed that our governments would remain in close touch to ensure that everything possible is being done to promote the prospects for peace in the Middle East. And speaking for myself and for the American people, I want to assure everyone that the United States is committed to promoting this goal.

## 34. Address by Secretary of State James Baker Before the American-Israel Public Affairs Committee, Washington, DC, 22 May, 1989 [Excerpts]

...You know, it's been said that AIPAC manages to bring together the Executive and the Congress in a way that they might not normally associate. I'd agree with that, and I would add only that we have a name for such coming together. We call it bipartisanship. And American bipartisan support for Israel is a great and an enduring achievement, not only for AIPAC, not only for Israel's supporters but also, above all, for America's national interest.

There have been many, many analyses of the US-Israeli relationship over the years, and most of them begin with the fact that we share common values of freedom and of democracy. That is the golden thread in the tapestry of United States-Israeli ties; and there are, if I might suggest it, other strands as well.

Ed [Ed Levy, President] has mentioned some of what I did in the Reagan Administration, but let me tell you that I was proud to work in that Administration, an Administration that recognized the importance of United States-Israeli strategic cooperation and an Administration that I think gave fiber and sinew to our strategic partnership.

I'm also proud to have had a small part to play in the historic free trade agreement which may well become a model for other nations. I really think we probably would not have gotten home on the Canadian-US free trade agreement had we not had a US-Israel free trade agreement. The President believes— President Bush believes—and I believe that on these issues there can only be one policy and that is a policy of continuity. American support for Israel is the foundation of our approach to the problems—the very, very difficult problems—of the Middle East.

This support has become all the more important as we approach what I think is a critical juncture in the Middle East. For many years we have associated that region with either the vanished glories of ancient history or the terrible costs of modern conflict. But now, I think, the world is changing. We have seen long-standing problems in other regions begin to abate. The President spoke last week of promising and hopeful, even though incomplete, developments in the Soviet Union. Everywhere there is a quickening consciousness that the globe is being transformed through the search for democracy, the spread of free enterprise and technological progress. And, of course, nowhere is that more true, as we meet here today, than in the People's Republic of China.

The Middle East should be able to participate fully in these new developments. Oftentimes we think of the region as a place full of precious resources, such as oil and minerals. But the area's most precious resource, if we really stop and think about it, is the lives of its peoples.

And that is the stake. Are the peoples of the Middle East going to safeguard their most precious resource? Are they going to join the rest of the changing world in the works of peace? Or is this region going to pioneer in conflict once more through the proliferation of chemical weapons and ballistic missiles?

The people of Israel are vitally concerned with these questions. Israel, of course, is a vigorous democracy. The Israelis are among the world leaders in communications, electronics and avionics—the new technological revolutions. And Israel understood long ago that the most important of her natural resources is the skill and the intelligence of her people.

This is the wider context in which we and Israel must consider the peace process. The outcome is of vital concern both to Israel's future and for our vision of a free and peaceful world.

Not so long ago, we marked a decade of the Camp David Peace Accords. That occasion reminded us not only of how far we have come but of how much further we have to go. I would like to report to you that we and Israel have taken some important steps forward.

Before Prime Minister Shamir visited Washington, we had called for some

Israeli ideas on how to restart the peace process. We did so based on our conviction that a key condition for progress was a productive United States-Israeli partnership. And I believe that the best way to be productive is through consultation rather than confrontation.

Let me assure you that we were not disappointed. The Prime Minister will, I'm sure, forgive me if I divulge to you a conversation at our very first meeting. The Prime Minister said, in preparing for his visit, he had studied President Bush and me, just as he suspected that perhaps we had studied him. I had been described by the media as an ever-flexible pragmatist. The Prime Minister, he said, had been described as an inflexible man of ideological principle. Then the Prime Minister volunteered that in his view the journalists were wrong, and they were wrong in both cases. "Yes," he said, "I am a man of principle, but I am also a pragmatist who knows what political compromise means." And he said that it was clear that I, although a pragmatist, was also a man of principle and that principle would guide my foreign policy approach. Needless to say, I didn't disagree with the Prime Minister.

If ever an opening statement achieved its goal of establishing a strong working relationship, this was it. I think it's fair to say that we understood each other to be pragmatists, but pragmatists guided by principle.

As we approach the peace process, together, we understand Israel's caution especially when assessing Arab attitudes about peace. I don't blame Israel for exercising this caution. Its history and, indeed, its geo-political situation require it.

At the same time, I think that caution must never become paralysis. Ten years after Camp David, Egypt remains firmly committed to peace, and Arab attitudes are changing. Egypt's re-admission into the Arab League on its own terms and with the peace treaty intact, I think, is one sign of change. Evolving Palestinian attitudes are another. Much more needs to be done—to be demonstrated—that such change is real. But I don't think that change can be ignored even now. This is surely a time when, as the Prime Minister said, the right mix of principles and pragmatism is required.

As we assess these changes, United States policies benefit from a longstanding commitment to sound principles, principles which have worked in practice to advance the peace process. Let me mention some of those principles for you.

First, the US believes that the objective of the peace process is a comprehensive settlement achieved through negotiations based on United Nations Security Council Resolutions 242 and 338. In our view, these negotiations must involve territory for peace, security and recognition for Israel and all of the states of the region, and Palestinian political rights.

Second, for negotiations to succeed they must allow the parties to deal directly with each other, face-to-face. A properly structured international conference could be useful at an appropriate time, but only if it did not interfere with or in any way replace or be a substitute for direct talks between the parties.

Third, the issues involved in the negotiations are far too complex, and the emotions are far too deep, to move directly to a final settlement. Accordingly, some transitional period is needed, associated in time and sequence with negotiations on final status. Such a transition will allow the parties to take the measure of each other's performance, to encourage attitudes to change, and to demonstrate that peace and coexistence is desired.

Fourth, in advance of direct negotiations, neither the United States nor any other party, inside or outside, can or will dictate an outcome. That is why the United States does not support annexation or permanent Israeli control of the West Bank and Gaza, nor do we support the creation of an independent Palestinian state.

I would add here that we do have an idea about the reasonable middle ground to which a settlement should be directed. That is, self-government for Palestinians in the West Bank and Gaza in a manner acceptable to Palestinians, Israel and Jordan. Such a formula provides ample scope for Palestinians to achieve their full political rights. It also provides ample protection for Israel's security as well.

Following these principles, we face a pragmatic issue, the issue of how do we get negotiations underway. Unfortunately the gap between the parties on key issues such as Palestinian representation and the shape of a final settlement remains very, very wide. Violence has soured the atmosphere, and so a quick move to negotiations is quite unlikely. And in the absence of either a minimum of good will or any movement to close the gap, a high-visibility American initiative, we think, has little basis on which to stand.

If we were to stop here, the situation would, I think, be gloomy indeed. But we are not going to stop with the status quo. We are engaged, as I mentioned a moment ago; we will remain engaged; and we will work to help create an environment to launch and sustain negotiations. This will require tough but necessary decisions for peace by all of the parties. It will also require a commitment to a process of negotiations clearly tied to the search for a permanent settlement of the conflict.

When Prime Minister Shamir visited Washington, he indicated that he shared our view that the status quo was unacceptable. He brought an idea for elections to—in his words—"launch a political negotiating process" which would involve transitional arrangements and final status. The Prime Minister made clear that all sides would be free to bring their preferred positions to the table and that the negotiated outcome must be acceptable to all. The United States welcomed these Israeli ideas and undertook to see whether it could help in creating an atmosphere which could sustain such a process.

Just last week the Israeli Cabinet approved a more detailed version of the Prime

Minister's proposal, indicating Israeli Government positions on some, but not all, of the issues which are involved. The Israeli proposal is an important and very positive start down the road toward constructing workable negotiations.

The Israeli Government *has* offered an initiative, and it *has* given us something to work with. It has taken a stand on some important issues, and this deserves a constructive Palestinian and broader Arab response.

Much work needs to be done—to elicit Palestinian and Arab thinking on the key elements in the process, to flesh out some of the details of the Israeli proposals, and to bridge areas where viewpoints differ. Both sides, of course, are going to have to build political constituencies for peace. Each idea, proposal, or detail, should be developed, if I may say so, as a deal-maker, not as a deal-breaker.

It may be possible to reach agreement, for example, on the standards of a workable elections process. Such elections should be free and fair, of course; and they should be free of interference from any quarter.

Through open access to media and outside observers, the integrity of the electoral process can be affirmed. And participation in the elections should be as open as possible.

It is therefore high time for serious political dialogue between Israeli officials and Palestinians in the territories to bring about a common understanding on these and other issues. Peace, and the peace process, must be built from the "ground up". Palestinians have it within their power to help define the shape of this initiative and to help define its essential elements. They shouldn't shy from a dialogue with Israel that can transform the current environment and determine the ground rules for getting to, for conducting, and indeed for moving beyond elections.

We should not hide from ourselves the difficulties that face even these steps here at the very beginning. For many Israelis it will not be easy to enter a negotiating process whose successful outcome will in all probability involve territorial withdrawal and the emergence of a new political reality. For Palestinians such an outcome will mean an end to the illusion of control over all of Palestine, and it will mean full recognition of Israel as a neighbor and partner in trade and in human contact.

Ladies and gentlemen, we do not think there is a real constructive alternative to the process which I have outlined. Continuation of the status quo will lead to increasing violence and worsening prospects for peace. We think now is the time to move toward a serious negotiating process, to create the atmosphere for a renewed peace process. Let the Arab world take concrete steps toward accommodation with Israel—not in place of the peace process, but as a catalyst for it.

And so we would say: end the economic boycott; stop the challenges to Israel's standing in international organizations; repudiate the odious line that Zionism is racism.

For Israel, now is the time to lay aside, once and for all, the unrealistic vision of a greater Israel. Israeli interests in the West Bank and Gaza—security and otherwise—can be accommodated in a settlement based on Resolution 242. Forswear annexation. Stop settlement activity. Allow schools to reopen. Reach out to the Palestinians as neighbors who deserve political rights.

For Palestinians, now is the time to speak with one voice for peace. Renounce the policy of phases in all languages, not just those addressed to the West.

Practice constructive diplomacy, not attempts to distort international organizations, such as the World Health Organization.

Amend the covenant. Translate the dialogue of violence in the *intifadah* into a dialogue of politics and diplomacy. Violence will not work. Reach out to Israelis and convince them of your peaceful intentions. You have the most to gain from doing so, and no one else can or *will* do it for you.

Finally, understand that no one is going to "deliver" Israel for you.

For outside parties—in particular, the Soviet Union—now is the time to make "new thinking" a reality as it applies to the Middle East. I must say that Chairman Gorbachev and Foreign Minister Shevardnadze told me in Moscow ten days ago that Soviet policy is changing. New laws regarding emigration will soon be discussed by the Supreme Soviet. Jewish life in the Soviet Union is also looking better, with students beginning to study their heritage freely.

Finally, the Soviet Union agreed with us last week that Prime Minister Shamir's election proposal was worthy of consideration.

These, of course, are all positive signs. But the Soviets must go further to demonstrate convincingly that they are serious about new thinking in the Arab-Israel conflict. Let Moscow restore diplomatic ties with Israel, for example.

The Soviets should also help promote a serious peace process, not just empty slogans. And it is time for the Soviet Union, we think, to behave responsibly when it comes to arms and stop the supply of sophisticated weapons to countries like Libya.

Ladies and gentlemen, I said at the beginning of these remarks that the Middle East had approached a turning point. I believe that this region, which is so full of potential, will not remain immune from the changes which are sweeping the rest of the world. These changes begin with the quest for democracy, for individual freedom and for choice. Long ago, of course, Israel chose this path. And long ago the American people decided to walk with Israel in her quest for peace and in her quest for security.

The policy I have described today reaffirms and renews that course. For our part, the United States will move ahead steadily and carefully, in a step-by-step approach designed to help the parties make the necessary decisions for peace. Perhaps Judge Learned Hand expressed it best when he said, "...we shall have to be content with short steps; ...but we shall have gone forward, if we bring to our task ...patience, understanding, sympathy, forbearance, generosity, fortitude and above all an inflexible determination."

## 35.   Letter to Secretary of State James Baker from 95 US Senators, Washington, DC, 8 June, 1989

The Honorable James A. Baker III
Secretary of State
Washington, DC 20520

Dear Secretary Baker:

We write to express our support for the peace initiative recently launched by the Government of Israel. We believe that holding free and democratic elections on the West Bank and the Gaza Strip would be indispensable in allowing a local Palestinian leadership to emerge as a first step toward a just and lasting peace between Israel and its Arab neighbors.

It is our conviction that Israel's offer is both sincere and far-reaching. The United States has a vital role to play in convincing others of the merits of Israel's plan. Israel's proposals have not always received the consideration they deserve by the other parties to the conflict or by the international community at large. To prevent that from occurring now, the United States must be fully supportive, both in fact and in appearance. While every detail of Israel's proposals may not yet be entirely in place, a strong endorsement by the United States would help ensure their serious consideration.

Israel's willingness to allow all options to be put on the table during the negotiations to be held after the elections and during the transition period demonstrates a real readiness to take risks for peace. We must keep in mind that Israel will be asked to give up politically what it won militarily by defending itself against attacks from outside Israeli borders in which thousands of Israelis died. Those aggressors, except for Egypt, remain in a state of war with Israel to this day. They possess far more sophisticated weapons than the stones of the Palestinian youths involved in the rioting. Israel is not simply being asked to make peace with the Palestinians on the West Bank and Gaza; the decisions Israel makes will greatly affect her ability to defend herself against other Arab enemies.

The Arab countries who have made war against Israel in the past now have the chance to make a real move toward peace. They can do so by urging the Palestinians in the territories to participate in the elections called for by this plan. While neither Egypt nor Jordan has rejected Prime Minister Shamir's proposal outright, their voices could be instrumental in persuading the Palestinians to accept this offer.

The Administration's reaction to this plan will undoubtedly have great influence over the Arab reaction. We urge you to strongly and publicly endorse the Israeli peace initiative.

Sincerely,

Adams, Brock (WA); Armstrong, William L. (CO); Baucus, Max (MT); Bentsen, Lloyd (TX); Biden, Joseph R., Jr. (DE); Bingaman, Jeff (NM); Bond, Christopher S. (MO); Boren, David Lyle (OK); Boschwitz, Rudy (MN); Bradley, Bill (NJ); Breaux, John B. (LA); Bryan, Richard H. (NV); Bumpers, Dale (AR); Burdick, Quentin N. (ND); Burns, Conrad (MT); Coats, Dan (IN); Cochran, Thad (MS); Cohen, William S. (ME); Conrad Kent (ND); Cranston, Alan (CA); D'Amato, Alfonse M. (NY); Danforth, John C. (MO); Daschle, Thomas A. (SD); DeConcini, Dennis (AZ); Dixon, Alan J. (IL); Dodd, Christopher J. (CT); Dole, Robert (KS); Domenici, Peter V. (NM); Durenberger, Dave (MN); Exon, J. James (NE); Ford, Wendell N. (KY); Fowler, Wyche, Jr. (GA); Garn, Jake (UT); Glenn, John (OH); Gore, Albert, Jr. (TN); Gorton, Slade (WA); Graham, Bob (FL); Gramm, Phil (TX); Grassley, Charles E. (IA); Harkin, Tom (IA); Hatch, Orrin G. (UT); Heflin, Howell, (AL); Heinz, John (PA); Helms, Jesse (NC); Humphrey, Gordon J. (NH); Inouye, Daniel K. (HI); Jeffords, James M. (VT); Johnston, J. Bennett (LA); Kassebaum, Nancy Landon (KS); Kasten, Robert W., Jr. (WI); Kennedy, Edward M. (MA); Kerrey, Bob (NE); Kerry, John F. (MA); Kohl, Herbert H. (WI); Lautenberg, Frank R. (NJ); Leahy, Patrick J. (VT); Levin, Carl (MI); Lieberman, Joe (CT); Lott, Trent (MS); Lugar, Richard G. (IN); McCain, John (AZ); McClure, James A. (ID); McConnell, Mitch (KY); Mack, Connie (FL); Matsunaga, Spark M. (HI); Metzenbaum, Howard M. (OH); Mikulski, Barbara A. (MD); Mitchell, George J. (ME); Moynihan, Daniel Patrick (NY); Murkowski, Frank H. (AK); Nickles, Don (OK); Nunn, Sam (GA); Packwood, Bob (OR); Pell, Claiborne (RI); Pressler, Larry (SD); Pryor, David (AR); Reid, Harry (NV); Riegle, Donald W., Jr. (MI); Robb, Charles S. (VA); Rockefeller, Jay (WV); Roth, William V., Jr. (DE); Rudman, Warren (NH); Sanford, Terry (NC); Sarbanes, Paul S. (MD); Sasser, Jim (TN); Shelby, Richard C. (AL); Simon, Paul (IL); Simpson, Alan K. (WY); Specter, Arlen (PA); Stevens, Ted (AK); Symms, Steve (ID); Thurmond, Strom (SC); Warner, John William (VA); Wilson, Pete (CA); Wirth, Timothy E. (CO).

## 36. Letter to Secretary of State James Baker from 68 US Senators, Washington, DC, 21 September, 1989

The Honorable James A. Baker III
Secretary of State
Washington, DC 20520

Dear Secretary Baker:

We are concerned that since the encouraging pronouncements by Yasser Arafat of the PLO in December, 1988, Arafat and the PLO have taken steps which substantially negate those pronouncements and directly undermine opportunities for progress in the Middle East peace process. We are opposed to the United States taking steps that could be seen as generally rewarding the PLO at this time.

Last December Arafat, ostensibly on behalf of the PLO, committed to recognize Israel's right to exist, renounce terrorism, and accept United Nations Resolutions 242 and 338. Based on these commitments and over the opposition of our strongest ally in the region, Israel, the US opened a "substantive dialogue" with the PLO. The past bloody record of terrorism by the PLO against Americans and others was, in effect, set aside in the hopes that the dialogue would lead to the transformation of the PLO and to significant gains in the peace process.

In the past nine months, the PLO has taken a number of actions that severely undermine the hopes for peace in the region:

*Condoning terrorism:* Arafat and the PLO have expressed understanding and sympathy for the terrorist who drove a bus off an Israeli highway in July, killing 16 people. Armed infiltrations into Israel from Lebanon and Jordan have not been condemned by Arafat. "Directives" issued by the PLO have encouraged the use of deadly "Molotov cocktails" of the type used in a bus attack that burned to death an Israeli woman and her three children.

*Terrorizing Palestinians:* The PLO has encouraged the killings of many Palestinians alleged to be Israeli "collaborators," including an individual whose only contact with Israel was possession of an identity card.

*Opposing dialogue:* Arafat and the PLO have called for an end to meetings between the West Bank and Gaza Palestinians and Israeli Prime Minister Shamir and other Israeli officials. PLO opposition to such meetings directly undermines American efforts—with strong support in the Congress—to negotiate plans for elections in the West Bank and Gaza.

*Fateh resolutions:* Recent resolutions of Fateh, the main component of the PLO called for an escalation of the "armed struggle," labeled the establishment of

Israel (referred to as the "barbarous Zionist entity") as a crime, and rejected the Shamir peace initiative. These resolutions contradict Arafat's December commitments.

The dialogue between the United States and PLO should not be an end unto itself: it must be a catalyst for, not an impediment to, a dialogue between Israel, her Arab neighbors, and Palestinians.

The PLO, through its recent statements and actions, is on a collision course with the peace process. Arafat and the PLO must reaffirm and implement, in deed and in word, the statements of just nine months ago. The more that the PLO moves in this direction, the more it can expect from the United States and Israel.

We applaud your efforts in seeking progress in the Arab-Israel conflict. We believe, however, that now is the time for the US to exert pressure on the PLO to move toward peace and away from terror. This is not the time for unearned concessions or rewards, such as reversing the current policy of denying a visa for Arafat to enter the United States, or elevating the PLO dialogue to higher levels. Rewarding the PLO at this time would undercut the peace process, call into question the seriousness of US anti-terrorism policy, be antithetical to American interests, and threaten the security of Israel.

We appreciate your consideration of our views.

(signed)

William Armstrong (R-CO), Max Baucus (D-MT), Lloyd Bentsen (D-TX), Joseph Biden, Jr. (D-DE), Christopher Bond (R-MO), David Boren (D-OK), Rudy Boschwitz (R-MN), Bill Bradley (D-NJ), John Breaux (D-LA), Richard Bryan (D-NV), Quentin Burdick (D-ND), Conrad Burns (R-MT), Dan Coats (R-IN), Thad Cochran (R-MS), William Cohen (R-ME), Kent Conrad (D-ND), Alfonse D'Amato (R-NY), Thomas Daschle (D-SD), Dennis DeConcini (D-AZ), Alan Dixon (D-IL), Pete Domenici (R-NM), Dave Durenberger (R-MN), James Exon (D-NE), Wendell Ford (D-KY), Albert Gore, Jr. (D-TN), Slade Gorton (R-WA), Bob Graham (D-FL), Phil Gramm (R-TX), Charles Grassley (R-IA), Orin Hatch (R-UT), Tom Harkin (D-IA), Howell Heflin (D-AL), John Heinz (R-PA), Jesse Helms (R-NC), Gordon Humphrey (R-NH), Daniel Inouye (D-HI), Bennett Johnston (D-LA), Robert Kasten, Jr. (R-WI), John Kerry (D-MA), Herb Kohl (D-WI), Frank Lautenberg (D-NJ), Carl Levin (D-MI), Joe Lieberman (D-CT), Trent Lott (R-MS), Connie Mack (R-FL), John McCain (R-AZ), Mitch McConnell (R-KY), Howard Metzenbaum (D-OH), Daniel Moynihan (D-NY), Frank Murkowski (R-AK), Don Nickles (R-OK), Bob Packwood (R-OR), Larry Pressler (R-SD), Harry Reid (D-NV), Donald Riegle, Jr. (D-MI), Charles Robb (D-VA), John Rockefeller (D-WV), William Roth, Jr. (R-DE), Warren Rudman (R-NH), Paul Sarbanes (D-MD), Jim Sasser (D-TN), Richard Shelby (D-AL), Arlen Specter (R-PA), Ted Stevens (R-AK), Steven Symms (R-ID), Malcolm Wallop (R-WY), John Warner (R-VA), Pete Wilson (R-CA).

## 37. Secretary of State James Baker's Five Point Plan, 10 October, 1989

1. The United States understands that because Egypt and Israel have been working hard on the peace process, there is agreement that an Israeli delegation should conduct a dialogue with a Palestinian delegation in Cairo.

2. The United States understands that Egypt cannot substitute itself for the Palestinians and Egypt will consult with Palestinians on all aspects of that dialogue. Egypt will also consult with Israel and the United States.

3. The United States understands that Israel will attend the dialogue only after a satisfactory list of Palestinians has been worked out.

4. The United States understands that the government of Israel will come to the dialogue on the basis of the Israeli government's May 14 initiative. The United States further understands that Palestinians will come to the dialogue prepared to discuss elections and the negotiating process in accordance with Israel's initiative.

The US understands, therefore, that Palestinians would be free to raise issues that relate to their opinions on how to make elections and the negotiating process succeed.

5. In order to facilitate this process, the US proposes that the foreign ministers of Israel, Egypt and the US meet in Washington within two weeks.

## 38. Statement by President George Bush on Jewish Settlements in the West Bank and East Jerusalem, Palm Springs, California, 3 March, 1990

*The following statement was made during a joint news conference with Prime Minister Toshiki Kaifu of Japan.*

My position is that the foreign policy of the United States says we do not believe there should be new settlements in the West Bank or in East Jerusalem. And I will conduct that policy as if it's firm, which it is, and I will be shaped in whatever decisions we make to see whether people can comply with that policy. And that's our strongly held view, and we think it's constructive to peace—the peace process, too—if Israel will follow that view. And so there's divisions in Israel on this question, incidentally. Parties are divided on it. But this is the position of the United States and I'm not going to change that position.

## 39.    Statement by President George Bush on Suspension of the Dialogue Between the US and the PLO, 20 June, 1990 [Excerpts]

Based on the recommendation of the Secretary of State, I have decided to suspend the dialogue between the United States and the PLO pending a satis- factory response from the PLO of steps it is taking to resolve problems associated with the recent acts of terrorism, in particular that May 30 [1990] terrorist attack on Israel by the Palestinian Liberation Front—a constituent group of the PLO.

By the way of background, on December 14, 1988, Yasser Arafat, speaking on behalf of the PLO Executive Committee, recognized Israel's right to exist. He accepted the United Nations Security Council Resolutions 242 and 338 and he renounced terrorism.

Now, subsequently, the United States announced that because the PLO had met our longstanding conditions for dialogue, we would begin a substantive dialogue with the PLO. And at the time we applauded Chairman Arafat for taking these essential steps and we have conducted such a dialogue with the PLO through our embassy in Tunis.

Over the past 18 months, representatives of the United States and the PLO regularly exchanged views about the political and security situation in the region.

On balance, we believed that these exchanges contributed to progress in the peace process.

On May 30, 1990, the Palestinian Liberation Front attempted a seaborne terrorist infiltration into Israel. Palestinian Liberation Front leader Abu Abbas represents the PLO [sic] on the Executive Committee of the PLO. The size of the force and the geographical target area strongly indicates that civilians would have been the target.

That day we issued a statement deploring this attempted terrorist attack. On May 31 we raised this incident with the PLO in Tunis. We told them that it could not avoid responsibility for an attempted terrorist action by one of its constituent groups and needed to take steps to deal with the matter by condemning the operation, disassociating itself from it and by also beginning to take steps to discipline Abu Abbas, the perpetrator.

We've given the PLO ample time to deal with this issue. To date, the PLO has not provided a credible accounting of this incident or undertaken the actions outlined above.

The US does take note of the fact that the PLO has disassociated itself from this attack and issued a statement condemning attacks against civilians in principle. But as we previously indicated, this is not sufficient. This alone is not suffi- cient.

## Viewpoint of US

The US-PLO dialogue has demonstrated that it can advance the Arab-Israeli peace process. And at the same time, the dialogue is based on the assumption that the PLO is willing to abide by the conditions it accepted in December 1988, including renunciation of terror.

At any time that the PLO is prepared to take the necessary steps, we are prepared to promptly resume the dialogue.

In the meantime, we would hope and expect, the peace process would proceed as intended and without delay.

We remain committed to the pursuit of a comprehensive settlement of the Arab-Israeli conflict and to a just and lasting peace. And as we've often stated, it is our view that such a peace must be based on those two resolutions—UN Resolution 242 and 338 and the principle implicit therein as territory for peace and provide for Israel's security and Palestinian political rights.

We believe that Palestinian participation is vital to any successful process and that there are real opportunities for Palestinians in this process. We strongly hope that Israelis, Palestinians and the Arab states will recognize these opportunities and take the necessary steps to create an environment in which a viable peace process can thrive. We denounce violence in the area and call upon all parties to eschew violence and terror and opt instead for dialogue and negotiation. We're prepared to continue working with the parties toward this end.

# Sadat's Visit and the Autonomy Negotiations

## 1. Statement to the Israeli Knesset by President Sadat, 20 November 1977

In the name of God, the Gracious and Merciful.

Mr. Speaker, Ladies and Gentlemen:

Peace and the mercy of God Almighty be upon you and may peace be for us all, God willing. Peace for us all on the Arab land, and in Israel as well, as in every part of this big world, which is so complexed by its sanguinary conflicts, disturbed by its sharp contradictions, menaced now and then by destructive wars launched by man to annihilate his fellow man. Finally, amidst the ruins of what man has built and the remains of the victims of Mankind, there emerges neither victor nor vanquished. The only vanquished remains man, God's most sublime creation, man whom God has created — as Ghandi the apostle of peace puts it: to forge ahead to mould the way of life and worship God Almighty.

I come to you today on solid ground, to shape a new life, to establish peace. We all, on this land, the land of God; we all, Muslims, Christians and Jews, worship God and no one but God. God's teachings and commandments are love, sincerity, purity and peace.

I do not blame all those who received my decision — when I announced it to the entire world before the Egyptian People's Assembly — with surprise and amazement. Some, gripped by the violent surprise, believed that my decision was no more than verbal juggling to cater for world public opinion. Others, still, interpreted it as political tactics to camouflage my intention of launching a new war. I would go as far as to tell you that one of my aides at the Presidential Office contacted me at a late hour following my return home from the People's Assembly and sounded worried as he asked me: "Mr. President, what would be our reaction if Israel should actually extend an invitation to you?" I replied calmly, I will accept it immediately. I have declared that I will go to the end of the world; I will go to Israel, for I want to put before the People of Israel all the facts.

I can see the point of all those who were astounded by my decision or those who had any doubts as to the sincerity of the intentions behind the declaration of my decision. No one would have ever conceived that the President of the biggest Arab State, which bears the heaviest burden and the top responsibility pertaining to the cause of war and peace in the Middle East, could declare his readiness to go to the land of the adversary while we were still in a state of war. Rather, we all are still bearing the consequences of four fierce wars waged within thirty years. The families of the 1973 October War are still moaning under the cruel pains of widowhood and bereavement of sons, fathers and brothers.

As I have already declared, I have not consulted, as far as this decision is concerned, with any of my colleagues and brothers, the Arab Heads of State or the confrontation States. Those of them who contacted me, following the declaration of this decision, expressed their objection, because the feeling of utter suspicion and absolute lack of confidence between the Arab States and the Palestinian People on the one hand, and Israel on the other, still surges in us all. It is sufficient to say that many months in which peace could have been brought about had been wasted over differences and fruitless discussions on the procedure for the convocation of the Geneva Conference, all showing utter suspicion and absolute lack of confidence.

But, to be absolutely frank with you, I took this decision after long thinking, knowing that is constitutes a grave risk for, if God Almighty has made it my fate to assume the responsibility on behalf of the Egyptian People and to share in the fate-determining responsibility of the Arab Nation and the Palestinian People, the main duty dictated by this responsibility is to exhaust all and every means in a bid to save my Egyptian Arab People and the entire Arab Nation the horrors of new, shocking and destructive wars, the dimensions of which are foreseen by no other than God himself.

After long thinking, I was convinced that the obligation of responsibility before God, and before the people, make it incumbent on me that I should go to the farthest corner of the world, even to Jerusalem, to address Members of the Knesset, the representatives of the People of Israel, and acquaint them with all the facts surging in me. Then, I would leave you to decide for yourselves. Following this, may God Almighty determine our fate.

Ladies and Gentlemen, there are moments in the lives of nations and peoples when it is incumbent on those known for their wisdom and clarity of vision to overlook the past, with all its complexities and weighing memories, in a bold drive towards new horizons. Those who, like us, are shouldering the same responsibility entrusted to us, are the first who should have the courage to take fate-determining decisions which are in consonance with the circumstances. We must all rise above all forms of fanaticism, self-deception and obsolete theories of superiority. The most important thing is never to forget that infallibility is the prerogative of God alone.

If I said that I wanted to save all the Arab People the horrors of shocking and destructive wars, I most sincerely declare before you that I have the same feelings and bear the same responsibility towards all and every man on earth, and certainly towards the Israeli People.

Any life lost in war is a human life, irrespecitve of its being that of an Israeli or an Arab. A wife who becomes a widow is a human being entitled to a happy family life, whether she be an Arab or an Israeli. Innocent children who are deprived of the care and compassion of their parents are ours, be they living on Arab or Israeli land. They command our top responsibility to afford them a comfortable life today and tomorrow.

For the sake of them all, for the safeguard of the lives of all our sons and brothers, for affording our communities the opportunity to work for the progress and happiness of man and his right to a dignified life, for our responsibilities before the generations to come, for a smile on the face of every child born on our land — for all that, I have taken my decision to come to you, despite all hazards, to deliver my address.

I have shouldered the prerequisites of the historical responsibility and, therefore, I declared — on 4 February 1971, to be precise — that I was willing to sign a peace agreement with Israel. This was the first declaration made by a responsible Arab official since the outbreak of the Arab-Israel conflict.

Motivated by all these factors dictated by the responsibilities of leadership, I called, on 16 October 1973, before the Egyptian People's Assembly, for an international conference to establish permanent peace based on justice. I was not in the position of he who was pleading for peace or asking for a ceasefire.

Motivated by all these factors dictated by duties of history and leadership, we signed the first disengagement agreement, followed by the second disengagement agreement in Sinai. Then we proceeded trying both open and closed doors in a bid to find a certain path leading to a durable and just peace. We opened our hearts to the peoples of the entire world to make them understand our motivations and objectives, and to leave them actually convinced of the fact that we are advocates of justice and peace-makers.

Motivated by all these factors, I decided to come to you with an open mind and an open heart, and with a conscious determination, so that we might establish permanent peace based on justice.

It is so fated that my trip to you, the trip of peace, should coincide with the Islamic feast, the holy Feast of Courban Bairam, the Feast of Sacrifice when

Abraham — peace be upon him — great-grandfather of the Arabs and Jews, submitted to God; I say when God Almighty ordered him, and to Him Abraham went, with dedicated sentiments, not out of weakness, but through a giant spiritual force and by a free will, to sacrifice his very own son, prompted by a firm and unshakable belief in ideals that lend life a profound significance.

This coincidence may carry a new meaning to us all, which may become a genuine aspiration heralding security and peace.

Ladies and Gentlement, let us be frank with each other, using straight-forward words and a clear conception, with no ambiguity. Let us be frank with each other today while the entire world, both East and West, follows these un-paralleled moments which could prove to be a radical turning point in the history of this part of the world, if not in the history of the world as a whole. Let us be frank with each other as we answer this important question: how can we achieve permanent peace based on justice?

I have come to you carrying my clear and frank answer to this big question, so that the people in Israel as well as the whole world might hear it, and so that all those whose devoted prayers ring in my ears, pleading to God Almighty that this historic meeting may eventually lead to the results aspired to by millions, might also hear it.

Before I proclaim my answer, I wish to assure you that, in my clear and frank answer, I am basing myself on a number of facts which no one can deny.

The first fact: no one can build his happiness at the expense of the misery of others.

The second fact: never have I spoken or will ever speak in two languages. Never have I adopted or will adopt two policies. I never deal with anyone except in one language, one policy, and with one face.

The third fact: direct confrontation and a straight line are the nearest and most successful methods to reach a clear objective.

The fourth fact: the call for a permanent and just peace, based on respect for the United Nations resolutions, has now become the call of the whole world. It has become a clear expression of the will of the international community, whether in official capitals, where policies are made and decisions taken, or at the level of world public opinion which influences policy-making and decision-taking.

The fifth fact: and this is probably the clearest and most prominent, is that the Arab Nation, in its drive for permanent peace based on justice, does not proceed from a position of weakness or hesitation, but it has the potential of power and stability which tells of a sincere will for peace. The Arab-declared intention stems from an awareness prompted by a heritage of civilization that, to avoid an inevitable disaster that will befall us, you and the entire world, there is no alternative to the establishment of permanent peace based on justice — peace that is not shaken by storms, swayed by suspicion, or jeopardized by ill intentions.

In the light of these facts which I meant to place before you the way I see them, I would also wish to warn you in all sincerity; I warn you against some thoughts that could cross your minds; frankness makes it incumbent upon me to tell you the following:

First: I have not come here for a separate agreement between Egypt and Israel. This is not part of the policy of Egypt. The problem is not that of Egypt and Israel. Any separate peace between Egypt and Israel, or between any Arab confrontation State and Israel, will not bring permanent peace based on justice in the entire region. Rather, even if peace between all the confrontation States and Israel were achieved, in the absence of a just solution to the Palestinian problem, never will there be that durable and just peace upon which the entire world insists today.

Second: I have not come to you to seek a partial peace, namely to terminate the state of belligerency at this stage, and put off the entire problem to a subsequent stage. This is not the radical solution that would steer us to permanent peace.

Equally, I have not come to you for a third disengagement agreement in Sinai, or in the Golan and the West Bank. For this would mean that we are merely delaying the ignition of the fuse; it would mean that we are lacking the courage to confront peace, that we are too weak to shoulder the burdens and responsibilities of a durable peace based on justice.

I have come to you so that together we might build a durable peace based on justice, to avoid the shedding of one single drop of blood from an Arab or an Israeli. It is for this reason that I have proclaimed my readiness to go to the farthest corner of the world.

Here, I would go back to the answer to the big question: how can we achieve a durable peace based on justice?

In my opinion, and I declare it to the whole world from this forum, the answer is neither difficult nor impossible, despite long years of feud, blood vengeance, spite and hatred, and breeding generations on concepts of total rift and deep-rooted animosity. The answer is not difficult, nor is it impossible, if we sincerely and faithfully follow a straight line.

You want to live with us in this part of the world. In all sincerity, I tell you, we welcome you among us, with full security and safety. This, in itself, is a tremendous turning point; one of the landmarks of a decisive historical change.

We used to reject you. We had our reasons and our claims, yes. We used to brand you as "so-called" Israel, yes. We were together in international conferences and organizations and our representatives did not, and still do not, exchange greetings, yes. This has happened and is still happening.

It is also true that we used to set, as a precondition for any negotiations with you, a mediator who would meet separately with each party. Through this procedure, the talks of the first and second disengagement agreements took place.

Our delegates met in the first Geneva Conference without exchanging a direct word. Yes, this has happened.

Yet, today I tell you, and declare it to the whole world, that we accept to live with you in permanent peace based on justice. We do not want to encircle you or be encircled ourselves by destructive missiles ready for launching, nor by the shells of grudges and hatred. I have announced on more than one occasion that Israel has become a *fait accompli,* recognized by the world, and that the two superpowers have undertaken the responsibility of its security and the defence of its existence.

As we really and truly seek peace, we really and truly welcome you to live among us in peace and security.

There was a huge wall between us which you tried to build up over a quarter of a century, but it was destroyed in 1973. It was a wall of a continuously inflammable and escalating psychological warfare. It was a wall of fear of the force that could sweep the entire Arab Nation. It was a wall of propaganda, that we were a Nation reduced to a motionless corpse. Rather, some of you had gone as far as to say that, even after 50 years, the Arabs would not regain any strength. It was a wall that threatened always with the long arm that could reach and strike anywhere. It was a wall that warned us against extermination and annihilation if we tried to use our legitimate right to liberate the occupied territories. Together we have to admit that that wall fell and collapsed in 1973.

Yet, there remained another wall. This wall constitutes a psychological barrier between us. A barrier of suspicion. A barrier of rejection. A barrier of fear of deception. A barrier of hallucinations around any action, deed or decision. A barrier of cautious and erroneous interpretations of all and every event or statement. It is this psychological barrier which I described in official statements as representing 70 percent of the whole problem.

Today through my visit to you, I ask you: why don't we stretch out our hands with faith and sincerity so that, together, we might destroy this barrier? Why shouldn't our and your will meet meet with faith and sincerity, so that together we might remove all suspicion of fear, betrayal and ill intentions? Why don't we stand together with the bravery of men and the boldness of heroes who dedicate themselves to a sublime objective? Why don't we stand together with the same courage and boldness to erect a huge edifice of peace that builds and does not destroy? An edifice that is a beacon for generations to come — the human message for construction, development and the dignity of man? Why should we bequeath to the coming generations the plight of bloodshed, death, orphans, widowhood, family disintegration, and the wailing of victims?

Why don't we believe in the wisdom of God conveyed to us by the Proverbs of Solomon:

> *"Deceit is in the heart of them that imagine evil; but to the counsellors of peace is joy. Better is a dry morsel, and quietness therewith, than a house full of sacrifices with strife."*

Why don't we repeat together from the Psalms of David:

> *"Hear the voice of my supplications, when I cry unto thee, when I lift up my hands towards the holy oracle. Draw me not away with the wicked, and with the workers of iniquity, which speak peace to their neighbours, but mischief is in their hearts. Give them according to their deeds, and according to the wickedness of their endeavours."*

To tell you the truth, peace cannot be worth its name unless it is based on justice, and not on the occupation of the land of others. It would not be appropriate for you to demand for yourselves what you deny others. With all frankness, and with the spirit that has prompted me to come to you today, I tell you: you have to give up, once and for all, the dreams of conquest, and give up the belief that force is the best method for dealing with the Arabs. You should clearly understand and assimilate the lesson of confrontation between you and us.

Expansion does not pay. To speak frankly, our land does not yield itself to bargaining. It is not even open to argument. To us, the national soil is equal to the holy valley where God Almighty spoke to Moses — peace be upon him. None of us can, or accept to, cede one inch of it, or accept the principle of debating or bargaining over it.

I sincerely tell you that before us today lies the appropriate chance for peace, if we are really serious in our endeavours for peace. It is a chance that time cannot afford once again. It is a chance that, if lost or wasted, the plotter against it will bear the curse of humanity and the curse of history.

What is peace for Israel? It means that Israel lives in the region with her Arab neighbours, in security and safety. To such logic, I say yes. It means that Israel lives within her borders, secure against any aggression. To such logic, I say yes. It means that Israel obtains all kinds of guarantees that ensure those two factors. To this demand, I say yes. More than that: we declare that we accept all the international guarantees you envisage and accept. We declare that we accept all the guarantees you want from the two superpowers or from either of them, or from the Big Five, or some of them.

Once again, I declare clearly and unequivocally that we agree to any guarantees you accept because, in return, we shall obtain the same guarantees.

In short, then, when we ask: what is peace for Israel, the answer would be: it is that Israel live within her borders with her Arab neighbours, in safety and security within the framework of all the guarantees she accepts and which are offered to the other party. But how can this be achieved? How can we reach this conclusion which would lead us to permanent peace based on justice?

There are facts that should be faced with all courage and clarity. There are Arab territories which Israel has occupied by armed force. We insist on complete withdrawal from these territories, including Arab Jerusalem.

I have come to Jerusalem, as the City of Peace, which will always remain as a living embodiment of coexistence among believers of the three religions. It is inadmissable that anyone should conceive the special status of the City of Jerusalem within the framework of annexation or expansionism, but it should be a free and open city for all believers.

Above all, the city should not be severed from those who have made it their abode for centuries. Instead of awakening the prejudices of the Crusaders, we should revive the spirit of Omar ibn el-Khattab and Saladdin, namely the spirit of tolerance and respect for rights. The holy shrines of Islam and Christianity are not only places of worship, but a living testimony of our uninterrupted presence here politically, spiritually and intellectually. Let us make no mistake about the importance and reverence we Christians and Muslims attach to Jerusalem.

Let me tell you, without the slightest hesitation, that I did not come to you under this dome to make a request that your troops evacuate the occupied territories. Complete withdrawal from the Arab territories occupied in 1967 is a logical and undisputed fact. Nobody should plead for that. Any talk about permanent peace based on justice, and any move to ensure our coexistence in peace and security in this part of the world, would become meaningless, while you occupy Arab territories by force of arms. For there is no peace that could be in consonance with, or be built on, the occupation of the land of others. Otherwise, it would not be a serious peace.

Yes, this is a foregone conclusion which is not open to discussion or debate — if intentions are sincere and if endeavours to establish a just and durable peace for ours and the generations to come are genuine.

As for the Palestinians' cause, nobody could deny that it is the crux of the entire problem. Nobody in the world could accept, today, slogans propagated here in Israel, ignoring the existence of the Palestinian People, and questioning their whereabouts. The cause of the Palestinian People and their legitimate rights are no longer ignored or denied today by anybody. Rather, nobody who has the ability of judgement can deny or ignore it.

It is an acknowledged fact received by the world community, both in the East and in the West, with support and recognition in international documents and official statements. It is of no use to anybody to turn deaf ears to its resounding voice which is being heard day and night, or to overlook its historical reality. Even the United States, your first ally which is absolutely committed to safeguard Israel's security and existence, and which offered and still offers Israel every moral, material and military support — I say — even the United States has opted to face up to reality and facts, and admit that the

Palestinian People are entitled to legitimate rights and that the Palestinian problem is the core and essence of the conflict and that, so long as it continues to be unresolved, the conflict will continue to aggravate, reaching new dimensions. In all sincerity, I tell you that there can be no peace without the Palestinians. It is a grave error of unpredictable consequences to overlook or brush aside this cause.

I shall not indulge in past events since the Balfour Declaration sixty years ago. You are well acquainted with the relevant facts. If you have found the legal and moral justification to set up a national home on a land that did not all belong to you, it is incumbent upon you to show understanding of the insistence of the People of Palestine on establishing, once again *(sic)* a state on their land. When some extremists ask the Palestinians to give up this sublime objective, this, in fact, means asking them to renounce their identity and every hope for the future.

I hail the Israeli voices that called for the recognition of the Palestinian People's rights to achieve and safeguard peace. Here I tell you, ladies and gentlemen, that it is no use to refrain from recognizing the Palestinian People and their rights to statehood and rights of return.

We, the Arabs, have faced this experience before, with you and with the reality of Israeli existence. The struggle took us from war to war, from victims to more victims, until you and we have today reached the edge of a horrifying abyss and a terrifying disaster, unless together we seize the opportunity today of a durable peace based on justice.

You have to face reality bravely as I have done. There can never be any solution to a problem by evading it or turning a deaf ear to it. Peace cannot last if attempts are made to impose fantasy concepts on which the world has turned its back and announced its unanimous call for the respect of rights and facts. There is no need to enter a vicious circle as to Palestinian rights. It is useless to create obstacles. Otherwise the march of peace will be impeded or peace will be blown up.

As I have told you, there is no happiness to the detriment of others. Direct confrontation and straight-forwardness are the short-cut and the most successful way to reach a clear objective. Direct confrontation concerning the Palestinian problem, and tackling it in one single language with a view to achieving a durable and just peace, lie in the establishment of their state. With all the guarantees you demand, there should be no fear of a newlyborn state that needs the assistance of all countries of the world. When the bells of peace ring, there will be no hands to beat the drums of war. Even if they existed, they would be soundless.

Conceive with me a peace agreement in Geneva that we would herald to a world thirsty for peace, a peace agreement based on the following points:

First: ending the Israeli occupation of the Arab territories occupied in 1967.

Second: achievement of the fundamental rights of the Palestinian People and their right to self-determination, including their right to establish their own state.

Third: the right of all states in the area to live in peace within their boundaries, which will be secure and guaranteed through procedures to be agreed upon, which provide appropriate security to international boundaries, in addition to appropriate international guarantees.

Fourth: commitment of all states in the region to administer the relations among them in accordance with the objectives and principles of the United Nations Charter, particularly the principles concerning the non-resort to force and the solution of differences among them by peaceful means.

Fifth: ending the state of belligerency in the region.

Ladies and Gentlemen, peace is not the mere endorsement of written lines; rather, it is a rewriting of history. Peace is not a game of calling for peace to defend certain whims or hide certain ambitions. Peace is a giant struggle against all and every ambition and whim. Perhaps the examples taken from ancient and modern history teach us all that missiles, warships and nuclear weapons cannot establish security. Rather, they destroy what peace and security build. For the sake of our peoples, and for the sake of the civilizations made by man, we have to defend man everywhere against the rule of the force of arms, so that we may endow the rule of humanity with all the power of the values and principles that promote the sublime position of Mankind.

Allow me to address my call from this rostrum to the People of Israel. I address myself with true and sincere words to every man, woman and child in Israel.

From the Egyptian People who bless this sacred mission of peace, I convey to you the message of peace, the message of the Egyptian People who do not know fanaticism, and whose sons, Muslims, Christians, and Jews, live together in a spirit of cordiality, love and tolerance. This is Egypt whose people have entrusted me with that sacred message, the message of security, safety and peace. To every man, woman and child in Israel, I say: encourage your leadership to struggle for peace. Let all endeavours be channelled towards building a huge edifice for peace, instead of strongholds and hideouts defended by destructive rockets. Introduce to the entire world the image of the new man in this area, so that he might set an example to the man of our age, the man of peace everywhere.

Be the heralds to your sons. Tell them that past wars were the last of wars and the end of sorrows. Tell them that we are in for a new beginning to a new life — the life of love, prosperity, freedom and peace.

You, bewailing mother; you, widowed wife; you, the son who lost a brother or a father; you, all victims of wars — fill the earth and space with recitals of peace. Fill bosoms and hearts with the aspirations of peace. Turn the song into a reality that blossoms and lives. Make hope a code of conduct and endeavour. The will of peoples is part of the will of God.

Ladies and Gentlemen, before I came to this place, with every beat of my heart and with every sentiment, I prayed to God Almighty, while performing the Curban Bairam prayers, and while visiting the Holy Sepulchre, to give me strength and to confirm my belief that this visit may achieve the objectives I look forward to, for a happy present and a happier future.

I have chosen to set aside all precedents and traditions known by warring countries, in spite of the fact that occupation of the Arab territories is still there. Rather, the declaration of my readiness to proceed to Israel came as a great surprise that stirred many feelings and astounded many minds. Some opinions even doubted its intent. Despite that, the decision was inspired by all the clarity and purity of belief, and with all the true expression of my People's will and intentions.

And I have chosen this difficult road which is considered, in the opinion of many, the most difficult road. I have chosen to come to you with an open heart and an open mind. I have chosen to give this great impetus to all international efforts exerted for peace. I have chosen to present to you, and in your own home, the realities devoid of any schemes or whims, not to manoeuvre or to win a round, but for us to win together, the most dangerous of rounds and battles in modern history — the battle of permanent peace based on justice.

It is not my battle alone, nor is it the battle of the leadership in Israel alone. It is the battle of all and every citizen in all our territories whose right it is to live in peace. It is the commitment of conscience and responsibility in the hearts of millions.

When I put forward this initiative, many asked what is it that I conceived as possible to achieve during this visit, and what my expectations were. And, as I answered the questioners, I announce before you that I have not thought of carrying out this initiative from the concept of what could be achieved during this visit, but I have come here to deliver a message. I have delivered the message, and may God be my witness.

I repeat with Zechariah, *"Love right and justice."*

I quote the following verses from the holy Koran:

*"We believe in God and in what has been revealed to us and what was revealed to Abraham, Ismail, Isaac, Jacob, and the tribes and in the books given to Moses, Jesus, and the prophets from their Lord. We make no distinction between one and another among them and to God we submit."*

## 2. Prime Minister Menachem Begin Knesset Speech, 20 November, 1977

Mr. Speaker, Mr. President of the State of Israel, Mr. President of the Arab Republic of Egypt, ladies and gentlemen, members of the Knesset: We send our greetings to the president, to all the people of the Islamic religion in our country, and wherever they may be, on this occasion of the feast of the festival of the sacrifice 'Id al-Adha. This feast reminds us of the binding of Isaac. This was the way in which the Creator of the World tested our forefather, Abraham, our common forefather, to test his faith, and Abraham passed this test. However, from the moral aspect and the advancement of humanity, it was forbidden to sacrifice human beings. Our two peoples in their ancient traditions know and taught what the Lord, blessed be He, taught while peoples around us still sacrified human beings to their gods. Thus, we contributed, the people of Israel and the Arab people, to the progress of mankind, and thus we are continuing to contribute to human culture to this day.

I greet and welcome the president of Egypt for coming to our country and on his participating in the Knesset session. The flight time between Cairo and Jerusalem is short, but the distance between Cairo and Jerusalem was until last night almost endless. President el-Sadat crossed this distance courageously. We, the Jews, know how to appreciate such courage, and we know how to appreciate it in our guest, because it is with courage that we are here, and this is how we continue to exist, and we shall continue to exist.

Mr. Speaker, this small nation, the remaining refuge of the Jewish people who returned to their historic homeland, has always wanted peace, and since the dawn of our independence, on 14 May 1948, 5 Iyar Tashah, in the declaration of independence in the founding scroll of our national freedom, David Ben-Gurion said: "We extend a hand of peace and neighborliness to all the neighboring countries and their peoples. We call upon them to cooperate, to help each other, with the Hebrew people independent in their own country. One year earlier, even from the underground, when we were in the midst of the fateful struggle for the liberation of the country and the redemption of the people, we called in our neighbors in these terms: In this country we will live together and we will advance together and we will live lives of freedom and happiness. Our Arab neighbors, do not reject the hand stretched out to you in peace."

But it is my bounden duty, Mr. Speaker, and not only my right, not to pass over the truth that our hand outstretched for peace was not grasped and one day after we had renewed our independence, as was our right, our eternal right, which cannot be disputed, we were attacked on three fronts, and we stood almost without arms, the few against many, the weak against the strong, while an attempt was made, one day after the declaration of independence, to strangle it at birth, to put an end to the last hope of the Jewish people, the yearning renewed after the years of destruction and holocaust. No, we did not believe in might and we have never based our attitude towards the Arab people on might. Quite the contrary, force was used against us. Over all the years of this generation we have never stopped being attacked by might, of the strong arm stretched out to exterminate our people, to destroy our independence, to deny our rights. We defended ourselves, it is true. We defended our rights, our existence, our honor, our women and our children, against these repeated and recurring attempts to crush us through the force of arms, and not only on one front. That, too, is true. With the help of God Almighty, we overcame the forces of aggression, and we have guaranteed existence for our nation. Not only for this generation, but for the coming generations, too. We do not believe in might. We believe in right, only in right. And therefore our aspiration, from the bottom of our hearts, has always been, to this very day, for peace.

Mr. President, Mr. President of Egypt, the commanders of all the underground Hebrew fighting organizations are sitting in this democratic house. They had to conduct a campaign of the few against the many, against a huge, a world power. Sitting here are the veteran commanders and captains who had to go forth into battle because it was forced upon them and forward to victory, which was unavoidable because they were defending their rights. They belong to different parties. They have different views, but I am sure, Mr. President, that I am expressing the views of everyone, with no exceptions, that we have one aspiration in our hearts, one desire in our souls, and all of us are united in all these aspirations and desires — to bring peace, peace for our nation, which has not known peace for even one day since we started returning to Zion, and peace for our neighbors, whom we wish all the best, and we believe that if we make peace, real peace, we will be able to help our neighbors, in all walks of life, and a new era will open in the Middle East, an era of blossoming and growth, development and expansion of the economy, its growth as it was in the past.

Therefore, permit me today to set forth the peace program as we understand it. We want full, real peace with complete reconciliation between the Jewish and the Arab peoples. I do not wish to dwell on the memories of the past, but there have been wars; there has been blood spilt; wonderful young people have been killed on both sides. We will live all our life with the memories of our heroes who gave their lives so this day would arrive, this day, too, would come, and we respect the bravery of a rival and we honor all the members of the younger generation among the Arab people who also fell.

I do not wish to dwell on memories of the past, although they be bitter memories. We will bury them; we will worry about the future, about our people, our children, our joint and common future. For it is true indeed that we will have to live in this area, all of us together will live here, for generations upon generations: The great Arab people in their various states and countries, and the Jewish people in their country, Eretz Yisrael. Therefore, we must determine what peace means.

Let us conduct negotiations, Mr. President, as free negotiating partners for a peace treaty, and, with the aid of the Lord, we fully believe the day will come when we can sign it with mutual respect, and we will then know that the era of wars is over, that hands have been extended between friends, that each has shaken the hand of his brother and the future will be shining for all the peoples of this area. The beginning of wisdom in a peace treaty is the abolition of the state of war. I agree, Mr. President, that you did not come here, we did not invite you to our country in order, as has been said in recent days, to divide the Arab peoples. Somebody quoted an ancient Roman, saying: Divide and rule. Israel does not want to rule and therefore does not need to divide. We want peace with all our neighbors: with Egypt, with Jordan, with Syria and with Lebanon. We would like to negotiate peace treaties.

And there is no need to distinguish between a peace treaty and an abolition of the state of war. Quite the contrary, we are not proposing this nor are we asking for it. The first clause of a peace treaty is cessation of the state of war, forever. We want to establish normal relations between us, as they exist between all nations, even after wars. We have learned from history, Mr. President, that war is avoidable, peace is unavoidable. Many nations have waged war among themselves, and sometimes they used the tragic term perennial enemy. There are no perennial enemies. And after all the wars the inevitable comes — peace. And so we want to establish, in a peace treaty, diplomatic relations as is the custom among civilized nations.

Today two flags are flying over Jerusalem: the Egyptian flag and the Israeli flag. And we saw together, Mr. President, little children waving both the flags. Let us sign a peace treaty and let us establish this situation forever, both in Jerusalem and in Cairo, and I hope the day will come when the Egyptian children wave the Israeli flag and the Egyptian flag, just as the children of Israel waved both these flags in Jerusalem.

And you, Mr. President, will have a loyal ambassador in Jerusalem, and we will have an ambassador in Cairo. And even if differences of opinion arise between us, we will clarify them like civilized peoples through our authorized envoys.

We are proposing economic cooperation for the development of our countries. These are wonderful countries in the Middle East. The Lord created it thus: oases in the desert, but there are deserts as well and we can make them flourish. Let us cooperate in this field. Let us develop our countries. Let us eliminate poverty, hunger, the lack of shelter. Let us raise our peoples to the level of developed countries and let them not call us "developing countries".

And with all due respect, I am willing to confirm the words of his majesty the king of Morocco, who said — in public too — that if peace arises in the Middle East, the combination of Arab genius and Jewish genius together can turn this area into a paradise on earth.

Let us open our countries to free traffic. You come to our country and we will visit yours. I am ready to announce, Mr. Speaker, this day that our country is open to the citizens of Egypt and I make no conditions on our part. I think it is only proper and just that there should be a joint announcement on this matter. But, just as there are Egyptian flags in our streets, and there is also an honored delegation from Egypt in our capital and in our country, let the number of visitors increase: our border will be open to you, and also all the other borders.

And as I pointed out, we want this in the south and in the north and in the east. And so I am renewing my invitation to the president of Syria to follow in your footsteps, Mr. President, and come to us to open negotiations for achieving peace between Israel and Syria and to sign a peace treaty between us. I am sorry to say that there is no justification for the mourning they have declared beyond our northern border. Quite the contrary, such visits, such links, such clarifications can and must be days of joy, days of lifting spirits for all the peoples. I invite King Hussein to come to us to discuss all the problems which need to be discussed between us. Also genuine representatives of the Arabs of Eretz Yisrael, I invite them to come and hold talks with us to clarify our common future, to guarantee the freedom of man, social justice, peace, mutual respect. And if they invite us to go to their capitals, we will accept their invitations. If they invite us to open negotiations in Damascus, in Amman or in Beirut, we will go to those capitals in order to hold negotiations with them there. We do not want to divide. We want real peace with all our neighbors, to be expressed in peace treaties whose contents I have already made clear. [interruptions indistinct from the audience].

Mr. Speaker, it is my duty today to tell our guest and the peoples watching us and listening to our words about the link between our people and this country. The president recalled the Balfour Declaration. No, sir, we did not take over any strange land; we returned to our homeland. The link between our people and this country is eternal. It arose in the earliest days of the history of humanity and has never been disrupted. In this country we developed our civilization, we had our prophets here, and their sacred words stand to this day. Here the kings of Judah and Israel knelt before their God. This is where we became a people; here we established our kingdom. And when we were expelled from our land because of force which was used against us, the farther we went from our land, we never forgot this country for even a single day. We prayed for it, we longed for it, we believed in our return to it from the day the words were spoken: When the Lord restores the fortunes of Zion, we will be like dreamers. Our mouths will be filled with laughter, and our tongues will speak with shouts of joy. These verses apply to all our exiles and all our sufferings, giving the consolation that the return to Zion would come.

This, our right, was recognized. The Balfour Declaration was included in the mandate laid down by the nations of the world, including the United States, and the preface to this recognized international document says: [speaks in English] "Whereas recognition has the Bible given to the historical connection of the Jewish people with Palestine and to the grounds for reconstituting their national home in that country", [ends English] — the historic connection between the Jewish people and Palestine [in English] — or, in Hebrew, Eretz Yisrael, was given reconfirmation — reconfirmation — as the national homeland in that country, that is, in Eretz Yisrael.

In 1919 we also won recognition of this right by the spokesman of the Arab people and the agreement of 3 January 1919, which was signed by Emir Faysal and Chaim Weizmann. It reads: [speaks in English] Mindful of the racial kinship and ancient bonds existing between the Arabs and the Jewish people and realizing that the surest means of working out the consummation of the national aspirations in the closest possible collaboration in the development of the Arab State and of Palestine. [ends English]. And afterward come all the clauses about cooperation between the Arab State and Eretz Yisrael. This is our right. The existence — truthful existence.

What happened to us when our homeland was taken from us? I accompanied you this morning, Mr. President, to Yad Vashem. With your own eyes you saw the fate of our people when this homeland was taken from it. It cannot be told. Both of us agreed, Mr. President, that anyone who has not seen with his own eyes everything there is in Yad Vashem cannot understand what happened to this people when it was without a homeland, when its own homeland was taken from it. And both of us read a document dated 30 January 1939, where the word "Vernichtung" — annihilation — appears. If war breaks out, the Jewish race in Europe will be exterminated. Then, too, we were told that we should not pay attention to the racists. The whole world heard. Nobody came to save us. Not during the nine fateful, decisive months after the announcement was made, the like of which had not been seen since the Lord created man and man created the Devil.

And during those six years, too, when millions of our people, among them one and a half million of the little children of Israel who were burned on all the strange beds [as heard], nobody came to save them, not from the East nor from the West. And because of this, we took a solemn oath, this entire generation, the generation of extermination and revival, that we would never again put our people in danger, that we would never again put our women and our children, whom it is our duty to defend — if there is a need for this, even at the cost of our lives — in the hell of the exterminating fire of an enemy. Since then, it has been our duty for generations to come to remember that certain things said about our people must be taken with complete seriousness. And we must not, heaven forbid, for the sake of the future of our people, take any advice whatsoever against taking these things seriously.

President el-Sadat knows, and he knew from us before he came to Jerusalem, that we have a different position from his with regard to the permanent borders between us and our neighbors. However, I say to the president of Egypt and to all our neighbors: Do not say, there is not negotiation, there will not be negotiations about any particular issue. I propose, with the agreement of the decisive majority of this parliament, that everything be open to negotiation. Anyone who says, with reference to relations between the Arab people, or the Arab peoples around us, and the State of Israel, that there are things which should be omitted from negotiations is taking upon himself a grave responsibility. Everything can be negotiated.

No side will say the contrary. No side will present prior conditions. We will conduct the negotiations honorably. If there are difference of opinion between us, this is not unusual. Anyone who has studied the histories of wars and the signing of peace treaties knows that all negotiations over a peace treaty began with differences of opinion between the sides. And in the course of the negotiations they reached an agreement which permitted the signing of peace treaties and agreements. And this is the road which we propose to take.

And we will conduct the negotiations as equals. There are no vanquished and there are no victors. All the peoples of the area are equal and all of them should treat each other with due respect. In this spirit of openness, of willingness to listen to each other, to hear the facts and the reasoning and the explanations, accepting all the experience of human persuasion, let us conduct the negotiations as I have asked and am proposing, open them and carry them out, carry them on constantly until we reach the longed-for hour of the signing of a peace treaty between us.

We are not only ready to sit with the representatives of Egypt, and also with the representatives of Jordan and Syria and Lebanon, if they are ready, we are prepared to sit together at a peace conference in Geneva. We propose that the Geneva conference be renewed, on the basis of the two Security Council resolutions: 242 and 338. If there are problems between us by convening the Geneva conference, we will be able to clarify them. And if the president of Egypt wants to continue clarifying them in Cairo, I am for it. If in a neutral place, there is no objection. Let us clarify anywhere, even before the Geneva conference convenes, the problems which should be clarified before it is convened. And our eyes will be open and our ears will listen to all proposals.

Permit me to say a word about Jerusalem. Mr. President, you prayed today in the house of prayer sacred to the Islamic religion, and from there you went to the Church of the Holy Sepulchre. You realized, as those coming from all over the world have realized, that ever since this city was unified, there has been completely free access, without interference and without any obstacle, for the members of every religion to the places sacred to them. This positive phenomenon did not exist for 19 years. It has existed for about 11 years, and we can promise the Moslem world and the Christian world, all the peoples, that there will always be free access to the sacred places of every religion. We will defend this right to free access, for we believe in it. We believe in equal rights for all men and citizens and respect for every faith.

Mr. Speaker, this is a special day for our legislative chamber, and certainly this day will be remembered for many years in the history of our nation, and perhaps also in the history of the Egyptian nation, maybe in the history of all nations. And this day, with your agreement, ladies and gentlemen, members of the Knesset, let us pray that the God of our fathers, our common fathers, will give us the wisdom needed to overcome difficulties and obstacles, calumnies and slander, incitement and attacks. And with the help of God, may we arrive at the longed-for day for which all our people pray — peace. For it is indeed true that the sweet singer of Israel [King David] said: "Righteousness and peace will kiss each other", and the Prophet Zachariah said: Love, truth and peace."

## 3.  Prime Minister Menachem Begin's Autonomy Plan, 28 December, 1977

*As announced in the Knesset*

1.   The administration of the Military Government in Judea, Samaria and the Gaza district will be abolished.

2.   In Judea, Samaria and the Gaza district, administrative autonomy of the residents, by and for them, will be established.

3.   The residents of Judea, Samaria and the Gaza district will elect an Administrative Council composed of 11 members. The Administrative Council will operate in accordance with the principles laid down in this paper.

4.   Any resident, 18 years old and above, without distinction of citizenship, or if stateless, will be entitled to vote in the elections to the Administrative Council.

5.   Any resident whose name is included in the list of candidates for the Administrative Council and who, on the day the list is submitted, is 25 years old or above, will be entitled to be elected to the Council.

6.   The Administrative Council will be elected by general, direct, personal, equal and secret ballot.

7.   The period of office of the Administrative Council will be four years from the day of its election.

8.   The Administrative Council will sit in Bethlehem.

9.   All the administrative affairs relating to the Arab residents of the areas of Judea, Samaria and the Gaza district will be under the direction and within the competence of the Administrative Council.

10.   The Administrative Council will operate the following Departments: education; religious affairs; finance; transportation; construction and housing; industry, commerce and tourism; agriculture; health, labour and social welfare; rehabilitation of refugees; and the administration of justice and supervision of local police forces; and promulgate regulations relating to the operation of these Departments.

11.   Security and public order in the areas of Judea, Samaria and the Gaza district will be the responsibility of the Israeli authorities.

12.   The Administrative Council will elect its own chairman.

13.   The first session of the Administrative Council will be convened 30 days after the publication of the election results.

14.   Residents of Judea, Samaria and the Gaza district, without distinction of citizenship, or if stateless, will be granted free choice (option) of either Israeli or Jordanian citizenship.

15.   A resident of the areas of Judea, Samaria and the Gaza district who requests Israeli citizenship will be granted such citizenship in accordance with the citizenship law of the state.

16.   Residents of Judea, Samaria and the Gaza district who, in accordance with the right of free option, choose Israeli citizenship, will be entitled to vote for, and be elected to, the Knesset in accordance with the election law.

17.   Residents of Judea, Samaria and the Gaza district who are citizens of Jordan or who, in accordance with the right of free option will become citizens of Jordan, will elect and be eligible for election to the Parliament of the Hashemite Kingdom of Jordan in accordance with the election law of that country.

18.   Questions arising from the vote to the Jordanian Parliament by residents of Judea, Samaria and the Gaza district will be clarified in negotiations between Israel and Jordan.

19.   A committee will be established of representatives of Israel, Jordan and the Administrative Council to examine existing legislation in Judea, Samaria and the Gaza district, and to determine which legislation will continue in force which will be abolished, and what will be the competence of the Administrative Council to promulgate regulations. The rulings of the committee will be adopted by unanimous decision.

20.   Residents of Israel will be entitled to acquire land and settle in the areas of Judea, Samaria and the Gaza district. Arabs, residents of Judea,

Samaria and the Gaza district who, in accordance with the free option granted them, will become Israeli citizens, will be entitled to acquire land and settle in Israel.

21.   A committee will be established of representatives of Israel, Jordan and the Administrative Council to determine norms of immigration to the areas of Judea, Samaria and the Gaza district. The committee will determine the norms whereby Arab refugees residing outside Judea, Samaria and the Gaza district will be permitted to immigrate to these areas in reasonable numbers. The rulings of the committee will be adopted by unanimous decision.

22.   Residents of Israel and residents of Judea, Samaria and the Gaza district will be assured freedom of movement and freedom of economic activity in Israel Judea, Samaria and the Gaza district.

23.   The Administrative Council will appoint one of its members to represent the Council before the Government of Israel for deliberation on matters of common interest, and one of its members to represent the Council before the Government of Jordan for deliberation on matters of common interest.

24.   Israel stands by its right and its claim of sovereignty to Judea, Samaria and the Gaza district. In the knowledge that other claims exist, it proposes, for the sake of the agreement and the peace, that the question of sovereignty in the areas be left open.

25.   With regard to the administration of the holy places of the three religions in Jerusalem, a special proposal will be drawn up and submitted that will include the guarantee of freedom of access to members of all the faiths to the shrines holy to them.

26.   These principles will be subject to review after a five-year period.

## 4. A Framework for Peace in the Middle East Agreed at Camp David, 17 September, 1978

*Following is the text of the Agreement reached at the Camp David Summit and signed September 17 at the White House.*

Mohammed Anwar el-Sadat, President of the Arab Republic of Egypt, and Menachem Begin, Prime Minister of Israel, met with Jimmy Carter, President of the United States of America, at Camp David from September 5 to September 17, 1978, and have agreed on the following framework for peace in the Middle East. They invite other parties to the Arab-Israel conflict to adhere to it.

The search for peace in the Middle East must be guided by the following:

— The agreed basis for a peaceful settlement of the conflict between Israel and its neighbors in United Nations Security Council Resolution 242, in all its parts.

— After four wars during thirty years, despite intensive human efforts, the Middle East, which is the cradle of civilization and the birthplace of three great religions, does not yet enjoy the blessing of peace. The people of the Middle East yearn for peace so that the vast human and natural resources of the region can be turned to the pursuits of peace and so that this area can become a model for coexistence and cooperation among nations.

— The historic initiative of President Sadat in visiting Jerusalem and the reception accorded to him by the Parliament, Government and People of Israel, and the reciprocal visit of Prime Minister Begin to Ismailia, the peace proposals made by both leaders, as well as the warm reception of these missions by the peoples of both countries, have created an unprecedented opportunity for peace which must not be lost if this generation and future generations are to be spared the tragedies of war.

— The provisions of the Charter of the United Nations and the other accepted norms of international law and legitimacy now provide accepted standards for the conduct of relations among all states.

— To achieve a relationship of peace, in the spirit of Article 2 of the United Nations Charter, future negotiations between Israel and any neighbor prepared to negotiate peace and security with it, are necessary for the purpose of carrying out all the provisions and principles of Resolutions 242 and 338.

— Peace requires respect for the sovereignty, territorial integrity and political independence of every state in the area and their right to live in peace within secure and recognized boundaries free from threats or acts of force. Progress toward that goal can accelerate movement toward a new era of reconciliation in the Middle East marked by cooperation in promoting economic development, in maintaining stability, and in assuring security.

— Security is enhanced by a relationship of peace and by cooperation between nations which enjoy normal relations. In addition, under the terms of peace treaties, the parties can, on the basis of reciprocity, agree to special security arrangements such as demilitarized zones, limited armaments areas, early warning stations, the presence of international forces, liaison, agreed measures for monitoring, and other arrangements that they agree are useful.

### Framework

Taking these factors into account, the parties are determined to reach a just, comprehensive, and durable settlement of the Middle East conflict through the conclusion of peace treaties based on Security Council Resolutions 242 and 338, in all their parts. Their purpose is to achieve peace and good neighborly relations. They recognize that, for peace to endure, it must involve all those who have been most deeply affected by the conflict. They therefore agree that this framework as appropriate is intended by them to constitute a basis for peace not only between Egypt and Israel, but also between Israel and each of its other neighbors which is prepared to negotiate peace with Israel on this basis. With that objective in mind, they have agreed to proceed as follows:

A.   West Bank and Gaza.

1.   Egypt, Israel, Jordan and the representatives of the Palestinian people should participate in negotiations on the resolution of the Palestinian problem in all its aspects. To achieve that objective, negotiations relating to the West Bank and Gaza should proceed in three stages:

(a)   Egypt and Israel agree that, in order to ensure a peaceful and orderly transfer of authority, and taking into account the security concerns of all the parties, there should be transitional arrangements for the West Bank and Gaza for a period not exceeding five years. In order to provide full autonomy to the inhabitants, under these arrangements the Israeli military government and its civilian administration will be withdrawn as soon as a self-governing authority has been freely elected by the inhabitants of these areas to replace the existing military government. To negotiate the details of a transitional arrangement, the Government of Jordan will be invited to join the negotiations on the basis of this framework. These new arrangements should give due consideration both to the principle of self-government by the inhabitants of these territories and to the legitimate security concerns of the parties involved.

(b)   Egypt, Israel, and Jordan will agree on the modalities for establishing the elected self-governing authority in the West Bank and Gaza. The delegations of Egypt and Jordan may include Palestinians from the West Bank and Gaza or other Palestinians as mutually agreed. The parties will negotiate an agreement which will define the powers and responsibilities of the self-governing authority to be exercised in the West Bank and Gaza. A withdrawal of Israeli Armed Forces will take place and there will be a redeployment of the remaining Israeli forces into specified security locations. The agreement will also include arrangements for assuring internal and external security and public order. A strong local police force will be established, which may include Jordanian citizens. In addition, Israeli and Jordanian forces will participate in joint patrols and in the manning of control posts to assure the security of the borders.

(c)   When the self-governing authority (administrative council) in the West Bank and Gaza is established and inaugurated, the transitional period of five years will begin. As soon as possible, but not later than the third year after the beginning of the transitional period, negotiations will take place to determine the final status of the West Bank and Gaza and its relationship with its neighbors, and to conclude a peace treaty between Israel and Jordan by the end of the transitional period. These negotiations will be conducted between

Egypt, Israel, Jordan, and the elected representatives of the inhabitants of the West Bank and Gaza. Two separate but related committees will be convened, one committee, consisting of representatives of the four parties which will negotiate and agree on the final status of the West Bank and Gaza, and its relationship with its neighbors, and the second committee, consisting of representatives of Israel and representatives of Jordan to be joined by the elected representatives of the inhabitants of the West Bank and Gaza, to negotiate the peace treaty between Israel and Jordan, taking into account the agreement reached on the final status of the West Bank and Gaza. The negotiations shall be based on all the provisions and principles of U.N. Security Council Resolution 242. The negotiations will resolve, among other matters, the location of the boundaries and the nature of the security arrangements. The resolution from the negotiations must also recognize the legitimate rights of the Palestine people and their just requirements. In this way, the Palestinians will participate in the determination of their own future through:

1) The negotiations between Egypt, Israel, Jordan and the representatives of the inhabitants of the West Bank and Gaza to agree on the final status of the West Bank and Gaza and other outstanding issues by the end of the transitional period.

2) Submitting their agreement to a vote by the elected representatives of the inhabitants of the West Bank and Gaza.

3) Providing for the elected representatives of the inhabitants of the West Bank and Gaza to decide how they shall govern themselves consistent with the provisions of their agreement.

4) Participating as stated above in the work of the committee negotiating the peace treaty between Israel and Jordan.

2. All necessary measures will be taken and provisions made to assure the security of Israel and its neighbors during the transitional period and beyond. To assist in providing such security, a strong local police force will be constituted by the self-governing authority. It will be composed of inhabitants of the West Bank and Gaza. The police will maintain continuing liaison on internal security matters with the designated Israeli, Jordanian, and Egyptian officers.

3. During the transitional period, representatives of Egypt, Israel, Jordan, and the self-governing authority will constitute a continuing committee to decide by agreement on the modalities of admission of persons displaced from the West Bank and Gaza in 1967, together with necessary measures to prevent disruption and disorder. Other matters of common concern may also be dealt with by this committee.

4. Egypt and Israel will work with each other and with other interested parties to establish agreed procedures for a prompt, just and permanent implementation of the resolution of the refugee problem.

B.   Egypt-Israel

1.   Egypt and Israel undertake not to resort to the threats or the use of force to settle disputes. Any disputes shall be settled by peaceful means in accordance with the provisions of Article 33 of the Charter of the United Nations.

2.   In order to achieve peace between them, the parties agree to negotiate in good faith with a goal of concluding within three months from the signing of this framework a peace treaty between them, while inviting the other parties to the conflict to proceed simultaneously to negotiate and conclude similar peace treaties with a view to achieving a comprehensive peace in the area. The framework for the conclusion of a peace treaty between Egypt and Israel will govern the peace negotiations between them. The parties will agree on the modalities and the timetable for the implementation of their obligations under the treaty.

C.   Associated Principles

1.   Egypt and Israel state that the principles and provisions described below should apply to peace treaties between Israel and each of its neighbors — Egypt, Jordan, Syria and Lebanon.

2.   Signatories shall establish among themselves relationships normal to states at peace with one another. To this end, they should undertake to abide by all the provisions of the Charter of the United Nations. Steps to be taken in this respect include:

(a)   Full recognition;

(b)   Abolishing economic boycotts;

(c)   Guaranteeing that under their jurisdiction the citizens of the other parties shall enjoy the protection of the due process of law.

3.   Signatories should explore possibilities for economic development in the context of final peace treaties, with the objective of contributing to the atmosphere of peace, cooperation and friendship which is their common goal.

4.   Claims Commissions may be established for the mutual settlement of all financial claims.

5.   The United States shall be invited to participate in the talks on matters related to the modalities of the implementation of the Agreements and working out the timetable for the carrying out of the obligations of the parties.

6.   The United Nations Security Council shall be requested to endorse the peace treaties and ensure that their provisions shall not be violated. The permanent members of the Security Council shall be requested to underwrite the peace treaties and ensure respect for their provisions. They shall also be requested to conform their policies and actions with the undertakings contained in this framework.

## 5. Government of Egypt Proposed Model of Full Autonomy for the West Bank and Gaza Strip, 28 January, 1980

**I — Introduction**

(a)   The Camp David Framework stipulates the withdrawal of the military government and its civilian administration, and the transfer of its authority to the self-governing authority which will replace it.

(b)   In reviewing the powers and responsibilities of the military government and its civilian administration, the working group was seeking to envisage, through a practical approach, the powers and responsibilities to be exercised by the SGA in the context of its replacement of the military government and its civilian administration as stated in the Camp David Framework. That was the purpose of the survey of the current situation, it was a way out of the deadlock caused by the conceptual discussions of the comprehensive approach, and a step to provide the parties with basic information for discussing the transfer of authority. Indeed, the presentations of the powers and responsibilities of the military government and its civilian administration were meant to lead the working group, in the light of these presentations, and in the context of the transfer of authority, to prepare a model for the powers and responsibilities to be exercised by the SGA.

This method was endorsed by the decision taken at the London meeting of the heads of delegation on October 26, 1979:

"... Presentations on the current situation will provide the parties with basic information for discussing transfer of authority as stated in the Camp David Framework."

This led subsequently to the call of the plenary on December 19, 1979 to the working group:

"To proceed to prepare for the plenary's future consideration a proposed model for the powers and responsibilities to be exercised by the SGA".

(c)   When the method is thus set in perspective, it becomes clear that when a model of the powers and responsibilities of the SGA is to be prepared, the guiding frame should be the powers and responsibilities of the military government and its civilian administration and that the focal points in discussing such a model should be:

1 — Withdrawal of the Israeli military government and its civilian administration.

2 — The transfer of authority.

3 — Organs of the SGA which will take over from, and replace, the military government and its civilian administration.

**II — The Military Government and its Civilian Administration**

(a)   On June 7, 1967, the Israeli military command published proclamation

No. 2 entitled "Laws and administration proclamation". A section of which is concerned with the assumption of government by the Israeli defence forces, and under the title "Assumption of powers" it reads:

"Any power of government, legislation, appointment, or administration with respect to the region or its inhabitants shall henceforth vest in me alone and shall be exercised only by me or a person appointed by me to that end or acting on my behalf."

(b)   The Israel military government currently existing in the West Bank and Gaza Strip has full comprehensive authority. It assumes the power of formulating all policies and coordinating all activities. Its decision making emanates from different and interconnected channels of Israeli cabinet and interministerial levels as well as a chain of military command leading to the area or regional commander (one for the West Bank and one for Gaza) who was vested with full legislative and executive authority in the area as shown in the aforementioned proclamation. Mandatory orders issued by the military commander presented legislative enactments and revisions. Policy is determined according to considerations adopted by the office of the coordinator of activities, the Israeli ministry concerned and the regional command.

(c)   Administrative authority is delegated to regional and district commanders. Routine administrative duties and conduct of ordinary activities are left to the relevant institutions that were already operating in the West Bank and Gaza or to newly organized units of administrative service.

The civil administration of the military government is carried out by branches, each branch supervising a number of units. The units carry out the conduct of every day life. Heads of units who operate in the areas are directly subordinated through the chief of branch to the military commander while they come, at the same time, under the corresponding ministries in Israel on professional matters. From the ministry they get instructions on professional matters, how to act, how to deal with the problems arising out of the daily life. From the commander, through the chief of branch, they get the policy, the command.

(d)   The military government and its civilian administration is therefore composed of different levels manifesting different layers of authority. One layer legislates and formulates policies while another layer executes and carries out the policies.

The Camp David Framework stipulates the transfer of both. It is not a matter of transferring the administrative set-up which implements the orders but first and foremost transferring the strata of authority which holds the power to issue the orders.

(e)   It may be recalled that the civil administration of the military government is mainly composed, even now, of local inhabitants. According to the figures of December 1978 there were in the West Bank 11,165 local employees in the civil administration (and only 980 Israelis) while in Gaza there are local director-generals heading 14 of the main units.

So, it may be said, that even now the Palestinian people in the West Bank and Gaza Strip are bearing most of the responsibility for running the affairs of their daily life but only carrying out decisions which were made for them and implementing policies which were formulated over their heads.

When the Camp David Framework promises them full autonomy, it can only mean that under the SGA they will be able to take their own decisions and formulate their own policies.

The full autonomy which the Camp David Framework provides for cannot amount to a reorganization of what the Palestinians in the West Bank and Gaza Strip already have, but rather the transformation of that set-up in an authority which is self-governing. Hence, the withdrawal of the military government and the transfer of its manifold authority to the inhabitants.

### III — Withdrawal of the Military Government and the Transfer of Authority

(a)   The first step in establishing the SGA should be the withdrawal of the military government, the Camp David Framework for peace states clearly that: "The Israeli military government and its civilian administration will be withdrawn as soon as a self-governing authority has been freely elected by the inhabitants of these areas to replace the existing military government."

The joint letter of March 26, 1979 states that: "The Military Government and its civilian administration will be withdrawn, to be replaced by the SGA."

(b)   Distinction is made in both the Camp David Framework and the joint letter between two kinds of withdrawals:

1 — The withdrawal of the military government and its civilian administration which is total and absolute. It is an unqualified withdrawal; and

2 — A withdrawal of Israeli armed forces which is going to be partial and there will be a redeployment of the remaining forces into specified security locations.

(c)   The withdrawal of the military government and its civilian administration, which occurs as soon as the SGA is elected, is the first step towards the assumption by the SGA of its powers and responsibilities. The transfer of authority takes place by handing over the powers and responsibilities of the military government and its civilian administration to the newly elected SGA. The SGA replaces the outgoing regime.

(d)   In this respect, the following elements should be stressed:

(1)   The transfer of authority implies the handing over of all powers and responsibilities presently exercised by the military government and its civilian administration.

(2)   The transfer of authority should be carried out in a peaceful and orderly manner.

(3)   Whenever Palestinian Institutions already exist in the West Bank and Gaza Strip, as part of the prevailing system of civil service, they will, in the course of such transfer of authority, take over the functions of, and replace, the military government and its civilian administration. It is only when new functions, or new powers, are transferred to the SGA which were not exercised before under the military regime by the Palestinian people that new organs should be sought.

(e)   Stress should be focused more on the powers and functions that are not exercised by the Palestinian people under the military regime so that the necessary relevant organs would be suggested. The Palestinian people already played the major role in the civil service which obeyed the commands and implemented the policies of the military regime. Under the autonomy there will be need for an organ to fulfill their newly acquired power to make their own decisions and formulate their own policies. The elected body of the SGA is obviously that organ.

## IV — Powers and Responsibilities to be Exercised by the Self-Governing Authority

For a model of powers and responsibilities to be exercised by the SGA, some keywords and guidelines from the Camp David Framework for peace should be stressed at the outset.

(a)   It is a self-governing authority, which means that it governs itself by itself. It is a self-generating authority. No outside source vests it with its authority.

(b)   It provides full autonomy, and not an impaired or partial autonomy.

(c)   This self-governing authority with full autonomy comes through free elections. It is a democratic structure of government by the people and for the people. As an elected body it has a representative character and its membership fulfill the functions and exercise the powers that an elected representative body usually does.

### 1 — Nature of the SGA

The SGA is an interim arrangement for a period not exceeding 5 years. This transitional process, at the outset of which the Israeli military government and its civilian administration will be withdrawn and the SGA established, can demonstrate that the practical problems arising from a transition to peace can be satisfactorily resolved. The transitional period is aimed at bringing about the changes in attitudes that can assure a final settlement which realizes the legitimate rights of the Palestinian people while assuring the security of all the parties. The purpose of this transitional arrangement is:

(a)   To ensure a peaceful and orderly transfer of authority to the Palestinian people in the West Bank and Gaza Strip.

(b)   To help the Palestinian people to develop their own political, economic and social institutions in the West Bank and Gaza Strip so as to give expression to the principle of full autonomy which the SGA provides.

(c)   To provide the proper conditions for the Palestinian people to participate in negotiations leading to the solution of the Palestinian problem in all its aspects and the realization of their legitimate rights including their right to self-determination.

*2 — Scope of the SGA:*

(a)   The jurisdiction of the SGA will encompass all of the Palestinian territories occupied after 5 June 1967 and which are delineated in the relevant armistice agreements of 1949 (Egyptian Israeli armistice agreement of 2 April, 1949 regarding the Gaza Strip and Jordanian Israeli armistice agreement of 24 February, 1949 regarding the West Bank including Arab Jerusalem).

(b)   Authority of the SGA extends to the inhabitants as well as the land in the West Bank and the Gaza Strip.

(c)   All powers and responsibilities of the SGA apply to the West Bank and Gaza Strip which shall be regarded under the autonomy as one territory and integral whole.

(d)   All changes in the geographic character, the demographic composition and the legal status of the West Bank and Gaza Strip or any part thereof are null and void and must be rescinded as they jeopardize the attainment of the legitimate rights of the Palestinian people as provided for in the Camp David Framework.

This applies in particular to:

1 — East Jerusalem, the annexation of which by Israel is null and void and must be rescinded. Relevant Security Council Resolutions, particularly Resolutions 242 and 267 must be applied to Jerusalem which is an integral part of the West Bank. Legal and historical Arab rights in the City must be respected and restored.

2 — Israeli settlements in the West Bank and Gaza Strip are illegal and, in the course of a final settlement should be withdrawn.

During the transitional period there should be a ban on the establishment of new settlements or enlarging the existing ones. After the inauguration of the SGA all settlers in the West Bank and Gaza will come under the authority of the SGA.

*3 — General Powers and Responsibilities of the SGA*
1 — Promulgation of laws and regulations
2 — Policy formulation and supervision
3 — Budgetary provisions
4 — Taxation
5 — Employment of staff

6 — Issuance of identity and travel documents

7 — Control of in and out movement of persons and goods

8 — Power to assume obligations and own property

9 — Power to hold title to public land

10 — Power to sue and to be sued

11 — Power to enter into contracts

12 — Power to participate in negotiations on the final status of the West Bank and Gaza Strip and to ascertain in the views of the Palestinians

13 — Assuming responsibility for:

(a) Public administration;

(b) Public services;

(c) Public order and internal security and police;

(d) Public domain and natural resources;

(e) Economic and financial fields;

(f) Social and cultural fields;

(g) Human rights and fundamental freedoms;

14 — Administration of Justice.

*4 — Structure of the SGA*

(a) The SGA will be composed of 80—100 members freely elected from the Palestinian people in the West Bank and Gaza Strip.

(b) The structure of the SGA contains two main organs:

— An assembly composed of all freely elected representatives from the West Bank and Gaza.

— A council composed of 10—15 members to be elected from among the membership of the assembly.

(c) The Assembly:

(1) It will take over, and replace, the authority of the military government in enacting laws and regulations, formulating and supervising policies, adopting the budget, levying taxes, etc...

(2) Its internal organization of a chairman with one or more vice-chairmen, its rules of procedure and the number and composition of its committees will be determined by the Assembly itself.

(d) The Council:

(1) It assumes the actual administration of the West Bank and Gaza and implements the policies formulated by the assembly in the different domains.

(2) It covers the whole range of activities and has full power in organizing, operating, employing staff and supervising the following executive branches; Education — Information and Culture — Transportation and Communications — Health — Social Welfare — Labour — Tourism — Internal Security — Housing — Religious Affairs — Agriculture — Economy and Finance — Commerce — Industry — Administration of Justice.

(3)   The Council will constitute its divisions as it deems necessary for the proper conduct of its functions and will determine the number of divisions, the internal organization of divisions and the machinery for coordination as befits the best and the most effective conduct of its activities. It may get in this respect, and if requested, expert help from the parties.

(e)   The Judicial authority will be manifested in a system of courts of law, courts of appeal and supreme court enjoying full guarantees for independence and efficiency in their administration of justice.

(f)   The SGA will have a representative, alongside with the representatives of Israel, Egypt (and Jordan), on the continuing committee in accordance with Article 3 of the Camp David Framework. Matters of common concern to Israel and the SGA which need mutual arrangements could be dealt with through the committee.

*5 — Seat of the SGA*
The seat of the SGA will be East Jerusalem.

*6 — Additional Arrangements*
(a)   As soon as the SGA is established and inaugurated in the West Bank and Gaza Strip, a withdrawal of Israeli armed forces will take place and there will be a redeployment of the remaining Israeli forces into specified security locations. Permission will be required for any movement of military troops into or through the territory.

(b)   The Camp David Framework requires the parties to negotiate an agreement which includes, inter alia, arrangements for assuring internal security and public order. Responsibility for security and public order will be decided jointly by the parties including the Palestinians, the Israelis, the Egyptians (and the Jordanians).

(c)   A strong police force will be established in the West Bank and Gaza Strip. It will be constituted by the SGA and composed of the people of the West Bank and Gaza Strip.

## 6.   Israel's Autonomy Proposal, January 1982

In the Camp David Agreement signed on 17 September 1978 between Egypt and Israel, with the United States signing as a witness, agreement was reached on a plan for the solution of the problem of the Palestinian Arabs, that includes a proposal for full autonomy for the Palestinian Arabs living in Judea, Samaria and Gaza. The manner of establishing this autonomy, as well as its powers, were to be determined in negotiations between the signatories (Jordan was invited to participate, but did not respond). It was Israel that first raised the idea of autonomy that was later to serve as the basis of the Camp David agreement. For the first time in the history of the Palestinian Arab inhabitants of Judea-Samaria and the Gaza district, they were offered an opportunity of this kind to conduct their own affairs by themselves. Since 1979, talks have been held for the implementation of this agreement; there were intermissions in the negotiations, but talks were resumed intensively in the summer of 1981, leading to a thorough-going clarification of the positions of the parties. At these talks Israel put forward its proposals with regard to the self-governing authority (administrative council), its powers, responsibilities and structure as well as other related issues. The main points of Israel's proposals, as submitted in the course of the negotiations were as follows:

### Scope, Jurisdiction and Structure of the Self-Governing Authority (Administrative Council):

1. The Camp David accords set forth the establishment of a self-governing authority (administrative council) that will comprise one body representing the Arab inhabitants of Judea, Samaria and the Gaza district, who will choose this body in free elections, and it will assume those functional powers that will be transferred to it. Thus the Palestinian Arabs will for the first time have an elected and representative body, in accordance with their own wishes and free choice, that will be able to carry out the functions assigned to it as an administrative council.

2. The members of the administrative council will be able, as a group, to discuss all subjects within the council's competence, apportioning among themselves the spheres of responsibility for the various functions. Within the domain of its assigned powers and responsibilities, the council will be responsible for planning and carrying out its activities.

### Powers of the Self-Governing Authority (Administrative Council):

1.a.  Under the terms of the Camp David agreement, the parties have to reach an agreement on the powers and responsibilities of the authority. Israel's detailed proposals include a list of powers that will be given to the authority and that, by any reasonable and objective criterion, represent a wide and comprehensive range of fields of operation. Without any doubt, the transferring of these powers constitutes the bestowal of full autonomy — in the full meaning of that term.

b.  The powers to be granted the authority, under these proposals, are in the following domains:

1.  *Administration of Justice:* Supervision of the administrative system of the courts in the areas; dealing with matters connected with the prosecution system and with the registration of companies, partnerships, patents, trademarks, etc.

2.  *Agriculture:* All branches of agriculture and fisheries, nature reserves and parks.

3.  *Finance:* Budget of the administrative council and allocations among its various divisions; taxation.

4.  *Civil Service:* Appointment and working conditions of the Council's employees. (Today, the civil service of the inhabitants of Judea-Samaria and Gaza, within the framework of the Military Government's Civilian Administration, numbers about 12,000 persons.)

5.  *Education and Culture:* Operation of the network of schools in the areas, from kindergarten to higher education; supervision of cultural, artistic and sporting activities.

6.  *Health:* Supervision of hospitals and clinics; operation of sanitary and other services related to public health.

7.  *Housing and Public Works:* Construction, housing for the inhabitants and public works projects.

8.  *Transportation and Communications:* Maintenance and coordination of transport, road traffic, meteorology; local postal and communications services.

9.  *Labour and Social Welfare:* Welfare, labour and employment services, including the operation of labour exchanges.

10.  *Municipal Affairs:* Matters concerning municipalities and their effective operation.

11.  *Local Police:* Operation of a strong local police force, as provided for in the Camp David agreement, and maintenance of prisons for criminal offenders sentenced by the courts in the areas.

12.  *Religious Affairs:* Provision and maintenance of religious facilities for all religious communities among the Arab inhabitants of Judea-Samaria and the Gaza district.

13.  *Industry, Commerce and Tourism:* Development of industry, commerce, workshops and tourist services.

2.  The council will have full powers in its spheres of competence to determine its budget, to enter into contractual obligations, to sue and be sued and to engage manpower. It will, moreover, have wide powers to promulgate regulations, as required by a body of this kind. In the nature of things, in view of the free movement that will prevail between Judea-Samaria and the Gaza district and Israel and for the general welfare of the inhabitants, arrangements will be agreed upon in the negotiations, in a number of domains, for cooperation and coordination with Israel. The administrative council will, hence, have full scope to exercise its wide-ranging powers under the terms of the autonomy agreement. These powers embrace all walks of life, and will enable the inhabitants of the areas concerned to enjoy full autonomy.

3.   Size: The size of the administrative council must reflect its functions and its essential purpose: it is an administrative council, whose representative character finds expression in its establishment through free elections, by the Arab inhabitants of Judea, Samaria and Gaza. Clearly, the criterion for determining the number of its members must be the functions that the council is empowered to perform. We propose, therefore, that the number of members will conform with the functions listed above.

4.   Free Elections: Elections to the administrative council, under Israel's proposals, will be absolutely free, as stipulated in the Camp David agreement. Under the terms of the agreement, the parties will agree upon the modalities of the elections; as a matter of fact, in past negotiations a long list of principles and guidelines has already been prepared in this matter. In these free elections, all the rights pertaining to a peaceful assembly, freedom of expression and secret balloting will be preserved and assured, and all necessary steps will be taken to prevent any interference with the election process. The holding of an absolutely free and unhampered election process will thus be assured in full, under the law, and in keeping with the tradition of free elections practiced in democratic societies. These elections will, in many respects, constitute a new departure in the region around us which in most of its parts is not too close to the ways of democracy, and in which free elections are a rare phenomenon. It is of some interest, therefore, to note that Judea-Samaria and Gaza, under Israel's Military Government since 1967, have exemplified the practical possibility of totally free elections in these areas. In 1972, and again in 1976, Israel organized free elections in these areas based on the tradition and model of its own democratic and liberal tradition and custom; voters and elected officials alike concede that these were free elections in the fullest sense. The elections in the administrative council will be organized and supervised by a central elections committee whose composition has been agreed upon by the parties.

5.   Time of elections and establishment of the self-governing authority (administrative council): The elections will be held as expeditiously as possible after agreement will have been reached on the autonomy. This was set forth in the joint letter of the late President Sadat and of Prime Minster Begin to President Carter, dated 26 March 1979, setting for the manner in which the self-governing authority (administrative council) is to be established, under the terms of the Camp David agreement.

6.   Within one month following the elections, the self-governing authority (administrative council) is to be established and inaugurated, and at that time the transitional period of five years will begin — again, in conformity with the Camp David agreement and the joint letter.

7.   Hence, every effort will be made to hold elections without delay, once an agreement is reached, to be followed by the establishment of the self-governing authority (administrative council).

8.   Following the elections and the establishment of the self-governing authority (administrative council) the military government and its civilian administration will be withdrawn, a withdrawal of Israeli armed forces will take place, and there will be a redeployment of the remaining Israeli forces into specified security locations, in full conformity with the Camp David agreement. Israel will present to the other parties in the negotiations the map of the specified security locations of the redeployment. It goes without saying that all this will be done for the purpose of safeguarding the security of Israel as well as of the Arab inhabitants of Judea-Samaria and Gaza and of the Israeli citizens residing in these areas.

9.   All of the above indicates Israel's readiness to observe the Camp David agreement fully and in every detail, in letter and spirit, while safeguarding the interests of all concerned.

# Israeli Documents

**1. Principles Guiding Israel's Policy in the Aftermath of the June 1967 War as Outlined by Prime Minister Eshkol. Jerusalem, 9 August, 1967 [Excerpts]**

(a)   The Government of Israel will endeavour to achieve peace with the neighbouring Arab countries. We shall never permit a return to a situation of constant threat to Israel's security, of blockade and of aggression.

(b)   The Government of Israel is prepared for direct negotiations with all the Arab States together, or with any Arab State separately.

(c)   The State of Israel strives for economic cooperation and regional planning with all States in the Middle East.

(d)   Israel will cooperate fully in the solution of the refugees problem . . . within the framework of an international and regional plan.

(e)   The Government endeavours to maintain fair and equitable relations with the population in the new areas, while maintaining order and security.

After our military victory, we confront a fateful dilemma; immigration or stagnation . . . By the end of the century, we must have five million Jews in Israel. We must work hard so that Israel may be able to maintain decent human, cultural, technical and economic standards. This is the test of Israel's existence as a Jewish State in the Middle East.

## 2. The Nine-Point Peace Plan, Israel's Foreign Minister Abba Eban, 8 October, 1968

*Statement to the U.N. General Assembly*

Mr. President, my Government has decided to give the members of the United Nations a detailed account of its views on the establishment of a just and lasting peace in the Middle East. Amidst the tumult of a rancorous public debate, the deeper motives of our policy have not always been clearly perceived. A structure of peace cannot, of course, be built by speeches at this rostrum. It may, however, be useful for the parties to clarify their intentions and to draw a picture of their policies beyond the routine vocabulary in which this discussion has been held down for sixteen months.

In the interest of peace, I shall refrain from detailed comment on the polemical observations made here by Foreign Ministers of Arab States. The total and unblemished self-satisfaction with which these Ministers have spoken, the complete absence in their worlds of any self-criticism or innovation, the lack of detailed and organized comment on concrete issues — all these illustrate the inhibition which still prevents Arab Governments from thinking lucid and constructive thoughts about their relations with Israel. Indeed, the Foreign Minister of Sudan actually recommended that Israel be dismantled and its people dispersed. Here we have the oldest and most tenacious link in all human history between a people and a land. And an Arab leader speaks of Israel as though it were a temporary international exhibition to be folded up and taken away! Such intellectual frivolity and self-delusion are not heard on any other international issue.

Israel cannot easily forget the immense loss and burden which it has borne through the implacable hostility directed against it for twenty years, culminating in the unforgettable summer of 1967. For there has not been a Six-Day War. There has been a twenty-year war conducted by the Arab States in varying degrees of intensity with the candid hope of Israel's ruin and destruction. The issue is whether this war is now going to be ended by a final peace or merely interrupted in order to be resumed in conditions more propitious for Arab success.

Our danger in 1967 was the climax and not the whole story of our predicament. No other people has had to live all its days with a mark of interrogation hanging over its collective and individual survival. And behind Israel's quest for secure life, there is a particular and hideous legacy of wholesale death in the European slaughter-house. In May 1967, we found ourselves beset by deadly peril which we faced in utter solitude of action and responsibility. Maritime blockade, murderous incursions, military encirclement, declarations of overt war, a frenzied torrent of violent threats and a formal announcement by President Nasser that the battle was joined for Israel's extinction, all came together in cumulative assault on Israel's life and security.

All the acts which fall under the widely supported definitions of aggression were simultaneously concerted against us. The universal conscience was deeply stirred. Millions across the world trembled for Israel's fate. The memory of those dark days broods over Israel's life. Our nation still lives intimately with the dangers which then confronted us. We still recall how the imminent extinction of Israel's statehood and the massacre of its population were seriously discussed across the world: in wild intoxication of spirit in Arab capitals, and with deep, but impotent, sorrow in other lands. To prevent the renewal of those dangers is the first law of our policy. The gravest danger is lest through a lassitude of spirit, or imprecision of diplomatic craftsmanship, or collapse of patience, we again revert to fragile, false and ambiguous solutions which carry within them the seed of future wars. Those of us who bear responsibility for our nation's survival and our children's lives cannot have anything to do with vague solutions which fall short of authentic and lasting peace. June 1967 must be the last of the Middle Eastern wars.

This resolve has moved our policy at every stage of the political discussion from the outbreak of hostilities to this very day.

In June and July 1967, the General Assembly rejected all proposals which sought to condemn Israel's resistance or to reconstruct the conditions which had led to the outbreak of war. A new milestone was reached when the Security Council adopted its unanimous Resolution on 22 November 1967. That Resolution was presented to us for our acquiescence, not as a substitute for specific agreement, but as a list of principles on which the parties could base their agreement. It was drafted, as Ambassador George Ball said on 11 September, as 'a skeleton of principles on which peace could be erected'. It was not meant to be self-executing. As Lord Caradon said on 22 November, it was not 'a call for a temporary truce or a superficial accommodation'; it reflected, as he said, a refusal 'to be associated with any so-called settlement which was only a continuation of a false truce'. Its author stated that any 'action to be taken must be within the framework of a permanent peace, and withdrawal must be to secure boundaries'. The term 'secure and recognized boundaries' had first appeared in a United States draft, the author of which pointed out that this meant something different from the old armistice demarcation lines. Secure and recognized boundaries, he said, had never existed in the Middle East. They must, therefore, be fixed by the parties in the course of the peacemaking process.

Now these were the understandings on which Israel's cooperation with Ambassador Jarring's mission was sought and obtained. Whatever our views might be on these formulations by other Governments, it has been evident at every stage that the two central issues are the establishment of a permanent peace and an agreement for the first time on the delineation of secure and recognized boundaries. These are the conditions prerequisite for any movement. It is here that the peacemaking process must begin. If these problems are solved, all the other issues mentioned in the Resolution fall into place. To seek a change in the cease-fire dispositions, without the framework of a just and lasting peace and the determination of agreed boundaries, is an irrational course for which there is no international authority or precedent. This would be a short and certain route to renewed war in conditions hostile to Israel's security and existence.

Our contacts with the Special Representative of the Secretary-General began in December 1967. At the end of that month, on 27 December, I conveyed a document to the Egyptian Foreign Minister, through Ambassador Jarring, proposing an agenda for a discussion on the establishment of a just and lasting peace. In this letter, I expressed a willingness to hear the UAR's views, and suggested that representatives of our two Governments be brought together informally in order to explore each other's intentions and to derive assurance and confidence for future contacts. In our letter we made it clear that the establishment of the boundary was fully open for negotiation and agreement.

The UAR made no reply, offered no comment, presented no counter-proposals. Indeed, from that day to this, the UAR has not sent us a single document referring to or commenting on any Israeli letters.

On 7 January, I conveyed to the Jordan Government, through Ambassador Jarring, a letter in which I sought to open a constructive dialogue. This letter reads in part:

"History and geography create an objective affinity of interest between the two countries. More than any other relationship between Middle Eastern States, this one involves human interests in a close degree of interdependence. A close and confident association would seem to be as necessary for Jordanian as for Israeli welfare.

"The major problems at issue between Jordan and Israel are closely interconnected. Territorial security, economic and humanitarian problems impinge directly on each other. Moreover, the political and juridical basis of this relationship is of overriding importance. If there is a prior agreement to establish relations of permanent peace, the specific problems at issue between the two countries can be effectively and honourably solved."

I went on to list the five major subjects on which we shall seek agreement. These included the establishment of the boundary and security arrangements. No reply was made to this approach.

On 12 February, I requested Ambassador Jarring to convey the following to the Governments of Egypt and Jordan:

"Israel has cooperated and will cooperate with you in your mission. We accept the Security Council's call, in its Resolution of 22 November 1967, for the promotion of agreement on the establishment of peace with secure and recognized boundaries.

"Once agreement is reached on a peace settlement, it will be faithfully implemented by Israel.

"As I indicated to you on 1 February 1968, Israel is prepared to negotiate on all matters included in the Security Council Resolution which either side wishes to raise. Our views on the problems of peace and our interpretation of the Resolution were stated by me in the Security Council on 2 November 1967.

"The next step should be to bring the parties together. I refer to the agreement which I expressed to you on 1 February for the Special Representative of the Secretary-General to convene the two Governments."

This message elicited no response. On February 19, I communicated another message to Ambassador Jarring for transmission to Cairo. This message assured the Secretary-General's Representative of Israel's full cooperation in his efforts to promote agreement and to achieve an accepted settlement for the establishment of a just and lasting peace in accordance with his mandate under the Security Council Resolution of 22 November 1967.

It further pointed out that the UAR is aware of Israel's willingness to negotiate on all matters included in the Security Council Resolution. It drew attention to the fact that the Resolution is a framework for agreement, and that it cannot be fulfilled without a direct exchange of views and proposals leading to bilateral contractual commitments. It accepted the sponsor's view that the principles recommended for inclusion in the peace settlement are integrally linked and interdependent, and it proposed to move forward to a more substantive stage and to embark on a meaningful negotiation for achieving a just and lasting peace called for by the Security Council.

Early in March 1968, Ambassador Jarring sought our reaction on a proposal to convene Israel, the UAR and Jordan in conferences under his auspices to seek an agreed settlement in fulfilment of his mandate under the Security Council's Resolution. We were later informed that the UAR had rejected and that Jordan had not accepted this course. On 1 May, Ambassador Tekoah was empowered to indicate, in the Security Council, Israel's acceptance of the November Resolution for the promotion of agreement on the establishment of a just and lasting peace. The Israeli Representative was authorized to reaffirm that we were willing to seek agreement with each Arab State on all the matters included in the Resolution, and that we accepted the proposal of Dr. Jarring of bringing about meetings between Israel and its neighbours under his auspices in fulfilment of his mandate for the purpose of peaceful and accepted settlement.

On 29 May, after a discussion in our Cabinet, I made a statement in the

Knesset proposing a method of implementing the Security Council Resolution through negotiation, agreement and the signature and application of treaty engagements to be worked out between the parties. In this, as in previous documents, it was made clear that we regarded the establishment of the boundary as a matter for negotiation and agreement.

On 14 June, I was informed that this proposal had been conveyed to the UAR's Permanent Representative, who had noted it without any reaction. At the end of August, I submitted to the UAR Foreign Minister, through Ambassador Jarring, a series of ideas and viewpoints on the implications of the term "a just and final peace". This was developed in further communications early in September. To all these detailed proposals, the UAR replied declining any specific comment, and limiting itself to a general reference to the text of the Security Council's Resolution. The UAR would recite the Resolution in a declaration of acceptance without any specification of how it proposed to reach concrete agreement. During this time, Egyptian policy was authoritatively defined by President Nasser in a formal utterance on 23 June. In that statement, the UAR President expressed willingness to attempt, as in March 1957, "a political solution" on condition that certain principles of Egyptian policy be recognized. He said:

"The following principles of Egyptian policy are immutable:

1) No negotiation with Israel

2) No peace with Israel

3) No recognition of Israel

4) No transactions will be made at the expense of Palestinian territories or the Palestinian people."

How one can build peace out of such negative and immutable principles defeats the imagination.

Mr. President, I have taken the General assembly into the knowledge of our initiatives and proposals. I leave it to my fellow delegates to judge whether their complete rejection was justified or compatible with a sincere attempt to explore the conditions of a permanent peace and to reach agreement.

In discussing the reasons for the lack of substantive progress, we cannot fail to perceive that the discussion on peace has revolved too much around semantic expressions, too little around the solution of contentious issues. There is no instance in history in which a stubborn and complex conflict has been brought to an end by the mere recitation of texts without precise agreement on the issues of which the conflict is composed. Israel has accepted the Security Council's Resolution for the establishment of a just and lasting peace and declared its readiness to negotiate agreements on all the principles mentioned therein. We hold that the Resolution should be implemented through negotiation, agreement and the joint signature and application of appropriate treaty engagements.

When the parties accept a basis for settlement — their least duty is to clarify what they mean by their acceptance.

To make identical and laconic statements with diametrically opposed motives and interpretations would come dangerously close to international deceit. All parties must say what they mean, and mean what they say. And the heart of the problem is not what we say, but what we do. The construction of a peaceful edifice requires sustained action in order to bring the vital interests of the parties into an acceptable harmony. There is no such thing as peace by incantation. Peace cannot be advanced by recitations accompanied by refusal to negotiate viable agreements. The Security Council's Resolution has not been used as an instrument for peace. It has been invoked as an obstacle and alibi to prevent the attainment of peace.

In these conditions, my Government has given intensive consideration to the steps that we should now take. Our conclusion is this. Past disappointment should not lead to present despair. The stakes are too high. While the cease-fire agreements offer important security against large-scale hostilities, they do not represent a final state of peace. They must, of course, be maintained and respected until there is peace. They must be safeguarded against erosion by military assault and murderous incursion. But at the same time, the exploration of a lasting peace should be constant. Unremitting, resilient and, above all, sincere, my Government deems the circumstances and atmosphere afforded by our presence here as congenial for a new attempt. We suggest that a new effort be made in the coming weeks to cooperate with Ambassador Jarring in his task of promoting agreements on the establishment of peace.

It is important to break out of the declaratory phase in which the differences of formulation are secondary and in any case legitimate, in order to give tangible effect to the principles whereby peace can be achieved in conformity with the central purposes of the United Nations Charter or the Security Council Resolution and with the norms of international law. Instead of a war of words, we need acts of peace.

I come to enumerate the nine principles by which peace can be achieved:

*1)   The establishment of peace*
The situation to follow the cease-fire must be a just and lasting peace, duly negotiated and contractually expressed.

Peace is not a mere absence of fighting. It is a positive and clearly defined relationship with far-reaching political, practical and juridical consequences. We propose that the peace settlement be embodied in treaty form. It would lay down the precise conditions of our co-existence, including a map of the secure and agreed boundary. The essence of peace is that it commits both parties to the proposition that their twenty-year-old conflict is at a permanent end. Peace is much more than what is called "non-belligerency". The elimination of belligerency is one of several conditions which compose the establishment of a just and lasting peace. If there had previously been peace between the States of our area and temporary hostilities had erupted, it might have been sufficient to terminate belligerency and to return to the previously existing peace. But the Arab-Israel area has had no peace. There is nothing normal or legitimate or established to which to return. The peace structure must be built from its foundations. The parties must define affirmatively what their relations shall be, not only what they will have ceased to be. The Security Council, too, called for the establishment of peace and not for any intermediate or ambiguous or fragmentary arrangement such as that which had exploded in 1967.

### 2)   Secure and Recognized Boundaries

Within the framework of peace, the cease-fire lines will be replaced by permanent, secure and recognized boundaries between Israel and each of the neighbouring Arab States, and the disposition of forces will be carried out in full accordance with the boundaries under the final peace. We are willing to seek agreement with each Arab State on secure and recognized boundaries within the framework of a permanent peace.

It is possible to work out a boundary settlement compatible with the security of Israel and with the honour of Arab States. After twenty years, it is time that Middle Eastern States ceased to live in temporary "demarcation lines" without the precision and permanence which can come only from the definite agreement of the States concerned. The majority of the United Nations have recognized that the only durable and reasonable solutions are agreed solutions serving the common interests of our peoples. The new peace structure in the Middle East, including the secure and recognized boundaries, must be built by Arab and Israeli hands.

### 3)   Security Agreements

In addition to the establishment of agreed territorial boundaries, we should discuss other agreed security arrangements designed to avoid the kind of vulnerable situation which caused a breakdown of the peace in the summer of 1967. The instrument establishing peace should contain a pledge of mutual non-aggression.

### 4)   The Open Frontier

When agreement is reached on the establishment of peace with permanent boundaries, the freedom of movement now existing in the area, especially in the Israel-Jordan sector, should be maintained and developed. It would be incongruous if our peoples were to intermingle in peaceful contact and commerce only when there is a state of war and cease-fire — and to be separated into ghettos when there is peace. We should emulate the open frontier now developing within communities of States, as in parts of Western Europe.

Within this concept, we include free port facilities for Jordan on Israel's Mediterranean coast and mutual access to places of religious and historic associations.

### 5) Navigation

Interference with navigation in the international waterways in the area has been the symbol of the state of war and, more than once, an immediate cause of hostilities. The arrangements for guaranteeing freedom of navigation should be unreserved, precise, concrete and founded on absolute equality of rights and obligations between Israel and other littoral States.

### 6) Refugees

The problem of displaced populations was caused by war and can be solved by peace. On this problem I propose:

*One:* A conference of Middle Eastern States should be convened, together with the Governments contributing to refugee relief and the specialized agencies of the United Nations, in order to chart a five-year plan for the solution of the refugee problem in the framework of a lasting peace and the integration of refugees into productive life. This conference can be called in advance of peace negotiations.

*Two:* Under the peace settlement, joint refugee integration and rehabilitation commissions should be established by the signatories in order to approve agreed projects for refugee integration in the Middle East, with regional and international aid.

*Three:* As an interim measure, my Government has decided, in view of the forthcoming winter, to intensify and accelerate action to widen the uniting of families scheme, and to process "hardship cases" among refugees who had crossed to the East Bank during the June 1967 fighting. Moreover, permits for return which had been granted and not used can be transferred to other refugees who meet the same requirements and criteria as the original recipients.

### 7) Jerusalem

Israel does not seek to exercise unilateral jurisdiction in the Holy Places of Christianity and Islam. We are willing in each case to work out a status to give effect to their universal character. We would like to discuss appropriate agreements with those traditionally concerned. Our policy is that the Christian and Moslem Holy Places should come under the responsibility of those who hold them in reverence.

### 8) Acknowledgement and Recognition of Sovereignty, Integrity and Right to National Life

This principle, inherent in the Charter and expressed in the Security Council Resolution of November 1967, is of basic importance. It should be fulfilled through specific contractual engagements to be made by the Governments of Israel and of the Arab States to each other — by name. It follows logically that Arab Governments will withdraw all the reservations which they have expressed on adhering to international conventions, about the non-applicability of their signatures to their relations with Israel.

### 9) Regional Cooperation

The peace discussion should examine a common approach to some of the resources and means of communication in the region in an effort to lay foundations of a Middle Eastern community of sovereign States.

Mr. President,

The process of exploring peace terms should follow normal precedents. There is no case in history in which conflicts have been liquidated or a transition effected from a state of war to a state of peace on the basis of a stubborn refusal by one State to meet another for negotiation. There would be nothing new in the experience and relationship of Israel and the Arab States for them to meet officially to effect a transition in their relationships. What is new and unprecedented is President Nasser's principle of "no negotiation".

In the meantime, we continue to be ready to exchange ideas and clarifications on certain matters of substance through Ambassador Jarring with any Arab Government willing to establish a just and lasting peace with Israel.

Mr. President,

I have expounded our views on peace in more detail than is usual in General Assembly debates. On each of these nine points we have elaborated detailed views and ideas which we would discuss with neighbouring States in a genuine exchange of views, in which we should, of course, consider comments and proposals from the other side. No Arab spokesman has yet addressed himself to us in similar detail on the specific and concrete issues involved in peacemaking. Behind our proposals lie much thought and planning which can bear fruit when our minds and hearts interact with those of neighbouring States.

We ask friendly Governments outside the region to appraise the spirit as well as the content of the ideas which I have here outlined. We urge the Arab Governments to ponder them in a deliberate mood, and to explore their detailed implications with us in the normal and appropriate frameworks.

The solutions which I have outlined cover all the matters mentioned in the Security Council's Resolution and would constitute the effective fulfilment of its purposes.

We base ourselves on the integral and interdependent character of the points at issue. Nothing is less fruitful than an attempt to give separate identity or precedence to any single principle of international policy, thus destroying its delicate balance.

Moreover, the obligations of Israel and the Arab States to each other are not exhausted by any single text. They are also governed by the Charter, by the traditional precepts of international law, by constructive realism and by the weight of human needs and potentialities.

Lest Arab Governments be tempted out of sheer routine to rush into impulsive rejection, let me suggest that tragedy is not what men suffer but what they miss. Time and again Arab Governments have rejected proposals today — and longed for them tomorrow. The fatal pattern is drawn across the whole period since 1947 — and before. There is nothing unrealistic about a negotiated peace inspired by a sense of innovation and constructed by prudent and flexible statecraft. Indeed, all other courses are unrealistic. The idea of a solution imposed on the parties by a concert of Powers is perhaps the most unrealistic of all. The positions of the Powers have not moved any closer in the last fifteen months than have the positions of the parties themselves. Moreover, the Middle East is not an international protectorate. It is an area of sovereign States which alone have the duty and responsibility of determining the conditions of their co-existence. When the parties have reached agreement, it would be natural for their agreement to receive international support. To the Arab States, we say: "For you and us alone, the Middle East is not a distant concern, or a strategic interest, or a problem of conflict, but the cherished home in which our cultures were born, in which our nationhood was fashioned and in which we and you and all our posterity must henceforth live together in mutuality of interest and respect."

It may seem ambitious to talk of a peaceful Middle Eastern design at this moment of tension and rancour. But there is such a thing in physics as fusion at high temperatures. In political experience, too, the consciousness of peril often brings a thaw in frozen situations. In the long run, nations can prosper only by recognizing what their common interest demands. The hour is ripe for the creative adventure of peace.

## 3. Israel's Foreign Minister Abba Eban Knesset Statement on Occupied Territories. Jerusalem, 13 May, 1969 [Excerpts]

Three demands which Israel will not waive are a permanent presence at Sharm el-Sheikh, a unified Jerusalem despite concessions to Jordan over the Holy Places, and a Golan Heights for ever out of Syrian hands.

## 4. Statement by the Israeli Government Embodying a Reaction to the U.S. Secretary of State Rogers' Address on United States Foreign Policy in the Middle East Tel Aviv, 11 December, 1969

The Israel Government discussed in special session the political situation in the region and the latest speech of the U.S. Secretary of State on the Middle East.

The Government states that the tension in the Middle East referred to by Mr. Rogers derives from the aggressive policy of the Arab governments: The absolute refusal to make peace with Israel and the unqualified support of the Soviet Union for the Arab aggressive stand.

Israel is of the opinion that the only way to terminate the tension and the state of war in the region is by perpetual striving for a durable peace among the nations of the region, based on a peace treaty reached through direct negotiations which will take place without any prior conditions by any party. The agreed, secure and recognized boundaries will be fixed in the peace treaty. This is the permanent and stated peace policy of Israel and is in accordance with accepted international rules and procedures.

The Six Day War, or the situation created in its wake, cannot be spoken of in terms of expansion or conquest. Israel cried out against aggression which threatened its very existence, and used its natural right of national self-defence.

In his speech, Mr. Rogers said that states outside the region cannot fix peace terms; only states in the region are authorized to establish peace by agreement among themselves. The Government states regretfully that this principle does not tally with the detailed reference in the speech to peace terms, including territorial and other basic questions, among them Jerusalem. Jerusalem was divided following the conquest of part of the city by the Jordanian Army in 1948. Only now, after the unification of the city under Israel administration, does there exist freedom of access for members of all faiths to their holy places in the city.

The position of Israel is: The negotiations for peace must be free from prior conditions and external influences and pressures. The prospects for peace will be seriously marred if states outside the region continue to raise territorial proposals and suggestions on other subjects that cannot further peace and security.

When the Four Power talks began, the Government of Israel expressed its view on the harmful consequences involved in this move in its statement of March 27, 1969. The fears expressed then were confirmed.

Peace was not promoted, Arab governments were encouraged by the illusion that an arrangement could be reached by the exertion of external influences and pressures with no negotiations between the parties. In this period Egyptian policy reached the most extreme expressions, especially in President Nasser's speech in which he spoke of rivers flowing with blood and skies lit by fire. In this period, the region has not become tranquil. In an incessant violation of the cease-fire arrangement, fixed by the Security Council and accepted by all sides unconditionally and with no time limit, the Egyptians have intensified their attempts to disturb the cease-fire lines. Conveniently, Arab aggression in other sectors continued and terrorist acts, explicitly encouraged by Arab governments, were intensified. Even the Jarring mission to promote an agreement between the parties was paralyzed.

The focus of the problem as stated by Mr. Rogers lies in the basic intentions and positions of the governments of the region to the principle of peaceful coexistence. The lack of intention of the Arab governments to move towards peace with Israel is expressed daily in proclamations and deeds. The positions and intentions of the parties towards peace cannot be tested unless they agree to conduct negotiations as among states desiring peace. Only when there is a basic change in the Arab position, which denies the principle of negotiations for the signing of peace, will it be possible to replace the state of war by durable peace. This remains the central aim of the policy of Israel.

In his forthcoming talks with the Secretary of State, the Foreign Minister will explain in detail the position of the Government of Israel concerning the situation in the region.

## 5. Resolution Adopted by the Israel Knesset Rejecting King Hussein's United Arab Kingdom Plan. Jerusalem, 16 March, 1972

The Knesset has duly noted the Prime Minister's statement of March 16, 1972, regarding the speech made by the King of Jordan on March 11, 1972.

The Knesset has determined that the historic right of the Jewish people to the Land of Israel is beyond challenge.

The Knesset authorizes the Government of Israel to continue its policy in accordance with the basic principles, as approved by the Knesset on December 15, 1969, according to which:

The government will steadfastly strive to achieve a durable peace with Israel's neighbours founded in peace treaties achieved by direct negotiations between the parties. Agreed, secure and recognized borders will be laid down in the peace treaties.

The peace treaties will assure cooperation and mutual aid, the solution of any problem that might be a stumbling-block in the path to peace, and the avoidance of any aggression, direct or indirect.

Israel will continue to be willing to negotiate — without prior conditions from either side — with any of the neighbouring states for the conclusion of a peace treaty. Without a peace treaty, Israel will continue to maintain in full the situation as established by the cease-fire and will consolidate its position in accordance with the vital requirements of its security and development.

The Knesset supports the Government in its endeavours to further peace by negotiating with the Arab states according to the resolutions of the Knesset.

## 6. The "Galili Plan" — Statement by Government Ministers of the Israeli Labour Party on Proposed Policy in the Occupied Territories. August, 1973

*Preamble:* These points of agreement are not decisions endorsed by the Party and the Labour Alignment, but recommendations by the Labour Party ministers. The Prime Minister has submitted these points of agreement to the authorized organizations (the Party, the Labour Alignment and the Government) for their approval. These points will be set out as guide-lines in the electoral programme of the Labour Alignment and included in the government's general plan of action. Once the basic lines of the plans of action have been approved the projects will be worked out in practical detail, and the budgets for their implementation will be included in the government's annual budgets. The plan of action in the occupied areas for the next four years will not be conditional on any change in the political status of these areas or the civil status of the inhabitants and the refugees.

A. *Principles:* The next government will continue to operate in the occupied areas on the basis of the policy pursued by the present government — development, provision of employment and services, economic links, open bridges, encouragement of initiative and the renewal of municipal representation, orders from the military government, village and town settlement, improvement of the refugee camps, specific and controlled work in Israel for

Arab workers from the occupied areas.

B. *Rehabilitation of Refugees and Economic Development in the Gaza Strip:* A four-year plan of action will be drawn up, and the necessary funds allocated for its execution, with a view to ensuring the rehabilitation of the refugees, and economic development. The main points of this plan of action will be: Changing the housing situation (establishing places of residence for the refugees near the camps, improving the camps and making the municipalities of neighbouring towns responsible for them); vocational training; improving health and livelihood in trades and industry; encouraging the population to take the initiative in improving their standard of living.

C. *Development in Judea and Samaria:* A four-year plan of action will be drawn up and the necessary financing for its execution ensured, with the object of ensuring the development of the economic infrastructure and improving the essential services (health, electrical, etc.); developing the water services to meet the requirements of the population; developing vocational and higher education; developing electrical communications and transport services; improving streets and roads; developing trade and industry as sources of employment for the inhabitants; improving the refugees' housing situation; and help to the municipal authorities.

D. *Financing for Judea and Samaria:* Once it is endorsed by the government, the agreement reached between the Ministries of Finance and Defence will constitute the basis of decisions as to how the plans of action in the Gaza Strip and the West Bank should be financed.

E. *International Financing:* Efforts will be made to obtain from external sources the means to finance projects for the rehabilitation of the refugees and development in the occupied areas.

F. *Encouraging Israeli Business in the Territories:* Facilities and incentives will be provided to encourage Israelis to establish industrial projects in the occupied areas (in accordance with the proposal submitted by the Minister of Trade and Industry to the Governmental Committee for Economic Affairs on August 1).

G. *Encouraging Local Residents' Initiative in Judea and Samaria:* Aid will be given for self-initiative of the inhabitants in the fields of education, religion and services, and in the field of developing democratic forms in social and municipal life. As far as possible local persons will be appointed to high civilian posts in the [Military] Government.

H. *The Policy of Open Bridges:* The policy of open bridges will continue.

I. *Work for the Inhabitants of the Territories in Israel:* Work for the inhabitants of the occupied territories in Israel and in Jewish economic areas in the occupied territories will be subject to control as regards both numbers and the areas in which workers are allowed to work. Necessary measures will be taken to ensure working conditions and wages similar to those in Israel.

J.  *Paramilitary and Civilian Settlements:* New settlements will be established and the network of settlements will be reinforced. Efforts will be made to increase their population by developing trade, industry and tourism. When the government's annual budget is drawn up from year to year it will be decided what means are necessary for the new settlements, in accordance with the recommendations of the Settlement Department, and after the approval of the Ministerial Committee on Settlement to establish new settlements in the next four years in the Rafah Approaches, the Jordan Valley and the Golan Heights. They will include a civilian-industrial settlement in the Golan Heights, a regional centre in the Jordan Valley, development of the north-east shore of the Sea of Galilee and the north-west shore of the Dead Sea and executing the planned water projects. Non-governmental organizations, both public and private will be included within the framework of the plans approved by the government for the development of sites for settlement.

K.  *The Regional Centre in the Rafah Approaches:* The continued development of the Regional Centre in the Rafah Approaches will be ensured so that it may comprise 800 housing units by the year 1977—1978. Industrial development for settlers prepared to settle at their own expense will be encouraged.

L.  *The Unification and Purchase of Land in the Territories:* 1. More intensive action to unify lands for the requirements of existing and planned settlement (purchase, state lands, absentees' lands, exchanges of lands, arrangements with the inhabitants) will be expanded. 2. The Israel Lands Authority will be recommended to expand purchases of land and real estate in the occupied areas for the purposes of settlement, development and land exchange. 3. The Lands Authority will lease to companies and individuals for the execution of approved projects. 4. The Lands Authority will also try to buy lands by all effective means, in particular through companies and individuals who buy lands, in coordination with the Lands Authority on its behalf. 5. Purchases of lands and real estate by companies and individuals will be approved only in cases where it is ascertained that the Directorate is unable to buy or not interested in buying the lands on its own account. 6. A special Cabinet Committee will be authorized to grant permits, on condition that the lands purchased are intended for constructive projects and not for speculation, and within the framework of the government's policy. 7. The Israel Lands Authority will also make a point of acquiring lands already bought by Jews.

M.  *Jerusalem and Environs:* Provision of housing and industrial development in the capital and its environs will be continued with a view to consolidation beyond the original area. To achieve this goal, efforts will be made to buy additional land; the government lands in the area to the east and south of Jerusalem which the government has decided to enclose will be exploited.

N.  *Nabi Samuel:* The government's decision taken on September 13, 1970, on the settlement of Nabi Samuel will be implemented.

O. *A Deep Sea Port in Southern Gaza:* In preparation for the rapid development of the Rafah Approaches studies will be carried out in the course of two or three years on the basic facts of the proposal to construct a deep sea port south of Gaza — the geographical situation, the economic viability and the political considerations. When the results have been obtained and a practical project has been submitted, the government will take a decision on the matter.

P. *An Industrial Center in Kfar Saba:* The necessary conditions will be ensured for the establishment of an industrial centre attached to Kfar Saba beyond the Green Line, as also for the development of Israeli industry in the areas of Tulkarm and Qalqilya.

## 7. Statement Issued by Israel's Cabinet Insisting that Jordan Represent the Palestinians in Negotiations. Jerusalem, 21 July, 1974

Israel will continue to strive for peace agreements with the Arab States within defensible borders to be achieved through negotiation without prior conditions.

The Government will work towards negotiations for a peace agreement with Jordan.

The peace will be founded on the existence of two independent states only — Israel with united Jerusalem as her capital and a Jordanian-Palestinian Arab state east of Israel within borders to be determined in negotiations between Israel and Jordan. This state will provide for expression of identity of the Jordanians and the Palestinians, in peace and good-neighbourliness with Israel.

The Cabinet endorses the Prime Minister's statement of June 3, 1974, in the Knesset, that the Government of Israel will not conduct negotiations with terrorist organizations whose aim is the destruction of the State of Israel.

The Minister for Foreign Affairs reported on the latest events in Cyprus.

## 8. Israel Knesset Statement, Prime Minister, Yitzhak Rabin, Following the Rabat Conference, 5 November, 1974 [Excerpts]

The meaning of [the Rabat] Resolutions is clear. The Rabat Conference decided to charge the organizations of murderers with the establishment of a Palestinian State, and the Arab countries gave the organizations a free hand to decide on their mode of operations. The Arab countries themselves will refrain, as stated in the Resolution, from intervening in the "internal affairs" of this action.

We are not fully aware of the significance of the fourth Resolution, which refers to "outlining a formula" for the coordination of relations between Jordan, Syria, Egypt and the PLO. It is by no means impossible that it is also intended to bring about closer military relations between them.

The significance of these Resolutions is extremely grave. The aim of the terrorist organizations is well known and clear. The Palestine National Covenant speaks bluntly and openly about the liquidation of the State of Israel by means of armed struggle, and the Arab States committed themselves at Rabat to support this struggle. Any attempt to implement them will be accompanied by at least attempts to carry out terrorist operations on a larger scale with the support of the Arab countries.

The decisions of the Rabat Conference are merely a continuation of the resolutions adopted at Khartoum. Only, further to the "no's" of Khartoum, the roof organization of the terrorists has attained the status conferred upon it by the presidents and kings at Rabat. Throughout this conference not a voice was raised expressing readiness for peace. The recurring theme of this conference was the aspiration to destroy a member-state of the United Nations. The content of this gathering has nothing whatsoever in common with social progress or the advancement of humanity among the Arab nations or in the relations with the peoples in the region and throughout the world.

There is no indication of any deviation from the goal and policy of the terrorist organizations, so let us not delude ourselves on this score. The terrorist organizations had no successes in the administered territories, but the successes they achieved at the U.N. General Assembly and at Rabat are encouraging them to believe that the targets they had so confidently set themselves are now within reach.

The policy laid down in Khartoum and Rabat shall not be executed. We have the power to prevent its implementation. The positions of the government of Israel in the face of these resolutions of the Rabat Conference is unequivocal:

A)  The government of Israel categorically rejects the conclusions of the Rabat Conference, which are designed to disrupt any progress towards peace, to encourage the terrorist elements, and to foil any step which might lead to peaceful coexistence with Israel.

B)   In accordance with the Knesset's resolutions, the government of Israel will not negotiate with terrorist organizations whose avowed policy is to strive for Israel's destruction and whose method is terrorist violence.

C)   We warn the Arab leaders against making the mistake of thinking that threats or even the active employment of the weapon of violence or of military force will lead to a political solution. This is a dangerous illusion. The aims of the Palestinian National Charter will not be achieved, either by terrorist acts or by limited or total warfare.

The Rabat Conference Resolutions do not justify the adoption of other resolutions, and merely add force to our determination. To anyone who recommends negotiations with the terrorist organizations, I have to say that there is no basis for negotiations with the terrorist organizations. It does not enter our minds to negotiate with a body that denies our existence as a State and follows a course of violence and terrorism for the destruction of our State.

Negotiations with such a body would lend legitimacy and encouragement to its policy and its criminal acts. The U.N. General Assembly's decision to invite this body to its debates is a serious error from the moral and political stand-points, but it has no substance as incompatible with the very existence of the State of Israel. Israel will grant no recognition to those who conspire against her existence.

Rabat is not a surprising innovation, but our policy will not be determined by its decisions. We shall carefully watch the steps the Arab States will take in the wake of this conference and, in particular, we shall watch the moves of those States with whom we were about to embark on negotiations on stages of progress towards peace. Above all, we shall see whether Egypt is in fact ready for this, or whether she has committed herself to the ban on reaching a separate agreement with Israel. We shall be watching Jordan's moves, too, to see whether she surrenders to Arafat.

In the face of this development, we believe that the strength and stability of the State of Israel, and the Israel defense forces, powerful and prepared for any test, are the guarantee for our safety. As long as we are strong and follow a wise and courageous policy, the chances will increase that our neighbors will be ready to seek ways of coming to terms with us.

## 9. The Allon Plan—Article by Israeli Foreign Minister Yigal Allon Reiterating his Plan for Peace, October 1976, [Excerpts]

The polarized asymmetry between the size and intentions of the Arab States and those of Israel, and the extreme contrast in the anticipated fate of each side in the event of military defeat, obliges Israel to maintain constantly that measure of strength enabling it to defend itself in every regional conflict and against any regional combination of strength confronting it, without the help of any foreign army. To our deep regret, this is the first imperative facing us, the imperative to survive. And I would venture to say every other state in our place would behave exactly as we do.

There are, of course, many elements constituting the essential strength that Israel must maintain, ranging from its social, scientific and economic standards, as well as its idealistic motivation, to the quality and quantity of its armaments. A discussion of all of these elements is not within the compass of this article; my concern here is with one of them — but one essential to them all and without which Israel might well lack the strength to defend itself. I am referring to the territorial element; to what can be defined as defensible borders that Israel must establish in any settlement, as an essential part of any effective mutual security arrangements and without any desire for territorial expansion per se.

The most cursory glance at a map is sufficient to ascertain how little the armistic lines of 1949 — lines which were never in the first place recognized as final — could be considered defensible borders. And even the most superficial fingering of the pages of history should be enough to demonstrate how attractive these lines have been to the Arab States as an encouragement to try their strength again against us. The truth of the matter is that Resolution 242 of the United Nations Security Council has already recognized, in its original English text, the need to provide Israel with secure and recognized boundaries — in other words, that changes must be introduced in the old lines of the armistice agreements.

It is no coincidence that this resolution does not speak about Israel's withdrawal from *all* the territories that came under its control in the war that was forced upon Israel in June 1967, nor even from *the* territories. In the original text (which was the outcome of long and exhaustive negotiation), Resolution 242 speaks only of withdrawal from territories. That the meaning was clear was demonstrated by the statement of the United States at the time, made by its U.N. Ambassador Arthur Goldberg on November 15, 1967, in the Security Council discussions that preceded the passage of Resolution 242. He stated:

"Historically, there never have been secure or recognized boundaries in the area. Neither the Armistice Lines of 1949, nor the Cease-Fire Lines of 1967, have answered that description."

As is known, Israel expressed more than once its willingness to withdraw from the cease-fire lines of 1967, within the framework of a peace agreement. On the other hand, it is clear — even according to the Security Council decision — that Israel is not obliged to withdraw to the armistice lines of 1949 that preceded the 1967 war, but to revised lines. The question is what borders will provide Israel with that essential minimum of security? And without such security it is difficult to expect to pacify the area and provide a lasting solution to the conflict within it.

If the sole consideration were the purely strategic-military one, then possibly the most convenient security borders would have been those Israel maintained following the Six-Day War, or perhaps those which it maintains today. There is even a basis for the claim that the 1973 Yom Kippur War — begun as a surprise attack in concert by the armies of Egypt and Syria — proves that these lines were ideally the best. Had the Yom Kippur War commenced on the 1949 armistice lines, for example, there can be little doubt that the price Israel would have had to pay in repelling the aggressors would have been unimaginably higher than that paid so painfully in October 1973. But we are not merely talking about purely military-strategic matters, to the extent that they ever exist in isolation. Nor are we discussing the maximum security that borderlines can provide Israel. As stated, our preoccupation is only with the essential minimum.

One does not have to be a military expert to easily identify the critical defects of the armistice lines that existed until June 4, 1967. A considerable part of these lines is without any topographical security value; and, of no less importance, the lines fail to provide Israel with the essential minimum of strategic depth. The gravest problem is on the eastern boundary, where the entire width of the coastal plain varies between 10 and 15 miles, where the main centers of Israel's population, including Tel Aviv and its suburbs, are situated, and where the situation of Jerusalem is especially perilous. Within these lines a single successful first strike by the Arab armies would be sufficient to dissect Israel at more than one point, to sever its essential living arteries, and to confront it with dangers that no other state would be prepared to face. The purpose of defensible borders is thus to correct this weakness, to provide Israel with the requisite minimal strategic depth, as well as lines which have topographical strategic significance.

Of course I do not wish to overlook the fact that there are some who would claim that in an era of modern technological development such factors are valueless. In a nutshell, their claim is that the appearance of ground-to-ground missiles, supersonic fighter-bombers, and other sophisticated instruments of modern warfare has canceled out the importance of strategic depth and topographical barriers. Personally, I do not know of a single state which is willing and ready to give up a convenient border line for this reason. At any rate, this argument is certainly invalid regarding Israel, and within the context of the Middle East conflict, where the opposite is true. Precisely because of dramatic developments in conventional weaponry the significance of territorial barriers and strategic depth has increased.

With all the heavy damage that warheads and bombs can inflict, they alone cannot be decisive in war, as long as the other side is resolved to fight back. Recent military history demonstrates this only too clearly. The German air "blitz" did not knock England out of World War II, nor did the heavy allied air bombardments bring Germany to its knees. This happened only when the last bunker in berlin fell. Even massive American air bombardments did not defeat North Vietnam which, in the final analysis, proved to be the victor in the war. At least as far as conventional wars are concerned, the following basic truth remains: without an attack by ground forces that physically overrun the country involved, no war can be decisive. This is all the more so in the Middle East where the Arab side is no less vulnerable to rocket and aerial bombardment than Israel, a factor that can greatly minimize the use of this kind of weaponry, and will leave to the ground forces the role of really deciding the issue.

## III

Fortunately, the geostrategic conditions that have existed in the Middle East over the past nine years permit a solution based upon a fair political compromise. This could provide Israel with the minimal defensible borders that are indispensible without impairing, to any meaningful extent, the basic interests of the other side, including those of the Palestinian community. As with every other compromise, so, too, is this one likely to be painful in the short term to both sides. But this compromise will, in the long run, grant advantages that both sides do not currently possess nor, without it, ever would in the future.

According to the compromise formula I personally advocate, Israel — within the context of a peace settlement — would give up the large majority of the areas which fell into its hands in the 1967 war. Israel would do so not because of any lack of historical affinity between the Jewish people and many of these areas. With regard to Judea and Samaria, for example, historical Jewish affinity is as great as that for the coastal plain or Galilee. Nonetheless, in order to attain a no less historically exalted goal, namely that of peace, such a deliberate territorial compromise can be made.

For its part, the Arab side would have to concede its claim to those strategic security zones which, together with a number of effective arrangements to be discussed below, will provide Israel with that vital element so lacking in the pre-1967 war lines: a defense posture which would enable the small standing army units of Israel's defense force to hold back the invading Arab armies until most of the country's reserve citizens army could be mobilized. These security zones would thus guarantee enough time to organize and launch the counter offensive needed to defeat any such aggression.

The armistice lines of 1949 extend along the foothills of the Judean and Samarian mountains and along the Mediterranean coastal plain — that is, flat territory without any topographical barriers. This leaves central Israel with a narrow area that comprises the Achilles heel of the lines prior to June 4, 1967. It serves as a constant temptation to a hostile army in possession of hilly Judea and Samaria to attempt to inflict a fatal blow against Israel by severing it in two in one fell swoop. Moreover, this weakness would permit such an army not only to strike at Israel's densest population and industrial centers, but also in effect to paralyze almost all of Israel's airspace with surface-to-air missiles with which the Arab armies are so abundantly equipped.

According to the 1949 lines, Jerusalem was pierced through its heart — the university and the principal hospital on Mount Scopus were cut off, while access from the coastal plain to Jerusalem was restricted to a narrow corridor, threatened on both sides by a pincer attack.

In the northeastern sector, the 1949 line left Syria on the dominating Golan Heights, controlling the Huleh Valley and the Galilee Basin at their foothills, and including the sources of the Jordan River and the Sea of Galilee from which Israel draws a vital part of its water supply. Moreover, after 1949 Syria not only repeatedly shelled the Israeli villages located at the Golan foothills but also attempted to divert the sources of the Jordan and thereby deprive Israel of a vital source of water. Even more important, the Golan Heights served in past wars as the most convenient base for the Syrian army to make swift and major attacks upon Galilee, ultimately aimed at the conquest of the entire northern part of our country.

According to the 1949 armistice agreements, signed by Israel in the naive belief that they would lead swiftly to peace, Egypt was given control of the Gaza Strip. This was a dangerous and needless anomaly. Bordering the unpopulated Sinai desert and without any affinity to Egypt proper, this zone came to serve as a base for large-scale terrorist raids launched at southern Israel. Should the strip be returned to Egyptian control it might easily resume its destructive function. Even worse, it might serve Egypt as a bridgehead for an offensive northward and eastward toward the very heart of Israel, following the historic invasion route from south to north. Another serious defect in the armistice agreements was that it left Israel's southern port entrance at Eilath on a tiny strip of shoreline only six miles long from its border with Egypt to that of Jordan. Moreover, Israel's maritime route to the Red Sea and Indian Ocean passes through the Straits of Tiran at Sharm-el-Sheikh, and the Egyptian blockade there against Israeli ships and cargoes constituted a *casus belli* in both 1956 and 1967.

A reasonable compromise solution can be found for all these weaknesses in the current geostrategic and demographic situation existing in the Middle East. Without going into details or drawing precise maps, an activity that must await direct negotiations between the parties themselves, in my opinion the solution in principle ought to be along the following general lines.

Both to preserve its Jewish character and to contribute toward a solution of the Palestinian issue, Israel should not annex an additional and significant Arab population. Therefore the strategic depth and topographical barriers in the central sector, so totally absent in the lines preceding the 1967 war, cannot be based on moving these lines eastward in a schematic manner, even though this would be logical from a purely strategic point of view. Rather, apart from some minor tactical border alterations along the western section of "the green line", this same goal can be achieved through absolute Israeli control over the strategic zone to the *east* of the dense Arab population, concentrated as it is on the crest of the hills and westward. I am referring to the arid zone that lies between the Jordan River to the east, and the eastern chain of the Samarian and Judean mountains to the west — from Mt. Gilboa in the north through the Judean desert, until it joins the Negev desert. The area of this desert zone is only about 700 square miles and it is almost devoid of population. Thus this type of solution would leave almost all of the Palestinian Arab population of the West Bank under Arab rule.

Cutting through this zone, which continues from north to south, it would be possible to delineate a corridor from west to east under Arab sovereignty. This would permit uninterrupted communication along the Jericho-Ramallah axis, between the Arab populated areas of the West and East banks of the river. In this manner the only realistic solution becomes possible — one that also helps resolve the problem of Palestinian identity that could then find its expression in a single Jordanian-Palestinian State. (After all, the population of both banks, East and West, are Palestinian Arabs. The fact is that the great majority of Palestinians carry Jordanian passports while almost all of Jordan's inhabitants are Palestinians.)

Jerusalem, Israel's capital, which was never the capital of any Arab or Muslim State, but was always the capital and center of the Jewish people, cannot return to the absurd situation of being partitioned. The Holy City and adjacent areas essential for its protection and communications must remain a single, undivided unit under Israel's sovereignty. Because of its universal status, however, in that it is holy to three great religions, as well as the mixed nature of its inhabitants, a solution for the religious interests connected with it can be found, a *religious* and not a political solution. For example, special status could be granted to the representatives of the various faiths in the place holy to them, just as it might be possible to base the municipal structure of the city upon subdistricts that take ethnic and religious criteria into account.

While the strategic zone in the central sector is crucial to Israel's security, so, too, is a zone on the Golan Heights. As past experience has demonstrated, a border not encompassing the Golan Heights would again invite the easy shelling of the villages below in the Huleh Valley, the Galilee Basin and eastern Galilee. More important than the danger of renewed Syrian shelling are sniping at Israeli villages and fishermen below, which is basically a *tactical* question, is that Israel needs an effective defense line on the Golan Heights for two cardinal *strategic* reasons: first, to preclude any new Syrian attempts to deny Israel its essential water resources and, second, to prevent a massive Syrian attack on the whole of Galilee, either independently or in coordination with other Arab armies on Israel's other frontiers.

In my view the city of Gaza and its environs, which is heavily populated by Palestinian Arabs, could comprise a part of the Jordanian-Palestinian unit which would arise to the east of Israel, and serve as that state's Mediterranean port. In this case, it would be necessary to place at the disposal of traffic between Gaza and the Jordanian-Palestinian State the use of a land route (as distinct from a land corridor) similar to that, for example, connecting the United States with Alaska. But Israel must continue to control fully the strategic desert zone from the southern part of the Gaza strip to the dunes on the eastern approaches of the town of El Arish, which itself would be returned to Egypt. This strategic zone, almost empty of population, would block the historic invasion route along the sea coast which many conquerors have taken over the generations to invade the land of Israel, and further north.

A number of border adjustments will also be essential to ensure security sensitive areas of the 1949 Armistice line between Israel and Egypt. These must be made in such a manner as to permit full Israeli control in a number of sectors of crucial importance to its defense and which lack any value for the security of Egypt. I am referring to such areas as those surrounding Abu Aweigila, Kusseima and Kuntilla, which comprise the principal strategic crossroads on the main routes from the desert to Beersheba, and to the Eilath shore line which is the gateway to Israel's maritime routes to the Indian Ocean and the Far East.

An especially sensitive point is that of the area of Sharm-el-Sheikh at the southern tip of the Sinai Peninsula. Although, from this vantage point, there is no danger of a massive surprise attack on Israel proper, a very concrete threat to Israeli freedom of navigation does exist. It should be repeated that Egypt has twice imposed blockades against Israeli ships and cargoes seeking passage through the Straits of Tiran. And, in both instances, Israel was compelled to break this blockade mounted from Sharm-el-Sheikh by capturing the place. In one way or another, unquestionable Israeli control over this corner of the

Sinai — and over a land route reaching it — is not only critical to Israeli defense, but also serves to neutralize a focal point that is liable to set the area on fire once again. Moreover, because of the threat of blockade to Israeli-bound traffic through the Bab-el-Mandeb Strait, which connects the Red Sea with the Indian Ocean, full Israeli control over Sharm-el-Sheikh might serve as a countervailing deterrent against such blockade attempts.

To sum up, there were numerous bitterly deficient points in the pre-1967 lines, and these proposals encompass minimal corrections to them required for an overall peace settlement. The necessity for these corrections is all the more apparent when it is realized that Israel not only faces the military strength of its contiguous neighbours, but may also have to face the combined strength of many other Arab countries. This has already happened to no small extent in the 1973 war, when contingents from Iraq, Libya, Algeria, Saudi Arabia, Morocco, Jordan and other Arab countries participated in the fighting, together with the armies of Egypt and Syria. Thus, in a very practical sense, solid defense lines are indispensible to Israel in order to withstand the attacks of the entire Arab world. In addition, these may well be supported by contingents of so-called volunteers who can be sent from certain countries from outside the area that are hostile to Israel.

Let me stress again that defensible borders are vital to Israel not out of any desire to annex territories per se, not out of a desire for territorial expansion, and not out of any historical and ideological motivation. Israel can compromise on territory but it cannot afford to do so on security. The entire rationale of defensible borders is strategic. This is also the only rationale for the selective settlement policy that Israel is pursuing, as an integral part of its unique defense system, in those strategic zones so vital to its security.

Of course, when the peace for which we strive is achieved, the borders will not divide the two peoples but be freely open to them. In short, good fences make good neighbors.

## IV

As I have pointed out, border adjustments essential for Israel's security, and hence for the long-term stability of the entire area, must also be linked with mutually effective security arrangements designed to prevent surprise attacks by one side on the other, or at least to reduce to a minimum the danger of such attacks. In the geostrategic circumstances of the Middle East, to reduce the possibility of surprise offensives is, in fact, to reduce the danger of all offensives. I am referring to such arrangements as the delineation of both totally and partially demilitarized zones under joint Arab-Israeli control, with or without the participation of a credible international factor; or such arrangements as the delineation of parallel early-warning systems like those functioning in the Sinai according to the terms of the 1975 Interim Agreement between

Israel and Egypt.

I will not enter here into the technical details of such arrangements, their nature, placement and scope. Not that they are unimportant or nonessential; on the contrary, without them, Israel could not permit itself to make the far-reaching territorial compromises which, in my opinion, it should be prepared to make within the context of peace agreements with its neighbors. Let me give one example, albeit, the most important, in order to illustrate this point. According to the principles I have already outlined, if Israel were to forfeit the densely populated heartland of Judea and Samaria, it would not be able to forego — under any circumstances — the effective demilitarization of these areas. Apart from civilian police to guarantee internal order, these areas would have to be devoid of offensive forces and heavy arms. In the same way as any other country, Israel would be unable to abandon areas so close to its heartland if they were liable once again to become staging areas for full-scale, limited or guerilla attacks upon its most vital areas.

In short, Israel cannot permit itself to withdraw from a large part of the West Bank unless the area from which it withdraws is shorn of all aggressive potential. For this purpose, absolute Israeli control, as proposed above, of a strategic security zone along the Jordan Basin will not be adequate. Effective demilitarization of the areas from which the Israel Defense Forces withdraw will also be essential. Here as elsewhere, the two elements are interwoven: without a security zone, Israel cannot be satisfied with demilitarization alone; without effective demilitarization, Israel cannot be satisfied with just the security zone.

It should be clear from what I have said, that Israel does not hold most of the territories that fell into its hands in the war, which was imposed on it in 1967, as an end in itself. Despite the paucity of its territory compared with the vast areas of the Arab countries, and despite the historical, strategic and economic importance of these areas, Israel would be prepared to concede all that is not absolutely essential to its security within the context of an overall peace settlement. It is holding most of these territories now only as a means to achieve its foremost goal — peace with all its neighbors.

## 10. Statement Issued by the Government of Israel Responding to the US—USSR Joint Declaration on the Middle East. Jerusalem, 1 October, 1977

1.  The Soviet Union's demand that Israel withdraw to the pre-June 1967 borders — a demand which contravenes the true meaning of Security Council Resolution 242 — is known to all.

2.  Despite the fact that the Governments of the U.S. and Israel agreed on July 7, 1977 that the aim of the negotiations at Geneva should be "an overall peace settlement to be expressed in a peace treaty", the concept of a "peace treaty" is not mentioned at all in the Soviet-American statement.

3.  There is no reference at all in this statement to Resolutions 242 and 338, despite the fact that the U.S. Government has repeatedly affirmed heretofore that these resolutions constitute the sole basis for the convening of the Geneva Conference.

4.  There can be no doubt that this statement, issued at a time when discussions are proceeding on the reconvening of the Geneva Conference, cannot but still further harden the positions of the Arab States and make the Middle East peace process still more difficult.

5.  As the Prime Minister has stated, Israel will continue to aspire to free negotiations with its neighbours with the purpose of signing a peace treaty with them.

## 11. Law Enacted by Israel's Knesset Proclaiming Jerusalem the Capital of Israel. Jerusalem, 29 July, 1980

1.  Jerusalem, whole and united, is the capital of Israel.

2.  Jerusalem is the seat of the President of the State, the Knesset, the Government and the Supreme Court.

3.  The Holy Places shall be protected from desecration and any other offense and from anything likely to prejudice the freedom of access of the members of the different religions to the places sacred to them or their feelings with regard to those places.

4.  (1)  The government shall preserve the development, the prosperity of Jerusalem and the welfare of its inhabitants by means of allocating special funds, including a special annual grant for the Municipality of Jerusalem (capitals' grant) [subject to] the approval of the Knesset Committee on Financial Affairs.

(2)   Jerusalem shall be given special priority as regards the activities of the state authorities for its development in the economic and other fields.

(3)   The government shall set up a special body or bodies for the implementation of this provision.

## 12. Fundamental Policy Guidelines of the Government of Israel as Approved by the Knesset, 5 August, 1981

*Articles Relevant to the Israeli-Palestinian Conflict:*

1.   Recognition of the common fate and joint struggle for the existence of the Jewish people in the Land of Israel and in the Diaspora.

2.   The right of the Jewish people to the Land of Israel, an eternal right that cannot be called into question, and which is intertwined with the right to security and peace.

3.   The government will continue to place its aspirations for peace at the head of its concerns, and no effort will be spared in order to further peace. The peace treaty between Israel and Egypt is a historic turning point in Israel's status in the Middle East.

4.   The government will continue to use all means to prevent war.

5.   The government will diligently observe the Camp David Agreements.

6.   The government will work for the renewal of negotiations on the implementation of the agreement on full autonomy for the Arab residents of Judea, Samaria, and the Gaza district.

7.   The autonomy agreed upon at Camp David means neither sovereignty nor self-determination. The autonomy agreements set down at Camp David are guarantees that under no conditions will a Palestinian State emerge in the territory of Western *Eretz Yisrael.*

8.   At the end of the transition period set down in the Camp David agreements, Israel will present its claim, and act to realize its right of sovereignty over Judea, Samaria, and the Gaza district.

9.   Settlement in the Land of Israel is a right and an integral part of the nation's security. The government will act to strengthen, expand, and develop settlement. The government will continue to honor the principle that Jewish settlement will not cause the eviction of any person from his land, his village, or his city.

10.   Equality of rights for all residents will continue to exist in the Land of Israel, with no distinction [on the basis] of religion, race, nationality, sex, or ethnic community.

11.   Israel will not descend from the Golan Heights, nor will it remove any settlement established there. It is the government that will decide on the ap-

propriate timing for the application of Israeli law, jurisdiction, and administration to the Golan Heights.

27.  Education will be based on the eternal values of Israel's Torah, on the values of Judaism and Zionism, love of the people of Israel and love of the homeland.

28.  The government will guarantee freedom of conscience and religion to every citizen and resident, will provide for community religious requirements using state means, and will guarantee religious education to all children whose parents so desire.

34.  The government will cultivate an attitude of respect toward the heritage of Israel, implant its values, strengthen the ties between the people in the Land of Israel and the Diaspora, and [strengthen] mutual responsibility and intergenerational ties.

35.  Jerusalem is the eternal capital of Israel, indivisible, entirely under Israeli sovereignty. Free access to their holy places has been and will be guaranteed to followers of all religions.

## 13. Text of Israel's Communique on the Reagan Plan, Jerusalem, 2 Sept, 1982

*Following is the text of the communique issued by the Israeli Cabinet on President Reagan's Middle East proposals.*

The Cabinet met in special session today and adopted the following resolution:

The positions conveyed to the Prime Minister of Israel on behalf of the President of the United States consist of partial quotations from the Camp David Agreement or are nowhere mentioned in the agreement or contradict it entirely.

The following are the major positions of the Government of the United States:

### 1.  Jerusalem

"Participation by the Palestinian inhabitants of East Jerusalem in the election for the West Bank—Gaza Authority."

No mention whatsoever is made in the Camp David agreement of such a voting right. The single meaning of such a vote is the repartition of Jerusalem into two authorities, the one — of the State of Israel, and the other — of the administrative council of the autonomy. Jerusalem is nowhere mentioned in the Camp David agreement. With respect to the capital of Israel letters were forwarded and attached to that agreement. In his letter to the President of the

United States, Mr. Jimmy Carter, the Prime Minister of Israel, Mr. Menachem Begin, stated that "Jerusalem is one city, indivisible, the capital of the State of Israel." Thus shall it remain for all generations to come.

## 2. Security

"Progressive Palestinian responsibility for internal security based on capability and performance."

In the Camp David agreement it is stated:

"A withdrawal of Israeli armed forces will take place and there will be a redeployment of the remaining Israel forces into specified security locations.

"The agreement will also include arrangements for assuring internal and external security and public order."

It is, therefore, clear that in the Camp David agreement no distinction is made between internal security and external security. There can be no doubt that, were internal security not to be the responsibility of Israel, the terrorist organization called P.L.O. — even after its defeat by the I.D.F. in Lebanon — would act to perpetrate constant bloodshed, shedding the blood of Jews and Arabs alike. For the citizens of Israel this is a question of life and death.

## 3. A Real Settlement Freeze

In the Camp David agreement no mention whatsoever is made of such a freeze. At Camp David the Prime Minister agreed that new settlements could not be established (though population would be added to existing ones) during the period of the negotiations for the signing of the peace treaty between Egypt and Israel (three months being explicitly stated). This commitment was carried out in full. That three-month period terminated on Dec. 17, 1978. Since then many settlements have been established in Judea, Samaria and the Gaza district without evicting a single person from his land, village or town. Such settlement is a Jewish inalienable right and an integral part of our national security. Therefore there shall be no settlement freeze. We shall continue to establish them in accordance with our natural right. President Reagan announced at the time that the "settlements are not illegal". A double negative makes a positive, meaning that the settlements are legal. We shall act, therefore, in accordance with our natural right and the law, and we shall not deviate from the principle that these vital settlements will not lead to any eviction.

## 4. The Definition of Full Autonomy

"The definition of full autonomy as giving the Palestinian inhabitants real authority over themselves, the land and its resources, subject to fair safeguards on water."

Such a definition is nowhere mentioned in the Camp David agreement, which states:

"In order to provide full autonomy to the inhabitants (underlined, our emphasis), etc."

In the lengthy discussion at Camp David it was made absolutely clear that the autonomy applies not to the territory (underlined) but to the inhabitants (underlined).

### 5.  Ties With Jordan

"Economic, commercial and cultural ties between the West Bank, Gaza and Jordan."

In all the clauses of the Camp David agreement there is no reference whatsoever to such ties.

### 6.  Israeli Sovereignty

There is nothing in the Camp David agreement that precludes the application of Israeli sovereignty over Judea, Samaria and the Gaza district following the transitional period which begins with the establishment and inauguration of the self-governing authority (administrative council). This was also stated by an official spokesman of the Government of the United States.

### 7.  Palestinian State

The Government of the United States commits itself not to support the establishment of a Palestinian State in Judea, Samaria and the Gaza district.

Regrettably, the visible reality proves this to be an illusion. Were the American plan to be implemented, there would be nothing to prevent King Hussein from inviting his new-found friend, Yasser Arafat, to come to Nablus and hand the rule over to him. Thus would come into being a Palestinian State which would conclude a pact with Soviet Russia and arm itself with every kind of modern weaponry. If the PLO could do this in Lebanon, establishing a state-within-a-state, how much more so will the terrorists do so ruling over Judea, Samaria and the Gaza district. Then a joint front would be established of that "Palestinian State" with Jordan and Iraq behind her, Saudi Arabia to the south and Syria to the north. All these countries, together with other Arab States, would, after a while, launch an onslaught against Israel to destroy her. It is inconceivable that Israel will ever agree to such an "arrangement" whose consequences are inevitable.

Since the positions of the Government of the United States seriously deviate from the Camp David agreement, contradict it and could create a serious danger to Israel, its security and its future, the Government of Israel has resolved that on the basis of these positions it will not enter into any negotiations with any party.

The Government of Israel is ready to renew the autonomy negotiations forthwith with the Governments of the United States and Egypt, signatories to the Camp David agreement, and with other states and elements invited at Camp David to participate in the negotiations, with a view to reaching agreement on the establishment of full autonomy for the Arab inhabitants of Judea, Samaria and the Gaza District, in total conformity with the Camp David Accords.

## 14. Basic Policy Guidelines of the Government of Israel, 13 September, 1984 [Excerpts]

At the center of the activity of the national unity government presented to the 11th Knesset are the following tasks:

1.   (a) Recognition of the shared fate and common struggle of the Jewish people in the homeland and the diaspora of exile;

(b) A sustained effort to create the social, economic and spiritual conditions to achieve the State of Israel's central objective—the return of diaspora Jews to their homeland;

(c) Boosting immigration from all countries, encouraging immigration from Western countries, and consistently striving to save persecuted Jews by bringing them to safety and realizing their right to immigrate to Israel.

2.   The central political objectives of the government during this period are: Continuing and extending the peace process in the region; consolidating the peace with Egypt; and withdrawing the IDF from Lebanon while ensuring the security of the northern settlements.

3.   (a) The government will act to cultivate friendly relations and mutual ties between Israel and all peace-loving nations;

(b) The government will continue to foster the deepening of the ties of friendship and understanding between the US and Israel;

(c) The government will strive for a resumption of diplomatic relations with the Soviet Union and with the countries of Asia, Africa, and Latin America that have severed their ties with Israel.

4.   Israel's foreign and defense policies will aim to ensure the nation's independence, to better its security, and to establish peace with its neighbors.

5.   The government will strive to increase the strength, deterrent capability and endurance of the IDF against any military threat, and will take firm action against terror, regardless of its source.

6.   United Jerusalem, Israel's eternal capital, is one indivisible city under Israeli sovereignty; free access to their holy places and freedom of worship will continue to be guaranteed to members of all faiths.

7.   The government will continue to place its desire for peace at the head of its concerns and will spare no effort to promote peace.

8.   The government will work to promote and strengthen the mutual ties with Egypt in accordance with the peace treaty. The government will call on Egypt to fulfill its part of the peace treaty with Israel and to give it substance and content in keeping with the spirit of the treaty and with the intentions of its signatories, including a full resumption of representation and diplomatic relations between the two countries.

9.   The government will work to continue the peace process in keeping with the framework for peace in the Middle East that was agreed upon at Camp David, and to resume negotiations to give full autonomy to the Arab residents in Judea, Samaria and the Gaza District.

10.   Israel will call on Jordan to begin peace negotiations, in order to turn over a new leaf in the region, for the sake of (the region's) development and prosperity. The Israeli Government will consider proposals raised by Jordan in the negotiations.

11.   The Arabs of Judea, Samaria and the Gaza District will participate in determining their future, as stipulated in the Camp David Accords.

12.   Israel will oppose the establishment of an additional Palestinian state in the Gaza District and in the area between Israel and Jordan.

13.   Israel will not negotiate with the PLO.

14.   During the term of office of the unity government, there will be no change in the sovereignty over Judea, Samaria and the Gaza District except with the consent of the Alignment and the Likud.

15.   (a) The existence and development of settlements set up by the governments of Israel will be ensured, and the extent of their development will be determined by the government;

      (b) Five to six settlements will be established within a year. The determination of their names will be made by mutual consent within a week of the date of the establishment of the government;

      (c) Implementation of the decisions of previous governments on the establishment of as yet unestablished settlements (whose names will be listed in an appendix that will be added within a week of the establishment of the government) will take place in subsequent years, as per a timetable to be determined by the plenum of the national unity government;

      (d) The establishment of new settlements will require approval by a majority of the Cabinet ministers.

16.   The government will do everything necessary to ensure peace for the Galilee. Security accommodations will be determined to enable an IDF withdrawal from Lebanon within a short period of time to be fixed by the government.

## 15. Statement by Prime Minister Shimon Peres on Negotiations with Jordan, Jerusalem, 10 June, 1985

During the 37 years of the state's existence, we have known five wars and one peace.

The wars had a price. The peace had a price. The wars cost the Jewish people and the Arab world heavy casualties. Thousands of young people fell on the battlefield. The national economies of the Middle East countries were severely damaged, and a heavy social price was paid. The wars ended with victories, but not with solutions.

The peace was also costly. But the price was in territory, not in human life. The economic cost was also high, but it was a one-time cost, and worthwhile.

Today, too, the alternative facing the countries of the region is not just between peace and war, but also between the price of peace and the price of war.

For wars—irrespective of who initiates them—all the sides pay a price; in peace—irrespective of who initiates it—all the sides enjoy its fruits.

Today, too, Israel is ready to pay a price for peace—but provided that the payment actually brings peace, and provided that the Arabs also pay its price; otherwise no one will believe that they genuinely want peace.

It's possible that there is a change of atmosphere in the Middle East. It's possible that an opportunity has arisen which must not be missed. We do not want to belittle such a possibility, or to slam the door on such an opportunity. And it is precisely out of a constructive approach that we must be careful that a negative tactic does not destroy a positive strategic change. Therefore, when we peruse Jordan's stands, we must examine not only whether they are acceptable to Israel, but also whether they lead to peace. To peace and not to evasion of peace.

The first, immediate Jordanian demand is for the supply of advanced American arms, as a down-payment on moves whose nature hasn't yet been made clear. The Jordanians—so they tell the Americans—need these arms so that they can cope with a possible Syrian threat.

I am pleased that Jordan does not sense—and it is right—the existence of an Israeli threat. But if there is actually an immediate Syrian threat—and I don't see Syria launching an attack on Jordan tomorrow morning—and I doubt whether three battle squadrons of F-20's and improved Hawk missiles will prevent Syria from going ahead. What's more, the supply and absorption of these planes is a matter of two to three years at least. And if an immediate Syrian threat has in fact arisen because of Jordan's possible move towards a strategy of peace, a different, immediate deterrent must be sought against such a threat.

Arms are meant to serve policy. And if these arms are not intended to serve a policy of belligerence vis-a-vis Israel, this should be stated authoritatively, unequivocally and publicly. Because the supply of American tanks to Jordan at the start of the 1960's is still fresh in our mind: when Jordan undertook that those tanks would not cross the Jordan River and would not be employed against Israel. But once an "environmental opportunity" arose, Jordan used those tanks to attack Israel in 1967, without any provocation whatsoever on Israel's part.

Our friends the Americans tried to explain this to Jordan, and also proposed, as the suppliers of the requested arms, that Jordan declare a policy of non-belligerence. The result was disappointing. Instead of declaring a policy of non-belligerence, Jordan declared a non-belligerent environment, meaning that non-belligerence is not a policy, but rather an environment. Instead of declaring a commitment for the future, it spoke in terms of a weather forecast.

Jordan's evasion from declaring a policy of non-belligerence effectively leaves it with a declared policy of a state of belligerence against Israel, and not a state of non-belligerence with Syria.

In this situation, Israel cannot regard additional arms [to Jordan] as a contribution to the peace momentum, but rather as an additional inducement [for Jordan] to refrain from withdrawing from its policy of belligerence. Israel is against such arms supplies.

The impression of the United States is that Jordan is approaching readiness for direct negotiations; but in the United States, Jordan's proposed stages for negotiations were published. The question is not only whether we accept them—a legitimate question in itself—but whether they pave the road to a peace process.

What is Jordan proposing?

In the first stage, talks between a Jordanian-Palestinian delegation and an American delegation headed by Mr. Richard Murphy, in Amman. The Palestinian contingent will not, at this stage, include Palestinians who are active in the PLO.

In the second stage, the head of the PLO is supposed to recognize 242 and 338, while simultaneously the United States is to announce its readiness to hold talks with a Jordanian-Palestinian delegation, with the Palestinian contingent being composed of PLO personnel.

The third stage is meant to commit the United States to hold talks with a Jordanian-Palestinian delegation, in order to prepare an international conference.

And only then would the fourth stage come. An international conference.

The first stage is designed to forge an American commitment vis-a-vis Jordanian-Palestinian delegation, and to [bring about] partial recognition of the PLO. This while the PLO continues to adhere to the Palestinian Covenant, rejects Resolutions 242 and 338, refuses to recognize Israel or to conduct negotiations with it, and while it continues to employ terrorism. The result of this stage might be a strengthening of the PLO which went to Amman only because it was weakened and reconciliation with the PLO's rejectionist policy which will then be able to cross the US door-step which is currently blocked.

In the second stage, according to the Jordanians, the PLO leader is supposed to recognize UN Resolutions 242 and 338. Then the United States would fully recognize the PLO despite the fact the PLO had not recognized Israel and had not stopped its terrorist actions. This is the Jordanian position but the PLO has other demands, including the right to self-determination. Jordan argues that it cannot advance on its own, without the Palestinians and the PLO. Were the entire problem just to make peace between Jordan and the PLO, even through US mediation, that would be all right. However, if the intention is to make peace with Israel rather than without Israel, this is an attempt to ignore Israel's positions and abrogate specific US commitments. Jordan proposed a third stage: A conference between the United States, Jordan, and the Palestinians in order to prepare an international conference. With all our due respect to King Hussein, I must tell him candidly, here and now, that he must make up his mind whether he does or does not want to make peace with Israel. If he wants to make peace with Israel—and Israel does not object to a Jordanian-Palestinian delegation that is not a delegation of the PLO—he must understand that he must sit with Israel rather than try time and again to make Israel sit in a dark and musty waiting room until everything is resolved without it. We respect Jordan and the Palestinians, but Jordan and the Palestinians must also respect us. Instead of negotiations with Israel, Jordan is proposing, as a fourth stage, holding an international conference. Among others, this conference would be attended by the United States, the Soviet Union, France, Britain, Syria, and the PLO.

What would happen at such a conference? The Soviet Union would be raised to the status of mediator despite the fact that it has severed relations with Israel and locked its gates to Jews seeking to leave. In other words, the Soviet Union would not recognize Israel diplomatically but Israel would have to publicly recognize the Soviet Union's objectivity. At the beginning of the conference, the Soviet Union might declare that it supports the Arab positions and the position of Syria, which is the most extremist among the Arab countries. It would justify Syria's goals and the Palestinian charter. What then would be the chances or possibilities that Jordan or a Palestinian delegation would adopt a position more moderate than that of the Soviet Union?

True, the Soviet Union is a huge superpower, while Israel is a small country; a small country but not one that will humiliate itself in the face of the grandiosity of a huge superpower.

The PRC would also be recognized as a participant, on the level of a mediator. The PRC has not even recognized Israel and, at least publicly, it supports the PLO's position. Israel does not pose a threat to the PRC and the PRC does not pose a threat to Israel. However, if the PRC wants to play a role in achieving peace in the Middle East it must recognize the supremacy of peace rather than prefer the interests of the countries that refuse to make peace.

According to this plan, the United States would have to come to the conference being semicommitted to the Jordanian and PLO position. Then, and only then, would Israel be asked to join in; it would be the last to be asked, it would be isolated, and it would be asked to supply territorial food to the patrons sitting around the conference table. This is a plan to defeat Israel rather than to hold negotiations with Israel.

Of course, we must distinguish between the Jordanian and US positions. I believe in the friendship of President Ronald Reagan and Secretary of State George Shultz, and even if we have an argument with them this is an argument between friends who are seeking a way to peace rather than an argument with enemies who want to bring Israel to its knees. Secretary of State George Shultz believes that the Jordanian and Palestinian positions have changed. He believes that Jordan and the Palestinians have opened new avenues for direct negotiations and peace. If that is true, then this change came about due to our fundamental and joint standing. An erosion in this standing might halt the process and reverse the achievement.

The United States has acceded to the first stage of the Jordanian plan but as far as recognizing the PLO based only on the latter's acceptance of UN Resolutions 242 and 338 and the PLO's demand for recognition of its right to self-determination, the United States had, according to what it has told us, remained faithful to its previous positions. Just like us, the United States is opposed to an international conference and insists on direct negotiations. Hence, the argument between us is about three fundamental issues: Holding a preliminary meeting with a Jordanian-Palestinian delegation, the composition of that delegation, and the supply of arms to Jordan as advance payment despite the fact that Jordan has—and the United States has also stated as much—abstained from declaring a non-belligerent policy.

Israel does not just criticize the positions adopted by Jordan or the US proposals. Israel also acts and makes proposals which will bring about a real change that will bring peace in our region closer. What is the Israeli plan?

First, Israel is currently completing its withdrawal from Lebanese soil and from Lebanese politics. Rumors have spread in the Arab world alleging that Israel covets parts of Lebanon's land, the waters of its rivers, and fragments of Lebanese politics. As everyone can see, all these rumors have proved to be false. The IDF's withdrawal from Lebanon not only concludes our presence in Lebanon, but it also puts an end to the groundless fears that this presence provoked. It was not the Amal organization that expelled the IDF from Lebanon, it was the Israeli Government that made the decision since, in any event, Israel did not plan to remain permanently in Lebanon. I remind Nabih Birri that terror from Lebanon brought Israel into Lebanon, rather than vice versa.

Second, the national unity government undertook not to change the sovereignty in Judea, Samaria, and the Gaza District. Moreover, it undertook and is committed to proposing far-reaching autonomy—that is, full autonomy—to the inhabitants of those territories. Israel promised, according to what is written in the

Camp David Accords, that the Arabs of Judea, Samaria, and the Gaza District would take part in determining their future.

Third, the government has adopted its own policy regarding the quality of life in the territories, and the settlements. This policy takes not only Israel's rights into account but also the feelings of the inhabitants of the territories.

Fourth, the dialogue with Egypt resumed after a freeze of several years. Ministers and emissaries on both sides visit Cairo and Jerusalem. We have launched a series of contacts in order to solve the disputed issues and to warm up the so-called cold peace. In fact, Egypt and Israel have reached a central and important conclusion that it would be best to solve all the problems simultaneously by weaving a common basket which would be filled with all the issues pending agreement.

From this podium, I would like to appeal to President Mubarak and his people and tell them candidly: The peace between Egypt and Israel, in which President Mubarak has a part, is the brightest ray that has illuminated the Middle East in the last few years, both us and the Egyptians have undertaken to promote this achievement, not just as an achievement on its own merit but as a move that will bring about the expansion of the process over the entire region. We undertook to act so that the strategy of peace has the upper hand over the traditional strategy of war. We did not look for a separate, but rather for a comprehensive peace, and we must strive to achieve this purpose. Therefore, and because of it, Egypt and Israel should prove to all the countries in the Middle East that peace between us has been successful and that it has enabled us to deal with the problems that emerge occasionally in a constructive fashion. Solving the disputes between us is therefore not a contribution to the past but a contribution to the future; it is not only a contribution to Egyptian-Israeli relations but also a contribution to the momentum of the peace process.

Fifth, we propose peace negotiations based on four principles: Negotiations between equals and under conditions of equality, direct negotiations, negotiations without preconditions, and negotiations with the parties interested in peace rather than with the parties interested in continuing the conflict.

Sixth, in order to achieve these aims, Israel proposes the following stages: First, continued talks between US representatives, Israel, Jordan, Egypt, and Palestinian representatives who are not PLO members; second, establishing a small Jordanian-Palestinian-Israeli team which will prepare an agenda for a Jordanian-Palestinian-Israeli summit with US participation; third, recruiting the support of the permanent members of the UN Security Council for direct negotiations between Jordan and a Palestinian delegation and Israel without asking them to undertake in advance to support the position of one of the sides; fourth, appointing authentic Palestinian representatives from the territories who will represent the positions of the inhabitants and who would be acceptable to all the parties; fifth, convening an opening conference within 3 months at a venue to be decided either in the United States, Europe, or the Middle East.

I believe that we can tell our friends across the ocean and our friends across the river that despite all the obstacles and difficulties in the way, Israel believes that we can reach direct negotiations which might bear fruit and that Israel is prepared to contribute a great deal in order to bring these negotiations as close as possible.

### 16. Address by Prime Minister Shimon Peres to the UN General Assembly, New York, 21 October, 1985 [Excerpts]

...From this rostrum I call upon the Palestinian people to put an end to rejectionism, to belligerency. Let us talk. Come forth, and recognize the reality of the State of Israel, our wish to live in peace and our need for security. Let us face each other as free men and women across the negotiating table. Let us argue, not fight...

When President al-Sadat came to Jerusalem the course of history for all of us was changed. He found Israel willing, open, and as courageous as he was in the pursuit of peace. The world looked on in wonder as a conflict, which had seemed insoluble for more than 30 years, turned soluble in less than 1 year. Between the 48 million Egyptians and 4 million Israelis there is today peace. Peace with Egypt was to accomplish several objectives: Sinai was returned to Egypt; a solution to the Palestinian problem in all its aspects was to be reached. It was agreed that full autonomy to the residents of the territories could be a promising step in that direction. Peace between Egypt and Israel never intended to be an isolated episode, it was to become a cornerstone of comprehensive peace strategy in our region...

Let us not allow gloom and doom to overshadow our worthiest accomplishment. Let us make our peace a success, a source of encouragement to others. Mr. President, the most complex issue, yet the most promising, involves our neighbor to the east, the Hashemite Kingdom of Jordan; an issue confined not only to borders, it reaches across people and state, if settlement should also comprise the resolution of the Palestinian issue. Middle East archives are filled with negotiating plans.

I invite this organization to depart from the tired and timid norm, and to fulfill its destiny as enshrined on its walls by ushering the parties to the conflict into a new diplomatic initiative. Let all parties to the dispute facilitate a new phase in the Arab-Israeli peace by renouncing and putting an end to the use of violence. The new initiative should be based on the following principles:

1) The objective of these negotiations is to reach peace treaties between Israel and the Arab states, as well as to resolve the Palestinian issue.

2) Neither party may impose preconditions.

3)   Negotiations are to be based on United Nations Security Council Resolutions 242 and 338, and on the willingness to entertain suggestions proposed by other participants.

4)   Negotiations are to be conducted directly between states.

5)   If deemed necessary, these negotiations may be initiated with the support of an international forum, as agreed upon by the negotiating states.

6)   This gathering can take place before the end of this year, in Jordan, Israel, or any location, as mutually agreed upon. We will be pleased to attend an opening meeting in Amman.

7)   Negotiations between Israel and Jordan are to be conducted between an Israeli delegation, on one hand, and a Jordanian, or a Jordanian-Palestinian delegation on the other, both comprising delegates that represent peace, not terror. Aware of the nature of this undertaking, I propose the following as a possible blueprint for implementation: Negotiations may produce immediate as well as permanent arrangements; they may deal with the demarcation of boundaries as well as the resolution of the Palestinian problem. The Camp David Accords provide a possible basis for the attainment of these objectives. The permanent members of the Security Council may be invited to support the initiation of these negotiations. It is our position that those who confine their diplomatic relations to one side of the conflict exclude themselves from such a role. This forum, while not being a substitute for direct negotiations, can offer support for them. Indeed, nothing should undermine the direct nature of these negotiations. In order to expedite this process, the agenda, procedure, and international support for negotiations can be discussed and agreed upon the meeting of a small working team to be convened within 30 days.

## 17.   "Outline for Advancement of Negotiations Between the Likud and the PLO," by Moshe Amirav, Jerusalem, September 1987 [Excerpts]

*The following is a report drawn up by Likud member Moshe Amirav for Israeli Prime Minister Shamir, prior to his trip to Romania.*

1.   The right of both peoples to the land is indivisible. It is equal. The injustice done to both peoples in our terrible and bloodstained history requires redress via the following equation: security and peace for the Jewish people, self-determination on part of the land and redress of the injustice done the refugees of the Palestinian people.

2.   Attempts over the past hundred years to solve this conflict by force have

failed. The Palestinians will not leave the country and will not surrender their right to it. The Jews will not dismantle the state they established within the 1948 borders and will not halt their buildup for maintenance of their security.

3.    Attempts to reach a settlement that do not include the Palestinians as a major partner to the negotiations or whose outcome is not the establishment of an independent Palestinian state are doomed to failure.

4.    The sole official representative of the Palestinian people in any settlement is the PLO without whose participation there is no point in reaching any settlement. Likewise, in Israel there is no point in reaching any settlement without the Likud.

5.    The present political situation does not permit an Alignment diplomatic initiative to be taken without the Likud. Thus the international conference cannot be held. However, a Likud counter-initiative vis-a-vis the Palestinians would be feasible, should the latter prove amenable. Such a move would not be rejected by either the Alignment or the Israeli left. Our assessment is that at the end of the Knesset's summer recess (i.e., around September) the Alignment will leave the government and a Likud government with a narrow Knesset majority (61 out of 120 seats) will be formed. In either case—with the Alignment in the government, or even more so if the Alignment goes into opposition—the Likud has a vested interest in embarking on a diplomatic initiative.

6.    Several top Likud members have now been presented with a proposed diplomatic settlement, based on the establishment of a region of Palestinian self-administration in Judea, Samaria, and Gaza. The Palestinian self-administration will cover this area—which encompasses some 5,000 sq. km.—and its capital will be in East Jerusalem.

Such an interim arrangement would guarantee Israel's security and enable it to maintain its settlements in Judea and Samaria at a fixed and unchanged level.

7.    It is proposed, under the plan for this interim arrangement, to advance within a year to the establishment of the Palestinian self-administration, which would wield powers approaching those of a state. Such an interim arrangement has clear advantages for both sides and also leaves open the option of halting negotiations and leaving the situation as it stands.

8.    Conditions for entering negotiations:

    a. Mutual recognition.

    b. Cessation of hostile actions. This means, as far as Israel is concerned:

    * Recognition of the right of the Palestinian people—not as refugees, but as a people—to its own state.

    * Recognition of the PLO as the representative of the Palestinian people.

    * Cessation of hostile actions toward Palestinians in the territories and cessation of any further Israeli settlement there.

The meaning, as far as the PLO is concerned, is as follows:

    * Recognition of Israel's existence within the 1948 borders and of its right

to exist within said borders in peace and security (i.e., 242 or amendment of the Palestinian Covenant).

&ast; Cessation of all hostile or terrorist actions everywhere.

9.   The negotiations will be held over a period of four years: the first year to deliberate the interim arrangement, and the ensuing three years to deliberate the final settlement. A "cease-fire" will be declared throughout this period, as is customary under international law.

10.   Egypt will be requested to host the negotiations for their entire duration. The delegates of both sides will consequently reside in Cairo.

11.   The initial contacts will be kept secret and will be held between un-authorized delegates until an understanding on this document has been concluded by both sides.

## 18.   Address by Foreign Minister Shimon Peres to the UN General Assembly, New York, 30 September, 1987 [Excerpts]

Mr. President, permit me to congratulate you on your assumption of the Presidency of the General Assembly.

Mr. President, I wish to take this opportunity to express our support for the relentless efforts of the emissary of peace and goodwill, Secretary-General Mr. Javier Perez de Cuellar.

In a world grown cynical of the superpowers' increased arms competition, and fearful of the technologies it has unleashed, the people of Israel appreciate the readiness of the United States and the Soviet Union to begin a process of nuclear disarmament. This is not just a technical accord. It is a political dictum: No longer can we find military answers to political problems—what is necessary are political answers to the military menace...

Indeed, two years ago, both Arabs and Israelis announced from this podium support for the current initiative for peace.

Moreover, since then, further progress has been made.

We have rekindled our peace with Egypt and intensified the dialogue with its leaders and people. We found President Mubarak to be a builder of better life for his people and of bridges for comprehensive peace in the region.

At the cedar groves of the mountain of Ifrane, we met courageous leadership: King Hassan of Morocco calling for peace.

Across the Jordan River, rich in history and poor in water, we hear the echo of the voice of King Hussein. An experienced leader who wishes, like us, to bring our peoples out of the darkness of old hostility into the new greenhouses of peace, security and development.

In the West Bank and Gaza we notice an unannounced change. Many

Palestinians seem to have concluded that violence leads nowhere, that dialogue should not be postponed. There is a readiness to negotiate in a joint Jordanian-Palestinian delegation.

We have all matured politically with the repeated failure at attempts to produce peace plans for our region; we have realized that none can be acceptable as a precondition for negotiation. For it is the object of negotiation to produce solutions otherwise unattainable. Hence, over the past three years, efforts have focused on the most promising plan: begin negotiations without pre-planning their outcome.

Five months ago these efforts crystallized and found expression in a document worked out with the support of American emissaries, whose tireless and creative efforts should be credited with much of what has been accomplished. It reflected a meeting of minds based on eight principles:

1.    The goal is peace; direct negotiations are the way to get there.

2.    An international conference is the door to direct negotiations. Once convened it should lead immediately to face-to-face, bilateral negotiations.

3.    The conference will not impose a settlement or veto agreements reached bilaterally.

4.    Those who attend the conference must accept Security Council Resolutions 242 and 338 and renounce terrorism and violence.

5.    Negotiations are to solve the Palestinian problem in all its aspects. This is to be done in negotiations between the Jordanian-Palestinian delegation and the Israeli delegation.

6.    Negotiations will be conducted independently in three bilateral/geographic committees:

—a Jordanian-Palestinian delegation and an Israeli delegation in one.

—a Syrian and Israeli delegation in another.

—a Lebanese and Israeli delegation in the third. All delegations, as well as an Egyptian one, will be invited to participate in a fourth, multilateral committee.

7.    Whereas the bilateral committee will be engaged in solving the conflicts of the past, the multilateral committee will deal with charting opportunities for the region's future.

8.    The five permanent members are to serve as the matchmakers; entrusted with bringing the parties together, and legitimizing the process whereby the parties negotiate freely and directly, without uninvited—and occasionally divided—external involvement. This is not a ceremonial task, but an essential role for facilitating negotiations.

Mr. President, Israel is united in its search for peace, in our desire to negotiate directly with our neighbors. We differ over how best to move the process forward. An international conference raises opposition in some Israeli quarters, while others see it as an opening.

The Israeli Cabinet is divided on the issue and is yet to make a decision. Much depends on the nature of the conference. Unless the permanent members of the Security Council respect the current consensus—rather than insist on their old preferences—the international conference will remain just a slogan.

We call upon the Soviet Union to credit us with the same good faith in our efforts for peace as we credit it in its readiness to make *glasnost* a way of life. The Soviet Union is not our enemy. It must be aware of our historical and family attachment to our brethren living on its land. We appeal to the new leadership in Moscow to allow the Jewish people to express their identity freely and to allow them to reunite with their destiny in the land of their ancestors.

We call upon the People's Republic of China, the great country that we respect, not to be timid or one-sided in its support for free negotiation.

To both Moscow and Beijing we say candidly, diplomatic relations are not the prize for peace but a channel for communication. Those wishing to participate in bringing peace cannot confine their relations to one side of the rivalry alone.

I would like to address the Palestinian people: The time for recrimination and blame is past. These have brought only violence and terror. Now is the time to turn from violence to dialogue, and travel jointly towards a different destiny. There your children, like ours, will live in self-respect, exercise self-expression and enjoy freedom and peace. We, who have experienced others' domination, do not wish to dominate others. We, who sought justice and security, do not wish to deny them to others ....

Mr. President, I welcome the forthcoming visit of Secretary Shultz to our region as an opportunity to negotiate the remaining obstacles.

I am convinced there are no conflicts without hope for solution—only people who have lost hope in their search for solutions. I am convinced that the real conflict today in the Middle East is not between Jew and Moslem; Arab and Israeli; Palestinian and Zionist. The conflict is between "past oriented" leadership and "future oriented" ones; between those resigned to the fatalism of belligerency and those determined to alter this fate. For the future of our children, for a better tomorrow, we must all stand up to the preachers of war....

## 19. Statement by Prime Minister Yitzhak Shamir on Yasser Arafat's Speech to the UN, Jerusalem, 13 December, 1988 [Excerpts]

*The following is a response by Prime Minister Shamir to Yasser Arafat's speech at UN General Assembly session in Geneva.*

Ladies and gentlemen: We are witnessing a deceitful PLO act of momentous proportions in Algiers, Stockholm, Strasbourg, and now in Geneva, aimed at misleading and creating the impression of growing moderation. At each of these events, particularly the convention of terrorist organizations in Algiers, the PLO reiterated its basic stand, the phrasing of which is altered each time, and which is a rejection of Israel's existence, the continuation of terrorism, and the encouragement of violent acts.

It is a well known fact that as far back as 1975 the United States promised Israel that it would not recognize the PLO and would not negotiate with it unless the PLO recognizes Israel's right to exist, accepts UN Resolutions 242 and 338, and renounces violence and terror. As far as we know the PLO did not accept these conditions. In his speech in Geneva, Arafat did not announce that he recognizes Israel's right of existence. He condemned terror, at the same time praising and encouraging what he termed the war of liberation.

In our view, the PLO is incapable of accepting the American conditions, which contradict the organization's very essence and its raison d'etre. I hope that for the sake of promoting the chance of peace and ending terror and violence, the United States will never form any official contacts with the PLO, since such a move will encourage extremists and violence and submerge the voices of those who are genuinely interested in promoting co-existence, negotiations, and peace between Israel and its neighbors.

Israel's policy is clear, and it is based on the guidelines of its governments since 1973. We have no conditions for negotiations or recognition of the PLO. From our point of view, the PLO is not a partner for any peace process. The PLO is a terrorist organization, or a group of terrorist organizations whose goal is to harm Israelis, undermine the existence of the State of Israel, and bring about its destruction.

Israel desires peace with all its might. We call again on our neighbors, including the Arabs of Eretz Israel, and propose true negotiations between equals without pre-conditions, breaks, or diversions, until a peace settlement is reached. Anyone who truly desires peace will find us willing and faithful partners in an effort toward the supreme goal....

I see no recognition of Israel's right to exist in Arafat's speech. There is no explicit statement to that effect. There is what they call in English double talk, various formulations aimed at camouflage, and the alleged call on Israel to come to Geneva is in fact an invitation to Israel to come to an international conference, rather than direct negotiations with anyone.

## 20.  Statement by the Israeli Foreign Ministry on the Decisions of the 19th Palestine National Council, Jerusalem, 15 November, 1988

Once again, the organization which claims to represent the Palestinian people has proven itself unable or unwilling to recognize reality. In its new statements, ambiguity and doubletalk are again employed to obscure its advocacy of violence, willingness to resort to terrorism, and adherence to extreme positions.

Hence, any recognition or legitimization of the declarations will not be conducive to peace in the Middle East.

No unilateral step can be a substitute for a negotiated settlement.

No gimmick can mask the tragedy inflicted upon the Palestinian people time and again by the absence of a reasonable, realistic, and peace-seeking leadership.

As it continues to shoulder its responsibility for tranquility in the territories, and the well being of the residents, Israel remains committed to the pursuit of a just, comprehensive, and lasting peace with all its neighbors—first and foremost Jordan and the Palestinians. Israel's policy remains equally firm in its adherence to, and insistence upon, UN Security Council Resolutions 242 and 338 as the only commonly accepted basis for peace negotiations.

### The PNC's Declaration of Independence—No Shift

1.   The PNC's declaration of Palestinian independence and the accompanying political statement do not indicate a significant fundamental shift in the PLO's approach regarding genuine peace with Israel.

2.   The PNC decisions continue to avoid criteria basic to advancing the peace process, such as:

*   Recognition of Israel's right to exist.

The PNC made no mention of this, nor was it even implicit. Palestinian statehood, especially along the lines declared by the PNC, is not a major departure from PLO decisions of the past which talked about a phased program or a "secular democratic" state in all of Palestine. Indeed, the current PNC formula is an integral part of these preceding PLO positions, which seek ultimately to eliminate Israel. The conditional manner in which the PNC dealt with 242 and 338 also shed light on the PLO's real intentions regarding Israel.

*   Unqualified acceptance of 242 and 338 as the basis for negotiations.

While mentioning 242 and 338 as a basis for an international conference, the PNC did so in conjunction with all other UN resolutions pertaining to the Palestinian issue since 1947. Many of those resolutions (e.g., equating Zionism with racism, stressing the right of return, calling for sanctions and severance of all ties with Israel) seek to delegitimize Israel's right to exist. Resolutions 242 and 338 are thereby emptied of content.

*   Abandonment of terror.

While, on the surface, condemning terror, the PNC has actually not abandoned terrorism, but has merely qualified its range and applicability. The PLO has essentially re-adopted Arafat's 1985 Cairo formula which allows terrorist acts inside Israel and the territories (indeed, simultaneously with the PNC conference, PLO terrorists attempted a number of infiltrations with the purpose of taking hostages in Israel).

3.   The PNC declaration is a unilateral act. It addresses issues which must be negotiated and not predetermined. While Israel recognizes the right of Palestin-

ians to participate in the determination of the final status of Judea-Samaria and Gaza, this must be done in the context of peace negotiations which would address Israel's needs and interests, above all those concerning security. An independent Palestinian state would pose a threat to Israel's security and to Middle East stability. Moreover, in view of its background and activities, including ongoing acts of terrorism, the PLO has disqualified itself from participation in the peace process. However, in negotiations with a Jordanian-Palestinian delegation Israel believes that a mutually acceptable mode of coexistence can be worked out.

## 21.  Basic Policy Guidelines of the Government of Israel, 23 December, 1988  [Excerpts]

At the center of the activity of the National Unity Government presented to the 12th Knesset are the following tasks:

1A.    Recognition of the shared fate and common struggle of the Jewish people in the homeland and the Diaspora.

B.    A sustained effort to create the social, economic and spiritual conditions to attain Israel's central aim: the return of Diaspora Jews to their homeland.

C.    Boosting immigration from all countries, encouraging immigration from western countries, and consistently struggling to save persecuted Jews by bringing them to safety and realizing their right to immigrate to Israel.

2.    The central policy objectives of the Government during this period are: continuing and expanding the peace process in the region, consolidating the peace with Egypt and ensuring the security of the Northern towns and villages.

3A.    The Government will act to cultivate friendly relations and mutual ties between Israel and all peace-loving countries.

B.    The Government will continue to foster the deepening of the ties of friendship and understanding between Israel and the United States.

C.    The Government will strive for a resumption of diplomatic relations with the Soviet Union, and for the establishment of diplomatic relations with China and other countries which have not yet formed diplomatic ties with Israel.

4.    Israel's foreign and defense policies will aim to ensure the country's independence, to strengthen its security, and to establish peace with all its neighbors.

5.    The Government will strive to increase the strength, deterrent capability and endurance of the Israel Defense Forces (IDF) against any military threat, and will take firm action against terrorism, regardless of its source. The IDF and the other security forces will continue to ensure the safety of all the residents, and will act forcefully in order to curb riots, prevent violence, and restore order.

6.    United Jerusalem, Israel's eternal capital, is one indivisible city under

Israeli sovereignty. Free access to their holy places and freedom of worship will continue to be guaranteed to members of all faiths.

7.   The Government will continue to place its desire for peace at the forefront of its concerns, and will spare no effort to promote peace.

8.   The Government will work to promote and strengthen the mutual ties with Egypt in accordance with the peace treaty. The Government will call on Egypt to fulfill its part of the peace treaty with Israel, and to give it substance and content in keeping with the spirit of the treaty and with the intentions of its signatories.

9.   The Government will work to continue the peace process in keeping with the framework for peace in the Middle East that was agreed upon at Camp David, and to resume negotiations to grant full autonomy to the Arab residents in Judea, Samaria and the Gaza District.

10.   Israel will call on Jordan to begin peace negotiations, in order to turn over a new leaf in the region, for the sake of [the region's] development and prosperity. The Government of Israel will consider proposals for negotiations.

11.   The Arabs of Judea, Samaria and Gaza District will participate in the determination of their future, as stipulated in the Camp David Accords. Israel will encourage representatives of Judea, Samaria and the Gaza District to take part in the peace process.

12.   Israel will oppose the establishment of an additional Palestinian state in the Gaza District and in the area between Israel and Jordan.

13.   Israel will not negotiate with the PLO.

14.   During the term of office of the unity government, no change will be made in the sovereignty over Judea, Samaria and the Gaza District except with the consent of the Labor Alignment and the Likud Party.

15A.   The existence and development of settlements set up by the governments of Israel will be ensured. An attached appendix (sections 'D', 'E' and 'F')* elaborates on various issues, whose execution will be agreed upon together with other issues in this framework.

B.   Between five and eight settlements will be established within a year. (Their names are elaborated on in the attached appendix, (section 'A')**.

C.   The settlements will be determined in an agreement between the Prime Minister and the Vice Premier, toward the conclusion of the first year.

16.   The Government will do everything necessary to ensure peace for the Galilee.

---

* Not included here.

** Not included here.

## 22.  Address by Prime Minister Yitzhak Shamir to the Knesset, 23 December, 1988 [Excerpts]

### The Peace Process

At the present stage in our nation's history, we urgently need national unity, a united appearance on international platforms and national consensus on basic and existential matters.  In addition, internal unity will help us greatly in fostering and strengthening the attachment of Jews still living in the Diaspora to the people of Israel and the land of Israel.  The Jewish communities abroad yearn for the message reflecting national agreement on basic issues in Israel, and it is our obligation to make every effort to consolidate this agreement and to unite around it both world Jewry and Israel's friends, by speaking clearly in one voice.

What are the immediate challenges before us?  In the diplomatic-security field we must first of all work to advance the peace process.  We are not doing this out of weakness, or out of fear of the pressures of time or the riots.  We have extended a hand to our Arab neighbors at all times and in all ways, and we have proved more than once that whoever really wishes to live in peace with us, will be met halfway by us with the greatest energy and good will.

This government is united in its call to the Arab countries to join us at the negotiating table in order to reach an honorable and lasting peace agreement. Nothing unites this entire nation, including all its strata and ethnic groups, more than the desire and yearning for peace.  There is no house in Israel that does not feel the pain of the tremendous human sacrifices made by this nation in its struggle for peace and security.

We will, therefore, strive tirelessly; we will spare no effort, and we will listen to every echo returning to us from beyond the borders of enmity, which bears a tiding of a readiness to coexist, to achieve mutual reconciliation and peace.  The peace for which we are striving must be two-sided, and it can be accomplished only as a result of direct talks.  It must explicitly express the Arab acceptance of the existence of Israel as a state with equal standing and equal rights with all the countries of the region.  It must enable Israel to ensure its security, and it must give the Arab residents of Eretz-Israel the ability to conduct their affairs with as much freedom as possible, and in conditions of peaceful coexistence with their Jewish neighbors.

I appeal to the Arab residents of Judea, Samaria and the Gaza District to listen to the voice of reason and common sense.  We are ready and willing to create conditions of peaceful coexistence with you which will assure liberty and prosperity for you and your children.  Those who have called upon you to take to the streets and use violent means will achieve nothing for you, except meaningless declarations and slogans.  Do not pay heed to suggestions of inciters and men of violence who only cause suffering and bereavement, and are not capable of dealing with and solving your problems. In the framework of negotiations with the neighboring Arab states, it will be possible to do a great deal to carry into effect practical plans for our common future in this country.

I call upon the King of Jordan to respond to our invitation and enter into negotiations with us immediately, together with representatives of the Arabs of Judea, Samaria and the Gaza District. The geographic, demographic, diplomatic and economic conditions in both our countries and on our common border, make dialogue necessary, in order to achieve a settlement and practical cooperation to the benefit of both nations. There is no justification for the continued rejection, estrangement and expressions of hostility toward the State of Israel. Peace between Jordan and Israel would strengthen the first level of the peace we made with Egypt, and bring prosperity and stability to the entire region.

Egypt was the first to enter into a peace agreement with us. This fact imposes a measure of responsibility on both countries to continue the efforts to widen the scope of peace and apply it to the entire region. The Egyptian government is at a crossroads in regard to this issue. It is able to reinforce the first bridge of peace between an Arab country and Israel, and to help expand it, so that other neighbors as well can cross it in order to arrive at a peace meeting.

There is only one way to achieve this goal, and it is through direct negotiations with Jordan with the participation of Palestinian-Arab representatives who are not connected with the terrorist organizations, with the PLO and similar bodies. We hope that Egypt will respond to our appeal and will choose to join us.

In historic Eretz-Israel two states arose, one Jewish and the other Arab. The two states give full expression to the aspirations of both nations for independence and a homeland of their own. There is neither room for, nor logic, in a second Arab state within Eretz-Israel, and it will never be established. The solution to the problem of the Arabs of Eretz-Israel will be found in the Camp David Accords. We are committed to them, and we are convinced that they contain a framework for a just and appropriate solution. We call upon Egypt to fulfill all the bilateral agreements with us that determine the framework of relations between the two countries in various domains.

The IDF, the security services, the Israel Police and all other security elements are courageously and devotedly guarding our country and fighting PLO terrorism and other manifestations of violence and disturbances. The government of Israel congratulates them and offers its encouragement.

There is a wide national consensus on the right of the Jews to live anywhere in Eretz-Israel. This does not contradict peace, nor does it harm the peace process. The Jewish settlements in Judea, Samaria and the Gaza District fulfill an important role in the realm of defense and in preventing the establishment of a PLO state within Eretz-Israel. The very fact that they are in these places contributes to the security and to the safety of movement throughout the country. It is imperative that the IDF and the security elements guarantee their security and defense. We will assure the promotion and development of these settlements, and of the settlements on the Golan Heights, and we will expand settlement throughout Eretz-Israel.

There are things about which it is unnecessary to speak. They are engraved not only in the pages of books and in history and in law; they are engraved, first of all, on our hearts. The heart of every Jew beats for Jerusalem. The basic principles of the Government define our policy toward Jerusalem, and they remove every evil thought from every heart. I quote from the Government's policy guidelines: "United Jerusalem, the Eternal Capital of Israel, is one city, under Israeli sovereignty, and cannot be divided. All religions will be guaranteed free access to the Holy Places and the freedom of religious practice." And as the Psalmist said: "May they prosper who love you. Peace be within your walls, prosperity within your palaces."

### Israel-US Relations

Israel-US relations naturally have a pivotal position in Israel's foreign policy. The years of the outgoing administration, the Reagan Administration, were marked by unprecedented developments in the bilateral relationship between Israel and the US. New dimensions were added to the historic commitment— based on common values and a common cultural and historical background—of a great power to a small country fighting for its existence. These included, first and foremost, strategic cooperation, accompanied by a constant broadening of the wide-ranging defense relations, in all their various forms: procurement, research and development, and yet others, leading to our being recognized for certain purposes, as a "major non-NATO ally." The economic aspect—the aid, the free trade area agreement, and other matters must also be noted. For all this we are grateful to President Reagan, to Vice-President Bush, to former Secretary of State Haig and, of course, to Secretary of State George Shultz, who was the guiding force in the main part of these developments, and to their other colleagues.

We are convinced that these new, qualitative dimensions will be continued, and will develop still more vigorously within the coming period, under President Bush's new administration. We convey our heartfelt congratulations to President-elect George Bush, to his Vice-President, Dan Quayle, to Secretary of State-designate James Baker and to their associates, and wish them every success in steering the ship of the leader of the free world. Their success will be the success of all who seek freedom and prosperity throughout the world.

It is true that in any relationship, occasional differences of opinion cannot be avoided. Even in recent years we have not always seen eye-to-eye with the US on certain issues, mainly those connected with the intricacies of the Israeli-Arab conflict. It is regrettable that we were forced to disagree strenuously with the recent US decision regarding a dialogue with the PLO which, as far as we see and know, has not changed its character or ways, its malicious covenant and the terrorism that it perpetrates. We know this from the statements of its main leaders, and from its actions in the field. The Government of Israel, in accordance with its guidelines will not negotiate with the PLO. We have paid close attention to statements by administration spokesmen regarding their approach to the issue of terrorism. We hope that, after due consideration, they will draw the necessary conclusions regarding the PLO.

For our part, we shall act so that Israel-US relations will continue to flourish in the future. The memorandum of agreement that both the president of the US and I signed on Israel's 40th Independence Day, reaffirms the close relations between the two countries, which is based on "shared goals, interests and values." I record appreciation for the achievements in the domains of strategic and economic cooperation, and in defense aid. I should like to mention the desire of both sides to promote and institutionalize their relations. We must work hard so that this process should develop further.

American Jewry, a faithful and vital ally, constitutes an important part of these relations. The bonds between us will continue, and will be fostered even more.

## 23. Statement by the Board of Trustees of the International Center for Peace in the Middle East, Tel Aviv, 14 January, 1989

We Israelis—Jews and Arabs—and Jews from democratic countries, committed to the welfare and security of Israel, are appalled at the grave crisis in the occupied territories. We are faced by a national uprising of the Palestinian people who seek to end the occupation. The crisis cannot be solved by military measures. The hope of a peaceful solution has been stifled by the rejection of all peace initiatives. This has been aggravated by those within and outside the Israeli government who wish to prolong the occupation of the territories indefinitely.

Security measures should be restrained and unprovocative. The use of the extreme measures such as expulsion, collective punishment, curtailment of the freedom of speech, and all other harsh measures should be stopped forthwith.

It is important to stress that we strive to terminate Israeli rule in the West Bank and Gaza, enabling the 1.5 million Palestinians to achieve self-determination in the framework of peaceful co-existence. A peace treaty achieved by direct negotiations under international auspices will bring an end to this bitter conflict, provide security for Israel, and end the corrosive effects of the occupation. By achieving peace, we will end the situation which is endangering the future of the state of Israel, its democratic principles, and its basic values.

## 24   "Israel, the West Bank and Gaza: Toward a Solution," Report by a Study Group, Tel Aviv University's Jaffee Center for Strategic Studies, 1989

The *intifadah*—the uprising waged by the Palestinians in the West Bank and Gaza since December 1987—and the diplomatic initiative launched by the PLO in late 1988, have added impetus to Israel's need to weigh its options with respect to the future of these territories. A comparative study of all relevant options was long overdue. *The West Bank and Gaza: Israel's Options for Peace* comprises the first attempt to meet this challenge. Six primary options comprise the core of this investigation. They were selected for analysis on the basis of one main criterion: they are currently on the Israeli public agenda.

**The Status Quo**
The first option studied is for Israel to maintain the status quo. Since the absence of change in the legal and political status of the West Bank and Gaza allows the IDF's disposition of forces to remain unchanged, Israel would continue to enjoy the strategic depth provided by the West Bank, with associated advantages for warfighting and deterrence. The status quo also allows Israel to await the appearance of desirable partners for peace, possibly with fewer concessions required.

Yet these advantages are increasingly offset by the progressive deterioration in Israel's strategic standing entailed by the continuation of the status quo. Elements of this deterioration include the likely growing radicalization of Palestinian Arabs and a possible intensification of the *intifadah*; radicalization among Israeli Arabs; and enhanced unilateral Palestinian state-building effort in the West Bank and Gaza, an increasing likelihood of deterioration in Israel's relations with the Arab world, and specifically with Egypt; growing domestic discontent and societal polarization in Israel; and increased strains in US-Israeli relations and in Israel's ties with Western Europe. The result may be a considerable erosion in Israeli deterrence, and the specter of an eventual Arab-Israeli war.

In the short-term, the potential costs of the status quo will be largely determined by the intensity of the *intifadah*, by the extent to which the PLO pursues a moderate political stance, and by the reactions of Israel and the Bush administration. Of these key elements, only the nature of Israel's reaction is under its own control. Hence it is difficult to assess Israel's strategic fortunes as a consequence of adherence to the status quo. Given that the status quo has proven to date to be quite resilient, it may be equally possible for Israel to "muddle through" for an undetermined period of time. Yet the potential dangers this entails for Israel and for the region require that Israel make a concerted search for alternatives.

## Autonomy

The second option is the establishment of autonomy in the West Bank and Gaza. Two principal versions of this option were considered. The first is a narrow autonomy similar to that developed by Israel in the course of the Camp David autonomy talks, that would be applied to all Arab residents of the two regions, but not to the land of those territories. Nearly all local matters that involve Arabs exclusively would be managed by the autonomous administration. The second variant is a "deep autonomy" offering the Palestinians extended self rule—including national symbols such as a flag and anthem—control over all state lands not occupied by the IDF or by Jewish settlements, and joint control (with Israel) over water, customs and immigration (of both Jews and Arabs). An additional variation on either of these two would involve unilateral imposition by Israel of elements of autonomy without prior negotiation with Palestinians.

In Israel, the Camp David autonomy option as a settlement agreed with the Palestinians would enjoy wide domestic acceptance, among Jews as well as Israeli Arabs. The security risks entailed in this option are minimal: since the IDF would be able to retain its present order-of-battle in the West Bank and Gaza, its capacity to withstand strategic threats would not diminish. In addition, the autonomy option would be supported by the United States and is unlikely to be opposed by the Soviet Union, provided that Palestinian acceptance is obtained. But the Palestinians would reject this option even as an interim arrangement, as long as a post-autonomy transition to sovereign independence were not agreed and specified in advance, as part of the autonomy agreement.

The second variation to this option, the establishment of deep or comprehensive autonomy, would not encounter fewer difficulties. Deep autonomy would not pose greater security threats to Israel than would the narrow variant, and the external reaction to its establishment—particularly in Washington—is likely to be even more supportive. But in Israel, autonomy schemes will elicit domestic opposition in direct proportion to the extent of self-government provided by them, and to the extent to which they would otherwise resemble state independence. Thus, opposition within Israel to an autonomy that comprised many elements of sovereignty could be considerable. Yet by the same token, a broader autonomy is unlikely to elicit greater Palestinian acceptance; for the Palestinians, the critical factor is not the extent of autonomous authority provided—though greater autonomy would be welcomed—but whether they receive a prior commitment that it will eventually, at an agreed date, lead to statehood.

As for unilaterally-imposed autonomy, in the current atmosphere of *intifadah* it most likely would neither encourage better Arab-Israeli relations nor reduce friction and violence. Quite the contrary, it might be understood as a sign of Israeli weakness. It would be nearly impossible to find local Palestinians willing to cooperate in good faith. Indeed, unilateral autonomy could well bring to power extremist Palestinians who would exploit it to bring about renewed escalation.

Moreover it may be perceived by the United States as a deviation from the Camp David agreements and an attempt to derail the American-Palestinian dialogue that commenced in mid-December 1988.

### Annexation

The third option considered in this study is the annexation of the West Bank and Gaza to Israel. In view of the presence of over 1.5 million Palestinians in the territories, Israel—assuming it wished to remain a Jewish-Zionist state—would have to either deny them political participatory rights, or eventually "transfer" most of them from the West Bank and Gaza to the surrounding Arab states.

Annexation is technically feasible; Israel requires no partners in order to carry it out. It offers Israel the ability to formalize its strategic presence throughout the Land of Israel, fulfilling the commitment of some Israelis to the concept of Greater Israel. But implementation of this option would end a decade-long trend of Arab accommodation with Israel, and would begin a spiral toward war, possibly with Soviet support for Arab belligerents. It presages a violent Palestinian reaction involving escalating and unrestrained terrorism. The United States and many others would likely see this as an attempt to preempt the peace process. The US would disassociate from Israel, minimize the "strategic relationship" and apply extreme sanctions. Annexation may induce Washington to expand its dialogue with the PLO, and to discuss with the Soviet Union the possibility of joint action designed to compel Israel to reverse its decision, and perhaps to try to impose a solution to the Israeli-Palestinian conflict. American Jewry, Israel's most important strategic ally, would be increasingly alienated. Economic damage to Israel would encompass not only a drastic reduction in American aid, but also the indirect effects of trade and tourism boycotts, and possibly the cost—in human lives and in billions of dollars—of a war with the Arab countries.

Annexation would also generate a crisis within Israeli society and the Israel Defense Forces, and would bring about accelerated radicalization among Israeli Arabs. And it would place upon Israel an unbearable demographic and economic burden. While a large scale "transfer" of Palestinians from the territories would alleviate the demographic problem, it is bound to exacerbate all other negative ramifications of annexation to an intolerable level.

### A Palestinian State

The fourth option considered is the establishment of an independent Palestinian state in most of the territory of the West Bank and Gaza. Israel and the PLO would agree that the Palestinian refugee problem would be solved by settling most of the refugees in Arab states, and the PLO would cancel the Palestinians' claim to the "right of return." Security provisions for Israel would include demilitarization of the territories, alterations to the pre-1967 borders, and the deployment of limited Israeli forces for early warning, air defense, and absorbing an initial Arab military move into the West Bank from the east. Israel would also retain control over West Bank air space. While some Jewish settlements located within the new borders and IDF deployment zones could be retained, others would probably be evacuated. The two countries would collaborate on sensitive issues of mutual importance such as internal security and counter-terrorism, and disposition of water resources.

The creation of an independent Palestinian state offers a greater possibility of resolving the Palestinian issue on terms acceptable to the Palestinians than does any other option considered. It more closely approximates the goals of the *intifadah* and the PNC's unilateral declaration of independence than any other option. But it entails serious risks for Israel. While the option could enjoy acceptance among the majority of Palestinians, it involves a danger that, in the long term, the Palestinian state would attempt to realize the Palestinians' aspirations for Greater Palestine (the "right of return") by terrorism, subversion and/or by catalyzing an Arab war coalition against Israel (the "strategy of stages"). It also projects the danger of Palestinization of Jordan, whereby a Palestinian state on the West Bank would collaborate with Jordan's large Palestinian population to engineer a Palestinian takeover of Jordan and elimination of the Hashemite Dynasty. Meanwhile, Palestinian extremists would likely opt for terrorism in an effort to prevent the establishment of a Palestinian state.

As a hedge against the danger that the Palestinians would attempt to invoke terrorism and subversion against Israel, the establishment of elaborate internal security arrangements in the West Bank following Israel's withdrawal would be an absolute prerequisite. Moreover, to ensure stability, extensive international economic aid would be required by the new state: some $1.5-2 billion per annum for the initial years to maintain its present standard of living, and an initial investment of $2-2.5 billion in essential infrastructure.

Most Arab states are likely to accept this option, with Syria and Libya remaining the most probable opponents of any separate Palestinian-Israeli accord. The Soviet Union would be highly supportive of this option, and is likely to attempt to constrain Syrian efforts to torpedo its implementation. Washington is likely to accept any deal concluded by Israelis and Palestinians, even if the Palestinian state is not its preferred option.

A Palestinian state is virtually the only choice of Palestinians. However, under existing circumstances most Israelis would regard this option as unacceptable, and it is highly unlikely that an Israeli government would contemplate its negotiation and implementation. Negotiations with Palestinians over statehood would elicit widespread opposition, some of it violent, among those Israelis who consider any Palestinian state option as an existential threat to the State of Israel. Actual implementation, requiring the forced evacuation of settlements, would result in further divisiveness among the public and within the IDF. Certainly without extensive transition stages to test Palestinian intentions, and confidence-building measures to improve the regional environment, Palestinian statehood is potentially extremely risky from a security standpoint, and is as dangerous for the fabric of Israeli society as is annexation.

## Gaza Withdrawal

The fifth option considered is a unilateral Israeli withdrawal from most of the Gaza Strip. The withdrawal would be followed by a complete severance of ties, including, possibly, a hermetic sealing of the border between Israel and the Strip. In order to prevent terrorist infiltration from Gaza and ensure Israel's security, the border would be fenced and mined. A few Jewish settlements in the Strip would be dismantled, but most—located near the border with Egypt—would remain in territory held by Israel which would serve as a security zone separating Egypt from the Gaza Palestinian population. The inhabitants of the Gaza Strip would be free to choose whatever political framework they wished, including a PLO-led Palestinian mini-state.

Unilateral withdrawal from Gaza would allow Israel to divest itself of a small section of territory in which over half of the inhabitants are refugees, and the rate of population growth is very high. The option would encounter limited Israeli domestic opposition, and is likely to be acceptable to Israeli Arabs as well. Implementation of this option would not present Israel with major military threats that are materially different from those presented by the continuation of the status quo. Most external parties—the Arab states, the superpowers—would not object strenuously to Israeli implementation of this option.

Yet Israeli unilateral withdrawal is likely to be perceived as a retreat, and an abdication by Israel of its responsibilities, in the face of cumulative Palestinian pressure. Hence it might result in some loss of Israeli deterrence, thereby producing increased unrest among Palestinians elsewhere. In addition, the option would amount to the creation of a Palestinian mini-state in Gaza that would constitute a precedent-setting realization of the Palestinian state ideal and would receive international recognition, yet would owe Israel nothing in return through negotiations or agreement. The Gaza mini-state would be destitute; its GNP could fall overnight by 75 percent. It could turn into a Lebanese-style base for terrorism and chaos; it would probably generate unrest in the West Bank, and would quickly constitute a source of friction between Egypt and Israel. Overall, this appears to be a very risky option.

## Jordanian-Palestinian Federation

The sixth option considered is the creation of a Jordanian-Palestinian feder-ation in most of the territory of the West Bank and Gaza Strip. Jordan would be predominant in such a federation, with responsibility for defense, internal security and foreign affairs resting in Amman. As in the case of the fourth option—a Palestinian state—security arrangements would be established to mitigate poten-tial strategic threats following Israel's withdrawal. Most important among these measures would be the complete demilitarization of the West Bank, security arrangements for Israel on the East Bank, and the deployment of Israeli forces for early warning, air defense, and absorbing an initial Arab military move into the West Bank from the east.

(Jordan, the PLO and some Israelis frequently refer to a *confederation* option. Yet they have different agendas in mind: King Hussein and most Israelis mean a federative structure of the type described here, in which Hussein controls security; the PLO means a genuine confederation between two independent states in which the King would be little more than a titular ruler. Here the option is analyzed as it appears on the Israeli agenda, and presumably on Hussein's covert agenda. The Palestinian variant is subsumed within the analysis of option IV, a Palestinian state.)

Like the creation of an independent Palestinian state, this "Jordanian option" would allow Israel to end its control over more than 1.5 million Palestinians. But given the envisaged predominant Jordanian role in maintaining internal security in the West Bank, and the fact that demilitarizing the area is likely to be far easier once it constitutes only part of a sovereign state's territory, this option seems to meet Israel's security requirements more efficiently. Moreover, Jordan would be effectively removed from membership in an Arab war coalition, thus further safeguarding Israel against strategic threats from the east. Indeed, Jordan and Israel would share a number of strategic interests that could contribute to peace and stability, such as resettlement of the Palestinian refugees.

For these and other reasons, on the Israeli domestic scene this option is potentially more acceptable than Palestinian statehood, although it too would elicit strong opposition from many quarters. Demographically and economically this option could be beneficial to the Palestinians. With appropriate economic aid, Jordan could take responsibility for the resettlement of a large number of refugees from Gaza and the West Bank. The United States is likely to support this option, but the Soviet Union is likely to accept it only if the PLO does so.

Yet the Jordanian-Palestinian federation option is not currently feasible, primarily because it is unacceptable to most of the Palestinians. Since the Palestinians believe that they can eventually achieve sovereign independence, they would oppose implementation of the federation option, employing terrorism against Israeli and Jordanian targets, as well as against Palestinian "collaborators." Given Jordan's refusal to conclude an agreement that does not receive the Palestinians' blessing, and in view of Jordan's progressive withdrawal during 1988 from responsibility for the West Bank, the option is not currently being advocated even by Jordan. Yet in view of Jordan's fundamental strategic interests, the Hashemite Kingdom will seek to be involved in any future Palestinian settlement, whatever the circumstances.

Even if the option were feasible, it is not entirely clear that it would be to Israel's long-term strategic advantage. Demographically, the Palestinians would constitute an overwhelming majority in a combined East-West Bank state. Should they later move successfully to establish majority rule in the federation, Israel would be faced with a far more potent Palestinian successor state along its eastern border, that is not committed by treaty to coexist with it. Hence, if and when this option does reemerge as a viable possibility, its many advantages for Israel would be valid only to the extent that long-term Hashemite rule is predicated. Thus Israel would have to weigh this option carefully against the risk of eventual Palestinian dominance over the East Bank—a risk that also exists in option IV, a Palestinian state. Finally, this option also involves heavy short-term risks, since Syria is likely to invest considerable effort to torpedo its implementation.

**Toward a Solution**

In the study entitled *The West Bank and Gaza: Israel's Options for Peace*, which is summarized above, the strategic ramifications for Israel of a variety of options for dealing with the West Bank and Gaza were examined in detail. These are the main options for a solution that are presently on Israel's political agenda.

The status quo bodes ill for Israel. Israeli society is already showing signs of deterioration under this reality, and the only reasonable prognosis is for worse to come. The Arab world might not tolerate the status quo indefinitely. The Palestinians, and Israeli Arabs, are liable to move increasingly toward political radicalization and/or Islamic fundamentalism. At the same time, Israel's relations with the United States and its Jewish community may well become increasingly strained. While compromise options appear to be either unfeasible or too risky for Israel; while its legitimate fears of the alternatives appear to be paralyzing Israel's capacity for bold initiative; while Israel may indeed "muddle through" for some time to come—it is equally possible that the foundations of Israel's society and its deterrence will begin to crumble, thus raising the specter of war. This is not a risk that either Israel or the Arab Middle East should wish to take.

Unilateral measures—annexation, or withdrawal from the Gaza Strip—are also potentially detrimental to Israel. Withdrawing without prior agreement with an Arab partner also risks damaging Israel's deterrent image. Moreover, Israel would probably be creating, single-handedly, a hostile Palestinian mini-state in Gaza that owes it nothing, and enjoys inter-Arab support while it seeks to subvert Israel. Annexation, even partial, would, by violating the Camp David agreements, jeopardize Egypt's treaty obligations with Israel, and would seriously threaten the very foundations of the Israeli-American alliance. It would pit Israeli against Israeli, demoralize large segments of the population, and drive a wedge between American Jewry and Israel. Were this act to be accompanied by mass deportation of Palestinians ("transfer"), acute internal strife might ensue, and the IDF—today a unifying factor in Israeli society—might eventually be torn from within. A new Arab-Israeli war would be inevitable.

Nor are the compromise solutions on the agenda likely to be implemented. A "Jordanian solution"—a Jordanian-Palestinian federation dominated by the Hashemite Kingdom and in which responsibility for security rests in Amman—

offers considerable strategic advantages for Israel. But it appears not to be feasible from the Jordanian standpoint at present, principally because it is unacceptable to the Palestinians. The limited autonomy that Israel has offered within the Camp David framework is also unacceptable to Palestinians; a more comprehensive version might be acceptable if a prior commitment were made— not necessarily by Israel—to eventual Palestinian independence. Under present circumstances, were autonomy to be imposed unilaterally upon the Arab inhabitants of Judea, Samaria, and Gaza, or negotiated with non-PLO Palestinians (in the highly unlikely event that one could find Palestinians willing to negotiate autonomy without prior commitment to a Palestinian state), it would encounter a combination of boycott by local Palestinians and an escalation of tensions.

A Palestinian state is virtually the only choice of Palestinians. Under present circumstances it is highly unlikely that an Israeli government would contemplate its negotiation and implementation. Certainly without transition stages to test Palestinian intentions and confidence-building measures to improve the regional environment, Palestinian statehood is potentially extremely risky from a security standpoint, and is as dangerous for the fabric of Israeli society as is annexation. But even with transition stages and confidence-building measures, many Israelis consider any Palestinian state option as an existential threat to Israel.

Thus all the options currently on Israel's agenda have been examined—and found wanting. Yet for radically different reasons. The unilateral initiatives that Israel could invoke are feasible, but they would produce immediate, disastrous consequences. The compromise solutions, on the other hand, bear some promise of mitigating the conflict. But in view of existing Israeli and Arab fears and predilections, they appear to be totally unacceptable to one of the sides to the compromise.

In the immediate term, and in view of the deadlock described here, it would seem that only a *deus ex machina* of some sort could catalyze a solution. Only a major event such as war, or the appearance of a Palestinian or Jordanian "Sadat," or superpower intervention, or a dramatic Israeli leadership initiative, might "loosen up" the system. Were, for example, Jordan to fall under Palestinian rule, this might open up a new agenda of options for Israel.

Alternatively, should the PLO sustain the move toward moderation that took on momentum in late 1988—should it cease its terrorist activity in deed as well as in word and commit its proposed independent Palestinian state to peaceful coexistence alongside the State of Israel—then many Israelis may well demonstrate increased willingness to contemplate the creation of such an entity. At best, this would be a gradual process. Meanwhile, the gap between Israelis and Palestinians remains very wide. For Israelis, under these circumstances, the status quo may continue to represent a kind of negative consensus; the least of all evils.

Indeed, in the most immediate sense, Israel had best invest considerable effort in searching for limited measures—probably of a unilateral variety—that hold out the prospect of even slightly alleviating the pressures and dangers inherent in the status quo. Otherwise, the status quo might generate a dynamic of international pressure upon Israel to implement a Palestinian state solution under conditions that are potentially highly detrimental to it.

Our analysis also implies that meaningful progress toward some resolution of the problems entailed in the West Bank and Gaza for Israel is both necessary and possible. It can be achieved only as an outcome of an Israeli-Palestinian agreement; yet all of the six options on Israel's agenda are either not feasible or not desirable. Hence, in order for progress to be achieved, Israelis and Palestinians would have to embark upon a course that is contingent upon, and, in turn, will induce change in their most fundamental perceptions. Such a confidence-building process does not offer an immediate solution; nor is it without danger for Israel. But it appears to be imperative, indeed inescapable, precisely because the status quo threatens to become intolerable, and alternative compromise solutions that might be preferable for Israel are not available.

Perhaps by elucidating the key sources of mutual rejection, as reflected in our analysis of the six options, it may be possible at least to point the way toward this new course. Currently, Israel perceives a Palestinian state as a threat to its existence, while the Palestinians see a state in Palestine as their primary aim, one over which they cannot make concessions. No progress toward a settlement appears to be possible without each side accepting that it must act to accommodate the other's basic needs, as well as to alter the fundamental approaches of the other.

For such change to happen, Israel would have to accept four premises:

1)    That remaining in all the territories and ruling over the Palestinians indefinitely will cause Israel to pay a heavy price, insofar as continued occupation will constitute a strategic disadvantage for it;

2)    That Israeli security can be maintained through continued military deployment but without physical control over all of the territories and all of their Palestinian inhabitants;

3)    That if at the end of the peace process some form of a Palestinian state were to emerge in most of the West Bank and Gaza Strip, such a state, given Israeli security measures, would not necessarily threaten Israel either strategically or by terrorism;

4)    That no settlement of the conflict is possible without direct negotiations with authoritative representatives of the Palestinians.

For their part, the Palestinians would have to accept:

1)    Israel's existence, with all that this implies: recognition of the legitimacy and permanency of a Jewish state in the Land of Israel for the Jewish people; renouncing the "right of return;" and renouncing any claim to pre-1967 Israeli territory or additional territory conceded to Israel within a final settlement;

2)    That they will have to enter a peace process that from the Israeli standpoint is open-ended. i.e., in which Israel itself offers no commitment regarding the nature of the ultimate settlement;

3)    An extended transition stage (10-15 years) in which there is no Palestinian state, and comprehensive Israeli security arrangements are maintained;

4)    That a final settlement with Israel will involve territorial concessions in Judea, Samaria, and the Gaza Strip, and permanent security arrangements.

As these changes in fundamental perceptions take place, the two parties can and should enter a dynamic of prolonged mutual confidence-building. This process would comprise the following elements and acts by both parties:

*Israel* would have to agree to offer genuine, comprehensive autonomy for the West Bank and Gaza; forego its control over most state lands in the territories; and cease—declaratively and in deed—the establishment of any new Jewish settlements in the territories.

The *Palestinians* would have to cease violence in the territories, and terrorism against all Israeli and Jewish targets; and accept a process of refugee resettlement outside the State of Israel.

In order to facilitate this process, and in view of the two sides' mutual suspicions of one another's ultimate intentions, the United States, possibly in conjunction with additional external parties, could play a critical role. This reflects the unique status enjoyed by the United States vis-a-vis the two parties: the Palestinians place great stock in American influence over Israel; Israel enjoys a special strategic relationship with the United States.

Consistent with this status, in the course of the process Israel would most probably need a commitment that, in the event Palestinian noncompliance with the aforementioned confidence-building measures, the US and associated external powers would support Israel in invoking unilateral corrective measures. And the Palestinians would most probably need a commitment that, if they complied with the aforementioned confidence-building measures, the US and associated external powers would support their quest for an independent state. Here it must be emphasized that Israel's vulnerability and consequent security requirements dictate that the Palestinian entity that would evolve in the course of the process be a highly constrained one, for which there are few precedents in modern history. In this sense, the solution would have to be as unique and unusual as the situation that produced it.

At the conclusion of the confidence-building stage—assuming it reached a successful conclusion—negotiations would be conducted between Israel and the Palestinians on the modalities of a final peace settlement, including the dimensions of territorial adjustments, the demarcation of final boundaries, and permanent ways in which Israel's security requirements and Palestinian sovereignty could be accommodated.

Thus we have described a course for a Palestinian-Israeli solution in which

Israel does not negate the possibility of the eventual emergence of a Palestinian state, but does not commit itself in advance to this outcome.

Here a crucial component of the process must be emphasized. It concerns the aforementioned requirements for Israel to negotiate with authoritative representatives of the Palestinians: under present and immediately foreseeable circumstances only the PLO or, at the very least, Palestinians identified with the PLO, meet this criterion. As long as the PLO maintains the moderate course it developed in late 1988, an Israeli policy that rejects unconditionally any dialogue with it does not appear to be sustainable over time. It would generate increasing unrest within Israel, a sharp conflict with world Jewry, and in Israel's own growing isolation. It would appear far wiser for Israel to proffer conditions of its own—primarily, the total cessation in deed as well as in word of all forms of PLO-sponsored terrorism and violence—for it to negotiate with Palestinian representatives associated with the PLO.

These, then, in brief outline form, are the elements of the dynamic that may break the deadlock. On a more general plane, our analysis appears to indicate that any negotiated solution to the Palestinian issue—whether those examined in depth in this report, or the elements described briefly above—would almost certainly require a number of fixed components.

The most important of these are far-reaching security arrangements for Israel that guarantee both its military preparedness and its control over potential Palestinian subversion; and extensive international financial aid in helping solve the water, refugee settlement, and development problems that threaten to cause any Palestinian solution to unravel.

As for the economic aid component, our analysis indicates that most solutions that are contemplated would have little effect on the Israeli economy, beyond the immediate costs of relocating IDF installations and possibly some of the Israeli settlers. But they might have far-reaching ramifications for the economy of the territories, and particularly that of the Gaza Strip. Hence immediate aid would be required to prevent economic collapse in the territories, and more long-range, extensive support would be needed to alleviate unemployment and infrastructure problems. Certainly agreed, successful resolution—in both political and socio-economic terms—of the Palestinian refugee issue is a sine qua non for any solution to succeed. Thus extensive American, Japanese, West European and Arab economic assistance would be needed, as well as the collaboration in refugee resettlement of some additional Arab states besides Jordan—collaboration that would have to be facilitated by the superpowers and Egypt, in a spirit of support for negotiated solution.

Under prevailing Middle East circumstances, one key Arab state that would probably attempt to obstruct almost any reasonable Palestinian solution is Syria. Any attempt to reach a settlement must provide for adequate dissuasion of Syria or, alternatively—if at all possible—its constructive involvement in a solution that deals with its own conflict with Israel.

An additional provision designed to diminish the danger of a future Israeli-Palestinian conflict should comprise constitutional prohibitions in both states against irredentist activity. Moreover, the two states should undertake to honor their contractual commitments to one another even in the event of regime or constitutional changes in one or both of them, or in Jordan.

In applying these fixed components of any negotiated settlement, as well as in assisting in negotiations themselves, the United States, and additional external powers as well, must play a key role. Moreover, the settlement must be ratified by the surrounding Arab world through the vehicle of peace treaties with Israel.

This applies particularly to Jordan. Any Israeli agreement with the Palestinians should be conditional upon Jordanian ratification and security collaboration in some form. This should involve not only the confederal arrangements that are acceptable to the PLO, but also a Jordanian-Israeli peace treaty. Eventually these could be expanded to comprise a tripartite Jordanian-Palestinian-Israeli confederation. These arrangements would mitigate some of the constraints imposed on a Palestinian state by Israeli security requirements. They would minimize the danger of a threat to Israel from east of the Jordan River by introducing appropriate nonbelligerency and demilitarization arrangements, such as reducing Jordanian force deployment near the border and preventing the introduction of Iraqi or Syrian forces into the Hashemite Kingdom.

This would add a Jordanian security dimension to the Palestinian political dimension of a settlement. True, if the parties succeeded in proceeding beyond the extended autonomy stage, to a form of Palestinian independence, a Jordanian-Palestinian confederal arrangement would leave the Palestinians, rather than the Hashemite Kingdom, in charge of Palestinian security. But both Israel and Jordan would find compensation for the risks this entailed in their own treaty relationship with its extensive security provisions. In this way even a malevolent Palestine, were it to emerge, would be deterred and constrained by an alliance of the stronger countries that completely surrounded it: Israel and Jordan and, adjacent to Gaza, Egypt.

The problems confronting Israel in the West Bank and Gaza are extremely grave. They do not lend themselves to risk-free solution. Indeed, as is the case with all options and possible courses of action, the path suggested here comprises a mix of risks and opportunities.

Whereas, from Israel's standpoint, other options might have been preferable—they are not feasible. The same holds true for the Palestinians. The course set forth here may constitute a realistic path for resolving the problems posed by the West Bank and Gaza for Israel, and a hope for progress toward a better future for the entire region.

## 25.   A Peace Initiative by the Government of Israel, 14 May, 1989

**General:**
1.   This document presents the principles of a political initiative of the Government of Israel which deals with the continuation of the peace process; the termination of the state of war with the Arab states; a solution for the Judea, Samaria and the Gaza District; peace with Jordan; and a resolution of the problem of the residents of the refugee camps in Judea, Samaria and the Gaza District.
2.   The document includes:
   a. The principles upon which the initiative is based.
   b. Details of the processes for its implementation.
   c. Reference to the subject of the elections under consideration.  Further details relating to the elections as well as other subjects of the initiative will be dealt with separately.

**Basic Premises**
3.   The initiative is founded upon the assumption that there is a national consensus for it on the basis of the basic guidelines of the Government of Israel, including the following points:
   a. Israel yearns for peace and the continuation of the political process by means of direct negotiations based on the principles of the Camp David Accords.
   b. Israel opposes the establishment of an additional Palestinian state in the Gaza District and in the area between Israel and Jordan.
   c. Israel will not conduct negotiations with the PLO.
   d. There will be no change in the status of Judea, Samaria and Gaza other than in accordance with the basic guidelines of the government.

**Subjects to be Dealt with in the Peace Process**
4.   a. Israel views as important that the peace between Israel and Egypt, based on the Camp David Accords, will serve as a cornerstone for enlarging the circle of peace in the region, and calls for a common endeavor for the strengthening of the peace and its extension, through continued consultation.
   b. Israel calls for the establishment of peace relations between it and those Arab states which still maintain a state of war with it, for the purpose of promoting a comprehensive settlement for the Arab-Israel Conflict, including recognition, direct negotiations, ending the boycott, diplomatic relations, cessation of hostile activity in international institutions or forums and regional and bilateral cooperation.
   c. Israel calls for an international endeavor to resolve the problem of the residents of the Arab refugee camps in Judea, Samaria and the Gaza District in order to improve their living conditions and to rehabilitate them.  Israel is prepared to be a partner in this endeavor.

d. In order to advance the political negotiation process leading to peace, Israel proposes free and democratic elections among the Palestinian Arab inhabitants of Judea, Samaria and the Gaza District in an atmosphere devoid of violence, threats and terror. In these elections a representation will be chosen to conduct negotiations for a transitional period of self-rule. This period will constitute a test for coexistence and cooperation. At a later stage, negotiations will be conducted for a permanent solution, during which all the proposed options for an agreed settlement will be examined, and peace between Israel and Jordan will be achieved.

e. All the above mentioned steps should be dealt with simultaneously.

f. The details of what has been mentioned in (d) above will be given below.

## The Principles Constituting the Initiative

### Stages:
5.   The initiative is based on two stages:

a. Stage A—a transitional period for an interim agreement.

b. Stage B—permanent solution.

6.   The interlock between the stages is a timetable on which the plan is built; the peace process delineated by the initiative is based on Resolutions 242 and 338, upon which the Camp David Accords are founded.

### Timetable:
7.   The transitional period will continue for five years.

8.   As soon as possible, but not later than the third year after the beginning of the transitional period, negotiations for achieving a permanent solution will begin.

### Parties Participating in the Negotiations in Both Stages:
9.   The parties participating in the negotiations for the first stage (the interim agreement) shall include Israel and the elected representation of the Palestinian Arab inhabitants of Judea, Samaria and the Gaza District. Jordan and Egypt will be invited to participate in these  negotiations if they so desire.

10.   The parties participating in the negotiations for the second stage (permanent solution) shall include Israel and the elected representation of the Palestinian Arab inhabitants of Judea, Samaria and the Gaza District, as well as Jordan; furthermore, Egypt may participate in these negotiations. In negotiations between Israel and Jordan, in which the elected representation of the Palestinian Arab inhabitants of Judea, Samaria and the Gaza District will participate, the peace treaty between Israel and Jordan will be concluded.

### Substance of the Transitional Period:
11.   During the transitional period the Palestinian Arab inhabitants of Judea,

Samaria and the Gaza District will be accorded self-rule, by means of which they will, themselves, conduct their affairs of daily life. Israel will continue to be responsible for security, foreign affairs and all matters concerning Israeli citizens in Judea, Samaria and the Gaza District. Topics involving the implementation of the plan for self-rule will be considered and decided within the framework of the negotiations for an interim agreement.

## Substance of the Permanent Solution:

12.   In the negotiations for a permanent solution, every party shall be entitled to present for discussion all the subjects it may wish to raise.

13.   The aim of the negotiations should be:

a. The achievement of a permanent solution acceptable to the negotiating parties.

b. The arrangements for peace and borders between Israel and Jordan.

## Details of the Process for the Implementation of the Initiative

14.   First and foremost, dialogue and basic agreement by the Palestinian Arab inhabitants of Judea, Samaria and the Gaza District, as well as Egypt and Jordan if they wish to take part, as above mentioned, in the negotiations on the principles constituting the initiative.

15.   a. Immediately afterwards will follow the stage of preparations and implementation of the election process in which a representation of the Palestinian Arab inhabitants of Judea, Samaria and Gaza will be elected. This representation:

1. Shall be a partner to the conduct of negotiations for the transitional period (interim agreement).

2. Shall constitute the self-governing authority in the course of the transitional period.

3. Shall be the central Palestinian component, subject to agreement after three years, in the negotiations for the permanent solution.

b. In the period of the preparations and implementation there shall be a calming of the violence in Judea, Samaria and the Gaza District.

16.   As to the substance of the elections, it is recommended that a proposal of regional elections be adopted, the details of which shall be determined in further discussions.

17.   Every Palestinian Arab residing in Judea, Samaria and the Gaza District, who shall be elected by the inhabitants to represent them—after having submitted his candidacy in accordance with the detailed document which shall determine the subject of the elections—may be a legitimate participant in the conduct of negotiations with Israel.

18.   The elections shall be free, democratic and secret.

19.   Immediately after the election of the Palestinian representation, negotiations shall be conducted with it on an interim agreement for a transitional period

which shall continue for five years, as mentioned above. In these negotiations, the parties shall determine all the subjects relating to the substance to the self-rule and the arrangements necessary for its implementation.

20.    As soon as possible, but not later than the third year after the establishment of the self-rule, negotiations for a permanent solution shall begin. During the whole period of these negotiations until the signing of the agreement for a permanent solution, the self-rule shall continue in effect as determined in the negotiations for an interim agreement.

## 26.    Statement by Prime Minister Yitzhak Shamir on the Israeli Peace Initiative, Jerusalem, 17 May, 1989

The Israel Government approved its peace initiative on 14/5/89, and I am hereby honored to present its main principles to the Knesset. The initiative's importance lies first and foremost in the fact that Israel has offered its own proposal, which is intended to lead to a peace settlement with our neighbors, in addition to Egypt. No less important is the fact that we are presenting a united stand by the Israel Government's major blocs and the other movements that comprise it, concerning an issue that heads Israel's political aims: attaining peace while guaranteeing Israel's security.

The government is saying to the nation in Israel, to our neighbors—first and foremost to the Arabs of Eretz-Israel—and to the countries of the world, that we are united in our aspiration for peace, we are united in proposing the channel for this, and we are of course united in recognition of the security requirements of Israel and its inhabitants.

With your permission, I will begin by presenting the main principles of the initiative, which concerns the peace process, an end to the state of war with the Arab countries, a solution for the Arabs of Judea, Samaria and the Gaza District, peace with Jordan, and a solution to the problem of the residents of the refugee camps in Judea, Samaria and the Gaza District.

The assumptions that lie at the foundation of the initiative are: The basis of national agreement, the aspiration to peace and a continuation of the political process through direct negotiations in accordance with the principles of Camp David; rejection of an additional Palestinian state and rejection of negotiations with the PLO; and a change in the status of Judea, Samaria and the Gaza District only in accordance with the government's basic guidelines.

In their treatment of the initiative, many in Israel and the rest of the world focused only on the subject of the proposal for elections in Judea, Samaria and the Gaza District for the selection of a representation for the Arab residents. This is an important part of it, but I must direct the Knesset's attention to the first three parts of the initiative:

Firstly, contrary to the claims of certain elements outside of Israel, the Camp David agreement, which is only 10 years old, has not been rendered obsolete. This is an agreement that is binding on Israel, Egypt and the US. If this agreement is to be considered invalid, why should we take seriously any future agreement that would be signed tomorrow and the day after would be claimed to be invalid? On the contrary: We call for the strengthening of the peace between Israel and Egypt, and for ongoing consultations between the two regarding a continuation of the peace process. It is unfortunate that Egypt did not agree to the proposal to hold a meeting between its president and myself on the recent 10th anniversary of the peace treaty. I hope that other opportunities will be found for this.

Secondly, the basis of the Israel-Arab conflict lies in the refusal of the Arab countries, except for Egypt since the signing of the peace treaty, to recognize Israel and to maintain peaceful relations with it. For example, each year we witness a futile Arab attempt in the UN to prevent recognition of Israel's credentials, the practical meaning of which is an attempt to expel Israel from the UN. The cessation of these negative phenomena—as well as, for instance, an end to the Arab boycott—is an integral, necessary part of the peace process. All those who seek peace must lend a hand in persuading the Arab countries to change their ways and to put an end to the state of war with Israel.

Thirdly, a human issue of the first order, which only callousness and hard-heartedness can continue to oppose: Without any connection to the political issue and without running contrary to the continuing political process, the inhabitants of the refugee camps in Judea, Samaria and the Gaza District deserve rehabilitation and proper housing. Israel has acted, and is acting, for the good of many of them with its meager means. A proper and complete solution, however, requires international cooperation in order to obtain the necessary resources, and for this we are calling without delay for an international financial effort to solve this human problem.

These points, as stated in the initiative, deserve to be promoted, together with the other part of the political process.

I will now move on to that part of the initiative that concerns elections in Judea, Samaria and the Gaza District. The initiative speaks of two stages: A transition period involving an interim settlement for a five-year period, to be followed by a permanent settlement, with the two being linked by a timetable and the principle of the process.

I must note here that the claim is sometimes made that Israel or elements within Israel are not interested in negotiations on a permanent settlement. There is no greater lie than this. First of all, Israel—contrary to what is perhaps acceptable among many of our neighbors—always fulfills its international obligations. This commitment exists in the Camp David agreement, and of course the initiative repeats it.

The difference between the initiative and the Camp David agreement is that the initiative proposes elections before a detailed agreement on an interim settlement; the purpose of this is to find appropriate interlocutors among the Arabs of Judea, Samaria and the Gaza District, with whom we must live. Tasks are being proposed in the various stages for the representation that will be chosen in these elections: As a negotiating partner for the interim agreement, as an authority for self-government after that agreement is reached, and—if it is agreed upon—also as a participant in negotiations on a permanent solution.

The transition period mentioned in the initiative will last for five years. Any period shorter than this absolutely cannot constitute the test of co-existence and cooperation that we need, and there are those who say that it is even too short.

During this transition period, the Palestinian Arab residents of Judea, Samaria and the Gaza District will be granted self-government to administer their affairs, while Israel will continue to be responsible for security, foreign relations and everything which concerns Israeli citizens in Judea, Samaria and the Gaza District. Of course, the issues that are connected with the transition period will be clarified in the detailed negotiations on the interim agreement with the representation that is chosen, including major issues concerning infrastructure and the economy. Egypt and Jordan will be able to join the negotiations if they so desire.

In negotiations on a permanent solution, which Jordan must naturally join, each side will be able to raise for discussion any subject that it wishes, inter alia because during negotiations, a peace treaty will also be contracted with Jordan. The goal of these negotiations will be to attain a permanent solution that will be acceptable to all participants. Until it is attained, the interim agreement will remain in force.

It should be noted that there will be no violence in Judea, Samaria and Gaza during the period of preparation and execution. I shall return to this point later on.

After an examination of the various options raised, the proposal of regional elections seemed to be the most reasonable alternative. It is obvious that we must work out the details, and they include significant questions.

The elections will be free, democratic and secret, something which is not a common phenomenon in the Middle East, and is actually unprecedented, except in Israel. Anyone who submits his candidacy to run in these elections in accordance with the rules that will be specified and agreed upon, and is elected, will be able to be part of the aforementioned representation.

These are the main points of the initiative.

The initiative is a totality whose various components are tied to each other. Our neighbors, who are invited to join the proposed process— and we will not spare any effort to convince them to do so—must know that the components cannot be isolated from one another. The various moves and stages of the suggested course are logical, fair and binding.

Furthermore, whoever joins the initiative should know that he must be committed—to us and to general agreement—to this outline and all that it implies. Of course, it will be necessary to conduct negotiations on the various details both before the elections, in order to hold them, and with the chosen representation regarding the interim agreement, but from our standpoint the outline itself is clearly binding from start to finish.

What are the next steps which follow from the initiative? First of all, as it states, a dialogue is needed in order to reach agreement with the Arabs of Judea, Samaria and the Gaza District. Of course, the US and other friendly countries that want to assist in the efforts at persuasion are invited to do so. Simultaneously, the details of proposals for various issues must be worked out, and all these issues, which are not simple, still require much internal work. We will also hear, at the same time, voices from our neighbors concerning their willingness to join the initiative.

Since this initiative was made public during my visit to the US at the beginning of last month, and until now, voices of refusal and rejection of the entire plan have reached us from the Arab side. We do not consider these voices the last word, since to the best of our knowledge this initiative includes fair, sincere and realistic proposals to settle the conflict between us and our neighbors.

Our neighbors face a dilemma: On what are they bent? The course of negotiations or a continuation of the violence? It will be our duty to do everything in order to prove to them that violence is not an alternative, and will only lead to disasters and destruction. The only path is the path of negotiations and peace. The PLO's announcement of rejection does not interest us; our proposals are not directed at them. We know that they are not interested in peace. Our call is directed at our neighbors in Judea, Samaria and the Gaza District.

The US, its government, its legislative institutions and public opinion there received the plan with clear support. American Jewry and all of world Jewry stand united by our side. There have been displays of interest in different countries, and even numerous displays of support.

Negotiations on implementation of the initiative have not yet begun with any outside element. All of it remains food for thought and discussion in the international arena. It is still too early to determine whether this initiative will indeed become a reality. Consequently, it is too early to turn the issue into an internal war among us, and there is no justification for this. Such a superfluous war will please and encourage only our enemies.

We are all aware of the feelings of the general public in Israel during this time; it is interested, above all, in a war to the death against terrorism and violence, which find their expression on the roads, along the highways and even in the heart of the cities. This war, which is being conducted by the IDF, the Israel Police and the other security forces, is an integral part of our historic struggle for survival in this land, in a conflict that was imposed on us and which does not end. This war will continue and we will also succeed in it, because contrary to the supposed examples of other nations that are mentioned to us, we are in our homeland, we have no other land, and we will utterly defeat—without hesitation—those who seek to kill us; they will also defeat themselves by murdering each other. True, we face restrictions that do not apply to the perpetrators of violence and terrorism; we are a law-abiding country and a society with values which unfortunately do not have counterparts among our neighbors. But we will emerge victorious in this war, and it is our duty toward our people and our future to do so. We should not get caught up in passing phenomena; our strength is with us, and we are stronger than our enemies. We will undoubtedly win.

All constructive criticism is legitimate. I accept with love the harsh comments I have heard from different quarters. There is a difference, however, between fulfilling the daily national mission which includes, inter alia, a responsibility to our international relations near and far and as much cooperation as possible among the different parts of the nation, and a person who is exempt from all this allowing himself to take positions.

There is no doubt that we have embarked on a path which contains both risks and opportunities. We will have to prevent and put an end to the risks, which are primarily attempts by elements that will be involved in the elections to deviate from the agreed-upon mandate. We will obviously see to this.

Concerning the risks along the way, however, it should be added that relative to the Camp David Accords, this time the level of risk is lower, because today we have 80,000 Jewish settlers in Judea and Samaria—may they multiply—much more than we had during the period of Camp David.

This past week we celebrated the 41st anniversary of our renewed independence. In another two weeks we will celebrate the 22nd anniversary of the reunification of our sovereign capital, Jerusalem. We are all united by the persistent effort toward the advancement and prosperity of the State of Israel. From here, from Jerusalem the capital, we say to all of Israel's citizens and inhabitants that the Israel Government will do everything humanly possible to ensure security in every area of Eretz-Israel with all the legal means at our disposal. We will, however, act untiringly to promote peace with our neighbors. There is no contradiction between these two. On the contrary, they complement each other.

I will permit myself to quote—don't be surprised—Ya'akov Hazan [one of MAPAM's Leuden], who several days ago received the Israel Prize for his special contribution to the state and society. He said at the awards ceremony—and I shall take this opportunity to wish him on his 90th anniversary, 'They shall still bring forth fruit in old age'—that: 'At the end of the Zionist Congress in [Eretz] Israel, Mr. [Menachem] Begin and I were assigned with concluding it. I ascended to the rostrum and stated that "we are united by a love for the Jewish people, and only on this basis are we capable of concluding it together." And now those with different—and sometimes even opposing—opinions are sitting here together, but a love for our people and concern for its future unites us all.'

I agree with every word of Ya'akov Hazan's comments.

I will add to this and mention what the Psalmist wrote: 'The Lord will give strength unto His people; the Lord will bless His people with peace.' This is indeed the proper combination of our national objectives: strength and peace.

In conclusion, I will permit myself to return to the matter of unity—Jewish and national unity—which I consider one of the primary motives for the establishment of the government in this format and for the formulation of the initiative before us. Throughout the history of our people, we knew prosperity and success when united, and we knew misfortune and tragedy when divided. Our strength lies only in our standing united against our enemies and those who seek to kill us, who delude themselves into thinking that they will soon be standing at the gates of Jerusalem. The truth is that it is we who will stand at the gates of a unified Jerusalem, now and evermore with God's help, united and adhering to our goals.

## 27.  Address by Prime Minister Yitzhak Shamir to the Likud Party's Central Committee, 5 July, 1989

*The following speech which contains the government's plan for elections in the territories touched off a government crisis by its endorsement of "four braces" restricting the plan as demanded by three leading members of the Likud: David Levi, Yitzhak Modai, and Ariel Sharon.*

My friend, the chairman of the session; dear acting Movement Chairman Minister David Levi; my friend, the Knesset speaker; fellow ministers; Knesset members; Central Committee members; friends; Dr. Bader [longtime Likud ideologue]; new and veteran mayors; dear guests; my friends—ladies and gentlemen. I would like to devote the beginning of my address to the Likud Central Committee to a very important issue, perhaps the most important one in the country's social system: By that I mean the plight of the development towns and their inhabitants.

The citizens of Israel who populate the development towns in the north, the south, and the central part of the country maintain the vital national decree of spreading the population throughout the homeland every day, 24 hours a day. They fulfill the edict of expanding urban settlement, and of building Eretz-Israel. Young and old, they ensure that the people of Israel will not be defenseless and exposed along the Mediterranean shores. They thereby constitute a democratic and geopolitical shield for the nation and the state in the various corners of the land. Their distress has recently reached dimensions that extend beyond the tolerance level of any human being. The state must stand by them and find practical solutions to the serious problems currently afflicting them.

Perhaps it would befit us to devote a special Central Committee session to the issue, but I find it my duty to emphasize, before I move on to the main topic of this session, that we will under no circumstances defer handling the problems of the development towns. We will muster all our efforts to help them!

Central Committee members: In my Knesset speech on 9 Iyar, 14 May, 1989, on the Israeli Government's peace initiative, I said, among other things: No negotiations with any external element on the implementation of the initiative have yet begun. The entire initiative is still good for thought and for deliberation in the international arena. It is premature to determine whether it will indeed become reality. Therefore, it is too early, and it is unjustified to turn the issue into a bitter, internal feud. Such an unnecessary war will only gladden and encourage our enemies.

I said all that out of my long-standing desire, which has guided me throughout my actions in the national arena, to avoid as much as possible any internal strife that may shatter our national unity. I said the same thing to the Cabinet as well, when I presented the peace initiative. I feared that even before the initiative could contribute anything toward reducing the hostility between us and the Arabs, it could—heaven forbid—lead to fighting, perhaps worse fighting, among us. This, both inside the overall, interpartisan national arena, as well as among the people.

When I said this, I never dreamed—I admit—that this initiative would become a source of friction within the national camp [the Likud] itself. I never imagined that such a move—which could promote the peace we all desire, and which could also strengthen our influence and standing at home—would result in a dispute among brothers. And when? At a time when we are so fortunate as to have gained strength in the public and scored further victories in the political conflicts with our opponents; when we are on the brink of promising chances for success in imminent conflicts in the elections to the Histadrut; and when I am hopeful that when the general elections come, our representation will increase. All this will happen if we continue to remain united in outlining our path and pursuing it.

After all, there is no doubt that the initiative which is today's topic for discussion has won us the sympathy of friends in Israel and abroad. Each one of us, who observes our continuing rise in power, prays every day that this process will continue!

I am no longer so young, for all my sins, and sometimes memories can be a burden. At the same time, they also illuminate the path. Many of my colleagues who are here with us this evening can remember a certain period during the 1930s when the national movement registered constant growth for a certain period of time—becoming a tidal wave which won increasing sympathy and persuaded many to join its ranks—until something happened which severed that upswing, leaving the political arena an empty front for our foes and opponents for a long time, until the 1977 Knesset elections, more than forty years. We spent more than forty years in the wilderness, in one move we forfeited forty years. Who can tell what could have happened during those forty years, what changes and processes we could have spurred or bred? One does not cry over spilled milk, but we must learn from this. We must learn how to draw the proper conclusions from the past, and make absolutely sure that we preserve a sober view and balanced considera- tion, and most importantly maintain adherence and faithfulness to the cause.

I read my speech to the Knesset before we reached a full consensus here, yet I find it necessary to repeat this portion. Let us not bring disaster upon ourselves, our nation. Let us continue to march forward assuredly, with determination and wisdom. I hope this forum and this argument will be the end, and finally close the door on our dispute rather than, heaven forbid, serve as the spark that lights an alien fire that could eat away at us. I call upon all our friends to do everything today, and tomorrow too, to extinguish the fire, and awaken tomorrow morning fresh, confident, and ready to continue to march along the path together, boldly, with mutual respect, and with faith in our strength and objective!

How was our peace initiative conceived? Over the past two years a dynamic to dispel tension and resolve conflicts peacefully has emerged. During that period we observed an improvement of relations between the United States and the Soviet Union, a Soviet withdrawal from Afghanistan, the cessation of war between Iraq and Iran, the resolution of the conflicts between the countries bordering on South Africa. All these have redirected world attention to the Middle East, increasing pressure for political solutions in that part of the world as well.

Since we had no doubt that we are the element working for peace in the region, we pursued our path, insisting on our argument that we are peace seekers. Yet Israel's peace declarations can no longer offer anything new, and they failed to garner any world attention. On the other hand, the declarations of moderation by Arab bodies—particularly the terrorist organizations—these did constitute a novelty. Thus the terrorist organizations jumped on the bandwagon of world sympathy thanks to deceitful declarations and promises, which merely distort reality. Thus a new method of warfare was added by the Arabs against Israel— that of daily violence, involving masses of women and children. Israel was obligated to give its political response, in addition to the measures it employed to curtail the violence and restore order. It became necessary for Israel to assume the political initiative, present the truth to one and all, and explain to everyone that its party is the path of peace, which it has pursued since the establishment of the state.

The initiative was timely. It presented in the proper light the necessity to contend with violence with one arm clutching the sword of defending ourselves, while the other is stretched out in an offer of peace. Much has been said about the components of the initiative, and I shall repeat them briefly:

Article One: The strengthening and expansion of the Camp David Accords. These Accords are not moribund; they must serve as the cornerstone for Middle

East peace. The cosignatories to these agreements—Egypt, Israel, and the United States—must all work to broaden the area of peace in this part of the world.

Article Two: Changing the nature of relations between the Arab countries and Israel by revoking the Arab boycott, granting diplomatic recognition to Israel, and ending the political fight against Israel in the international organizations—all this, in lieu of whispers by Arab leaders in the ear of Western politicians that they are seeking peace.

Article Three: Solving the problem of the Arab refugee camps in Judea, Samaria, and Gaza, where hundreds of thousands of Arabs suffer without any justification. They must be eliminated. That requires an international financial effort.

Article Four: Solving the problem of the Arab inhabitants of Judea, Samaria, and Gaza. In this we have followed the Camp David agreements. The initiative deals with two phases—a transitional period of a five-year interim arrangement, followed by a permanent solution. The two are interconnected through a timetable and the principles of the process.

The only difference between the initiative and the Camp David agreements is that elections are offered prior to the detailed interim arrangement. This was done in a bid to find appropriate interlocutors from among the Arabs of Judea, Samaria, and the Gaza District with whom we must live. The representation that will be elected in these elections will be given clearly-defined roles: to conduct negotiations on the interim arrangement; to constitute the authority for self-rule after the attainment of that arrangement; and also to serve as a participant in the negotiations on the permanent solution—if there is consent. The transitional period mentioned in the initiative is five years. During that time the Arab inhabitants of Judea, Samaria, and the Gaza District will be given self-rule in conducting their own affairs, while Israel will continue to be responsible for security in everything that pertains to the Israel residents of Judea, Samaria, and the Gaza District. Also, in the detailed negotiations over the interim arrangement, the problems relating to the transitional periods—including infrastructure and central economic issues—will be discussed. Jordan and Egypt could join these negotiations, if they should so desire.

The negotiations on the permanent solution should by nature also be attended by Jordan because a peace treaty with Jordan will be signed concurrently. In these negotiations each party will be permitted to raise for discussion all the issues it wants, yet the purpose of these negotiations will be the attainment of a permanent solution that will be acceptable to all its participants. Until its attainment, the interim arrangement will apply.

Certainly this path involves risks, if and when the Arabs consent to cooperate with us. It has already been said, and should be mentioned again: the same risks prevailed when we conducted the negotiations over the Camp David agreements. Now, as then, we have safety valves and measures against anyone who might try to violate or distort the fundamentals of the initiative. The IDF and the security forces will be in the area. They will constitute the guarantee that the negotiations on the implementation of the initiative will be conducted exclusively along the path acceptable to us.

Consequently, it is evident that the initiative is not different in substance from the Camp David Accords. Let me emphasize once again that we are talking about the problem of the Arab inhabitants of Judea, Samaria, and Gaza. We will therefore not agree to, nor allow the introduction into this process, of any element that cannot be called a permanent inhabitant of Judea, Samaria, and Gaza— whether directly or indirectly.

Now, before any negotiations with the Arab side have begun, it would be beneficial for us to stop and sum up where we are so far, six weeks after our decision to raise the initiative. What is the advantage we have already achieved within this short period of time?

First, the initiative highlighted and stressed before the whole world that it is the product of Israeli national unity; that it represents the aspirations of the vast majority of the people and their representatives. This carries enormous weight in the international community. Second, the publication of the initiative put an end to the dispute and rift that prevailed among the Jewish communities abroad, primarily among the US Jewry. Thanks to the initiative, the entire Jewish people in the diaspora united in firmly supporting Israel. This is a tremendous achievement of immeasurable importance. Third, the initiative registered one more enormous achievement on the tactical, diplomatic, and world media sphere: immediately upon its publication, it won a central position in the international arena. We forced the Arab countries, their supporters, the terrorist organizations, the Soviet Union, and the Arab countries to contend with our initiative first of all. They were pushed to a defensive position. Fourth, only a short time ago the international media teemed with views on suggestions and initiatives to activate the UN Security Council or convoke an international conference, and the like. Our initiative overshadowed all these proposals. If anyone raises any peace proposal for the middle East, we are capable of striking it from the world agenda in favor of our initiative.

Let us remember, friends, where has the international conference which we so strongly fought against disappeared? No one sees it, no one hears about it anymore! The initiative greatly improved our standing in the United States, among the administration members, in Congress, and in the public eye. The messages sent by the ninety-five senators and the two hundred and thirty-five congressmen have overturned the US political scene. Its attitude toward Israel has changed without Israel retreating one bit on any principle included in the government's basic guidelines. We have not budged and will not budge from the basic principles over which there is a general consensus in Israel. An arrangement with the Arabs of Judea, Samaria, and Gaza—yes. But there will be no negotiations with the PLO! Giving the Arabs of Judea, Samaria, and Gaza the opportunity to conduct their own affairs within the framework of an autonomy—yes; but never an Arab-Palestinian state! Third, any Jew who so wishes will be able to settle anywhere throughout Eretz-Israel. He will enjoy support from and protection by the Government of Israel.

We therefore offered a fair and reasonable plan. Every day that passes without a positive response by the Arab side adds to the suffering of the inhabitants of Judea, Samaria, and Gaza, and adds to their unnecessary casualties. It is not in our interest to cause suffering and bitterness to the Arabs residing there. But it is once more evident that Arabs from the outside—the Arab countries and the terrorist organizations—conduct their war against Israel on the back and at the expense of the Arabs of Eretz-Israel.

Those who think that continued violence will guarantee achievements and concessions from Israel are making a fatal mistake. They must understand that the fact that Israel treats them according to moral standards, evincing its respect for the principles of human rights, is not a manifestation of weakness or the outcome of international pressure. On the contrary: as long as the violence continues, it becomes clearer that its initiators, perpetrators, and the people who sustain it are cruel terrorists whose sole purpose is to burn, destroy, kill, and sabotage indiscriminately, drawing no distinction between Jew and Arab, soldier and civilian, man, woman, or child.

We tell our friends in the United States that their contacts with the PLO are a serious mistake which has already caused and will continue to cause serious damage to our interests and theirs, as well as to the chances for an arrangement. Any contact with the terrorist organizations, with the PLO, that grants further legitimacy to the terrorist organizations encourages the violent elements in the field, perpetuates the violence, further entrenches the Arab countries in their intransigence, and encroaches on US credibility in our eyes. It turns the Arab inhabitants of Judea, Samaria, and Gaza over to the hands of murderers and criminals who sow terror upon the residents of the Arab villages, pocketing hundreds of thousands [of dollars] in Arab aid intended for the population, and settling personal accounts by means of torture and cruel murders.

I call on the United States to stop contacts with the terrorist organizations which have not budged an inch from their despicable path.

Members of the Central Committee, I sympathize with those colleagues who ask today, before the negotiations with the Arab elements have begun, what our policy in the near and more distant [future] will be. They have tried to condense these questions into four clauses. I will try to give my answers to these questions, one by one.

First, regarding the elimination of violence. Our colleagues rightfully call for an end to violence and terrorism. The government's initiative, as endorsed, states that the elections offered in the proposal should be conducted in an atmosphere free of violence, threats, and terrorism. Can anyone conceive that elections could be held in a different atmosphere? Can anyone conceive of us lending a hand to a farce of elections, to elections under the threat of terrorism? Throughout the recent past, many people in Judea, Samaria, and Gaza have been assassinated by their brethren for the simple reason that someone thought that they had expressed readiness to engage in political negotiations with Israel. This is not new in the annals of the Palestinian Arabs. This was true in the 1930s, as well as later during the times of Camp David, when the government sought partners for negotiations. In fact, when did it ever stop!

The election process will be held only in complete calm, with everything that this entails. During my speech before the Knesset, when I first presented the initiative, I noted that we are all aware of the sentiments of the Israeli public at large, which wants first of all to conduct a bitter war against terrorism and violence. This war, conducted by the IDF, the security forces, and the Israeli police in the conflict that has been forced upon us as part of our struggle for survival in this land—this war will continue even more fiercely. Furthermore, we will succeed!

I pointed out then that, in contrast to the examples people try to present to us from other nations, for us this is the one and only homeland we have. We have no other, therefore we will be victorious in the struggle. That is why victory will be ours. The violence and terror, which have been the long-standing characteristics of Palestinian terrorism, will not be the gauge for the process of political negotiations or the elections. These will only be held in an atmosphere free of threats and assassinations. Otherwise, they will not be held at all.

Let me also point out that our peace initiative is based on control over security matters in Judea, Samaria, and Gaza. We do not have the ability to play around when it comes to this business. What can be a subject for foreign policy for other countries, including friends, for us means our very existence.

In conclusion, let me say the following: Ending violence is not subject to negotiation. This mission has been conducted by our security forces, and they will continue their job. We will end it! We hereby send the security forces and the IDF words of encouragement: The entire nation is united behind you, with you! Let me emphasize: the implementation of the initiative and the engagement in negotiations with the Arab side will never materialize as long as violence continues!

Second, Jerusalem. Some colleagues have raised various points regarding the peace initiative. They mentioned for example, the issue of Jerusalem. Jerusalem is not part of the initiative. Jerusalem is the eternal capital of our nation and our country. It is engraved in the Bible, on which the exiled in Babylon vowed: If I forget thee, O Jerusalem, let my right hand lose its cunning! Let my tongue cleave to the roof of my mouth, if I do not remember you; if I do not set Jerusalem above my highest joy! Pray for the peace of Jerusalem! These words are a holy tenet for all of us. The Basic Law: Jerusalem, the Capital of Israel, stipulates, in Article

One: Jerusalem as a single, united entity, is the capital of Israel. First and foremost, Jerusalem is imprinted in the hearts, in the heart of each one of us!

The Government of Israel's position regarding the participation of the East Jerusalem Arabs in the elections for the autonomy was stated in the resolution of the Cabinet under our leader, Menachem Begin, in whose Cabinet I had the honor of serving. The following is the phrasing of that resolution, listen! On 5 September, 1982, and I quote, the following was stipulated: The Camp David Accords never mentioned such a right to vote. By that he meant the vote of the Arabs of East Jerusalem. Such a vote can have only one interpretation: the repartitioning of Jerusalem, its redivision into two authorities—one Israeli, and the other belonging to the autonomy's administrative council. The resolution further states that in the letter appended to the Camp David agreement, which does not mention Jerusalem, Israeli Prime Minister Mr. Menachem Begin wrote that Jerusalem is the capital of Israel; that it is one indivisible city; and that it shall remain undivided for posterity.

I need not add that this is our position today as well. This is the binding position of the Government of Israel. Any change in this naturally requires a Cabinet resolution. There is no need to add anything to it. We will continue to guard Jerusalem in accordance with the government's basic guidelines, which stipulate that united Jerusalem, the eternal capital of Israel, is one city under Israeli sovereignty, indivisible. Free access in the city to the places holy to members of all religions, and freedom of worship will continue and will be guaranteed.

Another clause regards continued settlement activity in Judea, Samaria, and Gaza. We urge a continued Jewish settlement drive in Judea, Samaria, and the Gaza Strip. The right of Jews to settle throughout these regions can only be disputed by someone who believes that these zones should be another *Judenrein,* free of Jews, God forbid. This will never come to be! The government's basic guidelines state that the existence and development of the settlements established by the various Israeli governments will be guaranteed. It further specifies their number and the methods to set up additional settlements.

I am aware of the fact that we have certain political differences both at home and with friends outside. However, just as we honor the democratic process conducted by others, so we expect foreigners, friends, to respect our democratic procedure. Since this was agreed upon—and the universally accepted government basic guidelines so stipulated—there is no doubt in my mind that it will materialize, and that friends will also understand that. It is clear to me that there are differences of opinion on this matter between us and our friends in the United States. Yet the settlement activity will continue!

Let me take this opportunity to send our hearty and very warm congratulations to the settlers in Judea, Samaria, and Gaza. I tell you, your plight is not for nothing, your war is our war, and it will prevail. Have courage! This is a holy principle for us: Western Eretz-Israel will never again be repartitioned, and there will be no agreement to foreign sovereignty over parts thereof.

My friends, dear friends, the ideology we represent in the Cabinet is very well known to all. We remain faithful to these roots and fundamentals of our faith, and will continue to remain faithful to them as long as the spirit still lives within our bodies. Yet inside the unity government there is disagreement regarding the permanent solution insofar as Judea, Samaria, and the Gaza District are concerned. This is no secret. The initiative does not contradict the proposals for the permanent solution suggested by the various components of the government. Furthermore, it harmonizes with the government's basic guidelines, according to which during the term of the unity government no change will occur in the sovereignty over Judea, Samaria, and the Gaza District unless both the Alignment and the Likud agree.

Obviously, the supreme national need for unity in order to govern our country and our people was our prime consideration in forming the government, in formulating its basic guidelines, and in drawing up the peace initiative. We know that we can march together quite a distance. As far as the future is concerned, when the time comes we will have to reach an agreement on the matter, or else put the issue up to the people's vote. Yet at this stage there is no need to go beyond this. As I have said before: there is no contradiction between our desire and faith, and the peace initiative, which should start with an interim arrangement during which the nature of the permanent solution will be determined.

As to Eretz-Israel itself, I repeat what I told the US leaders: in the negotiations on the permanent solution, Israel's representatives will insist on Israeli sovereignty over areas that will be subject to negotiations. I cannot conceive any territorial component in the permanent solution which may, at the end of the process, be acceptable to us and our neighbors.

Let me add to these points further emphasis: We will not accept the establishment of an Arab-Palestinian state on Eretz-Israel land. The State of Israel will not be able to exist if such a state is established alongside it. As you can see, this is included not only in my statements, or the resolution we will propose, it is engraved upon our hearts. They will be the candle lighting our path, and we will fight for their implementation, and win.

Finally, Central Committee members: The initiative which is the cause for our gathering here today, and which we are debating, has a noble goal and purpose: to bring peace to the people of Israel, Eretz-Israel, and all those living among or around us. The people of Israel, who regard us today as the main and central political power, expect us to deliver the desired peace. Our people know very well that the job is not easy, that guaranteeing security takes precedence over everything else. There is no peace without security, and yet the national responsibility requires both peace and security. This is the mission and the duty which we must fulfill.

No negotiations with any external element on the implementation of the initiative have begun as of yet. It is still entirely theoretical food for thought on the international arena. It is too premature to tell whether this initiative will become reality. I therefore say to all of us, all the inhabitants of Israel: It is too early, and unjustified, to turn the issue into a bitter internal feud. Such an unnecessary war will only gladden our enemies. The psalmist says: the Eternal will give strength unto his people, the Eternal will bless his people with peace. This is indeed the proper combination of our national goals: might and peace.

Finally, I will permit myself to return to the issue of unity, which for me was one of the main motives for the establishment of the Cabinet in this format, and for the consolidation of the above-mentioned initiative. Throughout our history we have known prosperity and success during times of unity, and disaster and calamity when divided. Our strength lies solely in our standing united opposite foes and those who wish us harm, who delude themselves that they might soon stand at the gates of Jerusalem. The truth is that it is we who will stand at the gates of united Jerusalem, from now to eternity, God willing, united and steadfast in pursuing our goals.

In the most recent Central Committee meeting I stood before you, dear colleagues, attempting to explain the great importance I attribute to the national unity government. You agreed with me, and the unity government was established and still exists, despite its woes and weaknesses. I see it as a great asset these days. It may well be, however, that in the future we will have to withstand unsavory trends that will grow from within, trying to undermine national unity in order to make it possible for Israel to capitulate to disastrous foreign dictates. We will then have to stand fast—all of us, the entire national camp—with all our might in the face of the onslaught ...to grow stronger in order to be able to advance the nation and the country. For these future times of trial, we are duty-bound to preserve every morsel of strength and drop of energy. Our future depends on it. Therefore, friends and colleagues, let us preserve our unity. There is no better or stronger guarantee for our success and the success of the nation than unity in a strong and victorious bond!

Now, in conclusion, dear friends, we have all reached a joint draft proposal, agreed upon by all. Let me read out the text of the accepted draft proposal. Article One: In its session today, Wednesday, the 2d of Tammuz, 5749, 5 July, 1989, the Central Committee endorses the prime minister's political statement and the principles included in it, such as: Pursuing the peace process in accordance with the Camp David Accords and the government's peace initiative; the nonparticipation of the Arabs of East Jerusalem in the elections; an end to terrorism and violence before negotiations with the Arabs begin; the continuation of the settlement drive in Judea, Samaria, and Gaza; there will not be any foreign sovereignty over any part of Eretz-Israel; no Palestinian state will be established in Eretz-Israel; and no negotiations will be conducted with the terrorist organization, the PLO.

Toward the end of my speech, allow me, dear friends, to give thanks for the special effort made by Cabinet members, as well as many other rank-and-file members of the Central Committee and the Knesset, who felt strongly and deeply that there are no true differences of opinion between us, and thus that unity must be manifested in an agreed resolution.

Let me give special thanks to the acting chairman of the Movement. All the best, Shalom.

Friends, in the heat of the debate and due to the general commotion, I managed to overlook one article. The second article of the resolution states that the Likud representatives are obligated to work, in the Cabinet and in the Knesset, according to the principles included in the prime minister's address, and in accordance with the Likud's platform.

## 28.  The Government of Israel's "Assumptions" with Regard to Secretary of State James Baker's Peace Plan, 5 November, 1989

1.   That Israel will only negotiate with residents of Judea, Samaria, and Gaza, and only after it has approved the Palestinian delegation;
2.   Israel will not negotiate with the PLO;
3.   The Cairo talks will focus only on the Israeli elections proposal;
4.   The United States will publicly support Israel's position and will stand by Israel in the event that another party deviates from what has been agreed to;
5.   The United States and Egypt will declare their support for the Camp David Accords;
6.   One meeting will take place in Cairo and its results will determine if the talks will continue.

## 29.  Address by The Labor Party's Leader Shimon Peres Proposing a Non-Confidence Motion to the Knesset, 15 March, 1990

*The non-confidence motion was presented following the dismissal of Shimon Peres from the Cabinet by Yitzhak Shamir which led to the withdrawal of the Labor Party from the National Unity Government.*

Mr. Speaker, Honorable Knesset Members, I am not here to mourn or lament either national unity or the national unity government, or the chances for peace. I have come to point out that the prime minister, Mr. Yitzhak Shamir, has failed in these two tasks. The tasks did not fail, the man did. There is no presidential regime in the State of Israel, nor is there a premiership regime. The State of Israel operates based on a coalition system, which means elections. A genuine, respectable, and sincere effort was made to preserve the utmost unity, despite the divergence of opinion and the substance of the controversies.

For instance, we are divided on religious issues. There are religious and ultraorthodox parties, as there are secular, even atheist, parties. I do not consider myself a member of an ultraorthodox or a religious party, but I am concerned about the relations between the religious and secular populations. In my opinion—speaking as a representative of the secular sector—there are steps that have to be taken with respect to our relationship with the religious public: The slander must be stopped, and their real needs must be addressed. I see no reason in the world why a religious child should be discriminated against in matters of education only because he is religious. It should not happen. I believe we should strive for equality in the sphere of education. By the way, this is true regarding relations among Jews as it is regarding the Arab public. No kind of discrimination! And respect! I favored additional funds for the religious parties because they deserve it, not because I wanted to bribe them. I hold this view even now, as a member of the opposition. I am seeking no reward or payment for this. David Ben-Gurion established a status quo on matters of religion, and we will continue to respect it.

As for other issues and for peace, I will address them later. We have had arguments with Likud Knesset members. I would like to note that when Mr. Begin was prime minister, and when I was the opposition leader, I suggested to my Labor Party colleagues to vote for Mr. Begin's proposals. I did not request a seat in the Cabinet, although in my opinion, Mr. Begin went too far. Mr. Begin encountered opposition in his own party, and he found support in our opposition party. We did not underestimate things. Thus, unity under certain conditions, is acceptable to us. If unity can be maintained on issues of peace and for the sake of peace, or on issues of war in order to win one, it is to be preferred.

But then a man—Yitzhak Shamir—rose who, contrary to Menachem Begin, broke all the rules in the world. First of all, he believed this is a Shamir government, rather than a coalition government; that all voices will speak in Shamir's voice; that we are all objects to be trampled on by him; and that he will grade our performance, dismiss us, promote us, and demote us. Nothing like this has ever happened with any of the former prime ministers, neither regarding other parties or us. Regarding the other parties, he mindlessly broke every promise he made, whether written or oral, including promises to the sages in the ultraorthodox courts, whom he told: You can keep these promises in museums.

Yesterday, he voiced an antidemocratic and illegal pretext, an unbelievable one, saying: If I have broken promises, it was because I thought I was acting for the good of the country. Is Yitzhak Shamir the good of the country? Is there such a phrase—the good of the country—which is above the law? Which is above and beyond promises? Beyond keeping promises? Is every minister permitted to do whatever Yitzhak Shamir is permitted? Is every youth? Every child? Every judge? Is this a country where promises are not kept because the man who broke them says it was for the good of the country? A country where the end justifies the means is a communist regime, Mr. Yitzhak Shamir, not a democratic one. You are not above the law; you are part of it. You are not above promises; you are obligated to keep them.

But he did not merely break promises; he trampled crassly on the coalition agreement. We have belonged to this government for five years, but Mr. Yitzhak Shamir has not held even one single conversation with me in which he complained of my desire to topple the government. Not one word! Then I come to the Cabinet meeting and he fires a dismissal notice at me! Based on what? Are you some supreme president? Am I your clerk? There is an agreement between the two parties, and I am a party chairman; if you have complaints, they can be discussed. What are you doing throwing dismissal letters around? Who appointed you?

But whatever he did to me, he also did to Likud members. I heard what the Likud people said—for instance, what Eliyahu Ben-Elisar said about him. I also heard what Ariel Sharon said about him; what David Levi said about him.

Now, I would like to ask—why? Why had Mr. Begin kept his word, and why has Mr. Shamir not kept his? Mr. Begin launched a peace process despite the argument within the Likud. He did not fear the argument. He did not join the constraints camp at one time and turn against it the next. He did not say one thing on a trip to the United States and the opposite thing upon his return.

Mr. Shamir was against elections in the territories. In April, when he was about to depart for the United States, he had nothing to offer. He therefore proposed elections in the territories—a product of Alignment doctrine. He returned, the Likud Central Committee was convened, and he gave in to the constraints in contravention to what he had promised. We then asked him: Why did you give in to the constraints? It is against the Inner Cabinet resolutions! Mr. Shamir said: Whatever the Inner Cabinet decides is binding. Then, in November, when he had to go to the United States again, he decided to accept Baker's five points plus amendments. When he returned, a new constraint man was revealed, the man whom Mr. Yitzhak Rabin termed the national undertaker [allusion to Minister Moshe Nisim], and he again gave in to the constraints. This is not how Mr. Begin acted, and this is not how a democratic party acts. Nor is this the way to act toward democratic partners. National unity can be maintained, but not in this way and not in a way in which a word is not a word, a promise is not a promise, a commitment is not a commitment. It is impossible! It is Yitzhak Shamir's failure, not the failure of the national unity.

The same is true regarding the peace process. Gentlemen, Knesset Members! National unity is not designed to attain paralysis; national unity is not designed to glorify any one man; national unity is not designed to obtain general surrender to a man's title. National unity is possible for a mission. I believe it is possible to round up a vast majority in this Knesset for the sake of the peace process—unity for the sake of a mission, not for satisfaction, evasion, or the murder of the peace process.

I would like to tell Mr. Shamir his record arouses some genuine problems; I felt this from the first minute. I believe had Yitzhak Shamir and Moshe Arens headed the Likud in the Camp David era, there would have been no accord with Egypt. Arens voted against and Shamir abstained. Shamir described Al-Sadat as a Nazi. He kept frightening us.

Mr. Shamir was the prime minister and Arens was the defense minister when the IDF [Israel Defense Forces] was deployed in Lebanon. Why did they not pull the Army out of Lebanon? Why? Shamir said: If we pull the IDF from Lebanon, it will be a disaster.

The same is true regarding the Jordanian option, which he cut short.

I now would like to say a few words about peace. What is this peace founded upon? It is not founded on negotiations with the PLO. It is based on negotiations with a Palestinian delegation from the territories that is not made up of PLO members, although when we signed the Camp David Accords, we recognized the existence of a Palestinian people. What we are talking about are negotiations with a delegation from the territories that does not dabble in terror and does not belong to the PLO.

The second point we are discussing is autonomy as the first stage after the elections, which is acceptable to almost the entire Knesset.

The third point: We are speaking about a united and sovereign Jerusalem, on which autonomy will not be imposed and which will not be questioned.

The fourth point: We are speaking about the first stage of democratic elections, which are to replace the violence.

On behalf of the Alignment, I would like to add: We never suggested that existing settlements in the territories be evacuated. We were against the establishment of new settlements and in favor of developing the Negev. We tried to create genuine common grounds. But then came Mr. Shamir, who knew precisely with whom Egypt had consulted on its stands, with whom the United States holds talks, but who wanted us to say neither yes nor no to the two Baker questions.

I heard him say yesterday and the day before yesterday: We will discuss, we will discuss, we will discuss. What is there to discuss? Already while in the United States, you were asked by the president and by Baker whether you are ready to include a deportee or two, whether the delegation can include Palestinians from the territories who have a residence or a job in Jerusalem.

Knesset Members! On behalf of the Alignment, I am saying to the Knesset members it is possible to maintain national unity if there is mutual respect. It is inconceivable the prime minister would not summon me even once, and then, when I arrive at a Cabinet meeting, he would shell me with his dismissal letter! Who appointed you to do this in violation of the law, of the agreement! Who in this country will ever believe you again? Who? Is there a religious party that will believe you? A secular party that will believe you?

I always have strived for peace, and will continue to do so. Anyone who works against peace works against existence of the government. Mr. Shamir has made a joke of two things held sacred by most Knesset members: national unity and the peace process. Unity will be maintained in the future, too; peace is needed by the entire nation. Mr. Shamir now is saying something new: If I now launch the peace process, I have four conditions. The first is elections; second, the solution of the refugee problem; third, the improvement of our ties with Egypt; and fourth—I do not know to whom he presented it—the improvement of relations with all the Arab countries.

I now would like to tell the Knesset members that this morning, information was received from an authorized source saying the Syrians are offering to conduct peace negotiations. The demilitarization of the Golan Heights—is that what you now want? To enter negotiations with the Syrians before you achieve an agreement with the Palestinians? Is that your condition? In general, the idea you have that everyone is certain to adopt the Likud viewpoint... It is an excellent idea, and I am glad to hear it. I am hereby advising the Knesset members that we can launch peace negotiations with the Syrians if you are ready to discuss the Golan Heights. I suggest not to be so hasty. On the issue of refugees, they are saying: Okay, when Israel withdraws from Gaza, we will solve the refugee problem. So, whom is he presenting with these conditions?

Shamir has one problem: He represents an anachronism, an anachronistic fear; fear to move forward to peace, fear to make peace with Egypt, fear to make peace with Jordan, and fear to attain a dialogue with the Palestinians. Besides, he suspects everyone; everyone is suspect; his party colleagues, the constraints, the counter-constraints, his Cabinet partners, and the religious parties.

I would like to say to the religious comrades—not to all of them, only to those who vote confidence in the government today: Will you, who favor a broad-based government, a unity government, vote for a narrow government? Will you, who are for the peace process, vote for aborting the process? Will you, who favor an honorable relationship, vote for such a dismissal? One made without a discussion and in violation of agreements? What guarantee do you have that when Shamir signs any agreement whatsoever with you, he will keep it? Do you not know the truth? I know Shamir always has been spreading rumors about me, such as that I would not stick to the rotation agreement—which I did.

Today, I am telling the Knesset members: It is possible to maintain a peace process. The Arabs are doing us no favor, nor are we doing them one. The Palestinians need peace, just as we do. Peace with Egypt has saved us a lot. I would like to add that I do not regret the past year, nor do I regret the efforts made by the defense minister, because a chance for the emergence of a Palestinian party acceptable to them and to us has emerged—without constraints impeding both us and them. I am glad some Likud members agreed to things they earlier had rejected: to elections, autonomy, a tripartite gathering and Cairo talks. All these are no negligible achievements. We could sit down to talks even now—had someone had the courage to give Baker a reply without evasion. Baker's question was whether the Palestinian delegation can include a deportee or two, and one or two people with a dual address: one in the territories and one in East Jerusalem.

The Likud said it does not object to allowing East Jerusalem Arabs to vote in Jordanian Parliament elections. By the way, the validity of East Jerusalem Arabs' passports is limited. What will happen if they expire? Will it be suggested they vote in Knesset elections? Or would it be preferable to allow them to vote for autonomy? I also would like to point out the Alignment does not propose to impose autonomy on Jerusalem; it does not propose the Palestinians vote in Jerusalem—only outside it. I am telling Knesset members from all parties, including the Likud: We have attained so much accord, despite the coalition which has been so demanding and occasionally complex. We could have acted together—only one should not trample everything with such disregard.

We therefore are here to vote no confidence in the man who has stopped two processes: the peace process and the process of national unity. It was a national unity empowered with a mission, not one of silence or paralysis; national unity aimed at promoting the peace process, not national unity of intimidation; national unity with a character, not one that changes its mien when it moves from Washington to a Tel Aviv congress hall; unity that is determined democratically, rather than like a pendulum moving to and fro. Knesset Members: Peace does stand a chance, and every Jew, wherever he may be, needs that chance! Every Jew, wherever he may be, because peace will allow the absorption of mass immigration. Even now, we could have had direct flights from Moscow to Ben-Gurion Airport, had it not been for certain unnecessary prattle.

Now they are trying to make Jerusalem a piece in a chess game. There are no differences of opinion on the issue of Jerusalem. I am telling the comrades from the religious parties: Jerusalem, Israel's capital, within borders decided by the Government of Israel, will remain a united city where Israeli law will prevail, where autonomy will not be imposed—an eternal capital of Israel. Jerusalem will be built by deed, not rhetoric. I am warning the Knesset members not to turn Jerusalem into an artificial stumbling block for the purpose of elections! There is nothing that unites this house more than Jerusalem. The attempt to divide us on this issue is artificial.

I will repeat my point about the delegation: I know some colleagues are saying: Let us recognize the PLO. I told those colleagues: There is no need; the Palestinian party and the Egyptian party are not insisting on it. They accept an agreed delegation from the territories with whom it will be possible to launch a dialogue. To me, to us, negotiations with an elected delegation are preferable to negotiations with one that will be burned. Because in the present situation, who are the people who will be included in the delegation? All those who survive. Today the delegation is elected by gunfire, violence, and murder, with radicals shooting moderates most of the time. We want a delegation elected through free political elections, conducted with the democratic dignity they deserve.

The moment democracy penetrates the Middle East, peace will follow suit. It is a fact there almost is no war among democratic countries. What happened in East Europe will happen in the Middle East: Dictators will fall, antiquated methods of ends justifying means will disappear, economic and social aspects will replace the strategic one, and everything will be determined through elections.

Our nation has gone through a glorious time with the help of democratic elections. There is a second, less glorious chapter, and I am calling on all to unite for the sake of a mission; I am calling on all to create a relationship in which no one will simply disregard the other.

Mr. Speaker, we do not have confidence in this government headed by Mr. Shamir, and we are urging all Knesset members to vote as they really feel. Ge‘ula [Cohen from Tehiya] knows precisely how she feels, as does Raful [Tzomet's Refa‘el Eytan]: Vote for a government that will work to unite the nation and, while safeguarding the country's security, to bring to a new, additional horizon of peace between us and our neighbors.

## 30.  Address by Prime Minister Yitzhak Shamir at the Knesset in Response to the Non-Confidence Motion, 15 March, 1990

*Following the debate, the non-confidence motion passed: 60 for, 55 against, and led to the fall of the Shamir government.*

Mr. Speaker, Honorable Knesset: During the debate conducted today, mountains of slander, curses, and lies were poured on my head. I easily can turn back these false accusations, but I do not want to turn the Knesset into a wrestling arena of loathsome debates. That is why I will try, in my remarks, to refer strictly to the political and ideological framework of the issues in debate.

Knesset Members, the Jewish nation is undergoing revolutionary processes that only can be described in the most exciting terms. From the day the state was established, the course of Jewish history was changed. Here is the center, here is the heart. Here we are our own masters and are in control of our fate. Whatever is being done here has an effect on the Jewish nation throughout the diaspora. All the forecasts about this nation are being refuted. Who ever could have expected this nation would have to defend its very existence time after time and succeed in repelling its enemies? Who ever could have expected the earthquake of Israel's revival would be followed by waves of immigration to Eretz-Israel? Who ever could have believed the Iron Curtain surrounding the enormous Soviet bloc would fall, and that many of us would come here and return to the bosom of the Jewish nation on its land?

The nation in Israel is in the process of its formation and evolution as a sovereign nation in its sovereign state. The enemies still are at the gate. They as yet are far from beating their swords into plowshares. The state is being built, but the path toward settling all of its space still is long. Immigrants are coming in by the thousands. The national economy has not yet appropriately prepared for the tremendous challenge of their absorption and incorporation in the economy and society. In short, this gigantic operation still is being conducted.

One need not be a genius or very wise to know and realize the situation of the nation and the state requires us, the elected leaders in particular, to evince a great extent of loftiness and devotion, and above all, to remove barriers and demonstrate the utmost unity.

Ever since I first was nominated prime minister, I have not stopped preaching, demanding, begging, and urging the need for national unity. On more than one occasion, I gave up on certain stands and advantages for the sake of unity. This time I suffered false accusations and insults, and avoided responding to them for the sole reason of not breaking up national unity.

After the 1988 elections, my friends and I could have formed a government that was not a unity government. I decided to opt for unity, not to hurt other potential partners, but because I believed that to deal with the national challenges facing us required the government have as broad shoulders as possible.

Unfortunately, ever since the national unity government was formed some 16 months ago, I constantly have been attacked by certain elements, following the coalition negotiations that preceded the establishment of the government. These elements were in no way willing to accept that what I did, I did not for my own personal sake or for the sake of the movement I head, but only to enable establishment of the national unity government.

I have demanded on more than one occasion that Jewish communities and heads of Jewish organizations abroad avoid disagreement on various issues and aspire for unity, because only through unity could they help us—division only will serve our malefactors, those who want to save Israel from itself, as it were. That is why I can state, with all the weight of the responsibility bestowed on me, that I spared no effort, and gave up on no opportunity until the last moment, to maintain the national unity government.

The immediate reason for the crisis in the national unity government lies in the political activity in the promotion of the process that is to bring about peace between Israel and its neighbors. The pretext was the answer the Israeli Government was asked to provide to the question the US Secretary of State presented to Israel's foreign minister. The truth, however, is the background of the controversy which prevented us from providing an answer to this US question is broader and deeper than might be assumed from the question itself.

On 14 May, 1989, the Government of Israel endorsed and adopted a political initiative for the settlement of the Arab-Israeli conflict. This initiative had very important advantages and potential. It was the outcome of accord and balance between the stances of the two main blocs in the government. It reflected an agreed stance, a national consensus. It gave us an answer to all the pressures and attacks from inside and outside, and allowed Israel to assume the initiative, instead of being led into initiatives that others had made. It was based on the Camp David Accords, which laid the foundations for peace between Israel and its neighbors, and paved the way for peace between Israel and Egypt. It addressed all the components of the conflict, setting a realistic route for a comprehensive and all-embracing solution.

At the same time, the Israeli Government's political initiative contained a degree of risk and peril. Every plan proposing to settle this complex and profound conflict entails risks. It was clear a priori, therefore, that the initiative would bear fruit and that a certain success would be achieved if we move cautiously, if we stride together along the path of its implementation, if we avoid creating cracks that can be misused by our enemies, if we do not allow any deviation from its content, route, and goals.

The United States declared it was adopting our peace initiative. From the very start of its implementation, however, difficulties and problems arose. Repeated attempts were made to dismantle the initiative into fragments, to take whatever part that suited whatever party and leave the others aside, to be forgotten and left void of all meaning. This is when they began dubbing the initiative the Israeli peace initiative—in order to direct it uniquely at the implementation of the clause dealing with elections among the Arabs of Judea, Samaria, and Gaza, while ignoring all the other clauses that address the refugee problem, relations between Israel and the Arab countries, and relations between Israel and Egypt.

In connection with the above, I would like to say that today Mr. Peres leveled harsh criticism against those same clauses which are part of the peace initiative, treating them as if they were my inventions or the Likud's. They are organic parts of the peace initiative, which was endorsed by the government and for which he had voted. I cannot understand how he could come to the Knesset today to level criticism and mock the same clauses that had been adopted by the government and ratified by the Knesset.

In addition, there were attempts to divert the initiative toward the PLO in various ways. Egypt operated in full coordination with the PLO. To our deep regret, signals and disruptive chords emanated from the United States, too, regarding the status and future of Jerusalem, as well as the PLO's involvement in the political process. The dangers surrounding our initiative grew steadily, to a point when sometimes it seemed the name of Israel's peace initiative was attached to an entirely different creature, which contained components unacceptable to us. We need—and we are obligated—to stand united and consolidated against these trends.

This is where I want to broach the issue of the conduct of our coalition partners from the Labor party. I must say, first of all, that not all Labor ministers acted unanimously and in one direction, although what tipped the scales eventually was the voice of the Labor Party chairman, who led and guided the Labor Party institutions' resolutions all along the way until the present crisis.

He never has accepted the fact he is not the prime minister, although I always supported his economic measures in the framework of the state budget and in other frameworks. All along the way, the attitude I received from him was similar, I am sorry to say, to that which he has accorded all the prime ministers under whom he has served—most of them from his own party. All this is history written and recorded in history books and biographies. Mr. Peres spoke of the slander against him, but I am sorry to say Israeli leaders of the past can attest to his character.

From the moment the political initiative was endorsed, we discerned strident voices and divergent interpretations among Labor Party members that were incompatible with the initiative's content and goals. In the face of attempts from the outside to isolate the clause concerning the elections and ignore all other clauses, our partners in the government could have been expected to stress the need to take action on the broadest front possible that would encompass all the components of the initiative.

The leaders and foreign heads of state that I conferred with expressed understanding for our demand that the Arab countries should make some contribution to change the climate of hostility and the state of war with Israel. No one countered our argument that if the Arab countries made some kind of gesture of goodwill—such as terminating the economic boycott, issuing a declaration of intent to recognize Israel's right to exist, or ending the futile attempts to expel Israel's delegation from the United Nations—this would also have a positive effect on the Arab population of Judea, Samaria, and Gaza.

If so, why should the chairman of the Labor Party and some of his colleagues speak mockingly and scornfully to our demands on the issue, and signal to our enemies they should not take three of the clauses of our peace initiative seriously? Where is the minimal wisdom of conducting political negotiations? This phenomenon and similar events added to the dangerous deterioration that began during the term of the previous government, which spoke with two voices. We had hardly managed to overcome this disaster, which haunted us for several years, by a joint peace initiative—when the phenomena of speaking with two voices and of undermining the government's policy and performance resumed.

Since when does a Cabinet finance minister conduct his own foreign policy? Why should the government and the country, due to such behavior, thus shame itself in the eyes of the world? In each and every stage of the process, the Israeli Government and Inner Cabinet convened and conducted discussions within a reasonable and relatively short period of time whenever we were required to make a decision, take a position, or respond to the United States, which played a sort of mediating role in the process. In contrast, the Arab side, represented by Egypt, held up its response for weeks and months. The United States and others nevertheless displayed exceptional tolerance toward Egypt and occasionally even deemed fit to praise it. Those who deemed it fit to pass judgment on the Israeli Government, to cast doubts on its intentions, and time and again to accuse it of dragging its feet, were the chairman of the Labor Party and some of his colleagues and aides.

Once again they displayed a bizarre attitude toward the negotiations. They never said no to any proposal coming from the outside. On the contrary, at every opportunity they immediately started to put pressure on us, their partners in the government, to accept any proposal without any proper recompense. Any improvement in the negotiations, whenever it was achieved, came in the wake of the demands I and my colleagues posed.

When the United States proposed to give us assurances upon our acceptance of Baker's five points and when negotiations began with the United States over these assurances, according to the assumptions made by the Inner Cabinet on 5 December, 1989, the Labor Party chairman from the outset said there was no need for all these. This was not kept secret from the Americans and the Arabs; and of course, it had an impact on the results and progress in the negotiations.

On several occasions throughout the process we received proposals, and various initiatives from various quarters were published. First there were four points, later there were the 10 points of Egypt, and then came the five points of the United States. Each time we witnessed the same occurrence, when the Labor Party chairman hastened to respond positively to each of the proposals and the initiatives addressed to us even before they were discussed by an Israeli Government forum. Obviously, these occurrences prevented the government from functioning properly and from coping with the problems that cropped up at every stage of the process. The disruptive conduct of the Labor Party chairman and his colleagues played into the hands of the opposite side and encouraged it to demand a higher price from Israel at every step of the way, although he knew from the start...

I am talking about recent times; the day will come when we settle scores over Jordan and your international conference. Some brilliant invention!

He knew things had gone even further, and had it not been for security restrictions, the public would be apprised of the conduct of some members of the Labor Party on all these issues. I administer these issues more than you do, and when the day comes...

The horrid and shameful spectacle of extending tactical assistance and aid to our staunchest and worst enemies was not limited to this or another minister. This position was also taken by others, and the day of reckoning will yet come! All your screams will not silence the truth, and this is the truth!

Mr. Speaker, in view of this odd and irresponsible conduct by our partners in the government, we became increasingly worried and asked ourselves: How much of this undermining will we be able to put up with? How can we conduct negotiations on such sensitive and critical issues at a time when the actions of our partners in the government weaken the government? This was the background for the last stage in the process, on 23 February, 1990, when the US Secretary of State presented the Israeli Government with a question and an attendant interpretation. Our response would have enabled a meeting between the foreign ministers of Egypt, Israel, and the United States in which the arrangements and regulations would have been agreed on for the beginning of a dialogue between an Israeli delegation and Arab representatives of the inhabitants of Judea, Samaria, and Gaza.

The Inner Cabinet convened to discuss the Secretary of State's questions on Wednesday, 7 March, and on Sunday, 11 March. Likud ministers who attended the session stressed its decisive importance and its repercussions on the entire peace process. It was clear that our response to the Secretary of State's approach pertains to the issues most vital to Israel, which are the status of Jerusalem and the PLO's involvement in the process. We proceeded to hold the debate with a feeling of anxiety and utmost responsibility.

Mr. Speaker, anyone reading the Israeli Government's initiative of 14 May, 1989 will notice the words the Palestinian Arab residents of Judea, Samaria, and the Gaza District appear no fewer than 10 times in the document. It was not by coincidence we took pains to refer to the Arabs of Eretz-Israel who would take part in the process in such words. We wanted to prevent any misunderstanding and make it plain to all Israelis and others that Israel strives for an understanding and a solution with the Arabs of Judea, Samaria, and Gaza; that Israel believes such a solution may be attained according to the outline of our initiative; and that our proposal can significantly satisfy the desires of that population and, at the same time, be compatible with the interests of the State of Israel. By the same token, this formulation was meant to make clear beyond any shadow of a doubt the initiative is not addressed to Palestinian Arabs who are not inhabitants of Judea, Samaria, and Gaza. In other words, it is not meant for those residing in Tunis, Damascus, and Sidon, and not even for those residing in Jerusalem, the capital of Israel.

The PLO is the body representing all those who do not live in Judea, Samaria, and Gaza. Between us and them is an unbridgeable abyss, because they place at the top of their priorities what they call the right of return and the establishment of a Palestinian Arab state in Judea, Samaria, and Gaza as a first stage.

As for the Arab inhabitants of Jerusalem—and as far as we are concerned, there is no East or West Jerusalem: there is only one Jerusalem, the capital of Israel—they cannot be residents of the Israeli capital and at the same time belong to the areas of Judea, Samaria, and Gaza in any respect whatsoever. We heard the argument that if the Arab inhabitants of Jerusalem were allowed to vote in Judea, Samaria, and Gaza, this would not affect the status of Jerusalem as the capital of Israel. All these are theoretical formulas that can be used for self-persuasion and to ignore the reality around us.

Have the Labor Party ministers asked themselves: Why have the Arabs insisted from the outset on including deportees and inhabitants of Jerusalem in the

Palestinian delegation? Why did they rush to accept the Arab demand even before the Inner Cabinet debated the issue? The Arabs openly and clearly stated why they insist on including these two categories in the delegation. Not only PLO spokesmen, but also Egyptian officials did not conceal the fact including deportees was meant to introduce the PLO into the process, to use them to highlight the right of return, and to make clear the process as they perceive it is meant [to apply] to the Palestinian Arabs outside Judea, Samaria, and Gaza. As for Jerusalem, I will not go into the spate of declarations and statements from all quarters on the Arab side about Jerusalem being the capital of the Palestinian state, whose establishment they demand.

We were especially worried by declarations emanating from the US capital to the effect that sovereignty over Jerusalem is subject to negotiations, and that the neighborhoods set up in Jerusalem since the six-day war are considered settlements in occupied territory. It therefore turns out that as early as the outset of the talks about the elections scheduled to be held in Cairo, the Israeli delegation would have been faced by various sides which hold a totally opposite position to that of Israel regarding Jerusalem.

Given this state of affairs, would it not have been an illusion and a grave mistake on our part to call into question the status of Jerusalem as the capital of Israel by agreeing to grant its inhabitants voting rights concerning the autonomy in Judea, Samaria, and Gaza? I had the privilege of attending the debates on this subject during the negotiations on the Camp David Accords on the establishment of the autonomy. I had the privilege of hearing the harsh argument between the then-US President and Mr. Menachem Begin, the Israeli prime minister at the time.

I heard Mr. Begin categorically reject Mr. Carter's demand the inhabitants of East Jerusalem take part in those elections. Does anyone conceive of the possibility Israel today should agree to such a move, which would undermine our status in Jerusalem, the same Jerusalem to which everyone sings his praises that it will be the united capital of Israel forever? I am glad for the latter, but is it enough? We cannot declare we will insist the whole of Jerusalem forever will be the capital of Israel and, at the same time, allow the Arab inhabitants of East Jerusalem to take part in elections of the authorities and representatives of the inhabitants of Judea, Samaria, and Gaza. It then would be clear to all that there is no difference between East Jerusalem and Judea, Samaria, and Gaza. That is why we said a clear and unambiguous position should be adopted, and a decision should be made before going to Cairo, before an Israeli-Palestinian meeting.

On this issue, therefore, we declare once again: Jerusalem's status as the sovereign and united capital of the State of Israel cannot be called into question. The Arabs of East Jerusalem hence will not take part in the process related to the peace initiative, either by electing or by being elected. The inevitable meaning of any such participation is the partitioning of Jerusalem.

Mr. Speaker, we are grieved and deeply sorry about the developments that led to the disbandment of the national unity government, for whose establishment and existence we worked so hard. All Israelis know I was one of the people who conceived the notion of the national unity government. I fostered this notion and worked hard to maintain this unity. I feel very pained, therefore that I have to tell the Knesset today why the structure I helped build and maintain through such hard labor now is crumbling down.

Until the very last minute, including this morning, we tried to prevent the disbandment of the government. I welcomed the initiative of Religious Affairs Minister Zvulun Hammer and Rabbi Yitzhak Peretz to look for a compromise formula that would enable the survival of the government. They failed in their efforts because the Labor Party rejected all compromise proposals.

Mr. Speaker, in addition to the peace process, whose importance I do not ignore, we have to tackle the vast needs and challenges in the sphere of immigration and its absorption, the economy, and security. Each of these issues would necessitate and justify the establishment of a national unity government on its own merit. The continuous effort to disband the government therefore seriously affects our most vital national interests. History will pass judgment on those who acted and contributed to the disbandment of this government.

I must add some words on the recurring trick of raising the banner of the peace process and using it as a cover, camouflage, and excuse to undermine the government. I am convinced I speak for all Israelis when I say no one, not even the Labor Party chairman, has a monopoly on the desire for peace. Every honest Israeli will firmly reject the innuendos meant to create the impression the Alignment is in favor of peace while the Likud is against it. These are futile suggestions unworthy of those who voiced them, which did nothing to elevate the prestige of the State of Israel and its government. I categorically reject all remarks suggesting that a certain someone, rather than the entire Israeli people and Israeli Army soldiers, holds a monopoly on the battle for Jerusalem. No one holds a monopoly on these subjects.

You claim I voted against the Camp David Accords. That is not true, either! But no matter! Why did I abstain in the vote? Because I objected to setting the precedent entailed in the evacuation of Israeli settlements established on areas liberated by the Israeli Army. That was the only reason! But after the Knesset passed its resolutions, I too accepted them, and strove for their implementation in all the positions I have held in the government.

Let us please not forget it was not me, but Mr. Begin—the founder of the Likud, he and no one else—who signed the first peace treaty with an Arab country. Today you are praising Mr. Begin, but try to recall how you maligned him when he stood at this podium! How you slandered him and gave him hell. What hypocrisy to elevate Begin in order to bring down Shamir!

We are not afraid of peace or the peace process. We are afraid and apprehensive about the run to make concessions in an irresponsible and rash manner. We believe true and stable peace only can be attained when Israel is strong, united, self-confident, and when its government takes responsible action unanimously through mutual consultations.

Mr. Speaker, I therefore am proposing to the Knesset to reject all the no-confidence motions.

## 31. Basic Policy Guidelines of the Government of Israel, 10 June, 1990 [Excerpts]

*The following is the agreed program of the proposed government's policies:*

At the center of the activities of the national government being presented to the Knesset, will stand the following programs:

1.  (a) In recognition of a shared fate and of the common struggle for the existence of the Jewish people in Eretz-Israel and in the Diaspora, and in order to realize the central goal of the State of Israel—the ingathering of the Jewish people to its land—the government will place immigration and absorption foremost among its national objectives.

    (b) The government will act to accelerate immigration from all lands and will act to save persecuted Jews.

    (c) The government will act to create the social, economic and spiritual conditions for the speedy and successful absorption of the immigrants in their homeland.

2.  The eternal right of the Jewish people to Eretz-Israel is not subject to question, and is intertwined with its right to security and peace.

3.  The central political goals of the government in this period will be: ensuring the independence and sovereignty of the state, strengthening security, preventing war and achieving peace with all its neighbors. To these ends, the government will act as follows:

    (a) The government will be vigilant in increasing the strength of the IDF, its power of deterrence and its fitness to withstand threats from the states of the region, including threats of unconventional missile weaponry.

    (b) The government will act forcefully against terrorism, from all sources. The IDF and other security forces will act emphatically and with perseverance to ensure peace for all residents, to uproot the phenomenon of violence and disturbances and to generate calm throughout the country.

(c) The government will place the desire for peace at the top of its concerns and will not spare any effort in the advancement of peace.

(d) The government will act for the continuation of the peace process along the lines of the framework for peace in the Middle East, agreed upon at Camp David, and of its peace initiative of May 5, 1989, in its entirety.

(e) Israel will encourage representatives of the Arabs of Judea, Samaria and Gaza to take part in the peace process.

(f) Israel will oppose the establishment of another Palestinian state in the Gaza Strip and in the territory between Israel and the Jordan River.

(g) Israel will not negotiate with the PLO, directly or indirectly.

(h) Israel will call upon all the Arab states to enter into peace negotiations in order to turn over a new leaf in the region, so that it may prosper and flourish.

(i) The government will act for the furtherance and strengthening of bilateral relations with Egypt in accordance with the peace treaty between the two states. The government will call upon Egypt to fulfill its obligations as set forth in the peace treaty with Israel, including its commitments laid out in the Camp David Accords, and to bestow upon the peace treaty meaning and content as per its clauses, spirit and the intentions of its signatories.

(j)  (1) The government will act to foster relations of friendship and mutual ties between Israel and all countries which seek peace.

   (2) The government will continue to maintain the relations of friendship and understanding which exist between the United States and Israel and will seek to deepen them in all areas, including strategic cooperation.

   (3) The government will continue the movement of renewing diplomatic relations with the countries of Eastern Europe and other regions, especially with the Soviet Union, and will seek to establish diplomatic relations with China.

(k) United Jerusalem, Israel's eternal capital, is one indivisible under Israeli sovereignty; members of all faiths will always be ensured freedom of worship and access to their holy sites.

Jerusalem will not be included in the framework of autonomy which will be granted to the Arab residents of Judea, Samaria and the Gaza Strip, and its Arab residents will not participate, either as voters or as candidates, in elections for the establishment of representation of the residents of Judea, Samaria and the Gaza Strip.

4.   Settlement in all parts of Eretz-Israel is the right of our people and an integral part of national security; the government will act to strengthen settlement, to broaden and develop it.

# Platforms of Israeli Parties Represented in the Knesset

## 1.  AGUDAT ISRAEL Party Platform, 1988 [Excerpts]*

We are of the opinion that the myriad declarations and all the talk about the status of the territories and defensible borders do not benefit the state of Israel. On such sensitive matters, discreet action is to be preferred to loud declaration. Our guiding principle is the promise made by God to our forefathers, that we should inherit the land as stated in our Holy Bible. According to the eternal precept of our tradition: "the saving of life is above all else". However, we are loyal to the quest for peace as preached by our prophets; we demand the promotion of political initiatives on our side; and that no effort be spared in pursuing peace with our neighbors and establishing friendly relations with all nations and states. Until we attain the prophetic vision of "beat your swords into ploughshares", we have to maintain the military level and moral superiority of the Israel Defense Forces. This will be done in order to fulfil that biblical verse that "God walks in the midst of your camp to save you and to bring down your enemy; let your camp be holy."

## 2.  The ARAB DEMOCRATIC Party Platform, 1988 [Excerpts]**

a. Recognizing the right of self-determination of the Arab-Palestinian nation.
b. Convening an international conference for peace in the Middle East with the equal participation of all parties involved in the conflict including the PLO, which is the sole legitimate representative of the Palestinian people.
c. To end the Israeli occupation and the need for withdrawal of all Israeli occupation forces from all Arab lands which were forcibly occupied in 1967; and establishing a Palestinian state in the West Bank, Gaza Strip including East Jerusalem.

---

* All Party Platforms were provided by the information departments of the respective parties. AGUDAT ISRAEL is the Orthodox Religious Party.

** The Arab Democratic Party is represented by Mr. Abdel Wahab Darawshe.

## 3.  DEGEL HATORAH Party Platform, 1988*

Political questions shall be resolved in accordance with the pure Torah (i.e. Scriptural) approach, thereby sanctifying the name of Heaven among the nations. Foreign policy shall be made out of deep concern for the well-being of all Jews everywhere.

Our right to Eretz-Israel, as spelled out in the Torah, is unassailable. The government shall do its utmost to prevent bloodshed and achieve peace. Then shall we attain the promise: "They shall beat their swords into ploughshares." We should try, in the framework of international accords, to put a freeze on armament in the region and to maintain stability in our relations with the superpowers.

## 4.  HADDASH Party Platform, 1988**

**A Just Israeli-Palestinian Peace**

The peace will be based on a respect for the rights of all the peoples and states in our region, including Israel and the Palestinian Arab people, and on mutual recognition. The peace conditions will be anchored in treaties between the states, that will be the basis for peaceful coexistence between them.

The peace will be based on the following principles:

*    Israeli withdrawal from all territories occupied by Israel since the June war of 1967. The 4 June, 1967 lines will be the recognized and safe peace borders of the State of Israel.

*    Recognition of the right of the Palestinian Arab people to self-determination and to establish their own independent state in the West Bank, including East Jerusalem, and the Gaza Strip, alongside the State of Israel.

*    A just solution of the question of the Palestinian refugees according to the UN resolutions, that recognize their right to choose between return to their homeland and getting compensation.

*    Return of the Golan Heights to Syria.

*    Respecting the right of the State of Israel and of the Arab states, including the independent Palestinian state, to sovereign existence and development in conditions of peace and security.

*    Abrogation of every claim of a state of belligerency, guaranteeing recognized and safe borders, free of any threat or use of force.

---

* DEGEL HATORAH - The Flag of the Torah Party.

** HADASH is the Democratic Front for Peace and Equality.

* Within the framework of the peace settlement, West Jerusalem shall be recognized as the capital of the State of Israel and East Jerusalem as the capital of the independent Palestinian state. There is room for agreed arrangements, that will guarantee the cooperation between the two capitals in the municipal field, free access to the holy places, free movement between the two parts of the city and so on.

For the establishment of peace it is necessary to convene without delay an active and effective international conference under UN auspices with the participation of all the parties involved in the conflict, including Israel and the PLO—the sole authorized and recognized representative body of the Palestinian Arab people—as well as the five permanent members of the Security Council. Bilateral and multilateral committees can discuss various issues within the framework of the international conference.

In the conditions prevalent in the Middle East and due to the residues of many years of wars, hostility and mistrust—effective international guarantees on the part of the UN, with the participation of the Soviet Union, the USA and additional states, may greatly help the implementation of the peace settlement and also guarantee the peace and security of Israel, of the independent Palestinian state to be established and of all the other states involved in the Israel-Arab conflict.

To promote the cause of peace we shall fight:

* For the immediate termination of all actions of oppression in the occupied territories, for stopping the violation of human rights and the arrests and administrative detentions, and for the release of all political prisoners and detainees; for the termination of the tortures in the prisons, of the deportations, the demolition of houses, the collective punishments and the killing of demonstrators, strikers and prisoners; for the return of the mayors and Palestinian personalities who were deported; for the termination of the land expropriations and the return of the expropriated lands to the Palestinian inhabitants; for respecting the international conventions with regard to occupied territories.

* For the dismantling of all settlements in the occupied territories.

* For an immediate withdrawal of the Israeli army from South Lebanon and for the termination of every Israeli interference in this country. The Democratic Front for Peace and Equality will fight for a policy of national independence and of neutrality in foreign policy, which means active support of—

The international efforts initiated by the Soviet Union to relief from the nightmare of the nuclear weapons and of every weapon of mass extermination; peaceful coexistence between states with different social regimes.

* The demand that Israel signs the international convention for non-proliferation of nuclear arms and renounces its "nuclear option", and the efforts to demilitarize the Middle East of nuclear and chemical weapons.

* The abrogation of the strategical alliance between Israel and USA.

* The termination of the military, economic and political cooperation of the

Israeli government with states with racist regimes (in Latin America and else-where) and with the racist regime in South Africa.

\*   The struggle of the peoples for national and social liberation and for true independence, against colonialism and neo-colonialism in all its forms and for the liberation of the developing countries from the burden of debts.

## 5.   The LABOR-ALIGNMENT Party Platform, 1988

The principal objectives which guide the Alignment's defense and foreign policies are: security, peace, and the survival of a democratic Jewish state—with a large Jewish majority—that maintains full equality for all its citizens.

An Alignment-led government will regard a constant striving for peace as a major objective and vital interest.   It is critical to break through the political deadlock that has prevailed since the Likud torpedoed Shimon Peres's peace proposal.

To perpetuate the political deadlock would be to turn Israel into a binational Jewish-Arab state without peaceful coexistence and with the risk of a downslide into war.

An Alignment-led government will reinforce Israel's peace with Egypt and will work to further the peace process with Jordan and the Palestinians.   Israel's objectives in peace negotiations with Jordan and the Palestinians are:

a.   To maintain the existence of the State of Israel as a democratic Jewish state.   A Jewish majority in most of the land is preferable to holding onto the entire land and thereby losing the Jewish majority.

b.   To guarantee defensible borders.   This means that the IDF's security systems, along with the towns and villages of the Jordan Valley, the northwest Dead Sea, the Etzion Block and the environs of Jerusalem would, in peacetime, come under sovereign Israeli rule; that the Jordan River would constitute Israel's security boundary; that those areas to be evacuated would be demilitarized; that security arrangements vital to Israel would be made, and that no Arab or foreign army would cross the Jordan River or be stationed to the west thereof.   The Jewish settlements located in those areas to be evacuated would be allowed to remain in place, and the safety and security of their inhabitants would be guaranteed.

c.   To solve the Palestinian problem within a Jordanian-Palestinian political framework which would encompass the densely populated areas of Judea, Samaria, and the Gaza Strip.   The negotiations would also arrive at a solution to the refugee problem.

d.   To rule out the establishment of another separate state within the territorial area between Israel and Jordan.   A separate Palestinian state will not solve the conflict but will rather serve as a focus for antagonism and increased hostility.

e.   To end Israel's rule over the approximately 1.5 million Palestinian Arab inhabitants of Judea, Samaria and the Gaza Strip, and to ensure freedom of movement and transit across the borders agreed upon in the peace treaty.

As stated previously, an Alignment-led government will have as its top priority the resumption of dialogue and negotiation with Jordan, together with Palestinian representatives, in order to attain peace on its eastern border and settle the Palestinian problem.

In order to commence negotiations with a Jordanian-Palestinian delegation, Israel is willing to participate in an international conference that will not have the authority either to dictate the conditions for negotiation, to impose a solution, or to abrogate any agreement reached between the parties to the negotiation. The function of the international conference will be to enable direct bilateral talks to commence. The Labor Party advocates those conditions for holding a peace conference which were agreed upon by Israel, Jordan, and the United States in the London Document.*

The negotiations will be held without preconditions and will be conducted on the basis of UN Security Council Resolutions 242 and 338. Each delegation will be permitted to raise its own proposals and to respond to proposals made by others.

The Alignment is willing to hold talks with those Palestinian figures and elements that recognize Israel's existence, reject terrorism, and accept UN Security Council Resolutions 242 and 338. Any other organization which denies Israel's right to exist and denies the existence of the Jewish people as a nationality, or which employs terrorist methods, cannot be a partner to negotiations.

In the course of the peace process, Israel will both institute interim arrangements and be willing to discuss any interim arrangements proposed to it. Israel is willing to discuss interim arrangements with Jordan and the Palestinians, or with authorized representatives of the inhabitants of Judea, Samaria, and the Gaza Strip if Jordan does not take part in these talks. Under such an interim arrangement, Israel would hand over broad areas of responsibility and self-governing powers in the municipal and civil spheres to the local authorities and to civil elements in those areas. Israel would then concentrate on maintaining security and preventing sabotage and terrorism.

The December 1987 outbreak of rioting in the territories was due in part to the political paralysis forced on the government by the Likud. The IDF and the security forces will continue to take determined action in order to halt the rioting in the territories, prevent violence, ensure order and guarantee the inhabitants' safety.

---

* For the text of the London Agreement, see Chapter One.

## 6.  The LIKUD Party Platform [Excerpts]

The Jewish people's right to Eretz Israel is a perpetual and unassailable right which is intertwined with the right to security and peace. The State of Israel has rights and claims to sovereignty over Judea, Samaria, and the Gaza sector. Israel shall forward this claim and press for fulfillment of these rights.

The autonomy arrangements agreed upon at Camp David are a guarantee that there shall be no further territorial partition of the area of Western Eretz Israel, and that under no conditions shall a Palestinian state be there established. The autonomy agreed upon is neither state nor sovereignty nor self-determination. The Arab nation has already been granted self-determination through the existence of 21 independent Arab countries.

Israel is prepared to sit down with any Arab country and hold direct negotiations for a peace treaty. An international conference in the Alignment-proposed format would prevent any direct peace negotiations from taking place and therefore could not lead to peace. It would inevitably be a trap for Israel and would lead to its withdrawal to the boundaries of 1967. Any plan that includes handing over parts of Western Eretz Israel to foreign rule, as the Alignment is proposing, undermines our right to the land, leads ineluctably to the establishment of a Palestinian state, compromises the security of the civilian population, and ultimately jeopardizes the existence of the State of Israel and thwarts any prospect for peace.

There shall be no negotiations with organizations of assassins who seek to destroy the State of Israel. Israel shall instate law and order in the Judea, Samaria, and Gaza districts. Judicial, military, economic and administrative measures shall be taken so as to enable the population, Jewish and Arab alike, to live in peace and safety. Any resort to violence shall be punished to the full extent of the law, and if necessary, the law shall be made even more stringent.

Jerusalem, the eternal capital of Israel, is an absolutely indivisible city. The members of all faiths have been and shall always be guaranteed free access to their holy places.

The Tenth Knesset passed into law the bill submitted by the Likud-led government, imposing Israeli state law and administration on the Golan Heights, and thereby established Israel's full sovereignty over that area.

The Likud will resume the drive to settle all parts of Eretz Israel and will work to expand, develop, and fortify those settlements already established.

### A Summary of Principles
*The right of the Jewish People to the Land of Israel* is eternal and everlasting and is intertwined with its right to security and peace.

Zionism is the Jewish People's national liberation movement. The State of

Israel has a right and a claim to *sovereignty over Judea, Samaria, and the Gaza District*. Israel will raise this claim and act towards implementing this right.

The Autonomy arrangements agreed to at Camp David are a guarantee that west of the Jordan River there will be no territorial partition, no Palestinian state shall arise, and there shall be no foreign sovereignty or self-determination. *Israel will enforce law and order in Judea, Samaria, and Gaza.*

The Likud will continue to give priority to its quest for peace and will not spare any efforts to advance its cause. Israel is ready to *directly negotiate a peace treaty* with any Arab State. An international peace conference, as proposed by Labor, will not bring about peace negotiations, but will be a trap for Israel.

Israel will maintain its right to *self defense* and will fight the terrorists wherever they might be.

The Likud will renew the *settlement policy* in all parts of the Land of Israel.

The supreme objective of Israel's *defense policy* is to prevent war. The right combination of political and security means will thwart aggression.

*Jerusalem,* Israel's eternal capital, is a united city and will remain indivisible.

Full Israeli sovereignty has been applied to the *Golan Heights* as a result of a law passed in the tenth Knesset and proposed by the Likud-led government.

The campaign to save the remnants of Jews held as hostages by *Syria and other countries of persecution* will be increased.

### The State of Israel and the Jewish People

Aliyah is the spice of life for the State of Israel and the Jewish People. Our primary objective is to concentrate the *majority of the Jewish People in the Land of Israel*. The government will deepen the commitment between Israel and Jewish communities of the diaspora, will widen operations in the fields of education and information in the diaspora. Links with the Zionist federations will be strengthened. An effort will be made to simplify the absorption process and to prevent yerida (emigration).

## 7.   The MAFDAL Party Platform, 1988 [Excerpts]*

The NRP views the Jewish people's historic and religious right to sovereignty over all of Eretz Israel as a central tenet of its creed and of its educational message, whilst devoting the greatest care and responsibility to preserving the safety and unity of the Jewish people, and stressing that Zionism's true substance is the eternal triad of the Jewish people and Eretz Israel under Jewish law.

---

* MAFDAL is the National Religious Party

The NRP feels it important in these times to make a firm and unequivocal political statement that will make clear to the entire nation and to the world at large the precise nature of the bond between the Jewish people and Eretz Israel. Between the sea and the Jordan there will be but one state, the Jewish State.

The NRP views genuine peace as fulfilling the prophetic vision and as a vital necessity for the state. Peace agreements are to be reached in direct negotiations between Israel and its neighbor states. The NRP absolutely rejects the conduct of political negotiations with the PLO.

The movement regards the unbroken maintenance of a Jewish majority in Eretz Israel as the national mission of the entire Jewish people. The so-called "demographic" problem is a Jewish problem, and its solution depends upon the will of the Jewish nation to be the majority in the country—to immigrate and settle permanently here. The NRP does not see expulsion as a solution to the demographic problem, either from a Jewish ethical perspective or from the political standpoint. The key to solving the demographic problem lies in Zionist fulfillment, i.e. larger Jewish families and the resumption of large-scale immigration.

There will only be one state between the Jordan River and the Mediterranean Sea—the State of Israel.

No independent national Arab entity will exist within the limits of the Land of Israel.

No part of Israel will be given over to a foreign government or authority.

No Jewish settlement will be uprooted.

The State of Israel will strive for peace and make every effort to attain it.

## 8.   The MAPAM Party Platform, 1988 [Excerpts]*

### Political Plank
*Introduction*
• The Land of Israel is the common homeland of the Jewish people returning to it, and of the Arab-Palestinian people living in it. Both peoples have the right to realize their national self-determination in their homeland, on the basis of mutual recognition and within the framework of an agreed compromise, and in secure and recognized borders. Any agreement which will be signed, and any border which will be recognized during the course of negotiations, will be final and will not serve as a foundation for further claims.

In peace negotiations, representatives of the Palestinians must take part, and those representatives will be chosen by the Palestinians, themselves.

---

* MAPAM is the United Workers Party

## Principles for Peace in Our Region

• Comprehensive peace in our region depends on the solution to the problem of the security of Israel, and the solution to the national problem of the Palestinian people.

• Based upon our right and our duty to strive toward an agreement which will give us and the entire region a maximum chance of security and a durable and stable peace, Israel will aspire to an accord which will satisfy the Palestinian people's desire for national self-determination and will be realized within a common political framework, with Jordan, such as the Confederation Plan of February 1985.

The wide expanses of the common Jordanian-Palestinian framework will enable the Palestinian people to retain its unity, and to gather and rehabilitate its refugees. Furthermore, they will enable it to honor the right of the State of Israel to secure and recognized borders, and to suitable security arrangements, including the demilitarization of the territories west of the Jordan River.

• After the border corrections necessary for its security will have been determined, Israel will withdraw to secure and recognized borders, and the territories returned according to an agreed timetable will be demilitarized. Military forces will not cross the Jordan River. Jordanians and Palestinians will bear responsibility for the prevention of any act of terror emanating from their territory.

• The united city of Jerusalem is the capital of the State of Israel. Within the framework of a peace agreement, Israel will grant extra-territorial status to the sites holy to Islam and Christianity, and will make possible the expression of the national and cultural uniqueness of the inhabitants of the Arab sector of the city, within the framework of autonomous boroughs, and with the guarantee of their right to select the citizenship of their own choosing. If and when an Israeli-Palestinian-Jordanian confederation is established, a suitable center for the institutions of this confederation will be erected within the boundaries of Greater Jerusalem, which will symbolize the stable peace and ever-growing cooperation between all states in the region.

• A durable and stable peace in our region will be achieved through direct negotiations between Israel and the states in the region and an authorized representation of the Palestinians—including the PLO—which will announce its readiness to recognize Israel and make peace with it, in accordance with UN Security Council Resolutions 242 and 338, and will renounce terror.

• Israel will agree to any means of negotiations, including an international forum, which will guarantee that within that framework the conflicting sides will be able to reach final and binding agreements between them.

• Open dialogue between Israelis and Palestinians could well improve understanding between the two sides and pave the way for official negotiations between them. Israel should, therefore, remove the legal barriers to contact which have been placed upon its citizens and encourage Israeli-Palestinian dialogue.

*Peace and Security*

• In order to serve the peace-fostering process, Israel should: work toward removing the presence of atomic, chemical and biological weaponry from the Middle East; see in every present enemy a future partner in peace, and promote this attitude among its people; develop an attitude which combines security and political arrangements; and new technology as replacements for the areas which the IDF will evacuate in the future peace agreement.

• The Israel Defense Forces—the people's army—is the sole armed force defending Israel, responsible for its borders, sovereignty and the safety of its citizens. Any attempt to use the IDF for other purposes will disrupt the unity of the nation, damage the morale of the army and undermine its ability to perform its duties.

The IDF derives its strength from the democratic character of Israeli society, from the moral fighting principles of its soldiers and from the continuing economic, scientific and technological revitalization of the State of Israel.


## 9.   The MERKAZ-SHINUI Movement Platform, 1988 [Excerpts]*

The main aim of Israel's foreign policy must be to achieve a peace treaty between us and the Arabs. Although the Jewish people have a natural and historic right to Eretz Israel, it is incumbent upon us to keep the State of Israel from becoming a binational state—which aim may be achieved via compromise solutions, even via our withdrawal from Arab-inhabited areas in Judea, Samaria, and Gaza.

Under the present circumstances, no new settlements should be established, both for economic reasons and in order to promote the cause of peace talks.

The Center Party believes that a third state situated between Israel and Jordan could not provide a stable solution to the Palestinian question, would subvert the foundations of both Israel and Jordan, would serve as a base for terrorist activities, and would not solve the refugee problem. The Center party believes that those qualities that are uniquely Palestinian could obtain expression with a Jordanian-Palestinian state, thereby solving the Palestinian problem.

The State of Israel shall retain possession of the Golan Heights so as to guarantee the safety of the Galilee's inhabitants and to protect its sources of water.

---

* MERKAZ-SHINUI is composed of three parties: Shinui [change], the Independent Liberals and the Liberal-Center

United Jerusalem shall not be redivided and shall remain the capital of Israel under Israeli sovereignty. However, the value attached to this city by both Muslims and Christians requires that solutions be found which take this fact into consideration.

## 10.  The MOLEDET Movement Platform, 1988* [Excerpts]

In view of the political crisis in the Zionist movement and in the State of Israel; in view of the lurking perils to our maintenance of the achievements of the Six-Day War [following the withdrawal from Sinai]; in view of the Arab nationalist awakening, supported by international elements and by Jews here at home; in view of the demographic danger in our land; and in view of the leadership crisis and our clear belief in the justice of our course, the Moledet [Homeland] Movement has decided to run for election to the Knesset.

**Our guiding policies are as follows:**
Eretz Israel belongs to the Jewish people. Peace between Israel and the Arab countries will be attained via disengagement between the two peoples: the Jewish people in Eretz Israel, and the Arabs in the Arab countries. Exchanges of population will therefore be executed between Israel and the Arab countries. Most of the Jews from the Islamic countries have already moved to Israel; now we must work to move the Arab population out of the Judea, Samaria, and Gaza areas to the Arab countries.

## 11.  The PROGRESSIVE LIST FOR PEACE Platform, 1988 [Excerpts]

The Palestinian question is the crux of the prolonged conflict between the two peoples of this land, and the principles agreed upon outline the means for solving this conflict and paving the way for a just and comprehensive Israeli-Palestinian and Israeli-Arab peace.

**The following are our principles:**
1) The insurance of equal national and civil rights for the Jewish and Palestinian citizens of Israel within its boundaries of June 4, 1967; the implementation of a determined struggle against all aspects of national discrimination and racism;

---

*The HOMELAND Movement is led by General (Res.) Rehavam Ze'evi.

and the safeguard of these rights by means of a democratic constitution to be written for the State of Israel. This constitution will ensure the complete equality of all citizens of Israel, be they Jews or Arabs, Westerners or Orientals, men or women, religious or non-religious.

2) A mutual recognition of the right of both peoples—the Jewish-Israeli and the Palestinian-Arab—to national self-determination. The implementation of this principle requires Israeli evacuation from all the territories occupied in the 1967 war, including East Jerusalem, and the abolition of the occupation and all its implications. These territories should be returned to their legitimate owner, the Arab-Palestinian people, for the purpose of establishing there an independent Palestinian State alongside the State of Israel. The two states will maintain relations of peaceful neighborhood.

3) The mutual recognition between Israel and the future Palestinian State; the withdrawal of Israeli Forces from the occupied territories, and the peace treaty will be the outcome of negotiations between the government of Israel and the sole legitimate Representative of the Palestinian people, the Palestine Liberation Organization (PLO).

1) **The peace process: basic position.**
   A real Middle East peace process has yet to begin. The main obstacle is the rejectionist policy of the Israeli government, which does not recognize the Palestinian people's national rights—in particular, the right to establish an independent Palestinian state.

2) **An International Peace Conference.**
   An International Conference for peace in the Middle East should be convened with the participation of the five permanent members of the UN Security Council, Israel, the PLO and all other states who are party to the conflict.

3) **A Palestinian state.**
   An independent Palestinian state should be established, side-by-side with Israel. It would include *all* the Palestinian territories occupied by Israel in 1967, and its capital would be East Jerusalem.

4) **Negotiations with the PLO.**
   Negotiations on a political settlement are impossible without the participation of the Palestinian people. The Palestinian people have one, only one, representative: the Palestinian Liberation Organization (PLO).

5) **The Jordanian Option.**
   A Jordanian option for peace does not exist, has never existed and it never will. All talking and all "plans" based on this imaginary "option" are merely attempts to circumvent the Palestinian people and deny its right to a state of its own.

6) **Territories vital to Israel.**
   Vital to Israel is peace not territories. All talking about territories—such as the

West Bank, Gaza and the Golan Heights—as being "vital to Israel" is merely a cover for annexation plans.

7) **Annexations.**
All annexations should be opposed, and the annexation of East Jerusalem and of the Golan Heights should be annulled. Jerusalem, a city of two peoples and three religions, should be physically united under a divided sovereignty. East Jerusalem would be the capital of Palestine, West Jerusalem—the capital of Israel.

## 12.  The RATZ Party Platform, 1988*

### The Future Is In Peace
Peace is Israel's highest aspiration and a necessary condition for its secure existence.

The peace agreement between Israel and Egypt cannot remain an isolated phenomenon for long. Without similar agreements between Israel and its other neighbors, peace with Egypt will not last.

Two peoples live in the Land of Israel—the Jewish people and the Arab-Palestinian people. Both have natural and historical rights to this land. Therefore, the alternatives are clear: either compromise and partition, or endless war.

The long and bitter dispute between Israel and the Palestinians is presently the focus of the Middle East conflict. Our right to self-determination will be neither secure nor complete until the Palestinians are able to exercise the same right.

The Palestinian uprising in the occupied territories—the revolt of a people struggling for its rights and its freedom—cannot be suppressed by force. Without an effective peace initiative, the vicious circle of uprising and suppression will be exacerbated.

In the absence of peace, the next war is inevitable. Each war in this region is more difficult than the previous ones.

### Peace Is On The Way
Israel calls upon all the Arab states to start peace negotiations immediately, in any form or framework, in order to reach a settlement to the conflict by mutual-agreement.

Israel recognizes the Arab-Palestinian people's right to self-determination, and demands that the PLO recognize Israel's right to a secure and sovereign state, so that the PLO can represent the Arab-Palestinian people in peace negotiations while ending acts of hostility.

---

* RATZ is the Civil Rights and Peace Movement

The Arab-Palestinian people will choose the form of its self-determination. Whatever its decision—a federation, a confederation or an independent state—Israel will accept and honor that choice.

The territories occupied in 1967, which have been under military rule ever since, place a heavy burden on Israel, and endanger its democratic existence without being necessary to its national security. Therefore within the framework of a peace agreement, Israel will be willing to gradually withdraw from the West Bank and the Gaza Strip. These areas will be demilitarized to minimize any threats to Israel's security. Other security arrangements will be agreed upon between the two sides as needed.

The Jewish settlements are an obstacle to peace; thus the establishment of new settlements and the expansion of existing ones must be opposed. The peace agreement that will determine the sovereignty of the West Bank and the Gaza Strip, will also resolve the fate of these settlements.

Jerusalem—the capital of the State of Israel—shall not be divided again. In determining the final status of Jerusalem, the peace agreement will take into consideration the special religious and national attachments to the city.

**The I.D.F. is Israel's Security**

The Israel Defense Forces are among the best in the world, and they constitute the strongest guarantee of Israel's security.

The IDF is the army of the Israeli people and therefore should not be involved in a war whose nature is political, rather than defensive.

In this period of growing racist and aggressive nationalism, the IDF has a special duty to adhere to even higher standards of morality and ethics, and to function strictly according to the rule of law.

The policing duties, imposed upon the IDF in the occupied territories, endanger its values and high standards of conduct.

The IDF's deterrent capability, which was badly harmed during the Lebanon War and the current Palestinian uprising, must be restored. The IDF will not regain its deterrent capability through sporadic and fruitless actions but rather through the systematic development of advanced technologies and weapons' systems, original and updated combat strategies, and upgrading the level of the individual soldier.

**Until Peace Comes**

In order to advance the peace process and to improve its prospects for success, Israel agrees to interim agreements including Palestinian autonomy in the occupied territories.

The autonomy concept will be practical and effective only if Israel announces its intention to withdraw from the territories after the interim period, upon the signing of a final peace agreement, and if the Palestinians extend their recognition to the State of Israel.

Political activity in the West Bank and the Gaza Strip is a necessary condition for the normalization of life in these areas. Such activity will ease tensions; bring a measure of relative calm to the intifadah; reduce Israeli involvement in the territories to the bare minimum; and develop local leadership. Free municipal elections are now a vital step towards transferring civil authority into Palestinian hands.

Israeli military forces should be stationed outside of heavily populated areas—the cities and the refugee camps—so as to ensure the safety of main roads and other strategic points, without interfering in the daily life of the residents.

Collective punishment—curfews, area closures, closing down schools and stores, and mass detention—does not stop the uprising but rather exacerbates it. The deterrence and punishment system must adhere to the principle of punishing only the offenders for their acts.

Israel's rule of law is being undermined by repeated human rights violations in the occupied territories, and by the formation of two different judicial systems—one for Jews and one for Arabs. Efforts to restore order do not justify mass administrative detention, demolition of houses, deportations, and other punitive actions without due process of law, in violation both of international covenants and the Universal Declaration of Human Rights. Israel must conduct its rule over the West Bank and the Gaza Strip in accordance with Israeli law, international law and the rules of natural justice.

## 13.  The SHAS Party Platform, 1988 [Excerpts]*

### Jerusalem
The movement sees the holy city of Jerusalem as the eternal capital of the Jewish people. Everything will be done to secure Jerusalem's uniqueness and its character as the spiritual-scholarly center for the entire Jewish people.

### Foreign and Defense Policy
The borders of Israel were stipulated in our holy Bible and the longing for a return to Zion and a greater Israel has never ceased. It is, however, the duty of Israel's leaders to persist in putting an end to the bloodshed in the region through negotiations for peace.

The movement will work to prevent the recruitment of girls for military, or other forms of national service. The movement will prevent any obstruction in the postponement of military service for the yeshiva student whose knowledge is his art, because the yeshiva is "the nursery of the nation's soul."

---

* SHAS is the Torah Observing Sepharadim Party

## 14.   The TEHIYA Party Platform, 1988 [Excerpts]*

### The Land of Israel

The exclusive and eternal right to the Land of Israel lies with the Jewish people. This right is anchored in the heritage of the Jewish People and the Zionist vision.

This right cannot be surrendered, abrogated or transferred under any condition. No government has the authority to yield up any portion of the Land of Israel whatsoever.

Any political solution that includes the withdrawal from portions of the Land of Israel under our control is summarily invalid.   We will oppose all forms of territorial compromise or plans for autonomy.

Tehiya will continue to struggle in the Knesset as in the past to legislate the Law of Sovereignty that will apply Israel's sovereignty over Judea, Samaria and Gaza—(a law that was defeated three times by the combined votes of the Likud and Labor).

On the day that the Law of Sovereignty will be passed the name of the state will be changed from "Israel" to "Eretz-Yisrael"—the Land of Israel.

### Jerusalem

The fight over Jerusalem is not over.   United Jerusalem is not only the capital of Israel but is still at the front line that must be fortified and strengthened—diplomatically, security-wise, economically and demographically—in the face of enemies and "friends" who cast their eye over Jerusalem.

The Jerusalem Law (proposed by **Tehiya** in 1980) will be carried out fully.

Financial support will be directed on behalf of construction, industry and commerce in order to strengthen Jerusalem's economic status.

The Old City will be a Jewish city without displacing any Arab loyal to Jewish rule and without harming any of the Holy Places of other religions, whose rights will be honored.

We will increase the number of Jews living in all the quarters of the Old City.

We will renew and renovate the Old City alleyways that they will not serve as a security risk for Jews and tourists and to assure a safe passage to the Western Wall and the Temple Mount.

### Security

The essence of the conflict between Israel and its neighbors is not a Palestinian state but the desire of the Arabs to destroy the State of Israel.

---

* The TEHIYA Party is the Zionist Revival Movement

Israel's defense policy must be one of deterrence together with the strengthening of its arms arsenal. The IDF, as an army of defense and liberation, must be ready for a surprise war and to prepare the political-military aims in case of a preventive war.

**Tehiya** will act to halt the destructive attempts of movements and groups in Israel to malign the morality of the IDF, projecting it as an "army of repression and occupation" in Judea and Samaria and thus strike at the IDF's major strength—the motivation of its officers and soldiers.

Information activities in the army will be increased with the goal of deepening the Zionist-national education.

We will act to return to the IDF its deterrence in Judea and Samaria and thereby return to Jews the security to travel everywhere throughout the Land of Israel.

We will act to deepen the natural and traditional alliance between Jewish settlements and the IDF. To ease the burden on the IDF and to increase the security of the Jewish residents of Judea and Samaria, a settlement police force will be established under the auspices of the IDF, the sole responsible body in the sphere of the use of force or any security activity in Judea and Samaria.

**Tehiya** will campaign for clemency for Jewish prisoners who, out of security distress, erred in acting unlawfully, who were sentenced according to the law and are today eligible of clemency beyond the strict custom of the law.

An emphasis will be placed on the technological development of defense production such as the Lavie project which will bring about a renewed upswing for industry and defense and aid the IDF's deterrence capability.

An act of refusal to serve anywhere and any act of political subversion in the IDF will be severely punished and offenders will face increased penalties.

The politicization of the IDF will be halted and its officers will be asked to stop the improper habit of making political pronouncements. The IDF is the army of the people and must execute the decisions of the government.

## Peace

The aim of the Zionist State of Israel is the realization of the right of the Jewish people to all portions of the Land of Israel under our control; peace is an instrument in the attainment of that aim.

The policy of "peace for land" is a retreat from a Zionist and national approach and dangerous for our existence. Moreover, the willingness of all Israeli governments since the establishment of the state to surrender portions of the Land of Israel not only did not bring about peace, nor bring one Arab element to the negotiating table but, to the opposite, brought about wars.

A peace agreement with any Arab state will be made solely on the basis of "peace for peace" including the acquiescence of the Arab state to Israeli control over all portions of the Land of Israel now administered by Israel.

The Kingdom of Jordan, established by the British in 1922 on 75% of historic

Palestine and most of whose population and government are "Palestinian" Arabs is today the Palestinian state. But if this state initiates a war against Israel, the territories it loses will not be returned.

The continuation and expansion of Jewish settlements in Judea and Samaria is not an obstacle to peace but, rather the best guarantee for peace for the more "facts" are created, the more the dream of a Palestinian state will fade and the Arab states will become reconciled to the reality of the existence of Israel.

### The "Intifadah"

The "intifadah" did not break out in a vacuum. The political and military stammering of the Likud/Labor government regarding Judea and Samaria encouraged its eruption and continues to help it along today.

It is not only necessary but also possible to break the intifadah if we face its two aspects; the political and the military. Only a two-pronged approach can bear fruit and achieve the goal of breaking the uprising. The Arabs of Judea and Samaria must understand that the violence will bring them only damage and loss. Their situation will worsen. Their rights will be effected, their institutions closed and at the opposite pole, Jewish settlement will grow and flourish and the number of Jews throughout the Land of Israel will increase. For example:

> a new settlement site will be set up at a trouble spot: instigators and rioters, when they realize that the very act they do brings down upon them irreparable damage, they will think twice. As opposed to the political goals of the intifadah leadership, **Tehiya** sets forth these aims:

a) a clear and forthright message that Israel will never leave Judea and Samaria.

b) backing this message up, a renewed campaign of settlement to create new and immovable facts on the ground.

c) systematic acts to prevent the establishment of a Palestinian state in the area of Judea and Samaria.

In the security field, **Tehiya** views the intifadah as a continuation of the Arab wars that have attempted to liquidate the State of Israel. The violence of the intifadah must and can be broken through military and police means:

a) an unceasing and non-yielding war against the leadership and the terrorist organizations wherever they are;

b) legislation that will prevent exchanges of terrorists such as the Jabril exchange;

c) full implementation of the law prohibiting unauthorized meetings with PLO agents, a law initiated by **Tehiya;**

d) cancellation of the juridical reality that terrorists can appeal to the High Court of Justice;

e) in severe cases, the death penalty should be applied;

f) alteration of "open-fire" instructions in instances of self-defense to include stone throwers;

g) expulsion of terrorists including those allowed to stay in Israeli-controlled territory from the Jabril exchange;

h) punishments of deterrence including, in certain cases, of a collective nature;

i) temporary and permanent closures of associations, institutions, organizations, journals, information centers, universities and schools serving as focii of incitement and terrorist activity;

j) wide access roads will be built through the casbahs in the centers of the cities with alternate housing to be provided for the evacuees;

k) relocation of security nuisances exploited by terrorists for attacks on the roads;

l) mosques serving as cover for terrorists and centers for rioters will not be considered as sanctuaries and will pass to army or police supervision.

## 15. The TZOMET Party Platform, 1988 [Excerpts]*

Tzomet sees the solution to the Palestinian problem as lying to the east of the Jordan River, and will so propose in peace negotiations. The inhabitants of the refugee camps located within Eretz Israel will be rehabilitated in the Arab countries as part of any peace agreement, and the Jews who still reside in the Arab countries will come to Israel.

Any Arab in Eretz Israel who operates either on behalf of the terrorist organizations or at his/her own behest to subvert the state, shall be considered an enemy; his/her Israeli citizenship (if s/he has such) shall be revoked and property confiscated, and s/he shall be deported.

The Arab population of Eretz Israel must know that their presence in the country depends upon their full obedience to the laws of the country, and in case of insurrection, they run the risk of losing their citizenship and being transferred beyond the country's borders.

The Arabs of Judea and Samaria are Jordanian citizens living in Eretz Israel. Even once the entire area of Judea and Samaria is annexed to the State of Israel, the Arab population there will remain citizens of Jordan. The Arabs in the Gaza Strip will likewise become Jordanian citizens, or else retain their present status, following the annexation of the Gaza Strip to Israel.

The State of Israel will facilitate emigration by Arab inhabitants of Israel to any location of their choosing.

---

* TZOMET [Junction], the Movement of Zionist
Renewal is led by General (Res.) Raphael Eytan

# Palestinian Documents

## 1. Statement Issued by the Palestine Liberation Organization Rejecting U.N. Resolutions 242, Cairo, 23 November, 1967

Having studied the British resolution adopted by the Security Council on the Israeli aggression against Arab territories of June 1967, the Palestine Liberation Organization, in behalf of the Palestinian people, hereby defines its attitude to the said resolution as follows:

1. The resolution as a whole is in the nature of a political declaration of general principles, and is more like an expression of international intentions than the resolution of an executive power. Its treatment of the question of the withdrawal of Israeli forces is superficial, rather than being a decisive demand. It leaves Israel many loopholes to justify her continued occupation of Arab territories, and may be interpreted as permitting her to withdraw from such territories as she chooses to withdraw from and to retain such areas as she wishes to retain.

2. The resolution more than once refers to Israel's right to exist and to establish permanent, recognized frontiers. It also refers to Israel's safety and security and to her being freed from all threats, and, in general to the termination of the state of belligerency with her. All this imposes on the Arab countries undertakings and a political and actual situation which are fundamentally and gravely inconsistent with the Arab character of Palestine, the essence of the Palestine cause and the right of the Palestinian people to their homeland. This resolution completely undermines the foundations of the principles announced by the Khartoum Summit Conference held after the aggression.

3. The resolution ignores the right of the refugees to return to their homes, dealing with this problem in an obscure manner which leaves the door wide open to efforts to settle them in the Arab countries and to deprive them of the

exercise of their right to return, thereby annulling the resolutions adopted by the United Nations over the past twenty years.

4. The resolution recognizes the right of passage through international waterways, by which it means the Suez Canal and the Gulf of Aqaba. Granted that the Canal is an international waterway, this right cannot be exercised by a state which has engaged in usurpation and aggression, especially inasmuch as this usurpation and aggression were directed against an Arab country. The Gulf of Aqaba constitutes Arab internal waters, and its shores include a coastal area belonging to Palestine occupied by Israel through an act of usurpation and aggression. The principle of freedom of innocent passage is not applicable to the Gulf of Aqaba, especially as regards Israel.

5. The resolution includes provisions for the sending on a mission of a personal representative of the Secretary-General of the United Nations. This is no more than a repetition of unsuccessful attempts in the past, beginning with the dispatch of Count Bernadotte and ending with the formation of the International Conciliation Commission. All these attempts provided Israel with repeated opportunities to impose the *fait accompli* and to engage in further aggression and expansion.

6. The resolution as a whole validates Israel's attitude and her demands and disappoints the hopes of the Arab nation and ignores its national aspirations. The conflicting interpretations of the resolution made by members of the Security Council have weakened it even further, and it is not too much to say that the resolution is a political setback at the international level following the military setback which has befallen the Arab homeland.

For these reasons, the most important of which is that the Security Council ignores the existence of the Palestinian people and their right of self-determination, the Palestine Liberation Organisation hereby declares its rejection of the Security Council resolution as a whole and in detail. In so doing it is not only confirming a theoretical attitude, but also declaring the determination of the Palestinian people to continue their revolutionary struggle to liberate their homeland. The Palestine Liberation Organization is fully confident that to achieve this sacred aim the Arab nation will meet its national responsibilities to mobilize all its resources for this battle of destiny, with the support of all forces of liberation throughout the world.

## 2. The Palestinian National Covenant, 1968

This Covenant will be called The Palestinian National Covenant *(al-mithaq al-watani al-filastini).*

*Article 1:* Palestine is the homeland of the Palestinian Arab people and an integral part of the great Arab homeland, and the people of Palestine is a part of the Arab nation.

*Article 2:* Palestine with its boundaries that existed at the time of the British mandate is an integral regional unit.

*Article 3:* The Palestinian Arab people possesses the legal right to its homeland, and when the liberation of its homeland is completed it will exercise self-determination solely according to its own will and choice.

*Article 4:* The Palestinian personality is an innate, persistent characteristic that does not disappear, and it is transferred from fathers to sons. The Zionist occupation, and the dispersal of the Palestinian Arab people as a result of the disasters which came over it, do not deprive it of its Palestinian personality and affiliation and do not nullify them.

*Article 5:* The Palestinians are the Arab citizens who were living permanently in Palestine until 1947, whether they were expelled from there or remained. Whoever is born to a Palestinian Arab father after this date, within Palestine or outside it, is a Palestinian.

*Article 6:* Jews who were living permanently in Palestine until the beginning of the Zionist invasion will be considered Palestinians. [For the dating of the Zionist invasion, considered to have begun in 1917.]

*Article 7:* The Palestinian affiliation and the material, spiritual and historical tie with Palestine are permanent realities. The upbringing of the Palestinian individual in an Arab and revolutionary fashion, the undertaking of all means of forging consciousness and training the Palestinian, in order to acquaint him profoundly with his homeland, spiritually and materially, and preparing him for the conflict and the armed struggle, as well as for the sacrifice of his property and his life to restore his homeland, until the liberation of all this is a national duty.

*Article 8:* The phase in which the people of Palestine is living is that of national *(watani)* struggle for the liberation of Palestine. Therefore, the contradictions among the Palestinian national forces are of secondary order which must be suspended in the interest of the fundamental contradiction between Zionism and colonialism on the one side and the Palestinian Arab people on the other. On this basis, the Palestinian masses, whether in the homeland or in places of exile *(mahajir)*, organizations and individuals, comprise one national front which acts to restore Palestine and liberate it through armed struggle.

*Article 9:* Armed struggle is the only way to liberate Palestine and is therefore a strategy and not tactics. The Palestinian Arab people affirms its absolute resolution and abiding determination to pursue the armed struggle and to march forward towards the armed popular revolution, to liberate its homeland and return to it [to maintain] its right to a natural life in it, and to exercise its right of self-determination in it and sovereignty over it.

*Article 10:* Fedayeen action forms the nucleus of the popular Palestinian war of liberation. This demands its promotion, extension and protection, and the mobilization of all the masses and scientific capacities of the Palestinians, their organization and involvement in the armed Palestinian revolution and cohesion in the national *(watani)* struggle among the various groups of the people of Palestine, and between them and the Arab masses, to guarantee the continuation of the revolution, its advancement and victory.

*Article 11:* The Palestinians will have three mottoes: national *(wataniyya)* unity: national *(qawmiyya)* mobilization and liberation.

*Article 12:* The Palestinian Arab people believes in Arab unity. In order to fulfill its role in realizing this, it must preserve, in this phase of its national *(watani)* struggle, its Palestinian personality and the constituents thereof, increase consciousness of its existence and resist any plan that tends to disintegrate or weaken it.

*Article 13:* Arab unity and the liberation of Palestine are two complementary aims. Each one paves the way for realization of the other. Arab unity leads to the liberation of Palestine, and the liberation of Palestine leads to Arab unity. Working for both goes hand in hand.

*Article 14:* The destiny of the Arab nation, indeed the very Arab existence, depends upon the destiny of the Palestine issue. The endeavour and effort of the Arab nation to liberate Palestine follows from this connection. The people of Palestine assumes its vanguard role in realizing this sacred national *(qawmi)* aim.

*Article 15:* The liberation of Palestine, from an Arab viewpoint, is a national *(qawmi)* duty to repulse the Zionist, Imperialist invasion from the great Arab homeland and to purge the Zionist presence from Palestine. Its full responsibility falls upon the Arab nation, peoples and governments, with the Palestinian Arab people at their head. For this purpose, the Arab nation must mobilize all its military, human, material and spiritual capacities to participate actively with the people of Palestine in the liberation of Palestine. They must especially in the present stage of armed Palestinian revolution, grant and offer the people of Palestine all possible help and every material and human support, and afford it every sure means and opportunity enabling it to continue to assume its vanguard role in pursuing its armed revolution until the liberation of its homeland.

*Article 16:* The liberation of Palestine, from a spiritual viewpoint, will prepare an atmosphere of tranquillity and peace for the Holy Land in the shade of which all the Holy Places will be safeguarded, and freedom of worship and visitation to all will be guaranteed, without distinction or discrimination of race, colour, language or religion. For this reason, the people of Palestine looks to the support of all the spiritual forces in the world.

*Article 17:* The liberation of Palestine, from a human viewpoint, will restore to the Palestinian man his dignity, glory and freedom. For this, the Palestinian

Arab people looks to the support of those in the world who believe in the dignity and freedom of man.

*Article 18:* The liberation of Palestine, from an international viewpoint is a defensive act necessitated by the requirements of self-defence. For this reason the Arab people of Palestine, desiring to befriend all peoples, looks to the support of the states which love freedom, justice and peace in restoring the legal situation to Palestine, establishing security and peace in its territory, and enabling its people to exercise national *(wataniyya)* sovereignty and national *(qawmiyya)* freedom.

*Article 19:* The partitioning of Palestine in 1947 and the establishment of Israel is fundamentally null and void, whatever time has elapsed, because it was contrary to the wish of the people of Palestine and its natural right to its homeland, and contradicts the principles embodied in the Charter of the UN, the first of which is the right of self-determination.

*Article 20:* The Balfour Declaration, the Mandate document, and what has been based upon them are considered null and void. The claim of a historical or spiritual tie between Jews and Palestine does not tally with historical realities nor with the constituents of statehood in their true sense. Judaism, in its character as a religion of revelation, is not a nationality with an independent existence. Likewise, the Jews are not one people with an independent personality. They are rather citizens of the states to which they belong.

*Article 21:* The Palestinian Arab people, in expressing itself through the armed Palestinian revolution, rejects every solution that is a substitute for a complete liberation of Palestine, and rejects all plans that aim at the settlement of the Palestine issue or its internationalization.

*Article 22:* Zionism is a political movement organically related to world Imperialism and hostile to all movements of liberation and progress in the world. It is a racist and fanatical movement in its formation: aggressive, expansionist and colonialist in its aims; and fascist and Nazi in its means. Israel is the tool of the Zionist movement and a human and geographical base for world Imperialism. It is a concentration and jumping-off point for Imperialism in the heart of the Arab homeland, to strike at the hopes of the Arab nation for liberation, unity and progress.

*Article 23:* The demands of security and peace and the requirements of truth and justice oblige all states that preserve friendly relations among peoples and maintain the loyalty of citizens to their homelands to consider Zionism an illegitimate movement and to prohibit its existence and activity.

*Article 24:* The Palestinian Arab people believes in the principles of justice, freedom, sovereignty, self-determination, human dignity and the right of peoples to exercise them.

*Article 25:* To realize the aims of this covenant and its principles the Palestine Liberation Organization will undertake its full role in liberating

Palestine.

*Article 26:* The Palestine Liberation Organization, which represents the forces of the Palestinian revolution, is responsible for the movement of the Palestinian Arab people in its struggle to restore its homeland, liberate it, return to it and exercise the right of self-determination in it. This responsibility extends to all military, political and financial matters, and all else that the Palestine issue requires in the Arab and international spheres.

*Article 27:* The Palestine Liberation Organization will cooperate with all Arab States, each according to its capacities, and will maintain neutrality in their mutual relations in the light of and on the basis of, the requirements of the battle of liberation and will not interfere in the internal affairs of any Arab State.

*Article 28:* The Palestinian Arab people insists upon the originality and independence of its national *(wataniyya)* revolution and rejects every manner of interference, guardianship and subordination.

*Article 29:* The Palestinian Arab people possesses the prior and original right in liberating and restoring its homeland and will define its position with reference to all states and powers on the basis of their positions with reference to the issue [of Palestine] and the extent of their support for [the Palestinian Arab people] in its revolution to realize its aims.

*Article 30:* The fighters and bearers of arms in the battle of liberation are the nucleus of the popular army, which will be the protecting arm of the gains of the Palestinian Arab people.

*Article 31:* This organization shall have a flag, oath and anthem, all of which will be determined in accordance with a special system.

*Article 32:* To this covenant is attached a law known as the fundamental law of the Palestine Liberation Organization, in which is determined the manner of the organization's formation, its committees, institutions, the special functions of every one of them and all the requisite duties associated with them in accordance with this covenant.

*Article 33:* This covenant cannot be amended except by a two-thirds majority of all the members of the National Assembly of the Palestine Liberation Organization in a special session called for this purpose.


## 3. Palestine National Assembly Political Resolutions, 17 July, 1968

### II. Political Decisions:

(A) The Palestinian Cause at Palestinian Level:
Inasmuch as a definition of the objectives of the Palestinian struggle, the

methods it adopts and the instruments it employs, is essential for the unification of that struggle under one leadership, the Assembly, having debated the matter, endorses the following definitions:

*First — Objectives:*

1.  The liberation of the entire territory of Palestine, over which the Palestinian Arab people shall exercise their sovereignty.
2.  That the Palestinian Arab people have the right to establish the form of society they desire in their own land and to decide on their natural place in Arab unity.
3.  The affirmation of the Palestinian Arab identity, and rejection of any attempt to establish tutelage over it.

*Second — Methods:*

1.  The Palestinian Arab people have chosen the course of armed struggle in the fight to recover their usurped territories and rights. The current phase in their armed struggle started before the defeat of June, 1967 and has endured and escalated ever since. Moreover, despite the fact that this struggle renders a service to the entire Arab nation at the present stage, insofar as it prevents the enemy from laying claim to a *status quo* based on surrender, and insofar as it keeps the flame of resistance alive and maintains a climate of war, preoccupies the enemy and is an object of concern to the entire world community, that struggle is nevertheless a true and distinct expression of the aspirations of the Palestinian Arab people and is inspired by their objectives. In addition, we feel bound to declare quite frankly that this struggle goes beyond the scope of what it has become customary to call "the elimination of the consequences of the aggression", and all other such slogans, for the objectives of this struggle are those of the Palestinian Arab people, as set out in the preceding paragraph. The fight will not cease; it will continue, escalate and expand until final victory is won, no matter how long it takes and regardless of the sacrifices involved.
2.  The enemy has chosen *Blitzkrieg* as the form of combat most suitable to him, in view of the tactical mobility at his command which enabled him, at the moment of battle, to unleash forces superior to those deployed by the Arabs. The enemy chose this method in the belief that a lightning victory would lead to surrender, according to the pattern of 1948, and not to Arab armed resistance. In dealing with it, we must adopt a method derived from elements of strength in ourselves and elements of weakness in the enemy.
3.  The enemy consists of three interdependent forces:
    a)  Israel.
    b)  World Zionism.
    c)  World imperialism, under the direction of the United States of America.

Moreover, it is incontestable that world imperialism makes use of the forces of reaction linked with colonialism.

If we are to achieve victory and gain our objectives, we shall have to strike at the enemy wherever he may be, and at the nerve centres of his power. This is to be achieved through the use of military, political and economic weapons and information media, as part of a unified and comprehensive plan designed to sap his strength, scatter his forces, destroy the links between them and undermine their common objectives.

4. A long-drawn out battle has the advantage of allowing us to expose world Zionism, its activities, conspiracies, and its complicity with world imperialism and to point out the damage and complications it causes to the interests and the security of many countries, and the threat it constitutes to world peace. This will eventually unmask it, bringing to light the grotesque facts of its true nature, and will isolate it from the centres of power and establish safeguards against its ever reaching them...

5. An information campaign must be launched that will throw light on the following facts:

a) The true nature of the Palestinian war is that of a battle between a small people, which is the Palestinian people, and Israel, which has the backing of world Zionism and world imperialism.

b) This war will have its effect on the interests of any country that supports Israel or world Zionism.

c) The hallmark of the Palestinian Arab people is resistance, struggle and liberation, that of the enemy, aggression, usurpation and the disavowal of all values governing decent human relations.

6. A comprehensive plan must be drawn up to fuse the Arab struggle and the Palestinian struggle into a single battle. This requires concentrated ideological, information and political effort that will make it clear to the Arab nation that it can never enjoy peace or security until the tide of Zionist invasion is stemmed, and that its territory will be occupied piecemeal unless it deploys its resources in the battle, not to mention the extent to which the Zionist presence constitutes a drain on its resources and an impediment to the development of its society.

Palestinian action regards the Arab nation as a reserve fund of political, financial and human resources on which it can draw, and whose support and participation will make it possible to fight the successive stages in the battle.

7. The peoples and governments of the Arab nation must be made to understand that they are under an obligation to protect the Palestinian struggle so that it may be able to confront the enemy on firm ground and direct all its forces and capabilities to this confrontation, fully assured of its own safety and security. This obligation is not only a national duty, it is a necessity deriving from the fact that the Palestinian struggle is the vanguard in the defence of all

Arab countries, Arab territories and Arab aspirations.

8.   Any objective study of the enemy will reveal that his potential for endurance, except where a brief engagement is concerned, is limited. The drain
on this potential that can be brought about by a long-drawn out engagement
will inevitably provide the opportunity for a decisive confrontation in which
the entire Arab nation can take part and emerge victorious.

It is the duty of Palestinians everywhere to devote themselves to making the
Arab nation aware of these facts, and to propagating the will to struggle. It is
also their duty to endure, sacrifice and take part in the struggle.

*Practical Application in the Field of Armed Struggle:*

1.   The Palestine Liberation Organization is a grouping of Palestinian
forces in one national front for the liberation of the territory of Palestine
through armed revolution.

2.   This Organization has its Charter which defines its objectives, directs its
course and organizes its activities. The Organization also has a National Assembly and an Executive Command chosen by the National Assembly, which
Command forms the supreme executive authority of the Organization, as
defined by its constitution.

The Executive Committee shall draw up a unified general plan for Palestinian action at all levels and in all fields. This plan is to be implemented
through the instruments of the revolution gathered in this Council, each of
which must abide by the role assigned to it by this plan and by the decisions of
the Command.

Proposals for the Creation of a Spurious Palestinian Entity:

The Zionist movement along with imperialism and its tool, Israel, is seeking
to consolidate Zionist aggression against Palestine and the military victories
won by Israel in 1948 and 1967, by establishing a Palestinian entity in the territories occupied during the June, 1967 aggression. This entity would owe its
existence to the legitimization and perpetuation of the State of Israel, which is
absolutely incompatible with the Palestinian Arab people's right to the whole
of Palestine, their homeland. Such a spurious entity would in fact be an Israeli
colony and would lead to the liquidation of the Palestinian cause once and for
all to the benefit of Israel. The creation of such an entity would, moreover,
constitute an interim stage during which Zionism could evacuate the territory
of Palestine occupied during the June 5 war of its Arab inhabitants, as a
preliminary step to incorporating it in the Israeli entity. In addition, this
would lead to the creation of a subservient Palestinian Arab administration in
the territories occupied during the June 5 war on which Israel could rely in
combating the Palestinian revolution. Also to be considered in this context are
imperialist and Zionist schemes to place the Palestinian territories occupied
since June 5 under international administration and protection. For these

reasons, the National Assembly hereby declares its categorical rejection of the idea of establishing a spurious Palestinian entity in the territory of Palestine occupied since June 5, and of any form of international protection. The Assembly hereby declares, moreover, that any individual or party, Palestinian Arab or non-Palestinian, who advocates or supports the creation of such a subservient entity is the enemy of the Palestinian Arab people and the Arab nation.

*(C) — Palestinian Struggle in the International Field:*

The Security Council Resolution and the Peaceful Solution:

1. The Security Council resolution of November 22, 1967 is hereby rejected for the following reasons:

a) The resolution calls for the cessation of the state of hostility between the Arab nations and Israel. This entails the cessation of the state of hostility, free passage for Israeli shipping through Arab waterways, and an Arab commitment to put an end to the boycott of Israel, including the abrogation of all Arab legislation regulating that boycott. The cessation of the state of hostility also entails the relaxation of economic pressure on Israel, so that the door would be opened to an invasion of all Arab markets by Israeli goods, inasmuch as such goods could circulate, be traded in and flood the market regardless of whether or not economic agreements were concluded.

b) The resolution calls for the establishment of secure frontiers to be agreed upon with Israel. Apart from the fact that secure and mutually agreed frontiers involves the de facto recognition of Israel, and an encroachment on the unconditional right of the Palestinian Arab people to the whole of Palestine, which is totally unacceptable to the Arab countries, if the Arab countries agreed to secure frontiers for Israel, they would be committed to protecting Israel's security, after having first suppressed commando action, put an end to the Palestinian revolution and prevented the Palestinian Arab people and the Arab masses from discharging their sacred national duty to liberate and recover Palestine and to terminate the Zionist and imperialist presence there.

c) The resolution calls for the establishment of permanent peace between the Arab nations and Israel. This would have the following injurious consequences:

1. It would provide Israel with security and stability at domestic, Arab and international levels. This would throw the doors wide open to the Zionist movement, allowing it to entice large sections of Jewish communities in Western Europe and America into immigrating and settling in Israel. These communities have held back from doing so for the past twenty years because of misgivings about the security, future and continued existence of Israel.

2.   It would eliminate the reasons, including Arab influence, for which friendly nations have so far not allowed their Jewish citizens to immigrate to Israel, notably in the case of the millions of Jews in the Soviet Union.

3.   It would eliminate all reasons for which many countries friendly to the Arabs have refrained from recognising Israel or from dealing with Israel at all levels.

4.   It would strengthen the human and geographic barrier that separates the Arab homeland into east and west. This would be extremely injurious, as it would prevent the achievement of even partial, not to mention total, Arab unity.

5.   It would be a severe blow to the Palestinian armed struggle and to the Arab liberation movement whose objectives are liberation, social progress and unity. The consequence of this would be increased imperialist influence in the Arab homeland, accompanied by increased Zionist influence, in view of the organic political, economic, and other ties linking Zionism to imperialism. Arab policy would, as a result, be forced away from the line of neutrality and non-alignment.

6.   The resolution ignores the Palestine problem, which it does not even mention by name, and ignores the rights of the Arabs of Palestine to their territories and their homeland, referring to both as if the problem was merely a problem of refugees. This presages the final liquidation of the issue of Palestine as an issue of a land and of a homeland.

7.   It was not only territory that the Arab nation lost in June, 1967. Arab dignity and self-confidence were also involved. A peaceful solution might restore some, or even all of those territories to the Arabs, but it would not restore their dignity and self-confidence.

8.   The Arab nation must come to realise that it is under an inescapable obligation to defend its homeland, and not to rely on others for its protection or for the recovery of its territories and its rights. If the Arab countries accept a peaceful solution they will be renouncing the Arab will and agreeing that their destiny should be under the control of the Great Powers.

9.   A peaceful solution might lead the Arab countries to imagine themselves to be secure. Israel would certainly exploit this illusion to strike again, after creating a political situation more to her liking, and thus realize her expansionist designs on the territories of the Arab countries.

For these reasons the National Assembly calls on the newly elected Executive Committee to draft a comprehensive plan operative at Arab popular, official and international levels, designed to frustrate any political solution of the Palestine problem.

The Assembly affirms, moreover, that the aggression against the Arab nation, and the territories of that nation, began with the Zionist invasion of Palestine in 1917, and that, as a consequence "the elimination of the conse-

quences of the aggression" must signify the elimination of all such consequences since the beginning of the Zionist invasion and not merely since the
June, 1967 war. The slogan "the elimination of the consequences of the aggression" is therefore rejected in its present form, and must be replaced by the
slogan, "the destruction of the instrument of aggression". Thus, and thus
alone, will "peace based on justice" be established.

## 4. Palestine National Council Statement, 13 July, 1971

[Statement issued 13 July by the Palestine National Council on its ninth
session]

The Palestine National Council held its ninth session in Cairo from 7 to 13
July 1971 during extremely difficult conditions and amid increasing plotting
against the Palestine revolution. The council members discussed the demands
of the current stage of the Palestine revolution, at a time when the Jordanian
authorities are attacking the Palestine revolution bases and our heroic fighters
in 'Ajlun, Jarash, and the Ghazzah camp.

In addition to tackling the mission entrusted to it, the council adopted the
measures to deal with the situation. These measures have been announced.

The ninth session of the Palestine National Council was distinguished by
several progressive steps toward national unity. The following are the most
important:

1 — In its new form, the council is more representative of the various sectors
than past councils. All the fedayeen organizations without exception participated in it and representation of the trade union organizations has been increased.

2 — The council has affirmed the national unity formula as approved by the
eighth session and has adopted new practical decisions to achieve unity of the
revolution forces in all fields of command, organization, training, arms, and
combat orders. It has also approved the establishment of a unified council for
information and a unified system of collection and expenditure of funds.

3 — On the basis of and in complete response to these stands, the Executive
Committee was elected as supreme command of the Palestine revolution.
Representation of the various fighting organizations on the committee has
been widened to insure more collective action and bar individual action and
also to insure the participation of all forces in facing the dangerous conditions
threatening the Palestine revolution and people.

The first point the council dealt with was the serious situation facing the
revolution in Jordan. In view of the Jordanian regime's insistence on striking
and foiling the revolution, the council censured the policy of suppression and
terrorization exercised by the Jordanian authorities and the regional
fanaticism resulting from this policy. This policy has produced and continues

to produce serious negative effects on the cause of national unity in the Palestine-Jordanian arena, which in practice lead to the weakening of the masses' unity and the denial of the revolution's right to represent the Palestine people and to seek the realization of their aspirations for the liberation of their usurped land.

The council has censured the successive obstacles that the Jordanian authorities have been placing to prevent the fighters from proceeding to their occupied land. These obstacles include beseiging of the revolution bases and intercepting the revolution's supply convoys and armed men returning from military operations in the occupied territory.

The council condemns the recurrent disregard for the Palestine revolution's right to exercise its basic duty, and declares that several aspects of this duty have been regulated by the Cairo and Amman agreements. The council demands adherence to these agreements. It calls on the Arab States that signed these agreements to take the stands they pledged to take in order to guarantee implementation of the two agreements. It also calls on these states to stop financial aid to the Jordanian authority, which continues to disregard and violate these agreements, and to use this aid for its intended purpose — the liberation of Palestine from the imperialist onslaught against Arab land.

The council supports the efforts by the Jordanian nationalist forces to establish a cohesive nationalist front working to reinforce the march of the Palestine revolution and protect it against anyone plotting against it.

While it finds itself committed to the defense of the national rights of our people in Jordan and seeks to consolidate the unity of the two banks as one of its objectives, the Palestine revolution affirms through its National Council that the consolidation of this unity cannot take place through the practices of the Jordanian authorities, which encourage separatist and regional learnings, but only through strengthening the cohesion of the people and unifying their efforts for the sake of liberation. This cohesion and unity should be based on national and democratic foundations.

The second point the council dealt with was the danger of a political settlement. The council discussed the extensive current efforts to implement a settlement, particularly the activities of U.S. imperialism in imposing itself on the Middle East and creating deceptive conditions leading only to the liquidation of the palestine issue.

The council reaffirms its stand based on the permanent upholding of the Palestine people's full rights to liberate their land through popular armed struggle and on the reaffirmation of categorical rejection of all capitulationist settlements and of plans that harm the natural and historic rights of the Palestine people, including UN Security Council resolution No. 242 of 22 November 1967.

The Palestine National Council expresses the will of the Palestine people and their determination to continue their armed struggle until the achievement of all their national aims, despite the viciousness of the conspiratorial onslaught against the Palestine revolution.

While it is continuing its struggle and sacrifices, the Palestine revolution always looks to the Arab masses and their nationalist forces and the national liberation movements in the world to perform their duty in one of the most ferocious battles waged by a peaceful people against Zionist and imperialist forces and their agents in the Arab area.

## 5. Palestine National Council, Political Program, 12 January, 1973

### 1. The Palestinian Theatre

1. To continue the battle and the armed struggle for the total liberation of the soil of the Palestinian homeland and for the establishment of the democratic Palestinian society in which all citizens will enjoy the right to work and to a decent life, so that they may live in equality, justice and brotherhood, and which will be opposed to all kinds of ethnic, racial and religious fanaticism.

This society will also ensure freedom of opinion, assembly, demonstration, and the freedom to strike and form political and trade union institutions and to practise all religions, inasmuch as this Palestinian society will be part of the comprehensive unified Arab democratic society.

2. To struggle against the settlement mentality and the projects it harbours either for the liquidation of our people's cause as far as the liberation of our homeland is concerned or for the distortion of this cause by proposals for entities and for the establishment of a Palestinian State — in part of the territory of Palestine; and to resist these proposals through armed struggle and through mass political conflict linked with it.

3. To strengthen the links of national unity and unity in struggle between the masses of our countrymen in the territory occupied in 1948 and those in the West Bank, the Gaza Strip and outside the occupied territory.

4. To oppose the policy of evacuating the Arab population of the occupied territory, and to resist with violence the building of settlements and the Judaization of parts of the occupied homeland.

5. To mobilize the masses in the West Bank, the Gaza Strip and the whole of Palestinian territory, to arm them to continue the struggle, and to increase their ability to struggle against Zionist settler colonialism.

6. To assist the organizations of the masses to resist the attempts by the Histadrut to attract Arab workers to join it and strengthen it, and with this end in view to support the trade unions of Palestine and Jordan and to resist

the effort of the Zionist parties to establish Arab branches in the occupied territories.

7. To support the endurance of workers working in Arab territory and institutions, to provide safeguards to protect them against the temptation to work in enemy projects, and to resist the enemy's attempts to take over or smash Arab production projects.

8. To support the peasant masses and to promote national economic and cultural institutions in the occupied homeland, so as to attach Arab citizens to the land and check the trend to emigrate, and to resist Zionist economic and cultural aggression.

9. To show concern for the situation of our countrymen in the territory occupied in 1948 and to support their struggle to maintain their Arab national identity, to take up their problems, and to assist them to join the struggle for liberation.

10. To show concern for the interests of the masses of our people working in different parts of the Arab homeland, and to make every effort to ensure that they obtain economic and legal rights equal to those of the citizens of the societies they live in, especially as regards the right to work, compensation, indemnities, freedom for Palestinian action, both political and cultural, and freedom of travel and movement within the framework of maintaining their Palestinian personality.

11. To promote and develop the role of the Palestinian woman in the struggle at social, cultural and economic levels and to ensure that she plays her part in all fields of the struggle.

12. To show concern for the situation of our countrymen in the camps and to make every effort to raise their economic, social and civilizational levels, and to train them to manage their own affairs.

13. To regard anyone who cooperates with the enemy, joins him in his crimes against the people and the homeland, or neglects the established historical and natural rights of the people and the homeland, as a fit object for attack by the revolution, as regards both his person and his possessions, whether these be money, immovable property or land.

14. To show concern for the situation of our masses who live abroad as emigrants, and to make every effort to link them with their cause and their revolution.

15. In its official Arab relations the Liberation Organization concentrates on protecting the interests of Palestinian citizens in the Arab homeland and expressing the political will of the Palestinian people, and the Palestinian revolution, within the framework of the Palestine Liberation Organization, will continue to be the highest command of the Palestinian people; it alone speaks on their behalf on all problems related to their destiny, and it alone, through its organizations for struggle, is responsible for everything related to

the Palestinian people's right to self-determination.

16. Therefore the Palestine Liberation Organization consists of all the sections of the armed Palestinian revolution, of the Palestinian mass organizations, both trade union and cultural, and of all nationalist groups and personalities that believe that armed struggle is the principal and fundamental course to the liberation of Palestine, and that adhere to the Palestinian National Charter.

## II.  The Jordanian-Palestinian Theatre

It is the duty of the Jordanian-Palestinian national front to direct the struggle of the two people towards the following strategic objectives:

a)  To establish a national democratic regime in Jordan, and to liberate the whole of Palestinian soil from Zionist occupation and establish a national democratic regime that will ensure the protection of the national sovereignty of the Jordanian and Palestinian peoples and guarantee the renewal and restoration of the unity of the two banks on the basis of regional national equality between the two peoples. In this way it will fully safeguard the historical national rights of the Palestinian people and the established national rights of the two peoples, ensure their joint national development at economic, social and civilizational levels and strengthen brotherly relations and equality between the two peoples through equality of constitutional, legal, cultural and economic rights and by placing the human, economic and civilizational resources of each of the two peoples at the disposal of their joint development.

b)  To weld the struggle of the Palestinian and Jordanian peoples to the struggle of the Arab nation for national liberation and against imperialist projects designed to impose solutions and situations involving surrender of the Arab homeland, the struggle to liquidate the Zionist and imperialist presence in all its forms, economic, military and cultural, and all forces linked thereto, which play the role of go-between for neo-colonialist infiltration.

So that the Jordanian-Palestinian national front may be effectively established and be strengthened and grow, it is essential that an immediate start should be made on activating all kinds of day-by-day mass struggle, so that the movement of the masses on behalf of both their day-by-day- and general demands may lead to the emergence among them of organized leaderships and organizations that will express the interests of their various groups — leaderships and organizations that have been absent from the day-by-day battles of the masses in recent years.

Also, for the objectives of the Jordanian-Palestinian national front to be achieved, there must be a long and hard struggle, so that through day-by-day struggle and partial battles the masses may surmount all regional and social obstacles and be fused in a joint struggle. Such a struggle will enable the masses to play their part as fighters for the national cause, and will expose the subservient royalist regime whose basic support lies in the tribal relationships and regional bigotry which it employs as a mask to disguise its subservience to Zionism and colonialism.

The Jordanian-Palestinian national front which is striving to establish a national democratic regime in Jordan and to liberate Palestine must activate and direct the popular struggle on all the different fronts of the clash between the masses and the Jordanian authorities, employing appropriate slogans in the day-by-day battles, so as to forge a permanent link between these partial battles and its general objectives and so as to direct both the bayonets with which it fights and the consequences it achieves into the channel of the general struggle of the two peoples.

The Palestine Liberation Organization adopts the programme of action in the Jordanian theatre and submits it as a subject for serious comradely dialogue with the organizations in Jordan which are engaged in the struggle for the building of the Jordanian-Palestinian front, and which must engage in struggle:

1. To mobilize and organize the masses with a view to establishing a national democratic regime which will ensure that the revolution in Jordan is provided with all the means necessary for engaging in mass struggle.

2. To bring the members of the Jordanian people into the armed struggle against the Zionist enemy, this being a right at both local and Arab levels, and essential for the protection of Eastern Jordan in particular.

3. To struggle to achieve freedom for the Palestinian revolution to act in and from Jordan and to establish its bases in Jordanian territory, and to expose the conspiracies of the subservient regime and its misrepresentations in this connection, and to ensure protection by the masses of combatants who operate from and return to the territory west of the River.

4. To resist terrorist police measures and all aggressions against the freedoms and rights of citizens to expose and resist imperialist capitalists; to show up and resist the infiltration of Zionist political, economic and cultural domination; to resist all increases in taxes and prices; to expose the laws which disseminate a spirit of separatism between members of the two peoples; to disclose the deliberately repressive role of the army; to show up subservient and hostile elements and plans directed against the masses and other Arab countries instead of such efforts being directed to the battle of liberation; to make every effort to activate mass struggles of all kinds; to encourage the struggle of the workers, the agricultural, industrial, commercial and nationalist sectors, the peasants, the Beduin, the wage-earners, the intellectuals and students.

5. To make every effort to ensure that the Jordanian-Palestinian front has an active share in a single front of struggle to strengthen relations between the Palestinian and Jordanian national struggle and world revolutionary forces.

### 6. Statements by General Secretary of the PDFLP Naif Hawatmah Defending the Establishment of a Palestinian National Authority in Territories Liberated from Israeli Occupation, 24 February, 1974

We know that American imperialism seeks a settlement of surrender and liquidation to the detriment of the rights of the people of Palestine, a settlement that would, once again, expose our people to the dangers of dispersal and subjection, caught between Zionism, expansionism and subjection to the Hashimites. Imperialism believes that the interests of the Palestinian people are best served within the framework of Zionist expansion, with Israel not returning to the borders of June 4, 1967, and that they are best served by dissolving the Palestinian people once more in the proposed United Kingdom and in places of their exile in the Arab countries and abroad. Imperialism further presents schemes for dissolution, resettlement and relocation in the countries of the region. Our position with regard to these schemes is clear.

Yes, we are Arabs but we are, at the same time, Palestinians. Just as every Arab people has a full right to an independent national existence, so the Palestinian people too has a full right to an independent national existence and to fight all schemes which agree with American imperialist schemes, for these latter seek to obliterate our national existence and refuse to grant it prior recognition.

Knowing all this, we still find opportunistic currents of thought which at times counsel wisdom and at others call upon us to remain within the framework of nationalist unity, such as took place with the regime of King Hussein. We also find leftist opportunist Palestinian opinions attempting to obscure their true positions, which do not in the least lead to a clash with imperialism, Zionism and Arab and Hashimite reaction, by putting forth bombastic slogans ("The whole of Palestine at once", "Palestinian territories liberated from occupation are to go to the regime of King Hussein"). Our answer to these currents of thought is: They shall not succeed in directing the attention of the revolution from its objectives at this stage. Our people, our revolutionary bases and all the vanguard of the revolution know well that they must submit a pragmatic programme which puts the Palestinian people as a whole, the revolution as a whole and the movement for Arab national liberation against the American-Israeli-Hashimite solution of surrender and liquidation, together with any other solution presented by any Arab country which ignores our people's national and historic rights at this stage.

... We are fighting to end occupation and to stand effectively against imperialist solutions. We are fighting for our people's right to establish their national authority on their own land after the occupation has been ended. We also maintain that the logic of events in the world today demands that we inflict more defeats upon imperialism and racist regimes, whether in Palestine, Rhodesia or South Africa. And while these regimes came into existence at a certain historical stage, our own age is witnessing the end of that stage. We are entering upon a new age whose basic feature is further defeats for imperialism, local reaction and racist regimes. To inflict further defeats upon these regimes, we must follow a correct international policy which enables our people to become self-reliant and stand on its own land. This is a necessary step if the struggle is to continue on the long path ahead, the path of a long popular war of liberation. We know the road well and shall not allow these opportunistic currents, both of the left and the right, both in the Palestinian and in the Arab fields, to lead us astray by endangering the rights of our people and making us surrender.

These opportunistic forces do not have a leg to stand on. At times they claim that a national authority would not have the means necessary for economic subsistence and would not be able to survive on the West Bank and in the Gaza Strip. To these opportunists we answer that we are not at the stage of searching for a homeland. Over there is our homeland, even if it is a desert with nothing but thorn and sand. There is our homeland, whether it has the economic means of survival or not, although we should bear in mind that the economic potentialities of Palestinian territories occupied after 1967 are greater and more promising than those of many African and Asian countries, for example, Democratic Yemen. If we adopt this lunatic theory, half of Africa and the greater part of Asia would have been bound to fight to keep imperialism in their countries until such time as their economic means of subsistence would have allowed them to become independent.

## 7.   Palestine National Council, Political Program, 8 June, 1974

Proceeding from the Palestinian national charter and the PLO's political programme which was approved during the 11th session held from 3 to 12 January 1973, believing in the impossibility of the establishment of a durable and just peace in the area without the restoration to our Palestinian people of all their national rights, foremost of which is their right to return to and determine their fate on all their national soil, and in the light of the study of the political circumstances which arose during the period between the Council's previous and current sessions, the Council decides the following:

1.   The assertion of the PLO position regarding Resolution 242 is that it obliterates the patriotic [wataniyah] and national [qawmiyah] rights of our people and deals with our people's cause as a refugee problem. Therefore, dealing with this resolution on this basis is rejected on any level of Arab and international dealings, including the Geneva conference.

2. The PLO will struggle by all means, foremost of which is armed struggle, to liberate Palestinian land and to establish the people's national, independent and fighting authority on every part of Palestinian land to be liberated. This necessitates making more changes in the balance of power in favor of our people and their struggle.

3. The PLO will struggle against any plan for the establishment of a Palestinian entity the price of which is recognition, conciliation, secure borders, renunciation of the national right, and our people's deprivation of their right to return and their right to determine their fate on their national soil.

4. Any liberation step that is achieved constitutes a step for continuing [the efforts] to achieve the PLO strategy for the establishment of the Palestinian democratic State that is stipulated in the resolutions of the previous national councils.

5. To struggle with the Jordanian national forces for the establishment of a Jordanian-Palestinian national front whose aim is the establishment of a national democratic government in Jordan — a government that will cohere with the Palestinian entity to be established as a result of the struggle.

6. The PLO will strive to establish a unity of struggle between the two peoples [the Palestinian and Jordanian peoples] and among all the Arab liberation movement forces that agree on this programme.

7. In the light of this programme, the PLO will struggle to strengthen national unity and to elevate it to a level that will enable it to carry out its duties and its patriotic [wataniyah] and national [qawmiyah] tasks.

8. The Palestinian national authority, after its establishment, will struggle for the unity of the confrontation states for the sake of completing the liberation of all Palestinian soil and as a step on the path of comprehensive Arab unity.

9. The PLO will struggle to strengthen its solidarity with the socialist countries and the world forces of liberation and progress to foil all Zionist, reactionary and imperialist schemes.

10. In the light of this programme, the revolutionary command will work out the tactics that will serve and lead to the achievement of these aims.

A recommendation has been added to the political programme. The recommendation stipulates that the Executive Committee implement this programme. Should a fateful situation connected with the future of the Palestinian people arise, the Council will be called to hold a special session to decide on it.

During today's meeting, the Council approved by a large majority the political statement that asserted the Palestinian people's rallying around the PLO which is the only legitimate representative of the Palestinian people. The statement says: In the period from the time the Palestinian National Council convened its session from 3 to 12 January 1973 to the current session, from 1 to 8 July 1974, the Arab area witnessed a number of important and fateful events and developments, most prominent of which was the October war and its results which have strengthened the position and role of the Arab nation and which has been a step on the path of defeating the imperialist-Zionist enemy camp. In the wake of this, a sharp contradiction emerged between the Arab liberation movement and the enemies of our Arab nation who are trying to go around the achievements of the October war and to impose a political settlement at the expense of our Palestinian people's rights and jeopardize their future struggle and the struggle of our Arab nation.

On the level of our people's and revolution's movement, the Palestinian revolution emerged as a principal active force during and after the war. The movement of our masses inside and outside the occupied territories assumed important and new dimensions in confronting the imperialist, Zionist and reactionary plots by escalating the political and military struggle, especially after the bases of the Palestinian national front expanded in the occupied territories and after the PLO command expanded its political move resulting in a wide-scale world recognition of the PLO as the only legitimate representative of the Palestinian people. At the same time, the isolation of the Jordanian reactionary monarchical regime intensified, especially after the October war had revealed the regime's role of collusion with the enemies of our people and nation. This regime was not only content with its refusal to participate in the war but it also prevented the Palestinian revolution forces from playing their military role across Jordanian territory and it killed and captured many of our fighters.

In confronting these circumstances, our Palestinian people rally around the PLO, the only legitimate representative of the Palestinian people who adhere to the national charter, the political programme adopted during the 11th session, all the resolutions of the national councils, and the phasic political programme that is approved during this session. Therefore, they are determined to continue the struggle, to escalate the armed struggle and to strongly resist the Zionist occupation, the Jordanian reactionary monarchical regime's plots represented by the united Arab kingdom plan, and the imperialist schemes parallel to it.

Our people also resist any settlement that jeopardizes their rights and cause, and struggle to preserve their revolution's gains. In order to achieve this, the National Council believes that the following must be emphasized:

1. Achieving the unity of the aims of the Palestinian revolution by promoting the formulas for Palestinian national unity and implementing all the resolutions in respect in the various political, military, information and financial fields will be conducive to escalating the armed struggle, to achieving the unity of our Palestinian people inside and outside the homeland and to reinforcing the Palestinian national front inside the homeland so that it will

express our people's struggle and be a framework for all their struggles, especially because this front, as a fundamental base of the PLO inside the occupied territories, has played an effective role during the period following the October war. This calls for giving strong support to it and to all the popular establishments and organizations operating through it.

2.  As the Palestinian national movement is part of the Arab liberation movement, this calls for exerting all efforts to achieve greater cohesion between the Palestinian struggle and the Arab struggle and for achieving an advanced form of joint action between them through the Arab front participating in the Palestinian revolution and for translating the requirements of the fateful stage through which it is passing. This also calls for coordination among the nationalist Arab regimes to place them face to face with their responsibilities toward the cause of our Palestinians. It is necessary here to refer to the significance of the Arab solidarity which emerged during the October war and the need for its continuation and for adherence to the resolutions of the Arab summit conference held in Algiers in November 1973.

3.  The stand of the socialist countries and the forces of liberation and progress in the world in supporting the cause of our people and nation requires further efforts to achieve stronger cohesion with these forces. In this regard, we should concentrate on expanding the front of our friends.

4.  The Lebanese arena, which the Palestinian revolution is eager to keep strong and cohesive by strengthening the form of existing relations between the Lebanese and Palestinian peoples and out of the Palestinian people's care for the need to preserve the peace and security of fraternal Lebanon, requires constant and strong support by all the Arab countries to enable it to continue to stand fast against the enemy's aggression and expansionist ambitions and to enable our brothers in southern Lebanon and our people in their camps to stand fast against the enemy's aggression and his attempts to hit this steadfastness.

5.  The reactionary monarchical regime in Jordan, with all the history of its policy which is hostile to our people and nation, and which refused to fight the October war on the side on our Arab nation, is now plotting in complete coordination with Zionism and imperialism with the aim of liquidating and obliterating the Palestinian national character and in order to redominate our people in the occupied territory at any price. To confront this, the struggle must be intensified to isolate this regime and to make national democratic rule in Jordan.

6.  The Palestinian National Council appeals to all peoples and governments in the world which love peace and justice and all forces of liberation and progress in the world to struggle against the activities of world Zionism [seeking] further immigration of world Jewry to occupied Palestine which contributes to the strengthening of the colonialist Zionist military establishment,

the achievement of Zionist aggressive and expansionist dreams and the continued Zionist defiance of our people's national rights and of the national [qawni] and patriotic [watani] entity of our people and Arab nation.

At the conclusion of its 12th session, the Council addresses a greeting of esteem to the martyrs of the Palestinian revolution and the Arab nation and a greeting of appreciation to our fighters and strugglers in the enemy prisons and in the prisons in Jordan. The Council hails the Egyptian and Syrian armies, the forces of the Palestinian revolution and the Arab countries which took part in the October war of liberation with their forces or their resources. The Council also values the solidarity of the Palestinian masses who have been under the occupation since 1948, the masses of the Arab nation linked with the struggle of the Arab armies as well as the alliance of the Arab liberation movement with the Palestinian revolution and the Arab front participating in the Palestinian revolution, particularly the Lebanese national and progressive movement.

The Council stresses its appreciation for the role of the socialist camp, particularly the Soviet Union and the PRC, in supporting the struggle of the Palestinian people and the Arab nation. The Council also appreciates the support of the Islamic countries, the nonalined countries, the African countries and the world liberation and progressive movements for the Palestinian people.

The Council regards the victory scored by the Vietnamese people as an incentive to our revolution and to all liberation movements in the world in order to further intensity the struggle to achieve the will of our people in liberation, progress and self-determination.

## 8. Statement by the PFLP Announcing Its Withdrawal from the Executive Committee of the PLO. Beirut, 26 September, 1974 [Excerpts]

We therefore wish to set before our Arab and Palestinian masses the reasons for our withdrawal from the Executive Committee so that the situation may be absolutely clear and that we may perform our duty of opening up the revolutionary road to the movement of the masses.

1.  After the October war an international and Arab situation came into existence which was favourable to a so-called political settlement of the Arab-Israeli conflict. America was the power most enthusiastic for this settlement and made every effort to impose it, relying first and foremost on the approval of Egyptian and Saudi reaction. It was perfectly clear what results this settlement was likely to lead to: As the price for submitting Israel to every American pressure, America would be allowed to increase her influence and safeguard her interests in our territory. The price Israel would be paid for withdrawing

from all Arab territory would be support for her economy and armed forces, the reinforcement of her security and stability and steps towards the consolidation of the legality of her existence in the area. It is no longer possible to dispute this picture now that its consequences have taken tangible form before the eyes of the masses of our people.

In the light of this situation the Palestinian revolution should have submitted to all the Palestinian and Arab masses a precise analysis of this picture and its consequences, insisting that they be laid bare, fought against, and made known to all, so that our revolution might be the torch of the revolution for millions of Arabs rather than a cover for the laxness and surrenderism of certain of their rulers.

Since the October war ended and the picture of the imperialist liquidationist conspiracy has taken shape, the Front has called on the Palestine revolution to announce its analysis of the new political situation, to declare its opposition to the liquidationist settlement and to affirm that it would not permit the Liberation Organization to be used as a cover for the laxness of certain surrenderist Arab regimes. The Palestinian revolution should have revealed the truth about the Geneva conference and the consequences it would lead to. It should have placed itself unambiguously outside the framework of this liquidationist settlement and continued to mobilize the masses to continue fighting for dozens of years, whatever is involved.

The value of the Palestine revolution is that it should provide the pattern in accordance with which the masses of the whole Arab nation can settle their conflict with their enemies by force of arms through a people's war of liberation, rather than through laxness and surrenderism under the auspices of a balance of forces which means that the price paid for every piece of land we recover is higher than the value of the land itself.

The Front has made every effort to ensure that this period should provide an opportunity to strengthen the revolution and consolidate its national unity on the basis of the unambiguous and definitive rejection of the Geneva conference and the liquidationist conspiracy, and of continuing on the line of revolution. But the leadership of the Organization has persistently evaded defining any attitude, on the pretext that they have not been officially invited to attend the Geneva conference, although there has been every indication that many international and Arab forces want to contain the Organization and to frustrate its revolution by forcing it on to the road of surrender.

The Organization has maintained an attitude that is no attitude thereby losing its vigour for revolutionary action and influence in Palestinian, Arab and international circles.

2. On the eve of the twelfth session of the Palestine National Council which was held in Cairo last June, the leadership of the Liberation Organization started talking about national unity and its importance at this stage. It

showed that it was prepared to move from an attitude which was no attitude to an attitude of (temporary) refusal to attend the Geneva conference, employing a deceitful "tactic" aimed at suggesting to the forces that reject the settlement that it knew the truth about the liquidationist conspiracy but that it wanted to frustrate it by cunning rather than by confrontation. Profoundly aware as it is of its responsibility for taking any opportunity to achieve national unity seriously in this critical situation, the Front decided to show that such an opportunity existed and to see what actual consequences it would lead to. This is why it gave its approval to the ten points, although in fact they were a compromise and threadbare formula for national unity, after having placed on record in the minutes of the session our understanding of them to the effect that they involved rejection of the Geneva conference and set the Liberation Organization outside the framework of the liquidationist settlement.

At the end of the twelfth session of the Palestine National Council it was clear what the surrenderist leaderships intended by their acceptance of the ten point programme. They regarded it as legalizing their pursuit of the course of deviation and surrender. They started to interpret it as they wished, later making statements as they wished, in a manner incompatible with the Organization's charter and with the resolutions adopted at the sessions of its National Council, including those adopted at the eleventh and twelfth sessions.

The deception was disclosed and it became clear that what the surrenderist forces were talking of was the tactics misleading fellow-travellers and the masses, rather than misleading the enemy.

We continued to struggle within the framework of the Liberation Organization and the Executive Committee in the hope of establishing a sound understanding of the Organization's charter and the resolutions of its national councils, but it daily became clearer to us that the leadership of the Organization was involved in the settlement operation and hope to impose it on the masses piecemeal and to continue on their course of deviation step by step in the hope of ultimately confronting the masses with a fait accompli.

3. The Leadership of the Liberation Organization started to represent the possibility of its attending the Geneva conference — "the conspiracy" — as a great victory won by it over Jordanian reaction and Israel. They also started to talk of the possibility of coordination with the reactionary subservient regime in Jordan if certain conditions were met, thereby coming into conflict with the resolutions of previous sessions of the National Council which insisted that the regime should be overthrown and a democratic nationalist regime established in its place. At a session of the Executive Committee held before the issue of the Egypt-Jordan joint communique, the Executive Committee decided to coordinate with the subservient regime of Jordan on condition that it recognized firstly the Palestine Liberation Organization as the sole legitimate representative of the Palestinian people and, secondly, the Cairo

Agreements, although these agreements did not prevent the subservient regime from destroying the resistance movement and putting an end to its overt presence. It might have been thought that the Palestine revolution had not had a long history of experience of this regime, and that the National Council had never adopted resolutions calling for the regime to be blockaded until it collapsed totally.

4. It was not long after the National Council had ended its session, and the leadership of the Organization had interpreted its resolutions in so lax a manner that in fact they became the loyal followers of the surrenderist regimes, that the Egyptian-Jordanian communique came as a cruel slap in the face both to the leadership and its policy.

The issue of such a communique gave the leadership of the Organization a chance to face up to all the policies it had pursued since the October war in general and since the twelfth session of the National Council in particular. Three organizations represented on the Executive Committee of the Liberation Organization therefore presented a memorandum to the leadership of the Organization calling on it to conduct an operation of reappraisal and criticism, with a view to learning the lessons taught by past experience and defining its relations with the Arab regimes in the light of their attitudes to the imperialist liquidation proposal, and on the basis of reliance mainly on the masses of our Arab nation rather than on the agents of America in the area. But the leadership of the Organization persisted in its deviationist view of things. Heedless of the truth of the points raised in the memorandum, it refused to accept them, and maintained its previous policy. It conceived the idea that its principle battle was not that against the imperialist liquidation solution with a view to frustrating it and to insisting on the continuation of Palestinian and Arab combat, but a battle over its share in the settlement operation as compared with the share of the subservient regime in Jordan.

5. The leadership of the Liberation Organization is now trying to make our masses forget their essential national battle, which concerns the imperialist liquidationist settlement and the need to frustrate it. It is making every effort to distract the attention of the masses from their principal battle so that they may devote all their attention to the battles of the leadership of the Liberation Organization with the subservient Jordanian regime over its share in the settlement. It wants the masses to rally sympathetically around it if the Jordanian regime gets a larger share at its expense, and to applaud it if it gets a larger share at the expense of the subservient Jordanian regime — and all this within the framework of the imperialist liquidationist settlement.

The leadership of the Liberation Organization is at present making every effort to make out that the battle is exclusively between Israel and Jordan on the one hand and the Liberation Organization on the other and to suggest that in that battle it is entitled to seek any allies and to enjoy the support of the masses. We hereby declare most emphatically that this is a grave distortion of the battle and of the understanding of the conflicts. The battle is a continuous one and is being fought between Israel, Jordan, Arab reaction and the surrenderist forces on the one hand and the Palestinian and Arab revolution on the other, and no power on earth will be able to keep this fact from the masses.

The Palestinian masses do not want the leadership of the Liberation Organization to win their battles against Jordanian reaction within the framework of the settlement, so that it may compete with the subservient regime in negotiating with the Israeli enemy.

The Palestinian masses want the leadership of the Liberation Organization to win their battles against all the forces that are seeking to impose this imperialist liquidation settlement so that they may continue their popular revolution against Israel, the subservient regime in Jordan, imperialism and all reactionary surrenderist forces.

6. The leadership of the Liberation Organization ignored the memorandum of the three organizations, and when it had had time enough to anaesthetize and deceive the masses it attended a tripartite conference in Cairo. This the advocates of a settlement represented as being a major victory for the Liberation Organization, although the communique issued after the conference makes no mention of opposition to disengagement on the Jordanian front; indeed, it stresses the need for coordination with the other Arab countries, including the subservient regime in Jordan.

It was to be expected that the subservient rulers in Amman would make such an outcry and would suspend Jordan's political activities until the Arab summit conference meets. It can be easily understood in the context of the formula of competing over the share each party will obtain as a result of this settlement which America is conducting with the aim of imposing "permanent" stability in the area, while ensuring the continued existence of Israel and safeguarding her security and stability.

Our masses will not allow deceptions and play-acting to be foisted on them again. They are not prepared to allow our battle to be restricted to the framework that the leadership of the Liberation Organization is now establishing so as to ensure sympathy for itself if it gets a smaller share in the settlement and applause if it gets a greater share.

7. Nor is this all. The leadership of the Liberation Organization has denied that any secret contacts have been made with America, the enemy of peoples. But we have established that such secret contacts have been made, without the knowledge of the masses. We submitted these facts to the Central Council of the Liberation Organization at its recent session, and we now place them before the Palestinian and Arab masses.

We regard this as amounting to secret contacts with the imperialist enemy without the knowledge of the masses of the revolution and its forces and bases.

If some commands have started to regard such contacts as normal and natural, we leave it to the masses to decide their own view and understanding and to make their own appraisal of this matter.

The Popular Front for the Liberation of Palestine, having become acquainted with these facts, would be failing in its duty to the masses if it did not place them at their disposal so that they may judge the situation in the light of them. The time is past when the commands could regard the masses of our people and the bases of their revolution as so many sheep.

8. These are the most important reasons for our withdrawal from the Executive Committee. There are other reasons, but we do not wish, at this juncture, to touch on the organizational and administrative situation of the Liberation Organization. Nor do we wish to consider the repercussions of such a policy on a number of matters, such as the building of shelters, the fortification of the camps in Lebanon, and other issues.

In the light of the above, how can we continue to bear any responsibility within the framework of the Executive Committee?

Our withdrawal from the Executive Committee is now unavoidable.

## 9. Speech by Yasser Arafat to the UN General Assembly, 13 November, 1974

Yasser Arafat, as the Chairman of the Executive Committee of the Palestine Liberation Organization, addressed the United Nations General Assembly on November 13, 1974, during the debate on Palestine. The following is a translation of the speech, originally delivered in Arabic.

Mr. President, I thank you for having invited the Palestine Liberation Organization to participate in the plenary session of the United Nations General Assembly. I am grateful to all those representatives of United Nations member states who contributed to the decision to introduce the question of Palestine as a separate item on the Agenda of this Assembly. That decision made possible the Assembly's resolution inviting us to address it on the question of Palestine.

This is a very important occasion. The question of Palestine is being re-examined by the United Nations, and we consider that step to be as much a victory for the world organization as it is for the cause of our people. It indicates anew that the United Nations of today is not the United Nations of the past, just as today's world is not yesterday's world. Today's United Nations represents 138 nations, a number that more clearly reflects the will of the international community. Thus today's United Nations is more capable of implementing the principles embodied in its Charter and in the Universal Declaration of Human Rights, as well as being more truly empowered to support causes of peace and justice.

Our people are now beginning to feel that change. Along with them, the peoples of Asia, Africa and Latin America also feel the change. As a result, the United Nations acquires greater esteem both in our people's view and in the view of other peoples. Our hope is thereby strengthened that the United Nations may contribute actively to the pursuit and triumph of the causes of peace, justice, freedom and independence. Our resolve to build a new world is fortified — a world free of colonialism, imperialism, neo-colonialism and racism in all its forms, including Zionism.

Our world aspires to peace, justice, equality and freedom. It hopes that oppressed nations, at present bent under the weight of imperialism, may gain their freedom and their right to self-determination. It hopes to place the relations between nations on a basis of equality, peaceful coexistence, mutual respect for each other's internal affairs, secure national sovereignty, independence and territorial unity on the basis of justice and mutual benefit. This world resolves that the economic ties binding it together should be grounded in justice, parity and mutual interest. It aspires finally to direct its human resources against the scourge of poverty, famine, disease and natural calamities, toward the development of productive scientific and technical capabilities to enhance human wealth — all this in the hope of reducing the disparity between the developing and the developed countries. But all such aspirations cannot be realized in a world that is at present ruled by tension, injustice, oppression, racial discrimination and exploitation, a world also threatened with unending economic disaster, wars and crises.

Many peoples, including those of Zimbabwe, Namibia, South Africa and Palestine, among many others, are still victims of oppression and violence. Their areas of the world are gripped by armed struggles provoked by imperialism and racial discrimination. These, both merely forms of aggression and terror, are instances of oppressed peoples compelled by intolerable circumstances into a confrontation with such oppression. But wherever that confrontation occurs it is legitimate and just.

It is imperative that the international community should support these peoples in their struggles, in the furtherance of their rightful causes and in the attainment of their right to self-determination.

In Indo-China the people are still exposed to aggression. They remain subjected to conspiracies preventing them from the enjoyment of peace and the realization of their goals. Although peoples everywhere have welcomed the peace agreements reached in Laos and South Vietnam, no one can say that genuine peace has been achieved, for the forces responsible in the first place for aggression are determined that Vietnam should remain in a state of disturbance and war. The same can be said of the present military aggression against the people of Cambodia. It is therefore incumbent on the international community to support these oppressed peoples, and also to condemn the oppressors for their designs against peace. Moreover, despite the positive stand taken by the Democratic Republic of Korea with regard to a peaceful and just solution of the Korean question, there is as yet no settlement of that question.

A few months ago the problem of Cyprus erupted violently before us. All peoples everywhere shared in the suffering of the Cypriots. We ask that the United Nations continue its efforts to reach a just solution in Cyprus, thereby sparing the Cypriots further war and ensuring peace and independence for them instead. Undoubtedly, however, consideration of the question of Cyprus belongs within that of Middle Eastern problems as well as of Mediterranean problems.

In their efforts to replace an outmoded but still dominant world economic system with a new, more logically rational one, the countries of Asia, Africa, and Latin America face implacable attacks on these efforts. These countries have expressed their views at the special session of the General Assembly on raw materials and development. Thus the plundering, exploitation, and the siphoning off of the wealth of impoverished peoples must be terminated forthwith. There must be no deterring of these peoples' efforts to develop and control their wealth. Furthermore, there is a grave necessity for arriving at fair prices for raw materials from these countries.

In addition, these countries continue to be hampered in the attainment of their primary objectives formulated at the Conference on the Law of the Sea at Caracas, at the population conference and at the Rome food conference. The United Nations should therefore bend every effort to achieve a radical alteration of the world economic system, making it possible for developing countries to advance rapidly. The United Nations must resolutely oppose forces that are trying to lay the responsibility for inflation on the shoulders of the developing countries, especially the oil-producing countries. The United Nations must firmly condemn any threats made against these countries simply because they demand their just rights.

The world-wide armaments race shows no sign of abating. As a consequence, the entire world is threatened with the dispersion of its wealth and the utter waste of its energies. Armed violence is made more likely everywhere. Peoples expect the United Nations to devote itself single-mindedly to putting an end to the armaments race; to convert the vast sums spent on military technology until the stage is reached where nuclear weapons are destroyed, and resources go into projects for development, for increasing production, and for benefiting the world.

And still, the highest tension exists in our part of the world. There the Zionist entity clings tenaciously to occupied Arab territory; the Zionist entity is holding on to the Arab territories is has occupied and persisting in its aggressions against us. New military preparations are feverishly being made. These anticipate another, fifth war of aggression to be launched against us.

Such signs behoove the closest possble watching, since there is a grave likelihood that this war would forbode nuclear destruction and cataclysmic annihilation.

The world is in need of tremendous efforts if its aspirations to peace, freedom, justice, equality and development are to be realized, if its struggle is to be victorious over colonialism, imperialism, neo-colonialism and racism in all its forms, including Zionism. Only by such efforts can actual form be given to the aspirations of all peoples, including the aspirations of peoples whose states oppose such efforts. It is this road that leads to the fulfillment of those principles emphasized by the United Nations Charter and the Universal Declaration of Human Rights. Were the status quo simply to be maintained, however, the world would instead be exposed to the most dangerous armed conflicts, in addition to economic, human and natural calamities.

Despite abiding world crises, despite the powers of darkness and backwardness that beset the world, we live in a time of glorious change. An old world order is crumbling before our eyes, as imperialism, colonialism, neo-colonialism and racism, the chief form of which is Zionism, ineluctably perish. We are witnessing a great wave of history bearing peoples forward into a new world which they have created. In that world just causes will triumph. Of that we are confident.

The question of Palestine is crucial amongst those just causes fought for unstintingly by masses labouring under imperialism and oppression. I am aware that, if I am given the opportunity to address the General Assembly, so too must the opportunity be given to all liberation movements fighting against racism and imperialism. In their names, in the name of every human being struggling for freedom and self-determination, I call upon the General Assembly urgently to give their just causes the same full attention the General Assembly has so rightly given to our cause. Such recognition once given, there will be a secure foundation thereafter for the preservation of universal peace. For only with such peace will a new world order endure in which peoples can live free of oppression, fear, injustice and exploitation. As I said earlier, this is the true perspective in which to set the question of Palestine. I shall now do so for the General Assembly, keeping firmly in mind both the perspective and the goal of a coming world order.

Even as today we address this General Assembly from an international rostrum we are also expressing our faith in political and diplomatic struggle as complements, as enhancements of armed struggle. Furthermore we express our appreciation of the role the United Nations is capable of playing in settling problems of international scope. But this capability, I said a moment ago, became real only once the United Nations had accommodated itself to the living actuality of aspiring peoples, towards which this international organization owes unique obligations.

In addressing the General Assembly today our people proclaims its faith in the future, unencumbered either by past tragedies or present limitations. If, as we discuss the present, we enlist the past in our service, we do so only to light up our journey into the future alongside other movements of national liberation. If we return now to the historical roots of our cause we do so because present at this very moment in our midst are those who, as they occupy our homes, as their cattle graze in our pastures, and as their hands pluck the fruit of our trees, claim at the same time that we are ghosts without an existence, without traditions or future. We speak of our roots also because until recently some people have regarded — and continue to regard — our problem as merely a problem of refugees. They have portrayed the Middle East question as little more than a border dispute between the Arab States and the Zionist entity. They have imagined that our people claim rights not rightfully their own and fight neither with logic nor legitimate motive, with a simple wish only to disturb the peace and to terrorize others. For there are amongst you — and here I refer to the United States of America and others like it — those who supply our enemy freely with planes and bombs and with every variety of murderous weapon. They take hostile positions against us, deliberately distorting the true essence of the problem. All this is done not only at our expense, but at the expense of the American people and its well-being, and of the friendship we continue to hope can be cemented between us and this great people, whose history of struggle for the sake of freedom and the unity of its territories we honour and salute.

I cannot now forego this opportunity of appealing from this rostrum directly to the American people, asking them to give their support to our heroic and fighting people. I ask them wholeheartedly to endorse right and justice, to recall George Washington to mind — heroic Washington whose purpose was his nation's freedom and independence, Abraham Lincoln, champion of the destitute and the wretched, and also Woodrow Wilson whose doctrine of Fourteen Points remains subscribed to and venerated by our people. I ask the American people whether the demonstrations of hostility and enmity taking place outside this great hall reflect the true intent of America's will? What, I ask you plainly, is the crime of the people of Palestine against the American people? Why do you fight us so? Does this really serve your interests? Does it serve the interests of the American masses? No, definitely not. I can only hope that the American people will remember that their friendship with the whole Arab nation is too great, too abiding, and too rewarding for any such demonstrations to harm it.

In any event, in focusing our discussion of the question of Palestine upon historical roots, we do so because we believe that any question now exercising the world's concern must be viewed radically, in the true sense of that word, if a real solution is ever to be grasped. We propose this radical approach as an antidote to an approach to international issues that obscures historical origins behind ignorance, denial and a slavish obedience to the fait accompli.

The roots of the Palestinian question reach back into the closing years of the nineteenth century, in other words, to that period which we call the era of colonialism and settlement and the transition to the eve of imperialism. This was when the Zionist imperialist plan was born: its aim was the conquest of Palestine by European immigration, just as settlers colonized, and indeed raided, most of Africa. This is the period during which, pouring forth out of the West, colonialism spread into the furthest reaches of Africa, Asia, and Latin America, building colonies everywhere, cruelly exploiting, oppressing, plundering the peoples of those three continents. This period persists into the present. Marked evidence of its totally reprehensible presence can be readily perceived in the racism practised both in South Africa and in Palestine.

Just as colonialism and the settlers dignified their conquests, their plunder and limitless attacks upon the natives of Africa and elsewhere, with appeals to a "civilizing mission", so too did waves of Zionist immigrants disguise their purposes as they conquered Palestine. Just as colonialism used religion, colour, race and language to justify the people's exploitation and its cruel subjugation by terror and discrimination, so too were these methods employed as Palestine was usurped and its people hounded from their national homeland.

Just as colonialism used the wretched, the poor the exploited as mere inert matter with which to build and to carry out settler colonialism, so too were destitute, oppressed European Jews employed on behalf of world imperialism and of the Zionist leadership. European Jews were transformed into the instruments of aggression; they became the elements of settler colonialism and racial discrimination.

Zionist ideology was utilized against our Palestinian people: the purpose was not only the establishment of Western-style settler colonialism but also the severing of Jews from their various homelands and subsequently their estrangement from their nations. Zionism is an ideology that is imperialistic, colonialist, racist; it is profoundly reactionary and discriminatory; it is united with anti-Semitism in its tenets and is the other side of the same coin. For when what is proposed is that adherents of the Jewish faith, regardless of their national residence, should neither owe allegiance to their homeland nor live on equal footing with its other, non-Jewish citizens — when that is proposed we hear anti-Semitism being proposed. When it is proposed that the only solution for the Jewish problem is that Jews must alienate themselves from communities or nations of which they have been a historical part, when it is proposed that Jews solve the Jewish problem by immigrating to and settling the land of another people by terrorism and force, this is exactly the same attitude as that of the anti-Semites to the Jews.

Thus, for instance, we can understand the close connection between

Rhodes, who promoted settler colonialism in Southeast Asia, and Herzl, who had colonialist designs upon Palestine. Having received a certificate of good settler conduct from Rhodes, Herzl then turned around and presented this certificate to the British government, hoping thus to secure a formal resolution supporting Zionist policy. In exchange, the Zionists promised Britain an imperialist base on Palestinian soil so that imperial interests could be safeguarded as the most important chief strategic point in the Middle East.

So the Zionist movement allied itself directly with world colonialism in a common raid on our land. Allow me now to present a selection of historical facts about this alliance.

The Jewish invasion of Palestine began in 1881. Before the first large wave of settlers started ariving, Palestine had a population of half a million, most of these Muslims or Christians, and about 10,000 Jews. Every sector of the population enjoyed the religious tolerance characteristics of our civilization.

Palestine was then a verdant land, inhabited by an Arab people in the course of building its life and enriching its indigenous culture.

Between 1882 and 1917 the Zionist movement settled approximately 50,000 European Jews in our homeland. To do that it resorted to trickery and deceit in order to plant them in our midst. Its success in getting Britain to issue the Balfour Declaration demonstrated the alliance between Zionism and colonialism. Furthermore, by promising to the Zionist movement what was not hers to give, Britain showed how oppressive the rule of colonialism was. As it was then constituted, the League of Nations abandoned our Arab people, and Wilson's pledges and promises came to nought. In the guise of a mandate, British colonialism was cruelly and directly imposed upon us. The mandate document issued by the League of Nations was to enable the Zionist invaders to consolidate their gains in our homeland.

In thirty years the Zionist movement succeeded, in collaboration with its colonialist ally, in settling more European Jews on the land, thus usurping the properties of Palestinian Arabs.

By 1947 the number of Jews had reached 600,000; they owned less than 6 per cent of Palestinian Arab land. The figure should be compared with the [Arab] population of Palestine, which at that time was 1,250,000.

As a result of the collusion between the mandatory power and the Zionist movement and with the support of the United States, this General Assembly early in its history approved a recommendation to partition our Palestinian homeland. This took place on November 30, 1947, in an atmosphere of questionable actions and strong pressure. The General Assembly partitioned what it had no right to divide — an indivisible homeland. When we rejected that decision, our position corresponded to that of the real mother who refused to permit Solomon to cut her child in two when the other woman claimed the child as hers. Furthermore, even though the partition resolution granted the colonialists settlers 54 per cent of the land of Palestine, their dissatisfaction with the decision prompted them to wage a war of terror against the civilian Arab population. They occupied 81 per cent of the total area of Palestine, uprooting a million Arabs. Thus, they occupied 524 Arab towns and villages, of which they destroyed 385, completely obliterating them in the process. Having done so, they built their own settlements and colonies on the ruins of our farms and our groves. The roots of the Palestine question lie here. Its causes do not stem from any conflict between two religions or two nationalisms. Nor is it a border conflict between neighbouring states. It is the cause of people deprived of its homeland, dispersed and uprooted, the majority of whom live in exile and in refugee camps.

With support from imperialist and colonialist powers, headed by the United States of America, this Zionist entity managed to get itself accepted as a United Nations member. It further succeeded in getting the Palestine question deleted from the Agenda of the United Nations and in deceiving world public opinion by presenting our cause as a problem of refugees in need either of charity from do-gooders, or settlement in a land not theirs.

Not satisfied with all this, the racist state, founded on the imperialist-colonialist concept, turned itself into a base of imperialism and into an arsenal of weapons. This enabled it to assume its role of subjugating the Arab people and of committing aggression against them, in order to satisfy its ambitions of further expansion in Palestinian and other Arab lands. In addition to the many instances of aggression committed by this entity against the Arab States, it has launched two large-scale wars, in 1956 and 1967, thereby endangering world peace and security.

As a result of Zionist aggression in June 1967, the enemy occupied Egyptian Sinai as far as the Suez Canal. The enemy occupied Syria's Golan Heights, in addition to all Palestinian land west of the Jordan. All these developments have led to the creation in our area of what has come to be known as the "Middle East Problem". The situation has been rendered more serious by the enemy's persistence in maintaining its unlawful occupation and in further consolidating it, thus establishing a beachhead for world imperialism's thrust against our Arab nation. All Security Council decisions and calls by world public opinion for withdrawal from the lands occupied in June 1967 have been ignored. Despite all the peaceful and diplomatic efforts on the international level, the enemy has not been deterred from his expansionist policy. The only alternative open to our Arab nations, chiefly Syria and Egypt, was to expend exhaustive efforts to prepare, firstly, to resist this barbarous armed invasion by force and, secondly, to liberate Arab lands and to restore the rights of the Palestinian people, after all other peaceful means had failed.

Under these circumstances, the fourth war broke out in October 1973, bringing home to the Zionist enemy the bankruptcy of its policy of occupation and expansion and its reliance on the concept of military might. Despite all this, the leaders of the Zionist entity are far from having learned any lesson from their experience. They are making preparations for the fifth war, resorting once more to the language of military superiority, aggression, terrorism, subjugation and, finally, always to war in their dealings with the Arabs.

It pains our people greatly to witness the propagation of the myth that its homeland was a desert until it was made to bloom by the toil of foreign settlers, that it was a land without a people, and that the settler entity caused no harm to any human being. No, such lies must be exposed from this rostrum, for the world must know that Palestine was the cradle of the most ancient cultures and civilizations. Its Arab people were engaged in farming and building, spreading culture throughout the land for thousands of years, setting an example in the practice of religious tolerance and freedom of worship, acting as faithful guardians of the holy places of all religions. As a son of Jerusalem, I treasure for myself and my people beautiful memories and vivid images of the religious brotherhood that was the hallmark of our Holy City before it succumbed to catastrophe. Our people continued to pursue this enlightened policy until the establishment of the State of Israel and their dispersion. This did not deter our people from pursuing their humanitarian role on Palestinian soil. Nor will they permit their land to become a launching pad for aggression or a racist camp for the destruction of civilization, culture, progress and peace. Our people cannot but maintain the heritage of their ancestors in resisting the invaders, in assuming the privileged task of defending their native land, their Arab nationhood, their culture and civilization, and in safeguarding the cradle of the monotheistic religions.

By contrast, we need only mention briefly some instances of Israel's racist attitudes: its support of the Secret Army Organization in Algeria, its bolstering of the settler-colonialists in Africa — whether in the Congo, Angola, Mozambique, Zimbabwe, Rhodesia or South Africa — and its backing of South Vietnam against the Vietnam revolution. One can also mention Israel's continuing support of imperialism everywhere, its obstructionist stand in the Committee of Twenty-four, its refusal to cast its vote in support of independence for the African states, and its opposition to the demands of many Asian, African and Latin American nations, and several other states in the conferences on raw materials, population, the law of the sea, and food. All these facts offer further proof of the character of the enemy who has usurped our land. They justify the honourable struggle which we are waging against it. As we defend a vision of the future, our enemy upholds the myths of the past.

The enemy we face has a long record of hostility even towards the Jews themselves, for there is within the Zionist entity ugly racial discrimination against Oriental Jews. While we were vociferously condemning the massacres of Jews under Nazi rule, Zionist leadership appeared more interested at that time in exploiting them as best it could in order to realize its goal of immigration into Palestine.

If the immigration of Jews to Palestine had had as its objective the goal of enabling them to live side by side with us, enjoying the same rights and assuming the same duties, we would have opened our doors to them, as far as our homeland's capacity for absorption permitted. Such was the case with the thousands of Armenians and Circassians who still live among us in equality as brethren and citizens. But no one can conceivably demand that we submit to or accept that the goal of this immigration should be to usurp our homeland, disperse our people, and turn us into second-class citizens. Therefore, since its inception, our revolution has not been motivated by racial or religious factors. Its target has never been the Jew, as a person, but racist Zionism and aggression. In this sense, ours is also a revolution for the Jew, as a human being. We are struggling so that Jews, Christians, and Muslims may live in equality, enjoying the same rights and assuming the same duties, free from racial or religious discrimination.

a)   We distinguish between Judaism and Zionism. While we maintain our opposition to the colonialist Zionist movement, we respect the Jewish faith. Today, almost one century after the rise of the Zionist movement, we wish to warn of its increasing danger to the Jews of the world, to our Arab peoples and to world peace and security. For Zionism encourages the Jew to emigrate from his homeland and grants him an artificially-made nationality. The Zionists proceed with their destructive activities even though these have proved ineffective. The phenomenon of constant emigration from Israel, which is bound to grow as the bastions of colonialism and racism in the world falls, is an example of the inevitability of the failure of such activities.

b)   We urge the people and governments of the world to stand firm against Zionist attempts at encouraging world Jewry to emigrate from their countries and to usurp our land. We urge them as well firmly to oppose any discrimination against any human being, as to religion, race, or colour.

c)   Why should our people and our homeland be responsible for the problems of Jewish immigration, if such problems exist in the minds of some people? Why do the supporters of these problems not open their own countries, which are much bigger, to absorb and help these immigrants?

Those who call us terrorists wish to prevent world public opinion from discovering the truth about us and from seeing the justice on our faces. They seek to hide the terrorism and tyranny of their acts, and our own posture of self-defence.

The difference between the revolutionary and the terrorist lies in the reason for which each fights. For whoever stands by a just cause and fights for the freedom and liberation of his land from invaders, settler and colonialists would have been incorrectly called terrorist; the American people in their struggle for liberation from the British colonialists would have been terrorists, the European resistance against the Nazis would be terrorism, the struggle of the Asian, African and Latin American peoples would also be terrorism. It is actually a just and proper struggle of the Asian, African, and Latin American peoples, consecrated by the United Nations Charter and by the Declaration of Human Rights. As to those who fight against just causes, those who wage war to occupy the homelands of others, and to plunder exploit and colonize their peoples — those are the people whose actions should be condemned, who should be called war criminals: for the just cause determines the right to struggle.

Zionist terrorism which was waged against the Palestinian people to evict them from their country and usurp their land is on record in your documents. Thousands of our people have been assassinated in their villages and towns; tens of thousands of others have been forced by rifle and artillery fire to leave their homes and the crops they have sown in the lands of their fathers. Time and time again our children, women and aged have been evicted and have had to wander in the deserts and climb mountains without any food or water. No one who in 1948 witnessed the catastrophe that befell the inhabitants of hundreds of villages and towns — in Jerusalem, Jaffa, Lydda, Ramleh, and Galilee — no one who has been a witness to that catastrophe will ever forget the experience, even though the mass blackout has succeeded in hiding these horrors as it has hidden the traces of 385 Palestinian villages and towns destroyed at the time and erased from the map. The destruction of 19,000 houses during the past seven years, which is equivalent to the complete destruction of 200 more Palestinian villages, and the great number of maimed as a result of the treatment they were subjected to in Israeli prisons, cannot be hidden by any blackout.

Their terrorism fed on hatred and this hatred was even directed against the olive tree in my country, which they saw as a symbol of our spirit, a flag, and which reminded them of the indigenous inhabitants of the land, a living reminder that the land is Palestinian. Hence they uprooted or killed it by neglect, or used it for firewood. How can one describe the statement by Golda Meir in which she expressed her disquiet about "the Palestinian children born every day"? They see in the Palestinian child, in the Palestinian tree, an enemy which should be exterminated. For tens of years Zionists have been harassing our people's cultural, political, social and artistic leaders, terrorizing them and assasinating them. They have stolen our cultural heritage, our popular folklore and have claimed it as theirs. Their terrorism even reached our sacred places in our beloved city of peace, Jerusalem. They have endeavored to deprive it of its Arab (Muslim and Christian) character by evicting its inhabitants and annexing it.

I need not dwell on the burning of the al-Aqsa Mosque, the theft of the treasures of the Church of the Holy Sepulchre and the disfiguring of so many aspects of its culture and civilization. Jerusalem, with its beauty, and atmosphere redolent of history, bears witness to successive generations of our people who have lived in it, leaving in every corner of it proof of our eternal presence, of our love for it, of our civilization, of our human values. It is therefore not surprising that under its skies the three religions were born and that under that sky these three religions have shone to enlighten mankind so that it might express the tribulations and hopes of humanity, and that it might mark out the road of the future with its hopes.

The small number of Palestinian Arabs whom the Zionists did not succeed in uprooting in 1948 are at present refugees in their own country. Israeli law treats them as second-class citizens — even as third-class citizens since Oriental Jews are second-class citizens — and they have been subject to all forms of racial discrimination and terror after the confiscation of their land and property. They have been victims of bloody massacres such as that of Kafr Qassim; they have been expelled from their villages and denied the right to return, as in the case of the inhabitants of Iqrit and Kafr Bir'im. For 26 years, our population has been living under martial law and has been denied freedom of movement without prior permission from the Israeli military governor — this at a time when an Israeli law was promulgated granting citizenship to any Jew anywhere who wanted to emigrate to our homeland. Moreover, another Israeli law stipulated that Palestinians who were not present in their villages or towns at the time they were occupied are not entitled to Israeli citizenship.

The record of Israeli rulers is replete with acts of terror perpetrated on those of our people who remained under occupation in Sinai and the Golan Heights. The criminal bombardment of the Bahr al-Baqar School and the Abu Za'bal factory in Egypt are but two such unforgettable acts of terrorism. The destruction of the Libyan aircraft is another unforgettable act. The total destruction of the city of Quneitra is yet another tangible instance of systematic terrorism. If a record of Zionist terrorism in south Lebanon were to be compiled, and this terrorism is still continuing, the enormity of its acts would shock even the most hardened: piracy, bombardments, scorched earth, destruction of hundreds of homes, eviction of civilians and the kidnapping of Lebanese citizens. This clearly constitutes a violation of Lebanese sovereignty and is in preparation for the diversion of the Litani River waters.

Need one remind this Assembly of the numerous resolutions adopted by it condemning Israeli aggressions committed against Arab countries, Israeli violations of human rights and the articles of the Geneva Conventions, as well as the resolutions pertaining to the annexation of the city of Jerusalem and its restoration to its former status?

The only description for these acts is that they are acts of barbarism and terrorism. And yet, the Zionist racists and colonialists have the temerity to describe the just struggle of our people as terror. Could there be a more flagrant distortion of truth than this? We ask those who usurped our land, who are committing murderous acts of terrorism against our people and are practising racial discrimination more extensively than the racists of South Africa, we ask them to keep in mind the United Nations General Assembly resolution that called for the expulsion of South Africa from the United Nations. Such is the inevitable fate of every racist country that adopts the law of the jungle, usurps the homeland of others and oppresses its people.

For the past 30 years, our people have had to struggle against British occupation and Zionist invasion, both of which had one intention, namely the usurpation of our land. Six major revolts and tens of popular uprisings were staged to foil these attempts, so that our homeland might remain ours. Over 30,000 martyrs, the equivalent in comparative terms of 6 million Americans, died in the process.

When the majority of the Palestinian people was uprooted from its homeland in 1948, the Palestinian struggle for self-determination continued in spite of efforts to destroy it. We tried every possible means to continue our political struggle to attain our national rights, but to no avail. Meanwhile we had to struggle for sheer existence. Even in exile we educated our children. This was all a part of trying to survive.

The Palestinian people have produced thousands of engineers, physicians, teachers and scientists who actively participated in the development of the Arab countries bordering on their usurped homeland. They have utilized their income to assist the young and aged amongst their people who could not leave the refugee camps. They have educated their younger brothers and sisters, have supported their parents and cared for their children. All along the Palestinian dreamt of return. Neither the Palestinian's allegiance to Palestine nor his determination to return waned; nothing could persuade him to relinquish his Palestinian identity or to forsake his homeland. The passage of time did not make him forget, as some hoped he would. When our people lost faith in the international community which persisted in ignoring its rights and when it became obvious that the Palestinians would not recoup one inch of Palestine through exclusively political means, our people had no choice but to resort to armed struggle. Into that struggle it poured its material and human resources and the flower of its youth. We bravely faced the most vicious acts of Israeli terrorism which were aimed at diverting our struggle and arresting it.

In the past ten years of our struggle, thousands of martyrs and twice as many wounded, maimed and imprisoned have been offered in sacrifice, all in an effort to resist the imminent threat of liquidation, to regain the right to self-determination and our right to return to our homeland. With the utmost dignity and the most admirable revolutionary spirit, our Palestinian people have not lost their spirit either in Israeli prisons and concentration camps or in the great prison of Israeli occupation. The people struggle for sheer existence and continue to strive to preserve the Arab character of their land. Thus they resist oppression, tyranny and terrorism in their grimmest forms.

It is through the armed revolution of our people that our political leadership and our national institutions finally crystallized and a national liberation movement, comprising all Palestinian factions, organizations and capabilities, materialized in the Palestine Liberation Organization.

Through our militant Palestine national liberation movement our people's struggle has matured and grown enough to accommodate political and social struggle in addition to armed struggle. The Palestine Liberation Organization has been a major factor in creating a new Palestinian individual, qualified to shape the future of our Palestine, not merely content with mobilizing the Palestinians for the challenges of the present.

The Palestine Liberation Organization can be proud of having a large number of cultural and educational activities, even while engaged in armed struggle, and at a time when it faced the increasingly vicious blows of Zionist terrorism. We have established institutes for scientific research, agricultural development and social welfare, as well as centres for the revival of our cultural heritage and the preservation of our folklore. Many Palestinian poets, artists and writers have enriched Arab culture in particular, and world culture generally. Their profoundly humane works have won the admiration of all those familiar with them. In contrast to that, our enemy has been systematically destroying our culture and disseminating racist, colonialist ideologies; in short, everything that impedes progress, justice, democracy and peace.

The Palestine Liberation Organization has earned its legitimacy because of the sacrifice inherent in its pioneering role, and also because of its dedicated leadership of the struggle. It has also been granted this legitimacy by the Palestinian masses, which in harmony with it have chosen it to lead the struggle according to its directives. The Palestine Liberation Organization has also gained its legitimacy by representing every faction, union or group as well as every Palestinian talent, either in the National Council or in people's institutions. This legitimacy was further strengthened by the support of the entire Arab nation which supports it, and further consecrated during the last Arab Summit Conference, which affirmed the right of the Palestine Liberation Organization, in its capacity as the sole representative of the Palestinian people, to establish an independent national authority on all liberated Palestinian territory.

Moreover, the Palestine Liberation Organization's legitimacy has been intensified as a result of fraternal support given by other liberation movements and by friendly, like-minded nations that stood by our side, encouraging and aiding us in our struggle to secure our national rights.

Here I must also warmly convey the gratitude of our revolutionary fighters and that of our people for the honourable attitudes adopted by the non-aligned countries, the socialist countries, the Islamic countries, the African countries and friendly European countries, as well as all our other friends in Asia, Africa and Latin America.

The Palestine Liberation Organization represents the Palestinian people. Because of this, the Palestine Liberation Organization expresses the wishes and hopes of its people. Because of this, too, it brings these very wishes and hopes before you, urging you not to shirk a momentous historic responsibility towards our just cause.

For many years now, our people have been exposed to the ravages of war, destruction and dispersion. They have paid with the blood of their sons that which cannot ever be compensated. They have borne the burdens of occupation, dispersion, eviction and terror more than any other people. And yet all this has made our people neither vidictive nor vengeful. Nor have they caused us to resort to the racism of our enemies. Nor have we lost the true method by which friend and foe are distinguished.

For we deplore all those crimes committed against the Jews; we also deplore all the open and veiled discrimination suffered by them because of their faith.

I am a rebel and freedom is my cause, I know well that many of you present here today once stood in exactly the same position of resistance as I now occupy and from which I must fight. You once had to convert dreams into reality by your struggle. Therefore you must now share my dream. I think this is exactly why I can ask you now to help, as together we bring out our dream into a bright reality, our common dream for a peaceful future in Palestine's sacred land.

As he stood in an Israeli military court, the Jewish revolutionary Ehud Adiv said: "I am no terrorist; I believe that a democratic state should exist in this land." Adiv now languishes in a Zionist prison among his co-believers. To him and his colleagues I send my heartfelt good wishes.

And before those same courts there stands today a brave prince of the church, Archbishop Capucci. Raising his fingers to form the same victory sign used by our freedom-fighters, he said: "What I have done, I have done that all men may live in peace in this land of peace." This princely priest will doubtless share Adiv's grim fate. To him we send our salutations and greetings.

Why therefore should I not dream and hope? For is not revolution the making real of dreams and hopes? So let us work together that my dream may be fulfilled, that I may return with my people out of exile, there in Palestine to live with this Jewish freedom-fighter and his partners, with this Arab priest and his brothers, in one democratic state where Christian, Jew and Muslim live in justice, equality, fraternity.

Is this not a noble goal and worthy of my struggle alongside all lovers of freedom everywhere? For the most admirable thing about this goal is that it is Palestinian, from the land of peace, the land of martyrdom, heroism, and history.

Let us remember that the Jews of Europe and here in the United States have been known to lead the struggles for secularism and the separation of church and state. They have also been known to fight against discrimination on religious grounds. How can they reject this humane and honourable programme for the Holy Land, the land of peace and equality? How can they continue to support the most fanatic, discriminatory and closed of nations in its policy?

In my capacity as Chairman of the Palestine Liberation Organization and commander of the Palestinian revolution I proclaim before you that when we speak of our common hopes for the Palestine of tomorrow we include in our perspective all Jews now living in Palestine who choose to live with us there in peace and without discrimination.

In my capacity as commander of the forces of the Palestine Liberation Organization I call upon Jews to turn away one by one from the illusory promises made to them by Zionist ideology and Israeli leadership. They are offering Jews perpetual bloodshed, endless war and continuous thralldom.

We invite them to emerge into a more open realm of free choice, far from their present leadership's efforts to implant in them a Masada complex and make it their destiny.

We offer them the most generous solution — that we should live together in a framework of just peace in our democratic Palestine.

In my formal capacity as Chairman of the Palestine Liberation Organization I announce here that we do not wish one drop of either Jewish or Arab blood to be shed; neither do we delight in the continuation of killings for a single moment, once a just peace, based on our people's rights, hopes, and aspirations has been finally established.

In my capacity as Chairman of the Palestine Liberation Organization and commander of the Palestinian revolution I appeal to you to accompany our people in its struggle to attain its right to self-determination. This right is consecrated in the United Nations Charter and has been repeatedly confirmed in resolutions adopted by this august body since the drafting of the Charter. I appeal to you, further, to aid our people's return to its homeland from an involuntary exile imposed upon it by force of arms, by tyranny, by oppression, so that we may regain our property, our land, and thereafter live in our national homeland, free and sovereign, enjoying all the privileges of nationhood.

I appeal to you to enable our people to set up their national authority and establish their national entity in their own land.

Only then will our people be able to contribute all their energies and resources to the field of civilization and human creativity. Only then will they be able to protect their beloved Jerusalem and make it, as they have done for so many centuries, the shrine of all religions, free from all terrorism and coercion.

Today I have come bearing an olive branch and a freedom-fighter's gun. Do not let the olive branch fall from my hand. Do not let the olive branch fall from my hand. Do not let the olive branch fall from my hand.

War flares up in Palestine, and yet is is in Palestine that peace will be born.

## 10. Palestine National Council, Political Declaration, 22 March, 1977

Proceeding from the Palestine National Charter and the previous national council's resolutions; considering the decisions and political gains achieved by the PLO at the Arab and international levels during the period following the 12th session of the PNC; after studying and debating the latest developments in the Palestine issue; and stressing support for the Palestinian national struggle in the Arab and international forums, the PNC affirms the following:

1. The PNC affirms that the Palestine issue is the essence and the root of the Arab-Zionist conflict. Security Council Resolution 242 ignores the Palestinian people and their firm rights. The PNC therefore confirms its rejection of this resolution, and rejects negotiations at the Arab and international levels based on this Resolution.

2. The PNC affirms the stand of the PLO in its determination to continue the armed struggle, and its concomitant forms of political and mass struggle, to achieve our inalienable national rights.

3. The PNC affirms that the struggle, in all its military, political and popular forms, in the occupied territory constitutes the central link in its programme of struggle. On this basis, the PLO will strive to escalate the armed struggle in the occupied territory, to escalate all other concomitant forms of struggle and to give all kinds of moral support to the masses of our people in the occupied territory in order to escalate the struggle and to strengthen their steadfastness to defeat and liquidate the occupation.

4. The PNC affirms the PLO's stand which rejects all types of American capitulationist settlement and all liquidationist projects. The Council affirms the determination of the PLO to abort any settlement achieved at the expense of the firm national rights of our people. The PNC calls upon the Arab nation to shoulder its pan-Arab responsibilities and to pool all its energies to confront these imperialist and Zionist plans.

5. The PNC stresses the importance and necessity of national unity, both political and military, among all the contingents of the Palestine Revolution

within the framework of the PLO, because this is one of the basic conditions for victory. For this reason, it is necessary to co-ordinate national unity at all levels and in all spheres on the basis of commitment to all these resolutions, and to draw up programmes which will ensure the implementation of this.

6.    The PNC affirms the right of the Palestine Revolution to be present on the soil of fraternal Lebanon within the framework of the Cairo agreement and its appendices, concluded between the PLO and the Lebanese authorities. The Council also affirms adherence to the implementation of the Cairo agreement in letter and in spirit, including the preservation of the position of the Revolution and the security of the camps. The PNC refuses to accept any interpretation of this agreement by one side only. Meanwhile it affirms its eagerness for the maintenance of the sovereignty and security of Lebanon.

7.    The PNC greets the heroic fraternal Lebanese people and affirms the PLO's eagerness for the maintenance of the territorial integrity of Lebanon, the unity of its people and its security, independence, sovereignty and Arabism. The PNC affirms its pride in the support rendered by this heroic fraternal people to the PLO, which is struggling for our people to regain their national rights to their homeland and their right to return to this homeland. The PNC strongly affirms the need to deepen and consolidate cohesion between all Lebanese nationalist forces and the Palestine Revolution.

8.    The PNC affirms the need to strengthen the Arab Front participating in the Palestine Revolution, and deepen cohesion with all forces participating in it in all Arab countries, as well as to escalate the joint Arab struggle and to further strengthen the Palestine Revolution in order to contend with the imperialist and Zionist designs.

9.    The PNC has decided to consolidate Arab struggle and solidarity on the basis of struggle against imperialism and Zionism, to work for the liberation of all the occupied Arab areas, and to adhere to the support for the Palestine Revolution in order to regain the constant national rights of the Palestinian Arab people without any conciliation [*sulh*] or recognition [of Israel].

10.    The PNC affirms the right of the PLO to exercise its responsibilities in the struggle at the pan-Arab level and through any Arab land, in the interest of liberating the occupied areas.

11.    The PNC has decided to continue the struggle to regain the national rights of our people, in particular the right of return, self-determination and establishing an independent national state on their national soil.

12.    The PNC affirms the significance of cooperation and solidarity with socialist, non-aligned, Islamic and African countries, and with all the national liberation movements in the world.

13.    The PNC hails the stands and struggles of all the democratic countries and forces against Zionism as one form of racism, as well as against its aggressive practices.

14.   The PNC affirms the significance of establishing relations and coordinating with the progressive and democratic Jewish forces inside and outside the occupied homeland, since these forces are struggling against Zionism as a doctrine and in practice. The PNC calls on all states and forces who love freedom, justice and peace in the world to end all forms of assistance to and cooperation with the racist Zionist regime, and to end contacts with it and its instruments.

15.   Taking into consideration the important achievements in the Arab and international arenas since the conclusion of the PNC's 12th session, the PNC, which has reviewed the political report submitted by the PLO, has decided the following:

a.   The Council confirms its wish for the PLO's rights to participate independently and on an equal footing in all the conferences and international forums concerned with the Palestine issue and the Arab-Zionist conflict, with a view to achieving our inalienable national rights as approved by the UN General Assembly in 1974, namely in Resolution 3236.

b.   The Council declares that any settlement or agreement affecting the rights of our Palestinian people made in the absence of this people will be completely null and void.

## 11.  Six-point Programme Agreed to by the Various Palestinian Organizations Calling for the Formation of a "Steadfastness and Confrontation Front" in Opposition to Sadat's Negotiations with Israel, Tripoli, 4 December, 1977

In the wake of Sadat's treasonous visit to the Zionist entity, all factions of the Palestinian Resistance Movement have decided to make a practical answer to this step. On this basis, they met and issued the following document:

We, all factions of the PLO, announce the following:

*First:* We call for the formation of a "Steadfastness and Confrontation Front" composed of Libya, Algeria, Iraq, Democratic Yemen, Syria and the PLO, to oppose all capitulationist solutions planned by imperialism, Zionism and their Arab tools.

*Second:* We fully condemn any Arab party in the Tripoli Summit which rejects the formation of this Front, and we announce this.

*Third:* We reaffirm our rejection of Security Council resolutions 242 and 338.

*Fourth:* We reaffirm our rejection of all international conferences based on these two resolutions' including the Geneva Conference.

*Fifth:* To strive for the realization of the Palestinian people's rights to return and self-determination within the context of an independent Palestinian national state on any part of the Palestinian Revolution.

*Sixth:* To apply the measures related to the political boycott of the Sadat regime.

In the name of all the factions, we ratify this unification document:

— The Palestinian National Liberation Movement, Fatah: Abu Ayyad [Salah Khalaf].

— The Popular Front for the Liberation of Palestine: Dr. George Habbash.

— The Democratic Front for the Liberation of Palestine: Nayef Hawatmeh.

— The P.F.L.P. — General Command: Ahmad Jabril.

— Vanguards of the People's Liberation War, Saiqa: Zuhair Muhsin.

— Arab Liberation Front: Abdul-Rahim Ahmad.

— Palestinian Liberation Front: Talaat Ya'qoub.

— P.L.O.: Hamed Abu-Sitta.


## 12. Statement by West Bank Mayors on Sadat's Visit to Israel, 21 December, 1977 [Excerpts]

We state our dissatisfaction with this step taken by President Sadat, because of the results and dangers likely to arise from it and because in his speech to the Knesset he made no mention of the PLO as the sole legitimate representative of the Palestinian people. We also declare that the PLO had every right, and indeed the duty, to adopt the attitude it has taken to this visit. In adopting this attitude it was clearly expressing the view and the attitude of the Palestinian people. However, our sense of responsibility prompts us to record that President Sadat has committed himself not to resort to a separate solution with "Israel" and that he has declared that he insists on the Arab character of Jerusalem, "Israel" withdrawing from all the occupied territories, on the refugees returning to their homes and on the Palestinian people being granted their right to self-determination and to establish their independent state.

While recalling the world's commitment to the resolutions of the United Nations and, in particular, General Assembly resolution 3236, adopted on November 22, 1974 and the resolutions of the Algiers and Rabat summits which regarded the PLO as the sole legitimate representative of the Palestinian people wherever they may be, we affirm our adherence to these resolutions, as also to the resolutions of the Thirteenth Palestine National Council held in Cairo. We call on all quarters to respect the commitment of the peoples of the world, including our Palestinian people, and we condemn any attempt to prejudice the legitimate rights of our people and, first and foremost, their right to self-determination. In the light of the above we assert the following principles:

1.   While stating our attitude to President Sadat's visit to "Israel" we affirm our belief in the role Egypt has played and the sacrifices she has made on behalf of the Palestinian cause and the problems of Arab struggle. We stress the strength of the alliance between our people and the people of Egypt, and our unshakable belief in the central role occupied by Egypt in the battle of Arab liberation, and we salute the struggle and great sacrifices of her people.

2.   The ferocity of the battle that is being fought to counter the present imperialist attack on the achievements of our people and the Arab people requires the establishment of a broad Arab front comprising all the Arab countries that reject the imperialist attack on the area in all its forms. This front should also include the Arab popular organizations and the PLO. Also required is the mobilization of all economic, political and military resources to resist this attack and to put an end to the conspiracy against all the national gains in Arab lands, and to strengthen the alliance of this front with all forces opposed to imperialism and Zionism.

3.   The Palestinian people in the occupied territories unambiguously affirm their belief in the unity of the Palestinian people inside and outside the country. They also stress that all Palestinians are represented by the PLO alone, which is the only quarter entitled to speak on behalf of the Palestinian people. We condemn any attempt to establish an alternative or parallel leadership.

4.   The rights of the Palestinian people, as affirmed by the various resolutions of the UN, are not subject to bargaining, and first and foremost among these rights is their legitimate right to self-determination in their land and in full freedom.

We therefore reject any form of tutelage, whatever its source, and all kinds of solutions which detract from the independence of the Palestinian people and the independence of their will.

We therefore cannot agree that the Palestinian state should be forcibly linked to any other quarter, as such a trend is incompatible with our people's freedom to decide their own destiny.

5.   From the occupied territories we salute the struggle of all the Arab peoples. We also salute all the forces that have provided support for our just struggle. Above all we salute the struggle of our people outside the country under the leadership of the PLO and we call for resolute resistance to all attempts to shake the Arab solidarity which is based on the will of the Arab nation for delivery from the imperialist attack and Zionist aggression.

## 13. Statement by the West Bank National Conference, Beit Hanina, Jerusalem, 1 October, 1978

On this day Sunday, October 1, 1978, in the professional unions' centre in Jerusalem, Muslim and Christian religious leaders, mayors and city council members, representatives of the unions, clubs and national institutions, and leading personalities in Jerusalem and the rest of the occupied territories held a national conference and studied the results of the Camp David conference, its agreements, explanations, letters and the declarations of those who signed it. All those present have unanimously decided the following:

1. To totally reject and oppose these agreements, and all the documents, explanations and annexes related to them.

2. The Camp David agreements are in contradiction to the all-Arab character of our battle, as they actually constitute a separate treaty between Egypt and Israel, which will take Egypt out of the Arab arena in order to strike at the Arab and African liberation movements.

3. The above-mentioned agreements are a clear deviation from the resolutions of the Arab summit conferences in general and the Algiers and Rabat summits in particular, which clearly opposed separate solutions and demanded that the confrontation forces work jointly in all fields.

4. The above-mentioned agreements contradict the UN General Assembly resolutions on the Palestinian issue and are an open defiance on the international will and an attack on the Palestinian people's natural rights.

5. The above-mentioned agreements have denied the rights of the Palestinian people and ignored their just cause, which is the crux of the conflict in the Middle East, and ignored their usurped rights and their right of self-determination on their land. The agreements have also ignored the PLO, which is the sole legitimate leadership of the Palestinian people, and attempt to create an alternative leadership to the PLO under the auspices of occupation by establishing self-rule which time after time all sectors of our people have absolutely rejected.

6. The struggle of the Palestinian people was and still is an integral part of the struggle of the Arab peoples for freedom, unity and progress, and is part of the world liberation movement. And the Palestinian people inside and outside the occupied territory are a unified, inseparable whole.

7. No peace is possible in the area without the complete and genuine withdrawal of Israeli forces from all the occupied territories, nor without securing for the Palestinian people the right of return, self-determination and the creation of their own independent state on their land, with Jerusalem as its capital.

8. We reject the self-government plan both in its form and content. It is a plan to consolidate the occupation, to continue the oppression of our people

and the usurping of our legitimate rights. It is an open plot to bypass the ambitions of our people and our right to our own homeland and to self-determination.

9. From our beloved Jerusalem, the throbbing heart of Palestine, we appeal to our Arab people everywhere to retain their national unity, confirm their allegiance to their legitimate leadership, the Palestine Liberation Organization, and stand united in the face of all efforts to implement the proposed self-government plan and other capitulationist solutions.

On this occasion we salute our Palestinian people inside and outside [Palestine], the memory of our martyrs who sacrificed their lives for their country and the resisters in the Israeli prisons. We salute the Steadfastness and Confrontation Front and the resolutions of its summits in Tripoli and Damascus. These are an extension of the Arab people through their struggles. And we salute all friendly nations for their clear position in support of our national rights.

[96 signatories]

## 14. Palestine National Council, Political and Organizational Program, 23 January, 1979

The US settlement of the Arab-Zionist conflict embodied in the Camp David agreements poses grave threats to the cause of Palestine and of Arab national liberation. That settlement condones the Zionist enemy's continued usurpation of the national soil of Palestine, abrogates the inalienable right of the Palestinian Arab people to their homeland, Palestine, as well as their right to return to it and their right to self-determination and to the exercise of their national independence on their soil. It dissipates other Arab territories and overrides the PLO, the leader of our people's national struggle and their sole legitimate representative and spokesman expressing their will.

In addition, these agreements violate Palestinian, Arab and international legitimacy and pave the way for tighter imperialist and Zionist control over our Arab region and Africa, employing the Egyptian regime, in the context of its alliance with imperialism and Zionism, as a tool for the repression of the Arab and African national liberation movements.

Motivated by our awareness of the gravity of this new conspiracy and its implications and by our national responsibilities in the PLO, which represents our Palestinian Arab people with all their national groups and forces, we are obliged to reject this new conspiratorial scheme, to confront it and to defend our people and their inalienable national rights to their homeland, Palestine, as well as to safeguard our Palestinian revolution.

The courageous position adopted by our Palestinian masses inside and outside the occupied homeland and by the masses of our Arab nation through their rejection of the Camp David agreements and their open determination to confront this new conspiracy against our people and their inalienable national rights and our Arab nation strengthens our resolve to resist this conspiracy and our faith in defeating it.

At the same time, we shoulder a great responsibility which can be carried out only by adopting a united national and popular stand, within the framework of the PLO.

In response to the will of our people and to the challenges that we face, and motivated by our faith in national unity within the PLO as the sole means to achieve victory; basing ourselves upon the Palestine National Charter, the resolutions of the Palestine National Councils and the Tripoli document which established unity among the various organizations of the Palestinian revolution; believing in the right of our people to establish a democratic state on the whole of our national soil and in order to confront this critical and dangerous stage in the struggle of our people, we, the representatives of all organizations of the Revolution and Palestinian national forces, declare the following:

### In the Palestinian Sphere

1. [That we] adhere to the inalienable national rights of our people to their homeland, Palestine, and to their right to return and to self-determination on their soil without foreign interference, and to their right to establish their independent state on their soil unconditionally.

2. [That we shall] defend the PLO and adhere to it as the sole legitimate representative of our people, as leader of their national struggle and as their spokesman in all Arab and international forums; resist all attempts to harm, override or circumvent the PLO, or to create alternatives or partners to it as regards representation of our Palestinian people; adhere to the resolutions of the Arab summits of Algiers and Rabat and to UN resolutions — especially resolutions 3236 and 3237 — which affirm our inalienable national rights as well as Arab and international recognition of the PLO as the sole legitimate representative of the Palestinian people.

3. [That we] resolve firmly to continue and escalate the armed struggle and use all other forms of political and mass struggle, especially inside the occupied homeland which is the principal arena of conflict with the Zionist enemy, in order to achieve the inalienable and non-negotiable national rights of the Palestinian Arab people.

4. [That we] affirm that the problem of Palestine is the crux and the basis of the Arab-Zionist conflict, and [we] reject all resolutions, agreements and

settlements that do not recognize or that impinge upon the inalienable rights of our people to their homeland, Palestine, including their right to return, to self-determination and to the establishment of their independent national state. This applies in particular to Security Council resolution 242.

5. [That we] reject and resist the self-rule scheme in the occupied homeland, which entrenches Zionist settler colonization of our occupied land and denies the rights of our Palestinian people.

6. [That we] affirm the unity of our Palestinian Arab people inside and outside the occupied homeland, and their sole representation through the PLO; [we shall] resist all attempts and schemes that seek to divide our people or to circumvent the PLO; work to support the struggle of our people in the occupied territories and to fortify their unity and their steadfastness.

7. [That we shall] consolidate the framework of the Palestinian National Front inside Palestine since it is an integral part of the PLO, and [shall] furnish it with all means of political and financial aid so that it can mobilize our masses inside to face the Zionist occupation, its schemes and its projects which are inimical to our people and to their inalienable national rights.

8. [that we] cling to Palestine as the historic homeland of the Palestinian people for which there can be no substitute; resist all schemes for resettlement or for an "alternative homeland", which the imperialist and Zionist enemy is proposing in order to liquidate the Palestinian cause and Palestinian national struggle, and to circumvent our right to return.

### In the Arab Sphere

1. [that we] emphasize that the task of confronting the Camp David agreements, their annexes and their consequences, with the fateful dangers they pose to the cause of Arab struggle, is the responsibility of all the Arab masses and their national and progressive forces, that the Arab Front for Steadfastness and Confrontation, with Syria and the PLO as its central link, is the primary base from which to confront the US-Zionist conspiratorial settlement.

2. [That we must] work to fortify and strengthen the Arab Front for Steadfastness and Confrontation and to expand its scope on the basis of resistance to imperialist and Zionist settlement schemes; adhere to the objective of liberating the occupied Palestinian and Arab territories and to the inalienable national rights of the Palestinian people, and not dissipate or infringe upon these rights; [we must] furnish all possible mass and financial support to the Arab Front for Steadfastness and Confrontation, especially to the PLO and the Syrian Arab region.

3. The PLO calls upon all national and progressive parties, movements and forces in the Arab homeland to support the Arab Front for Steadfastness

and Confrontation and to furnish it with all possible mass and financial aid. It further calls upon them to unite and to struggle on the basis of resistance to the imperialist and Zionist schemes for settlement.

4.   a)   The PLO asserts its firm commitment to the unity, Arab character and independence of Lebanon, its respect for Lebanese sovereignty and its adherence to the Cairo Agreement and its sequels which regulate relations between the PLO and Lebanon's legitimate authority.

b)   The PLO highly values the role that has been and is being played by the Lebanese people and their national, progressive and patriotic forces in support of and in defence of the struggle of the Palestinian people. In expressing its pride in the solidarity between our Palestinian people and the people of Lebanon and their national, progressive and patriotic forces in defence of Lebanese territory and of the Palestinian revolution against Zionist aggression, its schemes and its local agents, the PLO emphasizes the importance of continuing and strengthening this solidarity.

5.   a)   The PLO affirms the special character of the relationship linking the two fraternal peoples, Palestinian and Jordanian, and its concern that the solidarity between these two fraternal peoples should continue.

b)   The PLO declares its adherence to the resolutions of the Arab summits of Algiers and Rabat which affirm that the PLO is the sole legitimate representative of the Palestinian people and that our people have a right to establish their national and independent state. The PLO considers that the commitment of the Jordanian regime to these resolutions, its rejection of the Camp David agreements and their aftermath as well as its refusal to be involved in them and its role in enabling the PLO to exercise its responsibility for militant and mass struggle against the Zionist enemy, constitute the basis that governs relations between the PLO and the Jordanian regime.

6.   The PLO affirms its right to exercise its responsibility for struggle on the Arab and national levels, and across any Arab territory, in order to liberate the occupied Palestinian territories.

7.   The PLO declares that its policies toward and its relations with any Arab regime are determined by the policy of that regime as regards adherence to the resolutions of the summits of Algiers and Rabat and to the rejection of and the opposition to the Camp David agreements with their annexes and their consequences.

8.   The PLO calls upon all Arab and national forces and all national and friendly regimes to support and aid the Egyptian people and their national movement to enable them to confront the Sadat conspiracy and to foil the Camp David agreement and its effect upon the Egyptian people, their Arabism and their history of struggle against Zionism and imperialism.

## In the International Sphere

1.   The role played by the US against our Palestinian people and their national struggle and against the Arab national liberation movement and its objectives of liberation and independence, whether this is manifested in its support of the Zionist entity or through its agents in the Arab region, constitutes a naked aggression against our people and their national cause. The PLO, by acting in solidarity with all groups in the Arab national liberation struggle and their national and progressive forces and regimes, declares its determination to resist the policy, objectives and actions of the US in the region.

2.   The PLO affirms the importance of alliance with the socialist countries, and first and foremost with the Soviet Union, since this alliance is a national necessity in the context of confronting American-Zionist conspiracies against the Palestine cause, the Arab national liberation movement and their achievements.

3.   The PLO affirms the importance of consolidating its cooperation with the non-aligned, Islamic, African and friendly states which support the PLO and its struggle to achieve the national rights of the Palestinian people to return to their homeland, to self-determination and to establish their independent national state.

4.   The PLO, as a national liberation movement, expresses its solidarity with national liberation movements throughout the world, especially with Zimbabwe, Namibia and South Africa, and its determination to consolidate relations of struggle with them since the fight against imperialism, Zionism and racism is a joint cause for all forces of liberation and progress in the world.

5.   The PLO declares its firm adherence to the achievements won by Palestinian struggle in the international sphere, such as the wide international recognition accorded to the PLO and to the inalienable right of the Palestinian Arab people to their homeland, Palestine, their right to return, to self- determination and to the establishment of their independent national state on their national soil. These are the achievements embodied in UN resolutions adopted since 1974 and up to the present, especially resolutions 3236 and 3237. It underlines the right of the PLO to participate in all meetings and conferences that discuss the Palestine question on these bases and considers that any discussion or agreement that takes place in its absence about matters related to the Palestine question are totally invalid.

## In the Sphere of Organization

1.   All the organizations of the Revolution and all Palestinian national forces participate in all institutions of the PLO, and principally in the National

Council and the Central Council and the Executive Committee, on a representative basis and in a democratic manner.

2.   Palestinian leadership is a collective one. This means that decisions are the responsibility of all, both through participation in the adoption of decision and in its execution. This takes place in a democratic manner where the minority adheres to the view of the majority, in accordance with the political and organizational programme and with the resolutions of the National Councils.

3.   [The PLO will work] to ensure that the departments, institutions and organs of the PLO carry out their functions in full, each within its own specific sphere as defined in the basic regulations of the PLO. The Executive Committee will form higher organs, composed on a representative basis, which will undertake to formulate the plans for the various institutions of the PLO and supervise their execution by them, especially in the military, informational and financial spheres.

4.   The Executive Committee and the Central Council are composed in accordance with what is agreed upon as stated in the basic regulations of the PLO and the resolutions of the National Council.

5.   The next Executive Committee undertakes as soon as it commences its activity to lay down the necessary plans to implement the interim programme and to review the departments and organs of the PLO in a manner that would take merit and quality into account in order to achieve optimal performance from these departments and organs.

## 15. Letter from PLO Executive Committee to Delegate Walter Fauntroy, 5 October, 1979

Walter Fauntroy,                                              Washington, D.C.
Chairman, SCLC,                                              October 5, 1979
Washington, D.C.

In response to Dr. Joseph Lowery and Congressman Walter Fauntroy and the Southern Christian Leadership Conference peace initiative as well as Reverend Jesse Jackson's People United to Save Humanity (PUSH) appeal, PLO Chairman Yasser Arafat after meeting with members of the Executive Committee of the Palestine Liberation Organization issued the following 6 point programme. (1) The PLO reaffirms its rejection of the Camp David process and the autonomy plan which only legitimizes the occupation and oppression of the Palestinian people.   (2) The PLO reaffirms the resolution of the Palestine National Council including the Palestinian people's right of self determination, their right of return, and their right to an independent state. (3) The PLO commits itself to a cease fire in Lebanon in line with the safety and security of Lebanon, at a time when Israel continues its ceaseless attacks by air, land and sea which have resulted in 600,000 refugees. (4) The PLO reaffirms its right to an independent state on any land Israel evacuates or is liberated. (5) The PLO reaffirms its respect for Judaism and the right of Jews to live in peace and its commitment to full equality of Jews, Moslems, and Christians and its opposition to all forms of racism. (6) The PLO appeals to all people to support the legitimate rights of the Palestinian people.

Chairman Arafat sends his best wishes to the SCLC delegation members and to the PUSH delegation.

## 16. The Fourth General Conference of the Palestinian Liberation Movement, Fatah, Political Programme, Damascus, 31 May, 1980

*I. At the Palestinian Level*

In the light of the unity of the Palestinian people, and the unity of their territory and their political representation, and in affirmation of their independent national will for the continuation and victory of their revolution;

Inasmuch as armed popular revolution is the sole and inevitable road to the liberation of Palestine, and inasmuch as the road to liberation is the road to unity; and in confirmation of the principle that democracy governs relations in the Palestinian arena and that democratic dialogue is the proper way to develop these relations, the Conference affirms the following:

1. Ceaseless efforts to consolidate Palestinian national unity at all levels inside and outside the occupied territory under the leadership of our Movement and within the framework of the PLO, so as to ensure the continuing escalation of all forms of Palestinian struggle.

2. The importance of stepping up our Movement's participation — with its proper weight — in the PLO, so as to ensure that it plays an effective role and so as to develop its internal regulations and organs in such a way as to guarantee the independence of all its institutions.

3. The escalation of armed struggle inside the occupied territory and via all lines of confrontation with the Zionist enemy.

4. Increasing concern for the organization of our people wherever they may reside, and expansion of the framework of the activities of popular and professional organizations and federations; protection of our people in their places of temporary residence and defence of them against persecution, exploitation or absorption.

5. Support at all levels for the steadfastness of our people inside the occupied territory, and provision of the necessary material support to enable them to maintain their steadfastness, escalate their struggle and develop all their national institutions and, in particular, efforts to strengthen the links

with the Palestinian masses in the territories occupied in 1948 to enable them to resist the plans to fragment their unity and suppress their Arab identity.

6. Stress on the necessity of independent Palestinian decision-making, and efforts to develop the ability of all organizations of the Palestinian revolution to abide by the independent Palestinian decision.

7. In conformity with the leading position occupied by our Movement in the PLO, with what the political programme outlines on this subject and with the legitimacy of the PLO in the Arab and international arenas, the resolutions of the PLO's Palestinian National Council currently in force are to be regarded as complementing the Movement's Political Programme, since they do not conflict with the goals and principles of our Movement and its political programmes.

8. Consolidation of the role of the Palestinian woman in all the fields of struggle, and efforts to ensure that she participates effectively in all frameworks and at all levels.

## II. At the Arab Level
A. At the Mass level:

Inasmuch as Palestine is part of the Arab homeland, and the Palestinian people are part of the Arab nation and their struggle part of its struggle, and inasmuch as the Palestinian revolution is the vanguard of the Arab nation in the battle for the liberation of Palestine, [the Conference affirms that:]

1. The relationship with the Arab masses is a strategic relation that enjoins more extensive participation by these masses in the protection of the revolution and in the conduct of all forms of struggle against the imperialist Zionist base in Palestine and against all the enemies of our people and our nation, and in the liquidation of imperialist and colonialist interests in the region.

2. There must be closer cohesion with the Arab national liberation movements and the Arab nationalist and progressive forces for the joint battle for the liberation of Palestine, and the achievement of the objectives of the Arab nation in the liberation of its regions and the building of a unified progressive Arab society.

4. [There must be] consolidation of the militant cohesion with the Lebanese national movement and all other nationalist forces that are valiantly fighting in the same trench as the Palestinian revolution against the enemies of the Palestinian and Lebanese peoples and the Arab nation, and participation with them in the struggle to protect Lebanon's unity, Arab character and territorial integrity. This requires strenuous efforts [both] to eliminate all negative manifestations that threaten relations with the masses, and to consolidate our relations with them by all ways and means.

4. The cohesion of the Lebanese masses with, and heroice support for, the Palestinian revolution in confronting the war of liquidation and annihilation

must be safeguarded, supported and developed so that it may become a model for relations with the masses throughout the Arab homeland on the basis of kinship ties; this requires further support with all our energies and resources.

5. The special importance of the Jordanian arena requires that special attention be devoted to its recovery as one of the principal bases of support in the struggle against the Zionist enemy; the energies of the masses must be harnessed for the achievement of this goal.

6. [It is necessary to] reinforce the common struggle with the Egyptian people, represented by their nationalist and progressive forces, to abort the Camp David conspiracy and its consequences, and to bring Egypt back into Arab ranks to assume its natural position in the Arab struggle.

B. At the level of Relations with Arab Regimes:

Inasmuch as the aim of relations with the Arab regimes is to develop their positive aspects, these relations must be governed by the following principles:

1. The principles, goals and methods of the Movement.

2. These relations must not conflict with the strategic relations with the masses.

3. The position of each regime with regard to the cause of Palestine and the armed revolution of its people and, in particular, recognition of and commitment to the PLO as the sole legitimate representative of the Palestinian people, and rejection of any attempt from any quarter to prejudice this.

4. No interference in our internal affairs, and confrontation of any attempts to impose tutelage on or to subjugate our people, or to persecute or exploit them, also confrontation of any attempt to settle [our people] in any land other than their homeland, Palestine.

5. Confrontation of any attempt to deny the revolution freedom of action within the ranks of our people, wherever they reside.

6. The revolution exercises its responsibilities at the pan-Arab level and via any Arab territory for the sake of [regaining] the occupied Palestinian Arab territories, and every effort must be made to mobilize the human and material resources of the Arab nation, in particular its oil wealth, as a weapon for the achievement of this goal.

7. Efforts to develop the Steadfastness and Confrontation Front so that it may become a primary instrument of action based on supporting the PLO, continuing the struggle against the Zionist enemy and confronting and thwarting all liquidationist solutions; efforts to harden Arab positions with a view to confronting and foiling the settlement in whatever form and under whatever name, and resolute resistance to any attempt to provide the Camp David agreements with a cover of legitimacy.

8. Efforts to create a broad Arab front, as stipulated by the resolutions of Steadfastness and Confrontation Front, for the confrontation of all imperialist and Zionist conspiracies, and first and foremost, the Camp David

conspiracy in all its forms.

*III. At the International Level*

Inasmuch as the cause of Palestine is the central cause of the Arab nation in its just struggle against the Zionist-imperialist enemy;

And inasmuch as the Middle East area is of international strategic importance, the cause of Palestine, in addition to its justice and the struggle of its people, has always had an important international dimension and [has always] been the focus of world conflict that has led to the emergence of two camps: that of the enemies, and that of the friends of the cause and the struggle of our people.

Our Movement is part of the international liberation movement in the common struggle against imperialism, Zionism, racism and their agents, and we establish our alliances with all international parties in conformity with our principles and with the Palestinian National Charter.

A. International Organizations:

[The Conference affirms the need for:]

1. Efforts through the PLO to secure the adoption of more comprehensive resolutions on the rights of the Palestinian Arab people in all international forums and organizations — in particular the UN — so as to increase the isolation of the Zionist-American enemy in these organizations and in the international arena.

2. Efforts to embody the UN General Assembly resolution condemning Zionism as a form of racism and racial discrimination in measures and sanctions against the imperialist and settler Zionist base in Palestine, as stipulated by the UN Charter.

3. Intensification of efforts to maintain the UN positions rejecting the Camp David agreements, and to develop these positions to involve the rejection of all forms of settlement reached at the expense of our people and their cause.

B. Friendly Forces:

[The Conference affirms the importance of:]

1. Consolidating the strategic alliance with the socialist countries, headed by the USSR, since this alliance is essential for the serious and effective confrontation of American and Zionist conspiracies against the cause of Palestine and liberation causes in the world.

2. Consolidating our relations with the world liberation movements that are fighting in the same trench with us against American imperialism, Zionism, racism, Fascism and reaction; Fatah supports the struggle of all liberation movements and all freedom-fighters against injustice, coercion and tyranny.

3. Consolidating our Movement's external relations and intensifying its

political activity on the basis of the Movement's principles and programmes, for the establishment of alliances with democratic and progressive political forces that support our just struggle and our legitimate rights.

4. Consolidating relations with the Islamic revolution in Iran which has swept away the most arrogant fortress of American imperialism in the region, and which supports us in our struggle for the liberation of Palestine.

5. Strengthening relations with the peoples and governments of the Islamic, African and the non-aligned countries, with a view to developing their positions towards greater support of the Palestinian cause and our struggle, and to winning greater recognition of the PLO as the sole legitimate representative of the Palestinian people.

C. The American Position:

The US heads the enemies of our people and our nation in that it pursues a policy hostile to our people, our revolution and the Arab nation, and to all Arab and international forces of liberation; it supports the Zionist enemy and its agents in the area, and establishes military pacts with the aim of subjecting the area to its military influence so that it may continue to plunder the wealth of our nation. It is, therefore, imperative to consolidate the international front opposed to US policy, to fight against it and abort it, and to strike at American interests in the area.

D. The Positions of Western Europe (EEC), Japan and Canada:

1. [The Conference affirms the need to] intensify political activity in these countries and benefit from the support of democratic and progressive political forces in them to reduce and then halt support for the Zionist entity, and achieve its isolation through the recognition by these forces of the PLO as the sole legitimate representative of the Palestinian people, and [the need to] achieve maximum political and material support for our cause, our struggle and our national rights.

2. Many of the Western European countries and Canada still pursue a policy that does not recognize the national rights of our people, and they provide support at all levels to the Zionist enemy. They are following a policy in conformity with that of the US and its schemes in the area, and Japan's policy is not dissimilar. Therefore, efforts must be intensified to resist and thwart any plan or initiative that conflicts with the national rights of our people.

In conclusion, the General Conference of our Movement stresses the need to safeguard and consolidate the political gains that have been achieved in the international political arena, and that have kept the cause of Palestine a living cause that enjoys such extensive international support that it is now the vanguard and standard-bearer of the world liberation movement.

## 17. Palestinian National Council Political Statement, Damascus, 21 April, 1981

The Palestine National Council [PNC] held its 15th session in Damascus, the capital of the Arab Republic of Syria, from 11-16 April 1981. His Excellency President Hafiz al-Assad, the president of the Syrian Republic, inaugurated the session with a speech in which he affirmed the cohesion of the Arab Syrian people with the struggle of the Arab people of Palestine and Syria's commitment to wage a struggle to liberate Palestine. President al-Assad pointed out the uniqueness of the Palestinian revolution in the Arab struggle movement and expressed Syria's intention to continue its support for the PLO in its confrontation with the Zionist-imperialist aggression and the Camp David designs and its signatories.

Ninety-two delegations representing Arab fraternal countries as well as friendly countries participated in the conference. Also attending were delegations from national liberation movements and from political organizations of a number of countries. These delegations delivered speeches expressing their countries' support for the Arab Palestinian people's struggle and its just cause. Also attending were a large number of observers representing the Palestinian people from various areas of their residence who are contributing to various spheres of the struggle; these observers interacted with the activities of the conference.

This session was convened at a time when the Palestinian struggle was waging an escalating struggle under the leadership of the PLO in various arenas inside and outside Palestine's soil in order to confront the imperialist-colonialist-Zionist aggression and to pursue its march along the path of liberation and return [to the homeland].

This aggression has been embodied by many forms represented by daily attacks that are being carried out by the Zionist enemy forces by land, sea and air against southern Lebanon and in which these forces are using the most deadly U.S. arms. This aggression is also embodied in the policies of persecution, despotism and settlement being practiced by the Zionist occupation in the Palestinian people's homeland. Another form of this aggression is represented by U.S. attempts to impose its domination and control over the Arab nation and the areas surrounding it by various means, foremost among which is the establishment of military bases and the call to sign pacts while brandishing the so-called Soviet threat.

The PNC conducted its activities in a democratic atmosphere, an atmosphere which the Palestinian people are very keen on and which the PLO adheres to and which the Palestinian revolution takes pride in.

The council debated the political and financial reports that were submitted by the Executive Committee and studied, by means of its committees, the various dimensions of the current situation in the Palestinian, Arab and international arenas. The PNC committees adopted the necessary organizational, military, political and financial resolutions with regard to various issues.

The PNC affirmed the organizational and political programs adopted in its previous session, the democratic bases and the collective leadership in various levels related to the PLO's activities and its bodies. The PNC also affirmed the need to have the PLO's offices and organizations exercise their full powers and establish specialized supreme councils on factional bases in order to draw up plans for the PLO's institutions in the military, information and financial spheres and to supervise their implementation.

The council expressed the need to work for completing national unity through the participation of the revolutionary squads and all the Palestinian national forces in all the institutions and in the various popular national organizations — inasmuch as this will constitute the basis for unifying the people's efforts. The council also called for developing the unified military activities under the responsibility of the Supreme Military Council and the Executive Committee in order to ensure the proper confrontation of the current perilous circumstances and as a step along the road to full military union.

The council stressed the importance of establishing consultative committees which will interact with the organization's offices wherever they may be and wherever Palestinian communities and aggregations exist.

The PNC also approved the proposal to declare a general military mobilization that will include the various sectors of our people in their places of congregation outside the occupied homeland. The council also called on the Arab and friendly countries to facilitate the implementation of the above and to enable the Palestinians residing in their countries to join the Palestinian revolutionary forces.

The council affirmed that the only alternative for resolving the Palestinian problem is the Palestinian alternative. The council rejected and denounced those alternative solutions proposed for solving the Palestinian problem by the imperialist-Zionist and those worked out by agents.

The PNC also affirmed that no country has the right to allege that it represents the Palestinian people or to negotiate the Palestinian problems — whether this refers to the Palestinian soil, people or rights. Anyone who violates this is taking a decision that is null and void and has no legal standing. The PLO alone has the right to choose the just and overall solution that will fully ensure the Palestinian people's firm national rights.

The council affirmed that the occupied city of Jerusalem is the capital of Palestine and that the council regards the Zionist occupation of Jerusalem as a violation of the Palestinian people's rights and a defiance of international laws as well as a provocation of all the believers in the world. The council called on all the world countries and organizations to refuse to carry out anything that will entail an implicit recognition of the Zionist aggression against Jerusalem or its actions therein.

In its debates and resolutions the council expressed its deep admiration for the standard of struggle which has been attained by our people's uprising in the occupied homeland, as well as their solid unity and their complete cohesion with the PLO. The council saluted the heroic struggle of our people in the Galilee, the triangle and the Negev as well as in Jerusalem, the West Bank and the Gaza Strip against the Zionist designs that aim at expanding the settlements, Judaization and the destruction of the national economy and education and the holy places.

The council also expressed its admiration for the steadfastness of those who are interned in the enemy's prisons and who are setting an example in their sacrifice in defending their people's right to liberate and return to their homeland. The council affirmed the exceeding importance of building the PNC inside the occupied homeland, considering that the PNC is a vital arm of the PLO and stressed the role of the national guiding committee and the various popular bodies and organizations in their national struggle against occupation and its designs.

The council stressed the importance of supporting the organizations encompassing students, unions and women as well as various vocational unions and municipal councils to enable them to carry out their tasks in enhancing the steadfastness of our people on their own soil and in bolstering their unity in the face of the Zionist enemy's practices and its expansionist policies.

The council considers the development and escalation of the armed struggle against the Zionist enemy as being the cardinal task that rests on the shoulders of the Palestinian revolution inside and outside [Palestine]. The council reiterated the importance of opening the various Arab fronts to the heroic fighters of our revolution.

The council debated social, economic, educational and health issues related to our people in their places of residence and the appropriate solutions for these issues. In this respect the council affirmed the importance of supporting the role of the institutions working within the framework of the organization which are dealing with the aforementioned problems.

the council also considered the continuation of UNRWA an international responsibility until the times comes for our refugees to practice their unshaken right in returning to their houses and taking over their properties. The council called for putting an end to the political blackmail being practiced by some Western countries, particularly the United States, which is embodied by threats of curbing the UNRWA services. The council affirmed the Arab League's resolution to work for integrating UNRWA's budget with the UN's regular budget.

The council also affirmed the importance of enhancing Arab solidarity by pledging enmity toward imperialism, Zionism and by rejecting the Camp David agreements and the Egyptian-Israeli pact and by implementing the Palestinian people's firm national rights, including their right to return to their homeland, their right to self-determination and the establishment of their independent state on their national soil under the leadership of the PLO.

The PNC also denounced Somalia, Oman and Sudan, which deviated from the Arab summit resolutions in Baghdad and Tunis. The council stressed the importance of the alliance between Syria and the PLO considering them the basic foundation of the Arab nation's struggle and its confrontation against its enemies. The council emphasized the importance of enhancing these fateful relations and providing the means that will achieve the joint national struggle.

The PNC stressed the importance of the deep-rooted struggle in the relations between the Palestinian and Jordanian fraternal people and the PNC's support for the Jordanian national movement in various spheres, particularly in its national struggle against any attempt to make Jordan deviate from the Arab and Islamic summit resolutions with regard to the Palestinian problem and the rejection of the Camp David agreements and the autonomy conspiracy. The council declared the PLO's adherence to the Arab summit resolutions in Algeria, Rabat, Baghdad and Tunis. The council regards the Jordanian regime's adherence to these resolutions — such as enabling the PLO to assume its popular responsibilities of struggle in the Jordanian arena — as the basis governing bilateral relations. The council also placed the blame on the Jordanian regime for not attaining positive results [with the PLO] that would practically enhance the PLO's role as the sole legal representative of the Palestinian people in their various places of residence.

The PNC also discussed the joint coordination committee's activities in bolstering steadfastness and stressed the need to work on the Arab level to let the PLO assume its full responsibility in this respect. The council also stressed the role of the Palestinian side in the committee and the need to draw a comprehensive plan, in accordance with predetermined priorities, in order to bolster the steadfastness of our people and their national institutions with the participation of the revolutionary squads as well as with national gatherings inside and outside the homeland.

Considering the fateful cohesion between the Lebanese and Palestinian people, the National Council stressed the importance of a unified political and military stance between the Palestinian revolution and the Lebanese National Movement and various other Lebanese forces as well as the importance of the joint struggle to thwart all the attempts that aim at sapping the strength of the Palestinian revolution in the Lebanese arena, at fragmenting Lebanon, and at endangering its security and Arab character.

The PNC saluted the Lebanese and Palestinian masses and the joint forces, which are standing fast in southern Lebanon, for their sacrifices and acts of heroism in their confrontation against the Zionist enemy and the separatist forces, which are armed to the teeth by the most modern U.S. weapons of destruction. The PNC also considers the Arab summit resolutions and the bases of national accord that were announced by President Ilyas Sarkis as the starting points for ensuring Lebanon's stability and for preserving the Palestinian revolution. The council also affirmed the continuation of the struggle, side by side with the heroic Lebanese people, under the leadership of their national movement and the various other national forces for the sake of the unity of Lebanon's territory, and their people's Arab character and democratic development.

The PNC affirmed its support for the Lebanese National Movement, which rejects all forms of outside intervention and the internationalization projects that aim at harming the Palestinian revolution's steadfastness, the Lebanese National Movement and Syria.

The PNC praised the efforts to unify the forces that are opposed to the separatist-Zionist designs into a broad Lebanese national front. The council affirmed the importance of the national role being played by the Arab Deterrent Forces in order to preserve Lebanon's security, Arab character, territorial safety and unity and in order to foil the partition plans. The council also expressed its rejection of all the resettlement plans and affirmed its full adherance to our people's right to return to their homeland — Palestine.

The PNC has also highly praised the patriotic and progressive forces in Arab Egypt for their heroic struggle waged to abort the Camp David accords and the Egyptian-Israeli treaty. The PNC emphasized its support for the patriotic forces and its belief in the inevitable triumph of the will of our Arab people in Egypt so that Egypt would resume its role of leading the Arab struggle against imperialism and Zionism and for the sake of liberating Palestine.

Regarding the Iraqi-Iranian war, the PNC called for the need to halt this war forthwith. The PNC blessed the efforts that the PLO command has exerted, and which it is still exerting, to halt this war so that the full potential of the two countries could be channeled toward buttressing the struggle that is being waged against the imperialist-Zionist aggression against our area and to liberate Palestine and holy Jerusalem. The reason is that the continuation of this war harms our cause and serves the enemies of our Arab nation and the Muslim peoples.

The PNC emphasized the importance of boosting the efficacy of the National Front for Steadfastness and Confrontation and the need to develop the existing relations among the members of this front in a way that would facilitate achieving its objectives to check all the imperialist conspiracies which are facing this area — first and foremost the Camp David designs and the parties to these designs. The PNC also stressed the basic role of the PLO and Syria, within the framework of the National Front for Steadfastness and

Confrontation, in seeking to discharge the national and pan-Arab objectives of the struggle prescribed by the resolutions passed by the steadfastness and confrontation summit conference.

The PNC expressed the importance it attaches to the Arab people's conference and the need to work to develop the formula for this conference so that this conference can constitute the framework for a popular Arab front dedicated to the achievement of the objectives of our Arab people and nation — liberation, unity and advancement.

The PNC affirmed that imperialist military provocations that are being made in the Arab Gulf and Red Sea areas are an integral part of the imperialist strategy geared to striking the national liberation movements, controlling the destinies and resources of the area and imposing political, military and economic mobilization against it.

The PNC also emphasized that it is imperative to use the Arab homeland's oil resources to ensure the prosperity and progress of the Arab nation and to serve this nation's present causes, particularly the Palestine cause.

The PNC delineated the importance of a strong alliance among the world's revolutionary forces. It expressed its desire to consolidate the relations of friendship and solidarity with the socialist countries — with the friendly Soviet Union in the forefront — with the national liberation movements and with the democratic and progressive forces hostile to imperialism and Zionism in the capitalist countries.

The PNC welcomed the announcement made by President Brezhnev at the 26th CPSU Congress on the Middle East crisis. In this announcement President Brezhnev emphasized the basic role the PLO is playing in the achievement of a just solution to the crisis, the need to put into practice the Palestinian people's inalienable national rights, including their right to set up their independent national state as confirmed by the UN resolutions passed on the Palestine question and the UN role in the resolution of this issue.

The council expressed its appreciation of the political and moral support extended by the socialist countries to the Palestinian revolution and the Palestinian people's struggle.

The PNC emphasized its interest in the unity of the Non-aligned, Movement on the basis of the movement's principles opposed to imperialism, Zionism and racism. It expressed its appreciation of the non-aligned states' solidarity with our people's struggle for their inalienable national rights and their confrontation with aggression. The council lauded the resolutions adopted by the non-aligned sixth summit conference in Havana and the recent resolutions of the foreign ministers in New Delhi on the Palestine and Middle East questions.

The council commended Arab-African solidarity in the struggle against the enemy and its ally the racist regime in South Africa. It also expressed its appreciation of the African states' solidarity with our people's struggle and it saluted the triumph scored by the people of Zimbabwe against racism and the emergence of the Zimbabwe nationalist state. The PNC expressed its full support for the struggle of the people of Namibia against the racist regime in South Africa and for freedom and independence.

The council underscored its firm support for the struggle of the peoples of Latin America and the Caribbean region. It condemned the aggressive practices of the U.S. Government in that region.

The council emphasized the importance of widening the circle of recognition for the PLO. It discussed the moves carried out by the EC states. It expressed its conviction that it is the right and the duty of the Palestinian revolution to continue its political and diplomatic moves and activity at the international level, including the states of Western Europe.

The PNC decided that the soundness of any initiative is measured by its nonrecognition of the Camp David accords and agreements as a basis of a settlement and the recognition of the PLO as the sole legitimate representative of the Palestinian people as well as our people's right to repatriation, self-determination and to their independent state on their national soil.

The PNC called on the Arab and Islamic States, especially the oil states among them, to use their capabilities and resources to make the industrial and capitalist states recognize the PLO and all the inalienable national rights of the Palestinian people.

The council saluted all the democratic and progressive forces opposed to imperialism, Zionism, recial discrimination, and fascism in the states of Western Europe as well as all the capitalist states.

The PNC strongly condemned terrorism and international terrorism, especially the Zionist official and organized terrorism against the Palestinian people, the PLO and the people of Lebanon, as well as American imperialist terrorism against the world liberation movements.

The council affirmed its adherence to the UN Charter and international legitimacy which has recognized the Palestinian people's national rights which are non-negotiable.

At the end of its meetings the PNC accepted the resignation of the Executive Committee in accordance with the basic laws. It elected a new Executive Committee manifesting national unity. The Executive Committee unanimously elected Brother Yasser Arafat as its chairman.

The council extended the term of the present National Council until the meeting of the 16th National Council and specified the way in which it is to be formed.

## 18. Committee for the Occupied Homeland Report on Contact with Jews. Damascus 21 April, 1981

The Committee discussed various subjects related to the development of activities within the occupied land, in all the military, economic and social spheres. . .

A number of most important matters were decided upon regarding the mobilization and concentration of all the potentials of our masses in the occupied homeland *(al-watan al-muhtall),* in order to intensify the armed struggle, and to confirm their commitment to the PLO. . .

The recommendations made a special point of saluting the heroic struggle of the Palestinian masses in that part of Palestine occupied since 1948, which thwarted the enemy plans for the liquidation of their identity, the Judaization of their land and the annihilation of their national culture. . .

Regarding the necessities of strengthening the steadfastness and intensifying the national struggle within the occupied land *(al-ard al-muhtall),* the Council emphasized the need for the mobilization and concentration of the masses' potentials, for the intensification of the armed struggle and the supplying of its necessities, insuring that the PLO is the sole party responsible for the matters concerning the strengthening of our people and its steadfastness in the occupied homeland. . .

The recommendations also confirmed the positive role which the democratic and progressive Jewish anti-Zionist forces play, both ideologically and practically, within the occupied homeland and their recognition of the PLO as the sole legitimate representative of the Palestinian people. . .

The recommendation condemned any contacts which would be held with the parties which follow the way of Zionism, both ideologically and practically. . .

## 19. Palestinian National Council Political Resolutions, Algiers, 22 February, 1983

### On the Palestinian Front

*1. Palestinian National Unity:*

The steadfast and heroic battle in Lebanon and Beirut embodied Palestinian national unity at its best. From the vantage point of the experience of struggle, the PNC affirms the strengthening of national unity between the factions of the revolution within the PLO and affirms the work to advance the structure of organizational relations in all PLO institutions and bodies on the basis of united front work and collective leadership and on the basis of the political and organizational programme approved by the fourteenth session of the PNC.

(A)   The Independent National Decision:

The PNC affirms the continued adherence to and protection of independent Palestinian decisions and resistance to all pressures from any side, aimed at influencing this independence.

(B)   Armed Palestinian Struggle:

The PNC affirms the need to develop and intensify armed struggle against the Zionist enemy. It also affirms the right of the Palestinian revolutionary forces to carry out military actions against the Zionist enemy from all Arab fronts. It also affirms the need to unite the Palestinian revolutionary forces within the framework of a united Palestinian national liberation army.

2.   *The Occupied Homeland:*

(a)   The PNC salutes our masses, steadfast in the occupied territories in the face of occupation, settlement and uprooting. It salutes their total national consensus and adherence to the PLO, the sole legitimate representative of the Palestinian people, *inside* and *outside* (the country).

(b)   The PNC denounces and condemns all suspicious American and Israeli attempts to strike at the Palestinian national consensus and calls on the masses to resist and confront them.

(c)   The PNC affirms the strengthening of the unity of popular, social and national institutions and unions and affirms the need to work to build and develop a national front *inside*.

(d)   The PNC affirms the need to double efforts to strengthen the steadfastness of our people inside the occupied homeland and to offer all the requisites for this steadfastness. Thus, to put an end to enforced emigration and to preserve the land and develop the national economy.

(e)   The PNC salutes the steadfastness of our people inside the areas occupied in 1948 and is proud of their struggle and stand, in the face of Zionist racism, to confirm their national identity as an inseparable part of the Palestinian people. The PNC also affirms the need to provide them with all means of support and to strengthen their unity and the unity of their national forces and institutions.

(f)   The council sends greetings of esteem and pride to prisoners and detainees in enemy prisons inside the occupied homeland and in South Lebanon.

3.   *Our People in the Diaspora:*

The PNC affirms the need to mobilize the energies of our people in all places outside our occupied land and to strengthen their adherence to the PLO as the sole legitimate representative of our Palestinian people. The council charges the executive committee to work to safeguard their (the Palestinian people's) economic and social interests and to defend their acquired rights and their basic freedom and safety.

*Relations with Jewish Forces*

Affirming resolution 14 of the political declaration issued by the PNC at its thirteenth session held on December 3, 1977, the PNC calls on the executive committee to study action in this framework, insofar as it is in keeping with and in the interest of the Palestinian cause and the national Palestinian struggle.

**On the Arab Front**

*1. Arab Relations:*

(a) Deepening the cohesion between the Palestinian revolution and the Arab national liberation movement in the whole Arab nation, in order to actively confront Zionist and imperialist conspiracies and plans of annihilation, especially the Camp David accords and the Reagan plan, and in order to end the Zionist occupation of Arab lands.

(b) Relations between the PLO and Arab States to be built on the following basis:

(i) Commitment to the cause of Arab struggle, headed by the Palestinian cause and struggle for its sake;

(ii) Adherence to the right of the Palestinian people, including the right of return, of self-determination and to establish an independent state under the leadership of the PLO. These are the rights endorsed by Arab summits' resolutions.

(iii) Determination on the unity of representation and national unity and respect for independent Palestinian national decision.

(iv) Rejection of all plans aimed at encroaching upon the right of the PLO as sole legitimate representative of the Palestinian people in any form such as power-of-attorney or agent or participant in the right of representation.

(v) The PNC calls for the strengthening of Arab solidarity on the basis of Arab summit conferences' resolutions and in the light of the above-mentioned principles.

*2. Resolutions of the Fez Summit: "The Arab Peace Plan"*

The PNC considers the resolutions of the Fez Summit as the minimum for political action by the Arab States which must be complimented by military action in all that it entails, in order to redress the balance of power in favour of the struggle and Arab and Palestinian rights.

The council affirms that its understanding of these resolutions does not contradict commitment to the political programme of the PNC resolutions.

## 3.  Jordan

(i)   Affirmation of the special and distinctive relations linking the Palestinian and Jordanian peoples. Affirmation of the need to work to develop this harmony and the national interest of the two peoples and the Arab nation to attain the firm national rights of the Palestinian people, including the right of return, self-determination and the establishment of an independent Palestinian State.

(ii)   Adherence to the resolutions of the PNC concerning relations with Jordan, starting with the PLO as the sole legitimate representative of the Palestinian people, *inside* and *outside* the occupied territories.

The PNC sees future relations with Jordan developing on the basis of a confederation between two independent states.

## 4.  Lebanon

(i)   Strengthening relations with the Lebanese people and their national forces and offering support to their brave struggle in resisting Zionist occupation and its tools.

(ii)   At the forefront of current tasks facing the Palestinian revolution is participation with the Lebanese masses and their democratic national forces in fighting and ending the Zionist occupation.

(ii)   The PNC calls on the executive council to work for holding talks between the PLO and the Lebanese government to achieve safety and security for Palestinian residents living in Lebanon and to ensure their rights to residency, freedom of movement, work opportunity and freedom of social and political activity.

(iv)   Work to stop the random collective and individual arrests on political bases and the release of detainees from prisons of the Lebanese authorities.

## 5.  Relations with Syria

Relations with Syria are based on PNC resolutions, in successive sessions, which affirm the importance of strategic relations between the PLO and Syria, in the service of patriotic and national goals of struggle in confronting the Zionist-imperialist enemy, and regarding the PLO and Syria — the front line before the common danger.

## 6.  Steadfastness and Confrontation Front

The PNC empowers the executive committee of the PLO to hold talks with all parties of the Steadfastness and Confrontation Front to discuss its revival on actual, clear and sound bases, considering that the front did not meet the tasks required from it during the Zionist invasion of Lebanon.

## 7.  *Egypt*

The PNC affirms its rejection of the Camp David accords and related plans for autonomy and civil administration. From its deep-rooted belief in the role of Egypt and its great people in the Arab struggle, the council affirms its stand alongside the struggle of the Egyptian people and their national forces to end the policy of Camp David, so that Egypt can return to its position of struggle at the heart of the Arab nation. The council calls on the executive committee to develop the PLO's relations with the Egyptian popular democratic national forces struggling against the normalization of relations with the Zionist enemy in various forms. It regards this (struggle) as expressing the basic interests of the Arab nation and supporting the struggle of our Palestinian people for their national rights. The council calls on the executive committee to define relations with the Egyptian regime on the basis of the latter's abandoning the Camp David policy.

## 8.  *The Iraq-Iran War*

The PNC holds in esteem the efforts of the PLO executive committee to end the Iraq-Iran war through the committees of the non-aligned countries and the Islamic countries. The council calls on the executive committee to continue its efforts to end this war, after Iraq declares the withdrawal of its forces from Iranian territory in response to the call of the Palestinian revolution, to mobilize all forces in the battle for the liberation of Palestine.

### On the International Front

## 1.  *The Brezhnev Plan*

The PNC expresses its esteem and support for the proposals contained in the plan of President Brezhnev published on September 16, 1980 and which affirm the inalienable national rights of our Palestinian people, including those of return, self-determination and the establishment of an independent Palestinian State under the leadership of the PLO, the sole legitimate representative of the Palestinian people. The council also expresses its esteem for the stand of the socialist bloc countries on the just cause of our people as affirmed by the Prague declaration on the Middle East situation, published on January 3, 1983.

## 2.  *The Reagan Plan*

The Reagan plan, in form and content, does not fulfill the inalienable national rights of the Palestinian people because it denies the right of return, self-determination, the establishment of an independent Palestinian State and that the PLO is sole legitimate representative of the Palestinian people and it contradicts international law. For these reasons, the PNC declares its refusal to consider the plan as a proper basis for a lasting and just solution to the Palestinian cause and the Zionist-Arab conflict.

### 3. International Relations

(i) Deepening and developing relations of the alliance and friendship between the PLO and the socialist countries, primarily the Soviet Union, and various international progressive and liberation forces opposed to racism, colonialism, Zionism and imperialism;

(ii) Deepening relations with non-aligned countries and Islamic and African countries for the sake of the Palestinian cause and other national liberation causes;

(iii) Strengthening relations with friendly countries in Latin America and working to widen the sphere of friendship there;

(iv) Activating political work with the countries of Western Europe and Japan, with the aim of developing their stand and widening the recognition of the PLO and the right of the Palestinian people to establish an independent Palestinian State.

The PNC salutes all progressive and democratic forces hostile to racial discrimination, Zionism and imperialism in Western European countries and various capitalist countries, considering them a basic ally in these countries. (The council) calls on the executive committee to work jointly with these forces for their countries to recognize the firm national rights of the Palestinian people and the PLO.

(v) Continuing the struggle to achieve the isolation of the Zionist entity in the United Nations in various fields;

(vi) Confronting American imperialism and its policy, regarding it as standing at the head of the camp hostile to our just cause and the causes of struggling peoples.

(vii) The council affirms the importance of continuing the struggle against racial discrimination which remains the prevailing practise in a number of regimes, especially South Africa, which has established the firmest relations with the Zionist enemy. The council salutes the struggle of the developing people, led by the SWAPO organization, for freedom and independence. The council also salutes the struggle of the people of South Africa against racial discrimination and oppression.

(viii) The PNC strongly condemns terrorism and international terrorism, particularly the organized and official terrorism of Israel and the US, against the Palestinian people, the PLO, the Lebanese people, the Arab nation and various national liberation movements.

(ix) The PNC affirms its adherence to the principles, charter and resolutions of the United Nations, which confirm the non-negotiable, inalienable national rights of the Palestinian people to establish a lasting and just peace in the Middle East and the right of all peoples subjugated by occupation to practice all forms of struggle for national independence and liberation. The council also affirms its decisive condemnation of all Zionist and imperialist practises which violate international law and the International Declaration of Human Rights and the principles and resolutions of the United Nations Charter.

(x)   The PNC values the activities and achievements of the special UN committee in enabling the Palestinian people to exercise their inalienable rights in Palestine. (The council) salutes the efforts of its members, especially the decision of the UN General Assembly to organize an international conference in the summer of 1983 to support the Palestinian people in achieving their inalienable rights.

The council likewise values the achievements of the secretariat of the international conference of the United Nations in preparing for the success of this conference. The council calls on all brother Arab countries and friendly countries to participate effectively in the work of the conference and likewise, in preparatory and regional meetings, to secure the success of the work of the international conference.

There is no doubt that the people's victory will come. The solidarity of peace-loving peoples is a solidarity we cherish and adhere to. The PNC sends salutations to all the heroic masses of our people, *inside* and *outside* (the occupied territories) and to our brave fighters who have preserved the honour of their revolution, arms and nation. (The council also salutes) the souls of the martyrs and fighters of our Palestinian people and of the Lebanese people who irrigated the national soil with blood and who affirmed that the cause of freedom will not die in our country.

The PNC also salutes our brothers in the Syrian forces who participated in the heroic battle in Beirut and other areas, and their martyrs. The PNC also values all the Arab and Muslim volunteers and friends who came to participate with the joint forces in the battles of Beirut and Lebanon. We salute their heroic martyrs.

The PNC values all countries and friendly forces who offered the support of weapons, money and military effort through equipment and training, particularly the Arab and Islamic States, the non-aligned countries, the African countries and the socialist countries.

—   Long live the victorious Palestinian revolution.

—   Long live the PLO, the unified framework of our people and leader of their struggle.

—   Long live the unity of the struggle of our Arab peoples and the peoples of the world for the sake of freedom and national independence the defeat of Zionism, racism and imperialism.

—Honour and eternal glory to our martyrs.
Revolution Until Victory.

In conclusion, the council warmly thanks and deeply appreciates the people, government and president of Algeria for hosting the council and its guests and for its great care for the success of (the council's) work. (We also thank them) for their effort to ensure the coverage of (the council's) activities in the mass media and in providing a suitable atmosphere for the progress of its discussions and ensuring the safety and comfort of its members and guests. The council especially thanks our brother, President Chadhli Ben Jadid, president of the republic and general secretary of the party, for his officially declared stand concerning the independence of Palestinian decision, and Algeria's readiness to support and further this decision by supporting the Palestinian struggle until it achieves victory and the establishment of an independent Palestinian State.

The council sends thanks and esteem to all popular and official delegations who participated in the work of our council and who declared their support for the PLO and the cause of the Palestinian people.

This international support of our revolution is, without doubt, one of the basic elements in the success of our march, in which the free peoples prove their solidarity in face of the joint enemy of Zionism and imperialism for the sake of the progress, independence and freedom of peoples.

As for our brother Arab delegations who have participated with our council, while thanking and saluting them for their presence and support, we also thank them in particular for their role and action in the Arab arena in creating more favorable conditions for supporting our struggle and for confronting Israeli plans.

The PNC, at the conclusion of its work, promises the Arab and Palestinian masses and all international forces for freedom and struggle, to continue the struggle in all political and military forms and to pursue them towards our people's goals. It considers this international, Arab and Palestinian cohesion to be one of the effective weapons of support and solidarity between peoples whose certain result must be the attainment of praiseworthy goals.


## 20.  Palestine National Council, Political Statement, Amman, 29 November, 1984 [Excerpts]

Our PNC held its 17th session on the hills of Amman, which overlook the hills of Jerusalem, and among our kinfolk and brothers in the Jordanian-Palestinian family. For one week, this council appealed to, consoled, and greeted our people in our occupied territory in Palestine. It deliberated with them, from across the river, on the issues of the revolution and of destiny, and on the cause of the successive generations—the sacred question of Palestine, which is the question of liberation in order to regain the usurped homeland and rights. In this particular session, the interaction and harmony between the two peoples were warmly and deeply felt.

Our session was opened in the presence of His Majesty King Hussein and the members of his government, as well as several Jordanian and Palestinian national figures. This is in addition to guest delegations from most world countries, and representatives of friendly national democratic forces that support our people's struggle. During the opening session, His Majesty King Hussein delivered a frank, noble speech in which he affirmed his concern for the Palestinian national identity and the PLO as the sole, legitimate representative of the Palestinian people. His Majesty also affirmed his government's stand that Jordan will not speak on behalf of the Palestinian people and will continue to exert every possible effort to save Palestine and Jerusalem, but without pursuing a separate solution. His Majesty also affirmed Jordan's respect for independent Palestinian decision-making, and proposed a formula for joint political action. The council has referred this formula to the Executive Committee for study, in accordance with the procedures approved by our National Council—especially in its 16th and 17th sessions—before undertaking a joint cooperative move with the Arab states.

Representatives of scores of fraternal and friendly states as well as representatives of official, popular, and party organizations addressed this session. All those speeches affirmed the Palestinian people's inalienable national rights; asserted that the PLO is the sole, lelgitimate representative of the Palestinian people; and asserted that nobody has the right to interfere in its internal affairs or to encroach on its legitimate institutions.

This session was also attended by a large number of observers from the sons of our Palestinian people who came from different places both inside and outside our occupied homeland. Their mere attendance at this session demonstrated their concern for and adherence to our revolution's democratic traditions, which are based on democratic dialogue in the PLO's legitimate institutions, headed by the PNC. They condemned the fascist conspiracies against the organization and its leadership.

The convocation of the PNC embodies the Palestinian national identity, the independent Palestinian decisionmaking, the free Palestinian will, and the legitimacy of the Palestinian resolution as expressed by the PLO, the leader of our people and the symbol of their struggle.

An Executive Committee has been elected to guarantee the normal operation and effectiveness of the PLO and its institutions, as well as the activity of our people's struggle on all levels and in all arenas, including the Arab and international arenas. Thus, by overcoming all the obstacles and pressures aimed at preventing its convocation, the PNC has achieved the principal objectives for which it held its 17th session. During this session, deep and comprehensive discussions and debates took place. They dealt with complete national and pan-Arab responsibility, with all the various problems, tragedies, and events to which our people and organization were subjected during the period that followed the convening of our 16th PNC session in Algiers in February 1983.

Through this responsible spirit and concern for the supreme national interest, and by placing it above all wounds, the PNC succeeded in making the decisions that will enable it to tackle the results of past painful events, confront future challenges, and find necessary ways of confronting these challenges—ways to guarantee the continuation and escalation of the effectiveness of our struggle, achieve our inalienable national objectives, and promote our pan-Arab action as well as regional and international cooperation in light of Arab and international developments.

From this premise, and as a result of all the speeches and views that were made, including the petitions, cables, and the messages from our kinfolk in the occupied land and from our friends in the world, this council's resolutions include, among other things, the following:

1. The need to continue efforts to achieve a national Palestinian unity of independent will and decisionmaking, and one that honestly and sincerely follows the objectives for which our struggle and organization began and for the sake of which our numerous martyrs have fallen. These resolutions stipulate the need to continue the constructive dialogue that took place in Aden and Algiers in order to achieve national unity. That dialogue and the subsequent agreements were characterized by a spirit that can be regarded as a sound basis for continuing the dialogue between the various national Palestinian forces and organizations. The council's resolutions also stipulate entrusting both the office of the chairman and the Executive Committee to form a committee from its members in order to participate in following up the comprehensive, national dialogue; to enrich it; and to guarantee it successful continuation in achieving and preserving Palestinian national unity.

2. While it considers the right to self-determination, repatriation, and the establishment of a Palestinian state as the introduction and the basis for any just political move toward our cause, the PNC reaffirms its previous sessions' resolutions concerning its stand on Resolution 242, which does not consider our question as one of a people and rights, but one of refugees. Therefore, it disavows our national rights. The PNC rejects all plans which do not contain these rights, particularly the Camp David Accords, the autonomy plans, the Reagan plan, and everything which does not recognize our national inalienable rights. The PNC also announced that its independent national decisionmaking is linked to the pan-Arab dimension. The PNC believes that any solution to the Palestine question can only be achieved in accordance with international legitimacy, on the basis of UN resolutions on Palestine, and in the framework of an international conference

in which the two superpowers would participate, under the auspices of the United Nations and the UN Security Council in the presence of all concerned parties, including the PLO on equal footing.

3. Inspired by the history of our people's Arab relations, out of its belief in the pan-Arab character of our cause, aware of the infringements on the Arab countries' security and sovereignty as a result of the Palestinian cause, and out of its realization of the importance of Arab solidarity in confronting the US-Zionist alliance which is hostile to our people and seeks to impose hegemony on our people's security and to exploit our resources, the PNC adopted a series of resolutions based on all of this. These resolutions seek to establish an Arab reality that will be capable of confronting the challenges of this alliance at this stage. With respect to Jordan, the PNC decided to continue the efforts to develop relations with Jordan in order to coordinate joint efforts to achieve our common objectives—the liberation of the Palestinian land and individual—on the basis of our firm convictions in the same fate, on the basis of what the Arabs agreed to in Fez, and in cooperation with Arab countries.

With respect to fraternal Syria—whose militant Arab history, geographical and political importance, and military power we appreciate—the PNC recommended the need to overcome the tension and subversion that have affected Palestinian-Syrian relations, and the need to rise above wounds, suffering, and feelings of bitterness in order to carry out a rectification of relationship on a clear and frank basis that will guarantee freedom of Palestinian will and national decisionmaking, as well as dealings on equal footing within the framework of the pan-Arab commitment and far from interference in the two parties' domestic affairs. This would mobilize all resources for confronting the US-Israeli alliance and its schemes.

With respect to fraternal Egypt, whose status and role we appreciate, the PNC explained the established facts in Arab-Egyptian relations and the new developments in Egyptian policy. The PNC asked the PLO Executive Committee to adopt a policy based on this rule, that fulfills the needs of our people in Egypt and the Gaza strip, and works to strengthen relations between the fraternal Egyptian and Palestinian peoples.

With respect to the Iraq-Iran war, which has been going on for more than 4 years, our PNC has urged the PLO Executive Committee and its chairman Brother Yasser Arafat to exert more efforts to immediately halt it. This is because ending it will stop the bloodshed of the two Muslim people, and will redress the balance of power in the interest of our nation in its confrontation of the Zionist enemy.

The council notes that the Palestinian revolution and the Lebanese nationalist forces were attacked while fraternal Iraq and its valiant Army as well as the rest of the region's countries were preoccupied. It also notes that fraternal Iraq responded to all exerted peace efforts to end the war and stop the bloodshed. The council affirms its special resolutions of bolstering and developing relations with the fraternal Arab countries in accordance with the resolutions of the 16th session. The council affirms the continuing support of the Palestinian people and the PLO for the Lebanese people's struggle to liberate their land, and to regain the unity of its territory and people as well as its national sovereignty.

4. The PNC hailed our people in the occupied land in appreciation for the glorious steadfastness in defending their freedom, land, and sanctities—particularly in Jerusalem, where the Al-Aqsa Mosque, the Ibrahimi Mosque, and our Islamic and Christian holy places are being desecrated and threatened with Judaization—against the Zionist occupation and its racist, terrorist practices. The council also hailed the rallying of our people in the occupied homeland around the PLO and its legitimate leadership, as expressed by the rallies in support for the convocation of the council which were crowned by the blood of martyrs. That is why the council decided to call this 17th session the session of the PNC martyrs. The council also hailed the prisoners and detainees in the enemy's prisons in the occupied land and southern Lebanon. The council adopted several resolutions to bolster our people's steadfastness and resistance until we liberate our land with various legitimate means, the foremost of which is escalating armed struggle.

5. The PNC affirmed all the resolutions governing the PLO's relations of friendship with the socialist countries, the foremost of which is the USSR, the Islamic Conference Organization countries, the Nonaligned Movement, the PRC, the OAU, the Latin American countries, and the various countries, forces, and movements struggling to achieve independence, freedom, justice, and peace and which oppose imperialism, colonialism, and racial discrimination—particularly the peoples of Namibia and South Africa—in our common just struggle against colonialism and racial discrimination.

## 21. Statement by the PLO's Executive Committee on the Amman Accord, 19 February, 1985

The Executive Committee of the Palestine Liberation Organization held a series of meetings between the 17th and the 18th of February 1985 under the chairmanship of Yasser Arafat, Chairman of the Executive Committee of the Palestine Liberation Organization.

The Executive Committee discussed the present issues on the agenda and the developments of the political and military situation in the area.

The Executive Committee discussed the Jordanian-Palestinian plan of action which was agreed upon on Monday, February 11th, 1985 between the PLO and the government of the Hashemite Kingdom of Jordan.

The Executive Committee discussed the detailed reports pertaining to the ongoing Palestinian-Jordanian talks which followed the agreement as well as the aide-memoire (explanatory memorandum) which was transmitted.

The Executive Committee of the Palestine Liberation Organization reaffirms that the joint action between the PLO and Jordan is based on the following:

1. Palestinian legitimacy as defined in the resolutions of the Palestine National Council, particularly in its 16th and 17th Sessions.

2. Arab legitimacy as defined in the resolutions of the Arab Summits, particularly the resolutions of the Rabat and Fez Summits.

3. International legitimacy as defined in the United Nations resolutions.

The joint action is based on all the previous resolutions which were approved, and which are:

1. Ending the Zionist occupation of the occupied Arab territories, including Jerusalem.

2. The realization of the inalienable rights of the Palestinian people, including their right to return, to self-determination and to the establishment of their independent state in their national homeland.

3. The rejection of all the plans of capitulation and separate deals, such as the self-rule plan, the Camp David Accords, the Reagan initiative and Security Council Resolution 242 which do not constitute a sound basis for a just solution which guarantees the national rights of the Palestinian people.

4. The rejection of the granting of mandates and representation (al-tafwid wal-inaba) or the participation in the right of representation to any other party.

The formula for joint Palestinian-Jordanian action aims at establishing a nucleus for common Arab action away from axis-building and for serious and effective action based on total Arab solidarity.

A reaffirmation of the privileges and specific relations between the Jordanian and the Palestinian people and the common aim of both peoples in conformity with the resolutions of the Palestine National Council are represented in the establishment of a Confederation between the two states of Jordan and Palestine. For the right framework to achieve the required aims is the convening of an international conference under the auspices of the United Nations, to be attended by the permanent members of states in the security council and with the participation of the PLO in its capacity as the sole legitimate representative of the Palestinian people and on an equal footing with the parties concerned in the conflict.

Based upon these foundations from which the joint Palestinian-Jordanian plan of action emanates, the Executive Committee of the Palestine Liberation Organization decided to approve the plan of action affirming that this action must include the parties concerned represented within a joint Arab Delegation, and that this plan of action receive total Arab support.

## 22.    Declaration by Yasser Arafat on Terrorism, Cairo, 7 November, 1985

The Palestinian people has and continues to struggle to liberate its occupied land, to exercise its right to self-determination, and to establish a state as a necessary condition for achieving a just and lasting peace in the region in which all peoples would coexist, free from acts of terrorism or subjugation.

Despite the political and military changes which the region has witnessed, especially in the last few years, beginning with the Israeli aggression against the PLO in Beirut, Lebanon in 1982 and the Israeli raid on Tunis against the PLO headquarters in 1985, the Palestinian people has continued to struggle and to cling to peace in pursuit of preparing the climate in the region and internationally for a just and peaceful solution.

The PLO has made good progress along this path in very important stages:

* The Arab summit in Fez which was held in 1982 and in which all the Arab parties, including the PLO, chose the peace option with Security Council guarantees and under the auspices of international legitimacy. These decisions were reaffirmed in Casablanca in 1985.

* The Geneva declaration regarding the international conference on Palestine in 1983, which reaffirmed the right of all states in the region to exist within safe and internationally recognized borders, including the right of the Palestinian people to self-determination on its land and to establish a Palestinian state.

* The Palestinian-Jordanian agreement of 11 February, 1985, which dealt with the specifics of the special relationship between the Jordanian and Palestinian peoples and which set down their adherence to a single line and a shared vision of goals and means.

* Continued adherence to the framework of an international conference on peace in the Middle East, to be attended by the USSR, the US, and the permanent members of the Security Council, as well as the other concerned parties in the region, including the PLO. And, in the framework of pursuing a just and peaceful solution, and given the PLO's struggle by all legitimate means to regain the established national rights of the Palestinians as well as their political freedom, the PLO condemns all violations of human rights, especially the right to life and security without discrimination on the basis of creed, gender, or color.

As an impetus to the efforts which have been exerted to convene an international peace conference, the PLO announces its criticism and condemnation of all acts of terrorism, whether they be those in which states become involved or those committed by individuals or groups against the innocent and defenseless, wherever they may be.

The PLO reaffirms its declaration issued in 1974 which condemned all operations outside [Palestine] and all forms of terrorism. And it restates the adherence of all its groups and institutions to that declaration. Beginning today, the PLO will take all measures to deter violators.

In view of the fact that this adherence cannot be achieved unilaterally, it is up to the international community to force Israel to stop all of its acts of terrorism both inside and outside [Palestine].

In this context, the PLO stresses its insistence upon the right of the Palestinian people to resist the Israeli occupation of its land by all available means, with the goal of achieving withdrawal from its land. For the right to resist foreign occupation is a legitimate right, not abrogated by the UN Charter, which calls for disavowing the use of force or threatening to use it to settle conflicts, and which considers the resort to force a violation of its principles and goals. The right of the Palestinian people to resist the occupation in the occupied territories has been stressed in numerous UN resolutions and in the rules of the Geneva Convention.

Events underline the certainty that terrorist operations committed outside [Palestine] hurt the cause of the Palestinian people and distort its legitimate struggle for freedom. From another perspective, these events deepen our conviction that terminating the occupation and putting limits on its policies is the one way to achieve peace and security in the region. The PLO implores all peace-loving powers in all parts of the world to stand beside it as it takes this step to participate in ridding the world of the phenomenon of terrorism and in freeing the individual from fear and protecting him from danger. For in the end, our goal is achieving a just, comprehensive, and lasting peace which will safeguard the affirmation of the enduring national rights of the Palestinian people in order to establish a safe society everywhere.

## 23. The PLO's Three Proposals on the Peace Process, Amman, 5 February, 1986

*The three proposals which follow were forwarded during the round of abortive talks between Jordanian and Palestinian officials in Amman in early February 1986.*

### I

In the event the Palestine Liberation Organization is extended an invitation to attend an international conference with effective authority to devise a peaceful solution for the Palestine question and to settle the Middle East conflict, and in which the permanent members of the UN Security Council and concerned Arab parties would participate, then the PLO would agree to participate in this conference on an equal footing within a joint Jordanian-Palestinian delegation and on the basis of securing the legitimate rights of the Palestinian people, including their right to self-determination, within a confederation with the Hashemite Kingdom of Jordan, as stipulated in the Jordanian-Palestinian accord signed in February 1985 and on the basis of implementing UN and Security Council resolutions pertinent to the Palestine question, including Resolutions 242 and 338.

In this context, the PLO reaffirms its condemnation and rejection of terrorism as confirmed in the Cairo Declaration.

## II

The Palestine Liberation Organization, the sole legitimate representative of the Palestinian people, affirms its steadfast belief that the peace process must lead to a just, comprehensive, and lasting peace in the Middle East and guarantee the realization of the legitimate rights of the Palestinian people, including their right to self-determination, within a Jordanian-Palestinian confederation.

In light of its sincere desire for peace, the PLO expresses its readiness to negotiate within the framework of an international conference attended by the permanent members of the Security Council with all the concerned parties, including Israel, on the basis of the Jordanian-Palestinian accord ratified on 11 February, 1985 and on the basis of UN resolutions pertaining to the Palestine question, including Security Council Resolutions 242 and 338.

In this context, the PLO reaffirms its condemnation and rejection of terrorism, which was confirmed in the Cairo Declaration of November 1985.

## III

The call for convening an international conference to settle the Middle East conflict and solve the Palestine question must be sponsored by the United Nations in its capacity as the international institution established after World War II to put an end to the suffering of peoples, to prevent aggression, and to safeguard justice and respect for human rights. The Preamble to the UN Charter issued in 1945 stipulates the realization of international cooperation to settle international disputes and to secure fundamental human rights and the right of peoples to self-determination.

Since the Palestine question is the core of our Middle East problems, the call to convene an international conference to resolve the conflict and establish peace in the region and to ensure the implementation of adopted resolutions and measures, the participation of the permanent members of the Security Council and concerned Arab parties including the PLO on an equal footing within a joint Jordanian-Palestinian delegation must be assured.

On the basis of the UN Charter, which affirms and determines respect for fundamental human rights and the right to self-determination of peoples, and on the basis of UN resolutions pertaining to the Palestine question and the Arab region, including Resolutions 242 and 338, the PLO shall participate in the international peace conference in its capacity as the sole legitimate representative of the Palestinian people, which is recognized (as such) on the Arab and international levels, and which has enjoyed observer status at the UN since 1974.

The participation of the PLO in the international conference shall be on the basis of securing the legitimate rights of the Palestinian people, including their right to self-determination within a confederation with the Hashimite Kingdom of Jordan, as stipulated in the Jordanian-Palestinian accord signed in February 1985.

In this context, the PLO reaffirms its condemnation and rejection of terrorism as confirmed in the Cairo Declaration of November 1985.

## 24.  PLO Executive Committee Statement, Tunis, 7 March, 1986

*The following statement was the official PLO response to the 19 February speech by King Hussein, terminating Palestinian-Jordanian coordination in the peace process.*

The PLO Executive Committee, with the participation of the Fateh Central Committee, has studied the current political situation from all its angles and dimensions. It has examined the new events and developments witnessed in the Palestinian and Arab arenas and the region. The most prominent aspect has been the US-Israeli onslaught against the Palestinian people and their national rights and the PLO, and the confiscation of the national achievements realized by the Palestinian Arab people through their struggle and sacrifices.

The Executive Committee in particular reviewed the developments of the situation in the occupied territory. It examined with pride the unified, comprehensive, and strong popular position which has firmly resisted the Zionist occupation and Zionist schemes and conspiracies, and which is standing up in a principled and firm manner in the battle to defend its existence, fate, and freedom, stressing its complete rallying around the PLO—the sole legitimate representative of the Palestinian people—and stressing its adherence to national constant factors which have been approved by PNC sessions and to which the Palestinian leadership has become committed.

The Executive Committee has also reviewed the course of the unification efforts which the PLO is undertaking with all Palestinian groups. It has studied the state of affairs in our Palestinian camps in Lebanon and the great popular steadfastness in the face of the deportation conspiracy, the fraternal and militant relationship with the heroic Lebanese people, and the escalation of resistance against Zionist occupation in southern Lebanon. The Executive Committee also reviewed the reports submitted to it on all political activities by the PLO and its chairman in the Palestinian, Arab, and international fields.

In the Arab field, the Executive Committee followed with great interest the developments and the course of the Iraqi-Iranian war in light of the recent attack by the Iranian forces against the soil of fraternal Iraq, and the Iraqi Army's heroic steadfastness and its courageous confrontation of the recent attack. It viewed with great satisfaction the decisive results recorded by this steadfastness in protecting Iraqi Arab territory, the positive effects this would have for the entire region, and the objective opportunities it provides to put an end to the war and settle the dispute with peaceful means in a way that safeguards the interests of the Iraqi and Iranian people, the Arab and Islamic nations, and the Palestinian cause.

Reviewing the results of the Palestinian-Jordanian talks and the state of affairs and new developments in the region, the leadership examined the speech by His Majesty King Hussein on 19 February, 1986 and the opinions contained in this speech. The Palestinian leadership sees that it is necessary to clarify the facts to our people and nation out of the PLO's keen desire to project the truth of its stand and to remove elements of distortion and ambiguity concerning a number of questions that were raised.

The PLO affirms the following:

1. The PLO at this time and this level does not see a need to return to the conditions which accompanied the representation of the Palestinian people during the stage which preceded the rise of the PLO in shouldering this national responsibility. In this connection, the basic definition of the right of the Palestinian people to choose their representatives must be stressed. No one else is entitled to argue or debate this question.

The shouldering by the PLO of this national responsibility is manifested in its complete, firm, and strong form through the cohesion of the armed Palestinian resistance and the political organizational framework of the Palestinian people— the framework of the PLO. The PLO, as a result of this, and thanks to the struggle of the heroic Palestinian people and their supreme sacrifices, has become a dynamic embodiment of resistance against occupation and of the struggle to achieve the national inalienable rights of the Palestinian people, who have wrested this representation in the Arab and international arenas under the PLO.

The Rabat summit in 1974 came to reinforce this militant reality, which was confirmed in resolutions by the United Nations and all its institutions and the resolutions of nonaligned, African, Asian, Islamic, and socialist countries and other friendly countries which recognized the PLO as the Palestinian people's sole, legitimate representative.

From the beginning, this representation would not have become a recognized political fact had it not been for the fact that the organization was an embodiment of the Palestinian national identity in all its dimensions and forms and an expression of the Palestinian national aspirations and aims, and because the Palestinian people have always affirmed in every way that the PLO is the national militant identity of every Palestinian. This fact has never contradicted, and will not contradict, the national dimension or framework of the Palestinian people, their cause, struggle, and destiny.

2. The Palestinian people's struggle, which is led by the PLO, is the achievement of all the sons of our Palestinian people inside and outside our occupied Palestinian land. Here, we should remember that the Zionist enemy would not have sent all of its army to Lebanon to strike at the PLO bases, or its planes across the Mediterranean to Tunis to strike at the PLO bases there, had it not realized that the source of danger exists here just as it does there, and everywhere the PLO and its militant people are present. Just as the Palestinian people's struggle and achievements are an indivisible whole, they cannot be transferred to others. This does not, of course, mean that our Palestinian people do not fully appreciate or are not fully grateful for all the Arab and friendly contributions toward bolstering their just struggle to achieve their inalienable national objectives.

3. The attempt to separate the organization from the people, or the organization from its leadership and institutions, constitute a futile attempt in the face of our great Palestinian people, who have gained experience in confronting challenges and conspiracies and who have affirmed with deep nationalist awareness their adherence to the PLO and its leadership, thus foiling all attempts to create alternative leaderships. In this our people recall the Algerian experience, in which the militant Algerian people succeeded in foiling the conspiracy aimed at isolating them from the Algerian Liberation Front at the height of the comprehensive national struggle against French colonialism. And just as the Algerian people raised the slogan "The people are the FLN and the FLN is the people," the Palestinian people today raise the same slogan: "The people are the PLO and the PLO is the people." This is the most convincing and deepest embodiment of the relation of the people with their cause, rights, leadership, and their national, independent Palestinian decisionmaking.

The relation emanates from the commitment to liberate the land and the people, which are physically linked. On the great path toward this commitment, the blood of martyred leaders in various positions and battles mixed with the blood of the strugglers, men and women, from the sons of these great sacrificing people during the march of the people with their leadership, cadres, and bases. This march was conducted by waves of martyrs and blood streams on the road to liberation, victory, and return.

4. The unity of struggle of the Palestinian people is an image of the unity of the people and cause. As a matter of elementary rule and principle, no one has the right to divide our Palestinian people into those who are inside and those who are outside, or into land and people, or people and organization, or organization and leadership, or into any other classification. The Palestinian cause is the cause of all the Palestinian people: it is their national cause and political right. Moreover, it

is a cause of the relation between the people to the homeland and man to land, whether the Palestinian is in his homeland and on his soil or exiled from his homeland and land.

Any partitioning of the Palestinian people or renunciation of their cause automatically means entering into the idea of an alternative homeland or homelands, an idea that carries with it a threat to the Palestinian question and the Palestinian people, and a threat to the lands and peoples of the proposed alternative homelands. Our brothers in Jordan realize that the danger of this conspiracy threatens them just as it threatens us. In this regard, the PLO is eager to point out that the idea of fragmenting the Palestinian people and their cause has been from the start a Zionist idea proposed by the enemy, from the beginning of Jewish immigration to Palestine and until the Camp David conspiracy with its Palestinian clause. Moreover, the idea of an alternative homeland is also an old Zionist idea which the Zionist leaders reiterate. The idea of an alternative leadership for part of the Palestinian people, especially in the West Bank and Gaza, is also a Zionist idea, which preceded the Village Leagues and will be proposed after these leagues. This remains a Zionist call and design.

Our people have stubbornly struggled and offered costly sacrifices in order to eliminate the conspiracy of settlement and alternative homelands. Historic testimony to this is still alive and decisive, facts about this are still there, and our people have been able to foil the conspiracy of settlement in Sinai, Jordan, the Syrian island (al-Jazirah), and southern Lebanon. They are now rejecting, with the same insistence and determination, the conspiracy of an alternative homeland once again, in fraternal Jordan, raising high their eternal emblem: Palestine is the homeland of the Palestinians; there is no homeland other than it; and it is the land of the Arabs. From these premises, which are considered of extreme importance and of delicate nature for the Palestinian people, the PLO is interested in clarifying its stand on the other issues being submitted concerning the Palestinian-Jordanian relationship, in its foundations and current line; the Palestinian-Jordanian joint move; the stand on Resolutions 242 and 338; and on the right of the Palestinian people to self-determination in the framework of the endeavor for a just and comprehensive settlement.

1. The PLO proceeds from its faith in the special relationship between the Palestinian and Jordanian people, with all the precision that this expression contains. Hence the organization's eagerness to overcome any negative aspects in its relations with Jordan. The current line of Palestinian-Jordanian relations was renewed in the second half of the seventies by the visit of Brother Abu 'Ammar [Yasser Arafat] and Col. Mu'ammar al-Qadhdhafi to Jordan, by the joint committee stemming from the Baghdad summit, and the continuous meetings between the two sides.

The PLO has always been the one to initiate this, and its motivation for such initiatives has been a fundamental conception of the fateful and special relationship between Jordan and Palestine. The PLO wanted to deepen this concept by working for a new framework that would embue the relationship with realistic substance and the necessary positiveness to face up to challenges and lay down steps for joint action.

The PLO's motivation was also the manifestation of a Zionist line openly calling for settling the Palestinian cause east of the River Jordan, the call for an alternative homeland. It was also motivated by the appearance of a second line to the effect that the settlement of the Palestinian issue must take place to the west of the river, in accordance with Israeli formulas that would be fulfilled at the Palestinian people's expense. This was expressed through conspiracies and attempts at imposing administrative self-rule.

The PLO saw that both calls represented a danger to Palestine and Jordan at the same time, and that the correct solution must come through concerted Palestinian-Jordanian efforts within a balanced relationship that would be able to constitute the core of a unified and effective Arab move. As a matter of fact, this fundamental stage initiated by the PLO—with all its contacts, talks, debates, or agreements—constituted the platform for all subsequent development of the relationship between the PLO and the Jordanian government. The concept—adopted by the PNC in its sixteenth session in 1983 and reaffirmed at the seventeenth session—of this special relationship and its future confederation-type framework was based on that serious Palestinian initiative. Furthermore, the political framework of this relationship has been based on the resolutions of the Arab summits, beginning with the 1974 Rabat summit.

2. From this fundamental stage, the Jordanian-Palestinian relationship progressed during the period that followed the Zionist invasion of Lebanon in 1982. Everyone recalls that this stage witnessed the appearance of Reagan's plan, which the PLO rejected. A positive strategic transformation also took place at this stage on the Arab level, embodied in the Arab peace plan adopted by the Fez summit, through which a comprehensive Arab concept of the question of a just peace was submitted. The PLO viewed this Arab peace plan as containing an important political dimension, particularly since it enjoyed widespread world support.

The PLO at the time focused on the importance of establishing a relationship with Jordan on the basis of common destiny, to be solidified by an agreement on principles that would define the formula of the joint move based on the Arab peace plan, particularly following the suspension of work by the seven-member committee entrusted with carrying out efforts to implement the Fez summit resolutions. However, the dissimilarity in stands between the Jordanian government and the PLO on the Reagan plan—to which the Jordanian government responded positively—brought about differences of opinion on the objectives of the joint move. Thus, the stage ended without reaching any agreement.

3. Late in 1984 and at the beginning of 1985, a new stage was initiated which began with King Hussein's initiative of accepting to hold the PNC session in

Amman. The results of the talks and the dialogue, which took place between the two sides at the time were contained in the 11 February, 1985 agreement, known as the Jordanian-Palestinian Joint Action Plan. On the basis of this agreement, and within the limits of its provisions, a joint political plan of action was formulated to be carried out on the international level to create suitable conditions for the convocation of an international peace conference in accordance with the Palestinian and Arab concept of the framework and prerogatives of this conference. The Jordanian side promised that it and its Arab brothers would exert their efforts with the United States to have it accept the formula of a just and comprehensive international solution. While the PLO was aware of the realities of the US stand, and the US intransigence toward it and toward the Palestinian people's national rights, it believed that this did not conflict with a Jordanian attempt to influence the US stand.

For its part, Jordan carried out attempts in this direction lasting several months. The results of these attempts, as Jordan told the PLO, were that the US stand continued to refuse to recognize the PLO and the Palestinian people's inalienable rights, including the right to self-determination; that it continued to insist on advance recognition by the PLO of Resolutions 242 and 338 and of Israel's right to exist within secure and recognized boundaries; and that the PLO must announce the suspension of armed struggle in exchange for US agreement to the PLO's participation in the international conference within a joint delegation. The United States also left the door open to Israel to reject all that it believed to be inappropriate, or all that it saw as being in conflict with its interests.

4. The PLO has reiterated its public stand toward Resolution 242, which it rejected from the beginning because it ignores the core of the Palestinian problem, whether on the level of the land, people, rights, or representation. The PLO explained that if it agreed to the resolution unaccompanied by the right to self-determination as the basis for an international conference to achieve a settlement in the Middle East, it would be agreeing to the striking of the Palestinian cause from the agenda of the international conference. The conference then would only deal with border issues. This resolution, which deals with the Palestinian cause as being a refugee problem, was explained in the Vance-Dayan statement in October 1977 as meaning that it deals with Palestinian and Jewish refugees.

The PLO stated that what is required, in accordance with international legitimacy, UN resolutions, Arab resolutions, and the Palestinian-Jordanian agreement, is to solve the Palestinian issue in all its aspects. Such a solution cannot be achieved except through guaranteeing the Palestinian people's right to self-determination in an explicit and clear manner, as has been the case with other peoples on earth.

The right to self-determination is a sacred right which is guaranteed by international conventions, particularly the UN Charter, and has been acknowledged as a right of the Palestinian people by all the resolutions and statements issued by the

United Nations, the Arab and Islamic summits, the nonaligned countries, African countries, and socialist countries. The EEC also expressed support for this right in the Venice Declaration in 1980. The highest Christian authorities also supported it, as well as the European Parliament, and Warsaw Pact statements. From this premise, the right of self-determination of the Palestinian people and their exercise of this right are not merely an internal and bilateral issue between Jordan and the PLO but a firm, natural, and sacred right which is being attained and entrenched through the huge sacrifices our people are making and through Arab world support for it.

The commitment of the Palestinian people and their leadership, the PLO, to the right of self-determination does not stop with the recognition of this right but extends to practicing it on the land liberated from occupation. The Israeli enemy, backed by the United States, is preventing the Palestinian people from exercising this right, not Jordan. Any Palestinian choice of the form of the relationship between the Palestinian state which emerges as a result of liberation and Jordan, or any other Arab country, will become an established fact when the right of self-determination is exercised on the land following the evacuation of the occupiers from it.

That is why the PLO insists that the right to self-determination must be one of the basic principles on whose basis the international conference would convene. This right must not be subject to disavowal, cancellation, or bargaining. This basis on which the PLO insists is the only factor that guarantees a just and comprehensive settlement that will not bring about any injustice or prejudice to the Palestinian people in the diaspora or under occupation.

5. The PLO rejects the US understanding of the international conference, which contradicts the Palestinian and Arab understanding with regard to its framework and suggested prerogatives. The US stand has remained confined to regarding it as a mere international umbrella for direct negotiations between the concerned parties. The PLO has rejected and continues to reject this, while affirming its stand on the need to adhere to the framework and prerogatives endorsed by the Casablanca summit for the international conference.

6. The PLO believes that the overall US stand has sought to ignore the main points that the PLO is eager to establish, and which Jordan said it was eager to establish, to achieve a permanent, just settlement. More specifically, Washington has sought to ignore the Palestinian representation through the PLO, by refusing to recognize the Palestinian people's inalienable rights—foremost of which is the right to self-determination—and by refusing to provide an international guarantee for the justice and durability of any settlement that can be achieved. A careful reading of the contents of King Hussein's speech confirms that the United States had intended to delude the Palestinian people into believing that an opportunity for peace existed in return for the PLO's response to its demand to give fundamental concessions. This was the point of difference which is essentially a difference with

the United States. On this basis, the PLO concentrated and planned that further steadfastness in the face of US prevarications and pressure was the sound course to obtain the necessary guarantees for achieving positive conditions for the settlement. But these positive conditions were not made available. The PLO expresses deep regret that King Hussein's speech, which concentrated on directing blame at the PLO, justified, in return, the US stand. Instead of blaming the US stand for foiling the move, the PLO was held responsible—a repetition of the stand which was previously announced regarding the joint delegation's visit to Britain. In fact, the PLO sees no reason to defend itself in this regard. However, it would be useful in this respect to refer to what was explained in the speech regarding the failure of all the meetings and initiatives in which Jordan took part and to which the PLO was not a party, starting with Jordan's acceptance of Resolution 242 in November 1967, the Rogers initiative, the Geneva conference, the disengagement of forces, and the Reagan plan. In all these cases, and others, the failure was due to the absence of US credibility and Washington's permanent bias toward the Zionist enemy.

7. With regard to what has been said about the PLO's course and credibility and the allegation that it accepted Resolutions 242 and 338 in August 1985, it should be noted that the resolutions of the emergency Arab summit in Casablanca which was held at that time, affirmed the need to adhere to the Fez summit resolutions and regarded these resolutions the basis of the Arab and the Palestinian-Jordanian moves. They also affirmed the Palestinian people's inalienable rights. This contradicts that allegation, which fundamentally conflicts with the resolutions to which we adhered at Casablanca—which mentioned the Jordanian-Palestinian efforts conducted through the Jordanian-Palestinian agreement signed on 11 February, 1985—and which provided that this move be based on the Fez summit resolution and be within the framework of seeking to convene an effective international conference with the participation of the USSR, and the United States, the permanent Security Council members, and the parties to the conflict in the region, including the PLO, to achieve a just, permanent, and comprehensive solution to the Middle East conflict and the Palestine question.

According to the agreement at the time following the Casablanca summit, a meeting was supposed to take place between a Jordanian-Palestinian joint delegation and [US Assistant Secretary of State Richard] Murphy. Agreement was reached with the Jordanian government to draft an integrated program that included US recognition of the PLO and the Palestinian people's legitimate national rights, including their right to self-determination, as well as other political guarantees for the PLO, in order to convene the international conference in return for the PLO's acceptance of international resolutions, including 242 and 338. However, as is known to everyone, the joint delegation's meeting with Murphy did not take place because the United States retreated from its promises to Jordan. How can our organization alone be asked to recognize Resolutions 242 and 338 while the United States refuses to recognize in return the Palestinian people's right to self-determination and refuses to provide all the political guarantees for the PLO which formed the crux of the talks with Jordan regarding the arrangement of the joint delegation's meeting with the US envoy? Moreover, how can the PLO be held responsible for the retreat while the PLO has never accepted Resolution 242 without its being linked to all the other UN resolutions and to the right to self-determination, starting with what it agreed upon with Jordan on 11 February and ending with its current firm stand on this issue?

There is no doubt that the responsibility for the failure rests with the US retreat, and that it is US credibility that has always been doubtful. The PLO has fulfilled its promise to its people and its Arab nation. It has never retreated from struggle to achieve the Palestinian people's rights and has spared no sacrifice for the continuation of armed struggle and for seeking any political move that might achieve a just and lasting solution. Therefore, the real criterion for its credibility is its firm commitment to its people's rights and its struggle for the sake of these rights.

8. What is being said about the mechanism of a solution and that the PLO does not care for priorities or for the restoration of the land is baseless. The PLO believes that its first and foremost goal is to achieve the Palestinian people's inalienable national rights. The restoration of the land is not merely a tactical option subject to priority calculations but a national goal to be achieved by the PLO, side by side with its people and its Arab nation. The PLO also exerts every effort to mobilize all Palestinian, Arab, and international energies to achieve it.

It has been the destiny of the Palestinian people and the PLO to inherit a great and accumulated burden (for which others were responsible). The PLO also spares no effort to seek its brothers' participation and to work with them to regain the land and the holy places. If there is somebody who needs militant proof, we can say that the Palestinian national struggle, recorded with Palestinian and Arab martyrs' blood, is decisive proof that the land is the base. Although that land was lost at a cheap price, our Palestinian people and our Arab nation are ready to liberate it at a high price, namely, at the cost of many martyrs.

9. Regarding talk about the sufferings of the people under occupation and about the issue of ending the sufferings by accepting the fait accompli and the time factor, as well as what is being described as the need to exploit the current opportunity, the PLO is concerned about clarifying matters that should be very clear. The foremost of these is the fact that the suffering of the Palestinian people should be viewed deeply, comprehensively, and objectively. It is suffering in which the Palestinians inside and outside the occupied land are unified. Those who are under occupation are suffering from the ferocity of repression, coercion, settlement, confiscation of land, and usurpation of the national identity. Those who are outside the land are suffering the pain of homelessness, persecution, and siege.

The PLO will never allow, and nobody has the right to agree to, partition [sic] of the suffering of the Palestinian people, or to deal with this suffering far from its essence and cause—the Zionist usurpation of the Palestinian homeland and its complicated consequences on all levels. In light of this, the PLO, as well as the entire Palestinian people and the entire Arab nation are aware that ending the suffering of the Palestinian people will take place only by recognizing their inalienable national rights, foremost of which is the right to self-determination. Without this, what is being proposed will only be a soothing and partial solution that will increase, deepen, and double the suffering and give license to those responsible for it to continue to impose that suffering in new contexts and under new titles, at the expense of the Palestinian people and their unity, destiny, land, holy places, and future.

10. Any hint that a settlement is ready, that there is real chance, or that all the complications of the crisis are resolved and that the PLO position is the last thing needed will be viewed in accordance with our information—including the Zionist and US positions—as a distortion of facts and a simplification of matters, far from political logic and from accurate and correct calculations of the overall complicated situation in the Middle East crisis. The United States, despite some people's efforts to stress a positive development in its stand, continues to insist on granting Israel the right to oppose any peace proposals that do not suit it. It also insists that it will not exert pressure on Israel to accept even a minimally balanced solution. Instead, it continues to put pressure on the Palestinian, Jordanian, and Arab sides to submit to Israel's conditions, based on power calculations and arrogance.

The PLO is interested in clarifying that logically and practically, the issue of peace in the Middle East should not be subject to transitory opportunities or vague hints that are not based on clear-cut, firm foundations, especially since repeated experience with the United States, tangible facts, and King Hussein's speech prove that peace efforts have always reached a stalemate. Retreat from US pledges has become a US characteristic. Hence, the PLO's insistence on providing firm bases for a just solution does not mean any haphazard intransigence, but—in essence and goal—it epitomizes a responsible move to crystallize just, real peace in which the Palestinian people's rights will be guaranteed, safe from changes, maneuvers, and conspiracies.

Proceeding from this, the PLO, during the recent talks in Amman, submitted three formulas for giving momentum to talks on bringing about a just, comprehensive, and lasting peace for the Palestinian question and the Middle East crisis, but these formulas were rejected by the US administration, as we were informed by Jordan.*

---

* See above

From the premise of its national and pan-Arab stance, and in accordance with the PNC resolutions and basic Palestinian principles, the PLO strongly affirms its desire to realize a positive course for the Jordanian-Palestinian relationship because this relationship, with its background, horizons, and distinctiveness, should be kept away from fluctuations and transient changes. This relationship should be first and foremost in the interest of the Palestinian and Jordanian peoples against the pressures and plots to which both peoples are subject. This is the basis of our view of the fateful, strategic relationship between the two peoples.

It is on its understanding of this fact that the PLO drew up its policy on its relations with Jordan and other Arab and non-Arab countries. It is on the basis of this understanding that the PLO is adopting stands and policies on all affairs pertaining to the Palestine question and the Palestinian people's rights. Many forms of suffering to which the PLO was exposed resulted from the PLO's adherence to its national decision making, on the basis of pan-Arab commitment. It had previously rejected, and continues to reject, all attempts to undermine his independence with the aim of ignoring our inalienable national rights.

In light of the above-mentioned facts, the PLO emphasizes the following:

1. From the position of its national and pan*Arab responsibility, the PLO continues its difficult and resolute struggle in all its forms, foremost being armed struggle, in order to achieve the Palestinian people's inalienable national rights, including their right to establish their national, independent state whose capital is Jerusalem as a solid basis for a just and lasting peace in our region.

2. Taking pride in the solidity of the deep-rooted popular stance inside and outside the occupied territory—a stance which very strongly expresses the Palestinian people's adherence to their national rights and their full support for the PLO—the PLO promises the Palestinian masses and the Arab nation that it will continue to struggle in all arenas. US-Zionist plotting and the forces and tools of pressure behind it will not prevent the PLO from keeping the national trust. The PLO's stance is in essence and strength derived from the Palestinian masses' stance, great steadfastness, and conscious insistence on continuing to struggle tirelessly and unhesitatingly until the just national objective is attained.

3. The PLO, along with all Palestinian people inside and outside the occupied territory, calls on the Arab nation to assume its national and pan-Arab responsibilities toward the central issue of Palestine by providing all forms of material and moral backing for the Palestinian people's struggle under the PLO's leadership and for the Palestinian people's national rights, as this is an Arab commitment.

4. While continuing its national struggle on all levels, the PLO takes pride in its firmly established alliances with the camp of friends as embodied in the stands of backing, support, and commitment expressed by international groupings such as the socialist countries, headed by the Soviet Union, and the nonaligned, Islamic, and African countries. It also realizes the importance of the positive development of the stands of several European countries. Therefore, the PLO will per-

severingly continue to work to entrench these alliances and promote their scope and positive outcome on the level of our rights and national struggle.

The PLO, while taking pride and having confidence in the firmly established national unity of our great people wherever they are, reiterates its call to all Palestinian factions to meet within the framework of the PLO to enhance unity and close all doors through which our people's enemies are trying to enter and tamper with our firmly established national edifice and our unified and glorious national march.

Long live the Palestinian people's struggle! Long live Palestine, both free and Arab! Glory and immortality to our righteous martyrs! Revolution until victory!

## 25.  Statement by the PLO Executive Committee Cancelling the Amman Accord, 19 April, 1987

On 11 December 1985 the PLO and the government of the Hashimite Kingdom of Jordan signed an agreement for a joint plan of action to achieve the mutual interests of the Jordanian and Palestinian peoples in accordance with the resolutions of the Arab summit in Fez; and following the termination of the work of the seven-member Arab committee as a new instrument of an Arab peace plan in order to secure the attainment of the established national rights of the Palestinian people through ongoing international and Arab efforts.

The agreement was based on resolutions of the PNC, especially those of the sixteenth and seventeenth sessions which affirmed the special, brotherly relations between the two peoples and which called for the establishment of future relations on a confederal basis between the two states (Jordan and Palestine) and for coordination of joint political efforts to thwart separate solutions and settlements and to foil the project for an "alternative homeland."

During the course of the joint work differences arose between the two parties as to the meaning of some of the text of the agreement and the means of implementing it. In addition, there were the pressures brought to bear by the United States and other circles in the aftermath of which Jordan, on 19 February, 1986, announced the suspension of political coordination with the PLO and took certain measures which froze the agreement and led to a period of rupture in relations.

Proceeding from its desire for the correct implementation of the resolutions of the PNC related to the special, brotherly relations between the Palestinian and Jordanian peoples and in the light of what practical experience has proven, that the above-mentioned agreement has become an obstacle to the development of these relations, and, since it is no longer standing in practice, the PLO Executive Committee considers it null and void.

At the same time the Executive in the context of its established policy will continue its efforts to find new bases for working with Jordan and other Arab countries in order to achieve a joint struggle in the framework of united Arab action and effective Arab solidarity to liberate occupied Palestinian and Arab land and to build Arab unity taking into consideration the resolutions of Fez in support of an international conference in which the Soviet Union, the United States and other permanent members of the Security Council would participate along with the parties to the Middle East conflict, including the PLO, on an equal footing with the other parties in the framework and under the auspices of the UN.

## 26. Palestine National Council, Resolutions of the Political Committee, Algiers, 26 April, 1987 [Excerpts]

Proceeding from the Palestine National Charter and in harmony with the PNC resolutions, we emphasize the following principles as a basis for Palestinian national action within the framework of the PLO, the sole legitimate representative of the Arab Palestinian people:

### I. *On the Palestinian Level*

1. Adhering to the Arab Palestinian people's national inalienable rights to repatriation, self-determination, and establishment of an independent state on Palestinian national soil, whose capital is Jerusalem. Commitment to the PLO's political program which is aimed at attaining these rights. Adhering to the PLO as a sole, legitimate representative for our people and rejecting deputization, procuration, and sharing of participation in Palestinian representation. Rejecting and resisting any alternatives to the PLO.
3. Adhering to the PLO's independence and rejecting trusteeship, containment, annexation, and interference in its internal affairs.
4. Continuing struggle in all its armed, popular, and political forms for the sake of attaining our national objectives; liberating Palestinian and Arab lands from Israeli occupation; and confronting the hostile schemes of the imperialist-Zionist alliance in our region, particularly the strategic US-Israeli alliance, as a genuine expression of our people's national liberation movement, which antagonizes imperialism, colonialism, and Zionism.
5. Continued rejection of the Security Council Resolution 242, which is not considered a good basis for a settlement of the Palestine question because it deals with it as if it were an issue of refugees and ignores the Palestinian people's national inalienable rights.
6. Rejecting and resisting all solutions and plans aimed at liquidating our

Palestine question, including the Camp David Accords, Reagan's autonomy plan, and functional partition in all its forms.

7. Adhering to the Arab summits' resolutions on the Palestine question, particularly the Rabat 1974 summit, and considering the Arab peace plan approved by the Fez 1982 summit and confirmed by the extraordinary Casablanca summit as a framework for Arab action on the international level to achieve a solution to the Palestine question and to regain the occupied Arab territories.

8. Taking into consideration UN Resolutions 35, 38, 48/41 regarding the convocation of an international conference for peace in the Middle East, and UN resolutions on the Palestine question, the PNC supports the convocation of an international conference within the framework of the United Nations and under its auspices to be attended by the permanent member states of the UN Security Council and the parties to the conflict in the region, including the PLO, on equal footing with the other parties. The PNC stresses that the international conference should have full powers. The PNC also expresses support for the proposal to form a preparatory committee, and calls for swift action to form and convene this committee. In this regard, the PNC expresses appreciation for the fifth ICO summit conference in Kuwait, the eighth nonaligned conference in Harare and the coordination committee stemming from it, and the OAU summit in Addis Ababa, which expressed support for the convocation of the international conference, the preparatory committee, and for the efforts to convene this conference.

9. Enhancing the unity of all the national institutions and forces inside the occupied homeland under the PLO, promoting their joint struggle action against the Zionist enemy, the Zionist iron-fist policy, the autonomy plan, functional partition, normalization, the so-called development plan, and the attempts to create alternatives to the PLO, including the establishment of municipal councils, and supporting the steadfastness of our people who are represented by their national forces and institutions.

10. Reinforcing the unity of action regarding reorganizing the situation in our camps in Lebanon; defending these camps; deepening the unity of our people in them under the PLO; insisting upon our people's rights in Lebanon regarding residence, work, movement, and the freedom of political and social action; rejecting the attempts to expel and disarm our people; stressing our people's right to struggle against the Zionist enemy, to protect themselves, and to defend their camps in accordance with the Cairo agreement and its annexes, which organize relations between the PLO and the Lebanese Republic; and contributing along with our Lebanese brothers and their nationalist forces to resisting the Israeli occupation in Lebanon.

11. Protecting our people; taking care of their affairs wherever they reside; insisting upon their rights of residence, mobility, work, education, health, and security in accordance with the Arab League resolutions and the declaration on human rights; guaranteeing the freedom of political action as embodied in Arab

brotherhood ties and pan-Arab affiliation; and bolstering their cohesion with their Arab brothers.

## II. On the Arab Level

1. Bolstering Arab solidarity on the basis of the Arab summit resolutions and adhering to the charters of the joint Arab action and the Collective Arab Defense Pact to mobilize potential to liberate the occupied Arab territories and to confront Zionist aggression and US schemes to impose control over the Arab nation.

2. Consolidating the relations of alliance with the Arab liberation movement forces on the basis of action to attain the objectives of joint pan-Arab struggle against imperialism and Zionism and to reorganize the Arab front, which participates in the Palestinian revolution to enable it to perform its pan-Arab role of supporting and protecting the revolution.

3. Supporting the struggle of the Lebanese people and their nationalist forces against the Israeli occupation of southern Lebanon and for the sake of Lebanon's unity, Arab affiliation, independence, and for enhancing the Palestinian-Lebanese militant struggle.

## Special Resolution

The PNC expresses pride in and appreciation for the fraternal Lebanese people; emphasizes the importance of pursuing the alliance with the heroic Lebanese National Movement under Walid Junblatt and the other nationalist and Islamic leaders and forces with which we have fought and continue to fight to liberate Lebanese territory from the Zionist occupation; and stresses to them that the Palestinian revolution will remain a support for their program and for the continuation of the joint confrontation against the Israeli aggression and occupation, and for Lebanon's unity, Arab character, and independence.

4. Correcting and establishing relations between the PLO and Syria on the basis of the struggle objectives hostile to imperialism and Zionism, and in accordance with Arab summit resolutions, particularly the Rabat and Fez summit resolutions, and on a basis of equality and mutual respect leading to militant Palestinian-Syrian relations as well as close Arab ties.

5. The Iraq-Iran war. Working to halt the Iraq-Iran war because it is a destructive war to the two neighboring Muslim people from which only imperialism and Zionism benefit. This war seeks to exhaust Arab efforts and resources from the principal arena of confronting Zionist aggression, which is backed by US imperialism against the Arab nation and the Islamic countries. While valuing Iraq's peace initiative seeking to halt this war, establishing relations of good neighborliness between the two countries based on total respect for the sovereignty of each, on the noninterference by either side in the domestic affairs of the other,

and with respect to their political and social potential, the PNC stands at fraternal Iraq's side in defending its land and any Arab land that is the target of foreign aggression and invasion. The PNC also condemns Iran's occupation of Iraqi territory and US-Israeli collusion to perpetuate this war through the US and Israeli arms deals to Iran.

6. Jordan. Reaffirming the special and distinctive relations that link the fraternal Palestinian and Jordanian people and working to develop these relations in a manner that will be in line with the pan-Arab interests of the two people and those of our Arab nation; consolidating their joint struggle to enhance Jordan's independence and against the Zionist designs of expansion at the expense of its territory, and for the attainment of the Palestinian people's inalienable rights, including their right to repatriation, self-determination, the establishment of the independent Palestinian state; abiding by the PNC resolutions pertaining to the relationship with Jordan on the basis that the PLO is the Palestinian people's sole and legitimate representative inside and outside the occupied territories, as was affirmed by the 1974 Rabat Summit resolution. Reaffirming that any future relationship with Jordan should be based on confederal bases between two independent states; and stressing adherence to the bases that were approved by the 15th PNC session and the Baghdad Summit resolutions concerning bolstering steadfastness, including the Palestinian-Jordanian Joint Committee.

7. Egypt. While stressing the historic role of Egypt and its great people within the framework of the Arab struggle against the Zionist enemy, the sacrifices of the fraternal Egyptian people and its heroic army in defense of the Palestinian people and their national rights, Egypt's struggle to achieve Arab unity and liberation from colonialism and Zionism, Egypt's struggle to liberate the occupied Arab and Palestinian territories in all circles and arenas, and while also appreciating Egypt's pan-Arab and international position and the importance of Egypt's return [to the Arab fold] and its assumption of its natural role in the Arab arena, the PNC has entrusted the PLO Executive Committee with the task of defining the bases for Palestinian-Egyptian relations in accordance with successive PNC resolutions, especially those of the sixteenth session, which contain certain positions and principles of Palestinian struggle, foremost of which are the right to self-determination, repatriation, and the establishment of an independent Palestinian state and that the PLO is the sole legitimate representative; as well as in light of the Arab summit conferences' resolutions to achieve the Palestinian people's goals and inalienable national rights, which have been stressed by these Arab resolutions in the service of the Palestinian and Arab struggle against the Zionist enemy and its supporters.

III.   *On the International Level*

   1. Bolstering relations of alliance with the world liberation movements.

2. Cooperating closely with the Islamic, African and nonaligned countries, and activating the PLO's action in these countries to promote relations with them and gain further support for the Palestinian struggle.

3. Strengthening militant relations of alliance with the socialist bloc countries, foremost of which is the Soviet Union, as well as with the PRC.

4. Supporting peoples struggling against imperialism and racism for the sake of their national liberation, especially in southern and southwest Africa, Central America, and Latin America; condemning the aggressive alliance between the racist regimes in Tel Aviv and South Africa against the Arab nation and the African peoples; strongly supporting the African frontline countries in their struggle against the Pretoria regime; and strongly supporting the South African and Namibian peoples.

5. Working with all means in the international arena to expose the Zionist racism exercised in our occupied homeland. This racism was confirmed by the historic UN Resolution 3379 in 1975 stating that Zionism is a form of racism; and working to abort the Zionist-imperialist move to cancel this resolution.

6. Working to develop positive positions toward our cause in West European circles, in Japan, in Australia, and in Canada, and strengthening relations with democratic parties and forces in the capitalist countries that support our established national rights.

7. Joining world peoples in the struggle for world peace and international detente; stopping the arms race; averting the danger of a nuclear war; supporting Soviet initiatives in this regard; and exposing the dangers of Israeli nuclear armament in cooperation with South Africa against the region and world peace.

8. Developing relations with Israeli democratic forces supporting the Palestinian people's struggle against Israeli occupation and expansion and the inalienable national rights of our people, including their rights to repatriation and self-determination as well as the establishment of their independent state; and recognizing the PLO as the sole, legitimate representative of the Palestinian people. Condemning all US imperialist-backed Zionist attempts to drive Jews in a number of countries to emigrate to occupied Palestine, and calling upon all honorable forces to stand up to these feverish propagandist campaigns and their harmful effects.

9. In its eighteenth session, the PNC appreciates the efforts made by the UN Committee to help the Palestinian people exercise their inalienable rights in cooperation with various UN bodies, especially in organizing periodic symposiums and news conferences with a view to educating world public opinion about the true objectives of the Palestinian people's struggle. The PNC appreciates the efforts of nongovernmental bodies throughout the world to bolster the struggle of the Palestinian people to realize their inalienable rights in Palestine.

## 27.  Communique of the Intifadah No. 1, 8 January, 1988

In the name of God, the merciful, the compassionate.

Our people's glorious uprising continues. We affirm the need to express solidarity with our people wherever they are. We continue to be loyal to the pure blood of our martyrs and to our detained brothers. We also reiterate our rejection of the occupation and its policy of repression, represented in the policy of deportation, mass arrests, curfews, and the demolition of houses.

We reaffirm the need to achieve further cohesion with our revolution and our heroic masses. We also stress our abidance by the call of the PLO, the Palestinian people's legitimate and sole representative, and the need to pursue the bountiful offerings and the heroic uprising. For all these reasons, we address the following call:

All sectors of our heroic people in every location should abide by the call for a general and comprehensive strike until Wednesday evening, 13 January, 1988. The strike covers all public and private trade utilities, the Palestinian workers and public transportation. Abidance by the comprehensive strike must be complete. The slogan of the strike will be: Down with occupation; long live Palestine as a free and Arab country.

Brother workers, your abidance by the strike by not going to work and to plants is real support for the glorious uprising, a sanctioning of the pure blood of our martyrs, a support for the call to liberate our prisoners, and an act that will help keep our brother deportees in their homeland.

Brother businessmen and grocers, you must fully abide by the call for a comprehensive strike during the period of the strike. Your abidance by previous strikes is one of the most splendid images of solidarity and sacrifice for the sake of rendering our heroic people's stand a success.

We will do our best to protect the interests of our honest businessmen against measures the Zionist occupation force may resort to against you. We warn against the consequences of becoming involved with some of the occupation authorities' henchmen who will seek to make you open your businesses. We promise you that we will punish such traitor businessmen in the not too distant future. Let us proceed united to forge victory.

Brother owners of taxi companies, we will not forget your honorable and

---

Note: Since the beginning of the Palestinian uprising in December 1987, dozens of communiques have been distributed by the clandestine Unified National Leadership of the Palestinian Uprising in the Occupied Territories. Space limitation has prevented the editor from presenting all the communiques in this volume. Most of the communiques are reprinted in *Foreign Broadcast Information Service, Daily Report*, Near East and South Asia. For the text of the first 28 communiques, see Zachary Lockman and Joel Beinin, eds., *Intifada: The Palestinian Uprising Against Israeli Occupation* (Boston: South End Press, 1989).

splendid stand of supporting and implementing the comprehensive strike on the day of Palestinian steadfastness. We pin our hopes on you to support and make the comprehensive strike a success. We warn some bus companies against the consequences of not abiding by the call for the strike, as this will make them liable to revolutionary punishment.

Brother doctors and pharmacists, you must be on emergency status to offer assistance to those of our kinfolk who are ill. The brother pharmacists must carry out their duties normally. The brother doctors must place the doctor badge in a way that can be clearly identified.

General warning: We would like to warn people that walking in the streets will not be safe in view of the measures that will be taken to make the comprehensive strike a success. We warn that viscous material will be poured on main and secondary streets and everywhere, in addition to the roadblocks and the strike groups that will be deployed throughout the occupied homeland.

Circular: The struggler and brother members of the popular committees and the men of the uprising who are deployed in all the working locations should work to support and assist our people within the available means, particularly the needy families of our people. The strike groups and the popular uprising groups must completely abide by the working program, which is in their possession. Let us proceed united and loudly chant: Down with occupation; long live Palestine as a free and Arab country.

## 28.   Statement by the PLO Central Committee, 9 January, 1988

The PLO Central Council held an extraordinary session in Baghdad from 7 to 9 January, 1988 under PNC Speaker Shaykh 'Abd al-Hamid al-Sa'ih and in the presence of Brother Abu 'Ammar [Yasser Arafat], PLO Executive Committee Chairman and Commander in Chief of the Palestinian revolution forces. This session was devoted to the heroic uprising of our steadfast people in our occupied territory. It also discussed what the PLO Executive Committee has done so far in this regard and the requirements of the next stage.

The PLO Executive Committee chairman has submitted a comprehensive and detailed report to the council on our people's all-encompassing uprising and the situation in the occupied homeland. The brother officials in charge of the committees and apparatuses of the occupied territories have also submitted detailed reports on the developments, escalation, and requirements of the uprising.

The situation was discussed in detail. The details of the procedural plans, the requirements to reinforce this blessed uprising, and the current developments on all levels regarding our people's just cause were reviewed. Also discussed was the fateful and positive reflection of these developments on all regional, Arab, and international levels and even on the level of confronting the racist, fascist Zionist enemy and its bestial crimes.

This great uprising has revealed the gigantic energies of our valiant people in the occupied homeland as a glowing and sublime link in our people's continuous national struggle under the PLO, their sole and legitimate representative. Our people are on the road to inevitable victory. They are struggling to liberate the Palestinian homeland from the racist Zionist occupation, to return to our homeland, to achieve our right to self-determination, and to establish our free independent Palestinian state.

This uprising constitutes the beginning of a new stage of confronting the Zionist-imperialist settlement onslaught. The major characteristic of this uprising is that it is continuous and comprehensive. Its waves will continue to escalate until liberation.

During the current uprising, our people have offered scores of martyrs, hundreds of wounded persons, and thousands of detainees. The bloodshed is continuing and confronting the Israeli-US war machine strongly, resolutely, and faithfully.

Our heroic Palestinian masses in the occupied territory, who escalated their uprising in support of the steadfastness of our masses in Lebanon's camps fifteen months ago, have now reached new heights in their present uprising. The overwhelming uprising is the product of continuing struggle and steadfastness within and outside the homeland. It is also the product of the cohesion of our people under occupation and in the diaspora—masses, cadres, revolutionaries, and leadership—in a revolutionary line. These are complementary tributaries which have joined forces to give momentum and strength to the triumphant march of our people.

It is a spectacular unity of all our people's forces, organizations, factions, and trends inside and outside occupied Palestine. This unity is inspired by a clear vision, self-confidence, and knowledge of the strengths and weaknesses of the enemy. It is propelled by enlightened and ingenious thought that innovates new styles of struggle against the enemy's tyranny with every battle.

Our people—men and women—are involving themselves in this blessed uprising, availing themselves of the militant experience of our masses over the years. The young generation of boys and girls has come to the frontline confronting tanks and armored cars with their bare chests. They are doing so alongside our workers, merchants, peasants, students, and intellectuals throughout our occupied homeland—in the camps, in the villages, in the cities, at schools and universities, at mosques and churches, and even in prisons and detention centers.

In these waves of confronting the Zionist enemy and its war machine, our children are making the stones of our country the epic of defiance just as our cubs are making the epic of steadfastness in Lebanon's camps and in southern Lebanon.

Our masses have thus commanded worldwide respect and brought to the fore our just cause on the political, diplomatic, and media fronts. They have also brought our cause to the fore on the Arab level and internationally. This includes

UN Security Council resolutions, which were passed despite Zionist attempts to keep our cause out of the international limelight and despite the pull of their strategic ally the United States, which stands by them and gives them all manner of unqualified support.

This blessed uprising is escalating and taking root to create new realities on the Palestinian land to pave the way to freedom and the removal of the hateful Zionist occupation, as well as to achieve a just peace. Such peace would be embodied by our people's return to their land and also by the establishment of a free and independent state on our Palestinian national soil with holy Jerusalem as its capital.

Welcoming the overall stands of Arab governments, the Central Council proudly appreciates the stand adopted by the Arab masses throughout the Arab homeland for embracing our people's blessed uprising and for reacting with it and supporting it. This stand expresses the extent of our Arab nation's adherence to the Palestine question, the Arabs' central cause. The Central Council calls on all honorable and free people, as well as all friends in the world, to do all that will enable us to supply this revolutionary uprising with all its requirements.

This is particularly necessary in the face of the unlimited aid our racist Zionist enemy is receiving from the United States. This nation extends all kinds of military, financial, political, and diplomatic support as well as the most sophisticated instruments of death, destruction, and war to the Zionist enemy.

US opinion and world public opinion have pressured the US government to adopt new stands at the Security Council, which we hope will not be transient stands. This pressure was accomplished in view of pictures showing thousands of detainees and hundreds of wounded and martyrs and also in view of the savage practices and crimes against mankind by Israel against our people, children, and women. Israel commits these crimes in the same manner of, and even competing with, the crimes by its twin, the fascist and racist Pretoria regime, against the peoples of South Africa and Namibia.

In this serious and fateful phase, the Central Council calls on all democratic forces and on the Israeli peace forces to play an effective role, as has always been the case, to confront the racist and fascist iron fist policy until we together establish a just peace on the land of peace.

O steadfast masses, the PLO Central Council has adopted a number of resolutions, measures, and moves to continue and protect the uprising's waves. Foremost among these measures is the meeting of all of our people's basic requirements. The council has emphasized the resolutions and measures adopted by the Palestinian leadership to recruit all revolutionary cadres and forces in view of the new priorities imposed by the current state of affairs. The starting point lies in further reaction and sacrifices by all our Palestinian cadres to provide capabilities, enhance our people's ability to stand fast, and shoulder the burden of successive confrontations.

We view this comprehensive confrontation inside and outside our occupied land as the way to a just solution on the road to victory, liberation, repatriation, and independence. Proceeding from this premise, we call for a speedy convening of an effective international conference under UN auspices with the participation of the five permanent Security Council members, as well as all parties to the conflict in the region, including the PLO, the sole, legitimate representative of the Palestinian people, on an equal footing with other parties.

This conference should be convened to achieve the Palestinian people's inalienable national rights on the basis of international legitimacy and in accordance with Arab summit resolutions, particularly those of the Arab summit held in Fez in 1982.

O our heroic steadfast masses, the Central Council has adopted several measures and resolutions to confront the accelerating developments and meet the necessary requirements of this blessed uprising. It has decided:

1. To form a higher committee, in addition to the Executive Committee, to follow up all uprising affairs and developments. This committee shall be formed from the PNC presidency, the Central Council Secretariat, the Occupied Homeland Affairs Committee, and representatives of the Higher Military Council. This committee will be in open session and a working committee, for everyday affairs, shall stem from it.

2. To urge Palestinian businessmen to perform their duty toward their people and our masses' uprising by extending material and moral support that will contribute to meeting the needs of our people's steadfastness and struggle.

3. To approve the Executive Committee's decision to establish an extraordinary budget and to ask it to take all necessary measures to set it up and to provide all requirements and commitments to continue the waves of the blessed uprising.

4. To demand that all Palestinian institutions, bodies, and organizations continue their efforts to bolster the blessed uprising on various levels and spheres and to continue contacts with all Arab and international institutions for this purpose.

5. The specialized committees will continue to exercise their daily tasks vis-a-vis the uprising and its developments on all levels and in all areas.

6. To bolster the popular and national action committees in all positions of confrontation in occupied Palestine—in camps, villages, towns, universities, institutes, schools, institutions, popular bodies, and other positions of popular struggle.

7. To ask the Executive Committee to set up a special fund to collect all donations for the continuation of the waves of the blessed uprising.

8. To call on the Arab masses and their national forces to form popular committees to back and support this blessed uprising.

9. To demand an immediate international protection of our people's masses, children, and women until the termination of occupation.

10. To emphasize to the sisterly Arab states that they should take a firm stand to foil the deportation and expulsion measures by the Israeli occupation authorities and to work with all friendly states so that they will contribute to stopping this crime.

The Central Council, while meeting on the land of proud sisterly Iraq, salutes the Iraqi people and their valiant army under the leadership of the Arab cavalier Saddam Hussein, who is defending the eastern flank of our Arab nation. We thank him for his noble initiative to embrace the uprising martyrs and treat them on an equal footing with their brothers, the martyrs of the valiant Iraqi army. [The Central Council] also thanks the Arab governments which adopted measures and decisions in support of this blessed uprising.

In this regard, it thanks all the friendly states and nations which supported our people's struggle and blessed uprising, especially the friends in the nonaligned, Islamic, African, Latin American, and socialist countries—headed by the Soviet Union—and the PRC. It also thanks the friendly European states, other friendly countries, and all friendly world forces, organizations, and parties which stood and continue to stand on the side of our people's just struggle and legitimate right to live free and sovereign over their free, independent land just like everyone else.

The Central Council, while addressing our people's masses inside and outside the occupied homeland, emphasizes its determination to pursue our people's victorious march along the road to free, independent Palestine, with the help of God the Almighty. We promise the martyrs' souls that we will continue along the revolutionary path until liberation and victory. Revolution until victory.

## 29. The Uprising Leadership's Message to the Arab Summit in Algiers, 7 June, 1988

We are confident the Arab nation will not disappoint the militant people of Palestine and will not refrain from supporting them with all means. We are also confident that our glorious nation's resources will deter the usurping enemy if some of these capabilities are used to support our struggle. Our people and the masses of the uprising expect your esteemed conference to shoulder the pan-Arab responsibility of supporting our heroic uprising and the leader of the Palestinian people's struggle and the PLO, their sole, legitimate representative, politically, materially, diplomatically, and morally.

We expect you to lend this support to enable them to achieve their goals, by defending our sanctities and the honor of Arabism, and to enable them to live in freedom on their national soil. While we expect your conference to take a clear-cut policy and support our struggle and our sole, legitimate representative, we pledge to you in the name of our masses in the occupied homeland and the masses of the uprising to continue to struggle to achieve the following:

1. Secure international protection for our masses from the crimes of the Zionist occupation to pave the way to end the occupation and achieve our people's freedom and independence.

2. Cancel emergency laws and achieve the withdrawal of the Zionist army from the cities, villages, and camps.

3. Foil all the suspected plans which deny our people's rights. These plans include the autonomy rule, Camp David, and Shultz' initiative.

4. Convene an international conference with full powers to be attended by the permanent Security Council member states as well as by the PLO independently and on an equal footing with all other parties, considering this conference as the only way to bring about a lasting, just, and comprehensive peace.

5. Establish an independent national state under the PLO, its sole, legitimate representative.

While we hope your conference will realize its cherished aims, we demand that your governments approve the following:

1. Persevere in carrying out a large-scale media campaign to expose the occupation authorities practices against our people.

2. Effect permanent and continuous coordination with our sole, legitimate representative, the PLO, based on equality and independence.

3. Release Palestinian detainees in some Arab jails.

4. Allow Palestinian communities in the host Arab countries to establish their institutions and unions to be devoted to permanent participation in the struggle against the Zionist entity.

5. Establish permanent supporting funds for the PLO and funneling all Arab assistance through them.

6. Open Arab frontiers to the fighters of the Palestinian revolution and establish military training camps.

As Palestinian people, our 70 years of struggle have been crowned with the present uprising. Our struggle has realized great achievements for our people and all of the Arab peoples, preserving the dignity of all of us and consecrating our persistent struggle to win our legitimate aspirations to live with honor. Your support for our struggle to establish an independent state is an essential factor for uniting the glorious Arab nation.

Long live the glorious Arab people. Long live our heroic Palestinian people. Long live the PLO, our sole, legitimate representative.

## 30. "PLO View: Prospects of a Palestinian-Israeli Settlement," by PLO Spokesman Bassam Abu Sharif, 18 June, 1988

Everything that has been said about the Middle East conflict has focused on the differences between Palestinians and Israelis and ignored the points on which they are in almost total agreement.

These points are easy to overlook, hidden as they are under a 70-year accumulation of mutual hostility and suspicion, but they exist nevertheless and in them lies the bone that the peace that has deluded this region for so long is finally within reach.

Peel off the layers of fear and mistrust that successive Israeli leaders have piled on the substantive issues and you will find that the Palestinians and Israelis are in general agreement on ends and means.

Israel's objectives are lasting peace and security. Lasting peace and security are also the objectives of the Palestinian people. No one can understand the Jewish people's century of suffering more than the Palestinians. We know what it means to be stateless and the object of the fear and prejudice of the nations. Thanks to the various Israeli and other governments that have had the power to determine the course of our people's lives, we know what it feels like when human beings are considered somehow less human than others and denied the basic rights that people along the globe take for granted. We feel that no people—neither the Jewish people nor the Palestinian people—deserve the abuse and disfranchisement that hopelessness inevitably entails. We believe that all peoples—the Jewish and the Palestinian included—have the right to run their own affairs, expecting from their neighbors not only non-belligerence but the kind of political and economic cooperation without which no state can be truly secure, no matter how massive its war machine, and without which no nation can truly prosper, no matter how generous its friends in distant lands may be.

The Palestinians want that kind of lasting peace and security for themselves and the Israelis because no one can build his own future on the ruin of another's. We are confident that this desire and this realization are shared by all but an insignificant minority in Israel.

The means by which the Israelis want to achieve lasting peace and security is direct talks, with no attempt by any outside party to impose or veto a settlement.

The Palestinians agree. We see no way for any dispute to be settled without direct talks between the parties to that dispute, and we feel that any settlement that has to be imposed by an outside power is a settlement that is unacceptable to one or both of the belligerents and therefore a settlement that will not stand the test of time. The key to a Palestinian-Israeli settlement lies in talks between the Palestinians and the Israelis. The Palestinians would be deluding themselves if they thought that their problems with the Israelis can be solved in negotiations with non-Israelis, including the United States. By the same token, the Israelis—and US Secretary of State George Shultz, who will soon return to the Middle East for further discussions on his peace proposals—would be deluding themselves if they thought that Israel's problems with the Palestinians can be solved in negotiations with non-Palestinians, including Jordan.

The Palestinians would like to choose their Israeli interlocutor. We have little doubt that we could reach a satisfactory settlement with the *Peace Now* movement in a month. We know, however, that an agreement with *Peace Now* would not be an agreement with Israel, and since an agreement with Israel is what we are after, we are ready to talk to Mr. Shimon Peres' Labor Alignment, and to Yitzhak Shamir's Likud Bloc, or anyone else the Israelis choose to represent them.

The Israelis and Mr. Shultz would also prefer to deal with Palestinians of their own choosing. But it would be as futile for them as for us to talk to people who have no mandate to negotiate. If it is a settlement with the Palestinians that they seek, as we assume it is, then it is with the representatives of that people that they must negotiate, and the Palestinian people, by the only means that they have at their disposal, have chosen their representatives. Every Palestinian questioned by diplomats and the newsmen of the international community has stated unequivocally that his representative is the Palestine Liberation Organization. If that is regarded as an unreliable expression of the Palestinians' free will, then give the Palestinians the chance to express their free will in a manner that will convince all doubters; arrange for an internationally-supervised referendum in the West Bank and the Gaza Strip and allow the population to choose between the PLO and any other group of Palestinians that Israel or the United States or the international community wishes to nominate. The PLO is ready to abide by the outcome and step aside for any alternative leadership should the Palestinian people choose one.

The PLO will do this because its *raison d'etre* is not the undoing of Israel, but the salvation of the Palestinian people and their rights, including their right to democratic self-expression and national self-determination.

Regardless of the satanic image that the PLO's struggle for those rights has given it in the United States and Israel, the fact remains that this organization was built on democratic principles and seeks democratic objectives. If Israel and its supporters in the US administration can grasp that fact, the fears that prevent them from accepting the PLO as the only valid interlocutor toward any Palestinian-Israeli settlement would vanish.

Those fears, as far as one can tell from what has been written and said in Israel and the United States, center on the PLO's failure of unconditionally accepting Security Council Resolutions 242 and 338 and on the possibility that a Palestinian State on the West Bank and Gaza would be a radical, totalitarian threat to its neighbor.

The PLO, however, does accept Resolutions 242 and 338. What prevents it from saying so unconditionally is not what is in the resolutions but what is not in them: neither resolution says anything about the national rights of the Palestinian people, including their democratic right to self-expression and the national rights of the Palestinian people, including their democratic right to self-expression and their national right to self-determination. For that reason and that reason alone, we have repeatedly said that we accept Resolutions 242 and 338 in the context of the other UN resolutions which do recognize the national rights of the Palestinian people.

As for the fear that a Palestinian State will be a threat to its neighbor, the democratic nature of the PLO—with its legislative, executive and other popularly-based institutions—should argue against it. If that does not constitute a solid enough guarantee that the State of Palestine would be a democratic one, the Palestinians would be open to the idea of a brief, mutually-acceptable transitional period during which an international mandate would guide the occupied Palestinian territories to democratic Palestinian statehood.

Beyond that, the Palestinians would accept—indeed, insist on—international guarantees for the security of all states in the region, including Palestine and Israel. It is precisely our desire for such guarantees that motivates our demand that bilateral peace talks with Israel be conducted under a UN-sponsored international conference.

The Palestinians feel that they have much more to fear from Israel, with its mighty war machine and its nuclear arsenal, than Israel has to fear from them. They would therefore welcome any reasonable measure that would promote the security of their state and its neighbors, including the deployment of a UN buffer force on the Palestinian side of the Israeli-Palestinian border.

Time, sometimes the great healer, is often the great spoiler. Many Israelis no doubt realize it and are trying to communicate it to the rest of their people. As for us, we are ready for peace now, and we can deliver it. It is our hope that the opportunity that presents itself today will not be missed.

If it is missed, we will have no choice but to continue to exercise our right to resist the occupation, our ultimate aim being a free, dignified and secure life not only for our children but also for the children of the Israelis.

## 31.    The Covenant of Hamas (The Islamic Resistance Movement in the West Bank), 18 August, 1988 [Excerpts]

*Strategies and Methods*
*Strategies of the Islamic Resistance Movement:*
*Palestine is Islamic Waqf [Trust]*

Article Eleven:

The Islamic Resistance Movement believes that the land of Palestine is an Islamic Waqf (Trust) consecrated for future Moslem generations until Judgement Day. It, or any part of it, should not be squandered: it, or any part of it, should not be given up. Neither a single Arab country nor all Arab countries, neither any king or president, nor all the kings and presidents, neither any organization nor all of them, be they Palestinian or Arab, possess the right to do that. Palestine is an Islamic Waqf land consecrated for Moslem generations until Judgement Day. This being so, who could claim to have the right to represent Moslem generations till Judgement Day?

This is the law governing the land of Palestine in the Islamic Sharia (law) and the same goes for any land the Moslems have conquered by force, because during the times of (Islamic) conquests, the Moslems consecrated these lands to Moslem generations till the Day of Judgement.

It happened like this: When the leaders of the Islamic armies conquered Syria and Iraq, they sent to the Caliph of the Moslems, Umar bin-el-Khatab, asking for his advice concerning the conquered land—whether they should divide it among the soldiers, or leave it for its owners, or what? After consultations and discussions between the Caliph of the Moslems, Umar bin-el-Khattab and companions of the Prophet, Allah bless him and grant him salvation, it was decided that the land should be left with its owners who could benefit by its fruit. As for the real ownership of the land and the land itself, it should be consecrated for Moslem generations till Judgement Day. Those who are on the land, are there only to benefit from its fruit. This Waqf remains as long as earth and heaven remain. Any procedure in contradiction to Islamic Sharia, where Palestine is concerned, is null and void.

"Verily this is a certain truth. Wherefore praise the name of thy Lord, the great Allah." (The Inevitable-verse 95)

*Homeland and Nationalism from the Point of View of the Islamic Resistance Movement in Palestine:*
*Article Twelve:*

Nationalism, from the point of view of the Islamic Resistance Movement, is part of the religious creed. Nothing in nationalism is more significant or deeper than in the case when an enemy should tread Moslem land. Resisting and quelling the enemy becomes the individual duty of every Moslem, male or female. A woman can go out to fight the enemy without her husband's permission, and so does the slave: without his master's permission.

Nothing of the sort is to be found in any other regime. This is an undisputed fact. If other nationalist movements are connected with materialistic, human or regional causes, nationalism of the Islamic Resistance Movement has all these elements as well as the more important elements that give it soul and life. It is connected to the source of spirit and the granter of life, hoisting in the sky of the homeland the heavenly banner that joins earth and heaven with a strong bond.

If Moses comes and throws his staff, both witch and magic are annulled.

"Now is the right direction manifestly distinguished from deceit: whoever therefore shall deny Tagut, and believe in Allah, he shall surely take hold on a strong handle, which shall not be broken; Allah is he who heareth and seeth." (The Cow-Verse 256).

*Peaceful Solutions, Initiatives and International Conferences:*
*Article Thirteen:*

Initiatives, and so-called peaceful solutions and international conferences, are in contradiction to the principles of the Islamic Resistance Movement. Abusing any part of Palestine is abuse directed against part of religion. Nationalism of the Islamic Resistance Movement is part of its religion. Its members have been fed on that. For the sake of hoisting the banner of Allah over their homeland they fight. "Allah will be prominent, but most people do not know."

Now and then the call goes out for the convening of an international conference to look for ways of solving the (Palestinian) question. Some accept, others reject the idea, for this or other reason, with one stipulation or more for consent to convening the conference and participating in it. Knowing the parties constituting the conference, their past and present attitudes towards Moslem problems, the Islamic Resistance Movement does not consider these conferences capable of realizing the demands, restoring the rights or doing justice to the oppressed. These conferences are only ways of setting the infidels in the land of the Moslems as arbitrators. When did the infidels do justice to the believers? "But the Jews will not be pleased with thee, neither the Christians, until thou follow their religion; say, The direction of Allah is the true direction. And verily if thou follow their desires, after the knowledge which hath been given thee, thou shalt find no patron or protector against Allah." (The Cow-verse 120).

There is no solution for the Palestinian question except through Jihad. Initiatives, proposals and international conferences are all a waste of time and vain endeavors. The Palestinian people know better than to consent to having their future, rights and fate toyed with. As said in the honourable Hadith:

"The people of Syria are Allah's lash in His land. He wreaks His vengeance through them against whomsoever He wishes among His slaves. It is unthinkable that those who are double-faced among them should prosper over the faithful. They will certainly die out of grief and desperation."

### The Three Circles:
### Article Fourteen:

The question of the liberation of Palestine is bound to three circles: the Palestinian circle, the Arab circle and the Islamic circle. Each of these circles has its role in the struggle against Zionism. Each has its duties, and it is a horrible mistake and a sign of deep ignorance to overlook any of these circles. Palestine is an Islamic land which has the first of the two kiblahs (direction to which Moslems turn in praying), the third of the holy (Islamic) sanctuaries, and the point of departure for Mohammed's midnight journey to the seven heavens (i.e. Jerusalem). "Praise be unto him who transported his servant by night, from the sacred temple of Mecca to the farther temple of Jerusalem, the circuit of which we have blessed, that we might show him some of our signs; for Allah is he who heareth, and seeth." (The Night-Journey-verse 1).

Since this is the case, liberation of Palestine is then an individual duty for every Moslem wherever he may be. On this basis, the problem should be viewed. This should be realized by every Moslem.

The day the problem is dealt with on this basis, when the three circles mobilize their capabilities, the present state of affairs will change and the day of liberation will come nearer. "Verily ye are stronger than they, by reason of the terror cast into their breasts from Allah. This, because they are not people of prudence." (The Emigration-verse 13).

### The Jihad for the Liberation of Palestine Is an Individual Duty:
### Article Fifteen:

The day the enemies usurp part of Moslem land, Jihad becomes the individual duty of every Moslem. In face of the Jews' usurpation of Palestine, it is compulsory that the banner of Jihad be raised. To do this requires the diffusion of Islamic consciousness among the masses, both on the regional, Arab and Islamic levels. It is necessary to instill the spirit of Jihad in the heart of the nation so that they would confront the enemies and join the ranks of the fighters.

It is necessary that scientists, educators and teachers, information and media people, as well as the educated masses, especially the youth and sheikhs of the Islamic movements, should take part in the operation of awakening (the masses). It is important that basic changes be made in the school curriculum, to cleanse it of the traces of ideological invasion that affected it as a result of the orientalists and missionaries who infiltrated the region following the defeat of the Crusaders at the hands of Salah el-Din (Saladin). The Crusaders realized that it was impossible to defeat the Moslems without first having ideological invasion pave the way by upsetting their thoughts, disfiguring their heritage and violating their ideals. Only then could they invade with soldiers. This, in its turn, paved the way for the imperialistic invasion that made Allenby declare on entering Jerusalem: "Only now the Crusades have ended." General Guru stood at Salah el-Din's grave and said: "We have returned, O Salah el-Din." Imperialism has helped towards the strengthening of ideological invasion, deepening, and still does, its roots. All this has paved the way towards the loss of Palestine.

It is necessary to instill in the minds of the Moslem generations that the Palestinian problem is a religious problem, and should be dealt with on this basis. Palestine contains Islamic holy sites. In it there is al-Aqsa Mosque which is bound to the great Mosque in Mecca in an inseparable bond as long as heaven and earth speak of Isra (Mohammed's midnight journey to the seven heavens) and Mi'raj (Mohammed's ascension to the seven heavens from Jerusalem).

"The bond of one day for the sake of Allah is better than the world and whatever there is on it. The place of one's whip in Paradise is far better than the world and whatever there is on it. A worshipper's going and coming in the service of Allah is better than the world and whatever there is on it." (As related by al-Bukhari, Moslem, al-Tarmdhi and Ibn Maja).

"I swear by the holder of Mohammed's soul that I would like to invade and be killed for the sake of Allah, then invade and be killed, and then invade again and be killed." (As related by al-Bukhari and Moslem).

## 32. Address of Yasser Arafat to the European Parliament, Strasbourg, 13 September, 1988

*Mr. Chairman,*
*Ladies and Gentlemen,*
It was a source of pleasure for me to receive and accept your invitation to this encounter in the hope that it will lead to greater mutual understanding over the problem of the Palestinian people and the Arab-Israeli conflict, the essence and crux of which is the Palestine cause.

As human beings, we need a genuine understanding which satisfies the heart and the conscience, for the interaction of the conscience and the mind enables us to take the right stand, the correct decision, and the proper action.

I want to address your consciences and your minds because I am fully convinced that the best weapon to be used in presenting the Palestine cause is the weapon of truth which addresses the mind while interacting with the conscience.

I also attach special importance to discussion and dialogue with you because, as parliamentarians, you represent the people—the natural source of authority—who have given you their confidence and, consequently, the prerogative to turn words into law.

That's why I do not view the parliamentarian only as a politician or a representative of his people. I also see in him a conscience or a mind with special responsibility. Whoever enacts laws cannot break with justice. Justice is the corollary of law; it is also the corollary of peace. There can be no peace without justice. There can also be no permanent stability without real peace.

Because I am convinced that the aforementioned points are human rules, hence universal, allow me to say this: the proof of truthfulness and seriousness about affinity to democracy, freedom, national independence, peace, and justice is the belief in the right of others to all that. To restrict these to one people or a group of peoples to the exclusion of others runs contrary to all what they mean, with preclusion becoming some sort of vicious selfishness concealing masked dictatorship. Democracy, freedom, national independence, human rights, peace, and justice are for all human beings. This is the course charted by the history of mankind.

It is only natural for our discussion then to revolve around the right of the Palestinian people to freedom, independence, peace, and stability after a near century-old struggle in that strategic and sensitive part of the world which interweaves with Europe and where one of the parties to the conflict, namely Israel, has become a nuclear force.

*Mr. Chairman,*

I realize you have a lot of queries, especially in the light of the historic steadfastness of the Palestinian people as manifested by the uprising of its masses to end the occupation and wrest independence.

Granted, they are legitimate queries: it is your right to get clear and specific answers to them from us outlining our overall line of thinking and action, without necessarily going into specific details, especially when they are sensitive. The final decision on these rests with our own parliament, the Palestine National Council, which expresses all trends and intellectual and political forces among our people, whether those under occupation or in the diaspora. We are proud of this parliament and its legislative stature among Palestinians and of the deliberations and democratic practices taking place under its roof.

I don't think it would be an overstatement on my part to say that we are a national liberation movement which has been able to intertwine the requirements of revolutionary endeavor with our commitment to the rules of democracy through a parliament endowed with full legislative prerogatives to oversee all executive powers without exception.

Our parliament meets regularly. This is probably because of the nature of the Palestine Liberation Organization, which is a revolution for liberation and peace, but with the role of a state.

In addition to exercising all means of legitimate struggle against occupation, the PLO assumes the responsibility— by virtue of legislation by the PNC and through various institutions for industry, agriculture, health, education, labor, social affairs, and the like—of catering to the needs of the homeland and of citizens, in all aspects of their lives and whether living under occupation or in the diaspora.

I hope you will understand us the way we are, not through the images in which we are portrayed by Israel and the US administration, who are linked by a strategic alliance, one of the main objectives of which is to dismiss the existence of the Palestinian people from history altogether, from today's reality, and from the future, and to disregard the Palestine Liberation Organization as the main party to the Arab-Israeli conflict.

*Mr. Chairman,*
*Ladies and Gentlemen,*

We are all happy to read into the looming international entente an end to a long period of cold and proxy wars, now that the two superpowers have realized the importance of settling regional disputes by peaceful means in order to secure comprehensive peace for all.

But it is painful to sense that American policy and that of others in the international community has been not to tackle a regional dispute unless it is hot and on the verge of exploding.

The people of Palestine have waited for justice from the international community for long, drawn out years. Unfortunately, the people of Palestine and their cause were forgotten and overlooked under one pretext or another. It was therefore natural for the people of Palestine to resume their struggle in 1965.

Our people within the occupied lands and outside had no choice but to continue their struggle, to face their destiny, and to pay a high price in the course of the confrontations and aggressions which were imposed on them, whether during the siege of Beirut, or in the massacres of Sabra, Shatila, and Burj [al-Barajinah], or in the air and naval raids, or in the course of the attacks currently underway on Lebanese villages and Palestinian refugee camps in south Lebanon, or in the course of what is now taking place against our women, children, and masses in the occupied territories.

The *intifadah* was an expression of the extent of our people's alertness and their determination to resist the occupation by all means at their disposal, exercising thereby their legal right under the UN Charter and resolutions.

Today, our people are confronting the iron fist policy and the Israeli war machine with stones, children, and youths, creating the image of a Palestinian David pitted against a Goliath armed to the teeth with the latest means of warfare and destruction.

We had hoped that the sight of children wielding stones to confront armored vehicles, gunfire, and suffocating gas would be sufficient to arouse the conscience of the Israeli occupiers and to open their minds to the future, realizing that recognition of the Palestinian people and their right to self-determination and independence is the only road to peace—away from the massacres and daily killings to which our men, women, and children are being subjected and in favor of a future built on peace and justice for all.

But Shamir refuses to use his mind and insists on using his muscles instead to crush what he calls "Palestinian grasshoppers." He insists on pressing ahead with plans to annex the occupied territories and on ordering both soldiers and armed settlers to fire at our children and kinspeople.

Peres, his partner in the coalition, continues to speak of the "Jordanian option" and of "alternative leaderships" while Rabin tries to overbid Shamir in his practice of the iron fist policy. More dangerous than that are the mounting voices among the Likud calling for the mass deportation of Palestinians to Jordan by force. There are others, too, clamoring for the expulsion of all Palestinians from throughout Palestine.

Sharon announces for his part a scheme to occupy Jordan and to create therein a substitute homeland for the Palestinians.

All this exposes political stands and inhuman practices which are unimaginable by human society, especially after the Second World War and in the era of international entente, disarmament, the settlement of regional conflicts by peaceful means, the technological revolution, and the impending challenges of the twenty-first century, which necessitate full cooperation among producing and consuming nations.

The people of the *intifadah* and the revolution of the "children of stones" are now confronting the iron fist policy, including the use of plastic and rubber bullets, live ammunition, internationally-banned suffocating gases, the burning and burial of people alive, miscarriages, the breaking of bones, the murder of prisoners, the torture of some detainees to death, the murder of children, the demolition of homes, collective punishments, inhuman mass detention centers, mass administrative arrests without trial or charge, deportation, desecration of Muslim and Christian sanctuaries, and a series of other practices which go against the principles set in Nuremberg.

When the occupation authorities realized the negative impact of these practices on world public opinion generally, and on Western public opinion in particular, and even on Jewish public opinion, they proceeded, on the advice of Mr. Kissinger, to kill Palestinians away from camera lenses. They also undertook to bar television and other media from recording and relaying events to the world, thus compounding their iron fist policy with the transformation of Israel into another South Africa. This exposed the true face of Israel, harming not only the Palestinians, but also Judaism and all democratic and progressive Israelis who reject these methods, practices, and crimes.

Here a question flies in the face of the motives behind this policy which runs counter to the course of history. It certainly is not insensitivity to the crime committed by these Israeli leaderships as much as fear from peace on their part.

They hope that their intransigent and negative policies and their aggressive practices will deepen hatred and grudge between Israelis and Palestinians, pushing the Palestinian people to despair of peace based on justice and ordinary Israeli citizens to shut themselves out and acquiesce in fascism and racism.

*Mr. Chairman,*
*Ladies and Gentlemen,*

I hereby declare that the people of the *intifadah*, the Palestinian people whom I represent, are committed to peace based on justice. Our heritage and culture and our Islam, Christianity, and Judaism disallow hatred and repudiate aggression. Inasmuch as they open our minds to peace based on justice, they shape our resolve to defend ourselves, uphold our rights, and resist the occupation.

We respect our international commitments. We also respect international legitimacy. At the same time, we believe that a just peace cannot be achieved through the selective application of half of what international legitimacy provided for and the dumping of the other half.

That is why it is imperative that we witness and sense the respect by Israel and the US administration of international resolutions, particularly those upholding the Palestinian people's right to self-determination and statehood, and which constitute the cornerstone of the proposed international peace conference.

I also declare from this rostrum that several contentious points as well as issues raised as preconditions in their minute details hinge on the success of negotiations at the international conference. Other points will figure on the agenda of negotiations to take place at the authoritative international conference under the auspices of the United Nations and with the participation of the permanent Security Council members and all the parties to the conflict in the region, including Israel and the PLO as the legitimate representative of the Palestinian people.

It would be possible at the said conference and through the negotiations which will take place within its framework to discuss and agree [upon] arrangements for international guarantees of peace among all states of the region, including the independent Palestinian state.

Israel has never defined the terms of reference for the settlement of the Palestinian-Israeli dispute. We wonder: Are they the UN Charter? Or the resolutions of the General Assembly and the Security Council? Or the US Declaration of Human Rights? Or the 1977 Vance-Gromyko statement? Or the natural right of peoples? Or international legitimacy with all its implications in as far as the establishment of the State of Israel is concerned?

As far as we are concerned, many of you wonder about our position vis-a-vis Resolutions 242 and 338 in view of our commitment to international legitimacy.

We endorse the Charter of the United Nations Organization and all its resolutions including 242 and 338. International legitimacy is an indivisible whole and no one can choose to accept only what suits him and discard what does not.

How can the United States and Israel accept the only birth certificate of the State of Israel, namely Resolution 181, which provided for the creation of two states in Palestine, and simultaneously reject, for instance, Resolution 194 (1948), which called for the repatriation of the Palestine refugees or the payment of compensation for the property of those choosing not to return?

How can we be asked to accept Resolution 242 and forget the other international resolutions, the most recent of which were Security Council Resolution 605, 607, and 608 as well as Resolutions 252, 446, and 465 and General Assembly Resolutions 3236 and 3237—especially since Resolution 242 concerned Israel and a number of Arab states and did not address the Palestine question or the rights of the people of Palestine? It only referred to the need to achieve a settlement of the refugee problem. Even this reference was interpreted in the US-Israeli (or "Vance-Dayan") statement of 1977 as meaning Jewish and Arab refugees.

Consequently, we declare our acceptance of one of the two following options as the basis for convening the international conference under UN auspices and with the participation of the Security Council's permanent members and all the parties to the conflict in the region, including the PLO and Israel:

a. All UN resolutions relevant to the Palestine question, including Security Council Resolutions 242 and 338.

b. Resolutions 242 and 338 along with the legitimate rights of the Palestinian people, foremost among which is their right to self-determination.

Allow me to cite another example where the selective application of international legitimacy led to distorted results, undermining international legitimacy as such. The example relates to Mr. George Shultz, the US Secretary of State, and his so-called Middle East initiative.

In the course of his fourth and last visit to the area, he stood up in Cairo to declare that he had discovered that the conflict in Palestine is one between two peoples over the same land and that the solution lies in the recognition of both people's rights.

We saw in this the first positive stand by Washington in terms of recognizing the Palestine people and their rights.

No sooner had Shultz made his statement than he reverted to the practice of partitioning international legitimacy by translating Israeli rights into an independent state, a government, and a people, while dismissing the Palestinian state, government, and people by speaking of Palestinian rights in terms of a mere entity attached to the Kingdom of Jordan and of Palestinian residents being absorbed within the Jordanian population.

In this context, and in order to create an atmosphere of good will conducive to a just peace, we responded positively—and still do—to all proposals calling for the withdrawal of the Israeli occupation forces from the Palestinian territories occupied in 1967 and placing these under UN administration or an internationally-supervised European force for a limited interim period. The proposed international force could stay on after the establishment of the independent Palestinian state for as long as the Security Council deems necessary to guarantee the security of everyone concerned.

*Mr. Chairman,*
*Ladies and gentlemen,*
We all know of the measures recently adopted by Jordan concerning the West Bank.

The PLO Central Council accepted these measures and decided to shoulder the responsibilities resulting therefrom, including the political among them, regardless of the timing and the manner in which the measures were introduced—without consultation or coordination with us—and irrespective of the difficulties which we found ourselves facing.

The Jordanian measures ended the European, American, and Israeli debate on Palestinian representation at the international conference. No one can claim any more that there is someone else to share with the PLO the representation of the Palestinian people, particularly after the cessation of the Jordanian option and the failure of the autonomy option. The only option left is the right, realistic, and irreplaceable one—namely, the Palestinian option, the essence of which is the independent Palestinian state.

The Jordanian measures also contributed to ushering in a new political phase which interacted with the achievements of the *intifadah* and the overall Palestinian struggle on the international level and within world public opinion, Israeli society, and the Jewish communities in the United States and Europe. The communities rejected the Israeli authorities' distortion of their Jewish beliefs, which do not condone aggression, oppression, and coercion.

The Central Council set up a legal-political committee to study all matters related to these developments. Once it ends its studies shortly, they will be put before the Palestine National Council, which will take the necessary decisions in its capacity as the Palestinian people's highest legislative democratic institute.

All those who genuinely believe in peace based on justice and in the right of peoples to self-determination and national independence were stunned by the Israeli outcry over the repercussions of the Jordanian measures, i.e., the moves to declare Palestinian national independence and to set up a provisional government for the forthcoming Palestinian state, or to place the occupied Palestinian territories under United Nations trusteeship.

I remind the Israeli leadership of what Mr. Nahum Goldmann, the late president of the World Jewish Congress, said about US policy in the region as conceived by Henry Kissinger. Mr. Goldmann said there was no point in avoiding the inevitable, because it is bound to come, no matter how long it is put off.

I would add that putting off the inevitable means more victims and an atmosphere poisoned by aggressive policies and organized state terrorism.

*Mr. Chairman,*
*Ladies and gentlemen,*

The people of Palestine do not fight for the sake of fighting. Like other peoples in the world who yearn for peace, freedom, democracy, and national independence, the Palestinian people played throughout history, and aspire to play in the near future, a role in achieving peace and progress for themselves and the rest of humanity. The Palestinian people are eager to contribute their share to human civilization, as they did in the past.

As a national liberation movement which took up arms against the oppression and illegitimate terrorism of the occupier, we have invariably, and in the clearest and strongest of terms, denounced terrorism in all its forms and from whatever source—be it by individuals, groups, or states.

Our people, including their leaders, cadres, and citizens, have invariably been the target of organized Israeli state terrorism as practiced directly or indirectly by armed settlers acting alongside troops in full view of all. In spite of this, we made the Cairo Declaration against terrorism in 1985 on the basis of international law and the United Nations Charter and resolutions.

But an unchecked Israel continued to practice all forms of terrorism, including state terrorism, against the Palestinian people and their leaders within the occupied territories and in every corner of the globe.

This terrorism reached its climax with the bombardment of my headquarters at Hammam al-Shatt in Tunis and the assassination of Brother Abu Jihad, my deputy and one of the most prominent symbols of Palestinian leadership, who was gunned down in front of his family in Tunis. Israel also perpetrated acts of piracy against civilian shipping in the high seas and in international waters and assassinated our leaders and cadres in Cyprus, Athens, and elsewhere.

We reaffirm our commitment to the Cairo Declaration made in 1985 in the presence of President Mubarak as well as to the relevant United Nations Resolution, No. 42/159 (1987).

We also reaffirm that we cling to our right to resist the occupation until Israel pulls out from our occupied territories and our Palestinian people achieve their national independence in their sovereign state, so our children can live in peace and liberty on their free soil, like other children of the world.

I would like to add here that we are working to set up an independent Palestinian state on the land liberated from Israeli occupation. This state will have a republican, democratic, and multi-party system; it will abide by the Universal Declaration of Human Rights and will not discriminate among its citizens on the basis of color, race, or religion.

*Mr. Chairman,*
*Ladies and gentlemen,*

I would like to conclude my address by dwelling on the Palestinian view of Europe's status and role in the present and future.

By virtue of historical ties, geopolitics, mutual interests, and the uninterrupted interaction between the two civilizations, Europe has always had, and still has, strong links with the Middle East in general, and the Arab world in particular.

This was evident throughout all crises and developments which occurred in the Middle East region in old and recent times. The most prominent recent example is the Iraq-Iran war, which is at the beginning of its end after Iran's acceptance of Security Council Resolution 598, the implementation of the cease-fire, and the opening of negotiations aimed at achieving comprehensive peace between the two countries and in the Gulf region as a whole.

## 33. The Palestinian Declaration of Independence, Algiers, 15 November, 1988

Palestine, the land of the three monotheistic faiths, is where the Palestinian Arab people was born, on which it grew, developed and excelled. The Palestinian people was never separated from or diminished in its integral bonds with Palestine. Thus the Palestinian Arab people ensured for itself an everlasting union between itself, its land and its history.

Resolute throughout that history, the Palestinian Arab people forged its national identity, rising even to unimagined levels in its defense, as invasion, the design of others, and the appeal special to Palestine's ancient and luminous place on that eminence where powers and civilizations are joined... All this intervened thereby to deprive the people of its political independence. Yet the undying connection between Palestine and its people secured for the land its character, and for the people its national genius.

Nourished by an unfolding series of civilizations and cultures, inspired by a heritage rich in variety and kind, the Palestinian Arab people added to its stature by consolidating a union between itself and its patrimonial Land. The call went out from Temple, Church and Mosque that to praise the Creator, to celebrate compassion and peace was indeed the message of Palestine. And in generation after generation, the Palestinian Arab people gave of itself unsparingly in the valiant battle for liberation and homeland. For what has been the unbroken chain of our people's rebellions but the heroic embodiment of our will for national independence? And so the people was sustained in the struggle to stay and to prevail.

When in the course of modern times a new order of values was declared with norms and values fair for all, it was the Palestinian Arab people that had been excluded from the destiny of all other peoples by a hostile array of local and foreign powers. Yet again had unaided justice been revealed as insufficient to drive the world's history along its preferred course.

And it was the Palestinian people, already wounded in its body, that was submitted to yet another type of occupation over which floated the falsehood that "Palestine was a land without people." This notion was foisted upon some in the world, whereas in Article 22 of the Covenant of the League of Nations (1919) and in the Treaty of Lausanne (1923), the community of nations had recognized that all the Arab territories, including Palestine, of the formerly Ottoman provinces, were to have granted to them their freedom as provisionally independent nations.

Despite the historical injustice inflicted on the Palestinian Arab people resulting in their dispersion and depriving them of their right to self-determination, following upon UN General Assembly Resolution 181 (1947), which partitioned Palestine into two states, one Arab, one Jewish, yet it is this Resolution that still provides those conditions of international legitimacy that ensure the right of the Palestinian Arab people to sovereignty.

By stages, the occupation of Palestine and parts of other Arab territories by Israeli forces, the willed dispossession and expulsion from their ancestral homes of the majority of Palestine's civilian inhabitants, was achieved by organized terror; those Palestinians who remained, as a vestige subjugated in its homeland, were persecuted and forced to endure the destruction of their national life.

Thus were principles of international legitimacy violated. Thus were the Charter of the United Nations and its Resolutions disfigured, for they had recognized the Palestinian Arab people's national rights, including the right of Return, the right to independence, the right to sovereignty over territory and homeland.

In Palestine and on its perimeters, in exile distant and near, the Palestinian Arab people never faltered and never abandoned its conviction in its rights of Return and independence. Occupation, massacres and dispersion achieved no gain in the unabated Palestinian consciousness of self and political identity, as Palestinians went forward with their destiny, undeterred and unbowed. And from out of the long years of trial in evermounting struggle, the Palestinian political identity emerged further consolidated and confirmed. And the collective Palestinian national will forged for itself a political embodiment, the Palestine Liberation Organization, its sole, legitimate representative recognized by the world community as a whole, as well as by related regional and international institutions. Standing on the very rock of conviction in the Palestinian people's inalienable rights, and on the ground of Arab national consensus and of international legitimacy, the PLO led the campaigns of its great people, molded into unity and powerful resolve, one and indivisible in its triumphs, even as it suffered massacres and confinement within and without its home. And so Palestinian resistance was clarified and raised into the forefront of Arab and world awareness, as the struggle of the Palestinian Arab people achieved unique prominence among the world's liberation movements in the modern era.

The massive national uprising, the *intifadah,* now intensifying in cumulative scope and power on occupied Palestinian territories, as well as the unflinching resistance of the refugee camps outside the homeland, have elevated awareness of the Palestinian truth and right into still higher realms of comprehension and actuality. Now at least the curtain has been dropped around a whole epoch of prevarication and negation. The *intifadah* has set siege to the mind of official Israel, which has for too long relied exclusively upon myth and terror to deny Palestinian existence altogether. Because of the *intifadah* and its revolutionary irreversible impulse, the history of Palestine has therefore arrived at a decisive juncture.

Whereas the Palestinian people reaffirms most definitively its inalienable rights in the land of its patrimony:

Now by virtue of natural, historical and legal rights, and the sacrifices of successive generations who gave of themselves in defense of the freedom and independence of their homeland;

In pursuance of Resolutions adopted by Arab Summit Conferences and relying on the authority bestowed by international legitimacy as embodied in the Resolutions of the United Nations Organization since 1947;

And in exercise by the Palestinian Arab people of its rights to self-determination, political independence and sovereignty over its territory,

The Palestine National Council, in the name of God, and in the name of the Palestinian Arab people, hereby proclaims the establishment of the State of Palestine on our Palestinian territory with its capital Jerusalem (Al-Quds Ash-Sharif).

The State of Palestine is the state of Palestinians wherever they may be. The state is for them to enjoy in it their collective national and cultural identity, theirs to pursue in it a complete equality of rights. In it will be safeguarded their political and religious convictions and their human dignity by means of a parliamentary democratic system of governance, itself based on freedom of expression and the freedom to form parties. The rights of minorities will duly be respected by the majority, as minorities must abide by decisions of the majority. Governance will be based on principles of social justice, equality and non-discrimination in public rights of men or women, on grounds of race, religion, color or sex, under the aegis of a constitution which ensures the rule of law and an independent judiciary. Thus shall these principles allow no departure from Palestine's age-old spiritual and civilizational heritage of tolerance and religious coexistence.

The State of Palestine is an Arab state, an integral and indivisible part of the Arab nation, at one with that nation in heritage and civilization, with it also in its aspiration for liberation, progress, democracy and unity. The State of Palestine affirms its obligation to abide by the Charter of the League of Arab States, whereby the coordination of the Arab states with each other shall be strengthened.

It calls upon Arab compatriots to consolidate and enhance the emergence in reality of our state, to mobilize potential, and to intensify efforts whose goal is to end Israeli occupation.

The State of Palestine proclaims its commitment to the principles and purposes of the United Nations, and to the Universal Declaration of Human Rights. It proclaims its commitment as well to the principles and policies of the Non-Aligned Movement.

It further announces itself to be a peace-loving State, in adherence to the principles of peaceful co-existence. It will join with all states and peoples in order to assure a permanent peace based upon justice and the respect of rights so that humanity's potential for well-being may be assured, an earnest competition for excellence may be maintained, and in which confidence in the future will eliminate fear for those who are just and for whom justice is the only recourse.

In the context of its struggle for peace in the land of Love and Peace, the State of Palestine calls upon the United Nations to bear special responsibility for the Palestinian Arab people and its homeland. It calls upon all peace- and freedom-loving peoples and states to assist it in the attainment of its objectives, to provide it with security, to alleviate the tragedy of its people, and to help it terminate Israel's occupation of the Palestinian territories.

The State of Palestine herewith declares that it believes in the settlement of regional and international disputes by peaceful means, in accordance with the UN Charter and resolutions. Without prejudice to its natural right to defend its territorial integrity and independence, it therefore rejects the threat or use of force, violence and terrorism against its territorial integrity or political independence, as it also rejects their use against the territorial integrity of other states.

Therefore, on this day unlike all others, November 15, 1988, as we stand at the threshold of a new dawn, in all honor and modesty we humbly bow to the sacred spirits of our fallen ones, Palestinian and Arab, by the purity of whose sacrifice for the homeland our sky has been illuminated and our Land given life. Our hearts are lifted up and irradiated by the light emanating from the much blessed *intifadah,* from those who have endured and have fought the fight of the camps, of dispersion, of exile, from those who have borne the standard for freedom, our children, our aged, our youth, our prisoners, detainees and wounded, all those whose ties to our sacred soil are confirmed in camp, village and town. We render special tribute to that brave Palestinian Woman, guardian of sustenance and Life, keeper of our people's perennial flame. To the souls of our sainted martyrs, to the whole of our Palestinian Arab people, to all free and honorable peoples everywhere, we pledge that our struggle shall be continued until the occupation ends, and the foundation of our sovereignty and independence shall be fortified accordingly.

Therefore, we call upon our great people to rally to the banner of Palestine, to cherish and defend it, so that it may forever be the symbol of our freedom and dignity in that homeland, which is a homeland for the free, now and always.

In the name of God, the Compassionate, the Merciful:
"Say: O God, Master of the Kingdom,
Thou givest the Kingdom to whom Thou wilt,
and seizest the Kingdom from whom Thou wilt,
Thou exaltest whom Thou wilt, and Thou
abasest whom Thou wilt; in Thy hand
is the good; Thou art powerful over everything."
Sadaga Allahu Al-Azim

## 34. Palestine National Council, Political Communique, Algiers, 15 November, 1988 [Excerpts]

In the name of God, the Compassionate, the Merciful

In the valiant land of Algeria, hosted by its people and its President Chedli Benjedid, the Palestine National Council held its nineteenth extraordinary session—the session of the *intifadah* and independence, the session of the martyred hero Abu Jihad—in the period between 12 and 15 November 1988.

This session culminated in the announcement of the rise of the Palestinian state in our Palestinian land, the natural climax of a daring and tenacious popular struggle that started more than seventy years ago and was baptized in the immense sacrifices offered by our people in our homeland, along its borders, and in the camps and other sites of our diaspora.

The session was also distinguished by its focus on the great national Palestinian *intifidah* as one of the major milestones in the contemporary history of the Palestinian people's revolution, on a par with the legendary steadfastness of our people in their camps in our occupied land and outside it.

The primary features of our great people's *intifadah* were obvious from its inception and have become clearer in the twelve months since then during which it has continued unabated: It is a total popular revolution that embodies the consensus of an entire nation—women and men, old and young, in the camps, in the villages, and the cities—on the rejection of the occupation and on the determination to struggle until the occupation is defeated and terminated.

This glorious *intifadah* has demonstrated our people's deeply rooted national unity and their full adherence to the Palestine Liberation Organization, the sole, legitimate representative of our people, all our people, wherever they congregate—in our homeland or outside it. This was manifested by the participation of the Palestinian masses—their unions, their vocational organizations, their students, their workers, their farmers, their women, their merchants, their landlords, their artisans, their academics—in the *intifadah* through its United National Command and the popular committees that were formed in the urban neighborhoods, the villages, and the camps.

This, our people's revolutionary furnace and their blessed *intifadah,* along with the cumulative impact of our innovative and continuous revolution inside and outside of our homeland, have destroyed the illusion our people's enemies have harbored that they can turn the occupation of Palestinian land into a permanent *fait accompli* and consign the Palestinian issue to oblivion. For our generations have been weaned on the goals and principles of the Palestinian revolution and have lived all its battles since its birth in 1965—including the heroic resistance against the Zionist invasion of 1982 and the steadfastness of the revolution's camps as they endured the siege and starvation in Lebanon. Those generations— the children of the revolution and of the Palestine Liberation Organization—rose to demonstrate the dynamism and continuity of the revolution, detonating the land under the feet of its occupiers and proving that our people's reserves of resistance are inexhaustible and their faith is too deep to uproot.

Thus did the struggle of the children of the RPG's outside our homeland and the struggle of the children of the sacred stones inside it blend into a single revolutionary melody.

Our people have stood fast against all the attempts of our enemy's authorities to end our revolution, and those authorities have tried everything at their disposal; they have used terrorism, they have imprisoned us, they have sent us into exile, they have desecrated our holy places and restricted our religious freedoms, they have demolished our homes, they have killed us indiscriminately, and premeditatedly, they have sent bands of armed settlers into our villages and camps, they have burned our crops, they have cut off our water and power supplies, they have beaten our women and children, they have used toxic gases that have caused many deaths and abortions, they have waged an ignorance war [sic] against us by closing our schools and universities.

Our people's heroic steadfastness has cost them hundreds of martyrs and tens of thousands of casualties, prisoners, and exiles. But our people's genius was always at hand, ready in their darkest hours to innovate the means and formulas of struggle that stiffened their resistance, bolstered their steadfastness, and enabled them to confront the crimes and measures of the enemy and carry on with their heroic, tenacious struggle.

By standing firm, continuing their revolution, and escalating their *intifadah,* our people have proved their determination to press ahead regardless of the sacrifices, armed with the great heritage of struggle, an indomitable revolutionary will, a deeply entrenched national unity that has been rendered even stronger by the *intifadah* and its attendant struggles inside and outside our homeland, and total adherence to the nationalistic principles of the Palestine Liberation Organization and its goals of ending the Israeli occupation and achieving the Palestinian people's inalienable right to repatriation, self-determination, and the establishment of the independent Palestinian state.

In all this, our people relied on the sustenance of the masses and forces of our

Arab nation, which have stood by us and backed us, as demonstrated by the wide popular support for the *intifadah* and by the consensus and resolutions that emerged at the Arab summit in Algiers—all of which goes to confirm that our people do not stand alone as they face the fascist, racist assault, and this precludes any possibility of the Israeli aggressors' isolating our people and cutting them off from the support of their Arab nation.

In addition to this Arab solidarity, our people's revolution and their blessed *intifadah* have attracted widespread worldwide solidarity, as seen in the increased understanding of the Palestinian people's issue, the growing support of our just struggle by the peoples and states of the world, and the corresponding condemnation of Israeli occupation and the crimes it is committing, which has helped to expose Israel and increase its isolation and the isolation of its supporters.

Security Council Resolution 605, 607, and 608 and the resolutions of the General Assembly against the expulsion of the Palestinians from their land and against the repression and terrorism with which Israel is lashing the Palestinian people in the occupied Palestinian territories—these are strong manifestation of the growing support of international opinion, public and official, for our people and their representative, the Palestine Liberation Organization, and of the mounting international rejection of Israeli occupation with all the fascist, racist practices it entails.

The UN General Assembly's Resolution 21L/43/1 of 4/11/1988, which was adopted in the session dedicated to the *intifadah,* is another sign of the stand the peoples and states of the world in their majority are taking against the occupation and with the just struggle of the Palestinian people and their firm right to liberation and independence. The crimes of the occupation and its savage, inhuman practices have exposed the Zionist lie about the democracy of the Zionist entity that has managed to deceive the world for forty years, revealing Israel in its true light—a fascist, racist, colonialist state built on the usurpation of the Palestinian land and the annihilation of the Palestinian people, a state that threatens and undertakes attacks and expansion into neighboring Arab lands.

It has thus been demonstrated that the occupation cannot continue to reap the fruits of its actions at the expense of the Palestinian people's rights without paying a price—either on the ground or in terms of international public opinion.

In addition to the rejection of the occupation and the condemnation of its repressive measures by the democratic and progressive Israeli forces, Jewish groups all over the world are no longer able to continue their defense of Israel or maintain their silence about its crimes against the Palestinian people. Many voices have risen among those groups to demand an end to these crimes and call for Israel's withdrawal from the occupied territories in order to allow the Palestinian people to exercise their right to self-determination.

The fruits that our people's revolution and their blessed *intifadah* have borne on the local, Arab, and international levels have established the soundness and realism of the Palestine Liberation Organization's national program, a program aimed at the termination of the occupation and the achievement of our people's right to return, self-determination, and statehood. Those results have also confirmed that the struggle of our people is the decisive factor in the effort to snatch our national rights from the jaws of the occupation. It is the authority of our people, as represented in the Popular Committees, that controls the situation as we challenge the authority of the occupation's crumbling agencies.

The international community is now more prepared than ever before to strive for a political settlement of the Middle East crisis and its root cause, the question of Palestine. The Israeli occupation authorities, and the American administration that stands behind them, cannot continue to ignore the national will, which is now unanimous on the necessity of holding an international peace conference on the Middle East and enabling the Palestinian people to gain their national rights, foremost among which is their right to self-determination and national independence on their own national soil.

In the light of this, and toward the reinforcement of the steadfastness and blessed *intifadah* of our people, and in accordance with the will of our masses in and outside of our homeland, and in fidelity to those of our people that have been martyred, wounded, or taken captive, the Palestine National Council resolves:

*First: On The Escalation and Continuity of the Intifadah*

A. To provide all the means and capabilities needed to escalate our people's *intifadah* in various ways and on various levels to guarantee its continuation and intensification.

B. To support the popular institutions and organizations in the occupied Palestinian territories.

C. To bolster and develop the popular committees and other specialized popular and trade union bodies, including the attack groups and the popular army, with a view to expanding their role and increasing their effectiveness.

D. To consolidate the national unity that emerged and developed during the *intifadah.*

E. To intensify efforts on the international level for the release of detainees, the return of those expelled, and the termination of the organized, official acts of repression and terrorism against our children, our women, our men, and our institutions.

F. To call on the United Nations to place the occupied Palestinian land under international supervision for the protection of our people and the termination of the Israeli occupation.

G. To call on the Palestinian people outside our homeland to intensify and increase their support, and to expand the family-assistance program.

H. To call on the Arab nation, its people, forces, institutions, and governments, to increase their political, material, and information support for the *intifadah.*

I. To call on all free and honorable people worldwide to stand by our people, our revolution, our *intifadah* against the Israeli occupation, the repression, and the organized, fascist official terrorism to which the occupation forces and the armed fanatic settlers are subjecting our people, our universities, our institutions, our national economy, and our Islamic and Christian Holy Places.

*Second: In the Political Arena*

Proceeding from the above, the Palestinian National Council, being responsible to the Palestinian people, their national rights and their desire for peace as expressed in the Declaration of Independence issued on 15 November, 1988; and in response to the humanitarian quest for international entente, nuclear disarmament, and the settlement of regional conflict by peaceful means, affirms the determination of the Palestine Liberation Organization to arrive at a comprehensive settlement of the Arab-Israeli conflict and its core, which is the question of Palestine, within the framework of the United Nations Charter, the principles and provisions of international legality, the norms of international law, and the resolutions of the United Nations, the latest of which are Security Council Resolutions 605, 607, and 608, and the resolutions of the Arab summits, in such a manner that safeguards the Palestinian Arab people's rights to return, to self-determination, and the establishment of their independent national state on their national soil, and that institutes arrangements for the security and peace of all states in the region.

Toward the achievement of this, the Palestine National Council affirms:

1. The necessity of convening the effective international conference on the issue of the Middle East and its core, the question of Palestine, under the auspices of the United Nations and with the participation of the permanent members of the Security Council and all parties to the conflict in the region including the Palestine Liberation Organization, the sole, legitimate representative of the Palestinian people, on an equal footing, and by considering that the international peace conference be convened on the basis of United Nations Security Council Resolutions 242 and 338 and the attainment of the legitimate national rights of the Palestinian people, foremost among which is the right to self-determination and in accordance with the principles and provisions of the United Nations Charter concerning the right of peoples to self-determination, and by the inadmissibility of the acquisition of the territory of others by force or military conquest, and in accordance with the relevant United Nations resolutions on the question of Palestine.

2. The withdrawal of Israel from all the Palestinian and Arab territories it occupied in 1967, including Arab Jerusalem.

3. The annulment of all measures of annexation and appropriation and the removal of settlements established by Israel in the Palestinian and Arab territories since 1967.

4. Endeavoring to place the occupied Palestinian territories, including Arab Jerusalem, under the auspices of the United Nations for a limited period in order to protect our people and afford the appropriate atmosphere for the success of the proceeding of the international conference toward the attainment of a comprehensive political settlement and the attainment of peace and security for all on the basis of mutual acquiescence and consent, and to enable the Palestinian state to exercise its effective authority in these territories.

5. The settlement of the question of the Palestinian refugees in accordance with the relevant United Nations resolutions.

6. Guaranteeing the freedom of worship and religious practice for all faiths in the holy places in Palestine.

7. The Security Council is to formulate and guarantee arrangements for security and peace between all the states concerned in the region, including the Palestinian state.

The Palestine National Council affirms its previous resolutions concerning the distinctive relationship between the Jordanian and Palestinian peoples, and affirms that the future relationship between the two states of Palestine and Jordan should be on a confederal basis as a result of the free and voluntary choice of the two fraternal peoples in order to strengthen the historical bonds and the vital interests they hold in common.

The National Council also renews its commitment to the United Nations resolutions that affirm the right of peoples to resist foreign occupation, colonialism, and racial discrimination, and their right to struggle for their independence, and reiterates its rejection of terrorism in all its forms, including state terrorism, affirming its commitment to previous resolutions in this respect and the resolution of the Arab summit in Algiers in 1988, and to UN Resolutions 42/195 of 1987, and 40/61 of 1985, and that contained in the Cairo declaration of 1985 in this respect.

## 35. Address by Yasser Arafat to the UN General Assembly, Geneva, 13 December, 1988

Mr. Chairman and Members: It never occurred to me that my second meeting since 1974 with this esteemed assembly would take place in the hospitable city of Geneva.

I believe that the position and the new political stands which our Palestinian people had adopted during the PNC meeting in Algiers, all of which were announced amid great international appreciation and welcome, would have behooved me to go to the UN Headquarters in New York to acquaint you with our resolutions and views regarding the cause of peace in our homeland as formulated by our PNC, which is the highest legislative authority in the Palestinian political body.

Therefore, my meeting with you in Geneva today after an unjust US decision which prevented me from going to you there is a cause of my pride and joy. My pride stems from the fact that I am with you and among you because you are the main platform for all issues of right and justice in the world.

My joy derives from the fact that I am present in Geneva where justice and neutrality are words on all tongues and are a constitution in a world in which the arrogance of the strong make them lose their neutrality and sense of justice.

Consequently, the resolution issued by your esteemed assembly, with the concurrence of 154 states to hold this meeting, was not a victory over the US decision but a victory for the international unanimity in upholding right and the cause of peace in an unparalleled referendum. It is also evident that our people's just cause has taken root in the fabric of the human conscience.

Our Palestinian people will not forget this noble stand by your esteemed assembly and these friendly states in support of right and justice to safeguard the values and principles for which the United Nations was established. This stand will be translated into feelings of confidence and reassurance by all peoples who suffer injustice, coercion, and occupation, and who are, like our Palestinian people, struggling for freedom, dignity, and life.

On this occasion, I express the deepest thanks to all the countries, forces, international organizations and world personalities that have supported our people and backed their national rights, particularly the friends in the Soviet Union, the PRC, the socialist countries, the nonaligned countries, the Islamic countries, the African countries, the Asian countries, the Latin American countries, and all the other friendly countries.

I also thank the countries of Western Europe and Japan for their recent stands toward our people. I call on them to take more steps on the course of positive development of these decisions in order to open the vistas for peace and the just solution in our region, the Middle East region.

I also underline our solidarity with and backing for the liberation movements in Namibia and South Africa in their struggle, and also our support for the African confrontation states against the aggressions of the racist South African regime.

I take this opportunity too to express my thanks and gratitude to the friendly countries that have supported us and backed our PNC resolutions, and also recognized the State of Palestine.

I also thank His Excellency UN Secretary-General Javier Perez de Cuellar and his assistants for their constant efforts to achieve the international detente sought by humanity and solutions for world problems, particularly those concerning the Palestinian issue.

I also express my thanks and appreciation to the chairman and members of the committee on the Palestinian peoples' exercise of their inalienable rights for their efforts toward our peoples' cause. I also greet and thank the nine-member committee of the nonaligned countries on the Palestinian issue for all its constructive work for our peoples' cause.

To you, Mr. Chairman, I express the warmest greetings on the occasion of your election as chairman of this assembly. I am fully confident of your wisdom and knowledge. I also greet your predecessor for his noble chairmanship of the former session.

Last, I express my greetings and deep thanks to the Swiss Government and people for the great help, facilities, and efforts they have extended for this session.

Mr. Chairman, members, on 13 November 1974—14 years ago—I received with gratitude an invitation from you to present the cause of our Palestinian people before this esteemed Assembly. Now I return to you here after all these years, which were fraught with grave events, to see that new peoples have taken their places among you, thus crowning their victories in the battles of freedom and independence.

To the representatives of these peoples I extend the warm congratulations of our people and to everyone I announce that I return to you with a louder voice, stronger determination, and greater confidence to emphasize that our struggle must bear fruit and that the State of Palestine, which we proclaimed in our National Council, must take its place among you, so it could take part with you in consolidating the charter of this organization and the human rights convention, in putting an end to the tragedies to which humanity is being subjected, and in laying down the bases of right, justice, peace, and freedom for all, for all, for all.

Fourteen years ago, when you said to us in the General Assembly hall yes to Palestine and the Palestinian people; yes to the PLO; and yes to the firm national rights of the Palestinian people, some thought your decisions would have hardly any effect. They failed to realize these decisions were among the most important springs that have watered the olive branch that I carried on that day. This branch, after we had it watered with blood, sweat, and tears, has become a tree whose root is in the ground and its branches in the sky, promising the yields of victory over repression, injustice, and occupation.

You have given us hope for the victory of freedom and justice and we have given you a generation from the sons of our people that have devoted their lifetime to achieving this dream. It is the generation of the blessed uprising which today is carrying the stones of the homeland to defend the honor of this homeland, so it can be worthy of belonging to a people that yearn for freedom and independence. Greetings to all of you from the sons of our hero people—men and women—and from the masses of our blessed uprising, which enters its 2nd year with huge momentum, meticulously planned tactics, and a democratic civilized method in confronting the occupation, oppression, injustice, and the bestial crimes which the Israeli occupiers are committing against them daily.

Greetings to you from our male and female youths in occupation prisons and mass detention camps. Greetings to you from the stonethrowing children, who are challenging the occupation and its aircraft, tanks, and weaponry, reminiscent of the new image of the defenseless Palestinian David versus the heavily-armed Israeli Goliath.

At the conclusion of my speech during our first meeting I said that as chairman of the PLO and leader of the Palestinian revolution, we emphasize our desire not to see a drop of Jewish or Arab blood spilled. We also do not want to continue the fighting for one more minute. At that time I appealed to you to end all this suffering and pain and to hasten to draw up the basis for the just peace based on the guarantee of our peoples' rights, aspirations, and hopes and the right of all peoples.

At that time I appealed to you to support the struggle of our people to exercise their right to self-determination to enable our people to return from their compulsory exile to which they had been pushed under bayonets of rifles and to help us end this injustice which generations of our people have been suffering for several decades so they could live free and sovereign in their homeland and country while enjoying all their national and human rights.

The last thing I said from this platform is that war erupts from Palestine and that peace starts in Palestine. Our dream then was to set up the democratic state of Palestine, in which Muslims, Christians, and Jews would live on an equal footing, in terms of rights and duties, under a single, unified society, similar to other peoples on this earth and in our contemporary world.

We were greatly astonished when we saw Israeli officials interpreting this Palestinian dream—which is inspired by the legacy of the heavenly messages that have illuminated the skies of Palestine and by the civilized and humane values that call for coexistence in a free and democratic society—as a scheme that aims to destroy and annihilate their entity.

It was our duty, Mr. Chairman, to learn a lesson from this difficult situation and to note the distance between this situation and the dream. We, in the PLO, began searching for the realistic alternative formulas, which are applicable, to find a solution to the question based on the possible and not absolute justice which would guarantee our peoples' rights to freedom, sovereignty, and independence; guarantee peace, security, and stability to all; and avoid the Palestine and Middle East wars and battles which have, regrettably, been going on for 40 years.

Mr. Chairman, did we not adopt the UN Charter and its resolutions, the human rights declaration, and international legitimacy as a basis for solving the Arab-Israeli conflict? Did we not welcome the 1977 Vance-Gromyko declaration as an initiative which could serve as a basis for a plan to solve this conflict?

Did we not agree to participate in the Geneva conference in accordance with the 1977 Egyptian-US statement to advance the process of peace and solution in our region? Did we not adopt the 1982 Fez Arab peace plan and later the call for an international peace conference under the auspices of the United Nations and according to its resolutions?

Did we not support Brezhnev's peace plan for the Middle East? Did we not welcome and support the statement issued by the EC countries in Venice concerning the establishment of just peace in the region?

Did we not welcome and support the initiative of Presidents Gorbachev and Mitterrand concerning the preparatory committee for an international conference?

Did we not welcome scores of political statements and initiatives put forward by African, Muslim, nonaligned, socialist, European, and other nations with the aim of finding a peaceful settlement in accordance with the principles of international law and with the goal of establishing peace and resolving the conflict?

What was Israel's reaction to all that? Please note that all these peace initiatives, plans, and statements to which I have referred were evenhanded. None of these initiatives ignored the demands and interests of any of the parties involved in the Arab-Israeli conflict.

Israel reacted to all that by building more settlements, by escalating its expansionist policies, and by exacerbating the conflict. Israel engaged in a policy of destruction and bloodshed and widened the front of hostility to include brotherly Lebanon.

The occupation armies of Israel swept over Lebanon in 1982. The invasion of Lebanon was accompanied by the slaughter and massacre of the Lebanese and Palestinian people, including the Sabra and Shatila massacres. Israel is still at this moment occupying a part of the Lebanese south. Lebanon is daily coming under Israeli land, air, and sea attacks and raids against its towns and villages, a fate shared by our camps in the south of that country.

It is painful and regrettable that the US government alone should continue to back and support these Israeli expansionist and aggressive plans; support Israel's continuing occupation of Palestinian and Arab territory; and support its crimes and iron-fist policy against our children and women.

It also is sad and painful that the US Government should continue to refuse to recognize the right of 6 million Palestinians to self-determination. This is a sacred right to the American people themselves and all the peoples of earth.

I remind them of President Wilson's stand, the architect of the two universal principles in international relations; namely, the inadmissibility of the occupation of the territories of others by force and the right of peoples to self-determination.

When the Palestinian people were consulted in 1919 by the King-Crane Commission, they chose the United States of America as the mandate country. But circumstances prevented this and Britain took its place.

I ask the American people; I ask the American people: Is it right, is it right that what President Wilson had decreed should not be applied to the Palestinian people? The subsequent US Administrations know that the only birth certificate for the establishment of the State of Israel is international Resolution 181, which was issued by the UN General Assembly on 29 November, 1947.

At that time, the United States and the Soviet Union approved this resolution. It stipulates the establishment of two states in Palestine—a Palestinian Arab state and a Jewish state.

How could the US Government explain its stand, which acknowledges and recognizes the same resolution which pertains to Israel, while, it simultaneously rejects the other half of this resolution which pertains to the Palestinian state?

How could the US Government explain its noncommitment to implementing a resolution which it had repeatedly sponsored at your esteemed Assembly, Resolution 194, which provides for the Palestinians' right to return to their homeland and property from which they were expelled or to compensate those who do not wish to return.

The US Government is aware that it is neither its right nor the right of others to divide international legitimacy and disintegrate the provisions of international laws.

Mr. Chairman and members of the Assembly, the continuing struggle of our people for the sake of their rights dates back scores of years, during which our people have presented hundreds of thousands of martyrs and wounded and suffered all kinds of tragic tortures. But these people have not relented and their determination has not faltered. But, rather, it has consolidated their determination to cling to their Palestinian homeland and to their national identity.

Israel's leaders, who were taken by deceptive intoxication, believed that, after our departure from Beirut, the sea would swallow the PLO. They did not expect that the departure into oblivion [rahil al-manasi] would turn into a road leading back to the homeland, the real arena of the struggle, and to occupied Palestine. The valiant popular uprising inside our occupied land broke out and will continue until our goals of freedom and national independence are realized.

I have the honor, Mr. Chairman, of being one of the sons of these people who record with the blood of their children, women, and men the most splendid epics of national resistance and who create daily miracles of which legends are made so that their uprising will continue and so this uprising will develop and grow stronger until they impose their willpower and until they prove that right can defeat might.

I extend greetings of admiration to the masses of our people who are now making this unique revolutionary and democratic experiment. Their faith has not been shaken by all of Israel's war machine, has not been terrorized by all kinds of bullets, and has not been affected by people being buried alive or having their bones broken, or by causing pregnant women to abort, or by the seizure of water sources.

The masses' resolution has not been weakened by detention, imprisonment, deportation, and expulsion outside the homeland. The collective punishment and demolition of houses, the closing of universities, schools, trade unions, societies and establishments, the suspension of newspapers, and the besieging of camps, villages, and cities have only established this faith more firmly. The revolution has spread to every house and taken root in every inch of the homeland's soil.

A people with such conduct and history cannot be defeated. All forces of repression and terrorism cannot dissuade the people from their firm belief in their right to their homeland and in the values of justice, peace, love, and tolerant coexistence.

The rebel's rifle has protected us and precluded our liquidation and the destruction of our national identity in the fields of hot confrontation. We are fully confident of our ability to protect the biggest olive branch in the fields of political confrontation.

That the world is rallying around our just cause to achieve just peace brilliantly indicates that the world realizes in no vague terms who is the executioner and who is the victim, who is the aggressor and who is aggressed upon, and who is the struggler for freedom and peace and who is the terrorist.

The daily practices of the occupation army's forces and fanatic armed settlers' gangs against our people, children, and women expose the ugly face and aggressive nature of the Israeli occupation.

This growing world awareness has affected the Jewish societies themselves inside and outside Israel. It has opened these societies' eyes to the reality of the problem and essence of the conflict, particularly to the inhuman daily Israeli practices which destroy the very spirit of the tolerant Jewish religion itself.

It has become difficult and almost impossible for a Jew to declare his rejection of racial oppression and his adherence to freedom and human rights while remaining silent over Israel's crimes and violations of the rights of the Palestinian man, the Palestinian people, and the Palestinian homeland, particularly over the abominable daily practices of the occupiers and gangs of armed settlers.

Mr. Chairman: We differentiate between the Jewish citizen whose awareness and conscience have been subject to the Israeli ruling circles' continual efforts to obliterate and falsify and between the practices of Israel's leaders.

Furthermore, we realize that both inside and outside Israel there are honorable and courageous Jews who do not agree with the Government of Israel over the policy of repression, massacres, expansion, settlement, and deportation and who admit the equal rights of our people for life, freedom, and independence. In the name of the Palestinian people, I thank them, thank them, thank them for this courageous and frank position.

Our people do not want any right to which they are not entitled and which is not compatible with international legality and laws. They are not seeking any freedom that encroaches upon the freedom of others or any destiny that cancels the destiny of another people.

Our people refuse to be more privileged than others, or for others to be more privileged than they are. Our people want equality with all other peoples, having the same rights and obligations.

Today I address this appeal to all the people of the world, particularly those who have suffered from the Nazi occupation and who have believed it be their duty to turn the page of repression and injustice by any people against another and to extend help to all the victims of terrorism, fascism, and Nazism, so that they could clearly see the responsibilities dictated by history upon them toward our suffering people, who want a place under the sun for their children in their homeland, in which they could live like the rest of the children of the world.

They want a place under the sun for their children in their homeland in which they can live like the rest of the children of the world, free on their liberated land.

Mr. Chairman, members, it is a cause for optimism that our march of struggle has climaxed into the ongoing uprising at a time when the international climate is one of earnest detente and prosperity.

We have been following with great satisfaction the successes of the United Nations and the UN Secretary-General in bringing about solutions to many problems and in many areas of tension in the world in this new atmosphere of international detente.

The improvement in the international atmosphere cannot be consolidated without attention being paid to regional problems and areas of tension. We need to forge a human conscience that is more sensitive and responsible in assessing the efforts of man and the policies of nations and more capable of carrying us into the next century.

We have new challenges and responsibilities to face away from, away from wars and destruction, and for more, for more freedom, prosperity, peace, and progress for all mankind.

Mr. Chairman, it is indisputable that the Palestinian issue is the most complicated problem of our time. It is the earliest problem on UN records, the most intricate issue, and the most menacing to international peace and security.

Therefore, the Palestinian issue, more than any other international problem, should be a reason of concern to the two superpowers and other world nations. Efforts should be made to find a solution to this issue. A just solution of the Palestinian problem would be the best guarantee for peace in the Middle East.

The PLO leadership, as it is responsible for the Palestinian people and its future, faithful to the struggle of the Palestinian people, loyal to the memory of the martyrs, responsive to the atmosphere of detente, aware of the need to engage in peaceful political efforts, and desirous of a political solution ending the course of war and fighting and opening the door to a peaceful existence governed by the norms of international law, had called the PNC for an extraordinary session in Algiers from 12 to 15 November of this year.

The goal was to define and clarify our position as a major party to the Arab-Israeli conflict; a party without the participation and endorsement of which a solution to this conflict cannot be achieved.

I am pleased to tell you with full pride that our National Council, through full democratic practice and under complete freedom, has once again proven its ability to shoulder its supreme national responsibilities and has made serious, constructive, and responsible decisions that have paved the way for deepening and showing our desire and our contribution toward finding a peaceful settlement that guarantees the national and political rights of our people and that ensures security and peace for everyone.

Mr. Chairman, the first and decisive resolution taken by our National Council was the declaration of the establishment of the Palestinian state with holy Jerusalem as its capital on the basis of the natural, historic, and legal right of the Palestinian Arab people to their homeland and the sacrifices of successive generations in defense of their homeland's freedom and independence.

It also stems from the resolutions of the Arab summits and from the strength of international legitimacy which is embodied by the UN resolutions since 1947. It is the Palestinian Arab people's exercise of their right to self-determination, political independence, and sovereignty over their land in accordance with your successive resolutions.

I would like to reiterate before the international community that this historic resolution—now that it has become an official UN document—is irreversible and that we will not stop to work until the occupation ends and our people exercise their sovereignty in their own state—the State of Palestine for all Palestinians wherever they are.

In this state they can develop their national and cultural identity, enjoy full equality of rights, and have their religious and political beliefs and their human dignity upheld in a democratic parliamentary system, established on the basis of freedom of opinion, the formation of parties, due regard by the majority for the rights of the minority, respect by the minority for the decisions of the majority, social justice and equality, and non-discrimination on the basis of race, religion, or color or between man and woman under a constitution that imposes legal supremacy—legal supremacy—and an independent judiciary and on the basis of full loyalty to Palestine's spiritual and cultural heritage of tolerance and generous coexistence among religions throughout the centuries.

The State of Palestine is an Arab state and its people constitute a part of their Arab nation in terms of heritage, culture, and hopes regarding social development, unity, and liberation. The state abides by the Arab League Charter, UN principles, the International Declaration of Human Rights, and principles of nonalignment.

It is a peaceloving state committed to the principles of peaceful coexistence and to working alongside all countries and peoples to establish a just, lasting peace based on justice and a respect of rights.

It is a state which believes in the settlement of international and regional problems through peaceful means in accordance with the UN Charter and resolutions.

It rejects threats of violence, force, or terrorism against its territorial integrity and political independence and the territorial integrity of any other state, as well as any encroachment on its natural rights to defend its territories and independence.

It is a state which believes that the future will only bring security to those who acted justly and even those who renounced justice. This, Mr. Chairman, is the State of Palestine, which we had proclaimed and which we will consolidate so it will assume its position among world countries and participate and excel in forming a free world in which justice will prevail and in which peace will be enjoyed.

Our state will have its own provisional government at the nearest possible opportunity, God willing.

The PNC has entrusted the PLO Executive Committee with the obligation of assuming the tasks of this provisional government until it is formed. To implement this decision, the PNC adopted several important decisions which emphasize our determination to seriously forge ahead in the just, peaceful settlement process and to exert utmost efforts to render it a success.

Our National Council stressed the need to convene an international conference on the Middle East problem, whose core is the issue of Palestine, under UN auspices and with the participation of the states which are permanent members of the Security Council and all parties to the conflict in the region including the PLO, the sole legitimate representative of the Palestinian people, on an equal footing since the international conference will convene in accordance with Security Council Resolutions 242 and 338 and on the basis of the guarantee of the national, political, legitimate rights of the Palestinian people, foremost being their right to self-determination.

Our National Council also has emphasized that Israel must withdraw from all Palestinian and Arab territories which it has occupied since 1967, including Arab Jerusalem; that the Palestinian state must be set up; that all the annexation decisions must be cancelled; and that the settlements which Israel has established in the Palestinian and Arab territories since 1967 must be removed. The Arab summits, particularly the Fez and Algiers summits, have endorsed this.

Our National Council has asserted that endeavors must be launched to place the occupied Palestinian territories, including Arab Jerusalem, under the supervision of the United Nations for a limited period to defend our people and to create the appropriate atmosphere to ensure the success of the activities of an international conference, to achieve a comprehensive political settlement, and to establish peace and security for all the peoples and states in the Middle East with their mutual consent to enable the State of Palestine to exercise its actual powers in their territories. This also has been emphasized by the resolutions adopted at Arab summits.

Our council also has emphasized the need to settle the issue of the Palestinian refugees in accordance with UN resolutions. It also has emphasized that freedom of worship and performance of religious rites in holy places in Palestine will be guaranteed to the followers of all religions.

The National Council has reaffirmed its previous decisions regarding the distinguished and special relationship between the two fraternal Jordanian and Palestinian peoples.

It affirmed the future relationship between the State of Palestine and the Hashemite Kingdom of Jordan will be established on a confederal basis and on the basis of a voluntary and free choice of the two fraternal peoples to strengthen the historical bonds and vital interests between them.

The council reasserted the need for the Security Council to lay down and guarantee the security and peace arrangements among all the states concerned with the conflict in the region.

I would like to point out here, Mr. Chairman, that these decisions reflect—as is clear from their contents and phraseology—our firm conviction with regard to peace and freedom and with regard to our deep understanding and appreciation of the climate of the international rapprochement and detente and of the eagerness of the world community to achieve balanced solutions responding to the basic interests and demands of the parties to the conflict.

These decisions also reflect the seriousness of the Palestinian stand toward the issue of peace, its eagerness for it, and the need to guarantee and ensure it through the Security Council and under the supervision of the United Nations.

These decisions carry the clear-cut and decisive answer to all the excuses, preconditions, and pretexts which some countries have used with respect to the positions and policy of the PLO.

At a time when our people have been voting for peace through their uprising and their representatives in the PNC and at a time when our PNC has been voting for peace, stressing its response to the prevailing trend which is being strengthened by the era of new detente in international relations to resolve world conflicts through peaceful means, the Israeli Government is nourishing aggressive and expansionist tendencies and religious fanaticism to stress its adherence to the option of aggression and of ignoring our peoples right.

The Palestinian side, for its part, has formulated clear-cut and responsible political stands that are in line with the will of the international community, in a bid to help convene an international peace conference and to ensure its success.

The courageous international support, as demonstrated by the recognition of the State of Palestine, which we appreciate, constitutes irrefutable evidence of the soundness of our course, the credibility of our decisions, and their compatibility with the international peaceloving will.

Despite our great appreciation for the free US voices which have hastened to explain and support our positions and decisions, the US Administration, however, still has no unified criterion to apply toward the parties to the conflict, requiring us alone to adopt positions that cannot be decided [la yumkin hasmaha] before negotiations and dialogue start within the framework of an international conference.

I would like to state that acknowledging the equality and rights of the two parties to the conflict on a mutual basis, is the sole prelude toward answering the clarifications requested by any quarter. If the policies and deeds are any indication of intentions, the Palestinian party has a better reason to worry and demand clarifications and assurances about its destiny and future with regard to the State of Israel, which is armed with the most modern weapons, including nuclear weapons.

Mr. Chairman, members, our PNC has reiterated its adherence to UN resolutions endorsing the right of nations to resist foreign occupation, imperialism, and racial discrimination, as well as the right of nations to struggle for freedom.

The PNC reiterated its rejection of terrorism; it reiterated its rejection of terrorism of all kinds—of terrorism of all kinds, including state terrorism—including state terrorism.

In this respect, the PNC underscored its commitment to its own previous resolutions, to the resolutions of the Arab summit in Algiers in 1988, to UN Resolutions 159/42 for 1987 and 40/61 for 1985, and to the Cairo Declaration issued on 7 November, 1985 in this regard.

Our position, Mr. Chairman, is clear and unambiguous. However, I, in my capacity as chairman of the PLO, declare from here once more—declare from here once more:

I condemn terrorism in all its forms, but, I, at the same time, salute all those before me in this hall who have been accused by their executioners and colonialists of being terrorists during the battles for the liberation of their land from the yoke of colonialism. They are today the faithful leaders of their people and sincerely devoted to the principles and values of justice and freedom.

I reverently salute the martyrs who have fallen at the hand of terrorism and terrorists, chief among those being my life long comrade, my deputy, Khalil al-Wazir, alias Abu Jihad, and the martyrs of the massacres which were inflicted on our people in many areas, towns, villages, and camps in the West Bank, Gaza Strip, and in south Lebanon.

Mr. Chairman, members, the situation in our Palestinian homeland can no longer be tolerated. The masses of our people, our heroes, are leading the way and holding high the torches of freedom. They die every day so the occupiers will leave and so peace will be established in their free and independent homeland and in the entire region.

Therefore, the PNC has based its resolutions on a realistic understanding of the conditions of both the Palestinians and the Israelis. The goal of these resolutions is to establish an atmosphere of tolerance between the Palestinians and the Israelis.

The United Nations has a historic and singular obligation toward our people, their cause, and their rights.  Over 40 years ago, the United Nations issued Resolution 181 setting up two states in Palestine, as I have mentioned—one to be an Arab Palestinian state and the other a Jewish state.

Today, despite the historic injustice that has been committed against our people, we still see that this resolution continues to provide international legitimacy to the right of the Arab Palestinian people to sovereignty and national independence.

Therefore, the acceleration of the peace process in the region requires additional efforts by all the parties concerned and by international powers, particularly the United States and the Soviet Union, both of which have a great responsibility toward the issue of peace in our region.

The United Nations, the permanent members of the UN Security Council, and all international groups and organizations have a vital and essential role to play at the current stage.

I hereby present the following Palestinian peace initiative in my capacity as the chairman of the PLO Executive Committee, which assumes the tasks of the provisional government of the State of Palestine:

1.  Serious work should be undertaken to convene the preparatory committee of an international conference for peace in the Middle East under the auspices of the UN Secretary-General in accordance with the Gorbachev-Mitterrand initiative, which has been supported by many countries and which President Mitterrand thankfully presented to your Assembly at the end of last September, preparatory to convening an international conference, which is being supported by all the world countries with the exception of the Government of Israel;

2.  Proceeding from our faith in the UN's vital role and international legitimacy, we believe the United Nations should assume temporary supervision of our Palestinian land; UN forces should be deployed to protect our people; and, at the same time, the UN forces should supervise the withdrawal of the Israeli forces from our country; and

3.  The PLO will work to reach a comprehensive peaceful settlement between the sides involved in the Arab-Israeli struggle, including the State of Palestine and Israel, as well as the other neighboring states, within the framework of an international conference for peace in the Middle East to realize equality and a balance of interests, particularly the right of our people to freedom and national independence, and the respect of the right to live, and the right of peace and security to everyone; namely, all the sides involved in the struggle in the area in accordance with Resolutions 242 and 338.

In the event these bases are recognized within the framework of such a conference, we would have made a principal stride toward a just solution, which would pave the way toward reaching an agreement over all the security and peace arrangements.

Mr. Chairman, I hope it is clear that to the extent they are eager to attain their legitimate national rights to self-determination and their return and to secure the termination of the occupation of the Palestinian land of their homeland, our Palestinian people also are eager to safeguard the peaceful process so as to achieve these goals within the framework of an international conference under UN auspices and in accordance with its charter and resolutions.

I stress that we are a people who yearn for peace like all the peoples on earth and, perhaps, more enthusiastically, because of our long endurance over the years; because of the harsh life that confronts our people and children; and because of their deprivation of an enjoyable, normal life without wars, tragedies, agonies, displacements, and harsh sufferings in their daily life.

Let the voices be raised in support of the olive branch, the policy of peaceful coexistence, and the climate of international relaxation. Let the hands unite in defense of an historical opportunity, which might not be repeated, to put an end to a long tragedy which has claimed the sacrifices of thousands of souls and resulted in the destruction of hundreds of cities and villages.

When we extend our hand with an olive branch and the peace branch, we do so because this branch stems from the tree of the homeland and freedom planted in our hearts.

Mr. Chairman, members, I have come to you in the name of our people to extend my hand so we may establish the real, just peace.

It is from this premise that I call on the leaders of Israel to come here, to come here, under UN auspices to create this peace. I also tell them that our people want dignity, freedom, and peace. They want peace for their state the same as they want it for all the countries and parties to the Arab-Israeli conflict.

I hereby address greetings to all factions, forces, and sects of the Israelis led by the forces of democracy and peace.

I tell them: Move away from fear and intimidation so we can make peace, make peace, make peace; move away from the spectre of the wars of this conflict, which have been raging for 40 years, and away from the flare-up of coming wars, whose fuel would only be their children and our children.

Come, let us make peace. Come let us create peace—the peace of the brave—and move away from the arrogance of the strong and the weapons of destruction, and away from occupation, coercion, humiliation, killing, and torture.

Say: O people of the book, come to common terms to establish peace on the land of peace—the land of Palestine. Glory be to God in the heavens, peace on earth, and joy to the people. God, you are peace, peace is from you, and peace returns to you. Make us live in peace, O Lord and admit us to paradise, the house of peace.

Finally, I tell our people: The dawn is coming and victory is coming. I see the homeland represented in your sacred stones.

I see the flag of our independent Palestinian state flying over the hills of the dear homeland. Thanks and God's peace and blessing be with you.

## 36.   Yasser Arafat's Geneva Press Statement, 15 December, 1988

Allow me to explain my viewpoints before you. Our desire for peace is strategic and not a temporary tactic. We work for peace regardless of whatever may happen.

Our state provides salvation for the Palestinians and peace for both the Palestinians and Israelis. The right to self-determination means the existence of the Palestinians and our existence does not destroy the existence of the Israelis, as their rulers claim.

In my speech yesterday, I referred to UN Resolution No. 181 as a basis for Palestinian independence. I also referred to our acceptance of Resolutions 242 and 338 as a basis for negotiations with Israel within the framework of the international conference.

Our PNC accepted these three resolutions at the Algiers session. Also in my speech yesterday, it was clear that we mean our people's rights to freedom and national independence in accordance with Resolution No. 181 as well as the right of all parties concerned with the Middle East conflict to exist in peace and security, including— as I said— the State of Palestine, Israel, and other neighbors in accordance with Resolutions 242 and 338.

Regarding terrorism, yesterday I announced beyond doubt— and nevertheless I repeat for the sake of recording stands, that we totally and categorically reject all forms of terrorism, including individual, group, and state terrorism.

We explained our stand in Geneva and Algiers. Any talk to the effect that the Palestinians must offer more— do you remember this slogan— or that what was offered is insufficient or that the Palestinians are playing propaganda games or public relations maneuvers will be harmful and unfruitful. That is enough.

All outstanding issues should be discussed on the table and at the international conference. Let it be perfectly clear that neither 'Arafat nor anyone else can stop the uprising.

The uprising will stop only when practical and tangible steps are taken toward the attainment of its national goals and establishment of its Palestinian state.

Within this framework, I expect the EEC states to play a more effective role in consolidating peace in our region. They assume a political and moral responsibility and they can deal with this.

Finally, I announce before you and ask you to convey these words on my behalf. We want peace, we are committed to peace, and we want to live in our Palestinian state and let others live.

Thank you.

### 37. Letter to Secretary of State George Shultz and Statement by Palestinian Institutions and Personalities from the West Bank and Gaza, Jerusalem, 27 January, 1988.

His Excellency George P. Shultz
*Secretary of State, Department of State, Washington, DC 20520*
Dear Secretary Shultz:

This meeting takes place at a crucial time when uncivilized and oppressive measures are being employed by Israeli occupation forces to quell the just uprising of our Palestinian people. This uprising comes as the inevitable national expression of our people's will to struggle until we achieve our freedom in our independent Palestinian state under the leadership of our sole legitimate representative, the Palestine Liberation Organization.

Our people are in urgent need of immediate international protection from the brutality of Israel's military authorities which have been unleashed against our unarmed civilian population to kill, maim and terrorize our women and children. To this end, we hope the international community will immediately authorize the provision of an international force to intervene in the occupied territories, to whose trusteeship our population can be delivered, as a first step towards the convening of an international peace conference. This conference is to be held under the auspices of the United Nations, and will be attended by all concerned parties to the conflict, including, foremost, the Palestinian nation through its legitimate representative, the PLO.

We look forward to your personal active involvement and that of the United States Government in the peace process, which we hope will bring an end to the suffering endured by our people for the past 20 years.

Yours respectfully,
Hanna Siniora
Fayez Abu Rahme
*Enc.: Copy of statement by Palestinian institutions and personalities from the West Bank and Gaza*

During the past few weeks the occupied territories have witnessed a popular uprising against Israel's occupation and its oppressive measures. This uprising has so far resulted in the martyrdom of tens of our people, the wounding of hundreds more and the imprisonment of thousands of unarmed civilians.

This uprising has come to further affirm our people's unbreakable commitment to its national aspirations. These aspirations include our people's firm national rights of self-determination and of the establishment of an independent state on our national soil under the leadership of the PLO, as our sole legitimate representative. The uprising also comes as further proof of our indefatigable spirit and our rejection of the sense of despair which has begun to creep to the minds of some who claim that the uprising is the result of despair.

The conclusion to be drawn from this uprising is that the present state of affairs in the Palestinian occupied territories is unnatural and that Israeli occupation cannot continue forever. Real peace cannot be achieved except through the recognition of the Palestinian national rights, including the right of self-determination and the establishment of an independent Palestinian state on Palestinian national soil. Should these rights not be recognized, then the continuation of Israeli occupation will lead to further violence and bloodshed and the further deepening of hatred. The opportunity for achieving peace will also move further away.

The only way to extricate ourselves from this scenario is through the convening of an international conference with the participation of all concerned parties including the PLO, the sole legitimate representative of the Palestinian people, as an equal partner, as well as the five permanent members of the Security Council, under the supervision of the two Superpowers.

On this basis we call upon the Israeli authorities to comply with the following list of demands as a means to prepare the atmosphere for the convening of the suggested international peace conference which will achieve a just and lasting settlement of the Palestinian problem in all its aspects, bringing about the realization of the inalienable national rights of the Palestinian people, peace, and stability for the peoples of the region and an end to violence and bloodshed:

1. To abide by the 4th Geneva Convention and all other international agreements pertaining to the protection of civilians, their properties and rights under a state of military occupation; to declare the Emergency Regulations of the British Mandate null and void, and to stop applying the iron fist policy.

2. The immediate compliance with Security Council Resolutions 605 and 607, which call upon Israel to abide by the Geneva Convention of 1949 and the Declaration of Human Rights; and which further call for the achievement of a just and lasting settlement of the Arab-Israeli conflict.

3. The release of all prisoners who were arrested during the recent uprising, and foremost among them our children. Also the rescinding of all proceedings and indictments against them.

4. The cancellation of the policy of expulsion and allowing all exiled Palestinians, including the four expelled to Lebanon on 13 January, 1988, to return to their homes and families. Also the release of all administrative detainees and the cancellation of the hundreds of house arrest orders. In this connection, special mention must be made of the hundreds of applications for family reunions which we call upon the authorities to accept forthwith.

5. The immediate lifting of the siege of all Palestinian refugee camps in the West Bank and Gaza, and the withdrawal of the Israeli army from all population centers.

6. Carrying out a formal inquiry into the behavior of soldiers and settlers in the West Bank and Gaza, as well as inside jails and detention camps, and taking due punitive measures against all those convicted of having unduly caused death or bodily harm to unarmed civilians.

7. A cessation of all settlement activity and land confiscation and the release of lands already confiscated especially in the Gaza strip. Also putting an end to the harassments and provocations of the Arab population by settlers in the West Bank and Gaza as well as in the Old City of Jerusalem. In particular, the curtailment of the provocative activities in the Old City of Jerusalem by Ariel Sharon and the ultra-religious settlers of Shuvu Banim and Ateret Kohanim.

8. Refraining from any act which might impinge on the Moslem and Christian holy sites or which might introduce changes to the status quo in the City of Jerusalem.

9. The cancellation of the Value Added Tax (V.A.T.) and all other direct Israeli taxes which are imposed on Palestinian residents in Jerusalem, the rest of the West Bank, and in Gaza; and putting an end to the harassment caused to Palestinian business and tradesmen.

10. The cancellation of all restrictions on political freedoms including restrictions on freedom of assembly and association; also making provisions for free municipal elections under the supervision of a neutral authority.

11. The immediate release of all funds deducted from the wages of laborers from the territories who worked and still work inside the Green Line, which amount to several hundreds of millions of dollars. These accumulated deductions, with interest, must be returned to their rightful owners through the agency of the nationalist institutions headed by the Workers' Unions.

12. The removal of all restrictions on building permits and licenses for industrial projects and artesian water wells as well as agricultural development programs in the occupied territories of their water resources.

13. Terminating the policy of discrimination being practiced against industrial and agricultural produce from the occupied territories either by removing the restrictions on the transfer of goods to within the Green Line, or by placing comparable trade restrictions on the transfer of Israeli goods into the territories.

14. Removing the restrictions on political contacts between inhabitants of the occupied territories and the PLO, in such a way as to allow for the participation of Palestinians from the territories in the proceedings of the Palestine National Council, in order to ensure a direct input into the decision-making processes of the Palestinian nation by the Palestinians under occupation.

*Palestinian nationalist institutions and personalities from the West Bank and Gaza, Jerusalem, January 14, 1988.*

## 38.   Address by Salah Khalaf to the International Center for Peace in the Middle East, 22 February 1989 (via videotape).

I look forward to a future in which our meetings will be face-to-face, and we can discuss the future of the lives of our two peoples as well as the future of real peace in direct meetings.

Although circumstances have prevented this on this occasion, I hope that in the near future we will address each other neither via the newspapers nor through video but through such personal contacts.

When I say these words, I say them on the basis of a fixed strategy which we now, and after a painful experience, work according to—and so that we may not deceive you. In the past we believed that this land is ours alone, and we did not believe in the idea of co-existence between two states, although we used to believe in the idea of co-existence as religious, or rather as people belonging to different religions. This kind of co-existence, that is, the co-existence between Muslims, Christians, and Jews, has been practiced by our people in this land. However, the idea of co-existence between two states was one that in the past was remote.

Everything that has happened to the Palestinian people and to the Israeli people—the blood which has been spilled, the victims, the maimed—all this has moved us to react naturally to the call of every Palestinian and Israeli child, so that we can take a serious step towards peace. Thus came the resolutions adopted in Algiers. These resolutions were not passed just by a leadership: they proceeded from a legislative council which represents the Palestinian people in its entirety. The council passed these resolutions after an arduous process of dialogue and discussion, and everybody was convinced that there is no path but the path of peace.

Some people asked us whether the Israeli leadership would respond to our call for peace and to our resolutions. We replied that this is not what is most important. What is important is that our Palestinian people and the Israeli people feel that the Palestinian leadership has responded to the most widely-supported call by our people for peace. What is important is that this call touch the heart and mind of every Israeli, whether child, woman, or man, because it is inevitable that peace will prevail, and that the two-state solution will be achieved.

So why the agony and the procrastination? The disagreement really is over the price. Are we prepared to pay the price of proceeding with courage and strength, inspired by the agony and suffering of our people? Or, would we rather drag our feet until there are more killed, more children who are subjected to terror, and until there are more disfigured and crippled victims, in this useless war?

It is on this basis that I address you, and say to you that the Algiers resolutions, and Arafat's statements at the press conference in Geneva, reflect the heart-felt convictions of every Palestinian. But we would remind you that just as you have some extremists, we also have many such people. However, the test of courage is when such extremism is countered head on, rather than surrendered to.

Does any Israeli really believe in his heart that it is possible to destroy five million Palestinians? We have asked a similar question of ourselves and have concluded that we cannot destroy the Israeli people. The realistic solution, therefore, is that we live side by side, and that we walk the path of peace.

Some people wonder whether this co-existence is only a first stage. We answer, no. We want a definitive settlement. But a definitive settlement will only come if its peace is just. Peace is not a piece of paper. All questions connected with peace and security have to be discussed in negotiations. The important thing is that the two peoples, the Palestinian and the Israeli, come to believe in the necessity of co-existence between two states. We are ready to reach any security arrangements through meetings: but believe me that real security lies only in the real belief in peace.

The real issue is not negotiations in which Israel seeks this piece of land or in which we seek that piece of land. This is a small geographic area, without much elbow room. We do not seek to have a Berlin Wall or any other wall separating us; we want there to be openness. The only thing we seek is that there be real—as opposed to verbal—normalization. I am confident that peace has now come to settle in the heart and conscience of every Palestinian. I am confident that if we search deeply in the hearts and minds of Israelis, we shall find peace there, too.

However it is important to take stock at some point and to admit that the ill-feelings that have accumulated in the past cannot be destroyed overnight. We must live with the idea of peace ourselves first if we are to transmit it to others. Without accepting it oneself, and living with it, we cannot transmit these ideas and beliefs to others.

I say truly that the Palestinian leadership and the Palestinian people want peace. The steps taken in Algiers and in Geneva reflect this conviction of the need for peace. But so that peace may be achieved, it is necessary that the Israeli leadership change its mentality of rejectionism, obduracy, the constant addition of further conditions, and seeking to win time.

I do not know why time should be won. Is it so that yet more conditions may be imposed on the Palestinians? This is absurd and will lead to nothing.

It is important that we capitalize on this historic opportunity. Each time our people hear of martyrs and of more wounded, the chances for peace will inevitably be pushed further away. This now is the opportunity that we must take. Let us be courageous and grasp it firmly. Let us put all the issues on the table. We believe in direct meetings; we are ready for such meetings, and we say it publicly, on any level. Let the Israelis come and meet us secretly, openly, or any other way. We are anxious for such meetings, not because we are in despair. Quite the contrary, it is because we are strong, because we have confidence in ourselves and in the need for peace, because we seek this peace with every faith in it, that we have arrived at a truth that we hope the Israeli leaders will also arrive at before it is too late. This is the truth which says that two peoples and two states must co-exist on this land.

All other matters are open to discussion. Our covenant and yours can be discussed. All security arrangements and guarantees can be discussed in direct meetings. Then, if we reach an agreement, as I am sure we shall, we can take this agreement to an international conference where the entire world can be a witness to these security arrangements, and so that not a single loophole will be left to spoil it.

Thus we do not see the international conference as an end in itself, but as a means to guarantee the safety of the two states in the context of an international agreement. And what is important for us is that these meetings and contacts and dialogues take place in advance of the conference, so that the conference itself becomes the forum in which to bring our agreement to fruition. Those who stand in the way of peace want the river of blood to continue to flow. Instead of seeking to achieve peace in order to avoid more victims, they seek more victims in order to achieve peace. I don't know what kind of peace it would be which is built on the mountain of corpses and skulls, and crippled, wounded, and killed. It would be a peace that is useless.

There are many peace movements, small and large, in Israel. To those I say, in the name of the Palestinian people, the PLO, and the Palestinian leadership: to every child in Israel, to every woman and every man, through you, that we are genuine in our desire for a strategic peace. A peace through which we shall bring security and stability to this region. A peace in which people can begin to devote their time and energy to making their lives prosperous and genuinely peaceful.

Why do the Palestinians and Israelis have to live in fear? How can we put an end to this fear, this state of mutual terror in which both Israelis and Palestinians live? There is no way out except through peace with the Palestinian people, whose suffering is the root of the problem.

Perhaps I need not mention the peace agreement with Egypt, or any other attempts at agreements with others. Perhaps all these agreements were good from the Israeli leadership point of view. But you should ask yourselves, why do these agreements not produce real peace? The answer is that the basic element required for such a peace was missing, namely, the Palestinian people.

As I said earlier, everything can be discussed with complete reassurance. We say this because, as I also said earlier, we are confident that our call for peace is a strategic call, and not just a call for useless talks. But we must note that real peace is just peace. When peace is just, it can be lasting. And just peace, now that we live in an age of rockets and long-distance artillery, cannot be linked with matters of technicalities and armaments. Rather, the condition for real peace is that there be a genuine desire to co-exist. We must work on our people to develop this desire, and you must equally work on yours. This is the road to real security and real peace.

The final question I wish to raise at this symposium in this context is, if this historic opportunity following the Algiers resolutions is missed, then what will the alternative be? Israel may be able to survive this situation for one more year, or two or even ten. But believe me, after these ten years, and after hundreds and maybe thousands more victims, we shall find ourselves back at this point: there can be no peace without the Palestinians. There can be no peace without co-existence with the Palestinians. There can be no peace without two states which will co-exist side by side, and which will be able to say to the entire world: the war in the Middle East has ended, and the tragedy is over.

Thank you.

## 39. Fateh Fifth General Congress, Political Program, Tunis, 8 August, 1989 [Excerpts]

*First: On the Palestinian level:*

1. The Palestine question is the core of the Arab-Zionist conflict.

2. Firm adherence to Palestinian Arab national inalienable rights in their homeland Palestine, including their right to repatriation, self-determination without foreign interference, and the establishment of their independent state with holy Jerusalem as its capital.

3. Asserting the unity of our Palestinian Arab people inside and outside Palestine and rallying around the PLO, the leader of their struggle and their sole, legitimate representative.

4. The fifth Fateh general congress affirms the historic importance of the resolutions of the 19th PNC session, particularly the document of independence. The congress supports the establishment of the independent state of Palestine and extends thanks to the Arab and friendly states that have recognized it. The congress authorizes the movement's Central Committee to work on all levels to implement the resolutions of establishing the Palestinian people's national inalienable rights, headed by the right to repatriation, self-determination, and the establishment of the state of Palestine on Palestinian soil with holy Jerusalem as its capital.

5. Continuing to intensify and escalate armed action and all forms of struggle to liquidate the Israeli-Zionist occupation of our occupied Palestinian land and guaranteeing our people's right to freedom and independence.

6. Bolstering national Palestinian unity on the various political and military levels, reiterating the PLO's leading role, and escalating the popular intifadah aimed at ending the Zionist Israeli occupation.

7. Reiterating that the PLO is the sole legitimate representative of our Arab Palestinian people wherever they are; the leader of their national resistance; their spokesman in Arab and international forums; and that it will resist all attempts to encroach on it, bypass it, surround it, or create alternatives or partners in representing the Palestinian people.

8. Rejecting and resisting the autonomy plan and the other liquidation plans aimed at entrenching the colonialist Zionist occupation.

9. The Fateh fifth congress rejects the Shamir plan on elections and affirms that any election in our occupied territory must take place in a free and democratic atmosphere under international supervision after the withdrawal of the Israeli forces, and that elections must be a link in an integrated plan for the final solution.

10. Taking into consideration the important achievements in the Palestinian arena as a result of our people's continuous struggle and their blessed intifadah as well as the new situations and facts created by the intifadah in the Arab and international arenas, the Fateh general congress stresses the PLO's right to participate—independently and on an equal footing with the other parties—in all the international conferences and efforts on the Palestine question and the Arab-Zionist conflict.

11. Providing all forms of support to reinforce the steadfastness of our masses in Lebanon's camps to stand in the face of the Israeli aggression and all its schemes aimed at scattering and displacing them and to consolidate the right of the sons of these camps to defend their presence, security, and natural right to join the people's militant march under the PLO.

12. Continuing the dialogue with the Israeli democratic forces that reject occupation; understand our people's inalienable rights, including their right to repatriation, self-determination, and establishment of the independent state of Palestine; and recognize the PLO as the sole, legitimate representative of the Palestinian people.

13. In light of the significant effect of the demographic factor on our conflict with the Zionist enemy, and in light of the huge efforts exerted by the Zionist movement to encourage Zionist immigration to Palestinian territory, the congress has decided to set up an ad hoc committee within the Revolutionary Council to oppose the Zionist immigration to our homeland and to assume all cultural, information, and political tasks to prevent the arrival of Jewish immigrants in our occupied homeland.

*Second: On the Arab level:*

1. The fifth general congress of the Fateh Movement salutes the solidarity of the Arab masses with our Palestinian revolution and the blessed intifadah of our people and calls on them to embody this solidarity within in practical ways on the pan-Arab level.

2. The congress appreciates the resolutions of the Arab summits on the issue of the intifadah and those that support it, particularly the Algiers and Casablanca summits. The Fateh congress calls on the Arab countries to abide by and implement all the resolutions and honor their financial commitments.

3. Promoting relations with all national and democratic parties, movements, and forces in the Arab homeland and working toward providing popular backing and support for the intifadah and the PLO. The congress also recommends the formation of support committees for the intifadah on the pan-Arab level.

4. Respecting the right of the Palestinian revolution to perform its militant tasks through any Arab land and mobilizing the Palestinian masses in a manner that serves our people's struggle for freedom, independence, and repatriation.

5. Our relationship with any Arab regime will be defined in light of its stand toward the Palestinian people's struggle, its noninterference in the internal affairs of the revolution, its respect of our national independent Palestinian decisionmaking, and its adherence to the resolutions of the Arab summits on the Palestine question.

6. Calling on the Arab countries, especially those on the confrontation lines, to unify their forces and mobilize their masses in order to confront the Israeli aggression.

7. Working toward protecting and looking after our people and their affairs wherever they live; adhering to their rights of residence, travel, work, education, good health, and security in accordance with the Arab League resolutions and world declaration on human rights; and guaranteeing the freedom of political activity as an embodiment of the fraternal Arab bonds and pan-Arab affiliation.

8. The fifth general congress of the Fateh Movement expresses its pride in, and appreciation of, the fraternal Lebanese people and affirms the importance of the militant and brotherly relations between the Lebanese and Palestinian peoples in order to continue the confrontation of the Zionist invasion for the sake of liberating the Lebanese and Palestinian territory from the Zionist Israeli occupation. The congress affirms that the Palestinian revolution shall remain a support for the Lebanese people in their struggle to achieve their national unity, preserve their independence and territorial sovereignty, and remove the Israeli occupation from their territory.

9. Stressing the special and distinguished relations linking the fraternal Palestinian and Jordanian peoples, and working toward developing them in harmony with the national interests of the two fraternal peoples. Any future relationship with Jordan must be based on a confederation between the States of Jordan and Palestine.

*Third: On the international level:*

1.  Adhering to an effective international conference with full powers for peace in the Middle East, which must be convened on the basis of international legitimacy under UN supervision and patronage, and with the participation of five permanent members of the Security Council and the concerned parties, including the PLO, on an equal footing and with equal rights as the other sides.

2.  The fifth general congress of the Fateh Movement stresses its adherence to the UN principles, charter, and resolutions which emphasized the Palestinian people's national inalienable rights and the right of all oppressed peoples under occupation to use all forms of struggle for their liberation and national independence. The congress also emphasizes its strong condemnation of all terrorist Israeli practices, which violate the principles of international law, the Geneva conventions and their appendices of 1949, the world declaration on human rights, and the UN Charter and resolutions.

3.  The congress calls on the United States to recognize the Palestinian people's right to self-determination and the establishment of their independent state; to abandon the policy of bias in favor of Israel; and to end its unlimited assistance of it as this would consecrate the Zionist Israeli occupation of our Palestinian territory and increase its violation of our Palestinian people's rights.

The congress calls on the United States to agree to holding an international conference for peace in the Middle East as soon as possible in accordance with the resolutions approved at the United Nations. The congress also calls on the United States to cancel all laws and legislation passed by the US Congress against the PLO so that its dialogue with us will lead to positive results.

## 40.  Statement by the PLO's Central Council, Baghdad, 16 October, 1989 [Excerpts]

The PLO Central Council held a session of meetings in Baghdad 15 to 17 October 1989. During this session, the Council discussed several political and organizational issues as well as developments in the Palestinian cause at this stage. The great intifadah of our people in their occupied homeland, and the requirements of their steadfastness and development were at the top of the Council's agenda. The Council noted a series of important developments that had taken place in the intifadah's march and in the march of the Palestinian national struggle in general since its previous session on 31 March 1989. Foremost among the developments witnessed over the past months are the following:

1.  The continued popular resurgence and its growth in confronting the Zionist occupation, and the enhancement of the militancy and popular nature of the intifadah.

2. The intensification of Israeli repression and its recourse to new methods, including the war of starvation and siege, comprehensive confiscations, orders to kill the sons of our people, the increase in arrests and deportations out of the homeland, and the destruction of houses—not to mention all the other forms of collective punishment.

3. The escalation and the spreading of popular defiance of the occupation's plans; and the enhancement of popular cohesion in major battles, such as the battle of the magnetic cards fought by the workers of the heroic Gaza Strip, the battle of Bayt Sahur's steadfastness, the courageous popular confrontation of Nablus, and the other battles of heroic defiance waged by our masses throughout our entire occupied land.

4. The enhancement of the unity of national ranks; the failure of the attempts by the enemy to damage national unity, particularly, following its announcement of what was called the Israeli government's election plan; the national consensus on rejecting this liquidatory plan; and the continued rallying around the PLO.

5. The growth of the intifadah has deepened its impact on Israeli society; inflicted tangible losses on the economy; increased the voices calling for a dialogue with the PLO; brought about disarray and division within the ruling institution and parties; and, in general, has increased the isolation of Israel and its rulers' policies inside and outside Israel.

6. In spite of the many forms of imperialist and Zionist conspiracy, and the media siege against the intifadah, the sympathy and support of international public opinion have increased. The most recent proof of this is UN General Assembly Resolution 140 supporting, against two opposing voices—those of the United States and Israel—and the abstention of six; as well as the EEC Madrid summit resolutions, the summit of the socialist countries in Bucharest, the positions taken by the PRC, Japan, the non-aligned summit, the Islamic summit, the African summit, the statement by the Scandinavian countries' foreign ministers, and other international positions.

World recognition of the State of Palestine has also increased. The US administration, in spite of its continued disavowal of our people's right to self-determination, and its support for Israel, its policies, and its crimes has, as a result of the intifadah and the Palestinian peace initiative, made statements calling for the termination of the Israeli occupation, the exchange of land for peace, and the abandonment of the idea of Greater Israel.

7. The Casablanca resolutions reflected Arab support for the Palestinian cause and for the PLO and its policy. The Arab summit's adoption of the Palestinian peace plan—which is based on the resolutions of the Palestine National Council—gave an important Arab dimension to these resolutions on the international scene.

8. Over the past few months, the PLO has conducted a tough dialogue with the US administration. Although this dialogue has failed to reach tangible political

results, it has helped to explain the aims of the PLO and its policy to large sectors of world public opinion, including US public opinion. It has emphasized that the US administration has actually and practically begun to deal with the PLO as a sole legitimate representative of the Palestinian people. The dialogue has also disclosed the US stances, which support the policy of Israel's rulers, and has further embarrassed Washington and tightened the noose around it. During this dialogue, the PLO adhered to its principled national line, and rejected the ideas and proposals that encroach upon the soleness of Palestinian representation and upon our sacred rights to repatriation, self-determination, and national independence. It exposed the premeditated intentions to pass liquidatory plans, such as Shamir's plan and any other proposals that harm our peoples' representation and their inalienable rights. For its part, the PLO presented a number of tangible proposals aimed at advancing the peace process and the movement toward the international conference.

O masses of our great people, masses of our heroic Arab nation: The continuation of the blessed intifadah and its firmness on the soil of the homeland; the management of the political battle in accordance with the right policy adopted by the PLO leadership on the basis of the PNC resolutions in Algiers; and the Palestinian peace initiative produced by this policy and unleashed by brother President Yasser Arafat in his speech before the United Nations in Geneva opened the way for the group of achievements that were scored. They also led to the growth of national victories toward realizing our peoples' aims of return, self-determination and the establishment of our independent state, with holy Jerusalem as its capital, on our sacred soil.

The current developments place before us a number of situations and basic tasks, foremost of which are:

— To adhere to the resolutions of the PNC and the Palestinian peace initiative and reject all alternative plans, projects, or proposals, because the Palestinian peace initiative includes the necessary elements for a just and comprehensive peace and is based on the resolutions of international legitimacy;

— To adhere to the resolutions of the Casablanca summit resolutions and endeavor to activate the Arab role to implement these resolutions and to highlight their contents, especially concerning the idea of elections, which must be conducted under international supervision, after the Israeli withdrawal from the occupied Palestinian territories, and as part of the comprehensive peace process, and the need for all Arab countries without exception to abide by these resolutions;

— To confront firmly the US policy, which continues to be based on rejecting our people's right to self-determination and on supporting and shielding the Israeli policy. This policy has recently been showcased by the US proposals, which aim to impose trusteeship on Palestinian representation, deny our people's rights and the PLO's role, and adopt the Shamir plan as a basis for a solution;

— To consolidate joint coordination and action in order to add further support to the Palestinian peace initiative and to prepare for an international conference with the Soviet Union, the socialist bloc, the European states and Japan, the non-aligned states, the Islamic group, the African states, the northern European states, and all the states that have recognized the State of Palestine and displayed solidarity with the Palestinian peace initiative. Regarding the proposal calling for Palestinian-Israeli talks, the required conditions to make these talks a step toward achieving a just solution are as follows:

1. Only the PLO has the right to select and declare a Palestinian delegation from inside and outside [the occupied territories] for talks with Israel.

2. The Palestinian stand during these talks will be based on the Palestinian peace initiative, which relies on and adheres to international legitimacy.

3. The agenda of the meeting must be open and without preconditions.

4. This meeting should be considered as preparatory talks between the Palestinian and Israeli sides and a step toward convening an effective international conference, which constitutes the only appropriate framework for negotiations that can lead to a comprehensive and just settlement of the conflict in accordance with the resolutions of the United Nations and international legitimacy.

5. This preparatory meeting should be attended by delegations from the UN Security Council permanent member states, the UN Secretary-General, and representatives for the other concerned parties, including Egypt and Sweden.

In its capacity as the sole, legitimate representative of the Palestinian people, the PLO affirms that it is the only authorized party to choose Palestinian representatives. It affirms that any matters related to the Palestinian cause and rights and the peace process and its steps cannot take place without the PLO's full and effective participation.

## 41. Reply by the PLO to Secretary of State James Baker's Five Point Plan, 1 December, 1989

The Palestine Liberation Organization (PLO) leadership studied the replies it received on November 16 and November 27, 1989 via the Egyptian Foreign Ministry from Mr. James Baker, the US Secretary of State, in response to Palestinian queries about his plan which he put forward November 6, 1989.

1. It is unfortunate that the (American) response ignores, right from the very beginning, the role of the PLO in forming the Palestinian delegation to the dialogue. (It) even completely denies the existence of the PLO by referring to "major and influential" Palestinian forces which would name the delegation. Where are these forces? On what basis has the American administration been holding a dialogue with the PLO since December 1988?

2. The American administration denies that Israel will have a veto power on names of the Palestinian delegation, but stresses that it will not pressure Israel to accept to talk with those it does not want to.

Stemming from the principle of equality, the PLO reiterates that it is not the right of any party to intervene, directly or indirectly, in the process of the formation of the (the PLO) delegation.

3. The American response concerning the dialogue's agenda contravenes what has been agreed upon between Egypt, Sweden, and the US. This (reply) constitutes an American concession to Israeli conditions to confine the agenda to elections and negotiate its procedures. We would like to refer here to the declaration made by US President George Bush stressing the need to end the Israeli occupation, and to the statement issued by Baker calling on Israel to drop its great dream of expansion and annexation.

4. The PLO was notified by the US administration's commitment to the statement made by former Secretary of State George Shultz on September 16, 1988.

5. The American response referred to an international peace conference on the basis of United Nations Security Council Resolutions 242 and 338. Taking into consideration that the Palestinian-Israeli dialogue is part of the preparatory process for the international peace conference, the PLO assumes that international sponsorship should include this dialogue.

6. The second American response, dated November 27, completely ignored the minutes of the Egyptian-Swedish, American meeting which took place at the Egyptian Foreign Ministry on September 16, 1989, and what we were officially notified at that meeting, of concerning [sic] international sponsorship and the PLO's right to name the Palestinian delegation and the open agenda.

7. The US administration's insistence that the dialogue be confined to the agenda to elections and to negotiations over its procedures—in response to the Israeli government's plan—contravenes what we were notified (by the American administration) regarding its commitment to the statement made by Shultz which contained a reference to open agenda for the dialogue and the right of the Palestinians and any other party to raise any issue, including the Palestinian demand for an independent Palestinian state.

8. We wonder: Does the US administration realize that no Palestinian delegation would be able to come to the negotiating table without being named and declared by the PLO? What would be the compulsory means deployed to bring any Palestinian outside this framework?

The PLO, referring to the Palestinian peace strategy and the Arab Casablanca summit resolutions, would like to reiterate willingness to seriously contribute to the international efforts exerted to push the peace process forward.

Stemming from this the PLO can accept to deal with Baker's plan, put forward on November 6, only according to resolutions endorsed by the PLO Central Council (held last October) as following:

a. Its readiness to conduct a dialogue between a delegation from the PLO, representing the Palestinian people inside and outside the occupied Palestinian land, and an Israeli delegation.

b. The dialogue's agenda should be open and without prior preconditions and each delegation should be able to raise any issues, including elections in the occupied territories and the Egyptian-proposed 10 points, in accordance to Shultz' statement issued September 16, 1988.

c. The dialogue would be conducted under the auspices of the United Nations and the five permanent members of the Security Council, Egypt and Sweden.

d. The dialogue should be a preliminary step towards the convening of an international peace conference on the Middle East which should convene under the auspices of the United Nations and on the basis of international legitimacy and (UN) resolutions, and will be attended by the five permanent members of the United Nations Security Council and all the parties concerned, including the PLO, the sole legitimate representative of the Palestinian people.

## 42. Letter Sent by Yasser Arafat to the Emergency World Jewish Leadership Peace Conference Organized by the International Center for Peace in the Middle East, Jerusalem, 17 February, 1990

Ladies and gentlemen,
Leaders of the Jewish communities around the world meeting in Jerusalem

Freedom, democracy and human rights. Those are the concepts that are bringing about the historic changes in the world around us at this turn of the century. Those are also the concepts that have fueled the struggle of the Palestinian people.

That there is a connection between my people's decades old struggle for its rights to existence, security and freedom like the rest of the peoples on this planet, and the political quakes that are rumbling through other parts of the world, I have no doubt.

While the Palestinian intifadan's quest for freedom played a role in inspiring today's global freedom fest, the brave new world of liberty that is dawning around us will in turn stiffen my people's determination to achieve the freedom that has now become the universal goal of humanity; the self-determination and democracy to which every nation, including the Palestinian nation, is entitled; the human rights that, by definition, no human being should be denied. The Palestinian popular uprising marks the ultimate steps of the march of our people in the diaspora to their land, to reaffirm their national identity and exercise their right to self-determination, freedom and national independence.

The objective of the Palestinian intifadah is peace, and the means we have so far assigned to the intifadah to attain that objective are peaceful. By resisting the occupation, the intifadah aspires to freedom, peace and coexistence on the basis of respect for the rights of all peoples in the region. Its sole creed is the Palestinian people's right, like all other peoples, to self-determination and independence. The ultimate authority it looks up to is international legitimacy.

Just over a year ago, the Palestine National Council, strengthened by the moral and political clout of the intifadah, met in Algiers and adopted a peace proposal. I assume that the thrust of this proposal is known to you, but I will reiterate that it embodies a strategic decision. It is not a tactical maneuver, as the opponents of peace claim. As a strategic decision, it has the full support of the Palestinian, Arab and international legal authorities.

It is truly regrettable that this proposal, which [can be translated into] peace and security for all the peoples of the region and end the occupation of Palestinian and Arab territories, has been subjected to so many campaigns of doubts and fears.

The apprehensions expressed by the Israelis, be they genuine or counterfeit, trouble us deeply, because they delay the historic settlement that awaits our two peoples.

But troubled as we are, we remain deeply convinced that the only real security guarantee for Israel lies in a peaceful settlement based on the termination of the Israeli occupation of the Palestinian and Arab territories and the acceptance of the two-state principle that the Palestinian people have already accepted in their peace proposal—a principle rooted in international law and supported by the Arab and international communities, including Arab summit conferences, the United Nations, the European Community, Japan, and the Socialist, Scandinavian, Non-Aligned, Moslem and African nations.

Let me add here that Israel's fears, whether they are real or fictitious, have an echo on the Palestinian side. Watching the convoluted maneuvers the Israeli government has engaged in and the massive obstacles with which it has littered the path to peace, the Palestinian people are not filled with confidence in the good intentions of the Israeli leaders. To them, the only guarantee of their own security and their political future lies in the full participation of the PLO in all stages of the peace process as the sole legitimate representative of the Palestinian people in the occupied territories and in exile.

In the final analysis, however, the fears of the Israelis and the Palestinians can only be quelled by international guarantees, which are attainable only in the context of an international peace conference on the Middle East.

Among the fears that the Israeli government says it has is fear of the Palestinian right of return.

Let me say at once that settlement of this issue lies in mutual recognition and the start of negotiations.

Having said that, I will tell you how we view the question of the Palestinian right of return.

It is a right enshrined in international law and reaffirmed by the United Nations in its Resolution 194 of December 11, 1948.

Let me draw your attention to the fact that UN Resolution 273 of May 11, 1949, which admitted Israel to the community of nations, includes an article that commits Israel to honor the United Nations Charter and accept all previous UN resolutions on the Palestine Question, including Resolution 194.

The right of return is sacred. However, we are ready to discuss the conditions of its application on the basis of Resolution 194.

Also among the fears that have been expressed by Israel is one that relates to the context of the peace process.

I have touched on this before, but I will repeat:

The Palestinian people need guarantees more than any other party to this conflict. Our people have been victims for decades. We have gone from crisis to catastrophe, from repression to dispossession, from siege to massacre. We need guarantees that can only be provided by the great powers and the United Nations, with the participation of the regional parties concerned. Hence our insistence on an international context for the peace settlement—a context that should not conflict with Israel's own requirement for guarantees.

However, because Israel, with American backing, has so far opposed the idea of an international peace conference, and because the Palestinians want to do everything in their power to create a climate of trust that will hopefully lead to an international peace conference, the PLO once more leaned over backward and approved the idea of dialogue between representatives of the Israeli government and representatives of the Palestinian people in the Occupied Territories and the diaspora, on the understanding that this dialogue would be part of a peace process aimed at a comprehensive and final settlement, and that its agenda would cover all the conceptual ingredients of that process, including the elections and the ten Egyptian points.

The Israeli government, by rejecting the idea of negotiating with the PLO and the principle of territory-for-peace, by blocking the implementation of UN Security Council Resolution 242 and by insisting on fragmenting the Palestinian people, is not only obstructing a peaceful settlement but is also confirming the propagandist nature of its election proposal, suggesting that the proposal was merely a maneuver to neutralize the Palestinian peace plan, mislead international and Israeli public opinion and gain time in order to perpetuate the suffering of the Palestinian people, stifle the intifadah and create new demographic and political facts in the occupied Palestinian land that would prevent a peaceful settlement.

In our view, these maneuvers will lead, whether we like it or not, to a new explosion in a region packed with nuclear, chemical and conventional weapons. Is this what the Israeli leadership wants?

The option we have chosen is peace. What we offer is the hand of a proud nation, not the surrender of a vanquished people.

The Palestinian Liberation Organization has made all the commitments it can make in favor of a settlement. It has laid the foundations of a comprehensive peace based on international legitimacy and a balance of the interests of all the parties to the conflict. In return, we have received from the Israeli government no positive response and no commitment to the peace process.

The Israeli government has been straining in the opposite direction, ignoring all international peace initiatives and the appeals of Jewish groups; trying to crush the promise of the future with the myths of the past; and insisting on swimming against the currents of change that have already swept away other ossified mentalities.

Still, we refuse to drop the olive branch we have raised for our sake and that of others, for the sake of our children and yours. We shall not be deterred by the arrogance of Israeli officialdom. We look forward to the outcome of your deliberations, hoping that it will mobilize the Israeli advocates of peace and world Jewry for a just and comprehensive settlement. We hope they will act as a pressure group to safeguard the Israeli people from the destructive obduracy of their leadership and uphold their spiritual and human values.

Your influence in Israel and elsewhere is great. That's why we pin great hopes on your meeting, confident that it will entice the Israeli government to press ahead with the peace process.

Throughout the history of mankind, Jews have played a pioneering role in the defense of freedom and human rights, and their great leaders have consistently taken noble stands.

I urge you to consider the Israeli Government's attempt to use Soviet Jews' newly acquired rights as a club with which to destroy the rights of the Palestinians.

Let me state unequivocally: we support the right of individuals to free movement and travel. We respect their freedom to choose the country in which they wish to reside. However, this right, like all others, has its limitations. It ends where other people's rights begin. The other people in this case are the Palestinians. They too have a right to live in their homeland and resist all attempts to uproot them.

Jewish emigrants have the right to choose their destinations, without being forcibly directed to any other place. Any attempt to deny them that right could provoke dangerous explosions and deal a fatal blow to peace efforts.

Ladies and gentlemen,

We have an opportunity to establish peace in our region. If we let it slip through our fingers, we will have many more years of death and destruction before another opportunity comes by.

There is no escape from peace. The only question is whether we accept it now or after thousands more of our children have been sacrificed at the altar of unrealistic ambitions.

The Palestinians have opted for peace now—peace for us and our children, peace for you and yours, peace in the land of the prophets and their message of peace.

Signed,
Yasser Arafat
Tunis, 17 February, 1990

# Arab Documents

## 1. The Arab League Summit Conference Resolutions, Khartoum, Sudan, 1 September, 1967

**Public Resolutions.** On 1 Sept, Sudanese PM Mahjub read out the following resolutions adopted by the Conference:

1) The Conference has affirmed the unity of Arab ranks, the unity of joint action and the need for co-ordination and for the elimination of all differences. The Conference affirmed the Arab Solidarity Charter which was signed at the Third Arab Summit Conference held in Casablanca, and undertook to implement it.

2) The Conference has agreed on the need to consolidate all efforts to eliminate the effects of the aggression on the basis that the occupied lands are Arab lands and that the burden of regaining these lands falls on all the Arab States.

3) The Arab heads of state have agreed to unite their political efforts at the international and diplomatic level to eliminate the effects of the aggression and to ensure the withdrawal of the aggressive Israeli forces from the Arab lands which have been occupied since the aggression of 5 June. This will be done within the framework of the main principles by which the Arab States abide, namely no peace with Israel, no recognition of Israel, no negotiations with it, and insistence on the rights of the Palestinian people in their own country.

4) The Conference of the Arab Ministers of Finance, Economy and Oil recommended that suspension of oil pumping be used as a weapon in the battle. However, after thoroughly studying the matter, the Summit Conference has come to the conclusion that the pumping of oil can itself be used as a positive weapon, since oil is an Arab resource which can be used to strengthen the economy of the Arab States directly affected by the aggression, so that these states will be able to stand firm in the battle. The Conference has,

therefore, decided to resume the pumping of oil, since oil is a positive Arab resource that can be used in the service of Arab goals. It can contribute to the efforts to enable those Arab States which were exposed to the aggression and thereby lost economic resources to stand firm and eliminate the effects of the aggression.

The oil-producing states have, in fact, participated in the efforts to enable the states affected by the aggression to stand firm in the face of any economic pressure.

5) The participants in the Conference have approved the plan proposed by Kuwait to set up an Arab Economic and Social development Fund on the basis of the recommendation of the Baghdad Conference . . .

6) The participants have agreed on the need to adopt the necessary measures to strengthen military preparation to face all eventualities.

7) The Conference has decided to expedite the elimination of foreign bases in the Arab States.

PM Mahjub then read the following additional resolution: "The Kingdom of Saudi Arabia, the State of Kuwait and the Kingdom of Libya have each agreed to pay the following annual amounts which are to be paid in advance every three months beginning from mid-October until the effects of the aggression are eliminated: Saudi Arabia, £ 50 m; Kuwait £ 55 m; Libya £ 30 m. In this way, the Arab nation ensures that it will be able to carry on this battle, without any weakening, till the effects of the aggression are eliminated."

## 2. Jordanian King Hussein's Peace Plan, 28 April, 1969 [Excerpts]

*Speech at the National Press Club, Washington D.C.*

1. The end of all belligerency; 2. Respect for, and acknowledgement of, the sovereignty, territorial integrity and political independence of all states in the area; 3. Recognition of the rights of all to live in peace within secure and recognized boundaries free from threats or acts of war; 4. Guarantees of freedom of navigation through the Gulf of Aqaba and the Suez Canal for all states; 5. Guaranteeing the territorial inviolability of all states in the area through whatever measures that were necessary, including the establishment of demilitarized zones; 6. Accepting a just settlement of the refugee problem.

In return for these considerations, Hussein said, the "sole demand upon Israel is the withdrawal of its armed forces from all territories occupied in June 1967 war, and the implementation of all the other provisions of Res. 242."

## 3. The Cairo and Melkart Agreements: Regulation of the P.L.O. Presence in Lebanon

### The Cairo Agreement, 3 November 1969

On Monday, 3 November 1969 the Lebanese delegation headed by Army Commander Emile Bustani and the PLO delegation headed by Yasser Arafat met in Cairo ... It was agreed to re-establish the Palestinian presence in Lebanon on the basis of:

1)   The right of Palestinians presently living in Lebanon to work, reside and move freely;

2)   The establishment of local committees from Palestinians living in the camps to look after the interests of the Palestinians there, in cooperation with the local authorities and within the context of Lebanese sovereignty;

3)   The presence of command centres for the Palestine Armed Struggle Command inside the camps to cooperate with the local authorities and guarantee good relations. These centres will handle arrangements for the carrying and regulation of arms within the camps, taking into account both Lebanese security and the interests of the Palestinian revolution;

4)   Permission for Palestinian residents in Lebanon to join the Palestinian revolution through armed struggle within the limits imposed by Lebanese security and sovereignty.

### Commando Operations

It was agreed to facilitate operations by [Palestinian] commandos through:

1)   Assisting commando access to the border and the specification of access points and observation posts in the border region;

2)   Ensuring the use of the main road to the Arqub region;

3)   Control by the Palestine Armed Struggle Command of the actions of all members of its organisations and to prevention of any interference in Lebanese affairs;

4)   The pursuit of mutual cooperation between the Palestine Armed Struggle Command and the Lebanese army;

5)   An end to media campaigns by both sides;

6)   A census of the complement of the Palestine Armed Struggle Command through its leadership;

7)   The appointment of representatives of the Palestine Armed Struggle Command to the Lebanese High Command;

8)   Study of the distribution of suitable concentration points in the border regions to be agreed upon with the Lebanese High Command;

9)   Organization of the entry, exit and movement of Palestine Armed Struggle elements;

10)   Abolition of the Jainoun base;

11)   Assistance by the Lebanese army in the work of medical centres, and evacuation and supply for commando operations;

12)   Release of all internees and confiscated arms;

13)   Acceptance that the civil and military Lebanese authorities will continue to exercise effective responsibility to the full in all regions of Lebanon and under all circumstances;

14)   Confirmation that the Palestine Armed Struggle acts for the benefit of Lebanon as well as for the Palestinian revolution and for all Arabs.

**The Melkart Agreement, 17 May 1973**

Both parties eagerly agree to serve the Palestinian cause and to continue its struggle, and to preserve the independence of Lebanon and its sovereignty and stability, and in the light of contracted agreements and Arab decisions, comprising: the Cairo agreement and all its annexes; agreements concluded between Lebanon and the leadership of the resistance forces; and decisions taken at the Joint Arab Defence Council; it was agreed on all points as follows:

*Presence in the Camps of Personnel*

1)   No commando presence;

2)   Formation of permanent Palestine Armed Struggle Command units;

3)   Confirmation of militia presence for the guarding and internal protection of the camps. By militia is understood Palestinians residing in the camps who are not members of the resistance force and who practice normal civilian duties;

4)   Establishment of a guardpost for Lebanese internal security forces at a location to be agreed upon close to each camp.

*Presence in the Camps of Arms*

1)   The militia will be permitted to carry light arms individually;

2)   No medium or heavy weapons will be permitted within the camps (e.g. mortars, rocket launchers, artillery, anti-tank weapons, etc.).

*Presence in the Border Regions*

1)   Western sector: presence and concentration outside the camps is forbidden . . .

2)   Central sector: According to agreements made at the meeting between the Lebanese High Command and the resistance forces leadership on 8 October 1972: Presence will be permitted outside Lebanese villages in certain areas by agreement with the local Lebanese sector commander. Resistance forces are not permitted east and south of the line running Al-Kusair/Al-Ghandouriya/Deir   Kifa/Al-Shihabia/Al-Salasel/Al-Saltania/Tabnin/Haris/Kafra/ Sadikin/Qana. This prohibition applies to all these points

inclusively. Concentration of resistance forces at a guardpost south of Hadatha is permitted. The number allowed is between five and ten men in civilian clothes, with all military appearance to be avoided. They will be supplied by animal transport. At all these places the total number permitted must not exceed 250.

3) Eastern sector: According to decisions taken by the Lebanese High Command and the resistance forces leadership, three bases will be permitted in the southern Arqub at Abu-Kamha Al-Kharbiya (Al-Shahid Salah base) and Rashaya al-Fakhar (Jabal al-Shahr). Each base will contain no more than 30 to 35 men each. Supply for these bases will be by motor-transport. Elements at these bases will be forbidden to proceed in the direction of Marjayoun unless they have a permit. The carrying of arms in Marjayoun is forbidden . . . In the northern Arqub and at Rashaya al-Wadi, presence is permitted at a distance from the villages, but not west of the Masnaa-Hasbaya road . . . At Baalbeck no commando presence is permitted except at the Nabi Sbat training base.

Note: Medium and light arms are permitted in these sectors; commando presence inside Lebanese villages is not allowed; all units which have been reinforced in Lebanon from abroad will be adjusted.

*Movement [in the camps]*

Movement will be allowed without arms and in civilian dress.

*Movement in the [frontier] areas*

Movement will be allowed by arrangement with local Lebanese commanders and according to agreement.

*Movement of Civilian and Military Leaders*

Military leaders will be allowed to move freely provided they are above the rank of lieutenant, carrying no more than a personnel weapon and are accompanied by a driver only. Civilian leaders will be supplied with numbered permits signed by the responsible joint liaison committee. The number of permits issued to area leaderships will be determined by the Lebanese liaison centre and supplied under the request of the Palestinian Political Committee in Lebanon.

*Military Training*

[Military] training is forbidden in the camps, but allowed at the training base at Nabi Sbat. Technical military training is permitted at points to be agreed upon by arrangement with the Lebanese High Command liaison centre. Practising with arms is forbidden outside the training base.

*Operations*

All [commando] operations from Lebanese territory are suspended according to the decisions of the Joint Arab Defence Council. Departure from Lebanon for the purpose of commando operations is forbidden.

*Command*

The Palestinian side reaffirms that the chief command base is Damascus, and that the Damascus office has representatives in other countries including Lebanon. The Palestinian side pledged to reduce the number of offices [in Lebanon].

*Information*

The Palestinian side affirmed that the resistance in Lebanon only produces:

a) *Filastin al-Thawra;* b) Wafa news agency, in addition to certain cultural and educational publications issued by Palestinian organizations publicly or for their own use; c) The Palestinian side pledged that these publications would not touch upon the interests and sovereignty of Lebanon; d) the Palestinian side adheres to the abstention from broadcasting in Lebanon; e) the Palestinian side pledges not to involve Lebanon in any of its publications or broadcast news items or announcements emanating from resistance sources in Lebanon.

*Controlling Contraventions and Offences*

Lebanese laws will be implemented on the basis of Lebanese sovereignty and offenders will be referred to the responsible courts.

1) Contraventions in military sectors will be submitted to local liaison committees. In cases where no result is achieved, they will be referred to the Higher Coordination Committee which will give an immediate decision.

2) Contraventions inside the camps will be the charge of the internal security forces in cooperation with the Palestine Armed Struggle Command, regarding the pursuit of all crimes, civil or criminal, which occur within the camps whoever the offender. They will also be responsible for delivering all legal notices and orders pronounced against persons residing in the camps. Incidents occurring in the camps between the commandos which have a bearing on the security and safety of the Palestinian revolution will be excluded from this procedure and be the responsibility of the Palestine Armed Struggle Command.

3) Contraventions outside the camps shall be subject to Lebanese law. The Palestine Armed Struggle Command will be informed of detentions and the procedures taken against offenders. In the case of commandos being apprehended in an offence and where the Lebanese authorities deem necessary the cooperation of the Palestine Armed Struggle Command, contact will be made through the liaison committee and the decision on the offender will be left to the Lebanese authority.

The Palestinian side condemned detention of any Lebanese or foreigners and the conduct of any investigation by resistance forces and pledged no repetition of such matters.

Regarding traffic offences, it has been agreed previously that a census would be taken of cars with Lebanese number plates under the auspices of the Internal Security Forces, and cars entering Lebanese territory under temporary licensing regulations of the customs authorities. Therefore any commando vehicle on Lebanese territory will be prohibited unless it carries a legal license according to Lebanese traffic regulations.

*Foreigners*

By the term foreigners it meant not Arab commandos.

The Palestinian side pledges to deport all foreigners with the exception of those engaged in non-combatant work of a civilian or humane nature (including doctors, nurses, translators and interpreters).

*Coordination*

Implementation will be supervised by the Liaison Committee and its branches in coordination with the Palestinian side.

*Highly Confidential*
*Aspirations of the Palestinian Side After the Joint Meetings*
—  Re-establishment of the atmosphere to its state before the incidents of 9 May 1973;
—  Gradual easing of armed tension;
—  Reduction of barriers of suspicion;
—  Aspirations towards the cancellation of the emergency situation;
—  Dealing with the matter of fugitives from the law, particularly those persons pursued as a result of the incidents of 23 April 1969;
—  Freeing of those persons detained as a result of the incidents of 2 April 1973;
—  Return of arms confiscated since 1970;
—  Facilitation of employment for Palestinians resident in Lebanon.

*For the Palestinian side*
Lt Col Abal Zaim
Abu Adnan
AlSayyid Salah Salah

*For the Lebanese side*
Lt Col Ahmad al-Hajj
Col Nazih Rashid (Col Salim Moghabghab)
Col Dib Kamal

# 4. Jordanian King Hussein's Federation Plan, 15 March, 1972

We are happy to declare that the bases of the proposed formula for the new phase are as follows:

(1)   The Hashimite Kingdom of Jordan will become the United Arab Kingdom and will bear this name [applause].

(2)   The United Arab Kingdom will consist of two regions: (a) The Palestine region which will consist of the West Bank and any other Palestinian territories which are liberated and whose inhabitants desire to join it [applause]. (b) The Jordan region which will consist of the East Bank.

(3)   Amman will be the central capital of the kingdom as well as capital of the Jordan region.

(4)   Jerusalem will be the capital of the Palestine region [applause].

(5)   The Head of State will be the king, who will assume the central executive authority with the help of a central cabinet. The central legislative authority will be vested in the king and an assembly to be known as the National Assembly. Members of this assembly will be elected by direct secret ballot. Both regions will be equally represented in this assembly.

(6)   The central judicial authority will be vested in a central supreme court.

(7)   The kingdom will have unified armed forces whose supreme commander is the king [applause].

(8)   The responsibilities of the central executive authority will be confined to affairs connected with the kingdom as an international entity to guarantee the kingdom's security, stability and prosperity.

(9)   The executive authority in each region will be assumed by a governor general from among its sons and a regional cabinet also from among its sons.

(10)   Legislative authority in each region will be assumed by a council to be called the People's Council (Arabic: majlis ash-sha'b). It will be elected by a direct secret ballot. This council will elect the region's governor general.

(11)   The judicial authority in the region will be in the hands of the region's courts and nobody will have power over them.

(12)   The executive authority in each region will assume responsibility for all the affairs of the region except such affairs as the Constitution defines as coming under the jurisdiction of the central executive authority.

Naturally, the implementation of this formula and its bases must be according to the constitutional principles in force. It will be referred to the [Jordanian] National Assembly to adopt the necessary measures to prepare a new constitution for the country.

The new phase which we look forward to will guarantee the reorganization of the Jordanian-Palestinian house in a manner which will provide it with more intrinsic power and ability to work to attain its ambitions and aspirations. Proceeding from this fact, this formula will bind the two banks with ties of stronger fibre and with closer bonds and will strengthen their brotherhood and march as a result of enhancing man's responsibility in each bank on bases more suitable for serving their national aspirations without prejudice to any of the rights gained by any citizen, whether he be of Palestinian origin living in the Jordanian region or of Jordanian origin living in the Palestinian region.

This formula gathers and does not disperse, strengthens and does not weaken, unites and does not divide. It does not contain anything to change anything gained by any person during a unity of 20 years [applause].

Every attempt to cast doubt on any of this or discredit it is treason against the unity of the kingdom, the cause, the people and the homeland. The experience, vigilance and ability gained by our people make them capable of facing the forthcoming responsibilities with greater confidence and more determination. If ability is a debt for a person to use for himself and others and if vigilance is a weapon to be used for his and other's welfare, then the time has come for that person to stand up and face his responsibilities, perform them sincerely and faithfully and practice them bravely and with dignity. For this reason this formula is the title for a new bright, shining and confident page in the history of this country in which each citizen has a part and responsibility. It is partly based on sound allegiance to his faithful country and sincere devotion to his glorious nation.

The armed forces which from the very beginning marched under the banner of the great Arab revolution [applause] and which includes and will always include in its ranks the best sons of the people in both banks, will always be prepared to welcome more sons of both banks. They will always be at peak efficiency, ability and organization, and will remain open to anyone anxious to serve the homeland and the cause with absolute loyalty to homeland and the cause and to the sublime aims.

This Arab country is the country of the cause, just as it is from the Arabs and for all the Arabs. The record of its sacrifices for the nation and the cause is long and well known. This record was written by its brave armed forces and free and loyal people with their blood and honourable sacrifices. Inasmuch as the attitudes toward this country change to attitudes of fraternity, assistance and support, this country will continue on the path of sacrifice with strength and hope until it and its nation regain their rights and achieve their objectives.

This Arab country belongs to all, Jordanians and Palestinians alike. When we say Palestinians we mean every Palestinian throughout the world [applause], provided he is Palestinian by loyalty and affinity. When we call on every citizen to rise to play his part and carry out his responsibilities in the new stage, we call on every Palestinian brother outside Jordan to respond to the call of duty — unaffected by appearances and attempts to outdo others and free from weaknesses and deviations — to proceed with his relatives and brothers in a march whose basis is this formula and to be united in rank and clear in aim in order that all may participate in attaining the aim of liberation and establishing the cherished edifice and strong structure.

If God helps you, none can defeat you. For God is mighty and strong. Peace be with you.

## 5. Arab League Summit Conference, Secret Resolutions, Algiers, 4 December, 1973 [Excerpts]

### a. The Current Goals of the Arab Nation

The Conference resolves that the goals of the current phase of the common Arab struggle are:

1. The complete liberation of all the Arab territories conquered during the aggression of June 1967, with no concession or abandonment of any part of them, or detrimental to national sovereignty over them.

2. Liberation of the Arab city of Jerusalem, and rejection of any situation which may be harmful to complete Arab sovereignty over the Holy City.

3. Commitment to restoration of the national rights of the Palestinian people, according to the decisions of the Palestine Liberation Organization, as the sole representative of the Palestinian nation. (The Hashemite Kingdom of Jordan expressed reservations.)

4. The Palestine problem is the affair of all the Arabs, and no Arab party can possibly dissociate itself from this commitment, in the light of the resolutions of previous Summit Conferences.

### b. Military

In view of continuation of the struggle against the enemy until the goals of our nation are attained, the liberation of the occupied territories and the restoration of the national rights of the Palestinian people, the Conference resolves:

1. Solidarity of all the Arab States with Egypt, Syria and the Palestinian nation, in the common struggle for attainment of the just goals of the Arabs.

2. Provision of all means of military and financial support to both fronts, Egyptian and Syrian, to strengthen their military capacity for embarking on the liberation campaign and standing fast in face of the tremendous amount of supplies and unlimited aid received by the enemy.

3. Support of Palestinian resistance by all possible measures, to ensure its active role in the campaign.

## 6. Arab League Summit Conference Communique, Rabat, Morocco, 29 October, 1974

The Seventh Arab Summit Conference after exhaustive and detailed discussions conducted by their Majesties, Excellencies, and Highnesses, the Kings, Presidents and Amirs on the Arab situation in general and the Palestine problem in particular, within their national and international frameworks; and after hearing the statements submitted by His Majesty King Hussein, King of the Hashemite Kingdom of Jordan and His Excellency Brother Yasser Arafat, Chairman of the Palestine Liberation Organization, and after the statements of their Majesties and Excellencies the Kings and Presidents, in an atmosphere of candour and sincerity and full responsibility; and in view of the Arab leaders' appreciation of the joint national responsibility required of them at present for confronting aggression and performing duties of liberation, enjoined by the unity of the Arab cause and the unity of its struggle; and in view of the fact that all are aware of Zionist schemes still being made to eliminate the Palestinian existence and to obliterate the Palestinian national entity; and in view of the Arab leaders' belief in the necessity to frustrate these attempts and schemes and to counteract them by supporting and strengthening this Palestinian national entity, by providing all requirements to develop and increase its ability to ensure that the Palestinian people recover their rights in full; and by meeting responsibilities of close cooperation with its brothers within the framework of collective Arab commitment;

And in light of the victories achieved by Palestinian struggle in the confrontation with the Zionist enemy, at the Arab and international levels, at the United Nations, and of the obligation imposed thereby to continue joint Arab action to develop and increase the scope of these victories; and having received the views of all on all the above, and having succeeded in cooling the differences between brethren within the framework of consolidating Arab solidarity, the Seventh Arab Summit Conference resolves the following:

1.  To affirm the right of the Palestinian people to self-determination and to return to their homeland;

2.  To affirm the right of the Palestinian people to establish an independent national authority under the command of the Palestine Liberation Organization, the sole legitimate representative of the Palestinian people in any Palestinian territory that is liberated. This authority, once it is established, shall enjoy the support of the Arab States in all fields and at all levels;

3.  To support the Palestine Liberation Organization in the exercise of its responsibility at the national and international levels within the framework of Arab commitment;

4.  To call on the Hashemite Kingdom of Jordan, the Syrian Arab Republic, the Arab Republic of Egypt and the Palestine Liberation Organiza-

tion to devise a formula for the regulation of relations between them in the light of these decisions so as to ensure their implementation;

    5.   That all the Arab States undertake to defend Palestinian national unity and not to interfere in the internal affairs of Palestinian action.

## 7. Statement by President Bourguiba of Tunisia Calling for a Settlement of the Arab-Israeli Conflict on the Basis of the 1947 UN Partition Resolution. Tunis, 26 October, 1976

It was intolerable that we should be blamed for the misdeeds of others and that the atrocities of Nazism should be atoned for in the heart of our land, our homes and our fields.

We therefore decided that we must fight to recover our usurped rights and to put an end to this injustice which is without precedent in modern history.

After nearly a third of a century we realized that this was impossible without exposing the security of the area — and perhaps world peace — to the gravest dangers.

We therefore decided that the maintenance of peace must be preferred to the cause of the homeland, to our love of it and our passionate attachment to it.

Therefore I have come to you today bearing an olive branch in both hands, calling for the implementation of the resolution adopted in 1947, hoping that the passage of time may gradually bring about detente between the two communities, that as the years go by links of mutual exchange and cooperation may be established between them and that rapprochement in one form or another may lead to the two groups coexisting in a single community. This at any rate is the one wager to which we should direct our hopes and energies. This is what I have said to the international community, although I know how heavy is the responsibility involved in this decision, and the reactions it may give rise to in certain circles of the Palestine revolution. In the past I staked all on just such a wager as regards Tunisia, thereby risking my reputation and my life.

But the leader must not be afraid to take decisions leading to peace which, although they appear to indicate weakness, are really, and in the sight of history, revolutionary decisions.

If Abu Ammar did this he would be entitled to as prominent a place in the register of freedom fighters as those who daily lay down their lives in Nablus, Acre and Jerusalem.

If he did this he would open up to Palestine a new era of hope for the building of honour and self-respect.

If he did this it would also be the prelude to many benefits for the Eastern Arab countries which have been trying since the fifties to achieve a reconciliation between two irreconcilable things, between war against Israel and war against backwardness, between the cost of armaments and planning for development. One of them is certainly important, but the second is vital as regards our destiny and it is therefore in my view more important, as without it the other goals and objectives cannot be achieved.

The most important of our duties as Arabs, in both the East and the West, is to give priority to organized and planned development so that we may rescue our peoples from backwardness and promote them to the ranks of the nations that are developing, growing and becoming strong enough to control not only their political destiny, but also, and in particular, their economic destiny, because in our times economic capacity is the key to political capacity.

## 8. Arab League Summit Conference Declaration, Tripoli, Libya, 5 December, 1977, [Excerpts]

In the name of God, the Merciful, the Compassionate: An Arab summit conference was held in Tripoli, the capital of the Socialist People's Libyan Arab Jamahiriyah, from 2 to 5 December 1977 at the invitation of Brother Colonel Mu'ammar al-Quadhafi. It was attended by the following:

1.   President Houari Boumediene for the Algerian Democratic and Popular Republic;

2.   President Hafiz al-Assad for the Syrian Arab Republic;

3.   Col. Mu'ammar al-Quadhafi, secretary general of the General People's Congress of the Socialist People's Libyan Arab Jamahiriyah;

4.   Brother 'Abd al-Fattah Isma'il, secretary general of the Unified Political Organization — National Front, for the FDRY;

5.   Brother Taha Yasin Ramadan, for the Iraqi Republic;

6.   Brother Yasser 'Arafat, chairman of the PLO Executive Committee and commander of the Palestinian revolution forces.

With a sense of complete pan-Arab responsibility, the conference discussed the dimensions of the current phase through which the Arab cause in general and the Palestinian question in particular are passing and the American-Zionist plans aimed at imposing capitulatory settlements on the Arab nation, prejudicing the established national rights of the Palestinian people, liquidating the national Arab accomplishments and striking at the Arab liberation movement as a prelude to subduing the Arab area and controlling its destiny and tying it to the bandwagon of world imperialism.

The conference also discussed the visit made by President el-Sadat to the Zionist entity as being a link in the framework of the implementation of the hostile schemes. The conference reviewed the results of the visit, which constituted a flagrant violation of the principles and objectives of the pan-Arab struggle against the Zionist enemy, a squandering of the rights of the Palestinian Arab people, a departure from the unity of the Arab ranks, a grave violation of the Arab League Charter and the resolutions of the Arab summit conferences and the withdrawing of Arab Egypt from the front of conflict with the Zionist enemy — a matter which the conference considered a great service by President el-Sadat to Zionism and American imperialism and their designs and a consecretion of the Zionist entity, which is their tool and base in the Arab area.

Those attending the conference studied the current situation with all of its dimensions and concluded that the objectives of the plot are as follows:

1. To undermine the possibility of the establishment of a just and honorable peace which would safeguard the national rights of the Arab nation and guarantee for it the liberation of its occupied territories, the foremost of which is Jerusalem, and for the Palestinian people their established national rights.

2. To isolate the Arab nation from its allies and friends on the African Continent who have adopted a historic stand in support of the Arab issue and exposed the organic link between the Zionist entity and the racist regime in South Africa.

3. To isolate the Arab nation from the group of non-aligned states and Islamic states which have supported the Arab issue in all of its stages and stood on the side of the just struggle of the Palestinian people.

4. To harm the relations of friendship and cooperation between the Arab States on the one hand and the Soviet Union and the countries of the socialist camp, which have given support and backing to the Arab nation in its historic struggle against the imperialist-Zionist enemy.

5. To enable the forces hostile to the Arab nation, headed by the United States, to realize gains that will upset the international balance in favor of the Zionist imperialist forces and Zionism and undermine the national independence of the Afro-Asian and Latin American countries.

6. To establish an alliance between the Zionist enemy and the current Egyptian regime aimed at liquidating the Arab issue and the issue of Palestine, split the Arab nation and forfeit its national interests.

Out of its belief in the nature of the Zionist and imperialist challenges aimed at weakening the Arab will for liberation and harming the firm national rights of the Palestinian people which have been confirmed by international legitimacy — the foremost of which is their right to return and decide their own destiny and build their independent state on the soil of their homeland under the leadership of the PLO, which is the sole legitimate representative of the Palestinian people — and proceeding from the reality of pan-Arab and historic responsibility, the summit conference decided the following:

1. To condemn President el-Sadat's visit to the Zionist entity since it constitutes a great betrayal of the sacrifices and struggle of our Arab people in Egypt and their armed forces and of the struggle, sacrifices and principles of the Arab nation. While appreciating the role of the great Egyptian people in the national struggle of the Arab nation, the conference stresses that Egypt is not the beginning nor the end and that if the Arab nation is great with Egypt, the latter's greatness is only possible within the Arab nation, without which it can only diminish in importance.

2. To work for the frustration of the results of President el-Sadat's visit to the Zionist entity and his talks with the leaders of the Zionist enemy and the subsequent measures including the proposed Cairo meeting. The conference warns that anyone who tries to pursue a similar line or to have any dealings with the said results shall be held responsible for his deed nationally and on the pan-Arab level.

3. To freeze [tajmid] political and diplomatic relations with the Egyptian Government, to suspend dealings with it on the Arab and international level and to apply the regulations, provisions and decisions of the Arab boycott against Egyptian individuals, companies and firms which deal with the Zionist enemy.

4. To decide not to take part in Arab League meetings which are held in Egypt and to undertake contacts with the Arab League member states to study the question of its headquarters and organs and the membership of the Egyptian regime.

5. The conference salutes the Palestinian Arab people, who are standing fast in the occupied homeland, including all of their national and other popular organizations which are struggling against the occupation and which reject the visit of el-Sadat to occupied Palestine. The conference also warns against any attempt to prejudice the legitimacy of the PLO representation of the Palestinian people.

6. The conference takes satisfaction in recording the preliminary positions taken by the Arab States which have denounced the visit and rejected its consequences. Out of its responsibility and in compliance with its commitment and collective resolutions, the conference calls on these states to adopt practical measures to face the serious character of this capitulatory policy, including the suspension of political and material support. The conference also condemns the disgraceful stands adopted by those who praise this visit or support it and warn them of the consequences of their despondent and defeatist policies.

7. The conference appeals to the Arab nation on the official and popular levels to provide economic, financial, political and military aid and support to the Syrian region, now that it has become the principal confrontation state and the base of steadfastness for dealing with the Zionist enemy and also to the Palestinian people represented by the PLO.

8. The conference greets our Arab people in sisterly Egypt and particularly their national and progressive forces, which have rejected the capitulatory policy being pursued by the Egyptian regime as being a betrayal of the sacrifices of the people and their martyrs and an insult to the dignity of their armed forces.

9. In asserting the importance of the relationship of struggle and nationalism between Syria and the Palestinians, the Syrian Arab Republic and the PLO announce the formation of a unified front to face the Zionist enemy and combat the imperialist plot with all its parties and to thwart all attempts at capitulation. The Democratic and Popular Republic of Algeria, the Socialist People's Libyan Arab Jamashiriyah and the PDRY have decided to join this front, making it the nucleus of a pan-Arab front for steadfastness and combat which will be open to other Arab countries to join.

10. Members of the pan-Arab front consider any aggression against any one member as an aggression against all members.

The conference pledges to the Arab nation that it will continue the march of struggle, steadfastness, combat and adherence to the objectives of the Arab struggle. The conference also expresses its deep faith and absolute confidence that the Arab nation, which has staged revolutions, overcome difficulties and defeated plots during its long history of struggle — a struggle which abounds with heroism — is today capable of replying with force to those who have harmed its dignity, squandered its rights, split its solidary and departed from the principles of its struggle. It is confident of its own capabilities in liberation, progress and victory, thanks to God.

The conference records with satisfaction the national Palestinian unity within the framework of the PLO.

Done at Tripoli on 5 December, 1977.


# 9. Summit of Anti-Sadat "Steadfastness and Confrontation Front". Algeria, Libya, South Yemen and the P.L.O. Damascus, 23 September, 1978

**Four-point Agreement**

There was agreement on four main points:

1. Economic and political relations with Egypt to be severed, and en-

couragement to be given to "progressive and nationalist forces" within Egypt to overthrow the Sadat government;

2.   The Arab League headquarters to be removed from Cairo or, failing that, a new league to be set up elsewhere in the Arab world;

3.   Closer relations with the Soviet Union, to which end Syrian President Assad would go to Moscow to strengthen co-operation between the front and the Soviet Union;

4.   A joint political and military command to be set up to co-ordinate moves against Israel and Egypt.

### Front as Basis for Arab Unity

The conference also voiced its wish to transform the Steadfastness and Confrontation Front into "a base for the Arab national struggle", a base which would be committed to the following goals:

1.   Arab unity and "support of all efforts aimed at removing obstacles in the way of ultimate unity of the Arab world".

2.   Recognition of the fact that the Palestinian problem is "the basic concern of all the Arabs and, consequently, no single Arab party may bargain on or undermine this commitment or take any action that would cause damage to the Palestine case and the national rights of the Palestinian people."

3.   Complete liberation of all Arab and Palestinian lands, no concession or abandonment of any part of these lands, and "no-one may undermine Arab sovereignty" over them.

4.   Commitment to the restoration of the "inalienable national rights of the Palestinian people, including its right to repatriation, self-determination and statehood."

5.   Support for the Palestinian people's struggle "under the leadership of the PLO, the sole legitimate representative of the Palestine people."

## 10. Arab League Summit Conference, Final Statement, Baghdad, Iraq, 5 November, 1978

The Arab summit conference issued a final statement at the conclusion of its meetings, which lasted for 4 days. The following is the text of the final statement:

By the initiative of the Government of the Republic of Iraq and at the invitation of President Ahmad Hasan al-Bakr, the ninth Arab summit conference convened in Baghdad 2-5 November 1978.

In a high spirit of pan-Arab responsibility and joint concern about the unity of the Arab stand, the conference studied confrontation of the dangers and challenges threatening the Arab nation, particularly after the results of the

Camp David agreements signed by the Egyptian Government and the effects of these agreements on the Arab struggle to face the Zionist aggression against the Arab nation.

Proceeding from the principles in which the Arab nation believes, acting on the unity of Arab destiny and complying with the traditions of joint Arab action, the Arab summit conference has emphasized the following basic principles:

First: The Palestinian question is a fateful Arab issue and is the essence of the conflict with the Zionist enemy. The sons of the Arab nation and all the Arab countries are concerned with it and are obliged to struggle for its sake and to offer all material and moral sacrifices for this cause. The struggle to regain Arab rights in Palestine and in the occupied Arab territory is a general Arab responsibility. All Arabs must share this responsibility, each in accord with his military, economic, political and other abilities.

The conflict with the Zionist enemy exceeds the framework of the conflict of the countries whose territory was occupied in 1967, and it includes the whole Arab nation because of the military, political, economic and cultural danger the Zionist enemy constitutes against the entire Arab nation and its substantial and pan-Arab interests, civilization and destiny. This places on all the countries of the Arab nation the responsibility to share in this conflict with all the resources it possesses.

Second: All the Arab countries must offer all forms of support, backing and facilities to all forms of the struggle of the Palestinian resistance, supporting the PLO in its capacity as the sole legitimate representative of the Palestinian people inside and outside the occupied land, struggling for liberation and restoration of the national rights of its people, including their right to return to their homeland, to determine their future and to establish their independent state on their national soil. The Arab States pledge to preserve Palestinian national unity and not to interfere in the internal affairs of the Palestinian action.

Third: Commitment is reaffirmed to the resolutions of the Arab summit conferences, particularly the sixth and seventh summit conferences of Algiers and Rabat.

Fourth: In light of the above principles it is impermissible for any side to act unilaterally in solving the Palestinian question in particular and the Arab-Zionist conflict in general.

Fifth: No solution shall be accepted unless it is associated with a resolution by an Arab summit conference convened for this purpose.

The conference discussed the two agreements signed by the Egyptian Government at Camp David and considered that they harm the Palestinian people's rights and the rights of the Arab nation in Palestine and the occupied Arab territory. The conference considered that these agreements took place outside the framework of collective Arab responsibility and are opposed to the resolutions of the Arab summit conferences, particularly the resolutions of the Algiers and Rabat summit conferences, the Arab League Charter and the UN resolutions on the Palestinian question. The conference considers that these agreements do not lead to the just peace that the Arab nation desires. Therefore, the conference has decided not to approve of these two agreements and not to deal with their results. The conference has also rejected all the political, economic, legal and other effects resulting from them.

The conference decided to call on the Egyptian Government to go back on these agreements and not to sign any reconciliation treaty with the enemy. The conference hopes that Egypt will return to the fold of joint Arab action and not act unilaterally in the affairs of the Arab-Zionist conflict. In this respect the conference adopted a number of resolutions to face the new stage and to safeguard the aims and interests of the Arab nation out of faith that with its material and moral resources the Arab nation is capable of confronting the difficult circumstances and all challenges, just as it has always been throughout history, because it is defending right, justice and its national existence.

The conference stressed the need to unify all the Arab efforts in order to remedy the strategic imbalance that has resulted from Egypt's withdrawal from the confrontation arena.

The conference decided that the countries that possess readiness and capability will coordinate participation with effective efforts. The conference also stressed the need to adhere to the regulations of Arab boycott and to tighten application of its provisions.

The conference studied means to develop Arab information media beamed abroad for the benefit of the just Arab issues. The conference decided to hold annual meetings for the Arab summit conferences and decided that the month of November will be the date.

After studying the Arab and international situation, the conference asserts the Arab nation's commitment to a just peace based on the comprehensive Israeli withdrawal from the Arab territories occupied in 1967, including Arab Jerusalem, the guaranteeing of the inalienable national rights of the Palestinian Arab people including the right to establish their independent state on their national soil.

The conference decided to embark on large scale international activity to explain the just rights of the Palestinian people and the Arab nation. The conference expressed appreciation to the Syrian Arab Republic and its heroic army, and to the Hashemite Kingdom of Jordan and its heroic army, and expressed its pride in the struggle of the Palestinian people and its steadfastness inside and outside the occupied territories, under the leadership of the P.L.O., the sole legitimate representative of the Palestinian people.

The conference praised the "charter for joint national action" signed by fraternal Syria and Iraq, and the conference regarded the charter as a great achievement on the way to Arab solidarity. The conference also expressed its great appreciation for the initiative of the Iraqi Government using President Hasan al-Bakr in calling for the convening of an Arab summit conference in Baghdad so as to unify Arab ranks and to organize Arab efforts to face the threats to which the Arab nation is currently exposed. The conference expressed its thanks for President Al-Bakr's efforts to make the conference a success.

## 11. Arab League Summit Conference Resolutions, Baghdad, 31 March, 1979

As the Government of the Arab Republic of Egypt has ignored the Arab summit conferences' resolutions, especially those of the sixth and seventh conferences held in Algiers and Rabat; as it has at the same time ignored the ninth Arab summit conference resolutions — especially the call made by the Arab kings, presidents and princes to avoid signing the peace treaty with the Zionist enemy — and signed the peace treaty on 26 March 1979;

It has thus deviated from the Arab ranks and has chosen, in collusion with the United States, to stand by the side of the Zionist enemy in one trench; has behaved unilaterally in the Arab-Zionist struggle affairs; has violated the Arab nation's rights; has exposed the nation's destiny, its struggle and aims to dangers and challenges; has relinquished its pan-Arab duty of liberating the occupied Arab territories, particularly Jerusalem, and of restoring the Palestinian Arab people's inalienable national rights, including their right to repatriation, self-determination and establishment of the independent Palestinian State on their national soil.

In order to safeguard Arab solidarity and the unity of ranks in defense of the Arabs' fateful issue; in appreciation of the Egyptian people's struggle and sacrifices for Arab issues and the Palestinian issue in particular; in implementation of the resolutions adopted by the ninth Arab summit conference that convened in Baghdad 2-5 November 1978, and at the invitation of the Government of the Republic of Iraq, the Arab League Council convened in Baghdad from 27 March 1979 to 31 March 1979 on the level of Arab foreign and economy ministers.

In light of the ninth Arab summit conference resolutions, the council studied the latest developments pertaining to the Arab-Zionist conflict, especially after the signing by the Government of the Arab Republic of Egypt of the peace [as-sulh] agreement with the Zionist enemy on 26 March 1979.

The Arab League Council, on the level of Arab foreign ministers, has decided the following:

1.  A.  To withdraw the ambassadors of the Arab States from Egypt immediately.

B.  To recommend the severance of political and diplomatic relations with the Egyptian Government. The Arab governments will adopt the necessary measures to apply this recommendation within a maximum period of 1 month from the date of issuance of this decision, in accordance with the constitutional measures in force in each country.

2.  To consider the suspension of the Egyptian Government's membership in the Arab League as operative from the date of the Egyptian Government's signing of the peace treaty with the Zionist enemy. This means depriving it of all rights resulting from this membership.

3.  A.  To make the city of Tunis, capital of the Tunisian Republic, the temporary headquarters of the Arab League, its General Secretariat, the competent ministerial councils and the permanent technical committees, as of the date of the signing of the treaty between the Egyptian Government and the Zionist enemy. This shall be communicated to all international and regional organizations and bodies. They will also be informed that dealings with the Arab League will be conducted with its secretariat in its new temporary headquarters.

B.  To appeal to the Tunisian Government to offer all possible aid in facilitating the settlement of the temporary Arab League headquarters and its officials.

C.  To form a committee comprising representatives of Iraq, Syria, Tunisia, Kuwait, Saudi Arabia and Algeria, in addition to a representative for the General Secretariat. The aim of this committee will be to implement this resolution's provisions and to seek the aid it requires from the member-states. The committee will have all the authorization and responsibilities from the Arab League Council necessary to implement this resolution, including the protection of the Arab League's properties, deposits, documents and records. It is also entitled to take necessary measures against any action that may be taken by the Egyptian Government to hinder the transfer of the Arab League headquarters or to harm the Arab League's rights and possessions.

The committee will have to accomplish its task of transfer to the temporary headquarters within 2 months from the date of this resolution. This period of time may be extended another month if the committee so decides. The committee shall submit a report on its accomplishments to the first forthcoming meeting of the Arab League Council.

D.  A sum of $5 million shall be placed at the committee's disposal to cover the transfer expenses. This sum shall be drawn from the credit accounts of various funds. The committee has the right to spend more than that amount if required. Expenditures for this purpose shall come under the supervision of the committee or of those it authorizes. The expenses shall be paid by the member-states, each according to the percentage of its annual contribution to the Arab League budget.

E. To transfer the Arab League General Secretariat officials who are employed at the time of the issuance of this resolution from the permanent headquarters to the temporary one during the period defined in paragraph 3C of this resolution. The committee referred to in the above-mentioned paragraph 3 will have the responsibility of paying them financial compensation compatible with the standard of living in the new headquarters and for settling their affairs until a permanent system is drafted for this purpose.

4. The competent and specialized Arab organizations, bodies, establishments and federations named in the attached list No. 1 will take the necessary measures to suspend Egypt's membership. They will transfer their headquarters from Egypt to other Arab States on a temporary basis, similar to the action that shall be taken regarding the Council General Secretariat. The executive councils and boards of these bodies, organizations, establishments and federations shall meet immediately following the implementation of this decision within a period not to exceed the period specified in Paragraph 3C above.

5. To seek to suspend Egypt's membership in the non-aligned movement, the Islamic conference organization and OAU for violating the resolutions of these organizations pertaining to the Arab-Zionist conflict.

6. To continue to cooperate with the fraternal Egyptian people and with Egyptian individuals, with the exception of those who cooperate with the Zionist enemy directly or indirectly.

7. The member-States shall inform all foreign countries of their stand on the Egyptian-Israeli treaty and will ask these countries not to support this treaty as it constitutes an aggression against the rights of the Palestinian people and the Arab nation as well as a threat to world peace and security.

8. To condemn the policy that the United States is practicing regarding its role in concluding the Camp David agreements and the Egyptian-Israeli treaty.

9. To consider the measures in this decision to be temporary and subject to cancellation by an Arab League Council decision as soon as the circumstances that justified their adoption are eliminated.

10. The Arab countries will pass legislation, decisions and measures necessary for the implementation of this resolution.

The Arab League Council, on the level of Arab foreign and economy ministers, has also decided the following:

1. To halt all bank loans, deposits, guarantees or facilities, as well as all financial or technical contributions and aid by Arab governments or their es-

tablishments to the Egyptian Government and its establishments as of the treaty signing date.

2.  To ban the extension of economic aid by the Arab funds, banks and financial establishments within the framework of the Arab League and the joint Arab cooperation to the Egyptian Government and its establishments.

3.  The Arab governments and institutions shall refrain from purchasing the bonds, shares, postal orders and public credit loans that are issued by the Egyptian Government and its financial foundations.

4.  Following the suspension of the Egyptian Government's membership in the Arab League, its membership will also be suspended from the institutions, funds and organizations deriving from the Arab League. The Egyptian Government and its institutions will cease to benefit from these organizations. The headquarters of those Arab League departments residing in Egypt will be transferred to other Arab States temporarily.

5.  In view of the fact that the ill-omened Egyptian-Israeli treaty and its appendices have demonstrated Egypt's commitment to sell oil to Israel, the Arab States shall refrain from providing Egypt with oil and its derivatives.

6.  Trade exchange with the Egyptian State and private establishments that deal with the Zionist enemy shall be prohibited.

7.  The Economic Boycott.

A.  The Arab boycott laws, principles and provisions shall be applied to those companies, foundations and individuals of the Arab Republic of Egypt that deal directly or indirectly with the Zionist enemy. The boycott office shall be entrusted with following up the implementation of these tasks.

B.  The provisions of paragraph A shall include the intellectual, cultural and artistic activities that involve dealing with the Zionist enemy or have connection with the enemy's institutions.

C.  The Arab States stress the importance of continued dealings with those private national Egyptian institutions that are confirmed not to be dealing with the Zionist enemy. Such institutions will be encouraged to work and maintain activities in the Arab countries within the framework of their fields of competence.

D.  The Arab countries stress the importance of caring for the feelings of the Egyptian people's sons who are working or living in the Arab countries as well as looking after their interests and consolidating their pan-Arab affiliation with Arabism.

E.  To consolidate the role of the Arab boycott and to enhance its grip at this stage, in affirmation of Arab unanimity, the assistant secretary general for economic affairs will be temporarily entrusted with the task of directly supervising the major boycott office in Damascus. He will be granted the necessary powers to reorganize and back the said department and to submit proposals on developing the boycott in method, content and scope. He shall submit a report in this regard to the first meeting of the Arab League Council.

8. The United Nations will be asked to transfer its regional offices, which serve the Arab region, from the Arab Republic of Egypt to any other Arab capital. The Arab States will work collectively toward this end.

9. The Arab League General Secretariat will be assigned the task of studying the joint Arab projects so as to take the necessary measures for protecting the Arab nation's interests in accordance with the aims of these resolutions. The General Secretariat shall submit its proposals to the Arab League Council in its first forthcoming meeting.

10. The Zionist plot must be faced by drafting an Arab strategy for economic confrontation. This will lead to utilizing the Arabs' own strength and will emphasize the need for realizing Arab economic integration in all aspects.

The strategy will strengthen joint Arab development and regional development within the pan-Arab outlook and will expand the establishment of joint Arab projects — projects that serve the aims of emancipating, developing and intergrating the Arab economy — and will promote the projects already in operation. The strategy will also develop the methods, systems and substance of the Arab boycott of Israel and will diversify and promote international relations with the developing countries. The Arab League General Secretariat shall rapidly submit studies relevant to the strategy of joint Arab economic action to the forthcoming session of the Arab Economic Council. This will be a prelude to the convention of a general Arab economic conference.

11. The above-mentioned committee shall be assigned the task of supervising the implementation of these decisions and of submitting a follow up report to the Arab League Council in its first forthcoming meeting.

12. The Arab States will issue the decisions and legislations pertaining to these decisions and will take the necessary measures to implement them.

13. These measures taken by the Arab and economy ministers are considered a minimal requirement to face the threats of the treaty. Individual governments can take whatever measure they deem necessary in addition to these measures.

14. The Arab foreign and economy ministers call on the Arab nation in all Arab countries to support the economic measures taken against the Zionist enemy and the Egyptian regime.

## 12. King Fahd of Saudi Arabia, Peace Plan, 6 August, 1981

1. Israeli evacuation of all Arab territories seized during the 1967 Middle East war, including the Arab sector of Jerusalem.

2. Dismantling the settlements set up by Israel on the occupied lands after

the 1967 war.

3.    Guaranteeing freedom of religious practices for all religions in the Jerusalem holy shrines.

4.    Asserting the rights of the Palestinian people and compensating those Palestinians who do not wish to return to their homeland.

5.    Commencing a transitional period in the West Bank of Jordan and the Gaza Strip under United Nations supervision for a duration not exceeding a few months.

6.    Setting up a Palestinian State with East Jerusalem as its capital.

7.    Affirming the right of all countries of the region to live in peace.

8.    Guaranteeing the implementation of these principles by the United Nations or some of its member states.


## 13. Arab League Summit Statement, Fez, Morocco, 6 September, 1982

### I.   The Arab-Israeli Conflict

The conference greeted the steadfastness of the Palestine revolutionary forces, the Lebanese and Palestinian peoples and the Syrian Arab Armed Forces and declared its support for the Palestinian people in their struggle for the retrieval of their established national rights.

Out of the conference's belief in the ability of the Arab nation to achieve its legitimate objectives and eliminate the aggression, and out of the principles and basis laid down by the Arab summit conferences, and out of the Arab countries' determination to continue to work by all means for the establishment of peace based on justice in the Middle East and using the plan of President Habib Bourguiba, which is based on international legitimacy, as the foundation for solving the Palestinian question and the plan of His Majesty King Fahd ibn 'Abd al-'Aziz which deals with peace in the Middle East, and in the light of the discussions and notes made by their majesties, excellencies and highnesses the kings, presidents and amirs, the conference has decided to adopt the following principles:

1.    Israel's withdrawal from all Arab territories occupied in 1967, including Arab Jerusalem.

2.    The removal of settlements set up by Israel in the Arab territories after 1967.

3.    Guarantees of the freedom of worship and the performance of religious rites for all religions at the holy places.

4.    Confirmation of the right of the Palestinian people to self-determination and to exercise their firm and inalienable national rights, under the leadership of the PLO, its sole legitimate representative, and compensation for those who do not wish to return.

5.  The placing of the West Bank and Gaza Strip under UN supervision for a transitional period, not longer than several months.
6.  The creation of an independent Palestinian State with Jerusalem as its capital.
7.  The drawing up by the Security Council of guarantees for peace for all the states of the region, including the independent Palestinian State.
8.  Security Council guarantees for the implementation of these principles.

## 14. Joint Jordanian — Palestinian Committee Communique, Amman, Jordan, 14 December, 1982

The joint Palestinian-Jordanian Committee ended a round of talks at noon today. Committee talks were conducted over the past two days. The committee issued the following communique to the press after the meetings:

"The Jordanian and Palestinian sides met with an understanding of the requirements of the current stage and for the effects that this stage will have on the Palestinian cause. The two sides met with a commitment to save the occupied territories and to restore the inalienable rights of the Palestinian people. The two sides met with an understanding of the historic and national dimensions which places the Palestinian and Jordanian peoples in a position which is directly affected by the continuous Zionist aggression against the Palestinian people and their national homeland.

"Joint continuous meetings have taken place since the historic meeting between PLO Chairman Arafat and Hussein on October 9, 1982. The Jordanian side was headed by Prime Minister Mudar Badran and the Palestinian side was headed by PLO Chairman Yasser Arafat.

"As a result of intensive deliberations the two sides agreed in the spirit of common understanding to develop a special and distinguished relationship between Jordan and Liberated Palestine.

"The two sides agreed to continue joint political moves on all levels and in conformity with the Fez Summit resolutions and within the framework of joint Arab moves which will guarantee the mobilization of Arab potentials to restore Arab and Palestinian rights.

"The two sides also agreed that the joint committee will continue further discussion on the question of bilateral relations and new political developments."

## 15. Iraqi President Saddam Hussein's Statements on Israel's Right to a Secure State. (Interview with Stephen Solarz, Member of US House of Representatives), 2 January, 1983

[Question] Mr. President, I do appreciate your frank answers. I would like to ask you the second question and I would like you to give, with all sincerity, your viewpoint: should Israel agree to return to the pre-1967 borders, but only within an objective framework, giving Jordan the primary responsibility for administrating the West Bank and Gaza Strip. (?Does) this represent an acceptable solution to the problem? Would it be sufficient for Israel to withdraw to the 1967 lines and to accept the establishment of a Palestinian State in the West Bank and Gaza Strip as a way to solve the conflict?

[Answer] I do not believe that forcing the Palestinians, under the current circumstances, to accept a constitutional formula with any Arab State is a sound action. However, I believe that the simultaneous existence of an independent Palestinian State acceptable to the Palestinians and the existence of a secure state for the Israelis are both necessary.

I believe that you will be committing a grave mistake, unacceptable of course to the Arabs and Iraq, if you think that Jordan is suitable as a Palestinian State. In other words, the state of Palestine would be on the east bank of the Jordan, as some Israeli officials have remarked. The Arabs would feel that their entire existence was threatened and that the political map of their national entity could be threatened any time by an international conspiracy or by the desire of this or that big power.

## 16. Jordanian Statement on End of Negotiations with the P.L.O, Amman, Jordan, 10 April, 1983

Ladies and gentlemen, the following is the full text of the communique issued today after the Jordanian Cabinet meeting presided over by His Majesty King Hussein:

Since the Israeli aggression of June, 1967 and through our awareness of the dangers and repercussions of the occupation, Jordan has accepted the political option as one of the basic options that may lead to the recovery of Arab territories occupied through military aggression. Consequently, Jordan accepted Security Council Resolution 242 of November 22, 1967. When the October 1973 war happened, it underlined the importance of continuing work on the political option while at the same time building our intrinsic strength. This war brought about Security Council Resolution 338 which put a stop to military operations and implicitly reemphasized Security Council Resolution 242.

Based on Security Council Resolution 338, disengagement agreements were concluded between Israel, on the one hand, and Egypt and Syria on the other. This process completed the Arab circle immediately concerned itself with the recovery of the occupied lands through political means. On this basis, Jordan, in cooperation with the Arab States, developed and adopted the concept of forming a United Arab delegation that would attend an international conference for the purpose of achieving a just and comprehensive peace settlement to the Middle East problem.

In 1974, the Rabat Arab summit conference designated the PLO the sole legitimate representative of the Palestinian people. Jordan went along with the Arab consensus, and has been committed to that decision ever since.

The ensuing period saw the disjointment of Arab unity as evidenced by the Camp David accords. Further disintegration in the overall Arab position followed, even between those directly affected by the Israeli occupation. All the while, Jordan kept sounding the alarm on the one hand, persevering in its course of action on the other. Jordan warned repeatedly of the dangers inherent in the continuation of the no-war and no-peace situation, and of the exploitation by Israel of this situation to perpetuate the status quo by creating new facts in the occupied Arab territories, to realize its declared ambitions, aided by Arab disunity and by its military superiority.

Jordan has also cautioned against letting time pass by without concluding a just and comprehensive peace settlement because time was, and still is, essential to Israel's aim of creating new facts and bringing about a fait accompli. Sixteen years have passed since the occupation, during which Israel established 146 colonies in the West Bank alone and has illegally expropriated more than 50 percent of that land.

Even today, Israel forges ahead, in defiance of all international conventions and of United Nations resolutions, with a systematic policy of evacuating the inhabitants of the West Bank to change the demographic composition of the occupied Arab territories, thus realizing its designs to establish the Zionist state in the whole of Palestine.

From the early days of the occupation, and through awareness of the Zionist aims, Jordan issued all these warnings and undertook the task of implementing all policies that may support the steadfastness of the Palestinian people and help them stay in their national soil.

With this objective in mind, we worked incessantly on all levels. Domestically, Jordan provides markets for the industrial and agricultural products of the West Bank and Gaza, and continues to extend support to the existing institutions in the West Bank. Also, we continue to attach great importance to building our intrinsic defense capability in cooperation with other Arab States, through the conviction held by all our nation of the danger posed by Zionist ambitions which threaten the Arab world and its future generations. Within this context, Jordan paid particular attention to building its Armed Forces, looked for new sources of arms within the available financial means, and enacted the military service law to mobilize all its national resources for self-defense and for the defense of the Arab world, because Jordan remains, by virtue of its geographic location, a constant target for Israeli aggression, and the first line of defense on the east flank of the Arab world.

On the Arab level, Jordan sought to provide financial support for the steadfastness of the Palestinian people, and formed a joint Jordanian-Palestinian Committee which continues to implement the policy of supporting our people in the occupied lands.

On the international level, Jordan worked to mobilize world opinion to bring pressure to bear on Israel, and in the United Nations, through cooperation with Arab and friendly countries, Jordan succeeded in passing resolutions condemning, isolating, and putting pressure on Israel. All the while, Israel continued with its expansionist colonization program, evicting the Arab inhabitants of Palestine and replacing them by Jewish immigrants. We strive to confront this program which stands to affect Jordan more than any other country, which threatens Jordan's identity and national security.

In June 1982, Israel launched its aggression on Lebanon, which resulted in that country joining the list of occupied Arab territories. Lebanon was not excluded from the ambitions of Israel, which had already annexed de facto the West Bank and Gaza.

Last September, United States President Ronald Reagan declared his peace initiative to solve the Middle East crisis, and shortly after the Fez Arab summit conference resumed its proceedings where the Arab peace plan was formulated. It was evident that both peace proposals were inspired by the provisions of Security Council Resolution 242 and by the United Nations resolutions that followed. Jordan, as well as other Arab and friendly countries, found that the Reagan plan lacked some of the principles of the Fez peace plan but at the same time, it contained a number of positive elements. Given the realities of the international situation, on the other hand, the Arab peace plan lacked the mechanism that would enable it to make effective progress. The Reagan peace plan presented the vehicle that could propel the Fez peace plan forward, and Jordan proceeded to explore this possibility.

We believe, and continue to believe, that this aim can be achieved through an agreement between Jordan and the PLO, on the establishment of a confederal relationship that would govern and regulate the future of the Jordanian and Palestinian peoples. This relationship would express itself, from the moment of its inception, through joint Jordanian-Palestinian action based on the Fez peace plan, Security Council Resolution 242, and the principles of the Reagan initiative. In addition, such a confederal relationship would be sought if only through the faith Arabs have in the joint Arab destiny, and in recognition of the bonds that have linked the peoples of Jordan and Palestine throughout history.

These concepts, and the ideas and assessments that follow from them, formed the subject of intensive discussions held over several meetings between His Majesty King Hussein and the PLO Chairman Yasser Arafat, as well as between the Government of Jordan and a number of senior members of the PLO, within the framework of a higher committee which was formed for this purpose and which held its deliberations over the 5 months between October 1982 and the recent PNC convention in 1982 [as heard]. In addition, a number of prominent Palestinians inside and outside the occupied territories took part in the discussions.

These deliberations resulted in the irrefutable conclusion that Jordan and Palestine are joined by undeniable objective considerations reflected by the common threat against them which united their interests and their goals. There also resulted a joint conviction in the soundness of our approach, and we agreed to form a joint stand capable of pursuing political action which, with Arab support, can take advantage of the available opportunity to liberate our people, land, and foremost of all, Arab Jerusalem.

Then, upon request of Mr. Yasser Arafat, we waited to see the results of the PNC meeting, where Mr. Arafat assured us he would act to secure the support of the council for the envisaged joint political action, on whose basic elements we agreed, pending their development in the PNC by declaring a confederate-union relationship between Jordan and Palestine.

In our latest meeting with Mr. Arafat, held in Amman between March 31 and April 5, we conducted a joint assessment of the realities of the Palestine problem in general, and in particular of the dilemma facing the Palestinian people under occupation. We also discussed political action in accordance with the Arab and international peace plans, including President Reagan's peace initiative, bearing in mind the resolutions of the PNC. We held intensive talks on the principles and the methods, and reemphasized the importance of a confederal relationship between Jordan and Palestine as being a practical conceptualization from which to work for the implementation of this initiative. We agreed to work together in this delicate and crucial time to form a united Arab stand that would enable us to deal with the practical aspects of these initiatives, in the hope of achieving a just, permanent, and comprehensive solution to the Middle East problem, especially the Palestinian problem.

We also agreed to start immediately joint political action on the Arab level to secure Arab support that would contribute enormously to the realization of the common goal of liberating the lands and people under occupation, thus fulfilling our duty to work in all possible ways and to take advantage of every possible opportunity to achieve our aims.

Together with PLO Chairman Yasser Arafat we laid the final draft of our agreement, which required us and Mr. Arafat to make immediate contacts with Arab leaders to inform them of its contents, seeking their blessing of and support for the agreement.

The PLO Executive Committee deliberated on this issue in the course of several meetings, and finally Mr. Arafat decided to discuss the agreement with other PLO leaders outside Jordan, and return to Amman after 2 days to conclude the joint steps necessary for the implementation of the agreement.

Five days later, a delegate was sent by the PLO Executive Committee chairman to Amman, to convey to us new ideas and to propose a new course of action that differed from our agreement and that did not give priority to saving the land, thus sending us back to where we were in October 1982.

In the light of this, it became evident that we cannot proceed with the course of political action which we had planned together, and to which we had agreed in principle and in detail, in answer to our historic responsibility to take the opportunities made available by Arab and international initiatives, and save our land and people.

In view of the results of the efforts we made with the PLO, and in compliance with the 1974 Rabat summit resolution, and through the strict observance of the independence of the Palestinian decision, we respect the decision of the PLO, it being the sole legitimate representative of the Palestinian people. Accordingly, we leave it to the PLO and to the Palestinian people to choose the ways and means for the salvation of themselves and their land, and for the realization of their declared aims in the manner they see fit.

We in Jordan, having refused from the beginning to negotiate on behalf of the Palestinians, will neither act separately nor in lieu of anybody in any Middle East peace negotiations. Jordan will work as a member of the Arab League, in compliance with its resolutions, to support the PLO within our capabilities, and in compliance with the requirements of our national security.

Being consistent with ourselves, and faithful to our principles, Arab Jerusalem, and holy shrines, we shall continue to provide support for our brothers in the occupied Palestinian territories, and make our pledge to them before the Almighty that we shall remain their faithful brother, and side with them in their ordeal.

As for us in Jordan, we are directly affected by the results of the continued occupation of the West Bank and the Gaza Strip through the accelerating colonization program and through the economic pressures systematically being brought on the Palestinian people to force them out of their land.

In the light of these facts, and in the no-war and no-peace situation that prevails, we find ourselves more concerned than anybody else to confront the de facto annexation of the West Bank and the Gaza Strip, which forces us to take all steps necessary to safeguard our national security in all its dimensions.

Both Jordanians and Palestinians shall remain one family that cares for its national unity to the same extent that it cares to stay on this beloved Arab land.

May God assist us in our aspirations.

## 17.  Address by King Hussein to the 17th Session of the Palestine National Council, Amman, 22 November, 1984 [Excerpts]

...After more than seventeen years, the West Bank and the Gaza Strip are still under occupation. Enemy programs and their implementation continue unabated. Jerusalem groans with fortitude under the weight of every Jewish fortress erected on its shoulders. Al-Aqsa Mosque and the Dome of the Rock are threatened with demolition and obliteration, a prey to the whims and designs of fanatics. Every day, the dear and sacred land is swallowed up either through outright expropriation or in the name of security and planning. The national features of the Palestinian economy have been blurred, having become part of the Israeli economy. The future, like the present, is engulfed in doubt, tension and uncertainty. But our people, through God's help, have remained steadfast, despite various forms of organized pressure. The question is: for how long will we allow time to serve a greedy enemy who every day eats up part of the remaining land while we dissipate our time in fruitless argument and recrimination?

How long shall we heed those among us who say: Leave it to future generations? Is this not a clear abdication of responsibility? Is each generation not responsible for the era in which it lives? What makes them believe that the circumstances of future generations will be more conducive to achieving what they are avoiding to achieve? Can they stop time and progress for the enemy and still keep them moving for themselves? What wisdom or morality is there in leaving future generations a heavy legacy which is apt to become more onerous than to recede? And will the Palestinians, who are lost in a sea of suffering under occupation, accept this kind of argument when they know better than anybody else the impact of granting the enemy even more time and the resulting impact on their existence and future?

The least that can be said about this argument is that it constitutes an escape from responsibility. The least that can be said about its advocates is that they are a breed which believe that the earth is coterminous with their own existence. This is not the way the world goes. Each generation has its own responsibilities. The justification of the existence of a ruler or leader rests on the fulfillment of his responsibilities with wisdom and courage, with vigor and sincerity. It is not indefinite suspension but proper utilization that endows time with meaning.

...In this presentation, my intention has been to delineate, with the utmost precision, the pace of the Palestinian cause in the Arab mind as well as on the political map. Perhaps you share with me the observation that the picture is bleak and that, in consequence, it requires a fresh outlook and a new approach. The new outlook must begin by defining a future course of action. Perhaps, again, the natural starting point would be to emphasize the special relationship which ties Jordan to Palestine, a relationship forged by purely objective factors of history, geography and demography, which have placed the two brotherly countries and peoples, since the beginning of the century, in the same boat of suffering and hope, of interest and harm, of history and destiny. The particularity of our relationship is not a whimsical self-description, but a scientific fact which has made the Palestinian question a daily and central concern in our lives and a basis of our defense, foreign and development policies. If to our brethren the Palestine question is one of their foreign and defense priorities, to us, as to you, it is the foremost priority. Consequently, Palestine has never been a political tool to serve our state objectives or our selfish ends. In its heart lies Jerusalem, the cradle of Jesus and the site of Mohammad's ascension to Heaven. It is the playground of Al-Shafi'i's youth, the battlefield of Saladin, the resting place of Al-Hussein Ibn Ali, and the martyr's stairway to glory. It is the threshold which the invaders of Jordan would cross, just as Jordan is the door of liberation for Palestine.

The defense of Palestine is a defense of Jordan, as the defense of Jordan is a defense of Palestine. Such is the special relationship which determines and will continue to determine Jordanian policy, and it is this distinctive bond that the enemy has tried to undermine. Also, there were some who tried to distort it by ascribing to it spurious notions of a desire by one flank to control the other. Be that as it may, it is within the framework of this relationship that the first Palestine Congress was held twenty years ago and that the Seventeenth Session of your Council holds its meetings today in Amman.

It is this relationship, ladies and gentlemen, that prompts me to be frank with you. In order that there be no shadow of a doubt about what I intend to say, let me emphasize at the outset that no new efforts have been offered for a peaceful settlement of the Palestine question. What I intend to express is no more than our opinion based on experience and an analysis of realities, capabilities and prevailing conditions. In this, I am encouraged by the fact that you too are people of experience. I hope that my words will not be construed as a desire to interfere in your affairs. The decision is yours, and Jordan will not speak for you, although it is fully prepared to join you in facing our common destiny. If the picture I have presented is bleak, one reason is that Arab and Palestinian action has dropped from its calculations the special relationship which ties Jordan to Palestine. This has led to a deviation of effort from its proper course. If things appear difficult at the moment, it is because of the time we wasted on disagreement, conflict and recrimination—despite our sincere efforts to rectify any errors, which the general Arab situation has prevented us from doing. The enemy was left free to utilize time in his favor on the soil of Palestine. We failed to strike a balance between the justice of our cause and our physical and strategic capabilities, with a view to reducing the effects of America's unquestioned support for Israel. We allowed the interests of our individual states to overshadow our national responsibilities. At the end of the day, we arrived at the present disarray in judgement and dissipation of capabilities.

...Let us be frank about your sacred cause. It holds the same interest to us as it does to you, and its repercussions affect us as they affect you. The international position at large is one that perceives the possibility of restoring the occupied territories through a Jordanian-Palestinian formula, which requires commitments from both our parties considered by the world as necessary for the achievement of a just, balanced and peaceful settlement. If you find this option convincing—recommended further by our ties as two families linked together by a united destiny and common goals—we are prepared to go with you down this path and present the world with a joint initiative for which we will marshall support. If, on the other hand, you believe that the PLO is capable of going it alone, then we say to you "Godspeed: you have our support." In the final analysis, the decision is yours. Whatever it is, we will respect it because it emanates from your esteemed Council, which is the representative of the Palestinian people.
Ladies and gentlemen.

...If you decide to adopt the first option I presented, namely the Jordanian-Palestinian formula, allow me to share with you our understanding of how the present situation can be transcended and effective action set in motion.

The existing facts in the Palestinian, Arab and international arenas require us to adhere to Security Council Resolution 242 as a basis for a just, peaceful settlement. The principle of "territory for peace" is the landmark which should guide us in any initiative we present to the world. This principle is not a precondition, but a framework within which negotiations will be carried out. As such, it is non-negotiable. Negotiations we deem necessary within the framework of an international peace conference should revolve around the means, methods and commitments which would guarantee the achievement of the principle of "territory for peace."

The international conference would be held under the auspices of the United Nations and would be attended by the permanent members of the Security Council and by all the parties to the conflict. The Palestine Liberation Organization would attend on an equal footing with the other parties, since it is the party empowered to address the most important and momentous aspect of the Middle East crisis, namely the Palestinian dimension.

Organizing the Jordanian-Palestinian relationship is a basic responsibility of the Jordanian and Palestinian people. No other party, be it foe, friend or brother, has the right to interfere or to decide for them, since such action would constitute an encroachment on Jordan's sovereignty and a blatant interference in the right of the Palestinian people to self-determination. In addition, introducing this issue into the efforts to restore the land will provide the enemy with an opportunity to disrupt any serious attempt at rescuing it from existing occupation and creeping annexation.

In our view, these broad lines may serve as the general framework for a Jordanian-Palestinian initiative to be presented to our Arab brethren for their support, in accordance with the Rabat resolutions. Then, together with our Arab brethren, we could go out to the rest of the world and seek widening support until it is adopted by the entire community of influential states.

We do not commit you to our vision, nor do we seek to impose it on you. The decision is yours, and so is the responsibility. We offer it to you out of a sense of sharing—whether in peace or in danger, for good or for bad. We are prepared to do anything for your cause—our cause—except conclude a separate peace.

Let us remember that the world—and the Arabs—will judge you by the results of your Council's present session. We do not seek to outbid one another, for it is an attempt to draw up a joint position to which people could be rallied. We have no differences as long as Palestine is the goal on which we meet.

...The occupied territories have reached the stage where neither outbidding nor excessive tact is feasible, as they both constitute weapons we would be delivering to Israel to carry through its plans and programs to annex the land and uproot the people. The scoring of points against you began when you announced your intention to hold your Seventeenth Session in Amman. The purpose was to freeze you in place and erode your legitimacy. Some have said that holding your meeting in Amman is indicative, implying that cooperation with Amman was an act of betrayal or treason. To these we say: "Yes, holding the meeting in Amman is indicative, because the people in the occupied territories see it and the Palestinian people welcome it." Its significance lies in the probability of drawing up a Jordanian-Palestinian position, a proper position leading to correct action in the right direction. In any case, it is up to you, for the decision is yours to make.

The issue is one of faith and self-confidence. There is either the will and the determination to act or there is not. The question put to us by our people is whether we are up to the task of formulating a cohesive Jordanian-Palestinian stand that would block any attempt to infiltrate our ranks and would pave the way for unified and effective action. History will record your answer, because in it lies the last feasible chance to save the land, the people and the holy places.

## 18.  The Jordanian-Palestinian Accord, Amman, 11 February, 1985

*Bid for Joint Action*

Emanating from the spirit of the Fez Summit resolutions, approved by Arab states, and from United Nations resolutions relating to the Palestine question,

In accordance with international legitimacy, and

Deriving from a common understanding on the establishment of a special relationship between the Jordanian and Palestinian peoples,

The Government of the Hashemite Kingdom of Jordan and the Palestine Liberation Organization have agreed to move together towards the achievement of a peaceful and just settlement of the Middle East crisis and the termination of Israeli occupation of the occupied Arab territories, including Jerusalem, on the basis of the following principles:

1. Total withdrawal from the territories occupied in 1967 for comprehensive peace as established in United Nations and Security Council resolutions.

2. Right of self-determination for the Palestinian people: Palestinians will exercise their inalienable right of self-determination when Jordanians and Palestinians will be able to do so within the context of the formation of the proposed confederated Arab states of Jordan and Palestine.

3. Resolution of the problem of Palestinian refugees in accordance with United Nations resolutions.

4. Resolution of the Palestine question in all its aspects.

5. And on this basis, peace negotiations will be conducted under the auspices of an International Conference in which the five Permanent Members of the Security Council and all the parties to the conflict will participate, including the Palestine Liberation Organization, the sole legitimate representative of the Palestine people, within a joint delegation (joint Jordanian-Palestinian Delegation).

## 19. Address by King Hussein to American Enterprise Institute, Washington, DC, 2 June, 1985 [Excerpts]

I will focus my remarks on where I think we stand today on the prospects for peace in the Middle East. This focus does not mean we are unmindful or indifferent to other problems we all face in the world; the nuclear threat, the famine in Africa, the danger-filled gap between the haves and have-nots, and the other conflicts around the world which are threatening lives and freedoms. We are concerned about all of these problems but our major concern at the moment is peace in the Middle East, and that is what I wish to discuss with you.

One cannot discuss the Middle East in a vacuum, divorced from power politics or accepted norms of national conduct. I have selected the United Nations Charter for such norms, because it is a common document we have all accepted and signed. There is thus, no room to argue principles, only their applications. It has particular applicability to the Middle East because more hours have been consumed, more documents produced and more resolutions enacted, by the United Nations, on the Middle East conflict than all other conflicts and issues combined. Specially, the accepted principles for a peaceful settlement of that conflict, are contained in two of those Resolutions: 242 and 338.

You might rightly ask, do the Palestinian people, who are obviously a principal party to any settlement, since it is, indeed, essentially the problem of their lives, land and future we are attempting to solve, accept these two resolutions which are to form the basis for peace? I will tell you what I assured President Reagan. The answer is yes, the Palestinians are willing to accept United Nations Security Council Resolutions 242 and 338, and the principles they contain, as the basis for a settlement.

This is an historic breakthrough. It is the first time in the thirty-nine year history of this conflict that Palestinian leaders, with the support of their people, have been willing to accept a negotiated peaceful settlement.

The evolution of this decision over thirty-nine years has its answer in some of the events which transpired during that period. I wish to remind you of some of them, not because I care to dwell on history, but because it will help explain the import of that decision and the ramifications it has on the peace process. I will summarize them briefly. Despite what may be the views and opinions in the west, this is how the Palestinian people view this problem.

In 1917, when Britain's Balfour promised a "Homeland for the Jews in Palestine", Jewish residents formed only nine percent of the population. By 1947, waves of Jewish immigrants increased their percentage of the population to thirty-five percent. In that same year, the United Nations partitioned the country, creating a Jewish and a Palestinian state. Fifty-five percent of the land was given to the Jewish minority, most of whom came from Europe. Forty-five percent went to the Palestinian majority, all of whom were born there. There were no Jews in the Palestinian state. There were almost as many Palestinians as Jews in the Jewish state. The most economically developed portion of Palestine was included in the Jewish state. All this was done without Palestinian consent or consultation. The shock and rejection of the Palestinian should not be difficult to understand.

During the 1948 war, Israel captured more land, ending up with seventy-eight percent. In 1967, it captured the remaining twenty-two per cent. The successive loss of land and lives, and the multitude of refugees it created, caused the shock, resentment, frustration, and rejection which persisted. The Palestinians' despair was coupled with dwindling hopes that the international community would somehow redress the injustice and restore their rights and land. It did not.

There has been a change of outlook over recent years and a change of attitude over recent months, which have combined to effect the change in Palestinian policy regarding a peaceful solution. The relative futility of armed struggle and the burdens of continuing military occupation, suffering and destruction, have increased the desire for a peaceful alternative. The new trust which has developed between Jordan and the PLO after the decisions of the Arab summit at Fez, culminating in the February 1985 accord, between the government of Jordan and the PLO, and subsequent understandings, has provided the Palestinians and Jordan, for the first time, with the means by which a peaceful alternative can be realized.

In effect, the Palestinians are turning from a past, despite the injustices, to a future, which will protect their lives, restore their liberty and permit their pursuit of happiness—all of which your nation considers to be rights that are universal and inalienable.

These are the reasons why the new Palestinian position is such an historical breakthrough—and opportunity. If we fail to seize this opportunity, the alternative is fore-ordained: further shock, deeper resentment, greater frustration and sharper rejection—not only by the Palestinians, but the entire area. Failure is bound to encourage and strengthen extremism on both sides. That is why time is essential and success imperative.

The Lebanese tragedy has caused both Israelis and Palestinians to begin to re-assess the validity of their previous policies. Both are now considering, simul-taneously, the need for a negotiated peace. Each is skeptical. The Palestinians need hope. The Israelis need trust. It is important for all of us to provide the hope and trust they need. If we fail to do so, hope will surely turn to deeper despair and trust to invincible suspicion. The dangers for all of us, including them, will be much worse than before.

We believe that as a result of Palestinian acceptance of the agreed principles by which peace is to be achieved, that the stage is now set to proceed toward a peaceful settlement. We believe the process must recognize and incorporate the willingness of the Palestinians to enter that process, and that, as a principal party, they must participate fully. It is their land and lives which are a major subject of negotiation and a major object of the settlement.

The peace process should be conducted under the auspices of an international conference attended by the five permanent members of the Security Council in addition to all the parties to the conflict, including the representatives of the Palestinian people, namely the PLO. The parties to the conflict must be the parties to the peace. If the PLO is not a party to the conflict, then who is? The conference will be based on United Nations Security Council Resolutions 242 and 338, to conclude a final peace settlement which would ensure the Palestinian people their right of self-determination within the context of a Jordanian-Palestinian confederation. This confederation has been approved by the Palestine National Council in its 16th and 17th sessions. The ultimate outcome must include: The exchange of territory for peace, defined and recognized borders, and a mutual commitment to peace and security by all the parties.

I believe this is a prescription for peace which is not only just, but also attain-able. I also believe the next step should be: a dialogue between the United States and Jordanian-Palestinian representatives to complete the understandings which must be reached in order to advance the process, and prepare the ground for a negotiated comprehensive settlement under the auspices of an international conference.

I should make it clear that when I speak of a comprehensive settlement and the exchange of land for peace, I am including Syria and the Golan Heights. The principles of Security Council Resolutions 242 and 338 apply to the occupied Golan with the same force and effect as to any of the territories under occupations. Its problem must be thus addressed in the context of peace.

Ladies and gentlemen:

Throughout the history of the Middle East conflict, most of the time and rhetoric has been devoted to the negative pursuit of analyzing the problem and objecting to obstacles. There is a positive pursuit which has been neglected, namely the vision of peace. If we achieve the miracle of peace, only our imagination will limit the horizons that will be opened to the nations and peoples of the area. Development of the resources, talent and energies, in an environment of peace and friendship, will assure all people in our area, the prosperity and tranquility to make it the holy land God surely intended. This is my vision.

This is my goal. It should be a powerful incentive for us all to redouble our efforts to achieve this goal.

Finally, the role of the United States is essential to the success of our peace efforts. America's ideals and moral leadership are being challenged and America's interests and reputation are at issue.

For our part—and I speak for both my own people and the representatives of the Palestinian people—we want peace. We are ready to pursue it now as earnestly and sincerely as is humanly possible. It is our hope and goal to turn our vision into a reality for all—Jews and Arabs alike. We want you as our partners in this sacred mission for peace. Let us attain our goal. Let us close the door on the bitter memories of the past, and let us look to the future—that after all, is the promise of peace. Thank you.

## 20.  Arab Summit League, Final Communique, Casablanca, 9 August, 1985 [Excerpts]

Within the framework of this discussion of the various developments, which the Palestinian issue is going through, the conference heard a detailed explanation from his Majesty King Hussein of the Hashemite Kingdom of Jordan, and brother Yasser Arafat, chairman of the Palestine Liberation Organization, regarding the Jordanian-Palestinian agreement which was signed in Amman on 11 February, 1985. The conference recorded with full appreciation the detailed explanation submitted by His Majesty King Hussein and brother Yasser Arafat about the compatibility between the Jordanian-Palestinian action plan and the Fez plan, and considers it an action plan for implementing the Arab peace plan for the realization of a peaceful, just and comprehensive settlement guaranteeing the withdrawal of the Israeli occupation forces from all the occupied Arab territories, at the forefront of which is Holy Jerusalem, and the regaining of the firm national rights of the Palestinian Arab people. And after dealing with this issue in an extensive study, from all aspects, the conference confirms the need to continue the collective Arab adherence to the spirit, principles and resolutions of the Fez summit conference.

The conference confirms its previous resolutions concerning the Palestine problem and its backing and support for the PLO in its capacity as sole legitimate representative of the Palestinian Arab people, and its support for its efforts aimed at securing the firm national rights of the Palestinian people. It also confirms the right of the Palestinian people to the independence of its national decision and not to allow any side to interfere in its internal affairs. The conference considers the holding of an international conference within the framework of the UN facilitates the achievement of peace in the Arab region, with the presence and participation of the USSR, the United States and other permanent members of the Security Council and with the presence and participation of the PLO, the sole legitimate representative of the Palestinian people alongside the other concerned parties.

The conference salutes the steadfastness of the Palestinian Arab people in the occupied Arab areas and their growing struggle against the forces of Israeli occupation, and the conference affirms its commitment to supporting this stead-fastness and its development to confront the expansionist plans which seek to Judaize Palestinian territory and render the sons of the Palestinian people homeless.

The conference affirms its condemnation of the terrorist and racist practices of the Israeli occupation authorities in occupied Arab and Palestinian territories, and it appeals to world public opinion to support the Palestinian and Arab people in their resistance to these practices which contradict international laws, and human rights. It also appeals to the world community to take practical measures to stand in the way of the Zionist practices.

It affirms previous commitments to giving material, political and media support for the PLO—the sole legitimate representative of the Palestinian people and leader of their struggle to recover their usurped rights. Regarding the suffering endured by the Palestinian camps after the Israeli invasion of Lebanon in 1982 and the massacres and slaughters that ensued; in order to guard against the dangers of displacement and destitution which threatened the Palestinian existence in those camps; and in order to ensure the safety of this existence and the rights of the Palestinian people to work and movement and to strengthen Lebanese-Palestinian fraternal ties, the conference calls on the Lebanese Government and the PLO to cooperate and coordinate between them in whatever concerns Palestinian affairs and protects the Palestinian camps in Lebanon, in accordance with the agreements concluded between them.

## 21.   Address by King Hussein to the 40th Session of the United Nations General Assembly, New York, 27 September, 1985 [Excerpts]

Mr. President, ladies and gentlemen, you will excuse me if I confine my speech to the Middle East, given the fact that Jordan lies in the heart of the Middle East and is directly affected by its events. Today there is a grinding war in the Middle East between Iraq and Iran. This war has entered its 6th year and has lost every justification and sense of continuity. All international attempts have so far failed to extinguish its fire or influence the Iranian authorities and make them respond to peace calls that Iraq is continuing to make so that the two neighboring countries can live in peace, safety, and stability. My country, which stands by Iraq in defending itself and its nation and supports its call for resolving the dispute by peaceful means, calls upon the Iranian leadership to respond to peace efforts and enter into peaceful negotiations with fraternal Iraq and end this tragedy once and for all.

As for the second explosive issue in the Middle East, it is the Arab-Israel dispute or the Palestine question. This is the fourth time I have spoken to this esteemed body on this issue. In my first speech in 1960 I drew attention to the inherent dangers in the international community's continued negligence of the legitimate right of the Palestinians to live a decent life. Seven years later, and following the 1967 war, I warned that the peace in the Middle East would not be realized unless it was combined with justice. In 1979 I criticized the stands of those who continued to refuse to recognize the Palestinians as a people just like other peoples who resided in a well-defined territory, that is, Palestine, for many continuous centuries.

Today, a quarter of a century after I spoke for the first time in the United Nations, the Palestinian rights of self-determination, a decent human living, justice, and free life in the fatherland still constitute the Palestinian problem. The absence of these rights continues to constitute the crux of the Middle East dispute. The Arab states and the Palestinian people are continuing to approach the United Nations to urge it to shoulder its responsibility in accordance with its charter and in implementation of its resolutions.

We approach the United Nations because it is the forum on which the Palestinian question was born as the Palestine partition resolution was adopted and because the Palestinian question and the United Nations have been linked from the very beginning. Both were influenced by the international trends of the world. They were influenced by the changes in the spheres of influence and the superpower rivalry. They were also affected by the process of liquidating colonialism and the appearance of national currents in developing states. No other issue presented to the United Nations attracted greater attention than the

Palestinian question. No other issue was able to place the United Nations before its responsibilities and challenged UN ability to adhere to its declared objectives more than the Palestine question.

The United Nations has issued more resolutions on the Palestine question than on any other world issue. The Palestine question and the United Nations are twins. They were conceived in the womb of war and born together. They suffered and grew up together in this world.

Nobody should think that we are pleased with this linkage. Our hope is to see it end with a just, lasting, and comprehensive solution to the Palestine question and its concomitants in accordance with the UN Charter and in implementation of the UN resolutions, especially four resolutions that constitute a balanced basis for any just and peaceful settlement: Resolution 181 of 1947, which provides for the partition of Palestine; Resolution 194 of 1948 concerning the resolution of the Palestinian refugee problem; Security Council Resolution 242 of 1967, which calls on Israel to withdraw from the occupied Arab territories and affirms the right of every state to live in peace within secure and recognized boundaries; and Security Council Resolution 338 of 1973, which calls for negotiations among the disputing parties under appropriate supervision.

The successive issuance of these and other similar resolutions on the same question for 4 decades and the outbreak of five wars in the same period because of this problem clearly point to the complications that have been created by some member-states by disregarding the principles of the United Nations and maintaining the problem with its tension, thereby threatening regional stability and world security.

I am telling you no secret, ladies and gentlemen, if I say that my country, which is part of the Arab community and a member that is trying hard to see that confidence in this world organization is not shaken, has suffered and is still suffering a great deal from the non-implementation of the resolutions concerning the Palestine question. I do not mean by these remarks to draw the curtain on the UN role, but to call for redoubled efforts and greater determination to achieve the objectives of the United Nations.

The late US President Eisenhower said only a short time after the outbreak of the Suez war in 1956: We are approaching a decisive moment. We either admit the United Nations' failure to restore peace to the region or call for renewed UN efforts with greater momentum to ensure Israeli withdrawal. If the United Nations does not do anything and remains silent on its successive resolutions concerning the withdrawal of the invasion forces, this means that it is admitting its own failure. In such a case, its failure would be tantamount to a blow to UN authority and influence in the world and to the hopes that mankind has pinned on it as an instrument for achieving peace and justice. The United Nations is at such a crossroads and, in my opinion, the future of this organization will be decided by its success or failure in its efforts to achieve world peace, especially in the Middle East.

Mr. President, friends, and colleagues, if the Palestine question and the United Nations have been linked to one another for 4 decades, the Jordanian and Palestinian peoples have been linked to one another by a common history and destiny for centuries. Ever since the first signs of the Palestinian problem after World War I, Jordan has been connected and affected by this question and involved with the Palestinian people. When the Palestine question emerged as an international problem, the United Nations assumed the responsibility of tackling this issue. Ever since, Jordan, with its distinctive relationship with the Palestinian people, has been coordinating and cooperating with the United Nations alongside its Arab and Muslim brothers in the hope of solving this problem. On this basis my country has adopted over the past 40 years a firm policy based on positive cooperation with UN efforts and endeavors, provided that these efforts are exerted for the sake of a just peace as defined by the Charter and principles of the United Nations.

When the 1967 war started, as is known, I personally participated in issuing Security Council Resolution 242. Our understanding was that just and permanent peace in the Middle East depends entirely on Israeli withdrawal. This conviction was reinforced through our contacts with many countries concerned, including the United States. This conviction was also reinforced by the fact that the principle of withdrawal cannot be divided and aggression should not be awarded.

When our efforts and demands failed to make Israel accept withdrawal from the occupied Arab territory in exchange for peace, this failure led to the outbreak of the 1973 war. The Security Council adopted Resolution 338, which resulted in a cease-fire, and asserted the need to implement Resolution 242. We supported the new Security Council resolution and participated in the Geneva peace conference.

The General Assembly then recognized the PLO as the legitimate representative of the Palestinian people. With this decision, the General Assembly opened the door for the Palestinian people, through their legitimate representative, to take part in the peace process. The Palestinian people, the first party to the conflict, should be the first party to peace.

In September, 1982 the Arabs reiterated their unanimous trend toward peace when, in the Arab summit conference held in Fez, Morocco, they adopted the Arab peace plan which the PLO helped formulate and agreed upon. The Arab group continued its activities in this regard through a seven-member Arab committee which was authorized to explain this plan to the five Security Council permanent members, hoping to revitalize peace efforts. His Majesty Moroccan King Hassan II led this committee on its visit to the United States and Washington, and I led the committee on its visits to the four other capitals. These capitals, together with the various world circles, expressed satisfaction over the Arab trend. However, the peace process remained inactive. Taking into consideration a number of realistic points, we found out that the peaceful endeavors needed a formula that would open the way for PLO participation in the peace process.

Accordingly, we held negotiations with the PLO which resulted on 11 February in an agreement organizing joint political action between the Jordanian Government and the PLO and providing a sort of mechanism for the Arab peace plan. It was part of joint Arab action and a link in Arab moves. This agreement called for implementing the UN resolutions on the Palestine question through an international conference in which the five permanent UN Security Council member-states would take part along with the other parties to the dispute.

Upon signing the agreement, Jordan and the PLO contacted a number of major capitals with the aim of reviving the peace process. Due to the special relationship between the United States and Israel, which is the side to the dispute that has hitherto been hindering peace efforts, Jordan made intensive efforts in Washington in the hope that the United States would shoulder its responsibilities as a superpower that cares about world peace, supports human rights, and is established on faith in freedom and the right of self-determination for peoples, so that it might use its weight and employ its influence and efforts along with the efforts and influence of the many other states that supported this agreement. This would lead to an international effort that would realize stability, peace, and prosperity for all peoples of the region and the world.

We are ready to negotiate with Israel under suitable, acceptable supervision, directly and as soon as possible, in accordance with Security Council Resolutions 242 and 338. These negotiations must lead to implementing Security Council Resolution 242 and solving all aspects of the Palestine question.

Jordan's stand is that suitable and acceptable supervision is represented in an international conference that the UN Secretary-General would call. The Secretary-General would invite to the conference the five permanent members of the Security Council and all sides to the dispute with the aim of reaching a comprehensive, just, and permanent peace in the Middle East.

My country, which believes that the Palestine question and the Middle East crisis are within the responsibility of the United Nations and of those states that have special interests in this issue, is of the view that any consultations between the United States and the USSR concerning the Middle East crisis are a necessary, positive element. Hence, my country is looking forward hopefully to the forthcoming meeting between the two leaders, Ronald Reagan and Mikhail Gorbachev, wishing their meeting complete success.

Friends and colleagues, we Arabs believe in peace just as we believe in justice; to us, peace is one of our sacred beliefs. It is our greeting in our prayers. In our spiritual concept, peace is the greetings of those in Paradise, as the Holy Koran verses say, Peace is so high in our souls that it becomes one of God's attributes. Peace signifies justice. Peace and justice mean a single thing.

With this spirit, the Arabs have moved toward peace since the June war in 1967, but so far without success. This is because, since its triumph in that war, Israel has put greed for expansion ahead of peace. Israel confiscated Arab

Jerusalem and the Syrian Golan, seized more than half the West Bank, and distributed settlements in all the occupied Arab territory. Israeli Government leaders openly announced their intentions not to relinquish this territory and adopted extreme policies that contribute to achieving this aggressive goal and obstruct peace efforts.

If Israel continues its opposition to peace trends by placing obstacles to these trends or if it can negatively affect the stands of the United States or others, this means that hopes for achieving a peaceful settlement of the Middle East crisis will collapse. This also means that Israel and any country that supports it in this negative course will be responsible for the opportunity that will be lost, for the escalation of extremism, and for other consequences that may result. The absence of justice and determination to prevent it will open the door for extremist parties to exploit such a situation in order to practice violence against defenseless people.

I announce before you Jordan's firm stand in condemning terrorism of any kind and from any source. Thus, I assert the decision adopted by the Arab leaders in the summit conference held in Casablanca last month. We also reject deceptive attempts by some parties to put terrorism on an equal footing with national liberation movements and people's right to resist occupation...

Much has been said about the city of holy Jerusalem being the main obstacle to peace. I can say that Jerusalem is the key to peace and the gate through which the glimmer of peace will emerge to hearten all inhabitants of the region. Jerusalem, which is the homeland of believers of the unity of God, will certainly bring God's sons together around peace, man's noblest goal. One of the prophets of the Jews, Christians, and Muslims went astray for 40 years, and 40 years after stumbling in the deserts of prejudice, hatred, and dispute, I hope that the desired future will be realized so that Palestinians and Jews can live in harmony in the land of peace, in hope instead of fear, in confidence instead of doubt, in accord instead of bitterness, and in understanding instead of enmity...

Ladies and gentlemen, the United Nations has a unique historic opportunity to bring about a just and comprehensive peace in the Middle East. We should not allow that opportunity to slip from our hands or be added to the other lost opportunities. We fear that without your effort and support the young flower of peace will wither before blooming. Let us mobilize our energies to wage the war of peace. Let us consider the future of generations the only firm element in our moves. Belief in it is the base for the United Nations; the United Nations is the base for peace; peace is the base for progress and prosperity.

## 22. Syrian-Jordanian Joint Communique, Damascus, 13 November, 1985 [Excerpts]

*The following is a communique issued at the end of Jordanian Prime Minister Zaid al-Rifai's visit to Syria.*

After a review of the situation in the region and the arena of the Arab-Israeli struggle, there was agreement, particularly on the following:

1. The need to strengthen joint Arab action in various fields in order to realize just, comprehensive, and permanent peace and confront the Israeli aggression.

2. Stemming from the two sides' conviction that the Palestinian cause is the central pan-Arab cause, they emphasized their rejection of partial and separate solutions as well as direct negotiations with Israel. They also emphasized that just, comprehensive, and permanent peace cannot be realized except by convening an international conference under UN auspices to be attended by all parties concerned and with the participation of the Soviet Union and the United States.

3. The two sides stressed that the political moves necessitate continuing serious efforts to build the Arab nation's strength and defense capability with the aim of realizing its aims of liberating the territories and restoring the rights.

## 23. Address by King Hussein on Middle East Peace, Amman, 19 February, 1986 [Excerpts]

*The following speech was delivered following the breakdown of the joint Jordanian-Palestinian peace initiative.*

We, in Jordan, having refused from the beginning to negotiate on behalf of the Palestinians, will neither act separately nor in lieu of anybody in Middle East peace negotiations.

Jordan will work as a member of the Arab League, in compliance with its resolutions, to support the PLO within our capabilities, and in compliance with the requirements of our national security for the sake of Palestine and the Arab East.

Further contacts between Jordan and the PLO ceased except within the framework of the Joint Committee for the Steadfastness of the Occupied Territories. The PLO became consumed by its internal differences, which resulted in the departure of the Palestinian leadership led by Arafat from Tripoli, Lebanon on 20 January, 1983. This was followed by attempts at reconciliation between the parties of the Palestinian coalition within the PLO, and between the PLO and other Arab states. It was then that the problem of convening the seventeenth PNC appeared, particularly the question of where to hold that meeting.

In early September, 1984, a member of the Palestinian leadership met with me and conveyed to me that the PLO hoped to convene the PNC in Amman. I welcomed their request.

On 27 September, 1984, I received Mr. Arafat, accompanied by other members of the PLO leadership, at al-Nadwah Palace in Amman. During our meeting, Mr. Arafat expressed the wish of the Palestinian leadership to convene the PNC in Amman. We officially notified him that Jordan welcomed such a convening.

On 22 November, 1984, I opened the seventeenth session of the PNC by delivering a speech which contained our assessment of prevailing Palestinian conditions and our conclusion that we needed to move politically outside the status quo of no peace-no war, which only helped to advance expansionist Zionist designs and posed serious dangers to the Palestinian issue, the Palestinian people, and Palestinian land, as well as a consequent threat to Jordan's national security. We proposed to the PNC members our view of future cooperation, should the PLO decide to work with Jordan to reach a joint Jordanian-Palestinian formula, and I said the following:

> Let us be frank about your sacred cause. It holds the same interest for us as it does for you and its repercussions affect us as they affect you. The international position at large is one that perceives the possibility of restoring the occupied territories through a Jordanian-Palestinian formula. This requires commitments from both parties, which the world deems necessary for the achievement of a just, balanced, and peaceful settlement. If you find this option convincing— recommended further by our ties as two families linked together by a united destiny and common goals—we are prepared to go with you along this path and present the world with a joint initiative for which we marshal support. If, on the other hand, you believe that the PLO is capable of going it alone, then we say to you: Godspeed, you have our support. In the final analysis, the decision is yours. Whatever it is, we will respect it because it emanates from your esteemed council, which is the representative of the Palestinian people.

I also pointed out in that speech the general guidelines which would constitute the framework for our proposed initiative. These were:

1. Security Council Resolution 242, of which I said:

> The existing facts in the Palestinian, Arab, and international arenas require us to adhere to Security Council Resolution 242 as a basis for a just and peaceful settlement. The principle of territory for peace is the landmark which should guide us in any initiative we present to the world. This principle is not a precondition but a framework within which negotiations will be carried out. As such, it is non-negotiable. Negotiations we deem necessary within the framework of an international peace conference should revolve around the means, methods, and commitments which would guarantee the achievement of the principle of territory for peace.

2. The international conference, of which I said:
   The international conference would be held under the auspices of the United Nations and would be attended by the permanent members of the Security Council and by all the parties involved in the conflict. The PLO would attend on an equal footing with the other parties, since it is the party empowered to address the most important and momentous aspect of the Middle East crisis, namely, the Palestinian dimension.
3. A formula defining the Jordanian-Palestinian relationship, of which I said:
   Organizing the Jordanian-Palestinian relationship is a basic responsibility of the Jordanian and Palestinian people. No other party has the right to interfere or decide for them.

Brothers and sisters, the PNC ended its meetings in Amman having provided an opportunity for our brothers in the occupied territories to view its deliberations on issues which bore directly on their existence and future. Their hopes were revived, and delegations representing them began to arrive in Amman, urging us and the Palestinian leadership to reach a common formula which could rally Arab and international support behind it. We left the Palestinian leadership to choose the path it wished to follow.

In January, 1985, we received the reply that the PLO Executive Committee had chosen to work with us on our proposal for joint political action. We started our consultations with Arafat's envoys on the third general outline—the Jordanian-Palestinian formula—since this formula constituted the base from which we were to move on the Arab and international arenas to convene an international peace conference.

In February, 1985, Arafat, accompanied by other members of the Palestinian leadership, arrived in Amman. An expanded meeting was held in al-Nadwah Palace, which was concluded by the signing of the Jordanian-Palestinian agreement, known as the 11 February Accord. This accord incorporated the following principles...*

Our assessment, which was also shared by the PLO, was that the accord constituted the beginning of collective Arab action to be followed by rallying the international community, which had become a mere spectator since the signing of the Camp David Accords and which had only paid polite lip service since the initiation of the Arab Fez Peace Plan.

We envisaged the Jordanian-Palestinian accord as one of the links in the chain of collective Arab efforts, providing a mechanism for the Arab Peace Plan while paving the path for facilitating the PLO to engage itself in the international effort aimed at establishing a just, permanent, and comprehensive peace.

---

* For the text of the accord, see above

As soon as the accord was announced, the wide international interest in the cause of peace in the Middle East reemerged after a period of democracy. More light was shed on the Arab peace principles, which became a central theme of discussion. The accord became the focal point of discussion both regionally and internationally. In other words, life was again breathed into the peace efforts after they were nearly buried in the grave of no peace-no war. The Palestinian people's hopes of salvation, particularly those under occupation, were revived.

The accord became a mover for the peace process because of the principles it contained. These were:

1. The accord's affirmation of a peaceful resolution to the conflict in accordance with the UN Charter;

2. The accord's conformity with the principles of the Arab Peace Plan, derived from United Nations resolutions concerning the Arab-Israeli conflict in general and the Palestinian problem in particular;

3. The agreement between Jordan and the PLO, the sole legitimate representative of the Palestinian people, to form a confederation between Jordan and Palestine.

This last item, while it reflects the objective considerations which require close institutional links between Jordan and a free Palestine to the mutual benefit of their peoples and the Arab nation at large, provides the key, or mechanism, to the peace process, for two main reasons.

First, it justifies PLO participation in the proposed international conference within a joint Jordanian-Palestinian delegation. Since confederation is the ultimate objective, why not have the two parties concerned assume one of the confederation's functions before it is established as a reality on the ground, particularly since this function allows for the participation of the PLO in the international conference, which in the past decade has posed one of the most difficult obstacles in convening an international peace conference?

Second, it lays the foundations for a responsible role for the PLO in realizing and safeguarding a just settlement through its links with Jordan, the sovereign state which enjoys credible international standing due to its serious and sincere efforts to achieve peace.

Dear brethren, after signing the 11 February accord and the agreement of the PLO Executive Committee, which was empowered by the PNC to arrive at a joint formula with Jordan, we embarked with the Palestinian leadership upon drawing up a plan for our proposed action. Two objectives were defined for this purpose:

1. To rally international support for the convening of an international peace conference, to be attended by the five permanent members of the Security Council and all parties involved in the conflict. This conference would be convened under the auspices of the United Nations and called for by the UN Secretary-General.

2. To ensure that an invitation will be extended to the PLO, representing the Palestinian people, to attend the conference within a joint Jordanian-Palestinian delegation.

Before embarking on our joint action, we needed to ascertain the position of the states concerned regarding the above-mentioned objectives. Our inquiries indicated the need for us to move on four fronts:

1. The Arab world, so that Arab positions could be shifted from making public statements to marshaling, coordinating, and organizing the elements of Arab potential to serve this cause through continuous and conscientious efforts. Our dialogue with our Arab brothers was conducted through bilateral contacts as well as collectively when Arafat and I jointly explained the dimensions, motives, foundations, and objectives of the 11 February Accord at the Casablanca Arab summit conference in August, 1985.

2. On the international front, in order to stimulate the interest of peace in the Middle East by reiterating the seriousness of our undertaking and the credibility of its expected results. Except for the two superpowers, which had their own calculations, our joint effort on the international arena was well received and encouraged, whether by the UN Secretary-General, regional organizations like the EEC, or the other three permanent members of the Security Council. Our dialogue with many states was achieved through bilateral contacts, either separately by the government of the Hashimite Kingdom of Jordan and the PLO, or through joint Jordanian-Palestinian delegations which visited Beijing, Paris, the Vatican, and Rome when Italy was the president of the European community. We had also planned for a joint delegation to visit London in October, 1985.

3. The Soviet Union, in an attempt to change its position regarding the international conference, since it held the position that only the two superpowers should participate in the conference and not all the five permanent members of the Security Council. There was also the issue of Palestinian representation at the conference in accordance with the Jordanian-Palestinian accord, to which the Soviet Union objected. Several contacts were made with Soviet officials aimed at explaining how the Jordanian-Palestinian accord could be employed to revitalize the peace process and requesting the Soviet Union to receive a joint Jordanian-Palestinian delegation in Moscow. However, the Soviet Union did not change its position despite our repeated attempts. On 9 November, 1985, in a meeting held at al-Nadwah Palace, we reiterated our firm position to hold an international conference.

4. The United States, which is close to the Israeli position. A special effort was therefore needed with the US side since, without the participation of Israel, the party in occupation of Arab territories, there could be no international conference. And since there were no direct channels of communications between the United States and the PLO, Jordan undertook the responsibility of dialogue with the United States, but in consultation with the Palestinian leadership. When we first briefed US officials on the accord and explained it to them, it became evident that we were facing a problem with the Americans on two points: the principle of convening an international conference, and the PLO's participation in this

conference as a representative of the Palestinian people. It also became evident that the US position on these two objectives to a large degree reflected the Israeli position. It was clear that our dialogue with the United States would require a major and concerted effort. In the face of these realities and facts, we began our difficult endeavor, which lasted one year and to which I referred earlier in my speech as the second phase of our coordination with the PLO leadership. This was the last chapter of our diplomatic efforts to reach a comprehensive, just, and permanent peace.

Brothers and sisters, in this last part of my speech I shall describe to you the important features of every phase of our efforts during this last year. In order to clarify the picture for you, a reference to three facts must first be made.

1. Every round of talks between us and the US administration was always preceded by consultation with the Palestinian leadership followed by further briefing and reassessment with that leadership.

2. Our discussions with the US administration in every round of talks dealt with two separate issues; the issue of the international peace conference, and the issue of Palestinian representation through the PLO.

3. When we started these discussions with the US administration in February, 1985, there was already another topic under discussion relating to Jordan's request to purchase US arms. This issue was started at the end of the Carter presidency, and continued through the Reagan presidency. Jordan adopted a very definite policy regarding this when we started our dialogue to revive the peace process. This position stipulated that there should be no linkage between the US arms deal to Jordan—a bilateral issue—and the peace effort, which has an international dimension.

Throughout all our meetings with US officials, we focused on two issues, as I mentioned earlier. However, during the period between the signing of the Jordanian-Palestinian accord and September, 1985, we concentrated our attention on the issue of Palestinian representation and the means to ensure the participation of the PLO in an international conference. I shall now review chronologically the stages pertaining to this issue.

We had agreed with the PLO leadership from the outset on the need to emphasize the concept of Jordanian-Palestinian partnership while dealing with the Palestinian dimension on the background of the larger Arab-Israeli conflict. On this basis, joint delegations visited world capitals, as I mentioned earlier. They also planned to visit Moscow and Washington. Moscow declined to receive the joint delegation, in keeping with the Soviet Union's position vis-a-vis the 11 February Accord. Washington, however, while not refusing the accord, did not endorse all its principles. Therefore, the need to concentrate on the United States became apparent to us, just as the need to concentrate on the Soviet Union became apparent.

We agreed with the Palestinian leadership on the following procedures for joint action:

1. We asked the US administration to start a dialogue with a joint Jordanian-Palestinian delegation composed of Jordanian government officials and members chosen by the PLO.

2. After this dialogue, the PLO would declare its acceptance of UN Security Council Resolutions 242 and 338.

3. If this took place, the United States would no longer be bound by its previous position not to conduct any talks with the PLO before the latter's acceptance of the two pertinent Security Council resolutions. Thus, the United States would recognize the PLO, a meeting between US officials and members of the PLO could be held in Washington to discuss the issue of a peaceful settlement, and relations between them would be normalized.

4. As a result of the normalization of US-Palestinian relations, a major political obstacle blocking the Arab Peace Plan, which gave an important role to the PLO, would have been removed. Arab efforts could then be channeled to pursue the efforts with the United States and other countries to convene an international peace conference.

After agreeing on this procedure with the Palestinian leadership, we accordingly contacted officials in the US administration at the end of March, 1985 and presented them with the idea of meeting a joint delegation in preparation for the next two steps which would follow as a result of the meeting.

In early April, 1985, we received the US reply which, in principle, accepted this proposal, provided that the Palestinian members of the joint delegation were not leading members of the PLO or any fida'iyyin organization.

We consulted with the Palestinian leadership, which provided us with the names of three candidates. The Americans refused them because they did not meet their criteria and asked that we provide them with the names of others who did.

In May, 1985, we met with the US Secretary of State in Qaba, who reiterated the administration's position regarding the subject of the names. However, he did not exclude those who were members of the PNC.

The US side expressed its government's doubts about the PLO's intentions and its government's fears that if the suggested meeting were to take place between a US official and a joint Jordanian-Palestinian delegation, a meeting after that would not be followed by the PLO's acceptance of Security Council Resolutions 242 and 338, and the PLO would obtain a political weapon as a result of its member's meeting with an American official. The US government would then be left to face criticism and political troubles resulting from this in the US arena. Thus, the serious political efforts would end at that point.

Our prime minister conveyed this recent US stand to Yasser Arafat in a meeting held at the Prime Ministry on 18 May, 1985. At that time, we were preparing for a visit to Washington. In order to remove the US fears, the prime minister agreed with Yasser Arafat on the text of a press statement which we would make at the end of our talks with the US president.

The statement which I made at the White House garden on 29 May, 1985 says: I also asserted to President Reagan that, on the basis of the Jordanian agreement with the PLO signed on 11 February, as a result of the talks which I recently held with the PLO, and in view of our sincere desire to achieve peace, we are determined to negotiate to achieve a peaceful settlement within the framework of an international conference on the basis of the related UN resolutions, including Security Council Resolutions 242 and 338.

The US officials affirmed, during my talks in Washington, their position regarding Palestinian participation in the joint delegation. They limited the number to four: two from the occupied territories and two from outside. They requested that we provide them with these names in advance and as soon as possible so that the US administration could make its decision at the appropriate time.

Upon our return to Amman in June, 1985, we conveyed to the Palestinian leadership our discussions in Washington. They, in turn, accepted this proposal and promised to provide us with the names of the candidates as soon as possible. We waited until 11 July, 1985, when some names were provided to us. We were then told that a meeting of the PLO Executive Committee and the Fateh Central Committee had discussed this subject and had agreed upon the names of the candidates.

On 12 July, 1985, we relayed a list of seven names to the US administration and waited for the administration to inform us of its approval of four of the names on that list. We agreed that no public announcement should be made on this issue. But a few days later, we were surprised when the world press began to discuss those names. Suddenly the issue turned into a US political issue. The press began to discuss it and the Zionist lobby activated influential political institutions in opposition to it, culminating in pressure on the US administration to justify, defend, and finally retract its position. As a result, we received American approval of only two names from the list, instead of four: one from the West Bank and the other from the Gaza Strip. After inquiries, we were told by the US officials that the administration was still not sure that the PLO would fulfill the second phase of the agreed scenario, namely, to accept Security Council Resolutions 242 and 338.

On 15 August, 1985, a meeting was held at our prime minister's residence in Amman attended by the prime minister, the chief of the Royal Hashimite Court, the minister of the court, and the foreign minister from the Jordanian side, and Yasser Arafat, accompanied by Khalil al-Wazir, 'Abd al-Razzaq al-Yahya, and Muhammad Milham from the Palestinian side. During that meeting, the prime minister again asked Arafat whether he was clear on the method of proceeding, particularly with regard to the second phase—PLO readiness to accept Security Council Resolutions 242 and 338. Arafat reaffirmed his acceptance of all steps and arrangements agreed upon between us, including the PLO's readiness to accept the above mentioned resolutions.

In light of Arafat's reply, we informed the US administration that the suspicions it had on this subject were not justified and that we were awaiting their positive reply concerning the date of the meeting between US officials and a joint Jordanian-Palestinian delegation.

On 7 September, 1985, we received the US reply, which said that it was not possible to hold the meeting, thus terminating this scenario before the first step, originally expected in June, was taken. This came at the time we were preparing for a visit to New York, to celebrate the fortieth anniversary of the United Nations, and Washington, to discuss bilateral issues and the peace process with the US administration.

Assessment of the situation prior to the visit led us to believe that we could pursue our dialogue with the United States by concentrating this time on the second phase of the process, the international conference, since not much progress had been achieved on the issue of Palestinian representation. Our reading of the US position led us to believe that further discussions could take place on that other issue, which was last discussed in May, 1985. I mentioned earlier that from the beginning, our dialogue with the Americans had dealt with two issues separately: Palestinian representation and the international conference, with emphasis on the subject of Palestinian representation.

I will now turn to our efforts on the second issue, the convening of an international conference.

In May, 1985, in our discussions with the US administration in Washington, we raised the issue of convening such a conference because we considered it to be the venue for all parties concerned to meet, including the PLO. The US position was a flat rejection of an international conference. Instead, the United States proposed that after the PLO was brought into the peace talks, a meeting should be set up between Israel and a joint Jordanian-Palestinian delegation, under the auspices of the United States, to be held in a US city. Upon learning this, we decided to cut our visit short and reaffirmed to them our definite and unequivocal rejection of seeking a unilateral approach similar to that of Camp David in the negotiations.

The US administration then changed its position and proposed that the talks could be held at the United Nations in Geneva. Once again, we informed the US administration that we rejected this proposal, like the one before it, as we did not see that the problem was one of where the talks should be held. We reiterated that Jordan's unwavering position was that it sought to reach a comprehensive settlement through the convening of an international conference attended by all the parties to the conflict, including the permanent members of the Security Council.

As a result, the US administration reconsidered its proposal and promised to ponder seriously the issue of convening an international conference. We accepted this and continued our discussions concerning the issue of Palestinian representation.

During talks in Washington in October, 1985, we again raised the issue of an international conference after having proposed it to the administration prior to our departure for the United States. Meetings were held between Jordanian and US officials in Washington. The United States submitted a proposal concerning the international conference, which, after careful examination, seemed to suggest a conference in name only. We, on the other hand, insisted that the conference should have clear powers.

Among the various US suggestions was the inclusion of the Soviet Union in the conference only after it restored diplomatic relations with Israel, because this was an Israeli condition. We argued for the rejection of this approach for the following reasons:

1. An international conference without the participation of the Soviet Union would be a flawed conference.

2. If the reason to exclude the Soviet Union from the conference was that it had not diplomatic relations with Israel, which is a party to the conflict, the United States on its part does not recognize the PLO, which is equally a party to the conflict. Thus, in this regard, the Soviet Union and the United States were in the same position.

3. It would be futile to plan seriously to convene an international peace conference if any party had the right to place conditions on who could attend. This applies to the five permanent members of the Security Council as well as the parties involved in the conflict. Therefore, it was imperative that an invitation be extended to Syria, the PLO, and the Soviet Union to attend the conference if the peace process was to continue and the efforts for a just and comprehensive peace were to produce fruitful results.

After extensive discussions lasting three days, the United States accepted the following points which we proposed:

1. The UN Secretary-General would issue invitations to an international conference under UN auspices.

2. Invitations to attend the conference would be issued to the permanent members of the Security Council, including the Soviet Union, in addition to the parties involved in the conflict.

3. Security Council Resolutions 242 and 338 would form the basis for the international conference.

4. The Americans held to their position of requiring acceptance by the PLO of Security Council Resolutions 242 and 338, since these formed the basis for the convening of the international conference. We agreed to this understanding on the basis that Arafat had himself agreed to this last August.

We continued our intensive discussions with the US administration concerning the powers of the conference and we insisted that it should not be a conference in name only but rather that it should be one that was effective and had a clear mandate. Despite prolonged discussions, we did not reach a final understanding with the US administration regarding this issue. We agreed to continue our discussions on this central point, and considered that what we had agreed upon constituted a basis from which to proceed. While we were still in Washington, the cycle of terrorism and counterterrorism began with the Larnaca incident, followed by the Israeli raid on the PLO headquarters in Tunis. This had a negative effect on the peace process, and our efforts were once again jeopardized by fears and suspicions.

Upon our return to Amman in October, 1985, we informed the Palestinian leadership of what we had accomplished during our talks in Washington. We informed them that the PLO would be required to accept Security Council Resolutions 242 and 338 in order to be invited to the international conference, to accept the principle of participating in negotiations with the government of Israel as part of a joint Jordanian-Palestinian delegation within the context of the international conference which would be convened to establish a comprehensive settlement, and to renounce terrorism. We also informed the Palestinian leadership that our discussions with the US administration regarding the question of the mandate of the conference were still inconclusive, and that further discussions would follow. We made it clear to the Palestinian leadership that a written statement of acceptance was needed from them, while leaving them to choose the appropriate time to announce that approval. The written acceptance was needed so that we could encourage the US administration to proceed earnestly to convene an international conference and to reassure them that the PLO was anxious to participate in the peace process. We had already made clear to the US administration that Jordan would not attend the conference unless invitations were extended to the PLO, sister Syria, and all other parties involved in the conflict, because we are after a comprehensive peace.

We also promised the Palestinian leadership that their acceptance would be kept confidential and shown only to the concerned US officials until they themselves decided to announce it.

On 7 November, 1985, after talks with President Husni Mubarak, Yasser Arafat issued a statement in Cairo denouncing terrorism in all its forms, irrespective of its source. The PLO Executive Committee then held a meeting in Baghdad, and as we were not officially notified of its decisions, we awaited Arafat's visit to Amman to hear from him, once again, the final position of the PLO on Security Council Resolution 242.

Meanwhile, I made a private visit to London on 7 January, 1986 for medical reasons. While I was there, the [US] Assistant Secretary of State for Near Eastern Affairs [Richard Murphy] arrived in London with a US delegation. He requested to see me to continue our discussions regarding the issue of the international conference. We held two rounds of talks in London, the first attended by the prime minister and the chief of the Royal Court on 18 January, and the second on 20 January, attended by the chief of the Royal Court. Throughout both meetings the discussion focused on defining the mandate of the international conference and the participation of the PLO, as both issues had become interwoven as a result of progress achieved in the peace process. The American position had developed to the extent of agreeing to the right of the concerned parties to submit any disagreements between them to the conference. However, we could not reach full agreement regarding the role of the conference in settling disputes among the negotiating parties.

Concerning the issue of PLO participation in the conference, the American delegation reiterated its previous position requiring that the PLO should first accept Security Council Resolution 242 in order for the United States to start a dialogue with it. The United States did not commit itself to accepting the inviting of the PLO to the conference. Our reply was that we wanted the United States to agree to have the PLO invited to participate in the conference if it accepted Security Council Resolution 242. This point became the subject of extensive discussions, during which I asked for a clear American position to relay to the PLO. The American delegation agreed to take this up at the highest level on its return to Washington.

On 21 January, 1986, I returned to Amman having achieved these results on the issues of an international conference and PLO participation. On 25 January, 1986, our efforts bore fruit when I received a final reply from the US administration concerning PLO participation in the international conference. Their reply came in a written commitment which said:

When it is clearly on the public record that the PLO has accepted Resolutions 242 and 338, is prepared to negotiate peace with Israel, and has renounced terrorism, the United States accepts the fact that an invitation will be issued to the PLO to attend an international conference.

The United States would then start contacts with the Soviet Union with the purpose of having them participate, together with the other permanent members of the Security Council, in the international conference, which would be convened by the Secretary-General of the United Nations.

On that same day, Arafat arrived in Amman with a Palestinian leadership delegation. We held four extensive meetings in four days. I presided over three of these meetings. The discussion concentrated on the subject of American assurances and the PLO's position regarding those assurances. We assumed that the PLO would accept these since:

1. The assurances met the PLO's requirements;
2. They reflected a significant change in the US position in favor of the PLO. The US position regarding the PLO when we first started our intensive year-long dialogue had been that the United States would only enter into talks with the PLO

after the latter's acceptance of Security Council Resolution 242. Now, by comparison, the present US position was that it was willing to go one step beyond talking to the PLO by agreeing to have the PLO invited to the international conference.

But our brothers in the Palestinian leadership surprised us by refusing to accept Security Council Resolution 242 within this context, while acknowledging what they described as our "extraordinary effort," which had caused a significant change in the US position and which would not have been possible had it not been for the respect, credibility, and trust which our country, Jordan, enjoyed in this world.

In spite of this, we continued our discussions with the PLO leadership in the hope of convincing them that their acceptance would cement a very important link in peace efforts leading to an international conference, which in the unanimous view of the Arabs and all peace-loving peoples constitutes the major venue for the establishment of a comprehensive, permanent and just peace. It is towards the objective of convening such a conference that we have worked tirelessly for the past nine years, but to no avail. Now that the opportunity presented itself, we hoped that it would not be wasted like other missed opportunities if we were to remain faithful to our goals of saving our people and liberating our land and holy places.

The answer of the brothers in the Palestinian leadership was that they wanted an amendment to the proposed text in return for acceptance of Resolution 242. The amendment would require the addition of a statement indicating the agreement of the United States to the legitimate rights of the Palestinian people, including their right to self-determination within the context of a confederation between Jordan and Palestine, as stated in the 11 February Accord. We reminded the Palestinian leadership that the subject of self-determination within the context of a confederation was a matter for Jordanians and Palestinians and that no other party had anything to do with it. Nothing was to be gained from the support of this or that state as long as we ourselves were committed to this text. The important thing was to achieve withdrawal first, then to proceed with what we had agreed upon. We reminded them that this had always been our position and that it had been clear all along, starting from my opening address in Amman at the seventeenth PNC session, in which I referred to the proposed Jordanian-Palestinian relationship, and continuing through all our discussions to date.

We also said to them that involving the United States, or others, in this matter meant that we were voluntarily opening the door to others to interfere in our common concerns and those of a people who had a sovereign right to their land and their own decision making—unless they were dealing with us on a basis of lack of confidence. But despite this, our brothers in the Palestinian leadership insisted on their position. And despite the fact that the most recent American position had satisfied PLO demands, we agreed to resume contacts with officials in Washington through the American embassy in Amman on the evening of 27 January, 1986.

The American response was as follows:

1. The 11 February Accord is a Jordanian-Palestinian accord which does not involve the United States.

2. The United States supports the legitimate rights of the Palestinian people as stated in the Reagan peace initiative.

3. The PLO, like any other party, has the right to propose anything it wishes, including the right of self-determination, at the international conference.

4. For all these reasons, the United States adheres to its position.

We relayed the American response to Yasser Arafat during an enlarged meeting at al-Nadwah Palace on 28 January, 1986, but he insisted that we try again. We indicated to him that we had gone as far as we could with the US administration at that stage, but he insisted. Thus, we got in touch once again, and the reply was still that the United States adhered to its position.

On the morning of 29 January, 1986, an enlarged meeting was held at the Prime Ministry and I headed the Jordanian side. I informed Yasser Arafat and his party of the American position as reaffirmed to us once again. The meeting ended with a statement by Yasser Arafat saying that he needed to consult the Palestinian leadership. We asked him to give us the final answer on the PLO position with regard to Resolution 242 while he was still in Amman, although we had ascertained, only then, that the PLO's decision to reject Resolution 242 had been made during the meeting of the PLO leadership in Baghdad on 24 November, 1985. We had not, however, officially been notified of that.

On the same evening, 29 January, 1986, we received a suggestion from the US administration to the effect that the United States felt that since the PLO could not presently decide to accept Resolution 242, the PLO could wait until a time it considered appropriate. The United States felt that the peace process could still proceed with Palestinian participation from the occupied territories. The opportunity would remain available for the PLO to take part in the international conference the moment it accepted Resolution 242.

In our reply to the United States, we rejected this suggestion, indicating that this time the suggestion concerned not only the PLO but Jordan as well, since our unwavering position was: no separate settlement.

President Reagan wrote to me on 31 January, 1986 explaining his inability to proceed in his efforts with Congress for the sale of sophisticated US arms to Jordan. We had sought to acquire the arms since 1979 in the face of fierce Zionist opposition. I had received assurances from the president that our requirements would be met.

On the evening of the same day, the minister of the court informed Yasser Arafat of the latest American suggestion to proceed with the peace process without the PLO until it met the set conditions. He also informed him of our categorical refusal of this suggestion and apprised him of President Reagan's letter explaining his inability to meet Jordan's requirements.

On 5 February, 1986, the American side presented a new text containing United States approval to convene an international conference on the basis of Security Council Resolutions 242 and 338, including the realization of the legitimate rights of the Palestinian people. We met with Yasser Arafat on the same evening at al-Nadwah Palace and we handed him the new American text. He promised to study it and at the same time gave us three differently worded texts* which were the same in substance, reaffirming the same PLO position which we had heard from the start of this round of meetings.

On 6 February, Yasser Arafat had a meeting with our prime minister at his residence. The meeting was attended by the chief of the Royal Court, and by 'Abd al-Razzaq al-Yahya and Hani al-Hasan from the Palestinian side. Arafat informed the prime minister that despite the positive development of the American position, recognition of the legitimate rights of the Palestinian people did not encompass the right to self-determination to which, the PLO insisted, the United States ought to give its prior approval.

On 7 February, Yasser Arafat left Amman still insisting on his position and on the reasons why the PLO was unable to accept Resolution 242. Hinging on this agreement, of course, was an immediate opening of an US-Palestinian dialogue on the basis of which we would have continued our efforts to convene an international peace conference in which the PLO would be invited to participate as a representative of the Palestinian people.

Thus, another chapter came to an end in the search for peace. Another extremely important and significant round of Jordanian-Palestinian action was terminated—after a full year of serious and persistent efforts to transform the PLO role, referred to in the Arab Peace Plan, into a significant reality that would go beyond a mere statement of positions. It would have led to the presence and participation by the PLO in an international conference at the invitation of the UN Secretary-General to represent its people and speak on their behalf with their adversary, under the eyes of the world, side by side with the other parties concerned and the five permanent members of the Security Council...

## 24. Statement by the Government of Jordan on Closing the PLO Offices, Amman, 7 July, 1986

The cabinet held a meeting at noon today under Prime Minister Zayd al-Rifa'i during which it discussed the contents of a statement issued by the Fateh Revolutionary Council on 19 June, 1986 and subsequent statements by a number of council members. The cabinet decided to issue the following statement and to implement the measures it contains:

---

* See Chapter VI.

1. The Fateh Revolutionary Council issued a statement on 19 June, 1986 assailing the Hashimite Kingdom of Jordan and its clear policy toward the Palestinian cause and the Palestinian Arab people. The statement said: "What we regard as tragic and highly dubious are certain proposals and practices being proposed and implemented by Arabs which are identical to US and Israeli aims. While the United States and Israel are presenting the issue of striking at the PLO and liquidating the Palestinian people's national rights as the first priority of US moves, the Jordanian government is taking a series of measures that fall within the same framework and which directly and seriously affect Palestinian national principles and pan-Arab guidelines defining the proper stances toward the Palestinian cause, the Palestinian people's national rights, and Palestinian national struggle under PLO leadership."

2. The Jordanian government has studied the significance, motives, and dimensions of this statement and has realized that the statement was not satisfied with using misleading expressions to interpret Jordan's firm, pan-Arab principles and its measures to preserve the steadfastness of the Palestinian people on their land, but it has also contravened the spirit of cooperation and understanding on whose basis the Jordanian government, upon the request of Mr. Yasser Arafat, has permitted for the past two years the existence of additional offices in Jordan which are officially not affiliated with the PLO and its institutions.

3. The Jordanian government expresses its regret at the contents of the Fateh statement, which contravenes the spirit of cooperation and understanding which the Jordanian government is eager to preserve despite the existing differences between it and the PLO leadership.

In view of the contents of the statement and the irresponsible, misleading utterances continually issued by some prominent council members against Jordan and its responsible pan-Arab stands, the government finds itself compelled to close down these additional offices, which it allowed to open, because these offices are working in accordance with policies drawn up for them by the side which has chosen to pursue this negative approach toward Jordan.

4. While taking this measure, the Jordanian government would like to affirm that the assaults and slanders launched against Jordan by certain sides will not divert it from its firm pan-Arab policy toward the Palestinian cause within the framework of joint Arab action or compel it to discontinue dealing with the PLO as the sole legitimate representative of the Palestinian people.

## 25.  Statement by the Government of Jordan on the PLO's Cancellation of the Amman Accord, 21 April, 1987

After becoming acquainted with the PLO Executive Committee's decision to abrogate the 11 February, 1985 agreement signed between the Jordanian Government and the PLO, the Jordanian Government would like to emphasize that the accord's principles, which reflect the distinguished relationship between the

Jordanian and Palestinian Arab peoples, will continue to be the beacon guiding Jordan in its serious, continuous efforts on the pan-Arab and international levels to liberate occupied Palestinian territory and enable the Palestinian people to regain their legitimate rights.

The 11 February agreement was basically the fruit of a shared Jordanian-Palestinian belief based on the Fez summit resolutions and was aimed at paving the way for PLO participation in the proposed international conference. It was also a pan-Arab step stemming from Jordan's sense of special responsibility toward our kinfolk, the Palestinian people.

As is known by all, Jordan continued to make intensive efforts for the holding of an international conference while insisting on laying the groundwork for PLO participation in that gathering as the Palestinian people's representative. This was despite the fact that coordination with the PLO leadership was suspended on 19 February, 1986.

The Jordanian Government emphasizes that it will not allow the Executive Committee's decision to be an obstacle to Arab efforts to reach a just and peaceful settlement of the Arab-Israeli conflict. This will be done through an international conference for peace in the Middle East in which the five permanent members of the Security Council will participate along with all parties to the conflict. Regardless of the circumstances, the Palestinian people will continue to have the last word in all matters pertaining to their future, since they are the ones primarily involved in getting rid of the Israeli occupation of their Palestinian land and in regaining their legitimate national rights.

## 26. Address by King Hussein to the Arab League Summit Conference, Amman, 8 November, 1987

My brother leaders, with regard to the other major issue—the Palestine question and the Arab-Israeli conflict—there is also need to go into its details, dimensions, and developments. These are already known to us and firmly entrenched in our consciences and minds. Perhaps what should be affirmed while in the process of assessing our position and rectifying the current situation, is the following:

1. UN Security Council Resolution 338 followed on the heels of the October, 1973 war to reaffirm Resolution 242. It calls for Israel's withdrawal from the occupied Arab territories in exchange for peace. This resolution is still awaiting implementation.

2. The Arab side has accepted Security Council Resolution 338 and expressed its readiness to implement it in its entirety and has worked toward that end. However, Israel has turned toward aborting and disrupting this resolution or at least depriving it of its essence. In pursuit of this objective, Israel has done the following:

a. It has obstructed the reconvening of an international conference for peace in the Middle East.

b. It has succeeded so far in diverting the role of the United States from that of a superpower with a special responsibility toward world peace into a role of a sponsor of Israel and Israeli interests. This has tied the United States' hands and made it view the peace process from the Israeli angle only, thus avoiding any contradiction with its view of Israel as a strategic ally.

c. It invaded Lebanon, where it achieved some of its objectives.

d. It has continued establishing settlements in the occupied Arab territories, announced the annexation of Jerusalem and the occupied Golan Heights, and is exerting efforts to liquidate the Palestinian Arab society in the West Bank and Gaza Strip by destroying its values and its economic, social, and cultural fabric.

3. To confront Israel's disruptive efforts, we in Jordan, in coordination with sisterly Syria, adopted the view of concentrating efforts on convening an international conference for peace in the Middle East and mobilizing resources and support for this conference. This approach realized noticeable progress with the result that an international conference has become acceptable worldwide as a formula to reach a just and comprehensive peace settlement for the Arab-Israeli dispute, especially as our proposal is based on international legitimacy since we called for convening it under UN auspices with the participation of the five permanent members of the UN Security Council and all the parties to the dispute including the PLO to implement Resolutions 242 and 338 and solve the various aspects of the Palestinian problem. However, this worldwide support for the conference is still facing disruptive Israeli attempts and US indulgence toward Israel's position.

4. Thus, these reasons make it important to formulate a unified Arab position supporting the call for an international conference for peace in the Middle East and the efforts exerted to convene it. At least, this will be a great contribution toward preventing Israel from exploiting Arab conditions and resolving the Palestinian problem its way while continuing to swallow Arab territories and beef up its military strength.

And while the Iraq-Iran war requires coordination among the GCC states and some Islamic states to seek effective ways to end it, the Palestinian problem, which is characterized by dynamism and change, also requires coordination and contacts among certain Arab sides that are directly concerned with the problem and a number of influential world powers. However, a unified Arab position and well-planned political action must be backed by the credibility of joint Arab action. In the Arab-Israeli dispute in particular, this credibility cannot materialize except through constant support, which is indispensable in continuing to build the military and economic resources of the states in direct confrontation with Israel and to provide systematic assistance for the Palestinian people under occupation.

## 27. Resolutions of the Arab League Summit Conference, Amman, 11 November, 1987 [Excerpts]

Their majesties, excellencies, and highnesses the kings, presidents, and amirs of the Arab states, meeting within the framework of the extraordinary Arab summit conference in Amman, the Hashimite Kingdom of Jordan, 8-11 November, 1987, considering that the Palestinian question is the Arabs' cause and the crux of the Arab-Israeli conflict and that struggle for the sake of regaining usurped Arab rights in Palestinian territory and other occupied Arab territories is a Pan-Arab responsibility; since the Zionist danger is not only targeted against the confrontation states but threatens the destiny and existence of the whole Arab nation; in view of Israel's continued perpetration of repressive practices in the occupied Arab and Palestinian territories; and in light of its persistent pursuit of its hostile and expansionist policy, decide:

1. To pool the Arab states' capabilities and resources for the sake of reinforcing the capabilities and energies of the states and forces that are confronting Israel on all levels to help end its continued aggression against the Arab nation and regain usurped Arab rights in Palestinian and occupied Arab territories.

2. To achieve strategic parity with Israel within the framework of an effective Arab solidarity to confront the Zionist danger, which threatens the Arab nation's destiny and existence, and to force Israel to accept the UN resolutions seeking to establish a just and comprehensive peace in the region.

3. To provide material and moral support to the persistent heroic struggle being waged by the Palestinian people in occupied Palestine, the Golan Heights, and southern Lebanon in their confrontation of Israeli occupation.

4. To urge all Arab parties to abide by Arab summit resolutions stipulating the inadmissibility of any Arab sides' unilaterally concluding any solution to the Arab-Israeli conflict, rejecting any peaceful settlement of the Arab-Israeli conflict that does not guarantee full and unconditional Israeli withdrawal from all occupied Palestinian and Arab territories and that does not call for enabling the Palestinian Arab people to exercise their inalienable national rights in accordance with Arab summit resolutions, especially those adopted at the Fez summit in 1982.

5. To condemn the US government's decision to close the Palestine Information Office in Washington.

*Resolution on an International Peace Conference:*

Their majesties, excellencies, and highnesses the kings, presidents, and amirs of the Arab states, meeting within the framework of the extraordinary Arab summit conference in Amman, the Hashimite Kingdom of Jordan, 8-11 November, 1987, out of commitment to the objectives and bases defined by the resolutions of Arab summit conferences concerning the Arab-Israeli conflict; in view of Israel's continued rejection of peace efforts as well as Israel's failure to accept UN resolutions to establish a just and comprehensive peace in the region; proceeding from the Arab nation's determination to pool its resources and capabilities to confront the Zionist challenge to its fate and existence; and out of commitment to the Arab nation's approach to peace defined in the Arab peace plan approved at the 1982 Fez summit with the aim of achieving a just and comprehensive settlement of the Arab-Israeli conflict guaranteeing the return of the occupied Arab and Palestinian territories as well as resolving the Palestine question in all its aspects on the basis of international legitimacy, decide:

The convening of an international conference for peace in the Middle East under UN auspices, called for by the UN Secretary-General and attended by the five permanent Security Council member states along with all parties to the Arab-Israeli conflict, including the PLO, the sole legitimate representative of the Palestinian people, on an equal footing, is the appropriate way to settle the conflict in a comprehensive, just, and peaceful manner.

This settlement will guarantee the return of occupied Palestinian and Arab territories, the resolution of the Palestine question in all its aspects, and the attainment of the inalienable national rights of the Palestinian Arab people.

*Resolution on Relations with Egypt:*

Their majesties, excellencies, and highnesses the kings, presidents, and amirs of the Arab states meeting within the framework of the extraordinary summit conference held in Amman, the Hashimite Kingdom of Jordan, from 8-11 November, 1987, discussed the third point on their agenda, concerning relations with Egypt. Following a detailed and fraternal discussion, they decided that the diplomatic relationship between any Arab League member state and Egypt is an act of sovereignty decided by every state in accordance with its constitution and laws and is not the jurisdiction of the Arab League.

## 28.  Resolutions of the Arab League Summit Conference, Algiers, 9 June, 1988 [Excerpts]

*The Uprising of the Palestinian People*

The Summit Conference hailed the uprising of the Palestinian people which constitutes an important phase in the long struggle it has been waging for more than half a century now, considering that it is an integral part of the Palestinian revolution which has contributed to the consolidation of Arab solidarity. The Conferees likewise expressed their great admiration for and their immense pride in the heroic acts which have marked the Palestinian people's resistance to Israeli occupation and its dauntless determination to liberate the occupied land and restore its right to return, self-determination and independent statehood on its national soil, under the leadership of the PLO, its legitimate and sole representative.

Similarly, the Summit saluted the combat of Syrian nationals in the Golan, as well as the Lebanese national resistance in South Lebanon to Israeli occupation of Arab land.

The Arab heads of state then investigated the proper ways and means of supporting the uprising, boosting its effectiveness and ensuring its continuity and further development. They reasserted their commitment to provide the Palestinian people with all forms and types of assistance it needs so that it may continue its resistance and carry on its massive revolt under the leadership of the PLO until the attainment of its inalienable national rights.

The Conference reiterated its commitment to support the confrontation states in their struggle against the Israeli enemy, so that they may boost their defensive capacities and reinforce their potential for liberating the occupied Arab territories and recovering spoliated Arab rights.

The Conference affirmed that Israel's continued occupation of Arab territories, its persistent denial of the Palestinian people's inalienable national rights and its growing repressive practices which have come to assume the form and content of war crimes against the armless Palestinian people, are so many clear cut illustrations of its racist and aggressive nature, as well as of its expansionist appetite.

The Conference called the UN Security Council to shoulder its responsibilities with a view to forcing Israel to comply with UN resolutions and the provisions of international conventions and to stop its repressive and inhuman practices.

The Conference also called the Security Council to work towards securing an immediate and total withdrawal of Israel from the occupied Arab territories and to place the Palestinian territories under a provisional UN mandate which provides the necessary protection for their citizens and guarantees for the Palestinian people the exercise of its inalienable national rights.

*International Conference*

The Algiers Summit Conference reviewed the developments relating to the efforts for peace in the Middle Eastern region and noted that those efforts were still marked with slow progress, lack of effectiveness and an incapacity to deal with the Israeli adamant rejection of peace. The Conference reaffirmed, once again, that the principles set forth in previous Arab Summit resolutions and, in particular, the 1982 Fez Summit, provide a base for solving the Arab-Israeli conflict and its essential component: the Palestinian problem. It renewed its support for the holding of an effective UN sponsored conference on peace in the Middle East, based on international legality and on UN resolutions calling for a total Israeli withdrawal from all occupied Palestinian and Arab territories and guaranteeing the Palestinian people's inalienable rights. Such a conference is to be held with the participation of the five permanent member states of the Security council and all the parties of the conflict in the region, including the PLO—the legitimate and sole representative of the Palestinian people—on an equal footing and with the same rights as the other parties.

### Arab Boycott of Israel

The Conference considers the legislations issued by some foreign countries to counter the Arab boycott of Israel as hostile measures meant to deny Arab rights, break off the isolation of Israel and enhance the economic potential of the Zionist entity at a time when the latter pursues its occupation of Arab territories. The Conference also reiterated the commitment of the Arab League member states to continue the application of this boycott, considered as a legitimate means which other states and international communities made and still make use of.

### US Policy and the Palestinian Problem

The Conference referred to the continued bias in the United States policy in favor of Israel and against the Palestinian people's inalienable national rights. Accordingly, the Conference condemned this policy which encourages Israel to continue its aggression and violations of human rights, hampers the efforts underway for achieving peace and contradicts the United States responsibilities, as a permanent Security Council member, for the preservation of international peace and security.

## 29. Address by King Hussein on Jordan's Disengagement from the West Bank, 31 July, 1988

In the name of God, the merciful, the compassionate, and peace be upon his faithful Arab messenger. Brother citizens: I send you greetings and am pleased to address you in your cities and villages, in your camps and dwellings, in your factories, institutions, offices, and establishments. I would like to address your hearts and minds in all parts of our beloved Jordanian land.

This is all the more important at this juncture, when we have initiated—after seeking God's help and after thorough and extensive study—a series of measures to enhance Palestinian national orientation and highlight Palestinian identity; our goal is the benefit of the Palestinian cause and the Arab Palestinian people. Our decision, as you know, comes after 38 years of the unity of the two banks and 14 years after the Rabat summit resolution designating the PLO as the sole legitimate representative of the Palestinian people. It also comes 6 years after the Fez summit resolution that agreed unanimously on the establishment of an independent Palestinian state in the occupied West Bank and the Gaza Strip as one of the bases and results of the peaceful settlement.

We are certain our decision to initiate these measures does not come as a surprise. Many of you have anticipated it, and some of you have been calling for it for some time. As for its contents, it has been a topic of discussion and consideration for everyone since the Rabat summit. Nevertheless, some may wonder: Why now? Why today and not after the Rabat or Fez summits, for instance? To answer this question, we need to recall certain facts that preceded the Rabat resolution. We also need to recall considerations that led to the debate over the slogan-objective which the PLO raised and worked to gain Arab and international support for, namely, the establishment of an independent Palestinian state. This meant, in addition to the PLO's ambition to embody the Palestinian identity on Palestinian national soil, the separation of the West Bank from the Hashemite Kingdom of Jordan.

I reviewed the facts preceding the Rabat resolution, as you recall, before the Arab leaders in the Algiers extraordinary summit last June. It may be important to recall that one of the main points I emphasized was the text of the unity resolution of the two banks of April, 1950. This resolution affirms the preservation of all Arab rights in Palestine and the defense of such rights by all legitimate means without prejudicing the final settlement of the just cause of the Palestinian people—within the scope of the people's aspirations and of Arab cooperation and international justice.

Among these facts there was our 1972 proposal regarding our concept of alternatives, on which the relationship between Jordan on one hand and the West Bank and Gaza on the other may be based after their liberation. Among these alternatives was the establishment of a relationship of brotherhood and cooperation between the Hashemite Kingdom of Jordan and the independent Palestinian state in case the Palestinian people opt for that. Simply, this means that we declared our clear-cut position regarding our adherence to the Palestinian people's right to self-determination on their national soil, including their right to establish their own independent state, more than 2 years before the Rabat summit resolution. This will be our position until the Palestinian people achieve their complete national goals, God willing.

The relationship of the West Bank with the Hashemite Kingdom of Jordan in light of the PLO's call for the establishment of an independent Palestinian state, can be confined to two considerations. First, the principled consideration pertaining to the issue of Arab unity as a pan-Arab aim, to which the hearts of the Arab peoples aspire and which they want to achieve. Second, the political consideration pertaining to the extent of the Palestinian struggle's gain from the continuation of the legal relationship of the Kingdom's two banks. Our answer to the question now stems from these two considerations and the background of the clear-cut and firm Jordanian position toward the Palestine question, as we have shown.

Regarding the principled consideration, Arab unity between any two or more countries is an option of any Arab people. This is what we believe. Accordingly, we responded to the wish of the Palestinian people's representatives for unity with Jordan in 1950. From this premise, we respect the wish of the PLO, the sole and legitimate representative of the Palestinian people, to secede from us as an independent Palestinian state. We say that while we fully understand the situation. Despite this, Jordan will continue to take pride in carrying the message of the Great Arab Revolt, adhering to its principles, believing in the one Arab destiny, and abiding by the joint Arab action.

Regarding the political consideration, since the June 1967 aggression we have believed that our action and efforts should be directed at liberating the land and the sanctities from Israeli occupation. Therefore, we have concentrated all our efforts, over the past 21 years of occupation, on that goal. We did not imagine that maintaining the legal and administrative relationship between the two banks could constitute an obstacle to liberating the occupied Palestinian land. Hence, in the past and before we took measures, we did not find anything requiring such measures, especially since our support for the Palestinian people's rights to self-determination was clear.

Of late, it has become clear that there is a general Palestinian and Arab orientation which believes in the need to highlight the Palestinian identity in full in all efforts and activities that are related to the Palestine question and its developments. It has also become obvious that there is a general conviction that maintaining the legal and administrative relationship with the West Bank—and the consequent special Jordanian treatment of the brother Palestinians living under occupation through Jordanian institutions in the occupied territories—goes against this orientation. It would be an obstacle to the Palestinian struggle which seeks to win international support for the Palestine question, considering that it is a just national issue of a people struggling against foreign occupation.

In view of this orientation, which was bound to stem from a purely Palestinian desire and an unflinching Arab determination to support the Palestine question, we have a duty to favorably respond to its requirements. First and last, we are part of our nation and we are eager to support its causes, foremost among which is the Palestine question. Since there is a unanimous conviction that the struggle for liberating the occupied Palestinian territory can be bolstered by disengaging the legal and administrative relationship between the two banks, then we must perform our duty and do what is required of us.

As we favorably responded to the appeals made to us by Arab leaders at the Rabat summit of 1974 which asked us to continue to deal with the occupied West Bank through Jordanian institutions to support the steadfastness of brethren there, we today favorably respond to the desire of the PLO, the sole legitimate representative of the Palestinian people, and also to the Arab orientation regarding consecrating the purely Palestinian identity in all of its elements in terms of form and content. We beseech God to make this step of ours a qualitative addition to the growing struggle being waged by the Palestinian people for the sake of attaining liberation and independence.

Brother citizens, these are the reasons, the considerations, and the convictions that prompted us to respond favorably to the PLO's desire and to the general Arab orientation which is in harmony with this desire, as we cannot continue to maintain this undecided situation which serves neither Jordan nor the Palestine question. We had to go out of the tunnel of fears and doubts to the atmosphere of tranquility and clarity where mutual confidence flourishes and blossoms into understanding, cooperation, and affection in favor of the Palestine question and also in favor of the Arab unity—which will remain a cherished objective sought and demanded by all Arab peoples.

However, it should be clear that our measures regarding the West Bank are connected only with Palestinian territory and its people, and not the Jordanian citizens of Palestinian origin in the Hashemite Kingdom of Jordan. All of them have citizenship rights and commitments just like any other citizen regardless of his origin.

They are an integral part of the Jordanian state to which they belong, on whose soil they live, and in whose life and various activities they participate. Jordan is not Palestine and the independent Palestinian state will be established on the occupied Palestinian territory after its liberation, God willing. On this territory the Palestinian identity will be embodied and the Palestinian struggle will blossom as confirmed by the blessed uprising of the Palestinian people under occupation.

If national unity in any country is dear and precious, it is for us in Jordan more than that. It is the basis of our stability and the cause of our development and prosperity as well as the foundation of our national security and the source of our faith in the future. It is also a living embodiment of the principles of the Great Arab Revolt which we inherited and whose banner we are proudly carrying. It is also a living example of constructive plurality and a sound nucleus for any formula of a more comprehensive Arab unity. Based on this, safeguarding national unity is a sacred matter that will not be compromised. Any attempt to tamper with it under any slogan will only help the enemy carry out its expansionist policy at the expense of Palestine and Jordan alike. Consequently, true nationalism and genuine pan-Arabism lie in bolstering and strengthening national unity. Moreover, the responsibility to safeguard it falls on every one of you. There should be no room among us for a slanderer or a traitor. With God's help, we shall always be one cohesive family whose members are joined by bonds of brotherhood, affection, awareness, and the common national and pan-Arab objectives.

Perhaps the most important thing to remember as we stress the need to preserve national unity is that the stable, productive communities are those in which order and discipline prevail. Discipline is the solid fabric that binds all people in a solid, harmonious structure that blocks all avenues before the enemies and opens the horizons of hope for the coming generations.

The constructive plurality which Jordan has been practicing since its establishment and through which it is witnessing progress and prosperity in all aspects of life, does not only increase our belief in the sacredness of national unity, but also in the importance of Jordan's pan-Arab role by presenting itself as a living example of the merger of various Arab groups on its soil within the framework of a good citizenship and one Jordanian people. This example, which we are experiencing on our soil, is the one which gives us confidence in the inevitability of attaining Arab unity, God willing.

If we closely examine this spirit of the age, we will see that self-assertion does not conflict with the achievement of institutional unity formulas that include all Arabs. There are living and existing examples in foreign countries. Perhaps the clearest example is the EC, which now seeks to achieve political European unity after it has succeeded in achieving economic integration among its members. As is known, the ties, relations, and basic elements that connect the Arabs are much greater than those connecting the European peoples.

O citizens, brother Palestinians in the occupied Palestinian territory, in order to eliminate any doubts that would be cast on our measures, we would like to stress to you that these measures do not mean the relinquishment of our pan-Arab duty toward the Arab-Israeli conflict or the Palestine question. These measures also do not mean a relinquishment of our belief in Arab unity. We have basically taken these measures, as I said, in response to the wish of the PLO, the sole and legitimate representative of the Palestinian people, and in response to the prevailing Arab conviction that such measures would contribute to supporting the Palestinian people's struggle and their blessed uprising.

Jordan will continue to support the Palestinian people's steadfastness and their valiant uprising in the occupied Palestinian territory within the limits of its capabilities. I will not forget to say that when we decided to cancel the Jordanian development plan in the occupied territories, at the same time we managed to contact the various friendly governments and the international institutions that expressed their desire to contribute to the plan. We urged them to continue to finance development projects in the occupied Palestinian territory through the concerned Palestinian circles.

Brothers, Jordan has not relinquished and will not relinquish its support for the Palestinian people until they achieve their national objectives, God willing. No one outside Palestine has ever had or will ever have connection with Palestine or with its cause that is stronger than the connection of Jordan or my family with it. This is on the one hand. On the other hand, Jordan is a confrontation state, and its border with Israel is longer than that of any other Arab state.

In fact, Jordan's border with Israel is longer than the borders of the West Bank and the Gaza Strip together with it. Jordan also will not relinquish its commitment to participation in the peace process. We contributed to the efforts to achieve an international unanimity on holding an international conference for peace in the

Middle East to reach a just and comprehensive peaceful settlement to the Arab-Israeli conflict, and to reach a settlement of all aspects of the Palestine question. We have defined our stands in this regard, as everyone knows, through the six principles that we previously announced to the public. Jordan, brethren, is a basic party to the Arab-Israeli conflict and the peace process. It shoulders its national and pan-Arab responsibilities accordingly.

I thank you and I repeat my heartfelt wishes to you, beseeching Almighty God to help us, guide us, make us please Him, and to grant our Palestinian brothers victory and success. He is the best of helpers.

May God's peace and blessings be upon you.

## 30. Statement by Jordanian Prime Minister Zaid al-Rifai on the Implementation of Jordan's Disengagement from the West Bank, 20 August, 1988

1. To further the interests of the Palestinian brothers in the occupied West Bank, Jordanian passports will be issued at their request. Such passports will be valid for two years.

2. Every person residing in the West Bank before 31 July, 1988 is considered a Palestinian, not a Jordanian national.

3. Citizens of the occupied West Bank will be given temporary passports valid for two years according to the same documents that were valid in the Civil Registration Department and the General Passport Department prior to the disengagement.

4. Every person who wishes to obtain a temporary Jordanian passport should report in person to the General Passport Department with the valid application form and documents. Applications will only be accepted from the person in question.

5. The documents required to obtain a temporary passport endorsed only by the Awqaf Department in the occupied West Bank will be valid.

6. Passports issued before 31 July, 1988 will remain valid until they expire. Their validity will be amended to two years when their holders report to the General Passport Department to conduct any transactions on the passport. In this case, a temporary passport will be issued without collecting the legal fees.

7. These instructions will not apply to citizens with family reunion cards.

8. Temporary passports for Gaza Strip citizens will continue to be renewed. They will be valid only for two years.

9. Issuance of new temporary passports for Gaza Strip citizens whose passports expired one or more years ago will cease.

10. Temporary passports, valid for two years, will still be issued for the persons listed in the passports which were given to the Gaza Strip citizens.

11.  The Civil Registration Department and the General Passport Department will cease to issue family books for citizens of the occupied West Bank.

12.  All family books held by citizens of the occupied West Bank, issued by the Civil Registration Department, will be considered invalid.  When they have occasion to call at the department, the family books will be stamped invalid, and the department will effect any additions or endorsements from that date.

13.  Having been cancelled, family books and identity cards will be kept by holders as means of identification.

14.  Certificates of birth, death, marriage, divorce, and inheritance will be valid if certified by the Chief, Qadi Department in the West Bank and the Palestinian Affairs Department at the Foreign Ministry.

15.  Bridge green or yellow cards will remain valid provided visits by green card holders do not exceed one month.  Students, workers abroad, and patients seeking hospital treatment in the Kingdom are exempted.

16.  Agricultural goods will still be imported from the West Bank and Gaza Strip subject to market needs.  The cooperative organization will be the body accredited to issue certificates of origin for agricultural goods allowed into the Kingdom from the West Bank.  The Gaza Strip Charity Organization will issue certificates of origin for agricultural goods imported from there.

17.  The Agriculture Ministry in Amman will issue permits required for bringing in agricultural produce in coordination with the Palestinian Affairs Department at the Foreign Ministry.

18.  Industrial goods will be imported subject to market needs according to the previous bases.

19.  West Bank establishments such as municipalities, trade unions, associations, youth centers and clubs may withdraw their deposits from the banks in the Kingdom upon presenting checks endorsed by the Palestinian Affairs Department.

20.  Previous regulations related to land registration will still be valid. Recommendations by the Awqaf Department to obtain land registration deeds for the West Bank citizens will be acceptable.  The Awqaf Department's endorsement of documents coming from the West Bank will also be acceptable.

21.  If the occupied West Bank schools adopt the Jordanian curriculum, the Ministry of Education will make the necessary arrangements to hold the General Secondary Education—Tawjihi—examination in the West Bank.  The examination papers will be marked and scrutinized and certificates issued by the Ministry of Education in Amman.

22.  The West Bank trucks will be allowed to enter the Kingdom provided they are subjected to temporary entry regulations for trucks.

## 31. Address by Iraqi Foreign Minister Tareq Aziz to the UN General Assembly, Geneva, 13 December, 1988 [Excerpts]

Mr. President, the major developments recently witnessed in the struggle of the Palestinian people makes the discussion of the Palestinian issue in this particular circumstance, and here in Geneva, an historic occasion that is most important for the Palestinian question to take the prominence it deserves among international concerns.

This occasion is also important for determining the responsibilities and duties which should be shouldered by the international community on this question in consonance with objectives and principles of the United Nation's Charter if the injustice and deprivation suffered by the Palestinian people throughout the past decades are to be removed.

The most important of these developments has been the valiant uprising of the Arab people of Palestine and the historic decisions made on 15 November at the nineteenth extraordinary session of the Palestine National Council in Algiers, the session that appropriately carried the name of the uprising.

The uprising and the fact that it has continued courageously for more than a whole year now all over the occupied territories, undaunted by the violence and repression perpetrated by the occupation authorities, offers eloquent and tangible evidence of the vitality and vigor of the intrepid Palestinian people, their attachment to the land of Palestine and their unwavering resolve to achieve self-determination on that land.

It was upon this solid foundation, concretely clear as it is to the whole world, that the Palestine National Council made the decision to announce the independent Palestinian state. The announcement came in free, vigorous exercise of the right of self-determination, an exercise very much in line with international legitimacy as reflected in the resolutions adopted by the United Nations since 1947, confirming the right of the Palestinian people to self-determination, political independence and sovereignty over their homeland.

By announcing an independent Palestinian state, the Arab People of Palestine have reaffirmed the democratic foundations of their state, their love for peace and their commitment to peaceful co-existence. The Palestinian people declared their resolve to work for an independent state and for the achievement of a lasting peace based on justice and respect for people's rights. The Palestinian people have also called upon the United Nations, which has a special responsibility towards the Palestinian question, to help them achieve their legitimate objectives.

The Palestinian people have also reiterated their belief in settling regional and international problems peacefully and according to the UN Charter and UN resolutions. They have also asserted their rejection of threatened or actual use of force, violence or terrorism against the territorial integrity and political independence of countries, without prejudice to the natural right of self-defense.

In addition to announcing independence, the Palestine National Council included in its political statement a balanced working program for ensuring the arrangement of security and peace in the region.

Mr. President, the entire world is obligated to view these decisions in a positive manner and to deal with them in earnest. It is most gratifying to note that a great number of states have welcomed and recognized these decisions. It is necessary to point out, at the same time, that those states which have hesitated so far to announce their support, should end their reluctance by declaring their support for the decisions of the Palestine National Council and their recognition of the new independent Palestinian state.

They should also come forward in clear support of the call for an international peace conference to be held with the full and equal participation of the Palestine Liberation Organization. In this context, we wish to say that, while we welcome the statement issued by the countries of the European Community on 21 November, we look forward to seeing these countries shake off whatever reluctance they may still have towards recognizing the independent Palestinian state and come forward in support of this state—the establishment of which constitutes a fundamental basis for achieving peace in the Middle East.

## 32. Address by Egyptian Foreign Minister Ismat Abd al-Maguid to the UN General Assembly, Geneva, 13 December, 1988 [Excerpts]

The Palestinian people have made great sacrifices for many years and the time has come for them to obtain their rights.

The decision taken by His Majesty King Hussein of Jordan at the end of July, 1988 to sever legal and administrative links with the West Bank was in harmony with this concept and has strengthened it, thus making Israel face the need to deal with the facts of the situation.

Mr. Chairman, the recent past has seen many meetings among the various Palestinian circles and groupings. They have discussed and studied the Palestinian people's demands and the uprising of their sons living under the occupation, in order to reach the appropriate decisions. Hence, the extraordinary PNC session was held. This session embodied the determination of the Palestinian people and their leaders to shoulder their responsibility wisely and courageously. A democratic and conscious exercise was carried out at the meetings and was crystallized by the pragmatic and reasonable trend that prevailed.

The PNC resolutions came at a time when the international atmosphere was propitious. They coincided with the emergence of positive indications and developments in many parts of the world beset by dangers of armed conflicts and tensions. We hope that the effects of this positive atmosphere will spread to include the Middle East too.

From this premise, I would like to underline the importance of the great step taken by the PLO through the three documents issued by the Algiers meeting to give an impetus to the peace efforts. They represent a substantial development in Palestinian thinking and in the attainment of a starting point for a Palestinian settlement, while taking into consideration all the regional and international circumstances and changes and their effects on the course of the conflict in the region. These are expressed by the following four factors:

1. The recognition of Security Council Resolutions 242 and 338 as a basis for holding an international conference for peace in the Middle East and a basis for according the Palestinian people their national legitimate rights.

2. The declaration of an independent Palestinian state within the framework of international legitimacy on the basis of General Assembly Resolution 181, which partitioned Palestine into two states; one Arab and the other Jewish. The framework of this resolution provides the conditions for the international legitimacy that ensures the Palestinian Arab people's right to sovereignty and national independence.

3. The move from the establishment of a Palestinian state to confederation with the Hashemite Kingdom of Jordan.

4. The rejection of violence and renunciation of terrorism. The Palestinian declaration was an affirmation of commitment to UN principles, particularly the settlement of problems by peaceful means, to the Universal Declaration of Human Rights, and to the principles of nonalignment. This deserves to be noted. These principles, in our opinion, represent a real achievement by the PNC. They also constitute, at the same time, an important basis for political activity in the coming period to strengthen efforts to achieve a just settlement acceptable to all the parties to the dispute.

I would like to affirm once again, and very clearly, that thereby the PNC has taken a realistic and practical course within the context of international legitimacy.

The Stockholm declaration was made with the same level of clarity and frankness. It reaffirmed the positive Palestinian commitment to the achievement of a just and final peaceful settlement of the problem.

Mr. Chairman, while the Palestinian party—which is the principal party—in the ongoing Middle East dispute has defined its position clearly, meeting the world demand that UN Security Council Resolutions 242 and 338 should be the basis for negotiations within the framework of an international conference for a comprehensive peaceful settlement, it should be underlined that the proclamation of the Palestinian state has included a recognition of the existence of the State of Israel. The Palestinians have made a decisive choice to engage in a peace process on the basis of UN General Assembly Resolution 181 concerning the partition of Palestine, as well as the relevant UN Security Council resolutions which refer to the situation as it was on 5 June, 1967.

This responsible stand by the PLO calls for a reciprocal response from other parties, particularly Israel. I call on Israel from this lectern to respond favorably to this positive Palestinian stand so that a just and comprehensive peace could be achieved, a peace which allows for the recognition of the State of Palestine as well as the State of Israel; a peace which allows for the respect of the Palestinian peoples' rights as well as the Israeli peoples' rights. International efforts must not be directed toward serving one party or endorsing the rights of that party. These efforts must be mobilized and resources marshalled to achieve a settlement according to the principles of justice and international law, so that ultimately justice may be obtained for all.

Mr. Chairman, we therefore have to adopt decisions which conform to the rules of international legitimacy and to the principles and objectives stipulated by the UN Charter and recognized by the entire world community.

Mr. Chairman, at this historic meeting, I would like to go further into a number of important points, and call things by their proper names. The international march toward a new era of international relations has started to move toward the establishment of relations marked by peace, understanding, and cooperation. The Middle East region is no exception to this rule. The Palestinian issue should not continue to represent the focal point of tension, dispute, and denial of basic rights.

The Palestinian declaration of independence stated that UN General Assembly Resolution 181 for the year 1947 still provides the basis for an international legitimacy guaranteeing the Palestinian people's right to national independence and sovereignty. This, in itself, is an acceptance of the idea of the partition of Palestine envisaged in that resolution. Moreover, the Palestinian acceptance of Resolution 242 is, in fact, a recognition of Israel's right to exist within safe, recognized, and secure borders. It is also an acceptance of an end to the war, a recognition of the right of Israel, as well as the parties to the dispute, to enjoy sovereignty, territorial integrity, and political independence...

Israel has the right to safeguard its security. However, this cannot be an absolute right. It is illogical, or rather a violation of the historic facts and basic principles of law and justice, to say that Israel's rights are above the rights of all the other parties to the dispute. Israel's rights must be parallel with others' rights and nothing more. It will never be possible to establish a just and lasting peace unless the rights and responsibilities are balanced.

Mr. Chairman, on this same basis, we call on the international community, particularly the major permanent members of the UN Security Council, to take the responsibility of preserving international peace and security and to embark on official consultations to prepare for the convocation of an international conference on peace in the Middle East. We also call on the UN Secretary-General to lead these consultations as soon as possible.

Egypt and other countries have made numerous positive initiatives to establish peace in the Middle East. All these initiatives include positive elements worthy of support. What is important is that these elements should be implemented and, should result in activating a process leading to a just settlement. A just peace is one in which every party that has a right will obtain it, and it is a peace which preserves the interests of all the concerned parties in a balanced matter...

Mr. Chairman, the United Nations and the international parties that are concerned with a peaceful settlement and are able to exert a decisive influence on it should perform the following role: They should maintain direct communication with the two parties to the conflict, and they should seek to obtain a mutual and simultaneous recognition between them. This can be done by paving the way for negotiations and the attainment of a settlement. In this respect these parties can exploit the recent positive developments and the favorable regional and international atmosphere, so that an effective international conference for peace may be held under UN supervision.

The UN Secretary-General would call for this conference, which would be attended by the permanent UN Security Council members, and in which all the parties to the conflict, particularly the PLO, the sole legitimate representative of the Palestinian people, would participate on an equal footing. Such a conference is the framework which the vast majority of the members of the international community have accepted and supported with the aim of attaining peace in the region.

Mr. Chairman, Egypt has been in the vanguard of the countries calling for peace and has taken it upon itself to urge all regional and international forums to support the Palestinian people's cause and enable them to exercise their legitimate rights, notably their right to self-determination and the establishment of an independent state. Egypt has exerted numerous efforts over the years under the leadership of President Muhammad Husni Mubarak. The most recent of these efforts was the Al-'Aqabah summit meeting in October, 1988, in which the Jordanian monarch and Yasser Arafat participated.

From the beginning, Egypt declared its support for the establishment of an independent Palestinian state and recognized this state at its birth. This formed part of Egypt's strategic commitment to pushing forward the efforts to establish a just, comprehensive, and lasting peace in the Middle East...

Mr. Chairman, we are now at a historic turning point. It is time for an active effort to solve this conflict on the part of all the parties concerned, regional, and international. In this regard, Egypt stresses several important and basic factors. They are:

1. All international forces should urge Israel to respond to the historic Palestinian achievement and to accept the idea of mutual and simultaneous recognition between the State of Israel and the State of Palestine.

2. The parties concerned should start consultations among themselves within the framework of the Security Council to prepare for the stage of negotiations,

which will be held directly through the convening of an international conference on peace in the Middle East on the basis of Security Council Resolutions 242 and 338, and what accompanies them in terms of recognition of the legitimate political rights of the Palestinian people.

3. It should be acknowledged that the goals of the settlement are defined by Israel's withdrawal from the Palestinian and Arab territories occupied since 1967, including the Syrian Golan Heights and Arab East Jerusalem; by the recognition of the right of all the peoples and states of the region, be they Arab states or Israel, to live in peace and within secure and recognized borders, free of threats and acts of violence; and by the provision to the Palestinian people of the opportunity to exercise their right to self-determination on their own land without external intervention...

## 33. Address by Jordanian Foreign Minister Tahir al-Masri to the UN General Assembly, Geneva, 13 December, 1988 [Excerpts]

Mr Chairman, the General Assembly is again debating the Palestine question while fully aware of the developments which have taken place during the past 41 years. It was the General Assembly which passed the 1947 resolution partitioning Palestine into two states; a Jewish state and an Arab state. That resolution constituted the birth of the Palestine question as the world knows it today and the beginning of its cumulations which are still continuing.

The Palestinian people, through their heroic uprising, have put their cause in its proper international perspective. The uprising has underlined the fact that Israel will not be able to maintain by force the status quo forever. Also, the Palestinian people have been capable of projecting, in clear black and white terms, its national identity as a colonized people aspiring to attain national independence through a genuine and sincere orientation toward peace and a desire to coexist with the other side on the basis of its ability to exercise its inalienable national rights, foremost of which is the right to self-determination and the establishment of its independent state on its national territory. This was expressed in recent PNC resolutions, which have stressed the PLO's commitment to reach a lasting and comprehensive peaceful settlement to the Palestine question.

Jordan has persistently, especially since 1967, advocated a peaceful, just, comprehensive, and lasting settlement of the Palestine question on the basis of the UN Charter and the relevant resolutions adopted by the world body.

In his speech before the General Assembly's 40th session, His Majesty King Hussein said that the resolutions, which constitute a balanced basis for any just peaceful settlement, are Resolution 181 issued in 1947 partitioning Palestine, Resolution 194 issued in 1948 on the refugees issue, Resolution 242 issued in 1967 calling for Israeli withdrawal from the occupied Arab territories and stressing the right of all countries in the region to live in peace within secure and recognized borders, and Security Council Resolution 338 issued in 1973 calling for negotiations among the disputing parties.

All the resolutions enjoy full international approval because they include the main important principles, which if successfully applied will guarantee the desired solution.

Jordan considered Security Council Resolution 242, right from the moment of its adoption, the chief basis for peace initiatives and international efforts to cope with the 1967 war. Accordingly, Jordan persisted in its efforts, both at the inter-Arab and international levels, to mobilize support for the compliance with, as well as implementation of, that resolution. Jordan's acceptance of the resolution was the beginning of an Arab movement toward efforts to reach a settlement of the Arab-Israeli dispute, the crux of which is the Palestine question.

This position has quickly advanced during the past few years and was epitomized in the Arab summit conference's resolutions in Fez in 1982, when the Arabs adopted a unified position committed to international legitimacy as a basis for settling the Arab-Israeli dispute. This was followed by joint Jordanian-Palestinian efforts as part of that trend. Then the Arab consensus during the two Arab summit conferences in Amman in 1987 and in Algiers in 1988 on the need to hold an international peace conference came as another confirmation of that trend.

Finally, all this led to the emergence of a serious and clear Palestinian position on peace expressed by the resolutions issued by the PNC during its recent session in Algiers. We believe this opportunity should not be missed. This opportunity, if coupled with the good intentions of the other side in the Arab-Israeli conflict, will constitute a very important contribution to the peace march, because there is no use in Israel's prevarication and the denial of the Palestinian's true eagerness to live in peace within an independent Palestinian state side by side with Israel.

We are confident that the international community, and even those who advocate the opposite, are fully aware that there is a high degree of a moderate and responsible position based on the principles stated in the international resolutions to which I have referred. Irrespective of whether the recent PNC resolutions literally meet the terms and conditions set by some powers, it is nonetheless essential to acknowledge that the formal Palestinian movement toward peace has now taken a distinct documented form so that any attempts to cast aspersions upon that are uncalled for and would prove pointless.

The question that must now be raised is if Israel is really ready to respond to this Arab and Palestinian position and whether the United States, which has been insisting on a specific recognition of Israel by the Palestinians, will be ready to request a similar recognition by Israel of the Palestinian side and its legitimate national rights. Mr. Chairman, regarding the double-dealing and selectivity which some sides practice towards the parties to the conflict, it is also regrettable to note that the United states does not respond to the important and positive develop-ments in the Palestinian stand which gained the satisfaction and appreciation of the whole world.

This negative US stand conflicts with frequent US promises and commitments to reconsider its stand toward holding contracts with the PLO if it accepted UN Security Council Resolutions 242 and 338, recognized Israel, and renounced terrorism. The PLO has done this through recent PNC resolutions which have just been reaffirmed by Arafat.

We hope that the new US Administration will shake itself loose from the legacy it has inherited, including the recent decision by the Secretary of State, so that it would contribute in a constructive fashion to the peace process both as a super-power and a power that has been providing a major party to the conflict with all means of strength and sustenance.

Mr. Chairman, Jordan, as a major party to the Arab-Israeli conflict and as a country with an organic association with the Palestine question, will continue its uninterrupted efforts to achieve a peaceful settlement guaranteeing desperately-needed security and stability for all the region's peoples. Jordan will also continue its constructive cooperation with the sincere international efforts, which we hope will be resumed immediately and in an intensified manner, to put the peace process on the right course and reactivate it toward convening the international peace conference.

In this regard, we hope that the UN Secretary-General's efforts will receive support and cooperation from all parties to the conflict and the UN Security Council five permanent member states so that the international conference is held as early as possible. Within the framework of such conference, efforts will be made to settle the Arab-Israeli conflict and its crux, the Palestine question, in all its aspects. This will serve security, peace, and stability not only in the Middle East, but in the whole world as well.

Thank you, Mr. Chairman.

## 34.    Resolutions of the Arab League Summit Conference, Casablanca, 26 May, 1989

The extraordinary Arab summit held in Casablanca, Morocco, from 17 to 20 Shawwal 1409 Hegira, corresponding to 23-26 May, 1989, out of its adherence to the principles and bases defined by the Arab Summits' Resolutions on the Palestine question and the Arab-Israeli conflict, and out of the Arab states' concern about continuing to work by all means to achieve a just and compre-hensive solution to the Middle East crisis and its crux, the Palestine question, and after discussing the situation in the Middle East, particularly in the light of the continuation of the heroic Palestinian intifadah against the Israeli occupation and its insistence on carrying out the policy of repression and persecution, the establishment of settlements, and the expulsion of citizens, and its refusal to recognize the Palestinian people's inalienable rights—and while expressing its great pride in the great popular intifadah in the occupied Palestinian territories and its glorification of the souls of its martyrs and the martyrs of all the occupied Arab territories; greeting the wounded hero and the steadfast detainees in the occupation prisons; highly appreciating the sacrifices, challenges, and steadfast spirit through which the Palestinian and Arab masses are confronting the Israeli forces of occupation and tyranny in the occupied Palestinian territories, the Syrian Golan Heights, and southern Lebanon; and stressing the importance of supporting the intifadah materially and politically and in all fields until it achieves its objectives of liberation and independence—decides:

1. To continue to work for the sake of achieving the objectives approved by the previous Arab Summits' Resolutions, particularly:

a) The achievement of the comprehensive Israeli withdrawal from all Palestinian and Arab territories occupied since 1967, foremost of which is Arab Jerusalem.

b) The restoration of the national inalienable rights of the Palestinian Arab people, including their right to repatriation, self-determination, and the establishment of their independent state in Palestine.

c) The mobilization of Arab resources in all fields to achieve comprehensive strategic parity in order to confront the hostile Israeli plans and to safeguard Arab rights.

2. a) To extend material and moral support for the Palestinian intifadah and the heroic and steadfast struggle of the Palestinian Arab people in occupied Palestine and for the Arab people's struggle in the occupied Golan Heights and in southern Lebanon.

b) To extend the aforementioned support for the valiant intifadah of the Palestinian people through the PLO in its capacity as the sole, legitimate representative of the Palestinian people, as follows:

* The payment of $128 million, which was approved by the Algiers summit, to be paid by the Arab states in accordance with their contributions to the Arab League budget.

* The commitment to pay $43 million a month, which was approved by the Algiers summit, to meet the needs of the intifadah and to guarantee its continuation. This shall be in accordance with what would be agreed on bilaterally.

c) To call on the Arab masses to reactivate popular donations to the intifadah.

3. To support the convocation of the international conference for peace in the Middle East with the participation of the UN Security Council's five permanent member states and all parties to the conflict, including an independent delegation of the State of Palestine, on equal footing with the objective of reaching a just and comprehensive settlement of the conflict on the basis of UN Security Council

Resolutions 242 of 1967 and 338 of 1973, on all the other related UN resolutions, and the Palestinian people's national inalienable rights, [and the objectives] of agreeing on security guarantees for all the region's states including the State of Palestine, and of solving the problem of the Palestinian refugees in accordance with UN General Assembly Resolution 194 of 1948 and considering all the related UN resolutions as still providing the conditions for international legitimacy which guarantee the right of the Palestinian people to establish their independent state.

4. To support the resolutions of the 19th Palestine National Council session, the intifadah session; to affirm support for the Palestinian peace initiative based on the Arab peace plan and on international legitimacy; and to welcome the positive international response to this initiative.

5. Any political settlement of the conflict must guarantee the comprehensive and unconditional Israeli withdrawal from the Palestinian and Arab territories occupied since 1967 and the enabling of the Palestinian people to exercise their national inalienable rights in accordance with the Arab summit's resolutions, particularly the Fez summit resolutions.

6. To support the establishment of the independent State of Palestine on Palestinian territories, to express the summit's appreciation of all the friendly states that officially recognized the independent State of Palestine, to call on the remaining world states to fully recognize this state, and to entrust the member states with the task of holding the necessary contacts to urge the states that have not yet recognized the establishment of the independent State of Palestine to do so.

7. To support the Palestinian stand toward the issue of elections to the effect that these elections should take place following the Israeli withdrawal from the occupied Palestinian territories and under international supervision and within the framework of the comprehensive peace process, especially since the Israeli plan is aimed at dealing a blow to the intifadah, bypassing the PLO, and circumventing the Palestinian people's national inalienable rights. The summit also stresses the need to adhere to ending the Israeli occupation of the occupied Palestinian and Arab territories and to putting the occupied Palestinian territories under the control of the United Nations for a temporary period in order to enable the Palestinian people to exercise their right to self-determination.

8. To set up a higher committee chaired by His Majesty King Hassan II of Morocco to follow up moves in the international arena and to hold the necessary contacts, on behalf of the Arab League, with the UN Security Council's permanent member states and the UN Secretary-General with the objective of reactivating the peace process and taking part in preparations for an international peace conference. The formation of this committee shall be completed through consultations with the president of the State of Palestine.

9. To call on the five Arab states—the Hashemite Kingdom of Jordan, the Syrian Arab Republic, the State of Palestine, the Republic of Lebanon, and the Arab Republic of Egypt—to intensify coordination among them and to follow up the international consultations and contacts to hold the international peace conference.

10. To firmly stand in the face of the inhuman crimes of the Israeli occupation authorities against the Palestinian people in the occupied Palestinian territories, against the Syrian citizens in the occupied Golan Heights, and against the Lebanese citizens in southern Lebanon, and to call on the UN Security Council to shoulder its responsibilities toward these crimes and practices that conflict with all the rules of humanitarian conduct and all the international laws that apply to military occupation of other people's land, including the possibility of imposing sanctions on Israel.

11. To call on the United States to develop its stand toward the PLO and the Palestinian people's national rights, and to frankly recognize their right to self-determination within the framework of a comprehensive peace process in implementation of the principles and objectives of the UN Charter, the related UN resolutions, and the principles of international legitimacy.

## 35. President Husni Mubarak's Ten Point Peace Plan, 2 July, 1989

1. The need for all inhabitants of the West Bank and Gaza, including those residing in East Jerusalem, to participate in the elections either by voting or contesting the elections. Any inhabitant should have the right to contest the elections provided that he has not been convicted of a crime by a court of law. This will allow persons under administrative detention to contest the elections.

2. Freedom to conduct electoral campaigns prior to and during the elections.

3. Acceptance of international supervision of the elections process.

4. Prior commitment by the Israeli Government to accept the results of the election.

5. The Israeli Government's agreement that the elections will be part of the efforts leading not only to a transitional period but also to a final settlement and that all efforts from start to finish will be based on the principles of solution as understood by the United States. These principles are: UN Security Council Resolutions 242 and 338, the principle of exchanging land for peace, and a guarantee of the security of all the countries in the region, including Israel, as well as of Palestinian political rights.

6. Withdrawal of the Israeli Army during the elections to a distance of at least 1 km from the polling centers.

7. Barring Israeli entry into the West Bank and Gaza on the day of the elections. Entry into these areas would be permitted only to those individuals working there and the inhabitants of the settlements.

8.  The preparatory period before the elections is not to exceed 2 months, and the preparations are to be conducted by joint Israeli-Palestinian committee which the United States and Egypt may help in forming.

9.  The United States should guarantee all the aforementioned points, and a prior declaration to this effect should be issued by the Israeli Government.

10. The creation of settlements is to be halted.

## 36.  Statement by Farouk Al-Shara' Minister of Foreign Affairs of the Syrian Arab Republic to the UN General Assembly, New York, 3 October, 1989 [Excerpts]

Despite the fact that few years have elapsed since the improvement of the atmosphere in international relations which has reflected positively on regional conflicts in the world, the Arab-Israeli conflict still winds in a different direction, and develops in an atmosphere imbued with tension and confrontation; the reason is clear and does not need a lengthy explanation.

The rulers of Israel—with their Zionist doctrine which is unmatched in its fanaticism and fundamentalism by any other doctrine—are still living out of this age, despite the fact that they possess the most advanced means and equipments, especially in the field of armament.

They still rely on myths and illusions to achieve their final objective in establishing the greater Israel from the Euphrates to the Nile, the objective that they neither hide nor can cover up. We all remember how furious the Israeli rulers were with their American friends who advised them to give up the dream of greater Israel.

When they fail to convince their closest allies with their false claims, the rulers of Israel resort, as did Moshe Arens in his statement to the General Assembly last week, to relying on colonial documents and promises in the files of the League of Nations to justify their continued occupation of the West Bank and Gaza, while flagrantly ignoring the Charter of the United Nations and its resolutions which call upon Israel to withdraw from the occupied Arab territories and to recognize the national inalienable rights of the Arab-Palestinian people.

The dilemma facing the peace process in the Middle East does not just lie in the dreams of Israel, but in its practices too. The rulers of Israel try to remind the world everyday of Nazi crimes against the Jews, though these crimes have ended fully with the end of the Second World War, forty-five years ago, and yet perpetrate in the meantime, their continued crimes against the Arabs until this very day to which there seems to be no near end in the horizon.

The rulers of Israel are trying to keep the so-called purity of the Jewish state and yet at the same time insist on continuing their occupation of the Arab land, the fact that has put them in a state of continuous confrontation to rid the land of its population, and has led them to practices as notorious as the racist practices of South Africa. It is a strange contradiction in terms for the Israelis to protest against the resolution of the United Nations which has equated Zionism with racism, while the rulers of Israel confirm the validity and credibility of this resolution through their continued repressive measures against the Arab population in the occupied territories.

The Israelis do not want peace because they want the land and peace together, and this is what they cannot achieve, and any initiative within the framework of these Israeli concepts is not destined to succeed. For the heroic Palestinian Intifadah, the brave resistance in the South of Lebanon and the steadfastness of our people in the occupied Syrian Golan were, first and foremost, a revolution against these concepts. Peace cannot be achieved except through a full Israeli withdrawal from the occupied Arab territories and the safeguarding of the inalienable national rights of the Palestinian people, including their right to self-determination, and the establishment of their state in Palestine in accordance with the resolutions of the United Nations.

The Syrian Arab Republic believes that the appropriate framework to achieve a just and comprehensive settlement in the Middle East is through convening an international conference under the auspices of the United Nations and with the participation of all parties concerned including the Palestine Liberation Organization.

## 37. The Government of Egypt's "Assumptions" With Regard to Secretary of State James Baker's Five-Point Plan, 5 December, 1989

1. The Palestinian delegation will represent all the Palestinians, including those living inside or outside the occupied territories.
2. The Israeli-Palestinian agenda will remain open, in accordance with the original version of Secretary of State Baker's five-point proposal.
3. The dialogue on the election process will be considered a first step toward a continuation of the process that will lead to the convening of an international peace conference on the Middle East with the participation of all relevant parties, including Israel and the PLO.

## 38. Statement by the League of Arab States on the Settlement of Soviet Jewish Emigrants in the Occupied Territories and South Lebanon, Tunis, 13 March, 1990

The Zionist entity has recently launched new efforts in its settlement design for the occupied territories by building two thousand units to accommodate the new emigrants from the Soviet Union. In addition, the occupying authorities have begun a process of surrounding East Jerusalem with a belt of new Jewish settle-ments, as a part of the Zionist plan aimed at altering the cities demography. Another new settlement has lately been established in the area of Kfar Kadom in the occupied Palestinian territories, as we witness an Israeli attempt to build a settlement around Rashaya Al-Fakhar, in Southern Lebanon, near an already existing one in Al-Arkoub for the Falash Jews (Ethiopian).

The Council of the League of Arab States strongly condemns this colonial and expansionist policy that constitutes a threat to the national rights of the Palestinian and Lebanese people. The Council calls upon the international community to recognize the grave consequences of such policy and its adverse effects on the peace process as well as on world peace, because it violates Arab rights, inter-national treaties, UN resolutions, and the Geneva Conventions.

The Council strongly urges the international community to force Israel to stop its illegal settlement activities and to abide by international legitimacy, thus protecting the inalienable national rights of the Palestinian people and the integrity of a sovereign, independent Lebanon.

### 39. Arab Summit League Final Statement, Baghdad, 30 May, 1990 [Excerpts]

The conference welcomed the approach of securing international detente, achieving cooperation among peoples, bringing an end to the arms race, putting an end to destructive wars, and building a foundation for international peace and security on the basis of the balance of mutual interests, equal respect, sovereignty, and independence. Moreover, the conference fully realizes that these changes—in their negative and positive aspects—mandate, more than ever, the Arab nation's dependence on its own capabilities, whether in confronting the direct threats to pan-Arab security or in dealing with the international environment which is being reshaped. Therefore, the Arab nation should maintain a status commensurate with its time-honored history and civilized contribution.

The conference hailed, with great appreciation, the Palestinian Arab people's steadfastness under the unjust Israeli occupation; the valiant Palestinian intifadah's escalation in face of the Israeli authority's brutal oppression; and the Palestinian people's daily heavy sacrifices in their quest to liberate their occupied homeland and build their independent state on their national soil, with Holy Jerusalem as its capital, under the leadership of its sole, legitimate representative, the PLO.

Furthermore, the conference stressed the need to make available all forms of official and popular material and political support which ensures the continuation and developing of the intifadah so that it can attain its noble objectives—liberation, independence, and sovereignty—and to reinforce assistance of the intifadah on the pan-Arab, regional, and international levels.

The conference also discussed the grave dangers resulting from the planned, organized Jewish immigration to Palestine and other occupied Arab territories and what this entails; the violation of the Palestinian people's rights in their homeland and Zionism's plans, which aim to deport the Palestinians from their national land, strengthen the Israeli occupation, and widen its range through the processes of intensified settlement, deportation of Palestinian people, seizure of their properties and lands in order to absorb the Jewish immigrants and fulfill the scheme of the so-called Greater Israel, which has been confirmed by Israeli officials' statements and the new maps they have drawn to implement their known expansionist ambitions.

The conference is fully convinced that the immigration of Soviet Jews and others to Palestine and the other occupied Arab territories is a new aggression against the Palestinian people's rights and a serious danger to the Arab nation as well as a gross violation of human rights, the principles of international law, and the fourth Geneva Convention of 1949. The conference affirms that this massive and premeditated process represents a dangerous threat to pan-Arab security and that it thus deserves to be tackled in accordance with this perspective and on a collective basis. The conference also believes that all necessary measures must be taken to safeguard the rights of the Palestinian people and pan-Arab security.

While strongly condemning Jewish immigration to Palestine and the other occupied Arab territories, the conference asks the countries directly concerned with immigration in particular and the international community in general to immediately end the Israeli immigration and settlement scheme. Furthermore, the conference calls for guaranteeing the national rights of the Palestinian people, including their right to repatriation on the basis of UN Resolution 194 of 1949. In addition, the conference affirms that the building of Israeli settlements is illegal, that this building must be halted, that the settlements already built must be dismantled, and also that an international mechanism must be found to monitor and detect Israeli settlement activities.

The conference calls on the various states to stop offering any aid or loans to the Israeli Government to facilitate the settling of emigres in Palestine and the other occupied Arab territories. The conference also affirms the need to reassess Arab relations with other states in light of their stand toward Palestinian national rights and Jewish emigration. The conference urges the United Nations to shoulder its responsibilities in accordance with the UN Charter, UN General Assembly and Security Council resolutions, and international agreements to guarantee that Jewish immigrants are not settled in the occupied Palestinian and Arab territories, including Jerusalem. The conference also urges the United Nations to launch an international monitoring effort to implement this and to issue a UN Security Council resolution to this effect.

The conference analyzed the current Arab situation and reviewed the political efforts to achieve a comprehensive and just peace in the region. The conference expressed the conviction that the escalating tension, which gives signs of leading to an explosion, is the result of the continued Israeli occupation of Palestine and other occupied Arab territories, of the continuing denial of the inalienable national rights of the Palestinian Arab people, and also of the continuing policy of aggression, terrorism, and expansion by the Israeli authorities.

In this regard, the conference holds the United States primarily responsible for this situation, in its capacity as the power which provides Israel with military capabilities, financial aid, and political cover. It believes that without these things, Israel could not continue these policies or to defy with such arrogance the will of the international community.

Out of its commitment to the Palestinian peace initiative and Arab summit resolutions, especially those adopted at the 1988 Algiers summit and the 1989 Casablanca summit, the conference affirms that the call for convening an international conference under UN auspices and with the participation of all parties to the conflict, including the PLO on an equal footing, is now a pressing and urgent matter. The conference also reiterates the Arab states' commitment to the Palestine question as the crux of the Arab-Zionist conflict and that a just and lasting solution to the plight of the Palestinian people and to the regional crisis lies in restoring the inalienable national rights of the Palestinian people, including their right to repatriation, to self-determination, and to the establishment of an independent Palestinian state with Holy Jerusalem as its capital.

The conference has also saluted the Palestinian masses' steadfastness alongside their Lebanese brothers in southern Lebanon and their contribution to confronting the air, ground, and naval Israeli attacks against villages and Palestinian camps in the south.

In view of the developments in the East European countries, the conference recommended that Arab relations with these countries be assessed in light of these countries' positions on the Palestine question and on the basis of mutual interests.

The conference expressed satisfaction with the outcome of the Arab-European ministerial meeting, which was held toward the end of last year, and the member states' determination to participate actively in promoting the Arab-European dialogue with a view to bolstering the relations of cooperation and friendship between the two groups.

The conference registers with satisfaction and appreciation the growth of world support for the Palestine people's just cause and the increase in the number of states that recognized the young Palestinian state. The conference expresses its indignation and denouncement of the prejudice, political protection, and big military and economic support for Israel that characterize the US Congress' positions and resolutions, the latest among which were the null resolutions on Jerusalem and the support for and finance of Jewish emigration, which helps settlement in the occupied territories.

The conference underscores the religious and political status of holy Jerusalem and considers the city an integral part of Palestine and capital of its state. It dismisses any change to the city's religious and legal status as a flagrant violation of international conventions and resolutions. The conference also underlines the Islamic Jerusalem Committee's resolution on the convening of the Islamic Christian conference to protect Islamic and Christian sanctities. The conference condemns the US Senate and the House of Representatives resolutions in this respect. The conference affirms that the Arab states will take the necessary political and economic measures against any state that considers Jerusalem the capital of Israel.

And because the Israeli authorities are going far in their terrible crimes against Palestinian citizens, the conference demands that the Palestinian people be protected against the scheme of genocide and transfer. This should be done under international supervision, under the auspices of the United Nations until the Palestinian people exercise their right to self-determination and national independence.

The conference is fully confident that the protection of rights, maintenance of lands, and defense of sanctities can only be achieved through achieving unity of positions and goals, bolstering Arab solidarity, clearing Arab atmosphere, engaging in constant struggle by all means, mobilizing all Arab resources in service of the pan-Arab destiny, and moving actively on all levels and on both regional and international scenes.

On this occasion, our conference registers its full gratitude for all states, organizations, and figures that supported and are still supporting the national and pan-Arab rights of the Palestinian people and the Arab nation. It urges further material and moral support in the interest of world justice and peace and in order to curb Israel's arrogance and inhumane practices.

The conference strongly opposes the US attempts to repeal the UN General Assembly Resolution 3379, which considers Zionism a form of racism and racial discrimination, and called for the intensification of efforts to abort those attempts.

The conference paid extreme attention to the threats, the hostile tendentious political and media campaigns, and the scientific and technological ban against Iraq. It discussed the threats these pose to the sovereignty of an Arab League member state and their effects on pan-Arab security.

While affirming its adherence to the Arab League Charter, the Collective Arab Defense Pact, and economic cooperation, the conference strongly condemns these aggressive threats, campaigns, and measures and affirms its effective solidarity with fraternal Iraq. The conference warns against the continuation of these campaigns against its sovereignty and pan-Arab security and warns that there are preparations to facilitate aggression against it.

The conference affirms Iraq's right to take all the appropriate measures to safeguard and protect its national security and provide the requirements for

Israeli-Palestinian Conflict: A Documentary Record

development, including the possession of advanced science and technology and using them for internationally legal purposes.

The conference affirms the right of Iraq and all the Arab states to reply to aggression by all means they deem fit to guarantee their security and sovereignty.

Proceeding from the full understanding of the organic link between national and pan-Arab security, and in appreciation of Jordan's steadfast and firm stand along the longest confrontation lines with the enemy, the conference condemns the settlement policy and Israeli expansionist schemes, including schemes to settle the new Soviet Jewish immigrants in the occupied Arab territories. This poses a direct threat to the Hashemite Kingdom of Jordan, and therefore, a threat to, and aggression against, the whole Arab nation. The conference affirms its total adherence to defending and protecting national Jordanian security, because it is an indivisible part of the Arab nation's pan-Arab security. Support for and solidarity with Jordan, as well as providing it with its needs for steadfastness, is a pan-Arab duty stemming from the fact that Jordan is a frontline base of the Arab nation protecting its borders, defending it, and helping to avert dangers from it. The conference has decided to provide support for Jordan through bilateral negotiations to enable it to strengthen its steadfastness and bolster its capabilities in various fields. This would thus form the main support for the Palestine cause, the glorious Palestinian intifadah, and for the Palestinian people to remain steadfast in their occupied territory.

# Notes

## I. International Documents

1. *The Search for Peace in the Middle East, Documents and Statements 1967-1979.* Report prepared for the Subcommittee on Europe and the Middle East of the Committee on Foreign Affairs, US House of Representatives (Washington, DC; US Government Printing Office, 1979), p. 93.
2. *Ibid.,* pp. 124-139.
3. *Ibid.,* p. 92.
4. Meron Medzini, (ed.), *Israel's Foreign Relations, Selected Documents 1947-1974.* (Jerusalem: Ministry of Foreign Affairs, 1976), pp. 1064-1065.
5. *The Search for Peace, op. cit.,* p. 101.
6. *Ibid.,* pp. 159-160.
7. *Ibid.,* p. 176.
8. *The New York Times,* 14 June, 1980.
9. *Documents and Statements on Middle East Peace, 1979-1982.* Report prepared for the Subcommittee on Europe and the Middle East of the Committee on Foreign Affairs, US House of Representatives (Washington, DC: US Government Printing Office, 1982), p. 58.
10. *F.B.I.S. USSR International Affairs, Middle East and North Africa,* 16 September, 1982.
11. *F.B.I.S. Daily Report, Soviet Union,* 30 July, 1984.
12. *F.B.I.S. Daily Report, Middle East and North Africa,* 24 July, 1986.
13. *Journal of Palestine Studies,* Vol. XVI, No. 1 (Autumn 1986): 199.
14. Michael Simpson, (ed.) *United Nations Resolutions on Palestine and the Arab-Israeli Conflict, Vol. 3, 1982-1986* (Washington, DC: Institute of Palestine Studies, 1988), pp. 182-183.
15. *Journal of Palestine Studies,* Vol. XVI, No. 4 (Summer 1987): 185-186.
16. *F.B.I.S. Daily Report, Near East and South Asia,* 4 January, 1988.
17. *F.B.I.S. Daily Report, Soviet Union,* 28 April, 1987.
18. Congressional Research Service, Library of Congress, *Documents on Middle East Peace,* 1982-1988, Report Prepared for the Subcommittee on Europe and the Middle East of the Committee on Foreign Affairs, US House of Representatives (Washington, DC: US Government Printing Office, 1989), pp. 43-44.
19. *Ibid.,* p. 45.
20. *Ibid.,* p. 46.
21. *F.B.I.S. Daily Report, Soviet Union,* 3 June, 1988.
22. *Washington Post,* 8 December, 1988.
23. United Nations Information Office, Washington, DC.
24. *Ibid.*
25. *F.B.I.S. Daily Report, Soviet Union,* 15 December, 1988.
26. *Ibid.,* 19 December, 1988.
27. *F.B.I.S. Daily Report, Soviet Union,* 24 February, 1989.
28. *New Outlook,* May/April 1989, p. 9.
29. *Journal of Palestine Studies,* Vol. XIX, No. 1 (Autumn 1989): 121-122.

II. **US Documents**

1. *The Search for Peace, op. cit.,* pp. 288-289.
2. *Ibid.,* p. 292.
3. Israel Ministry of Foreign Affairs, Information Division, Jerusalem, 1975.
4. *The Search for Peace, op. cit.,* pp. 305-307.
5. *Ibid.,* pp. 155-156.
6. *Ibid.,* pp. 309-310.
7. *Ibid.,* p. 311.
8. *Ibid.,* p. 316.
9. United States Information Services, Embassy of the United States of America.
10. Israel Government Press Office.
11. US Department of State Bulletin, Vol. 83, No. 2079 (October 1983), pp. 33-34.
12. *American Foreign Policy, Current Documents,* 1984 (Washington, DC: Government Printing Office, 1985), p. 492.
13. *American Foreign Policy, Current Documents,* 1985 (Washington, DC: Government Printing Office, 1986), p. 496.
14. US Department of State, *Current Policy,* No. 715.
15. *American Foreign Policy: Current Documents,* 1986, (Washington, DC: Government Printing Office, 1987), p. 375.
16. US Department of State, *Outgoing Telegram,* 19 February, 1987, "Unclassified."
17. US Department of State, Office of Press Relations, Press Release, Vol. 191, April 1-July 30, 1987, No. 78-166.
18. *Toward Arab-Israeli Peace: Report of a Study Group,* (Washington, DC: The Brookings Institute, 1988), pp. 3-7.
19. *Building for Peace: An American Strategy for the Middle East,* The Washington Institute's Presidential Study Group, (Washington, DC: Washington Institute for Near East Policy, 1988), xi-xxi.
20. *Journal of Palestine Studies,* Vol. XVII, No. 4 (Summer 1988): 188-189.
21. *Journal of Palestine Studies,* Vol. XVII, No. 4 (Summer 1988): 189-190.
22. *Ibid.,* pp. 190-191.
23. "This is the Plan," *Washington Post,* 18 March, 1988.
24. *US Policy in the Middle East, Selected Documents,* No. 27, June 1988.
25. US Department of State, Bureau of Public Affairs, Press Release No. 199, 19 September, 1988.
26. US Department of State, Daily Press Briefing, DPC No. 209, 16 November, 1988.
27. *Documents on Middle East Peace,* 1982-1988, pp. 79-80.
28. *New York Times,* 14 December, 1988.
29. US Mission to the United Nations, Press Release, USUN 178-(88), 14 December, 1988.
30. *New York Times,* 15 December, 1988.
31. Ibid., 15 December, 1988.
32. The White House, Office of the Press Secretary, Press Release, 3 April, 1989.
33. *Ibid.,* 6 April, 1989.
34. US Department of State, Bureau of Public Affairs, Press Release No. 96, 22 May, 1989.
35. *Journal of Palestine Studies,* Vol. XIX, No. 1 (Autumn 1989): 176-178.
36. *Ibid.,* Vol. XIX, No. 2 (Winter 1990): 167-169.
37. *Washington Post,* 7 December, 1989.
38. *New York Times,* 4 March, 1990.
39. *Ibid.,* 21 June, 1990.

### III. Sadat's Visit and the Autonomy Negotiations
1. *Israel's Foreign Relations op. cit.,* 1977-1979, pp. 182-190.
2. *Ibid.,* pp. 191-201.
3. *F.B.I.S. Middle East and North Africa,* 29 December, 1977.
4. *The Search for Peace, op. cit.,* pp. 20-3.
5. *Documents and Statements, op. cit.,* pp. 16-20.
6. *Ibid.,* pp. 38-42.

### IV. Israeli Documents
1. Fuad A. Jabber (ed.), *International Documents on Palestine, 1967,* (Beirut: Institute on Palestine Studies, The University of Kuwait, 1972), p. 156.
2. *Israel's Foreign Relations, 1947-1977, op. cit.,* pp. 849-857.
3. *The Jerusalem Post,* 14 May, 1969.
4. *Ibid.,* 12 December, 1969.
5. *Ibid.,* 17 March, 1972.
6. *International Documents on Palestine, op. cit.,* 1973, pp. 269-271.
7. *Ibid.,* 1974, pp. 314-315.
8. Anne Sinai and Allan Pollock (eds.), *The Hashemite Kingdom of Jordan and the West Bank, A Handbook,* (New York: American Academic Association for Peace in the Middle East, 1971), pp. 352-353.
9. *International Documents on Palestine, op. cit.,* 1976, pp. 323-328.
10. *Ibid.,* 1977, p. 256.
11. *Ibid.,* 1980, p. 211-212.
12. Hillel Schenker (ed.), *Beyond Lebanon,* (New York: The Pilgrim Press, 1983), pp. 496-498.
13. Israel Government Press Office.
14. *F.B.I.S. Daily Report, Middle East and North Africa,* 14 September, 1984.
15. *Ibid.,* June 1985.
16. *Ibid.,* 22 October, 1985.
17. *Journal of Palestine Studies,* Vol. XVII, No. 3 (Spring 1988): 184-186.
18. *F.B.I.S. Daily Report, Middle East and North Africa,* 2 October, 1987.
19. F.B.I.S. Daily Report, Near East and South Asia, 14 December, 1988.
20. Embassy of Israel, Information Bureau, Washington, DC.
21. *Ibid.*
22. *Ibid.*
23. *Journal of Palestine Studies,* Vol. XVII, No. 3 (Spring 1988): 194.
24. Tel Aviv: The Jaffe Center for Strategic Studies, 1989.
25. Embassy of Israel, Information Bureau, Washington, DC.
26. *Ibid.*
27. *Journal of Palestine Studies,* Vol. XIX, No. 1 (Autumn 1989): 148-156.
28. *Ibid.,* Vol. XIX, No. 2 (Winter 1990): pp. 161-162.
29. *F.B.I.S. Daily Report, Near East and South Asia,* 15 March, 1990.
30. *Ibid.,* 16 March, 1990.
31. Embassy of Israel, Information Bureau, Washington, DC.

### V. Platforms of Israeli Parties Represented in the Knesset
All party platforms were provided by the information department at the respective parties.

## VI. Palestinian Documents

1. *International Documents on Palestine, op. cit.,* 1967, pp. 715-716.
2. *Middle East Record, op. cit.,* pp. 432-436.
3. *International Documents on Palestine, op. cit.,* 1968, pp. 399-403.
4. *F.B.I.S. Daily Report, Middle East and North Africa,* 14 July, 1971.
5. *Journal of Palestine Studies* (Spring 1973): 169-172.
6. *International Documents on Palestine, op. cit.,* 1974, pp. 410-411.
7. *F.B.I.S. Daily Report, Middle East and North Africa,* 10 June, 1974.
8. *International Documents on Palestine, op. cit.,* 1974, pp. 500-503.
9. *Journal of Palestine Studies* (Winter 1975): 181-192.
10. *B.B.C. Summary of World Broadcasts,* 22 March, 1977.
11. *International Documents on Palestine, op. cit.,* 1977, p. 462.
12. *Journal of Palestine Studies* (Summer 1978): 195-196.
13. *Ibid.,* (Winter 1979), pp. 194-195.
14. *Ibid.,* (Spring 1979), pp. 165-169.
15. *Congressional Record,* 11 October, 1979, p. 267.
16. *International Documents on Palestine, op. cit.,* 1980, pp. 154-157.
17. *F.B.I.S. Daily Report, Middle East and North Africa,* 22 April, 1981.
18. *Ibid.*
19. *Al-Fajr,* (English Edition), 4 March, 1983.
20. *F.B.I.S. Daily Report, Middle East and North Africa,* 30 November, 1984.
21. *Journal of Palestine Studies* Vol. XIV, No. 3 (Spring 1985): 204-206.
22. *Ibid.,* Vol. XV, No. 2 (Winter 1986), pp. 214-215.
23. *Ibid.,* Vol. XV, No. 4 (Summer 1986), pp. 241-243.
24. *F.B.I.S. Daily Report, Middle East and North Africa,* 10 March, 1986.
25. *Journal of Palestine Studies* Vol. XVI, No. 4 (Summer 1987): 195-196.
26. *F.B.I.S. Daily Report, Middle East and North Africa,* 27 April, 1987.
27. Zachary Lockman and Joel Beinin, (eds.), *Intifadah: The Palestinian Uprising Against Israeli Occupation* (Boston: South End Press, 1989), pp. 328-329.
28. *F.B.I.S. Daily Report, Near East and South Asia,* 12 January, 1988.
29. *Documents on Middle East Peace,* 1982-1988, pp. 60-61.
30. *Al-Fajr,* (English Edition), 19 June, 1988.
31. Embassy of Israel, Information Bureau, Washington, DC.
32. *Journal of Palestine Studies* Vol. XVIII, No. 2 (Winter 1989): 206-213.
33. *Ibid.,* pp. 213-216.
34. *Ibid.,* pp. 216-223.
35. *F.B.I.S. Daily Report, Near East and South Asia,* 14 December, 1988.
36. *Ibid.,* 16 December, 1988.
37. *Documents on Middle East Peace,* 1982-1988, pp. 48-50.
38. *Journal of Palestine Studies* Vol. XVIII, No. 3 (Spring 1989): 152-155.
39. *F.B.I.S. Daily Report, Near East and South Asia,* 10 August, 1989.
40. *Ibid.,* 18 October, 1989.
41. *Ibid.,* 26 December, 1989.
42. *New Outlook,* March 1990, pp. 44-46.

## VII. Arab Documents

1. *International Documents on Palestine, op. cit.,* 1967, pp. 656-657.
2. *Middle East Record,* 1969-1970, *op. cit.,* 1970, p. 15.
3. *Arabia and the Gulf,* 16 May, 1977, pp. 12-13.

4. *B.B.C. Summary of World Broadcasts,* 17 March, 1972.
5. *Documents on Israel's Foreign Relations, op. cit.,* 1974-1976, pp. 1076-1077.
6. *The Search for Peace..., op. cit.,* p. 273.
7. *International Documents on Palestine, op. cit.,* 1976, p. 503.
8. *The Search for Peace..., op. cit.,* pp. 274-276.
9. *Arab Report and Record,* 16-30 September, 1978, p. 700.
10. *F.B.I.S. Daily Report, Middle East and North Africa,* 6 November, 1978.
11. *Ibid.,* 2 April, 1979.
12. Saudi Press Agency, 1981.
13. *F.B.I.S. Daily Report, The Middle East and North Africa,* 7 September, 1982.
14. *American Arab Affairs,* (Winter 1982), No. 3.
15. *F.B.I.S. Daily Report, Middle East and North Africa,* 4 January, 1983.
16. *Ibid.,* 11 April, 1983.
17. *Journal of Palestine Studies* Vol. XIV, No. 2 (Winter 1985): 253-257.
18. *Ibid.,* Vol. XIV, No. 3 (Spring 1985): p. 206.
19. *Documents on Middle East Peace,* 1982-1988, pp. 22-25.
20. *F.B.I.S. Daily Report, Middle East and North Africa,* 12 August, 1985.
21. *Ibid.,* 30 September, 1985.
22. *Ibid.,* 14 November, 1985.
23. *Ibid.,* 20 February, 1986.
24. *Ibid.,* 8 July, 1986.
25. *Ibid.,* 21 April, 1987.
26. *F.B.I.S. Daily Report, Near East and South Asia,* 12 November, 1987.
27. *Documents on Middle East Peace,* 1982-1988, p. 47.
28. The League of Arab States, Arab Information Center, Washington, DC.
29. *F.B.I.S. Daily Report, Near East and South Asia,* 1 August, 1988.
30. *Ibid.,* 22 August, 1988.
31. *Ibid.,* 14 December 1988.
32. *Ibid.*
33. *Ibid.*
34. *Ibid.,* 30 May, 1989.
35. *Ibid.,* 29 November, 1989.
36. Embassy of the Syrian Arab Republic, Information Department, Washington, DC.
37. *F.B.I.S. Daily Report, Near East and South Asia,* 8 December, 1989.
38. The League of Arab States, Arab Information Center, Washington, DC.
39. *F.B.I.S. Daily Report, Near East and South Asia,* 31 May, 1990.